4 875

CLAUS   HIRSCH

Economic Forecas

Economic

Forecasting

V LEWIS BASSIE

Director, Bureau of Economic and Business Research
University of Illinois

1958

McGraw-Hill Book Company, Inc.

NEW YORK
TORONTO
LONDON

THE MAPLE PRESS COMPANY, YORK, PA.

Preface

It is common in the economics profession to think of forecasting as an art, or as a field of endeavor that is at best pseudoscientific. This view is unfortunate, though not without justification. A great deal of what forecasters have done has not been even pseudoscientific. The impostures and errors of the past—sometimes the consequence of detours by reputable economists into unfamiliar territory—tended to keep forecasting on the fringe of what was supposed to be the science of economics. Even when efforts met with success, those who succeeded often refused to disclose their methods, so that there was no way to determine if anything of scientific value had been achieved.

The fault, however, has not been all on the side of the forecasters. Partly it lay in the traditional notion of what constituted scientific method in economics. Much of what has been built onto the structure of this intellectual discipline through the generations has represented an unscientific retreat from reality. In some of its aspects economics became preoccupied with "principles of behavior" no better founded than the forecasts that were rejected. There was one important difference: The forecasts could be checked, but the principles could not. No discipline has a right to call itself scientific except as its theory meets the test of explaining what happens, and what will happen, in the world of things and people.

It is the custom among writers of books on economics—a custom not followed here—to conclude with a section on public policy and control of business fluctuations. Sometimes these discussions are filled with brilliant, though perhaps overly abstract and impractical, ideas. Most of them ignore human relations and the mechanisms by which things actually get done. It may be perceived that control is possible only if the results of action can be foretold; but there may at the same time be a failure to perceive that persuasive foretelling is possible only in terms of the realities which tend to be ignored.

This is not to say that forecasting must be a final goal of action for

v

people in general or for businessmen and economists in particular. There are various passages in this volume stating the contrary. These consistently indicate that most of the activities of living and, indeed, of building a better future can proceed without forecasts. The world neither relies on predictions nor accepts dictates. It wants better knowledge of what must be done, and when, if certain other things are to follow. Whatever control is possible will come almost automatically with understanding of the forces that move the economy. It is my hope that this book will contribute something to such understanding.

Making it a book on forecasting rather than on economic analysis is partly just a matter of emphasis. What the book attempts to show is that forecasting is simply good analysis, and insistence that analysis should embody substantial elements of predictive value is just a means of ensuring a realistic approach. The book goes beyond the demonstration of this identity in describing many of the research techniques that can be used to deal with the kind of workaday problems of planning for the future that are continually being encountered.

The book is not designed to teach elementary economics and statistics. It does review some aspects of those subjects with the dual purpose of describing their basic logic and of presenting a minimum background to make the main topic understandable to the reader not trained in the field.

A good part of the volume deals with such mundane matters as sources of information and rules of research procedure. These are often not treated in the textbooks. They have to be learned. The analyst must know how to obtain and how to interpret statistical data in order to do a good job; he must understand the necessity for care in arriving at conclusions and in presenting them for use by others. The costs of endlessly repeated trial and error in learning some of the most elementary aspects of the task are altogether too high.

The development of the forecasting method discussed in Part 2 was begun during the late 1930s, while I was in the government service. My first experience in the field came from certain projects begun at the Federal Reserve Board in 1938, under the direction of Lauchlin Currie, and carried through to completion at the Department of Commerce by mid-1940, under the direction of Richard Gilbert. The broad outlines of the approach described in Part 2 retain much the same form as the original procedure worked out in that period.

As director of the Bureau of Economic and Business Research at the University of Illinois since 1948, I have been able to command the services and facilities that made possible much of the research whose results are included in this volume. University policies have provided unstinting support for the research efforts of my colleagues as well as myself.

I am grateful to my wife, Janet M. Hooks, for untold hours spent in reading and commenting on the manuscript. Her thoroughgoing efforts have resulted in numerous improvements throughout the book.

Exceptional thanks go also to Donald Streever, Jr., who carried out a number of subsidiary research projects and assumed most of the burden of checking, reviewing, and revising the statistical material presented throughout the book. His efforts went beyond the usual role of a research assistant. He was preceded in that capacity by several others, among whom Robert Wolff and Sidagouda Khot bear special mention.

I am grateful also to all the friends and colleagues who reviewed for me one or more separate chapters. Among those who offered substantive comments are Garfield Cox, Edward Dennison, Robert Ferber, Marvin Frankel, C. Addison Hickman, George Kleiner, Walther Lederer, Dorothy Newman, Donald Paden, Hersey Riley, Walter Salant, and George Steiner. This list by no means exhausts the acknowledgments due those who have contributed ideas or suggestions. A beginning is all I can make in accounting for all the assistance I have had in making this book what it has come to be.

V Lewis Bassie

Contents

PART ONE

The Essentials
of Forecasting

CHAPTER 1

The Role
of Judgment

Predictions of future events or conditions vary greatly in character. Some are of necessity sheer guesses, like attempts to call the toss of a coin. Others are in effect statements of plans or decisions, since the outcome is subject to control. The most important forecasts refer to real events, like weather, which are not subject to control but are determined by forces at least partially known, so that the outcome can be defined to a satisfactory degree of probability.

The popular notion of forecasting—in business and economics as in other fields—is a long, intent look into the crystal ball. Sometimes the magic takes more mundane forms, such as a statistical formula or the crossing of lines on a chart. The forecasts that arise from such processes may even work out fairly well for a while. Nevertheless, all that magic can contribute is essentially a guess, dependent upon the ability of the guesser. Nothing can be obtained from short-cut devices that is not put into them, and in most cases the result will be something less than the full value of the clues and indications that were initially available.

In contrast to such subjective or pseudoscientific procedures, the essence of a sound approach to forecasting is common-sense analysis of the important forces making for economic change. To appraise the relative importance of those forces and put them into proper relationship with each other, they must be expressed quantitatively on a coordinated basis of timing. To minimize the probability of error, the estimates of their separate values must be modified in the light of their mutual interrelationships and integrated in an internally consistent pattern of ongoing economic development.

In this approach, as in any other, judgment is one of the prime requisites. Two others are information and analysis. All three are, of course, interacting.

At the very outset, the role of judgment must be emphasized. Any forecast is itself essentially a judgment or involves a judgment that the method used in making it is appropriate to the task. Whenever a statistical series is projected into the future, a judgment, or perhaps a whole series of judgments, is made. When a forecast is based on expected changes in one dominant factor, such as government expenditures, other factors are judged to be relatively unimportant. Every step requires a decision among possible alternatives. Frequently the component elements are in conflict and are so evenly balanced on each side as to provide little basis for choice. Nevertheless, one or another must be judged appropriate for use under the circumstances.

It is necessary to know what is happening, as quickly and accurately as possible. Without adequate information about the current situation, there are bound to be errors of judgment and of statistical projection.

It is also necessary to isolate the strategic factors in the current situation and relate them effectively to other factors and developments. Without techniques for analyzing the course of business, for projecting important statistical measures into the future, and for assessing the quantitative importance of the various forces affecting the level of activity, there can be no consistent validity to judgments about the future.

Accurate information and valid analytical techniques bolster judgment. But these are assets that cannot be acquired without it. Judgment is necessary both in interpreting the information that defines the starting point and in selecting methods of analysis and appraising their applicability to the specific problem.

As far as possible, all decisions of this kind should be conscious, informed judgments, and not decisions made on the basis of superficial appearances without full consideration of relevant facts and relationships. Only judgment so informed can produce consistent results.

In speaking of informed judgment it must be made clear that what is meant is judgment that is broadly informed rather than narrowly specialized. There are, of course, numerous specialists, such as commodity experts, who are very able and know their special fields very well. The hunch of one of these competent analysts, well informed about the developments and special factors operating in his particular field, is far more valuable than the hunch of a person who is operating by snap judgments on the basis of what he is told or otherwise happens to pick up. By reason of their special knowledge and experience, many of these experts are able to provide forecasts in a limited field that could not be obtained in any other way.

On the other hand, one reason such experts do not always make the best judgments in their own field of specialization is that they tend to ignore other important developments in the economy whose repercussions may have far-reaching consequences even for the particular industries or commodities in which they are interested. What is needed is a means of accounting for the repercussions, both direct and indirect, of all the important changes that are currently taking place.

Even the expert can form sound judgments only if he has found a means of getting and ordering information, of selecting the significant items from the mass of information confronting him, and of weighing their importance on one side of the question or the other. When confronted with new situations, when new factors are driving familiar indicators beyond the previous range, he may find himself completely at sea. When developments not encompassed by the scope of his experience occur and they are not explained by his usual sources of information, he may be unable to cope with the problem. For only a systematic technique of analysis, working through principles rather than cases, can deal with the new situations that are continually arising.

Most people, lacking the perspective of the expert, cannot even understand the significance of current information unless it is put into a context in which it is properly appraised in relation to other things. For the forecaster who has many fields to consider, such a context involves a framework for quantitative analysis. Understanding in the significant sense is understanding in quantitative terms, and this is the primary basis for good judgment.

Judgment as such is still needed to obtain a practical solution. It is, in fact, required at all stages of the forecasting process. But judgment applied at various stages in a process of quantitative analysis is quite a different thing from judgment used to pull a general answer out of nowhere.

Technical judgments on methods or on points of information can be made in routine fashion by the trained forecaster. The chances are that most such judgments will be reasonably valid; and if there is relative freedom from bias, the errors will tend to offset each other. The possibilities of going wrong are thus greatly reduced, in comparison with the case where an intuitive process is relied upon to provide an answer in the form of a single, complete, and final conclusion as to the outcome. Judgment, to take full advantage of what experience can contribute, must operate in the sphere in which knowledge and experience can be expected to give consistent results.

In other words, the role of judgment, though important, is limited. It is necessary, both in marshaling facts and in utilizing techniques of analysis, but without facts and a technique of analysis no dependable judgment is possible. It is because of the tripartite character of the relationship that these are referred to as the essentials of forecasting. The balance among them necessarily varies from one forecasting situation to another, but combining the three as effectively as possible, impartially and without preconceptions, provides in highest degree the kind of wisdom that offers the possibility of reliable forecasts.

JUDGMENT IN INTERPRETING INFORMATION

A great deal of information about the business situation is currently being made available by statistical agencies, corporation reports, statements of business or government executives, and day-to-day newspaper, radio, or television reports. It might be said that there is too much information—partly because there are just too many facts to handle effectively and partly because there is too much misinformation mixed in with the facts presented.

Nobody can follow all the sources from which relevant information is obtained, and nobody is always in a position to know whether a statement is representative of more than the specific case or item referred to or even whether it is factually correct. Perhaps the first task of judgment is that of sorting out the important facts about the current situation from the mass of irrelevancies and errors constantly being forced on the forecaster's attention.

Practically everyone who is putting out data or making statements about the business situation has his own view of the outlook. What he says is likely to be slanted to fit that view. The distortions of interpretation may be minor, or they may be of crucial importance. Perhaps they are in conflict with other interpretations of the same facts. Then the forecaster, or indeed anybody who has an interest in the business outlook, has to decide how much weight to give the statements coming from the various sources.

In particular, the handling of the news by the press, television, and radio makes it difficult for the individual to arrive at a calm, reasoned conclusion. Newsmen and commentators inevitably tend to play up certain angles, those which in their view are considered to be most newsworthy. Their constant effort is to select whatever seems most exciting and dramatic and to feature that particular aspect. In this way some minor element may be played up to such an extent as to exclude anything on the other side of the question. The result is that the reader, viewer, or listener gets a biased view.

What intensifies the effects of such reporting is that there is so much concert running through all the media of communication. Certain lines of thinking are handed out in waves, and during each wave conflicting views have hardly a chance of being heard. For a period of months everything seems to be going one way, and then there will be a switch in the line and everything seems to be going the other way.

The danger of falling in line with the consensus of economic opinion when a certain aspect of the situation is played up to the exclusion of everything on the other side of the picture poses a real problem for the forecaster. Hence the ability to make an independent decision on the basis of the facts rather than on the basis of what everyone is saying is one of the qualities that go into the make-up of sound judgment. There is no virtue in standing out from the crowd just to be different. There is a definite need for holding to a correct position, which has the support of facts and analysis, no matter how often or how severely it may be criticized by other observers.

To assist in the process of segregating accurate facts as a basis of analysis, it is desirable to rely on certain tested statistics rather than on spot facts or statements of opinion. Even opinions coming from people in important positions may not be firmly founded and should be regarded with something of the skepticism ordinarily reserved for those of a less informed but more opinionated person. Much greater reliability attaches to the data obtained from one of the regular statistical reporting agencies. The data actually reported may be quite different from the results expected by the individual who expressed the earlier opinion, and it is essential to avoid jumping to conclusions before there is a fairly definite indication that the situation has changed or is different from what it had been thought to be.

Even when one does insist on pinning decisions or conclusions to statistics rather than to statements of opinion, there are problems that cannot be solved except with a considerable exercise of judgment. Consider, for example, the difficulty of interpreting the significance of a change in trend shown by one of the statistical indicators. Suppose there is a downturn. When the decline first occurs, one does not have the perspective he will have at a later date, after he sees where it has ended. It is just a minor decline. But it presents a problem. What does it mean? On the one hand, it may be the beginning of an important development. On the other hand, it may be due to any number of temporary and inconsequential factors.

Very often further information is needed before a change of this kind can be correctly interpreted. There can be no doubt that statisticians now show much greater appreciation than formerly of the need for providing information about the nature of the changes that affect the published statistics. Hence interpretations of the various statistical series are now generally released with the data. This is true, for example, of practically all the government statistics. It does not mean, however, that complete reliance can always be placed on the official explanations. They should be evaluated just as other statements are.

For example, the situation in the early part of 1947 was affected by the widespread belief that inventories had been piling up rapidly and had become excessive. It is true that the dollar value of inventories was rising rapidly at that time, but the fear that inventories were excessive was largely a misinterpretation of the situation, fostered in part by a reporting agency. Stocks of goods on hand were really quite limited, having been much too low at the end of the war, so that a substantial increase was needed to bring them into line with normal business requirements. However, the accumulation was not so rapid as it appeared, consisting in large part of revaluation of existing stocks in line with the upsurgence of prices following the abandonment of controls.

Such pitfalls in our information may not always be easy to avoid, but certainly experienced judgment can hold them to a minimum. It is important always to make some attempt to get at the reasons for a change —sound reasons being defined as those which offer an acceptable explanation in the broad perspective of past and current economic events and not those which merely provide a superficial, ready explanation of immediate change.

JUDGMENT IN SELECTING AND APPRAISING METHODS OF ANALYSIS

The availability of information in the quantity and detail in which it is now available opens the door to use of an almost unlimited variety of techniques of analysis. Each new statistical measure makes possible a new method of dealing with problems, particularly if it spotlights a significant element in the economic picture. Such a series may even result in the solution of what has previously seemed to be one of the baffling mysteries of the economic outlook.

With new data, one may be in a position to make analyses that were not previously possible. But the fact that data are available with which to make analyses does not mean that any analysis made with them is valid. At the outset, new data may merely create a problem of deciding what is the best approach to follow. For example, one of the supposed mysteries in the business outlook has been the outlook for producer's investment in new capital goods. After the war, a new approach to the problem was opened by surveys of planned investment expenditures. This approach put before the forecaster a decision requiring judgment. Should it be substituted for the older approach, which proceeds in terms of analysis of past situations and interrelationships? It was necessary to make a choice of approaches.

In other cases, the choice may lie between statistical techniques. Will the best results be obtained by projecting a trend or cyclical pattern, or will a correlation with some other variable offer greater rewards? Obviously the answer depends upon the type of activity under discussion, the character of its normal behavior in similar situations, and the nature of its relationship to other variables. To answer such questions requires at a minimum a considerable degree of familiarity with the data themselves and with the results to be obtained by the use of alternative techniques of analysis in similar circumstances.

Appraising an analysis already made may present almost as grave a problem of judgment as starting a new one from scratch. Even established techniques present such questions from time to time. Sometimes a method that has long been established and has been successfully used suddenly seems to go haywire. Perhaps there is a seeming aberration in the current data that seems to invalidate the whole procedure; then a judgment must be made about the range of tolerance under the circumstances. To answer such a question, considerable study and perhaps further information may be needed. Just as appropriate data and wise decisions are needed if certain approaches or techniques are to be used, so likewise availability of data and sound judgment are essential in trying to determine their continuing validity under changed conditions.

The importance of judgment in the solution of all these problems cannot be overestimated. It may even be stated as a general rule that any attempt to make forecasts mechanically, as by projecting cyclical patterns or by relying solely on correlation formulas, must eventually result in failure. The person who says, "I have found this method to be successful, and nothing else is worth considering," is bound to fall into error at one time or another. Each time an analysis is reused, a new opportunity for appraising its validity is presented, and each time the reappraisal should be made without preconceptions, to ensure the best results.

Although trained judgment is thus regarded as providing a basis for dealing with various forecasting problems, it must be taken for granted that some errors will be made. Error can creep in at any point in the process of working out a forecast. There may be errors in the data being used or in the processing of such data. There may be errors in method, not only because invalid techniques are adopted but also because valid techniques may be too mechanically applied.

Error can also creep in from outside the forecasting process itself. What is not taken into account at the time the forecast is made, what cannot possibly be foreseen at that time, may have a greater influence on the outcome than the various forces specifically analyzed. Changes of this kind are usually referred to as "disturbances," and they may arise entirely outside the sphere of economic affairs. Characteristically, these exogenous changes are unexpected—not necessarily by everyone, but by the great majority—so that their effects take the form of sharp movements that do not flow out of what went before.

For all these reasons, the history of forecasting has not been encouraging. Those who have studied it commonly conclude that forecasting is an art rather than a science, and they frequently add that it can never be anything but an art.

The thinking of those who voice such conclusions is sometimes cast in a perspective of predictive accuracy that is entirely inappropriate to the problem. What is scientific in the natural sciences, where accuracy may be demanded to the nth decimal place, has no necessary relation to the province of economics, in which even our observations of the recent past are subject to an error that may run to several billion dollars. All that can be expected is that the general character of the situation be accurately portrayed and that the margin of error in any specific measure of activity be limited to a reasonable range for that measure in that kind of situation.

EVALUATING FORECASTS MADE BY OTHERS

When one sets out to answer the question: "Why did forecasts go wrong?" he finds any number of reasons but little basis for generalizing from them. Usually there is only a limited number of instances in which forecasts can be compared with the actual outcome, and these have special features not characteristic of other situations, so that any conclusion drawn from them may not apply elsewhere. In any such situation, the reason why one forecast was wrong may be precisely the reason why another was right, and that fact may offer no basis whatever for preferring the second to the first in the following year.

It is fairly common to say of a forecast that "it was right, but for the wrong reasons." This may imply a high degree of superficiality in thinking. On any particular occasion, the sheer guess of a novice might happen to be successful. The momentary appearance of accuracy certainly provides no basis for relying on forecasts from the same source in the future.

The potential user of a forecast may not feel that he is in a position to judge the validity of the reasoning underlying it, but he should recognize that he is acting on faith when he accepts it on any other basis. If a forecast cannot be explained in clearly understandable terms, if it has to be derived from mystic mumbo jumbo, even though this is presented as esoteric statistical manipulation, it is fundamentally untrustworthy.

There are two problems in using forecasts: the first is determining what is likely to happen; the second is deciding how much confidence to place in what is predicted. When the forecast is received from someone else in finished form, the second of these problems must still be faced, and it may be very troublesome. Unless this problem can be solved, the forecast may be useless. Hence an understanding of users' attitudes is basic to good work on the part of the forecaster.

One of the most common methods of getting a forecast accepted is to support it with a record of past performance. Such a record, however, cannot provide a reliable test, for it can never be established that either the methods or the conditions that led to a given performance will be repeated. Hence no particular set of forecasts can be considered to establish a valid probability, in the sense of one derived from a large number of trials in which the same method is used under conditions of random variation. It is therefore practically meaningless to state that a set of forecasts were right three times out of four, implying that the method used will continue to produce as good results in the future. Such claims may well be looked upon with skepticism.

Commercial forecasters try, of course, to build up a good performance record as a way of fostering sales of their services. The better consulting firms own up to a certain amount of inaccuracy in their forecasts. Others seem to feel that they have to be right all the time. The general tendency is to rely on various kinds of devices for avoiding errors or for covering up or explaining away errors already made. This may be good business, but it certainly does not lead to good forecasting.

One way to avoid making errors is simply not to make forecasts. It is not that something resembling a forecast will not be presented; it is rather that the thing presented will be so vague and indefinite that it can never be tested and either proved or disproved. Many definite points may be made, of course, but they do not necessarily have to add up to anything definite in the aggregate. Even a seemingly definite forecast may be preceded by qualifications that assume away the most important of the conflicting possibilities and thus leave escape holes for use when any of those "exceptions" puts in an appearance.

One of the most common statements of this kind is hedged with the expression, " . . . if only we don't let our fears get the better of us." This type of hedge is a favorite of the public official who wants to offer reassurances about the soundness of the situation but just can't bring himself to a definite commitment on the outlook. It tends to destroy the value of the forecast to which it is attached. For most people seem to have little confidence in the public's stability and calmness under stress, and to leave them with such a statement as the basis for their appraisal of the future leaves them with nothing at all. It also, as a rule, has the wrong effect. The audience quickly draws two conclusions: first, that the speaker has no real confidence in his predictions, and, second, that the situation cannot really be secure or he would not feel the need to reassure them about it. The negative impression derived from these conclusions is so strong that the effect is the opposite of the reassurance intended.

Another way of avoiding a forecast is to straddle. This is done in either of two ways. The first is by saying enough on both sides of the question so that the forecaster can always claim he was right. The second is by explaining that there are two possibilities, neither of which can be completely ruled out. Discussions of the latter kind may be useful at times, if they contain enough information and present it logically; but since the decision is left to the listener, what value they have must be considered as of a reporting rather than a forecasting character.

The chances of getting away with any of these substitutes for a forecast are greatly enhanced by the opportunities for bringing in irrelevancies of one kind or another. These provide good material for a smoke screen to cover up the fact that nothing definite has been said about the outlook. Another device of this kind takes the form of statements and policy recommendations designed to show that the forecaster's heart is in the right place. He may avoid making a forecast, and that point may be overlooked, if his presentation is cluttered up with ideas about how ridiculous it is to be drifting into a mess the way we are, when the application of a few "sound" policies would turn things around and get them headed in the right direction.

For all these reasons, it would seem desirable for the user of forecasts to follow some definite rules in appraising them. First of all, he should try to determine just what is forecast. Precisely what kind of movement is projected? If next year is to be a little lower, will there be a steady, slow retreat, a sharp decline followed by a partial recovery, or a period of comparative stability followed by a plunge? When the projection is so vaguely stated and hedged about with qualifications in such a way as to avoid almost any possibility of error, it may well be disregarded.

Furthermore, how definitely is the timing specified? Just when will the predicted changes take place? What is the nature of the situation at the terminal point, and how does it relate to what has happened in the meantime? Some forecasts that may look reasonably good in terms of annual averages will be exposed if considered in this light, especially if knowledge of what has already occurred is used in judging the change still to be experienced.

Next the user should try to determine what method or procedure underlies the forecast. Is the forecaster relying on judgment, business-cycle indicators, opinion surveys, or other techniques? Does he apply those techniques rigorously or attempt to make appropriate allowances where needed to deal with special characteristics of the current situation? There is a sound basis for suspicion of any method so complicated that its logic cannot be explained in relatively simple terms.

It may also be helpful to consider the purpose for which the forecast is being made. Does it confuse what "should be" with what is? Does it sound good merely because it tells you what you want to hear? It is a good idea in listening to any "forecast" to make sure that what you are receiving is not propaganda. In some cases, forecasting is definitely a secondary purpose, the primary objective being to influence a favorable decision on a matter almost entirely unrelated to the outlook. This is the approach of the quack who describes everybody's trivial failings as symptoms of the disease his medicine "will cure." If a receptive climate of opinion can be created in favor of a product or policy that the forecaster is trying to promote, his prestige as well as his financial interests may be advanced.

In short, the listener should analyze the forecast, try to tear it apart, and subsequently check up on the outcome, because some of the answers can only be obtained after the fact.

AVOIDING ERROR

If such rules are important for the user of forecasts, they are even more so for the forecaster. His ability to do an effective job is likely to depend on his being honest with himself, however much he may wish to conceal his weaknesses and mistakes from his clients. By the nature of the situation with which he deals, he is an investigator with much to learn, and the better he learns each lesson as it occurs, the better will he be able to handle the problems that arise in the future. Preservation of the attitudes of the learner, the unbiased investigator, is essential to consistent results.

One of the first things that should be recognized is that hedging and similar devices are not means of avoiding error. They are merely ways of not forecasting. The person who has built a lucrative practice in the business of *not* forecasting is unlikely, of course, to wish to abandon it, and it is not suggested here that he should. That is a matter between him and his clients. The person who wants to make accurate forecasts, on the other hand, cannot afford to mislead himself into thinking he was right when he covered up in this manner.

The best thing he can do, in private at least, is to put himself in the position of the user and ask: "Is this what I would want if I were on the receiving end of the line? If not, why not, and why can't I give myself what I would like?" The mere definition of deficiencies and uncertainties in this way will help to eliminate them.

Even if the weaknesses in a forecast cannot be eliminated immediately, the user may find it quite useful to be warned about them. The forecaster may perform a useful function by indicating their specific nature and describing the time when or conditions under which certain contingencies might be expected and the items of information to watch in order to detect them at an early stage. It is desirable to make each forecast as unequivocal as possible, but such a frank explanation of uncertainties is always legitimate.

When the character of the current situation is in doubt, it may be wise to call to the listeners' attention inconsistencies or other points of uncertainty about the preliminary information. One of the reasons why the situation might at first appear different from what actually exists arises from the possibility of outright error in the reported information. However careful research workers or organizations may be in compiling statistics, errors are bound to creep in once in a while. Hence part of the equipment of the good forecaster is the ability to spot errors in published reports.

In part, facility in detecting errors in data is just a matter of familiarity with the statistical series under observation. To the experienced observer, mere unexpected movements in a direction or of a magnitude that seldom occurs in the item measured become a kind of warning signal. The casual attitude that disregards anomalous movements is never appropriate for the statistical analyst.

Frequently it is possible to use other inconsistencies than those within the reported data themselves to uncover an error. Thus in a period when prices and production both rose, a decline in manufacturers' sales would be suspect. Again, in a period when consumption rose and production declined, there could hardly be an increase in the rate of inventory accumulation. The experienced forecaster who has the basic facts of the situation in mind will recognize such inconsistencies at a glance.

A special case of detecting error in this way arises when an observation is out of line with a relationship that has been validly used in the past. A striking example of this was provided when the *National Income* supplement to the *Survey of Current Business* was released in July, 1947, containing an error in the data for 1936. Anyone investigating the relationship between disposable income and consumers' expenditures was almost bound to run across a large discrepancy. At first it would appear as no more than an almost incredibly large deviation from the usual relationship. The only way to verify that it was an error was to communicate with the Department of Commerce. The error was, of course, readily acknowledged, and correct data were provided. Also a revised edition of the supplement was quickly published.

This, by the way, is the kind of experience undergone at some time or other by almost every large statistical organization. The National Income Division of the Department of Commerce regularly gets correspondence from people interested in its data. As a rule, the data are valid and the writer's questions about them are readily cleared up. Occasionally a report from someone who has special information indicates that there is something not quite right about one or another of the series being used, so that at least a certain amount of revision is necessary. The process of revising statistical series as new information comes in is an everyday routine in good statistical work.

It should perhaps be made clear that these comments represent only a caution and not in any sense a suggestion that the facts be discounted. The occasions on which a forecast will prove correct in the light of revised data, though not earlier, will probably be exceptions, and perhaps rare ones at that. Yet in the early stages of a shift, before the situation is clearly defined, all the possibilities should be considered.

In the more usual case, any discrepancy in the better statistics will be the result not of error but rather of some unusual development. The forecaster's reaction in this case should be the same as in that where error is suspected. The question is: "Why did this occur?" The search for an answer to this question will determine both the accuracy of the data and the causes responsible for the deviation from the expected pattern of development. If the data prove correct, arriving at the explanation for the extraordinary movement may enrich understanding of the situation to an important degree.

Other errors are of a kind for which the forecaster himself is wholly responsible. The statistician, like everyone else, is only human, and one of the first things he must learn is to protect himself from his own errors as well as those of others. He therefore disciplines himself in checking everything he does, from beginning to end, and even to double-checking, using alternative procedures if available.

An analysis may go wrong from the very start if data are carelessly transcribed from the original reports. New data may not only be preliminary, they may also be presented on a revised basis; and if they are obtained from newspaper or radio reports, this fact may not be stated in the earliest release available. Hence the latest report should be checked against earlier reports in which there are overlapping periods—just as past data are checked from one volume of a statistical record to the next in order to ensure that a continuous series is being compiled. Sometimes a revision will produce a distinct break in the data, and any projection over the break, from the old to the new, will be far off the mark.

Errors in transcription and reporting tend to be most frequent nowadays, because computations are usually protected by automatic checks of one kind or another. The electronic computer, for example, may check by doing each computation twice and comparing the results. Other procedures are usually set up as parts of the statistical methods taught. But there is nothing automatic to ensure accuracy in the forecaster's own input and output operations.

Another common source of error arises from too mechanical an application of statistical devices to a future situation without consideration of whether the result would be reasonable in the light of all the relevant information available. The idea that mechanically contrived indicators or charts are a substitute for analysis and judgment is a frequent misconception, one that particularly seems to affect stock-market forecasters. There comes to mind an incident in mid-1949 concerning two market analysts whose charts showed that there would be a serious decline throughout 1950. They did indeed have an impressive set of charts, which, in their view, revealed "all the secrets of market action." Actually the charts, though a masterpiece of art, were an embodiment of complete economic confusion. The indicators on which they mainly relied had hardly any relation at all to the mass of other statistics portrayed, and nowhere was there a summing up to give effect to the various factors included.

This illustration is not intended to detract from the importance of charts to the forecaster. They distinctly assist in viewing developments in perspective, they help to provide a correct interpretation in some cases, and they afford a ready check on the reasonableness of results, however the results were obtained. Nevertheless, they are no more suitable to provide answers by themselves than any other device.

Charts should be regarded as an adjunct of the process by which a forecast is produced, not the essence of the process itself. They are not a substitute for fundamental research. They cannot be used mechanically, to eliminate judgment; they merely help judgment avoid the errors that arise from too mechanical an application of other methods. Their usefulness is greatest when the characteristics of the series under consideration are well understood, on the basis of observation and study covering a period of years.

In many cases the information that must be relied on will not be as precise as the statistician might desire. This is particularly true in delineating the course of events in such fields as government, international affairs, and speculation in commodities or securities. By the nature of the case, all that can be done is to work up a hypothetical projection that will be in approximately the right order of magnitude. Charting will not guarantee correct results, nor will any of the precise methods of statistical analysis. Any notion that such a projection is the one and only answer is pure nonsense. This fact is likely to be understood by business executives and other informed observers whose interests are largely nonanalytical, and it explains their impatience with the pretense that a single, exact answer is possible. What really pays off is the combination of both points of view. When the forecaster applies the more flexible attitude toward his own work, he steals the thunder of the practical man. For the latter is seldom capable of determining for himself just when the precise methods of analysis are applicable.

It should become almost a matter of principle with the forecaster to regard results as provisional, regardless of how they are obtained. Experience will, of course, indicate that some techniques are relatively trustworthy and others the reverse. Yet even the most reliable will not hold good in all situations. A relationship that is perfectly sound in most situations cannot be applied in those where patterns are distorted by serious abnormalities. Conversely, a wholly unsatisfactory relationship for use in the usual kind of situation may happen to give an excellent result under abnormal circumstances.

All this leads to a reformulation of the role of judgment: judgment has to be used at innumerable points in the process of working out a forecast; but since judgment is subject to error, its use should be confined to the points where it will do the least harm to the over-all result. Judgments should as far as possible be made on specific points only, and then only in a technical, disinterested way. Each and every one of such decisions should be as independent of the others as possible.

GUARDING AGAINST BIAS

The question may be asked: "Do errors of judgment average out?" The answer is: "As a rule, no!" The forecaster who is inclined to be optimistic is likely to be optimistic everywhere, and the corollary is true of the pessimist. Only in the absence of systematic bias can such a result be expected. A second condition for the counterbalancing of errors is that there must be enough specific decisions so that the process of averaging can operate effectively. This condition is likely to hold in most forecasting situations, the exceptions being those where the outcome is determined by one overriding factor. But the existence of bias is a possibility inherent in the basic processes of thinking and doing, and it represents a potential danger in any situation.

Psychology has shown that there are irrational elements in the make-up of everyone and that people's attitudes about the future are in large part emotionally rather than logically derived. Guarding against bias must therefore be a primary effort at all times. Among the most important of all the rules governing the conduct of the forecaster are those aimed at this objective.

The sources of bias in attitudes and judgments are indeed numerous.

Some are deeply rooted in the social and cultural structure of the community. Many aspects of the individual's environment are so important to him that he cannot help being influenced by changes in it. He associates with others whose fortunes are tied up with his in various ways. He wants to think well of himself, and, by and large, this means that he must receive recognition from others. He has goals and objectives that he hopes to realize, and he tends at times to merge the imaginary world in which his plans are formulated into the realities he observes.

These problems are, of course, more acute for some than for others. The infant begins life with a mind that is completely open. As he develops, he acquires prejudices, dogma, and other attitudes that interfere with this quality of open-mindedness in various ways. Efficiency in learning demands that certain ideas or patterns of thought be accepted in order to eliminate the necessity for constantly thinking things out anew. By the time most people reach adulthood, their attitudes are set. Some persons are basically independent and objective. Others lack self-confidence, seek the dictates of authority, or refuse to recognize realities.

To state that independence is a quality of good judgment is not to imply that originality is requisite. Anyone interested in the economic outlook will find all the elements of a sound forecast freely offered in the news and other reporting services. Many forecasts or hypotheses will actually be thrust upon him.

In this situation, judgment may operate in complete absence of originality, and it should, ideally, operate independently with regards to one's own ideas as well as those of others. Independence implies an attitude, or method of approach, which accepts no authority other than the cold logic of the facts known about the situation. If the source from which information is obtained is considered generally reliable, if the analysis is that of a reputable agency, there is a probability that it is correct. But it is not necessarily so! If it is in conflict with other facts or hypotheses, it should be questioned. The appeal is not to the degrees of authority of the various sources but to the implication of the known facts.

To appraise the facts independently of what everyone is saying about them is to free judgment from the errors that are bound to be made when any particular source or consensus is accepted as valid without question. For the forecaster, skepticism is a healthy attitude of mind. But skepticism cannot perform the constructive function of putting together a sound forecast.

Some people are so firmly set in their attitudes that they could never change. Others are still flexible and plastic enough so that they can overcome established habits and prejudices if they really try. It makes a tremendous difference just to recognize that these irrational elements may exist in one's thinking. From recognizing such attitudes to bringing them under control by trying to determine how much a conclusion derives from them and how much from logical reasoning is perhaps a shorter step. But it is a long step toward working out good forecasts.

Current events no doubt have a considerable influence on attitudes toward the future. Optimism typically reaches its peak when business is booming and security prices are near the ceiling, and pessimism flourishes in the trough of recession, just before the upturn. There is a tendency to focus attention too exclusively on anti-inflationary considerations during a boom and on remedies for unemployment during a depression and these attitudes are likely to be maintained too long. The problem here evidently lies in lack of perspective. The temporary, special character of those situations has to be appreciated in order that stability of outlook may be achieved. It is a shortcoming that tends to disappear with improved understanding of the forces that make each kind of situation what it is. The person who is otherwise a good forecaster will overcome this deficiency as his knowledge and experience increase.

The character of a person's job also tends to produce a distinct occupational bias in his analysis. Among the findings of Livingston's study[1] of the forecasts reported to him are the following: Business economists tended to be pessimistic and "conservative" because their "bread was buttered on the side of caution." Bank economists also have a conservative bias, deriving from an institutional "desire for disinflation." Government economists generally displayed a strong political bias, resulting from the support of official policies: "To get the cure, they promised the disease." Economists for investment and brokerage firms tended to be optimistic about stock prices but rather less so about general business conditions. Finally, economists for labor unions "usually showed an inflationary bias, . . . no doubt related to collective bargaining . . . when the cost of living was a major argument for wage boosts." Livingston concludes with a psychoanalytical definition of forecasting: "the projection of one's hopes and fears." The question here is: "Can these irrational elements in forecasting be avoided?" If the answer has to be: "No," or "Not entirely," then at least much can be done to minimize them.

Isolating oneself from the influence of other people may be even more difficult. The forecaster cannot completely disregard the opinions of other forecasters. He wants to please the boss. He wants to make himself agreeable, not to argue with and perhaps antagonize friends or other people he considers important. When others feel strongly enough on a certain

[1] *The Reporter*, May 26, 1953, pp. 18–19.

point, argument may do no more than strain personal relations. Yet he knows he can accomplish nothing by going to the extreme of being a yes man.

Sometimes a person may be put in a position where he is forced to support a policy recommendation or other proposal dependent upon a view of the outlook that he does not fully agree with. This happens in business as well as in government. The person in such a position will probably do a better job if he does it with tongue in cheek, recognizing that he is writing propaganda and not forecasting at all. It is said that the best advertisers are cynical about their own products.

One of the easiest mistakes for the analyst and writer to make is to be deceived by his own propaganda. Realistic forecasting can never be doctrinaire, because the acceptance of doctrine or dogma that restricts the possibilities considered destroys the necessary objectivity of attitude.

Moreover, efforts to line up support by means of a forecast are futile, unless the forecast is so long range that it can never be checked. It is an almost complete fallacy to think that any forecast will greatly influence world affairs. It may be possible to achieve a moderate success of this kind when the situation is turning in the indicated direction and the threat exists quite apart from the forecast. In early 1946, when full-employment policy was under discussion, the real threat of unemployment appeared not from any forecasts made but from what was happening. Millions of men were being discharged from the Armed Forces. The production index had fallen by approximately one-third. The wave of strikes confused the situation and made a sound appraisal of developments difficult for some months. In these facts lay the basis for action. Policies adopted to stimulate recovery were agreed upon because it was easy to perceive a danger to which all had been sensitized by years of depression.

The forecasts of large-scale unemployment circulated at that time may have contributed something to the passage of the Full Employment Act, but if so, it was at best a fruitless victory. It may perhaps be argued that that one act is enough of an achievement to compensate for the years of ridicule that followed. The better view is simply that the forecasts represented an honest mistake—one in which nearly everyone shared, even some who, not being on record, could later claim they had nothing to live down.

Most people are suspicious of forecasts and do not pay much attention to them anyhow. But even when a forecast is widely accepted, it has only limited effects. What actuates business is not what people think but what they do, and what they do depends upon what happens, not upon what anyone tells them.

When a mistake has been made, there is a tendency to cover it up or, failing that, to explain it away. This is just a little human weakness shared by everyone. Most people forgive, and even sympathize with, the batter who "only struck out because his spikes caught in the dirt!" Hardly anything, however, will be so damaging to a forecaster's future work as this reluctance to own up to error and the attitude of misinterpretation which it engenders.

A forecaster has to be prepared to recede from a position previously taken whenever it is shown to be wrong, though not necessarily before that time. Working up a rationalization to interpret a previous position as correct when it was not will almost invariably get him off on the wrong foot in making new predictions. That kind of attitude will continue to make a forecaster wrong as long as it is maintained. Year by year, it adds to the number who have gone broke insisting that they know they are right and will show everybody they were right all along.

There is no need to advertise one's mistakes. There is a need to recognize why the mistakes occurred in order that they may be prevented from happening again.

The attitude that one has to be right is most likely to develop in the heat of controversy. Whenever a forecast is made, there is a good chance that the forecaster will be put in the position of having to defend it. Someone may say he thinks it is all wrong. The forecaster may bristle, but he should retain the attitude that he is willing to be shown. It is a situation in which heat does not produce light. In most cases the future will be along to settle the dispute soon enough.

Other ways of getting one's thinking set too firmly in a single mold should also be avoided. It is frequently proposed, for example, that a forecast be backed up with a bet. Such a bet is obviously pointless from the standpoint of affecting the outcome. It is no more than an indication of confidence; and since a forecast may turn out to be right for the wrong reasons, or wrong even though the reasoning was correct, it may not even provide a good indication of whether or not the confidence was misplaced. Perhaps there would be some point to betting if this were merely a way of getting the forecast recorded in order to ensure future checking, but even this advantage would be missing in the event that the forecast had already been made a matter of open record. On the other hand, there is the danger that it might confirm and reinforce the attitude that what was predicted had to be right, thus ruling out the exploration of alternatives.

The forecaster should always realize that he has to take his chances. Since there are many indeterminate elements in a complex economic situation, he is in effect engaged in a game of chance. There are only certain probabilities of success, and those are not necessarily modified by what he thinks or does. The professional gambler learns to isolate decisions from his personal feelings during a streak of bad luck because he knows that the only sound procedure is to play the odds. There is no reason why the forecaster should not act as rationally. He must take his losses or gains as philosophically as possible and get away from the notion that his personal fortunes have a bearing on what will happen next in the broader sphere of business activity.

The general rule to follow at all times has already been indicated: Consider the possibility that the forecast may be wrong. Opposed views should generally be taken seriously, at least until it is known what goes into their make-up. Make concessions to those views, if only mentally for the moment, and see how much difference they make quantitatively. If the worst they do still leaves the over-all result on the same side, the position is stronger than when the concessions swing the forecast clear over to the other side.

This is just part of the procedure of working up a good forecast in the first place. It is a process of integrating the valid elements from many sources into a comprehensive analysis. In this process, there can be no automatic or routine concessions to other people's points of view. The approach cannot be eclectic in the narrower sense. It is as important to reject wrong theories as it is to pursue correct ones. Otherwise it will be impossible to keep from being constantly led astray. Frequently, however, it may be desirable to moderate an extreme forecast. The more moderate forecast may well leave a position basically unchanged in the eyes of other people but gain greater acceptance because it does not seem so wholly out of line. The thought here is not to give up a position because the weight of opinion on the other side is heavy but rather to consolidate that position by opening possible weaknesses to scrutiny and remodeling where necessary to make it invulnerable.

TESTING ONE'S OWN FORECASTS

After a forecast has been completed and issued, it still cannot be regarded as final and unchangeable, as if the future were in fact known. Even before it can be put to effective use, new developments or new information may partly invalidate it. The big, dramatic changes will hardly ever be missed. Nobody will blame the forecaster for his failure to anticipate the collapse of France in 1940 or the entry of the United States into the Korean War a decade later. However, more gradual changes in the domestic scene may also produce unpredictable deviations of as much as a year in duration, and these are likely to be regarded as within the forecaster's area of responsibility. Some of the best forecasters looked bad in 1928 and early 1929, because they knew the stock market was far too high, but it kept going up anyway.

When something begins to go wrong with a forecast, the forecaster should be the first to know about it. It is an essential part of his task to watch current developments and see whether they are conforming to or departing from the forecast. This constant review has the advantage of keeping him up to date on developments. It also enhances his ability. For it is only when he knows what has happened, and why it has happened, that he is in a position to go on to the next step of making a suitable revision.

When the new appraisal of the outlook appears to be significantly different, the only sound procedure is to correct the forecast in as objective a manner as possible. There is ordinarily no point in standing by a forecast previously made when developments have made known a better alternative; and when such a change appears to be reasonably firm in the light of what is happening, it is usually desirable to issue the new forecast as quickly as possible.

This need for continual revision is one of the reasons why it is desirable to make a forecast continuous, quarter by quarter, from the present to the most distant period forecast. Unless these early points of reference have been established, it may be difficult to tell whether or not developments are consistent with the more distant conditions of the forecast date.

Early deviations from a forecast do not rule out the possibility that it will ultimately prove correct. They do call attention to the possibility of error and should be looked at with that possibility in mind. If a new development merely postpones expected conditions, the basic forecast may be retained or even made more extreme. If, on the other hand, it appears that some important element was in error, the forecast must be modified accordingly.

Sometimes, when a forecast seems to be proving wrong, it may be better to scrap it entirely and reforecast than to attempt revisions. If one of the basic elements is in error, there is a probability that others will be also. One important change in any situation is likely to modify the whole pattern. Reasoning previously relied upon can be reviewed and compared, but it should not be permitted to restrict the thinking needed to analyze and integrate the implications of the unexpected development.

This implies that each forecast, as made, including any revisions, should be made a matter of record, and as a rule the subsequent analysis of this record will be very enlightening. Acceptance and understanding of last year's mistakes will lead to the improvement of next year's forecast.

As the forecast is being worked out, therefore, the basis on which each decision is made should be spelled out and set down for future reference. The record need not be elaborate. Informal notes will ordinarily be sufficient, but even at this minimum the charts and tables used on any occasion will tend to resemble research work sheets. Notations of various kinds will call attention to sources of information, adjustments or other procedures used, and significant considerations leading to a conclusion. Even the record of discarded alternatives may be retained for a while, as it hardly ever pays to discard research work sheets. When such procedures are followed, what was done can always be checked, and by observation of the results techniques can constantly be improved.

This is also an easy way to obtain insurance against any tendency toward instability. If the basis of a former conclusion is forgotten when a new argument is presented the whole orientation may be illogically changed, at least for a while. Reference to what was previously done may quickly reveal the inadequacies of the new argument. At times even new developments will be best interpreted in the light of the broader perspective established by all that went into the make-up of a comprehensive forecast.

Where the object is to evaluate methods rather than specific forecasts as such, the requirements are much the same. The only way to ensure the accuracy of a forecasting method is to test it in various situations and appraise the results it produces in each. Different methods sometimes produce results so nearly alike that it is hard to choose between them. One method may have given better results in some past situations, another in others. With margins of error about the same on the average, there may be little basis for preferring the one to the other. In the end, the question will probably have to be decided pragmatically, by observing how well each works in future tests.

Whether a method is being tested against past data or in new situations, it is desirable to set up well-defined testing standards to ensure that results will be free of bias. The primary test is, of course, a comparison of forecasts with actual results. As far as possible, tests should apply to predictions made under conditions of actual use. Since judgment will ordinarily be used under these conditions and hindsight inevitably affects judgment, only the forward tests can be considered to meet this requirement fully. For this reason, tests based on past data are usually set up mechanically, to rule out the judgment factor—for example, by comparing projected levels of year-to-year changes without allowances or adjustments for the special factors known to have influenced the outcome in each period.

It should be recognized that any comparison of actual and predicted values provides only a relative measure—one that varies not only with the method used but also with the item being forecast and the character of the over-all situation. When it is found that an error amounted to, say, $6 billion, or 3 percent, that fact may in itself be meaningless. If such a result was the average error in a large number of trials conducted in various kinds of circumstances, it would give a somewhat better indication of the deviation that might generally be expected. But it would still leave open the question whether or not such a deviation is a good or bad result for that item. This question can only be answered by comparison with the same kind of test results obtained from other methods. In other words, a method is considered good if it produces errors that are small not only in relation to the item being forecast but also in relation to those obtained from the available alternatives.

Where only one method is known, so that comparisons are lacking, a basis for judging the test results may be established by the construction of a *naïve model*. This term is used to describe any of a number of simple statistical methods of projecting the original series, relying mainly on the serial correlation it displays. The simplest of such models assumes that next year's result will be the same as this year's observed value. Only a little more flexible is the assumption that next year will conform on the average to the fourth quarter of this year. More commonly, difference procedures are applied; then next year may be taken to exceed this year by the same amount that this year exceeded last, by some fraction of that amount, or by some other modification of recent changes arrived at in a fairly straightforward manner. In suitable form, the naïve model may itself become a forecasting method. Even if two or more other methods are available, it may be worthwhile to test all of them against some such device, as a rough criterion of the magnitude of the errors that could be expected. In the effort to apply such devices, however, attention should not be diverted from the primary objective of quantifying test results in an impartial manner.

If this is done systematically, it may be found not only that one method works better but also that its advantage lies in certain kinds of situations, and the character of those situations may suggest hypotheses about new factors to be taken into account or other modifications that will result in further improvement.

From the testing of methods as well as from the actual making of forecasts, the forecaster should continue to learn about the workings of the economy. As his analysis becomes increasingly realistic, his ability to make valid projections will grow. It is not something he can pick up in a day or in the time it takes to read a book, but it can be expected as an outgrowth of experience obtained in the application of intelligent effort over a period of time.

Recently, after these general considerations had come up in a discussion of forecasting procedure, one member of the group charged "What you have is not a forecasting method at all. It's just a set of rules of conduct." The truth was out! There is no time machine, no fixed formula, no sure solution. Forecasting is no more than an attempt to utilize the most promising techniques available in solving the specific problem presented by the current situation. By the nature of that problem, there can be no guarantee of accuracy in any structure of specified methodology, in any system of facts or indicators. For what emerges in each situation is a future that is always new in significant aspects. To apply ourselves with rules of conduct that make the most of the intelligence with which we have been endowed is to work for the best we can reasonably expect.

CHAPTER 2

Information for Forecasting Use

For even a fair degree of accuracy and consistency the kind of hypothetical projection which a forecast represents must be based on factual information about the current state of the economy. Without such information a forecast can hardly be anything but an uninformed guess, and there is little more to be said for uninformed guessing about the future than for reading tea leaves.

Anyone who is not careful in making a current interpretation of the immediate situation and of its implications for the future outlook can go very badly off even on the short term. When important elements in the current situation are not known, when observed changes are not understood and there is no means of clearing up questions about them, an area of uncertainty is immediately introduced into the forecast. On the other hand, when the current situation is fully understood, its elements of strength and weakness analyzed, and the changes currently taking place fully revealed, an accurate forecast of the immediate future is practically at hand, and the basis for appraising longer-term prospects is tremendously improved.

It is not merely a question of having some knowledge of the economy and of the relations between various phases of economic activity. The knowledge must be definite and quantitative. It is not sufficient to know that there are certain tendencies toward expansion and others toward decline. The quantitative balance between these tendencies is precisely the item of information needed.

Examples illustrating one tendency or the other can never provide a sufficient basis for deciding what the situation really is. There are always examples that can illustrate practically any point, even the contrary of what is then taking place. For example, on days of acute crisis in the stock market, when the most extreme breaks were taking place, as in the fall of 1929, there were always some stocks that moved up against the trend. As an expository technique it may be quite desirable to present examples, but as a method of analysis the use of examples illustrating the particular forces or tendencies at work is hopelessly inadequate.

Sometimes it is known that changes in particular segments are likely to occur, and such knowledge is helpful in understanding the general situation. But as a rule it is not helpful just to know that something or other is going to change, for only by getting at the changes in quantitative terms can one assess their value for forecasting purposes.

Insistence on definition and measurement does not mean that there has to be a whole series of censuses before a forecast can be made or even that any new data have to be compiled at all. On the contrary, the information available for this purpose today is much better than ever before. There is a great variety of statistical series relating to the important phases of economic activity.

It is true that some of the available series are only partial, covering only a limited portion of the activity measured. Also some are not entirely accurate, and perhaps they cannot be made so, because of the conditions of reporting or other factors that restrict the operations of the organization compiling them. Sometimes they are based on samples too small to give entirely dependable results. Yet with all their disadvantages, even the weaker statistical series may be useful in giving estimates well within the tolerable margins of error.

The important thing is not that any statistical series should be perfectly accurate and dependable but rather that its imperfections should be understood and that these should not be of such a magnitude as to invalidate the more inclusive totals into which they enter. Knowing that certain defects exist should be sufficient to put the analyst on guard.

Difficulties with the statistical record will never be entirely eliminated, but this fact should not divert the analyst from insistence on the use of statistics and quantitative methods. Use of such methods in no sense implies that each and every phase of economic activity must be measured in detail or that all the detailed segments must be regularly considered in working out an over-all forecast. Such an approach could end only in confusion, with the analyst bogged down in a welter of detail. Consider the numerous statistical series available in such publications as *Survey of Current Business,* the *Federal Reserve Bulletin* and the *Monthly Labor Review,* and it will be apparent that there are more statistical series than can be effectively used. The releases of the government alone present more material than the average person can assimilate. In addition there are a good many private organizations and state- and local-government agencies that put out statistics of relevance to some aspects of the business situation. There are also innumerable items reported in the press just as a matter of business interest.

Anyone concerning himself with all this detail as a regular routine will never arrive at valid conclusions about the general situation. Certainly any sound conclusions he does reach will not be founded on his observations of detail but rather on his ability to pick out the important points and analyze them without regard to all the other detail coming to his attention.

Detail is useful only as it fits into and makes up part of a coordinated whole. This is true even of the specific series that are commonly billed as good barometers of business. In the past any number of specific series —such as the price of iron and steel scrap—have been used this way. Such business barometers may have some validity for a time, but at best they provide a shaky kind of basis for appraising the situation; and when the situation changes in some relevant aspect, they may lose their validity entirely. They can be considered valid only as long as they are understood in the light of the situation that makes them behave as they do. If they have to be depended upon as the sole basis for understanding the situation, the forecaster will be just as much at sea as the barometer is —and any barometer is subject to unusual fluctuations.

As a general rule, therefore, it may be stated that the best procedure is one which analyzes the economy in terms not of all its parts but merely of its most important parts and which falls back upon investigation of detail only to the extent that it is needed for understanding the behavior of the more important major segments.

Occasions when detail has to be studied to obtain answers to specific questions usually occur when some particular economic problem has temporarily assumed unusual importance, so that it may be necessary to get the answer to a specific problem in order to clarify the broader developments that have been observed. There are innumerable sources of variation in each major segment. There are also many changes produced by interrelationships among subsegments of the major segments, and many of these could not be fully described in terms of the totals. Data that take account of the interrelations, that automatically relate the parts of the expenditure stream to each other and to the whole, are by their nature preferable to any detailed collection of facts; no matter how comprehensive. The facts themselves must be known, but they must be fitted together in a logical manner that systematically brings out their significance for the entire economy as it is portrayed in a few broad measures of activity.

It takes only limited experience in economic analysis to realize that no single set of statistical data can satisfy all the criteria of usefulness or meet all the needs of analysts working in this field. It could not, for example, be both up to the minute and wholly accurate. Moreover, each problem, each new situation, presents its own special questions, which can be answered only in terms of data suitable to the occasion. The most that can be asked of any set of data is that it should have substantial validity with reference to all the problems ordinarily dealt with. Data of this kind may be termed *general-purpose* or *basic data*. In practice, basic data constantly have to be supplemented with more timely or other special data that meet the specific needs of the occasion.

The detail must also, of course, be available at all times as the raw material for making up the more comprehensive and significant aggregates upon which judgments and forecasts may be based. Fortunately, most of the detail work necessary in constructing basic measures of activity is being done by the agencies that compile such over-all statistics as the national income, the index of industrial production, and the indexes of wholesale and consumer prices. The numerous subseries included in such comprehensive measures are constantly being worked up, adjusted in various ways, and assigned a reasonably proper weight in the composition of the total. Ordinarily the forecaster will do well to leave these phases of data handling to the statisticians trained and regularly employed in that work.

From the agencies that perform such work the forecaster gets not only the total measure but also usually some statement of the particular segments which account for the changes in the total and perhaps even some explanation for the changes in those segments. He can even draw upon the specific knowledge of the specialists. In the event that there are some peculiarities in the reported statistics or that relevant detail is lacking, he may be able to obtain the answers to his specific question by making inquiries of the reporting agency.

In brief, the basic informational need for forecasting consists of dependable, quantitative data on various aspects of the economic situation. These data should cover the economy as a whole, but with detail related to the major parts of the economy which represent important sources of change, and they should in so far as possible organize the various segments of the total in a way that is meaningful for analytical purposes. This means, in essence, that each segment should be so presented as to bring out its relationships to the total and to the other segments which its movements affect or by which they are affected. Beyond this, it is necessary only that additional information should be available for use on the occasions when specific problems are encountered that can only be solved by resorting to detail that is not an integral part of the regular forecasting procedure.

NATIONAL-INCOME AND GROSS-PRODUCT DATA

Judged in the light of these criteria, the best general-purpose data available for forecasting are the gross-national-product and national-income data compiled by the Department of Commerce. It is recognized that designating any data as best, or basic, for forecasting implies a method or procedure of forecasting in which such data can be effectively used. The validity of any kind of data is clearly dependent upon the forecaster's ability to get results from them. What is basic from one point of view is not necessarily so from another.

The procedure implicit in the present discussion is that of broad, common-sense analysis of economic developments. For other forecasting methods, other data suitable to those methods are needed. This an analysis of leads and lags involves the use of sensitive indicators, and a projection of cycles involves data with as dependable a cyclical movement as possible. In each case data of the relevant character would be considered basic by the forecasters using them. Discussion of such methods may be postponed to subsequent chapters, but it may here be stated merely that these alternative procedures have weaknesses inherent in the partial character of their approach to the forecasting problem.

One of the reasons the national-income and product data are considered basic for the present approach is that they are the most comprehensive measures of economic activity. They present a complete accounting of the money flows that take place in connection with the production of real goods and services. These money flows are presented in their dual aspect—first, as measures of the values of goods and services produced and, second, as incomes to the individuals, business firms, and other organizations producing them. Table 2–1 presents these totals in this dual form: the column on the left shows the total goods and services produced; that on the right shows the disposition of income and other receipts derived from production and sale of those goods and services.

The dual aspect of money flows derives from the fact that every payment is also a receipt. A payment made by one person for goods or services is a receipt of income by another person who furnishes those goods or services, and the money payment is assumed to measure the value of the items transferred. The gross-national-product data in the left-hand column of Table 2–1 summarize payments or expenditures according to the objects for which payment is made. The income data in the right-hand column distribute the same total value considered as receipts. A receipt by any one person is a reimbursement for the goods and services he supplies, but part of it may go to others, who supplied materials or labor, and thus becomes income to them. Ultimately all of it appears as income except the portions reserved for taxes or for replacement of the capital equipment used up in the process of production. Together the two distributions represent a kind of double-entry accounting.

In compiling the gross national product, only the value of final products is included, in order to eliminate duplication. Raw materials like steel and components or parts like bearings, gears, engines, and wheels are included in the value of the final product into whose make-up they

Table 2–1.   National Income and Product Account, 1954*

In billions of dollars

Expenditures or product		Income and charges	
Personal-consumption expenditures	$236.5	National income	$299.7
Durable goods	29.3	Wages and salaries	196.2
Nondurable goods	120.9	Supplementary labor income	11.7
Services	86.4	Proprietor's income†	$ 37.9
Gross private domestic investment	$ 47.2	Business and professional	25.9
		Farm	12.0
Residential construction......	13.5	Rental income of persons	10.5
Nonresidential construction	14.3	Net interest	9.5
Producers' durable equipment	22.3	Corporate profits†	$ 33.8
Change in business inventories	$−2.9	Corporate profits before tax	$ 34.0
Farm	−3.2	Tax liability	17.1
Nonfarm	0.4	Dividends	10.0
		Undistributed profits	7.0
Net foreign investment	−0.3	Corporate-inventory-revaluation adjustment	−0.2
Government purchases of goods and services	$ 77.0	Indirect business taxes‡	31.6
Federal	49.2	Capital-consumption allowances	30.0
Less government sales	0.4	Statistical discrepancy	−0.8
State and local	27.8	Charges against gross national product	$360.5
Gross national product	$360.5		

* Details do not necessarily add to totals because of rounding.

† Adjusted for inventory revaluation.

‡ Includes business-transfer payments and current surplus of government corporations minus subsidies.

SOURCE: *Survey of Current Business*, July, 1955.

go, except to the extent that they accumulate as inventories. If the items used were separately counted at earlier stages, when they were sold to producers who converted them into other products, most materials and many of the bits and pieces would be counted several times.

The total unduplicated value obtained in this way is gross in the sense that it includes something more than the net return to the producers engaged in the processes of making and delivering things to their final users. There are two reasons for this. First, productive processes consume capital in the form of plant, equipment, and other productive facilities. The expense involved in the gradual wearing out of these capital items has to be charged against the things produced, and this is usually done by business in the form of depreciation charges; but these charges could be allocated to the various final products making up the total only with difficulty, so that the result would at best be only a modification of what is in its present form a very useful measure of economic activity. An alternative way of looking at this matter regards part, or even all, of the equipment and other capital items produced each year as replacements of existing worn-out facilities rather than as new production. But there is no way to distinguish replacement items from similar new goods, and there is no correspondence between the total real capital used up and the new capital produced in any given year. So the "gross" measure which includes all the new capital produced is in many ways a clearer concept.

Second, the prices at which things are sold to final users include taxes on the goods produced or the facilities producing them, and these taxes frequently cannot be segregated from the price as such, or even allocated to one group of products rather than another. Such taxes are not properly a part of value produced in the narrower sense, but since they cannot be readily segregated with respect to the various types of product, it is easier and more straightforward to adopt the measurable total in which they are included as the gross national product.

It will be noted from Table 2–1 that the two items just discussed—capital-consumption allowances and indirect business taxes—appear in the right-hand column as "charges" against gross product and make up most of the difference between gross national product and national income. One other item in the difference between gross national product and national income may be called to attention at this point—that is, the statistical discrepancy. Except for this item, which is merely the difference between the total of all the items above it in the table and the gross national product, all the items are independently measured or estimated. In compiling such a variety of statistics from literally a multitude of sources, each of which is subject to some error, it must be expected that the final results will fall short of complete agreement. The amount of the discrepancy is carried as a means of balancing the two sides of the account.

On the income side, the approach is to make a complete accounting of the earnings of everyone receiving legitimate payment for his services or for use of things he owns. Such activities as gambling and such various kinds of distinctly antisocial activities as robbery and fraud, though they may be profitable to the people engaging in them, are excluded as not being productive. Some of these payments or receipts could not enter into the statistics on the product side but might be reported as income in conformity with the income tax laws. Even if reported, however, the sources of such income probably could not be identified, making it virtually impossible to obtain a strict segregation of economic income from gains obtained in noneconomic pursuits.

It should be clear from this that the line between things included in these general measures and things excluded is necessarily fuzzy; but although this may leave room for debate about the theoretical validity of the results, it creates no great practical problem, since the important condition for the forecaster is merely that a consistent approach be used throughout.

On the income side also it is necessary to eliminate duplications, though by definition of income as net income most of the problem is taken care of automatically. The income earner who incurs certain costs in the process deducts them from his total receipts, and double counting of these payments, which appear as income earned in earlier stages of production, is thus excluded.

Each February the Department of Commerce publishes an annual review number of the *Survey of Current Business*, which gives the previous year's national-income and gross-product data by quarters, in a preliminary summary with somewhat greater detail than that shown in Table 2–1. Then in each succeeding quarter these figures are brought up to date by the addition of data for the preceding quarter. The data published quarterly do not present all the detail of the accounts but are confined mainly to the major breakdowns of income and product. Those major breakdowns present enough detail to work with on an interim basis.

Each July the Department of Commerce publishes the National Income Number of the *Survey*, which includes the full details of these statistics for the preceding year. It provides "final" quarterly figures, which take account of any revisions since the publication of the preliminary data, as well as the annual totals. In all, about 50 tables are required for the presentation of the full detail. Many of the subsidiary tables are of service primarily in bringing certain detail up to date and in straightening out certain questions never answered by the quarterly data. For the most part, they are not current enough for use in making forecasts.

From time to time, even the annual estimates previously published have to be revised on the basis of later information. Periodic compilations of basic statistics commonly termed "bench marks," such as the census of business reports and the income tax returns, are available only after a long lag, and they usually reveal that the situation in the years to which they apply was different in some respects from what it had previously been thought to be. Usually these revisions affect the data for only a few recent years. The basic series for earlier years have developed to the point where there is practically no untapped source of additional information.

Progress through the years has meant that changes in concepts and manner of presentation as well as in specific data have had to be made, and some further changes of this kind are contemplated. However, the present annual series, which go back to 1929, may be regarded as essentially stable both in concept and in content. They cover all the activities that change significantly over periods appropriate for realistic economic analysis; and although not all are measured with equal adequacy, the over-all results portray the pattern of change in the broad stream of economic affairs adequately for most purposes.

The fact that these data are so comprehensive is just one of the reasons why they are basic for forecasting purposes. Their completeness is, of course, an important fact in itself. It provides the only assurance that all sources of change are taken into account. But the manner of taking things into account is also important, and it is in this respect that the other advantages of national-income and product data are revealed.

Not only do these data cover all the important aspects of economic activity, but also they bring in each segment on an adjusted basis, to ensure as far as possible that each series has the essential qualities of good statistics. These adjustments are designed to make the various segments of the total consistent in concept and comparable over extended periods of time. This does not mean that there are not compromises in both concept and comparability; it merely means that the compromises do not affect the working validity of the data as analytical tools. Any alternative compilation of similar scope would involve similar compromises.

The importance of the adjustments becomes quickly evident to anyone engaged in quantitative economic analysis. Any number of false conclusions have been reached because invalid comparisons or relationships were involved in unsound statistics. In the present instance, the peculiarities and problems of measurement involved in compilation of these data may on the whole be disregarded for forecasting purposes. Sharp shifts that would invalidate comparisons or introduce false impressions are practically excluded. Within their limits in time, the national-income data provide reasonable assurance against such difficulties.

Another source of advantage in these data derives from the almost unlimited possibilities of working out meaningful relationships between the various segments, between particular segments and the whole, and between either the totals or the segments and statistical series obtained from other sources. The relationships are partly built into the data, by reason of the way they are constructed: outputs and efforts that produce them are immediately identified as part of the same process. Other relationships derive from the fact that the data describe all forms of economic activity in money terms. Being in the universal terminology of dollar values, the data embrace all the aspects of activity that help to make up values—such as physical units of output, prices, wage rates, employment, and man-hours of labor. Hence any segment of the total of particular interest to the forecaster can be further analyzed by relating it to other economic measures. There is sufficient detail, particularly as regards all the important segments of the total, so that any independently derived statistics on an important segment can be brought into relationship with its income or product counterpart and thus with the whole.

Finally, the data provide a number of analytical advantages arising from the fact that they are constructed from the standpoint of the goals of human action. In economic terms, these goals are expressed most clearly in terms of the end products that comprise the gross national product and the income that conveys the power of command over such end products. How this point of view provides an effective approach for the forecaster will be explained in detail in succeeding chapters. At this point two important points may be stated without elaboration. First, analysis in these terms is almost inevitably directed toward the important sources of change. Second, the requirement that the accounts must be balanced forces internal consistency in the over-all results and protects against certain kinds of errors.

There are, of course, weaknesses in these data, as there are bound to be in any comprehensive statistics. The weaknesses are in a sense beyond remedy, being tied up with important points of strength. The most important weakness, lack of timeliness, derives from limitations imposed by the task of compiling and making meaningful a mass of diverse statistics. Another weakness, the possibility of interim error, derives from the requirement of completeness, since some of the original data needed are inadequate or long delayed.

As stated above, timeliness is the most important weakness, even though the data are much more timely than they used to be. Compiling all these statistics and making all the adjustments that are necessary to put them in the form in which they are finally released is a time-consuming process. Results are necessarily delayed until the basic data come in, and allowance has to be made for variation in the time when tabulations are received. Then additional time is required for processing the data and preparing reports for publication.

The mere fact that all but limited parts of the data are available only quarterly is itself a serious handicap with respect to timeliness. With quarterly data, it sometimes takes over half a year to discover that a reversal has occurred. For example, suppose a certain measure has been going down rapidly but turns up moderately in the last month of a quarter. The quarter as a whole will, of course, be lower than the preceding quarter; and if the decline through the first 2 months was rapid and the subsequent upturn was comparatively slow, the succeeding quarter may well average lower, even though each month in that quarter was higher than the preceding month. In such a case, not until data for the third quarter are in, some 7 or 8 months after the actual turning point, will the reversal be definitely revealed. Some protection against such a development is afforded by the fact that a major component of total income—personal income—is available monthly.

Even in the absence of an unusual development of this kind, quarterly data are too slow for best results. The forecaster must be sensitive to new developments in their early stages if he is to avoid being left in an exposed position at times through lag alone. An illustration may be found in the *Report of the Council of Economic Advisers* of January, 1949. This report was prepared in the preceding quarter, largely on the basis of discussions beginning in the summer months, and its main focus was the inflationary situation prevailing up to that autumn. When it was made public in January, however, the situation had changed drastically, and some of the recommendations were already outdated.

Other weaknesses in the national-income and product data relate mainly to problems of the availability of original data and consequent inaccuracies in preliminary reports. Current statistics are not available on all the activities included in these totals. When minor series come in too late to meet publication deadlines, or when they are available only annually, and then perhaps only after a long lag, it is necessary to make estimates to fill in the gaps, since the data are necessarily published as complete totals. In some instances such provisional estimates have to be made on a very sketchy basis. To the extent that there are elements of guesswork in them, there are bound to be errors, and it is possible that at times these may mislead. This would be particularly true when specific segments being forecast were dependent upon the data in question. On the whole, however, it represents a minor problem to the general forecaster, one that need be given only occasional attention.

Effective use of the data is also complicated by the major revisions that have to be made from time to time as new data become available. In less than a year after the publication of the basic 1951 *National Income* supplement, data for 1949 and 1950 had to be revised on the basis of new source material—particularly the Bureau of Internal Revenue tabulation of 1949 income tax returns. Since some of these sources are consistently very late, this is a recurring problem.

A study conducted in 1950 by the Federal Reserve Bank of New York compared preliminary estimates of the gross national product with the final data for the years 1945 to 1948. The study revealed that revisions were consistently small on such large, relatively stable aggregates as personal income but were large on such hard-to-measure items as personal savings and business investment. Of 64 items examined, 25 showed a revision of 10 percent or more in at least 1 year of the 4. Some of the largest revisions occurred in gross-private-domestic-investment items, particularly inventories, which are of key importance to the forecaster. These facts point up the need for caution in using even the best statistics.

The revisions create a secondary nuisance at times because they may make it necessary to reformulate an entire forecast. But it is clearly better to undertake the necessary work than to risk the errors into which inaccurate data may lead one. Moreover, forecasting itself is essentially a continuous process, requiring modification and adjustment with each change in the economic scene. Correcting a forecast to take account of revisions in the basic data is therefore as much a part of the forecaster's task as is correcting a forecast to take account of new developments whenever the situation has proved different in any significant aspect from what was anticipated.

TIMELY DATA ON CURRENT DEVELOPMENTS

One of the first problems of current analysis is to "forecast" the present. It is necessary to foretell what the current situation will prove to be after data are available to define it adequately. The quarterly income and product data, when first issued, are themselves estimates of this provisional character; they attempt to predict what the final estimates will be after all possible information is in. But in current analysis, it is necessary to move ahead of the preliminary quarterly estimates. This has to be done, in general, by methods similar to those used by the Department of Commerce in moving the quarterly data ahead of the annual, and the annual ahead of the periodic bench marks. Monthly or weekly data related to various important components are used to give provisional indications or clues to what is happening, but of necessity there remain large elements of prediction in the forecaster's first knowledge of what the current situation may be.

A variety of series, some monthly, some weekly, can be used to keep the forecaster up to date on what is happening. They reveal changes or tendencies that would not become apparent for some time in the national-income and product data. From them, any number of inferences can be drawn in the interim before the next basic quarterly accounting of our economic position is available. Foremost among the comprehensive measures of activity available promptly are the monthly personal-income series, the employment and unemployment data published by the Bureau of the Census and the Department of Labor, and the Federal Reserve Board's Index of Industrial Production. Still more timely are a number of significant weekly indexes, such as electric-power production, freight-car loadings, and wholesale prices. All of these, and others, are used by analysts as general indicators, or "barometers," for keeping pace with the latest developments.

In addition to utilizing these general indicators, it is desirable to keep current on changes in all the major components of gross national product. For this purpose, a good deal of supporting data is available, such as retail sales, construction contracts, inventories, and foreign trade. These statistics not only are more current but also in many cases provide a basis for understanding why the major components of gross national product are moving as they are. The following brief summary is not intended to be complete, either in coverage or in detail, but is intended merely to give selective comments on the nature and usefulness of some of the more important current statistics available.[1]

The Monthly Personal-Income Series. This series has already been mentioned as an important indicator of the interim movements of total income and product. The personal-income data not only show the total flow of money income into personal accounts but also provide a break-down of the total by source. It is a limited breakdown but a useful one. It not only divides the total into various types of income, such as wages, proprietors' income, dividends, and transfer payments, but also divides total wages into the major segments of the economy in which they are earned.

Personal income differs from national income by excluding the items in national income that are not directly paid to individuals and by including certain payments for which there is no corresponding contribution to production. The former items consist of social security contributions, by both employer and employee, and corporate profits other than those paid as dividends. The latter consist of net interest paid by government and transfer payments, which are made up of such "unearned" income as social security and veterans' benefits, relief payments, gifts to nonprofit institutions, and individuals' bad debts to business.

The only serious difficulty in translating personal income into national income is the lack of data on corporate profits. This is a deficiency of the current national-income and product data generally, as corporate-

---

[1] A more extended discussion with charts portraying past movements of the various series may be found in *Selected Economic Indicators*, Federal Reserve Bank of New York, New York, 1954.

profits data are ordinarily omitted from preliminary reports and do not become available until a full quarter later. Nevertheless, some preliminary estimates of this item may be obtained from scattered reports and from movements of sales and price indexes (see Chapter 17). Such estimates must be used carefully, with some judgment, since this is one of the most difficult items to forecast. Assuming that a satisfactory estimate can be worked out, the over-all movement of national income is fairly well portrayed by adjusting personal income. The other items needed to complete the translation from personal income to national income either are known or are fairly stable and can be estimated with reasonable accuracy over the short term (see Chapter 13).

The Combined Employment and Unemployment Release. This publication, issued by the Bureau of the Census and the Department of Labor, is outstanding in usefulness, not only because the information it contains is so important but also because it is so timely. It is available almost a month before either the personal-income statistics or the production index. This is possible because of the fact that it is really a compilation of weekly data covering the week or payroll period ending nearest the 15th of each month. This report presents data from three major sources—the Census Bureau's monthly survey of the labor force, the Bureau of Labor Statistics' compilation of industrial-payroll statistics, and the Bureau of Employment Security's unemployment-insurance statistics.

The Census Bureau's *Monthly Report on the Labor Force* is based on personal interviews with a representative sample of households to obtain information on the employment status of the adult population. It shows how many of the entire population fourteen years and over are in the labor force, dividing them between active workers, other jobholders, and the unemployed; it also divides those not in the labor force between housekeepers, students attending school, and others who for one reason or another cannot or do not wish to work. The survey is based on a rather limited sample—about 35,000 households in 330 areas—and obtains answers to only a limited number of questions, so that results for the week containing the 8th day of the month can be processed and released near the end of the month.

The unemployment figure is widely used as a basic indicator of the economic state of health of the nation. It is sensitive because any change in employment usually results in a much larger percentage change in unemployment. Unemployment is in a sense a residual from the much larger labor force and employment totals, and absolute changes in these over-all aggregates are large when considered in relation to the residual. The unemployment estimate is not actually computed in this way, of course, being reported by the unemployed or by the family member interviewed—usually the housewife, who is at home when the interviewer calls.

Reasons for important changes are given in the initial releases, where it may be stated, for example, that an increase in unemployment was due to bad weather, which prevented outside work, and consequently should not be interpreted as a decline that will continue. Small changes may be of little or no significance, since potential errors are substantial. The probable magnitude of sampling errors is clearly indicated in the reports, but there is no basis for judging response errors. Moreover, partial sample changes are made every month, and these introduce an element of erratic variation into the data which may lead to difficulty of interpretation on occasion. The survey provides a fairly accurate and sensitive indication of changes in employment, but not in sufficient detail for analytical purposes.

Better suited to such needs are the employment data compiled from industry reports by the Bureau of Labor Statistics. These cover a long list of manufacturing industries and, somewhat less adequately, major non-manufacturing activities. Each month's reports are obtained from a large sample of cooperating establishments, covering manufacturing industries to the extent of roughly two-thirds of all production workers and other lines of business not so adequately but on the whole fairly well.

The value of the employment data as such is greatly enhanced by co-ordinate reports on hours of work, payrolls, and wage rates, though only hours of work are reported in the initial release. The full details on employment and the other items of information are available only after a considerable time lag, apparently as a result of unavoidable delays in obtaining and compiling the reports. Nevertheless, appraisal of the character of over-all changes first reported in the preliminary releases may have to await this more detailed information.

The unemployment-claims data published by the Bureau of Employment Security represent a regular weekly series, based on the unemployment-compensation program, and they provide the earliest reports on changes in unemployment. The worker who becomes unemployed must file a claim before he can draw benefits. When the number of such claims rises, it indicates that unemployment is increasing. The new-claims data may be taken in conjunction with continuing claims, that is, the total number of workers who are claiming compensation for unemployment which is continuing into the week of the report. In periods when there is a distinct change in unemployment, these reports give somewhat of an advance indication of what the Census Bureau's monthly reports will show.

The difficulty with these data is that they display erratic movements deriving from the administrative rules by which the unemployment-insurance program is governed. Compensation ends after a limited period of weeks, usually 26, and then ineligible claimants are removed from the rolls, so that the number of continuing claims no longer advances even though unemployment is still rising. Subsequently, many of those discontinued may be restored to the rolls as soon as a new benefit year begins, and the number of claims will then advance, even though no change in unemployment has occurred. Movements of this kind must be watched for in interpreting these data.

Production Data. The Federal Reserve Index of Industrial Production is another fairly sensitive indicator of over-all changes. It is strategic because the amplitude of short-term fluctuations in the industrial sector is much greater than in the rest of the economy and its movements usually carry the rest of the economy along. The monthly reports include not only the combined index and its major components—durable and nondurable manufacturing and mineral production—but also a detailed list of component series that go into the make-up of those major indexes. Weights are assigned in accordance with the value added by manufacture in each industry for which production data are available.

The monthly index is based on about 175 individual statistical series that vary greatly in quality and timeliness. Coverage also varies greatly, and in many areas information on end products is lacking. A good many of the component series do not represent physical units of production but rather man-hours or materials consumption, and these are types of data that require special adjustment to represent physical units of production. Inasmuch as the necessary adjustments cannot be well founded over short periods of time, the portrayal of changes in physical volume is imperfect. Despite these difficulties, however, the index is a very useful short-run indicator of general activity, one that is widely relied upon as a basic barometer of business.

Each year the index is adjusted to take advantage of the fact that annual statistics are available in much greater volume than usable monthly series. The annual data in many cases provide bench marks to which the monthly series are adjusted, and the coverage in terms of direct production data is improved.

The movements of the components may at times give information of greater importance than the movements of the total. They reveal points of unusual strength or weakness in industrial activity and thus may suggest hypotheses about future developments or provide a quantitative basis for appraising hypotheses originating in other sources.

Still greater timeliness in production information may be obtained from a number of weekly series available from various sources. Among the most important of these are steel, automobiles, electric power, coal, petroleum, lumber, and paper products. The electric-power series is of

special significance as a general indicator because the use of electricity
is so pervasive throughout the economy. Freight-car loadings are not
production figures in the usual sense but are often included in weekly
indexes of activity. Their significance has dwindled greatly over a quarter of a century as traffic has shifted from the railroads to the highways.

Indexes compiled from data of this kind are published each week by
Business Week, Barron's, and *The New York Times.* Such indexes can
be effectively used in predicting the movements of the more comprehensive Federal Reserve index. Chart 2–1 shows the relationship between
The New York Times weekly index and the Federal Reserve monthly
index during the postwar period.

Price Indexes. These are the third important type of data commonly
used as indicators of general economic changes. Prices are not, of course,
a measure of activity as such, but are rather a measure of the relationship between the flow of goods and services and the funds being spent
on those goods and services. Nonetheless, they provide a sensitive and
early indication of changes in businessmen's attitudes concerning the
general outlook. Prices move most rapidly when businessmen anticipate
cost changes and abandon the usual caution in their buying and selling
activities. The movements of the price indexes may therefore be taken
as one of the best indicators of changes in business attitudes that will
affect such important activities as investment in new facilities or changes
in inventories.

Perhaps the most useful of the price indexes are the wholesale price
indexes of the Bureau of Labor Statistics. These indexes are available
both monthly and weekly. The weekly series is prepared from a much
smaller sample of prices—200 as compared with over 2,000 in the
monthly index—but provides a fairly accurate indication of the comprehensive movements.

The history of this weekly series provides an illustration of how better
results can be obtained by critical selection of data than by massive accumulation of detail. In revising this index in 1949, the Bureau
of Labor Statistics greatly reduced the number of component prices. As
a result of more careful selection of the items included and the omission
of those that tended to overrepresent special influences, the short-term
movements of the weekly index were made more representative of
changes in the comprehensive monthly index than before. In using the
weekly index as an indicator of current changes, attention should be
directed toward finding out what is making the index move and not
merely what its movement happens to be.

An even greater degree of analytical caution is needed in using daily
or weekly indexes of sensitive commodity prices which represent a limited group of industrial raw materials, farm products, imports, and the

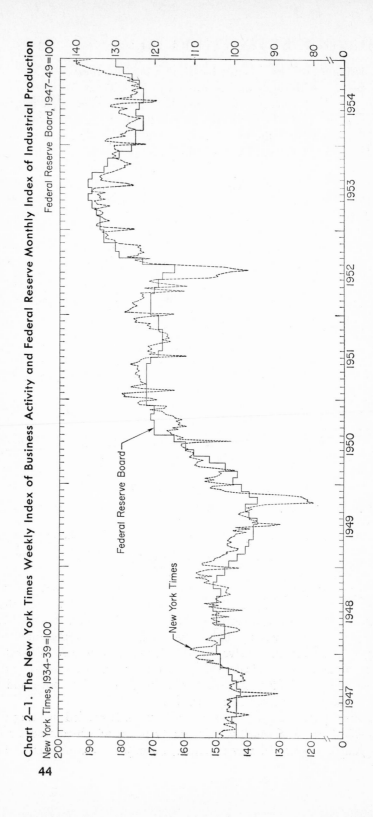

Chart 2–1. The New York Times Weekly Index of Business Activity and Federal Reserve Monthly Index of Industrial Production

New York Times, 1934-39=100

Federal Reserve Board, 1947-49=100

44

like, whose prices fluctuate widely. In these indexes each commodity is heavily weighted, and by the nature of such commodities explosive movements may occur in individual prices or groups. The index as a whole tends, therefore, to be rather unstable and may on occasion move in ways that are of little or no general significance.

In contrast, consumer or retail-price indexes tend to be too stable and slow moving to perform the functions of a good indicator. There are other uses for such indexes, of course, such as deflating consumption expenditures to obtain a measure of the physical volume of goods flowing to consumers. Even in this respect, however, the analyst finds himself less well off than first impressions of the wealth of price data would lead one to believe. Coverage has been deficient in many areas, particularly durable goods and services, and quoted prices of such items as automobiles often deviate widely from the actual charge to the buyer, when trade-ins, discounts, installment terms, and other considerations are taken into account. The field of price information is one on which attention was early focused, providing the most comprehensive statistical records over a long period of years, but various shortcomings in the early data, many of which were perhaps unavoidable, illustrate the need for an analytical framework to guide statistical compilations by reference to the way the final data are to be used.

Bank Loans, Prices, Orders, and Inventories. Weekly data on bank loans combine with price changes to provide a kind of rough early indication of changes in inventory policy. Bank loans in some respects represent a kind of counterpart to inventories, being the immediate resort when funds are needed to finance the accumulation of inventories. In other words, business commonly borrows from the banks as a means of financing inventory expansion, and such loans are paid off when inventories are liquidated.

Changes in inventory holdings are also likely to be reflected quickly in wholesale commodity prices, as indicated above. Any increase in demand for most sensitive commodities immediately tends to push prices up, and if demand falls because business wishes to reduce inventories, weakening of prices in these markets quickly occurs.

There is a kind of inherent instability in the data on inventory changes, arising from the role of inventories as the immediate equalizer compensating differences in rates of production and consumption, and for this reason only limited reliance should be placed upon an abrupt change reported in any one month. If a sharp inventory change occurs, the forecaster will want quickly to investigate the possibility of a change in inventory policy, because both erratic and more basic changes may take place with disconcerting suddenness. From this point of view, the most adequate current indications may sometimes be obtained from data other than inventories themselves.

Prices, being the most readily adjustable of all these items, reflect such changes most quickly—though it should be recognized that not all price changes are the result of changes in inventory policy. On the other hand, commercial loans more clearly coincide in timing with the actual movements of inventories, because inventory policy cannot be made effective immediately, and for a time inventories may even run contrary to policy if consumer purchases change rapidly. In the usual case, however, if prices turn up, followed shortly by business loans, inventories are or will soon be moving in the same direction (see Chart 2–2). Hence some of the best immediate clues to inventory policy may be obtained from these sources.

The monthly estimates of manufacturers' new orders, sales, and inventories compiled by the Department of Commerce must be included in any discussion of timely indicators. Although these data go back only to 1939, their value as a current business indicator has been demonstrated. The inventory series is a basic contribution in this field. The new-orders series has the value of an advance indicator in an important area, bearing a direct relation to future production, and it is therefore given close attention by industry analysts.

More complete reports on the book value of business inventories are also issued monthly by the Department of Commerce, which brings together the available information from other sources, such as the Federal Reserve data on department-store inventories. The samples on which these reports are based are not entirely satisfactory but appear to give a fairly good indication of inventory changes. A more serious difficulty in using them arises from the fact that they are book-value figures rather than value of physical-volume changes similar to those included in the gross-national-product totals. A method of adjusting to the latter basis is described in Chapter 7, but the result is necessarily rough, providing only a general indication of current changes.

The data on new and unfilled orders for durable manufactures are widely used as indicators of prospective business changes. The relationship between sales and orders provides a measure of the need for adjustment of current operations and at times gives definite warning of changes in rates of activity in this important segment of the economy.

Manufacturers' sales and orders represent useful measures of interim and prospective changes in output of producers' durable equipment, which is one of the weakest areas in the current statistical picture. These data are reported for corporations whose major products are electrical machinery, other machinery, motor vehicles, and other transportation equipment. In the postwar period, they have been relied upon as a basis for interim estimates of producers' expenditures for durable equipment included in the gross national product. However, the data have to

Chart 2–2. Business Inventories, Bank Loans, and Wholesale Prices

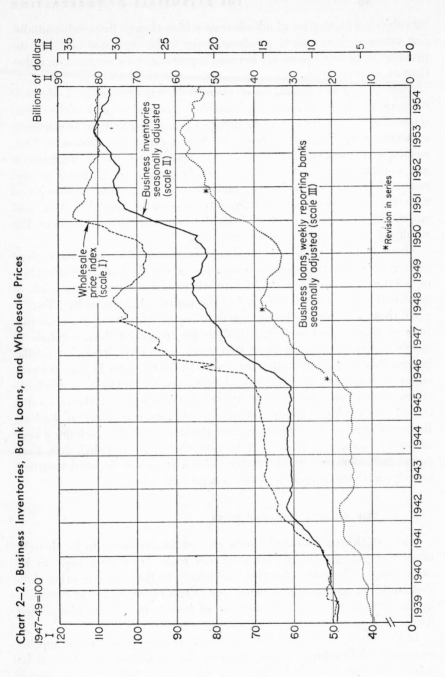

be subjected to a series of adjustments which change them substantially. For example, government purchases have to be separated out, and the problem is made more severe because reports are on a corporation rather than an industry basis.

Another advance indication of changes in this component is obtained on a quarterly basis from the survey of planned capital outlays conducted by the Securities and Exchange Commission and the Department of Commerce. The survey result itself is a projection subject to forecasting errors and does not make the separation between construction and equipment. Nevertheless, it is widely used as an indicator of current activity in this field. New and unfilled orders may be compared with the projections obtained from the survey of capital outlays, and where the indications received from the two sources are consistent, the result may be accepted as conclusive.

These and other statistical indicators are useful in keeping current with general developments on a monthly or weekly basis. Consideration of a number of additional series relating to the major components of gross national product is deferred to the various chapters of Part Two.

All these statistical series are listed as important tools for the economic forecaster. For quick review, it is desirable to receive them regularly in graphic form. For this purpose, two government chart books are available monthly. *Economic Indicators,* prepared for the Joint Economic Committee of Congress by the Council of Economic Advisers, is available on an annual subscription basis. It contains practically all the series discussed above plus a number of others. The other publication, *Federal Reserve Chart Book on Financial and Business Statistics,* includes a very useful historical supplement. It is somewhat more detailed than *Economic Indicators* and in addition contains a wealth of financial statistics, more than is usually needed by the general forecaster.

THE SEARCH FOR KEY DATA

These statistical data and charts are not in any sense to be thought of as the forecaster's sole informational tools. He cannot hope to be successful by directing attention exclusively to these or any other data that could be specified in advance, for in this changing world there can be no security in any fixed structure of knowledge or any blueprinted forecasting procedure.

As the situation changes, new problems constantly put in an appearance and relationships change. Most of the significant changes will be reflected in the basic indicators that are used to follow current developments. Some may not—at least not for overly long intervals during which decisions must be made. In other cases, the effects of changes may be so indirect and veiled that their nature is not revealed or their significance cannot be interpreted without additional information. At the outset, it may be possible only to note the occurrence of developments that are vaguely inconsistent or puzzling in some dimly understood way.

It therefore becomes an almost basic rule relating to observation of the economy, through statistical data or otherwise, that movements which are anomalous, movements that do not fit into the unfolding pattern of economic and political developments, must be investigated. Brief investigation may produce a ready explanation. On the other hand, what seemed at first a minor question may developed into an extended research project, with ramifications in lines that had not been thought to be even remotely involved.

In pursuing almost any such specific inquiry, there can be no thought of restricting the scope of the investigation. Specific questions can only be answered by the specific information appropriate to the problem. Each new situation imposes its own informational demands, and the discovery of the statistics or other information that meets those demands is the essential purpose of the investigation.

It frequently happens that needed information is not available in the desired form. This is likely to be the case in a great variety of practical problems faced by business concerns. What they are interested in depends upon the specific characteristics of their own business, with its peculiarities of product, of growth, and of relations to other businesses. These may be sufficiently unique, or so lacking in common qualities with other economic operations, that the collection of relevant data is not justified from the standpoint of more general needs. In many such cases, there may be no alternative to special surveys or other work in the field of operations, and the most effective way of conducting such necessary surveys may be to employ consultants or survey agencies specially organized for such work.

Yet it should not be assumed without investigation that collection of new data is necessary. Possibly the problem cannot be solved with current data alone but requires back data which no current survey could produce. Possibly also time limitations may preclude extensive compilations of new data. In these cases it may be that existing data can be discovered which are closely enough related to those originally desired so as to provide answers within a degree of accuracy acceptable for most practical purposes.

The process of working out a substitute for direct information becomes a kind of adventure in statistical exploration. When all the partial, scattered information that bears on the immediate problem has been brought together, the possible ways of utilizing it have to be considered. The manner in which the Federal Reserve Board utilized employment and working-hours data to fill gaps in its production index illustrates what can be done. Production data might in other cases be derived from sales records if a suitable price series is available. Volume of sales might be derived from output adjusted for changes in inventories. Or where two products are typically used or produced together, either might be derived from knowledge of the other.

Whenever indirect measures are obtained by such procedures, it is desirable to find periodic data of a direct character against which the derived series can be checked. This is in addition to the requirement that whenever an alternative utilizing such indirect measures or related data is adopted there should be some justification for using it, something to guarantee results in addition to the mere historical coincidence revealed by the past record. The nature of the specific item, the method by which it is produced, or the way in which it is used may furnish clues to the relationships that can be explored and perhaps put to use in this way. Safeguards are necessary, but the possibilities of discovery and invention are almost infinite. It is a field in which imagination and ingenuity can pay high returns.

When one speaks of imagination and ingenuity, it is obviously difficult to lay down any rules for the operation of such processes. Sometimes the solution comes as a sort of inspiration, full-blown at its conception. At other times there may be no alternative to the hard routine of plugging away at testing hypotheses—some original, others obtained by consultation or discussion—each of which must be confirmed or eliminated. Frequently, there may be no wholly satisfactory answer, so that the whole effort becomes just a matter of arriving at the best combination or compromise under the circumstances. But even such a compromise is likely to be much better than nothing at all.

Handling data in this way is not a matter of training in the use of high-powered statistical techniques, though knowledge of the principles of statistical procedure is helpful. What is mainly required is a common-sense approach to the problems and information at hand. Certain results are desired. Certain data are available. How can the latter be adapted to provide the former? If the statistics are regarded as working materials, the problem is to shape them to the need. In this as in other fields, it should be clear that a functionally satisfactory product can often be made from substitute materials.

Here again the attitude of open-minded independence that builds good judgment assists and protects the forecaster. He regards data as materials or tools of value but credits them with no more than that. For "facts" are not always what they seem. What is first perceived as incontrovertible fact may upon investigation turn out to have far different implications. Inventories may appear to remain in line with sales on a decline; but if the decline in inventories is merely the result of their being marked down to a lower market-price basis, a substantial surplus may be accumulating. Preliminary minor movements may be no more than the prelude to more important changes of a quite different character. There are innumerable cases in which partial information can be completely misleading.

Nevertheless, partial information can be, and typically must be, used in economic analysis. A good number of the series regarded as parts of our basic historical statistics are derived from such information, and the first indications of what is currently happening also consist of bits and pieces of the whole picture. The procedures that have been and are used to establish the statistical position of the whole economy apply with equal validity to the specific subsidiary segments of interest to the individual firm or forecaster.

Whenever a series is based on a sample, it is of course subject to all the errors that are involved in sampling procedure and may in addition embody the same kind of errors that would appear in a census report. In the typical situation, where the sample is judged to be satisfactory, it is simply blown up to the level of the whole population, and the straight proportionate increase needed to accomplish this in the period of the last basic report is carried forward.

Most samples, however, vary in relation to the totals they represent. If the sample of reporting units is constant, no account is taken of changes in the number of units not included in the sample, that is, the units that are properly in the whole population or universe but for one reason or another are omitted from the sample. This is one of the most typical situations in the reporting of business data. Changes in such a sample do occur from time to time. Some firms drop out as reporting units. Additional firms may be sought out, and if their cooperation can be obtained, they may be included in the sample. Even if adjustments are made for the dropping of some firms and the inclusion of others, there may be no telling in this kind of situation whether the changes reported by the firms in the sample are in line with the actual changes in the total, that is, in the population as a whole.

Where the sample of reporting units varies from month to month as well as over longer periods of time, a fairly common procedure for getting around the problem is to base the monthly changes on the reports of "identical firms," that is, to use the reports of only those firms that report in both months. The firms reporting only in the first month or only in the last are dropped, and the change may be reported as a percentage change in the total for the remaining firms. These percentage changes are then chained together to obtain a continuous series.

This procedure gives results that are similar in character to those given when a fixed sample is used but may introduce biases of its own if reporting firms consistently fail to report under special circumstances. Moreover, inconsistencies in a series of this kind may be revealed where month-to-month and year-to-year percentage changes are reported. If the month-to-month changes are chained for 12 months and then compared with the reported change from year to year, the results are sometimes found to be quite different. Over a long succession of months, it may be found that the chaining process gives results which in some periods are higher than those obtained from the year-to-year changes and which in other periods are lower. The differences may vary rather irregularly, or there may be a fixed pattern of divergence that cannot be corrected without additional information.

When a series is constructed by chaining, seasonally adjusted data may give a more valid indication than the index originally obtained in unadjusted form. The sampling and chaining processes tend to introduce spurious seasonal fluctuations. This is true both when month-to-month changes are chained from an arbitrary starting point and when year-to-year changes are chained in both directions to assumed constant monthly figures for any year in which operations were relatively stable. In either case, after a sufficient number of years has been covered, an adjustment may be made to eliminate the spurious seasonal variation, and the result may be a monthly series representing the underlying movements within each year, as well as longer-term changes, with a high degree of plausibility.

In recognition of the difficulties of maintaining accuracy in a sample of monthly reports and of obtaining cooperation from a fixed group of respondents over an extended period of time, the Census Bureau has moved away from fixed sample techniques in recent years. The reports making up the *Monthly Report on the Labor Force* involve a shift in 25 percent of the sample every month, so that no respondent is asked to report for more than 4 months at a stretch; however, a sample that has reported for 4 months is again interviewed in the same months of the following year, a procedure that holds the year-to-year changes in the sample to 50 percent and minimizes discontinuities from this source. In other surveys, concerning such topics as family formation and retail inventories, new samples are selected annually. These are then blown up to represent the entire populations from which they are derived, and the published reports include a statement of the probable sampling errors involved.

The latter method also produces difficulties for the forecaster. Even though sampling errors are small, they may importantly modify the movement from one period to the next, and it is precisely this fact that is of primary concern to the forecaster.

It is often necessary to carry an analysis back into the past by means of less dependable data than those currently available. To do this, it may be necessary to splice on a series from another source—perhaps a smaller sample, perhaps just a part of the improved recent series, or perhaps only a related series whose movements are representative enough to justify the expedient. The data may dwindle by stages as the series is pushed further and further back into the past. It is likely to be found that fewer and fewer parts of a total are covered by data of any kind or that samples become smaller and smaller.

Any series constructed in this way is obviously subject to limitations. The analysis may help to determine the degree of reliance to be placed on the data, but the mere fact that data fit a pattern called for by a certain analytical approach does not ensure their accuracy. The validity of the analysis as well as the facts upon which it is based must be checked in the broadest possible terms against other available information, nonstatistical as well as statistical; and in the absence of substantiating evidence, the entire picture presented must be regarded as hypothetical.

To the extent that the data he has constructed improve his understanding of what has happened and what is happening, the forecaster will have gained one of the keys to the future. But from a broader point of view, the advantages gained derive not from the facts as such but from the inquisitive, skeptical attitude of mind of the research analyst.

Methods of Projecting Statistical Series

As the attempt to shape available information into a meaningful pattern progresses through the successive stages of working out a forecast, it becomes apparent that judgment and information are not by themselves sufficient for the task. Judgment cannot be informed merely by being encyclopedic, and even the best statistical series are just accumulations of detail that become meaningful as they convey something more than the bare facts which they present.

Both must be supported by techniques for analyzing and integrating knowledge about economic objects and operations into a pattern in which the significant forces are viewed as a coordinated whole. Only by means of these techniques is it possible to arrange and organize the available data in such a way as to bring out the implications of their movements and their interrelationships for the future course of economic activity.

Although at some stage all the series must be combined to make the over-all forecast, many of them have to be dealt with individually. Some are important in their own right, for the specific contribution they make to the over-all result; others must be converted or adjusted in some way before their import is clear; still others must be considered in relation to each other and projected with reference to the specific movements of the related series.

In short, a comprehensive forecast inevitably requires a good deal of work with individual statistical series, or even subparts of such series. In various stages of the process, a number of analyses and projections have to be made on the basis of substantial independence for the simple reason that no over-all forecast is yet available. The basis on which these separate projections are made is likely to be of critical importance —even allowing for the fact that it is possible to adjust and correct them after the broader outlines of the forecast have been worked out. In this chapter some of the techniques commonly used will be discussed briefly from the standpoint of their forecasting value.

Methods of making projections vary greatly. Perhaps the basic distinction is between statistical methods as such, which utilize past data in a rather rigorous manner, and less formal methods of extrapolation, which merely extend various series from the latest reported date into the future, utilizing any available clues to their probable behavior. Both approaches are useful in the particular situations to which they properly apply, but the latter method is subject to a higher degree of error and requires a greater degree of judgment.

Becoming proficient in making informal projections is likely to impress the forecaster with the necessity of observing principles like those underlying the more formal statistical methods, except as he finds adequate reason for a procedure that is seemingly in violation of them. It is of some importance, therefore, that the forecaster have an understanding of the methodology of formal statistics, even though he does not plan to depend primarily on those methods in his day-to-day work.

The reader who lacks formal training in this field would be well advised to gain some familiarity with the techniques of rigorous statistical treatment. Although necessarily subject to limitations, these techniques are the results of extended investigation and provide the best tools available for dealing with the problems for which they are adapted. They have shortcomings for forecasting, as will be seen, but the shortcomings are a reflection not so much of their own inadequacies as of the complexity of the situation in which they are being used. Since these techniques have been so thoroughly worked out and their uses and validity explained in such detail elsewhere, they will not be considered in detail here.[1]

Since forecasting is necessarily concerned with the movements of variables through time, practically all the methods used fall in the category of *time-series analysis*.[2] The problem is usually to estimate the probable value of the next term, or terms, in a sequence describing

[1] A brief, general discussion of the concepts and uses of statistics may be found in L. C. H. Tippett, *Statistics*, Oxford University Press, London, 1956. A more extended treatment from the nonmathematical approach is W. Allen Wallis and Harry V. Roberts, *Statistics: A New Approach*, Free Press, Glencoe, Ill., 1956.

[2] All the standard statistical textbooks devote some space to time-series analysis. Two that give this topic greater than usual emphasis are Frederick Mills, *Statistical Methods*, 3d ed., Henry Holt and Company, Inc., New York, 1955; and Frederick Croxton and Dudley Cowden, *Applied General Statistics*, 2d ed., Prentice-Hall, Inc., Englewood Cliffs, N.J., 1955.

the past behavior of a given variable or set of variables. It is thus a kind of problem in probabilities. But it differs from the usual probability problem in that causes are uncontrolled and underlying conditions are variable, so that the factors determining the outcome cannot be considered to remain the same from one period to the next. True probabilities apply only when the relevant determining causes and conditions are stable. Here the causes are not just indeterminate; they are undependably indeterminate.

All the controlling factors vary, and it is generally more important to get at these underlying sources of change than to apply any accepted rules of probability. The past data give some indications of what is likely to happen, either in the continuation of movements currently in progress or in the recurrence of movements observed in the past. Other indications are obtained from other information—from the relations of any given variable to others, which have some predictive value, or from special information, perhaps nonquantitative in character, which applies to the specific situation but does not represent a statistical time series carrying back over an extended period.

The degree of confidence to be placed in any projection is not easily definable in this field. The statistical tests usually relied upon are carried over by analogy from other fields in which the uncontrolled variation is random so that the rules of probability may be considered to hold good. Since those rules do not apply in strict logic to time-series analysis, the usual statistical tests of validity must be considered crude approximations only. They are useful as indications of what might be expected in subsequent observations but do not afford the same kind of test of hypothesis that is obtained when the results of further trials will be determined by stable factors and by "chance" alone. No effort will be made to deal with this problem here in a detailed or rigorous way. Use of a certain amount of judgment in appraising the probability of an economic prediction is unavoidable.

METHODS INTERNAL TO THE DATA

In the narrow definition of the term, *time-series analysis* refers to methods that take account only of the data given in the specific time series being projected. As usually presented, this form of analysis ignores other series to which this specific series may be related and also other outside information that may be useful in understanding its past movements. The object is essentially to analyze the past behavior in such a way as to segregate various components of the observed past movements and then to apply those components in projecting the future movements. The procedure may be wholly internal to the data themselves, and to the extent that this is true it involves a high degree of abstraction from the real situation in which those data were produced.

The four components usually considered in this approach are seasonal variation, cyclical movements, secular trends, and the residual irregular or random fluctuations. The last is held to be the result of unknown or indeterminate causes and therefore is seldom considered a basis for predicting the future. The other three kinds of variations or movements are those ordinarily applied in making projections. The first two project patterns established by analysis of the past data; the third projects continuous growth or decline, although curved trend lines may be used in some cases. The time intervals covered are progressively longer: forecasts produced by the first usually cover just several months; those produced by the second, several years; and those produced by the third, much longer periods.

As a rule, these techniques are not presented from a forecasting point of view in the statistical textbooks. The primary concern is with descriptions of the past behavior of the data, and there may be little or no consideration of the causes or influences responsible for the observed results, this being part of another "discipline." Techniques therefore tend too much toward pure empiricisim. Data are sometimes put through a series of computations without regard to the logic of handling them in this way, and the student may be left with the impression that he can obtain the answers to practical problems by a kind of mechanical manipulation of a set of data.

In statistical research, as in other work, tools do not produce satisfactory results unless they are adapted to the task. Hence, before one proceeds with any analysis, it is usually desirable to give a little thought to the nature of the variable that is being studied. Some variables are dominated by the forces that produce cyclical movements; others are apparently independent of those forces and move along in a fairly regular way through substantial declines and recoveries in the general economy. Other variables are relatively erratic or unpredictable with respect to time, so that techniques based on time changes throw little light on their movements. Attention should also be given to the suitability of the data for the kind of analytical treatment to which it is proposed to put them. The discussion will return to this point later in this chapter. Only when sensible answers can be given to these general questions is it wise to begin putting the rules of statistical procedure to work.

Seasonal Variation. Fluctuations of a "seasonal" nature are, as the word implies, the results of changes from one season of the year to the next. Thus most of the fuel for home heating is consumed during the winter months, and the heaviest vacation travel comes in the summer. Holidays like Christmas and Easter also have important effects on some series. The characteristic of such movements is that they flow from specific conditions of operation that vary over regular calendar intervals and do not represent changes in the underlying position of the activity when viewed in a longer perspective.

Since seasonal changes are confined to months within a single year and since only one phase of the movement is likely to be in question for a forecast, the use of these movements is confined to very short-term forecasting—usually to the kind referred to in business concerns as sales forecasting. Some seasonal movements are consistent enough to be very useful in this context. As a rule, they have to be used in conjunction with other elements of change.

Although seasonal movements may be so strong as to represent by far the greatest source of short-term variation, they nevertheless may be lacking in significance from the forecaster's point of view. The nontypical changes are usually of greatest interest to the concern. Moreover, the effects of disturbances or other external factors may override the seasonal movements in a given forecast period. Hence the effort is usually to eliminate them, and with them the distortions they convey, in order that other kinds of changes may more readily be appraised.

The most popular procedure for making seasonal adjustments is that developed and used by the Federal Reserve Board. The first step is to adjust for the number of working days. A 12-months moving average of the data corrected in this way—including first the months January to December, then February to January, and so forth—is used to eliminate the seasonal variation and most of the irregular month-to-month fluctuations but is assumed to retain all the longer-term movements.

Next, a smooth line approximating the 12-months moving average is drawn through the data to represent trend and cyclical components. Such a line may be adjusted to take account of known changes in the course of activity in a way that the 12-months moving average cannot, because the month-to-month changes of the latter are determined mechanically by differences between specific months a year apart. Then, the ratios of the actual data to the smooth curve are averaged for each month to select the specific month's ratios for all the years available; this step is designed to eliminate the effects of random fluctuations by averaging them out. The result, when adjusted to average 100 percent for the year as a whole, is a set of factors representing the seasonal movement.

On the whole, this is a good method of making seasonal adjustments. It is neither an entirely foolproof method nor by any means the only valid one for making seasonal adjustments. Substantially as good results can be obtained, for example, from the link-relative method, which uses month-to-month percentage changes as links between one part of the year and another. This method may be a real short cut in cases where the month-to-month links are already computed. When projections are being made, it also has the advantage of focusing attention on the changes likely to occur in the months immediately ahead, introducing an element of flexibility in the adjustment process.

In making seasonal adjustments, it is usually desirable and sometimes important to correct the adjusted data so that they produce the same annual totals as the unadjusted data. Although the seasonal factors average out to 100 percent, they will not necessarily produce a neutral result in the aggregate. The observed data are in effect weighting factors, and the weighted average will not be the same as the unweighted average. Where there has been an unusual pattern of movement within the year, particularly in the months at the seasonal peak or seasonal low, quite a discrepancy is likely to be introduced. The adjusted average might then be several percent greater or lower than the unadjusted unless it is corrected. Such a correction can be made by means of a suitable interpolation formula.

In many economic series, a precaution that must constantly be observed is to make sure that the seasonal adjustment is satisfactory. The character of seasonal fluctuations does change from time to time, or with changing conditions, so that a single adjustment may not soundly portray what is happening. During World War II, for example, when industries were operating at capacity, as in the case of the steel industry, or at the peak of the available labor supply, as in the case of the textile industry, the usual seasonal movements tended to disappear. Business concerns could sell everything they produced and therefore operated through the year at the peak rate they could attain under the existing conditions. After the war the seasonal movements reappeared, though with varying lags, and both in the early war period and immediately after the war incorrect conclusions were drawn because these shifts in seasonal movements were not accurately accounted for. It is precisely at the ends of the periods covered by the data—primarily the most recent months—that such errors are likely to be greatest.

Whenever a moving seasonal adjustment is necessary, the reasons for the shifting of patterns should be investigated. In the usual treatment, this shifting is regarded as a function of time. It may, however, be a function of some internal variable, such as the degree to which the industry's operations approach capacity. If this can be established, then, as operations drop away from the capacity level, the seasonal factors can be automatically shifted, without waiting for evidence that a change in time trends has taken place.

If the data are received in adjusted form, judging of the validity of the seasonal factors may still be necessary, as even the best reporting agencies cannot always keep their adjustments up to date. The Federal Reserve Board, for example, which has over the years gained a pre-eminent reputation in this field, carried many series in its production index through the early postwar years without seasonal adjustment and did not begin adjustments promptly after the seasonals reappeared.

When adjusted data are delayed, there may be a problem of keeping up with current changes in the interim, and for this purpose it is not essential to use a formal seasonal adjustment. There are at least two short-cut ways of obtaining a sound idea of what is taking place without developing explicit adjustment factors. The first consists of charting the data so that successive years are plotted on a single scale of 12 months; then, by observing the course of developments through the year in comparison with other recent years—years in which the general character of changes is already known—a fairly good appraisal of the current movement can be made. This technique is particularly effective in following weekly data, where the problems of making seasonal adjustments in the usual way would be multiplied. Examples of this kind of chart may be found in the *Federal Reserve Chart Book,* under the heading "Weekly Series on Production, Selected Years."

The second way of keeping up to date is by comparing current percentage changes with those for the same months in past years. This comparison may be especially fruitful if the character of past situations is well known. Recent changes may then be compared not with a single seasonal factor but with the whole series of past changes and particularly with the changes that occurred in similar situations. The usual rule of averaging out random variations in computing seasonal indexes is to take averages for the various months only after the elimination of the extreme cases on either side, because it is feared that some unique development might be permitted to influence the seasonal adjustment if they are included. But when the reasons for past changes are known, the extreme cases may be exactly the ones that provide the best comparison for analysis of current developments.

In forecasting beyond very short intervals of several months, it is desirable to carry out a formal seasonal adjustment so that adjusted data will be available through the latest month. Generally speaking, this is the basis on which data can be most effectively used in forecasting. Once the seasonal movement is eliminated, other techniques of projection can be applied with greater facility. If data in unadjusted form are desired as the end product, it is usually the best procedure to make the projection in adjusted form and then reverse the adjustment process to put the seasonal movement back into the series. There are exceptions to this procedure, occurring mainly in series where the seasonal movement is limited and relatively erratic, and in those cases it becomes in effect necessary to forecast the seasonal movement itself. But as a rule the forecaster can work best with adjusted data.

It should be evident from the preceding discussion that seasonal movements play no great role in forecasting. They tend to be either undependable or trivial in significance. The department-store executive, for example, wants to know not that sales will rise sharply from September to December but rather that they will rise by more or less than the usual amount. With some minor exceptions in the field of moving seasonals, this is a kind of information the adjustment process cannot provide.

Cyclical Movements. These are quite different in character from the fluctuation produced by changes in seasons. In particular industries or activities, they result either from changes in the general level of economic activity that react upon the particular segment or from changes and reactions within the particular segment that tend consistently to over-carry the points of stability or equilibrium and thus produce the recurring, wavelike movements known as "business cycles."[3]

Data representing cycles in general activity are of little use to the forecaster when considered as purely statistical devices suitable for projection. Many of the forces producing cycles do not change in any periodic or regular manner. Other forces do exhibit such tendencies, but in combination they vary so greatly in timing and magnitude that it is well-nigh impossible to obtain dependable results by projecting any fixed pattern of over-all activity from an existing position.

Attempting such projections in making forecasts may be considered not only impracticable but also theoretically unsound. "The business cycle" is not a single entity but the result of a coincidence or conjuncture of specific forces which combine to produce the over-all movement, and unless the analysis can get at those specific forces it cannot produce accurate forecasts. It may indeed be helpful to know the stage of "the business cycle" and the sequence of changes that would ordinarily be expected in that stage, but using this kind of knowledge effectively is in no sense a mechanical process.

Of the cycles in specific segments or industries, perhaps the best known is the construction cycle. It covers a span of 15 to 20 years and is sometimes referred to as "the long cycle." Another cycle well defined by data going back more than half a century is that found in the number of cattle on farms. This cycle, portrayed in Chart 3–1, averages about

---

[3] The most extended scientific description of business cycles is found in the works of the National Bureau of Economic Research. See, for example, Wesley Mitchell, *Business Cycles, the Problem and Its Setting*, National Bureau of Economic Research, Inc., New York, 1927; and Arthur Burns and Wesley Mitchell, *Measuring Business Cycles*, National Bureau of Economic Research, Inc., New York, 1946.

14 years in length. In this case, the process of building up herds involves withholding a substantial portion of the current supply from the market. It takes the biggest part of 3 years from the time a cow is bred until an offspring steer is ready for market. As cows and heifers are held for breeding, the flow to market falls, and this aggravates the demand-price conditions promoting the expansion. Subsequently, on the decline, the reduction of herds increases the current supply. Cows are marketed in large numbers, and the heavy slaughter adds to the meat surplus, depressing prices and stimulating further efforts to correct the situation by reduction of herds.

In cases where there is a direct independent cycle of this kind, it results basically from the fact that long periods of time are required

Chart 3–1. Cattle on Farms

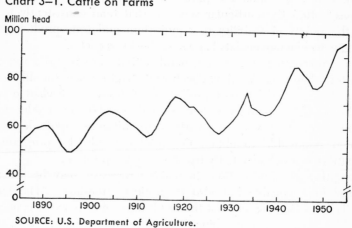

SOURCE: U.S. Department of Agriculture.

for adjustment of the processes of production and consumption. Because it takes time to build up supplies, an increase in demand cannot be quickly met. Conversely, because it takes time to use up or consume existing supplies, a surplus cannot be quickly worked off. Thus a movement in either direction is likely to continue for some time before it is corrected, and typically it continues long enough so that a reverse imbalance requires at least the beginning of a movement in the opposite direction.

When shorter cycles are considered, the case is usually less clear, because adjustments can be made more quickly and the response to outside forces is stronger. Much emphasis was once put on a hog-corn cycle of about 3½ years' duration, but the hog-corn price ratio is now regarded mainly as a correlation device for estimating the next season's hog crop rather than as an element in a fixed cycle as such.

Chart 3–2. Cotton-consumption Cycle*

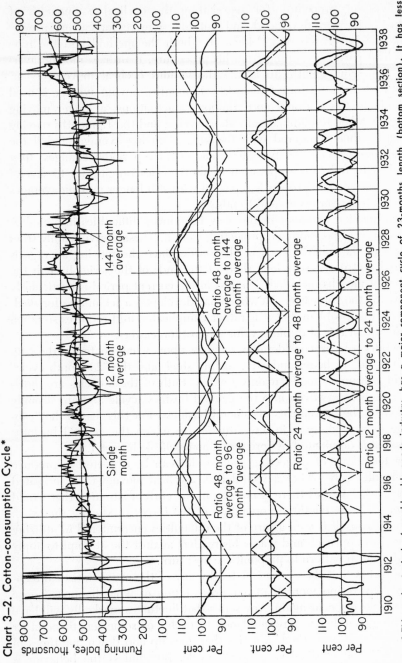

* This cycle, typical of semidurable-goods industry, has a major component cycle of 23-months length (bottom section). It has less important components of 40-months length (next to bottom section) and an irregular 7- to 10-year component (next to top section).
SOURCE: By permission from Business Forecasting: Principles and Practice, by Frank D. Newbury, McGraw-Hill, New York, 1952, p. 148.

63

A short-cut procedure for segregating the cyclical components of various series was developed and put to extensive forecasting use by Frank Newbury.[4] Chart 3–2 illustrates both the method and the type of cyclical pattern resulting from his procedure. It utilizes moving averages of varying lengths to isolate the various cyclical movements incorporated in the historical record. A 12-months moving average is used to eliminate the seasonal and "random" fluctuations; a longer moving average is taken to eliminate any short cycles; and the 12-months moving average is then compared with the longer moving average, and if the differences between the two show any regular periodic changes, they are taken to reflect the operation of short cycles ranging up to several years' duration. The process is repeated with still longer moving averages to segregate longer cycles and trends.

Using moving averages in this way introduces difficulties into analyzing the current position and projecting from it. These derive mainly from the loss of data at the ends of the series, since the moving average is centered and necessarily falls short of the ends of the series by half the number of months included. The loss in the current period is particularly serious for the forecaster. Newbury has developed a technique for dealing with this problem, but it is rather complicated and requires so much judgment that it is of dubious value to most forecasters.

Newbury places considerable reliance upon what he terms the "40-month cycle" in heavy industry, mainly steel, and the "23-month cycle" in light consumer goods, mainly textiles. Both of these cycles are, however, closely interwoven into the general business cycle and are strongly affected by the movements of general business. For this reason they cannot be depended upon in any situation in which the general business movement is dominated by forces of a noncyclical character.

The technique of projecting such cycles can be expected to produce valid results only where a well-defined cyclical movement is indicated by the past data and there is nothing in the current situation that would conflict with the continued operation of the forces producing the cycle. Newbury himself is well aware of the difficulties encountered in utilizing the cyclical approach and warns his readers against the attempt to apply a fixed cyclical pattern to pinpoint the next turn.

The fact is that the cycles isolated by any of the usual statistical techniques may be no more than a representation of what happened once and may never occur again. Any series that fluctuates markedly will have something that bears a resemblance to cycles of some length or other if appropriately smoothed. A series that goes up and down five times in 10 years in effect displays a 2-year cycle. But, unless the behavior is

---

[4] Frank D. Newbury, *Business Forecasting: Principles and Practice,* McGraw-Hill Book Company, Inc., New York, 1952, p. 148.

truly regular and can be attributed to continuing causes, that cycle may be entirely worthless as a basis for forecasting.

Rather definite sequences in inventory accumulation and liquidation, for example, produce general business movements with all the characteristics of what we ordinarily refer to as "cycles." These, however, cannot be regarded as regular in character but vary considerably in extent and in duration from one period to the next. They both initiate changes and respond to changes in other parts of the economy. In so far as the "cycles" in particular industries are phases of the more general swings in inventory investment, they cannot be projected effectively in their own right.

There remain the general indications that knowledge of the cycle can convey. In a boom or a depression, a reversal is likely to set in, and, once started, the new movement is likely to run for some time. Such indications can indeed provide useful information at times, as will be shown later, but it is information that has to be interpreted with judgment.

To summarize the evidence on cyclical movements, it may be said that there is hardly a fixed cycle anywhere in economic experience, and even the best cyclical pattern is subject to substantial variation. If such cycles are short enough to make an important difference in a near-term forecast, they are likely to be so irregular as to be quite unreliable. If they are quite long, about all they can indicate for the near term is a continuation of what has been happening in the recent past. The latter is true, for example, of the construction cycle. Hence fixed cycles as such have very little value in short-term forecasting.[5]

Trends. Trends present a distinct contrast to the surges and reversals of cyclical movements. They portray changes that take place consistently from year to year—usually in a single direction and with little change in magnitude from one year to the next. When such steady progress is observed in the past data over a considerable period of years, there is some basis for projecting "the trend" into the future. Presumably the forces that have been bringing about the gradual shift in level will continue to operate for some time subsequent to the period of observation.

One of the fields in which trends are often used is that of population, because rates of birth and death and the other factors affecting the number of people in a country are ordinarily stable enough to produce fairly steady growth. Chart 3–3 illustrates how a straight-line trend

[5] This view is obviously in sharp conflict with that of forecasters who rely mainly upon projection of cycles as the basis for their forecasts. For a forceful statement of the philosophy of this approach, see Edward Dewey and Edwin Dakin, *Cycles: The Science of Forecasting*, Henry Holt and Company, Inc., New York, 1949. Their forecast of a depression on the grounds that cycles of varying periodicity would simultaneously reach lows in the early 1950s illustrates the dangers of relying heavily on fixed-cycle techniques.

fitted to the period 1900 to 1930 might have been projected into the future. The actual population fell behind the trend during the 1930s, but after 1940 and especially after the end of the war it advanced more rapidly, recovering the trend position by 1953.

The chart also shows the 1954 Census Bureau projections to 1960. These projections are computed not from this kind of trend line but by much more detailed analysis of probable births and deaths. Projections

Chart 3–3. Midyear Continental Population

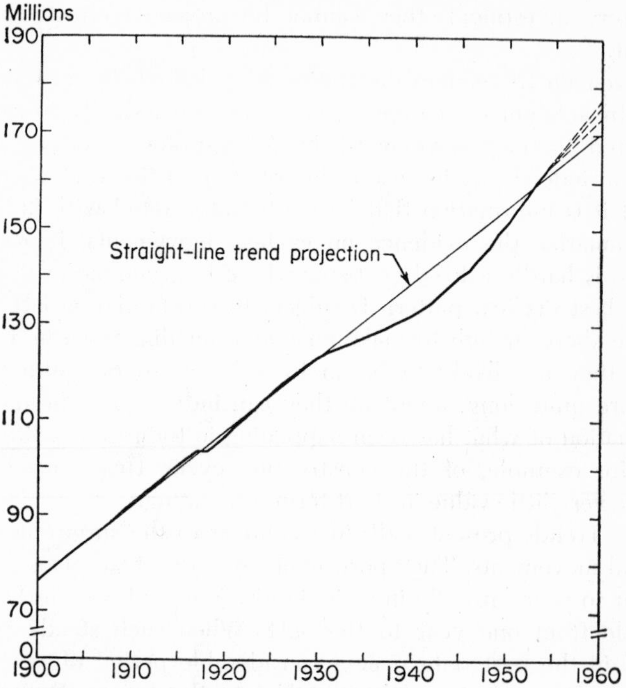

SOURCE OF DATA: U.S. Bureau of the Census.

made in terms of similar detail in the late 1930s fell far short of the numbers actually realized in the early 1950s and to that extent lacked superiority over the simpler straight-line trend. Although total population was for many years regarded as one of the easiest series to project, the history of population projections during the last quarter century provides numerous examples of how even the most carefully compiled projections can be wide of the mark.

Another illustration of a long-term trend, fitted in this case to production data for periods of peacetime prosperity, is presented in Chart 3–4. A semilogarithmic scale is used, so that the trend represents a constant percentage rate of increase rather than a constant rate of advance in absolute volume of output. Noteworthy are the wide deviations in the depression and war years. These are regarded as "disturbances," since rates of change in the labor force, in technology, and in other factors affecting output imply relatively continuous advances in over-all ability

Chart 3–4. Real Gross National Product

THE NATION'S MARKET

● **Grows about 3 percent per year**

● **Real output has doubled since 1929**

● **Since 1941 —**

⟶ Real output increased by nearly one-half

⟶ Real output per capita is up one-quarter

⟶ Real output per capita for private use is up one-fifth

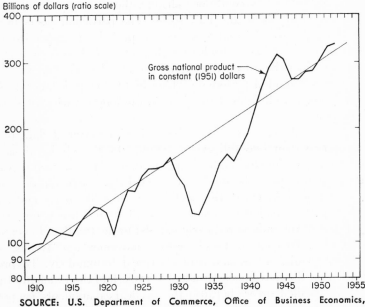

Billions of dollars (ratio scale)

SOURCE: U.S. Department of Commerce, Office of Business Economics, Markets After the Defense Expansion, 1952.

to produce. The fact that output in the postwar years is back on the line is the kind of evidence used in placing reliance on such a trend as a basis for making projections into the future. Resumption of such a trend after serious disturbances like depression and war provides a measure of confidence that growth in output will continue in the future, at least in years of prosperity.

What the trend does not tell is whether there will be prosperity in any particular future period. Almost the first thing that should be understood about a trend is that it tells nothing about the short-term cyclical or irregular movements that run counter to it. These short-term movements, departing from the trend and perhaps returning to it after a while, are essentially independent of anything that goes into the make-up of the trend. The trend must, in fact, abstract from the influences producing such movements. It can, therefore, tell practically nothing about what will happen next to such cyclical variables as production, employment, and income. Perhaps activity will actually conform to the trend in a year 10 or 20 years beyond the last shown on the chart. The trend cannot by itself offer any assurance that business conditions will remain good through the intervening period.

Even for use over the longer term, it is not safe to project trends without testing their underlying assumptions. Just because a trend has fitted well in the past is not a sound reason for thinking that it will continue to fit well in the future. As conditions change, the course of developments may deviate widely from the past trend. The particular years used in fitting it may be so different from future periods—or even from still earlier periods—as to be entirely unrepresentative. This is particularly true if the trend is based on the experience of relatively few years, but there are even extended periods in which highly cyclical data will seem to be following a well-defined trend, as in the long upswing of the construction cycle.

Generally speaking, a trend can be defined in cyclical data only if there are more than two full cycles covered by the observations, and then only by selecting the ending and starting points in such a way as to eliminate completely the effects of cyclical swings. In the downward phase of the business cycle, the declines are usually sharp, cutting directly across the trend. The recoveries tend to be drawn out over a greater interval, running more nearly parallel to the trend and eventually rising above it. To speak of these recovery movements as "trends," such as "postwar trends," is an abuse of statistical terminology. To project those based on the movements of a single cycle into the indefinite future involves an implicit error, because the cyclical components cannot be treated in this way. In other words, the rates of growth temporarily attained during cyclical recoveries are usually much greater than the long-term rates of growth computed over a number of cycles, and there is no sound basis for projecting these exaggerated rates of increase. Yet this is exactly the error often made by analysts who support optimistic views with trend projections.

The selection of an appropriate time period over which to fit the line is of critical importance. It has frequently been asserted in recent years that the long-term trend of prices is upward. Such statements can be supported statistically, in these years of postwar inflation, by trend lines going back to the beginning of the century. Chart 3–5 shows a trend line A fitted in this manner. This line takes advantage both of the all-time low at the beginning of the century and the all-time high of the post–Korean War inflation. It ignores both the hump of World War I and the

Chart 3–5. Wholesale Prices

Bureau of Labor Statistics Index, 1947–1949 = 100

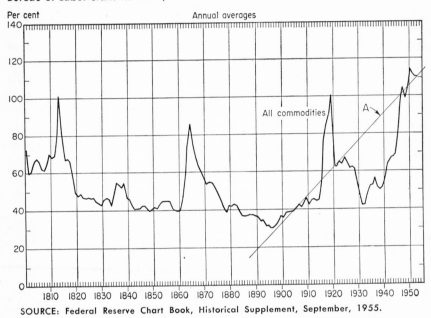

SOURCE: Federal Reserve Chart Book, Historical Supplement, September, 1955.

deep trough of the Great Depression; fitting between these points would give a steep downward slope. Looking at the longer period, including the nineteenth century, there is nothing to suggest that trend A could appropriately be projected beyond 1950. If there is any continuing tendency toward inflation, the evidence for it must be found elsewhere.

There are times when forces of an exceptional nature produce changes that resemble for some years a fairly stable trend movement. During the nineteenth century, there were two periods of over 30 years each in which downward "trends" in prices could have been obtained. In projecting any such trend it is essential either that the nature of the causes producing it is sufficiently understood to justify the projection or that the period of years covered is not only long but also of such a character as to create a presumption that continued stability of change may be expected.

Again, to speak in terms of stock-market prices, the long cyclical up-swings and declines are commonly referred to as the "primary trends" in bull and bear markets. This terminology leaves no place for the long-term trend as such, though trends of the latter type are also computed by market analysts, particularly for purposes of formula plans worked out as a guide for investment policy. The fallacies of attempting to use trends to forecast stock prices over shorter periods are quickly apparent to anyone who attempts to make a profit in that manner.

It follows from this that trends, too, are of limited usefulness in short-term forecasting. If the trend is flat, its significance for practical purposes is that of a constant; and although it may represent an element of stability in the over-all economic picture, the important elements of variation lie elsewhere. If the trend component is larger, though still small relative to the cyclical or random components, it contributes little to our knowledge of what lies immediately ahead. Even if the trend component is large and these other types of movements are limited, problems will be encountered whenever the data deviate significantly from the trend, for the steeper the trend the more important the errors of estimate are likely to be.

It is only in projecting over long periods that trend lines play a valid role. In making long-term forecasts, no other device available offers anywhere near a comparable degree of reliability. The forecaster who uses it can always hope that if there are departures from the trend in the interim the series will come back into line by the more distant data forecast. Possibly he can supplement the trend with a tentative projection of the long cycle, but this does not offer the same possibility of eventual accuracy, because the shifts in timing and magnitude of such cycles are likely to be so substantial as to invalidate the projection. Beyond this, the result obtained from the trend line can be modified by certain hypotheses or assumptions about important special factors, such as military programs, but these are likely to be of a still lower order of dependability in long-range work.[6]

[6] In recent years, there have been published a succession of carefully worked out long-range projections based essentially upon trends in basic economic factors, particularly the labor force and its productivity. The most elaborate of these is *America's Needs and Resources*, The Twentieth Century Fund, Inc., New York, 1955. This book provides a wealth of background material. It makes a distinct contribution in its discussion of the problems and assumptions involved in long-range projections, which is both frank and relatively complete. It also implicitly reveals how little can be done to make a realistic forecast for a specific date over a long period. A brief perusal of this volume will indicate to the short-term forecaster that the projections are of little help in his work.

From an a priori point of view, there is no "ideal" trend or method of projection. Nevertheless, it may be stated as a general rule that the most useful and generally the safest trend to use in situations where the nature of the trend is not predetermined is the straight line. It is simplest to fit and easiest to understand. It excludes abrupt or extreme rates of change in either direction—in contrast to more complex curves, which sometimes make sharp turns not far beyond the range of the observations. It has in practical situations a greater theoretical validity than its simplicity might suggest. It may be true that "there are no straight lines in nature," but some things that are not "naturally" straight lines tend toward a practically linear course when other things change in a related manner.

The intercorrelation between economic forces and variables is such that a straight line may be appropriate in many cases where it never could if it were operating in isolation from such intercorrelations. Thus a single variable like population might tend in a static environment toward a fixed upper limit but under the actual dynamic conditions of economic growth may continue to rise indefinitely; and with a growth in population and a growth in living standards—that is, in real consumption per capita—a product that can at best command only a limited portion in the consumer's budget may obtain a constantly expanding market for many years. A straight-line trend may then appropriately represent the product demand.

Differences in the results obtained by various trend lines are brought out on Chart 3–6, which presents estimates of steel requirements made by three analysts just after World War II. This chart brings out several points. The first is that the specific observations to which the curve is fitted must be appropriate to the problem. Smith, in fitting his curves to production for all years—the upper curve includes the war years, the lower excludes them—overlooks this point. As Bean points out, the depression years contribute little to an analysis of steel requirements for full employment. Sykes, in holding one important element of variation constant, also artifically restricts the level of future requirements. It might have been possible, as he felt, that only as much steel as the 1929 per capita production would have been needed *on the average,* but this argument ignores the fact that we live in a boom economy, which demands materials when it wants them, not when an industry is ready to produce them. The actual steel output in 1953, for which capacity had been built, was fairly close to the projection made by Bean. By that time the industry, given the special character of the international situation, had lost its earlier reluctance to expand and was becoming enthusiastic about its future prospects.

An interesting aspect of Bean's projection is the manner in which he runs a curve into a straight line. This reduces rather than increases the validity of his analysis, as each element of flexibility in a curve must be supported by additional evidence to support its use. In testing the validity of a line of estimate, the degrees of freedom—that is, the number of parameters which give the curve its shape and thus determine its flexibility—are subtracted from the total number of observations. A straight line would fit all the full-employment points except the first two

Chart 3–6. Three Estimates of Steel* Production per Capita Required for Full Employment, United States

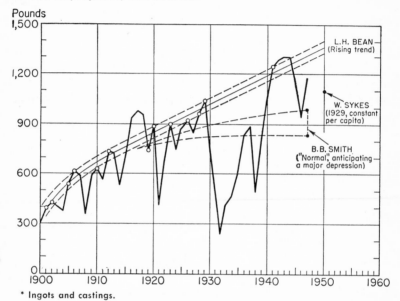

* Ingots and castings.

SOURCE: Louis H. Bean, The Dependence of Industrial-Agricultural Prosperity on Steel Requirements for Full Employment (mimeographed), U.S. Department of Agriculture, June, 1948.

—1901 and 1902—fully as well as the complex curve. Only two points are added, and at least three degrees of freedom are used up, so that the curve as a whole gains nothing in theoretical validity. Moreover, the curved part of the line contributes nothing at all to the projection, which has to be made from the straight line itself. Altogether, it would have been better to omit the first two points and use the straight line alone.

Nonlinear trends are, of course, useful and should be used where theoretical considerations or the data themselves indicate that a different type of curve would be appropriate. Thus, exponential or logarithmic curves have demonstrated usefulness in cases where rates of change rather than absolute amounts are being measured and projected. In the absence of a compelling reason for some other type, the preference usually lies with the simpler trend. If doubts are resolved in favor of the straight line, the forecaster is likely to go wrong less frequently than with more flexible or complex types of trends. When a complex curve is used, its use must be justified logically, in terms of the particular segment being analyzed, and it should be projected outside the range of actual data only with reservations.

Another aspect of this problem arises from breaks in the trend—usually representing a distinct turn or an abrupt change in level from one period to the next. The causes of such breaks vary: some derive from nonhomogeneity in the data, which it may be possible to adjust and thus bring into conformity with a continuous trend. Others derive from changes in underlying conditions; for example, in specific firms, when a new management takes over the business or new uses for its product are discovered, the old trend may no longer apply. The reasons for the break must be investigated, and where circumstances indicate the desirability of such treatment, a broken trend may be utilized. This is hardly ever true in the case of general economic series, because over-all conditions hardly ever change sharply except in circumstances where trend projections are inappropriate. In any case, the justification for special treatment cannot be found in the data themselves but must be sought in the form of evidence that supplements the statistical record.

Residual Variation. After the other three components have been extracted, the unexplained portions of the observed are the residual commonly referred to as "irregular" or "random fluctuations." Although this residual variation may be erratic in character, it may not be random in the true sense. All that the term ordinarily implies is that it does not conform to seasonal indexes, cyclical patterns, trend lines, or other patterns of behavior definable in terms of the data themselves.

By "definition" there is no way to account for this kind of variation and therefore no way to utilize it in future predictions, except to the extent of making allowance for some indicated margin of error. If the residual variation were truly random in character—derived from truly indeterminate forces like those governing the results of tossing a coin— the hypothesis implicit in this narrow definition would be meaningful. Actually the reasons for many of the residual movements can often be determined without difficulty. This calls, of course, for further analysis by means of other information, perhaps partly statistical and partly nonstatistical, that can be helpful in explaining the past behavior of the variable. If such information is helpful in explaining the past, the chances are that it can also be used to advantage in explaining movements yet to come.

CORRELATION

The primary statistical procedure for bringing additional information to bear on the analysis of any variable is to investigate its relations to other variables. If two variables consistently move together, whether in the same direction or inversely, the movements of one may be used to estimate those of the other. Such patterns of interrelated movements may be very useful in forecasting, particularly when one variable follows the other with a time lag or when estimates of one are logically obtained at an earlier stage in the analysis. The patterns of relationships used in this way are established by correlation techniques.

"Correlation" is similar to trend analysis in that it attempts to estimate a statistical series, designated the "dependent variable," by means of a fitted line of relationship. However, instead of using regularly spaced intervals to locate the points on the line at which this dependent variable is estimated, it uses another variable called the "independent variable," to which the first is related. Since the independent variable may change irregularly, moving down as well as up, there is much greater flexibility in the estimates derived from such a line of relationship than from a trend.

It is sometimes convenient to think of the changes in the dependent variable as being "caused" by those in the independent variable. However, strict causal relationships can hardly ever be established in the field of economics, and mere similarity of past movements, unexplained and perhaps unexplainable, is no assurance of corresponding results in the future. A multiplicity of forces is usually acting on each of the variables. At best, both may be governed by a common set of forces, so that they move together to a dependable degree. Moreover, the variables themselves commonly interact with each other, so that the "effects," in reacting upon the "causes," themselves become causes and make their "causes" also effects. Frequently no causal connection can be shown to exist, and in strict logic many correlations of economic variables have to be regarded as purely empirical fits to specific data.

Lack of logical validity need not, however, destroy the usefulness of such interrelationships from the forecaster's point of view. As a practical necessity, he is often forced to disregard many questions of pure logic or theory. As long as knowledge of one thing helps him to predict another, he can use it to obtain the desired result and may consider it appropriate to refer to the former as "causal," even though the statement is not strictly accurate.

Correlation, like the establishment of a trend, is a curve-fitting procedure. It sets up a fitted line of relationship as the basis for estimating probable values of the dependent variable. The trend line is in effect the special case of correlation in which the independent variable time changes in one direction only and by constant increments. Cyclical projections may also be considered a variant of curve-fitting technique; in this case the dependent variable is related to a complex, time-determined variable that repeats a pattern of changes through successive periods. Correlation, in the specific meaning of the term, introduces the maximum flexibility into the estimating process.

Two methods of curve fitting are most commonly used when a single variable is to be projected. The first is the least-squares method, in which the solution is arrived at by mathematical procedures that ensure the same results for anyone using them. The second is the graphic method, in which a line is simply drawn on a graph by visual inspection of the data and judgment is relied on to place the line properly.[7]

"Least squares" is the traditional method of the statistics textbooks. It provides the line that is theoretically most nearly correct under appropriate conditions. These may be described by the following assumptions: first, that the lines of causation are correctly represented by considering the specified variable as dependent; second, that errors and other sources of "random" variation are confined to the dependent variable; and, third, that the effects of any supplementary or conditioning variables not directly included in the relationship are comparatively unimportant. Since these assumptions are not justified in many cases, statisticians have turned to the maximum-likelihood method to obtain a more rigorous mathematical solution. The latter—again assuming the correct selection of variables and the appropriate form of relationship—gives the most probable result in the sense that the observed data are more likely to have been derived from that particular relationship than from any other line of the indicated type.[8]

In practical work, the analyst is likely to make a preliminary graphic analysis of the problem, even though he intends to reach a final solution by mathematical methods. This enables him to decide such questions as the form of the relationship, the period of observations to be included, and the effects of disturbances or peculiarities of the data. The preliminary decisions may, of course, be modified as the analysis proceeds to an evaluation of the results, which is also best handled in graphic terms. It often happens that the results obtained by various methods—graphic, least squares, or maximum likelihood—differ only slightly for most of the observations; and in the years where differences

---

[7] For a more detailed discussion, see Mordecai Ezekiel, *Methods of Correlation Analysis*, 2d ed., John Wiley & Sons, Inc., New York, 1950.

[8] The reader interested in pursuing this theoretically more accurate technique is referred to L. R. Klein, *A Textbook for Econometrics*, Row, Peterson & Company, Evanston, Ill., 1953.

occur, each method may have advantages in some years and disadvantages in others. This kind of experience may lead the analyst who is interested in results rather than procedures to make the graphic method the only, and not just the preliminary, solution.

The graphic method is in general subject to the unavoidable inadequacies of the mathematical methods. It also has some disadvantages of its own. Although with judgment a good fit may be obtained, without it a very poor fit may be obtained. A good deal of restraint is necessary on the part of the forecaster to avoid meaningless results.

The graphic method has several advantages when it is properly used. First, it is simpler and relatively easy to use. Much of the work involved, such as charting, is necessary even when the other methods are used. Second, at all times the analyst is close to the data; unusual observations are immediately seen in relation to other data, perhaps leading to checking or to explanations that provide a better understanding of the data themselves or of the kind of relationship that is appropriate. Third, this method provides greater flexibility: unusual observations may be given less weight than others in determining the best fit, or some points may be given greater or less weight than the average when specific reasons for doing so are known. Finally, the results obtained by the experienced analyst are likely to be about as good as those obtained by the mathematical methods, since minor differences within the general range of forecasting error are likely to be of small consequence.

Whether mathematical or graphic methods of fitting are employed, the degree of correlation is measured by the improvement in the estimate obtained by using the fitted curve as compared with just the average value, or mean, of the original data. There is no correlation when the line is horizontal, the line then being in effect no more than a graphic representation of the mean. The correlation is perfect when all the points lie on the fitted line, so that there are no errors of estimate, or residuals —in which case all the variation in the dependent variable is said to be "explained" by the movements of the independent variable. Usually, of course, there is at least some improvement in the estimates; and in recognition of the fact that this improvement may be accidental or spurious, a series of tests has been worked out to determine whether the observed improvement and the corresponding degree of correlation are significant or whether they should be considered to have resulted from "chance" alone.

It is desirable for the forecaster to know that the correlations he has developed are significant in the statistical sense. However, the tests of significance, like the relationships themselves, are not strictly valid when applied to time series. For this and other reasons, these tests are not adequate protection against accidental or spurious correlation. A correlation that is seemingly of a high level of significance may have no validity beyond the actual observations from which it was derived. Mere unrelated growth in two variables, perhaps only temporary in one or the other, may give the appearance of a high degree of correlation over the period in which it occurred. Other sources of possible fallacy are numerous, and the dangers of spurious correlation have been thoroughly established, for example, by deriving nonsense correlations from random numbers.

The only basis for relying on a correlation, therefore, is knowledge that the changes in the variables are in fact related. Unless it can be shown that there are common forces operating on both variables, or it is otherwise established that a valid relationship exists, there can be no basis for confidence in the result. Such knowledge may be available a priori, but at times the interconnections may be obscure. In any case, developing the rationale of the relationship is an important part of utilizing a correlation effectively.

In short, the analyst is faced with a logical dilemma. He is required to make the maximum use of logic in order to assure the validity of the techniques he uses and at the same time is forced to acknowledge that the results do not stand up in strict logic. What this logical dilemma forces him to do is to treat each established relationship as provisional. He knows that because it is not a true causal relationship it is subject to error. He therefore expects to find it going wrong at times and to make changes or revisions as may be appropriate. What is appropriate can be determined only through special efforts to discover why the unsatisfactory results were being obtained.

It may readily be seen that the nature of the correlation set up as a basis for the projection is highly important. The variables must be selected with due regard to lines of causation. The type of curve to be fitted must be selected with a view to correctly representing the relationship. The period of past observations used in fitting must be long enough and sufficiently homogeneous with the future in which the relationship is to be used to offer some probability of success. And the results have to be interpreted with caution at all times. For even when a valid relationship can be shown to exist, reliance on it as a basis for projection into the future has to be limited. When there are serious disturbances in the economy, the usual relationships may be made inoperative for a while, and over longer periods of time changes in the structure of the economy may bring about changes in the relationships of specific variables to each other.

Two other kinds of considerations are likely to be of practical importance. A consideration that modifies the selection of dependent and independent variables concerns the ultimate conditions of use. In general, the independent variables should be capable of being forecast in advance of their use in the correlation function. This means that if they are not independently forecast they should at least be derivable at an earlier stage of the forecasting process.

Care should also be taken in setting up any correlation to ensure that the data are suitable for such treatment. Various adjustments of the original source material may be necessary in this connection, as will be indicated below. Another kind of adjustment frequently required is to remove the effects of price movements. This requirement appears in most cases where value data are correlated with physical volume or other nonprice variables, such as population. Even if both series are in dollar terms, the problem may persist if the relative price movements show substantially different variation. This holds in trend and cycle analysis also, since wide or erratic movements of prices in the past may result in very inaccurate projections.

Both of these points are illustrated by Chart 3–7.[9] In setting up the correlation, it was assumed that forecasts of gross national product in constant dollars would be available for use in applying the relationship. The fit obtained in relating industrial production to deflated gross national product as a whole was not very good. The solution depended upon finding a form of the independent variable that would produce satisfactory results. This was obtained by excluding services, that is, by confining the independent variable to those portions of gross national product which more specifically derive from industrial operations.

In the correlation of cyclical variables, the period of observation should cover more than one cycle. This is not absolutely essential, as it is in fitting a trend, but is highly desirable from the standpoint of establishing the validity of the relationship. Many correlations covering the depression and recovery of the 1930s show near-perfect fits between series which in prior or subsequent periods display different relations to each other or none at all.

At this point it may be worth while to contrast the position of trends and correlations in the logic of forecasting. The trend is more completely lacking in causal significance, because time itself can hardly be regarded as a force that will produce dependable changes in the future. On the other hand, the trend may, when suitable to the data, be safer for projecting a year or two ahead, because the projection made in terms of it is

---

[9] The calculated values shown in the lower panel of the chart were computed from the line of relationship shown in the upper panel. The equation is

$$O = 0.716F - 11$$

where O = FRB index of industrial production

F = flow of goods and inventory changes from deflated gross-national-product data; see Table 7–2

Chart 3–7. Relation of Industrial Production to Flow of Goods Plus Inventory Changes

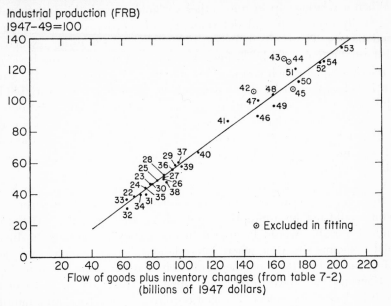

Industrial production (FRB)
1947–49=100

⊙ Excluded in fitting

Flow of goods plus inventory changes (from table 7-2)
(billions of 1947 dollars)

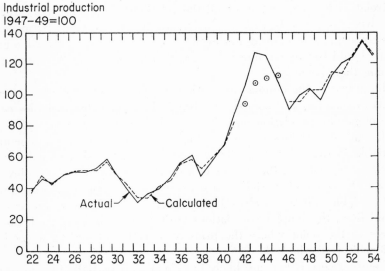

Industrial production
1947–49=100

Actual   Calculated

restricted to a well-defined range. In correlations the independent variable may fluctuate more widely in such a brief interval, and this may call for a projection far beyond the range of observed data, thereby magnifying the potential error in the dependent variable. Consideration of potential errors in the light of the past behavior of the variables, particularly if similar past situations can be identified, may be helpful in deciding the validity of the alternative procedures.

When a relationship to some other variable is used, this fact does not necessarily exclude partial determination of the dependent variable by trend factors. There are many correlations where the estimates may be substantially improved by fitting a trend to residuals from the basic line of relationship. In such cases, where a considerable portion of the variation is not explained by the movements of the independent variable but exhibits an independent regularity of movement, time may be introduced as a second independent variable. In this use, time is treated as a catch-all. It not only accounts for factors that vary smoothly through the years but also may serve as a way of eliminating persistent bias in the series being correlated.

A relationship using time and one other independent variable is one of the simplest forms of multiple correlation. In other cases the time factor would not be appropriate, but other variables that affect the dependent variable would be useful in estimating its movements. In the usual economic situation, where interrelationships are complex and many factors may affect the movements of each, it is not strange that multiple relationships may have to be called upon to explain the behavior of the one it is desired to project. The first requirement in setting up a multiple correlation is investigation of all the relationships among the variables involved. This investigation is partly carried out, of course, by means of the correlation techniques; but even before the latter are applied, a great deal should be known about the variables included and the forces governing their behavior.

Inasmuch as the dangers of spurious results are multiplied as correlations are made more complex by the addition of extra variables or by use of nonlinear relationships, it is particularly desirable to confine the independent variables to those actually known to affect the dependent variable in some fairly specific way. As Frisch has shown in his work *Confluence Analysis,* the danger of a spurious result in any complex correlation of economic variables arises when two or more of the independent variables are themselves highly intercorrelated. As in the case of trend lines, the simpler correlations are usually to be preferred, though never to the point where the primary objective of getting a good relationship is overlooked.

Complex correlations are likely to give at least partially invalid results whenever the data are subject to error. As an illustration, the experience of a colleague of the author may be cited. He attempted to reconstruct the weights used in calculating a complete income distribution from sample data. With the original data and the final results given, a simultaneous solution should have produced the weights used in the translation. Although errors in this instance were presumably limited to rounding in the final estimates, the results of the "correlation" showed serious misbehavior, with the calculated weights coming out negative in some extreme income groups. The required weights were subsequently derived by a more flexible approach—reliance on trial and error through several approximations—with sufficient accuracy that they could be proved out in computations like the original. Since even the best of our economic statistics incorporate a certain amount of error, it should be kept in mind that the dangers of spurious results may be multiplied by the introduction of additional variables or by other refinements in technique, and any peculiarities in the results obtained should be investigated.

The complexity of the analysis must, of course, be partly a matter of personal preference. But actual experience indicates what might be stated as a general rule: the more a function is complicated by additional variables or by nonlinear relationships, the surer it is to make a good fit with past data and the surer it is to go wrong at some time in the future.

Usually the degree of correlation is improved in the more complex relationships. Any measure of the improvement, however, offers little assurance of validity when the relationship is applied in making forecasts. It is usually said that a coefficient of correlation r of .9 indicates that 81 percent of the squared variance is "explained." This does not mean either that this proportion will continue to hold good or, even assuming it does on the average, that it will hold good in any particular year.

When absolute values of economic variables are correlated, coefficients of correlation are likely to be very high, but even values of r above .99 may produce faulty forecasts. When year-to-year changes are correlated, much lower degrees of correlation may be useful, but dealing with the residual variation becomes increasingly difficult as the coefficient falls. When r is .7, only about half of the squared variance is "explained," and the other half has to be "determined" on some other basis. At still lower levels, the correlation becomes of so little help and the other means of arriving at an estimate so much more important that the forecaster may be almost as well off with no correlation at all.

Another appropriate word of warning relates to the use of relationships incorporating a time lag. There is nothing to delight the heart of the forecaster so much as a good, dependable lag which automatically produces a future estimate of one variable as soon as the current value of another is known. Unfortunately, few lags can be expected to provide dependable forecasts. Thus the stock market has been used for many years as an indicator that moved ahead of general business conditions;

but in the last two decades it has failed so frequently, or the timing has been so undependable, that its value as an independent variable has been close to the vanishing point. Any such lag is likely to show similar shifts beyond an initial period of observation. Exceptions are found in those cases where one series, such as building contracts, is virtually just an earlier aspect of another, such as value of construction put in place. Unless there is some clear-cut reason of this kind underlying the relationship, reliance on lags cannot be recommended.

In deriving any correlation, it would seem clear almost without saying that every care should be exercised to get the best possible fit. But what represents the best fit for purposes of projection is seldom considered. The aim of correlation procedures is usually to get the best fit to the past data, in the sense that the differences between the observed and the calculated values will be at a minimum and will conform to a random distribution. Although this is a good standard for the analyst who knows nothing beyond the data with which he is working, it is not necessarily "best" from the standpoint of estimating future values of the dependent variable.

Often it is better if the relationship does not fit some of the past points quite so well and fits others somewhat better. In fact, a relationship that purports to "explain" all the past observations, whether or not there were disturbances affecting particular years, is likely to be distorted and therefore fallacious in comparison with one that deliberately fails to fit the observations in the disturbed years. For this reason, it is common practice to exclude the war years in correlating economic variables. But even in other years disturbances may be important. In a rather erratic series, the relationship should miss the mark at times rather than hit it precisely. Automobile sales, for example, were stimulated in 1950 by the Korean outbreak and were depressed in 1952 by production quotas and a prolonged steel strike. The best relationship should therefore underestimate 1950 and overestimate 1952. To make such a determination requires that other information than the statistics themselves be brought to bear on the problem. It requires research into the nature of the causes or influences that have produced the observed deviations.

After the mathematical equation expressing the relationship has been derived, it is usually desirable to review the results. Mathematical methods of obtaining a solution always provide an answer, and this is the best answer conforming to the assumptions underlying it. But the validity of that answer cannot be determined without considering the appropriateness of the calculated relationship in the light of everything else known about the behavior of the variables. Unless the analysis goes beyond the data themselves, the forecaster may be misled on many points.

An essential part of the testing process consists of analysis of the devia-

tions from the fitted line. This "residual variation" may be very revealing. Statistical theory usually puts the emphasis in analyzing it on the
character and distribution of the deviations from the standpoint of deciding how much reliance can be placed on the statistical tests of significance. But these tests are not good enough from the forecaster's point
of view. Differences between various relationships, all of which are well
within the range of statistical significance, may be of critical importance
in future applications.

Considered from the statistical point of view, the residuals, to be truly
random, not only must be distributed in accordance with the kind of
patterns that governs the behavior of variables influenced by chance
alone but also must be unsystematic in behavior through time. It frequently appears in analysis of economic time series that the residual
deviations will approximate a normal distribution if the order in which
they appear is disregarded. But when taken in sequence, they may display systematic variation that is inconsistent with the hypothesis that
their behavior is random, which implies that the variation in the dependent variable is not adequately explained. This happens when the
residuals are serially correlated, that is, when each tends to resemble the
preceding one in direction and magnitude. It might also be true in other
cases: for example, if the deviations followed a 4-year cycle, with two
pluses being consistently followed by two minuses, there would be no
serial correlation, but there would be a need to explain this additional
pattern of variation.

The unexplained behavior stands as a question mark on the validity
of the original analysis. A line of relationship whose deviations are
serially correlated cannot be considered as reliable as one whose deviations are truly random, because the forces that produce the systematic
variation in the residuals may also be responsible in large measure for
other aspects of the relationship itself. If they fail to behave like the
independent variable in the future, the relationship may be rendered
worthless.

Nevertheless, systematic patterns of deviation do appear at times in
otherwise sound correlations, perhaps in one subperiod under the influence of special conditions, and not in others; and such discrepancies
do not necessarily represent a sufficient fault to invalidate the relationship. In time-series analysis one should not expect a truly random distribution of the residuals, and if it has been obtained in the past, it should
not necessarily be expected to hold good in the future. The important
thing is to ensure that the abnormal behavior appears in the right periods
and not in others and that its effects are isolated and not spread out over
all the observations in such a manner as to create an illusion of random
behavior where it does not really exist.

The primary concern of the practical forecaster, therefore, is with the logical rather than with the statistical character of the residuals. No matter what method of fitting he has used, the final test is whether the line of estimate arrived at will give the best set of future estimates, with account being taken of all that is known about the nature of the variable being forecast and what has happened elsewhere in the economy to make that variable behave as it did. There are many occasions when he may be justified in using a relationship that does not appear to be entirely satisfactory or dependable in a statistical sense. He may, in fact, "adjust" a relationship in such a way as to create a larger average "error" of estimate in the past in order to improve its fit in the particular situations where it appears logically to hold good.

It is entirely proper, in other words, to modify the relationships first obtained by correlation procedures in order to take account of any factors known to have been operating toward abnormal results. A relationship may validly be shifted in such a way as to produce the pattern of deviations called for by the special circumstances prevailing at various times within the period of observation as a whole. Modifications made in this way by the experienced analyst may distinctly improve the forecasting validity of a relationship. They should be made, however, only when two criteria apply: first, when there is definite justification for the change in terms of what is known to have produced the past results; and, second, when there is reason to believe that the modified relationship will be the better one to work with in the future.

With these qualifications in mind, correlation may be regarded as one of the forecaster's most useful tools. It enables him to move from one point of analysis to another, both in working out an over-all forecast and in applying it to specific problems after the over-all result is obtained. In fact, once a decisive change in any variable can be forecast, it may be no more than a matter of working out its repercussions on other variables in order to project the movement of the over-all economy. Similarly, many particular segments of the economy can be forecast only in relation to over-all activity or some other broad measure, and forecasts made on any other basis may be subject to a wide margin of error.

Many estimating devices that are not correlation procedures as such in reality imply correlations. For example, most of the procedures relating inputs to outputs involve a kind of correlation analysis, whether it is consciously used or not. Again, such an operation as breaking down a broad aggregate into components by means of past percentage distributions could often be more appropriately carried out by correlation techniques. Even a seasonal that needs to be adjusted as an industry approaches capacity operations involves a correlation approach, although in practice some other method may be adopted.

The extreme flexibility of the method is shown by the ease with which it may be applied in situations that require attention to time lags or other relationships between the results of one period and another. The whole field of linear programming, which seeks to ensure the necessary inputs to provide a general program of final outputs, consists of formulating the series of relationships involved in terms of all the lags and wastage factors applicable in the various stages of production and distribution. Similarly, rate of change analysis, which relies upon the acceleration of one variable to determine the movements of another, involves exploration and testing by correlation methods.

ADJUSTMENT OF DATA

In the usual discussion of statistical methods, it is assumed that the data used are satisfactory for the application of those methods. In practice, however, this is likely not to be the case, at least not unless precautions are taken to ensure their suitability. There are always imperfections in time series, no matter how carefully they are compiled, and these imperfections make necessary adjustments before the data can effectively serve the purposes of analysis.

The question: "How sound are the data?" is one of the first points to be considered in practical work. As a rule it should be taken up before one proceeds with any analysis of cycles, trends, or correlations. Possibly the current observations are entirely sound, but if the earlier data are not also sound, there will be a tipping of the correlation or trend line that may invalidate the projection. Since there are various reasons why even a single series may not be comparable from one year to the next, it is extremely important to make every effort to ensure accuracy over the entire period covered by the analysis.

The raw data available from most reporting sources require some adjustments to make them analytically meaningful. The history of the data themselves and comparisons with partial information available from other sources are among the primary means of evaluating them for this purpose. If an effort is made to find out what made the statistical record what it is, the reason why one treatment should be applied rather than another may be apparent.

Important in this is an understanding of how current series are constructed, because the agencies compiling current statistics face the same problem as part of their regular work. The procedures for reconstructing the entire population from a sample are an essential aspect of the task. But in time-series analysis, difficulties arise: samples are not truly random, variations in the samples are troublesome, and even when constant samples are available from period to period, the populations to which they belong are continually changing. An almost unavoidable type of adjustment consists of those designed to correct sample deficiencies. Fortunately most basic current reports are handled in a satisfactory way today, but where the reporting agencies have not attempted the necessary adjustments, the forecaster is left to work them out to the best of his ability.

Underlying each current series is usually a set of basic data which is depended upon as a measure of absolute magnitude in the current period and as a measure of the relationship of various past periods to the present. These basic data, commonly referred to as "bench marks," may take the form of periodic censuses or of reports to the Bureau of Internal Revenue under the income tax laws. They seldom cover all years in the past and usually are available only after considerable delay, so that at least the latest year and perhaps the last several years must be covered by interim reports of a less comprehensive nature.

In the past these basic data were often regarded as beyond question. Today, however, it is recognized that they too have deficiencies. Both the war experience of registration for the draft, which turned up something like a million men who had not been counted in the 1940 census, and more recent studies by the Census Bureau, which amounted in effect to retaking the 1950 census on a more accurate basis in selected areas, have revealed important errors in the basic census data themselves. There are, in other words, enumeration errors and response errors even in what purports to be a complete census; and where sample surveys are used, these errors may be more important than the sampling errors. Hence even the most comprehensive reports may require analysis and adjustment in certain parts.

In any case, it is necessary to fill in gaps in the periods between past bench-mark reports and to bring the series up to date in the interval since the last report. In some cases current data may be available for this purpose. Perhaps there is a monthly series based on reports from a panel or sample of respondents among the population as a whole, or there may be a closely related type of information in terms of which the desired data may be carried forward. In other cases no satisfactory data can be found, interpolation has to be used to fill the gaps, and the current series has to be extrapolated or projected from the last basic report in the light of whatever is known about its behavior. For certain relatively stable series these may be fairly satisfactory expedients.

In some cases it will be found that there are no basic data which can be relied upon, but merely one or more sample or partial sources, and in the usual case of this kind such sources vary greatly in quality and dependability. Not only are there important differences between sources, but also the quality of reports from a given source may vary greatly from period to period. Hence there are innumerable situations where adjustments to current or back data are needed.

Then, too, errors and omissions may create an important problem. Anyone who has been engaged in a large-scale reporting operation knows the practical impossibility of obtaining accurate reports from all respondents or of coding, editing, and tabulating the returns with complete accuracy. Although a good statistical organization will hold errors to a relatively insignificant level, nevertheless they will be encountered, and at least some thought should be given to what might be done about them. Here again the advantage of plotting the data may be quickly apparent, because inspection may reveal important differences between the data for different periods and call attention to this particular period in which the difficulty is critical. This problem is quite likely to be encountered in following any series back over a great many years, because some of the techniques for ensuring comparability have only recently been put to use. Hence the older part of the series may be subject to a much greater degree of error than the recent, but errors in the older part of the series may produce as big an error in a projection into the future as any likely to arise from ignoring the older data entirely.

Splicing. The difficulties of making adjustments are multiplied when data from several sources have to be relied upon. Many of our best statistical series go back only 10 to 25 years. Sometimes a reasonably good analysis can be carried out on the basis of a period as short as this, but at other times results would be in considerable doubt because of the various disturbances that have had such important effects since 1929. Bench-mark reports may be very helpful in extending the record but tend to be of very little use analytically. Partial reports covering the intervals between bench marks may be available, but before any adjustment of interim levels can even begin to be made, it is necessary to splice together the various partial data available.

Very frequently in these cases the question is asked: "What is the best method of joining two series?" Experience teaches that there is no single best method. If both the series to be joined are available during an overlapping period, it pays to investigate their relationship during that period. This may require no more than charting the two series together, but in special cases it may require much greater effort—for the purpose of determining the characteristics of the two series and testing their validity in terms of consistency with other information. If the overlapping period is long, a definite relationship between the series may be established. One may represent a relatively fixed proportion of the other, the two may be intercorrelated but with quite different amplitudes of fluctuation, or they may differ by a fixed absolute amount.

In all such cases the observed relationship may serve as a basis for making the splice. Then again, it may not. There is, for example, a need for great caution in making fixed absolute adjustments, especially if the adjusted series covers a long period in which it changes level substantially.

On occasion the overlapping period may reveal no definite relationship but perhaps just an irregular but growing divergence. Possibly, then, the history of the statistical series, the procedures used in compiling them, and their make-up in terms of reporting samples may indicate the best procedure for splicing. One series may reflect a growing sample, the other a dwindling sample, making both too low during the period of overlapping. Then the early part of the current series could be modified in the light of the average movements of the two series during the overlapping period, and the whole series could then be spliced to the modified new series at an appropriate point.

Perhaps some shorter period within the period of overlapping may provide the best basis for the splice. If one or both of the series are found to be undependable in some years but relatively dependable in others, the dependable period would be the appropriate one for making the adjustment.

In other cases there may be no real overlapping, just one year or month in which both of the two series are reported. That period would seem to provide the only basis for the splice. This is in fact a fairly common situation where two series are generally comparable in quality but some change in concept, in reporting method, or in classification has produced a break. Such breaks may be observed for example, in the Federal Reserve series on bank loans shown in Chart 2–2.

If the changes in the reports are clearly understood, the kind of adjustment method appropriate may be indicated. In a commonly encountered case of this kind the only expedient may be a simple adjustment by a fixed ratio. Yet such a simple splicing technique should not be applied blindly, even in cases where the alternatives are or seem to be quite limited. One alternative that should be explored is the possibility of making back estimates of the particular component responsible for the break.

An important consideration in making adjustments of this kind has to do with seasonal effects. If the seasonals in the two series are different, it may be necessary to eliminate seasonal variation before making the adjustment, and at the very least it is important not to make an adjustment in seasonally unadjusted data in any period when differences in seasonal position would affect the outcome. Thus, if a series with little seasonal variation is spliced to one where such variation is important—which is likely, for instance, when data from different regions or cities are being used—a splice made at a seasonal high or low could introduce a large error into the earlier or later part of the series. Possibly there may be some means of checking whether the earlier and later levels of the resulting series are consistent, as in cases where census or other basic information is available for both but only at rather substantial intervals and not in the intervening period.

Again, there may be a gap between two series with no overlapping. Even then, it is sometimes possible to splice them together into a continuous series. There are three possibilities. First, if the earlier or later levels can be established, then an interpolation can be made to fill the gap. Second, if a series of a similar nature can be constructed from hitherto utilized sources, it may be adequate for bridging the gap. Third, closely related series may be used to estimate the desired series over the intervening period, or other knowledge obtained from special studies may produce some kind of reasonable basis for setting earlier and later levels. Obviously any such adjustment raises a question about the validity of the series, and any trends or relationships should be projected with that qualification in mind.

Interpolation Formulas. There are almost innumerable uses of interpolation techniques in adjusting, translating, or projecting statistical data. Two situations are common. In the first, bench marks are available in the form of basic reports at rather infrequent intervals. In the second, comprehensive reports are available annually, but the series that must be used currently is a monthly series distinctly less dependable in character. The movements of the current data in these cases may be undependable in that they tend to drift away from the basic data over a period of time but nevertheless present a more realistic picture of interim changes than any smoother interpolation or extrapolation of the basic series. In either case, a satisfactory result may be obtained by using interpolation formulas to adjust the current series to the level of the basic reports.

It is usually desirable to preserve the monthly pattern of the current data in the adjusted series. To accomplish this, the ratios of the basic annual data to the annual averages of the monthly or quarterly data for the same years are computed. Then a smooth curve is applied to these ratios, and monthly values of the ratios are read off the curve. When the monthly series is multiplied by these ratios, the result is a series which has much the same month-to-month movements but corresponds in level to the basic data in the years for which such data are available.

Where such an adjustment is made, the fitting of the smooth curve may be done either graphically or by mathematical methods. A discussion of the problem is contained in Appendix A. To summarize the principles involved: the adjustment factors should be smoothly changing from month to month; at points where one adjustment ends and another begins, the juncture in the factors should be smooth, and the earlier adjustments should be modified as may be necessary to accomplish this; extreme shifts should be avoided, and the factors should be confined as far as possible to the range established by the bench-mark ratios; and the extent of the adjustment should be restricted at the end of the period, as by assuming that the bias being corrected has halted at that time.

In one respect this solution oversimplifies the problem. It assumes that the appearance of errors is a function of time alone. There are cases, however, when it may be preferable to assume that the errors are a function of the changes that have occurred. Then the over-all error may be assigned in proportion to the absolute magnitude of each of the interim changes that has occurred in the period between the basic reports. Or if special knowledge of the situation suggests still another hypothesis about the source or timing of errors, that hypothesis might be put to work as the basis for an interpolation specifically designed to meet the needs of the situation.

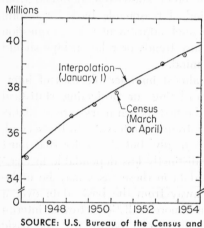

Chart 3–8. Married Couples

SOURCE: U.S. Bureau of the Census and Appendix C.

Interpolations are not confined, of course, to adjusting data to a specified level. They may satisfactorily be used to fill gaps in statistical series or to break down known annual totals into monthly or quarterly parts. If, for example, an expenditure of known amount has been made in a specified period of months, it may be possible to portray the results with a degree of accuracy that is acceptable for most practical purposes. If the total amount of the program, the month in which it began, and the approximate peak rate reached in a subsequent month are known, an interpolation would be almost bound to give results similar to the actual monthly expenditures. Or if annual totals are known and it is also known that the program tended to fluctuate inversely with some other measure, such as unemployment, a monthly representation of what happened could be made with a substantial degree of dependability.

When related data are available, the short-term movements may sometimes be portrayed more effectively by an interpolation than by an original compilation of new data. An illustration is provided by the data on married couples presented in Chart 3–8, where estimates based on an interpolation of marriages, divorces, and deaths are compared with the Census Bureau estimates for selected postwar years. Whenever new data have to be based on a limited sample or are weak in other respects, an interpolation from other related data of a comprehensive character might work fully as well in measuring year-to-year changes. Even though the sampling variation in the newly developed survey is small, it may produce erratic and illogical movements from any one year to the next.

The person who is familiar enough with these techniques of reproducing past situations by reference to the sheer logic of the known facts will be in a much better position to project series into the future. Knowing how certain series behave and putting that knowledge to work in constructing a hypothetical portrayal of their future behavior is as sound a way of forecasting certain series as it may be possible to obtain. A device capable of portraying effectively something that happened in the past can be turned to just as effective use for indicating what will happen in the future if the conditions for it are specified to the same degree. In other words, interpolation is one of the keys to extrapolation.

EXTRAPOLATION PROCEDURES

The practice of extending series from the latest reported date merely on the basis of what they seem likely to do in the light of current information has become fairly widespread. In simplest form the procedure consists simply of extrapolating a line on a chart to depict expected changes from the latest reported date to some future period for which a forecast is desired. Projection of the gross-national-product and national-income accounts in this way provides an easy "forecast" of what the economy "will do" in the period covered by the projection. That the attractiveness of such an easy solution tends to be offset by a corresponding lack of validity is less frequently taken into account.

Consider the projections on Chart 3–9, which portrays the postwar movements of personal income. The line portraying the "trend" for the entire period 1946 to 1954 seemingly provides a basis for projecting into 1955 and beyond. However, even limited consideration of what happened will indicate that it has little more validity than the short-term projections indicated by the dotted lines, which resulted in errors at points A, B, C, D, and E. These, by the way, represent actual forecasts that were commonly accepted 9 months earlier.

The method does produce good results in some instances, particularly over the very short term, because there is sufficient continuity in most economic activities that a simple projection for several months cannot give much different results from those which would be obtained by more complicated methods. The projection *D*, for example, which was widely accepted at the end of 1950, gives a good estimate for the first half of 1951. The difficulty is that the period over which continuity can be relied upon is so short that the forecast will be lacking in significance for that reason alone.

Much of the "success" achieved by analysts using this approach suffers this disadvantage. Projecting a stable series like gross national

Chart 3–9. Projections of Personal Income

Quarterly Data at Seasonally Adjusted Annual Rates

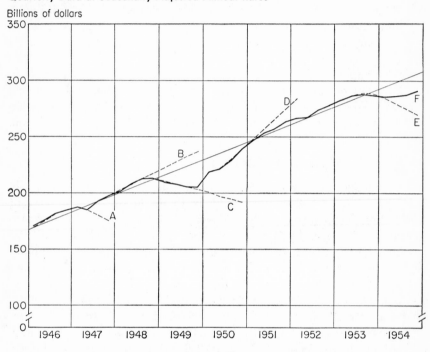

product 1 month ahead would generally be regarded as inconsequential. Projecting the next quarter's average level at the beginning of the quarter represents substantially the same accomplishment, but this fact is not so generally recognized. Estimating the gross national product for the year at the mid-point of the second quarter is hardly more of a feat. It definitely is not a process of forecasting 7½ months ahead. The averaging of so much that is already known with any reasonable estimate for the remainder of the year reduces the margin of error in the annual estimate to only a fraction of what it might be in terms of the annual rate at the year end.

Even a forecast made just after the beginning of a year in terms of totals for the whole calendar year does not qualify as more than a short-term forecast. Its potential error is in fact equivalent to that of a forecast for something less than 6 months, because the level of the early months is already fairly well defined.

As a rule, a forecast is more useful the further into the future it reaches. As the forecaster looks into the future, however, there is less and less that can definitely be said about anything that will be important in determining the level of activity. There are some exceptions to this, but ordinarily we are moving from something that is known to something that is at best dimly perceived. Just ahead, many things are fairly well defined, being, as they are, no more than extensions of what is here and now. Further along, everything merges into the shadows.

What, then, is the optimum period for forecasting? Obviously this depends in large measure on the circumstances confronting the forecaster. For most who are interested in general economic conditions rather than in some particular industry or branch of activity, a year ahead may be taken as the best objective. Beyond a year, so many things can happen that it becomes very difficult to define the situation with any assurance. On the other hand, anything less than a year may leave the user of the forecast with too little time to operate, for before the year is out the general nature of the situation is likely to be so widely understood as to remove the advantage of foreseeing it.

A period described as "a year" should refer to a full year from the time the forecast is made. This means something like 5 quarters from the last basic data reported, and if the nature of the situation at the end of the year is to be defined in terms of the way things are changing, it may be necessary to include the sixth quarter in the forecast also.

Using annual data alone may make it impossible to produce this kind of forecast. An additional disadvantage of working in terms of annual data is that it tends to conceal important movements within the year. Sometimes an annual estimate looks entirely reasonable in terms of past annual data, but when taken in relation to the existing situation as revealed by quarterly or monthly data, it is readily seen to be inconsistent with the situation that is developing or is thought likely to develop. In a period of advance, for example, an estimated 5 percent increase for the next year over the year just closed might seem reasonable; but when it is known that the closing months of the year were already more than 5 percent above the average, then it is clear that 5 percent on an annual average basis is much too small if the advance is expected to continue.

This brings out one of the advantages of projecting each series from the latest period actually reported, no matter what other considerations are used in arriving at the final estimate. Continuity may thus be utilized to the extent appropriate for the specific series, by obtaining the explanation of current movements, including any temporary developments, and then going on to a consideration of the intermediate movements that might occur on the way to the terminal point. Moreover, failure to consider the intervening period tends to leave the forecaster in the dark about the nature of the situation at the forecast date. He has little idea of what the direction or rate of change in the over-all movement is likely to be at that time. A correct forecast of a higher level is made much more useful by distinguishing whether the economy will then be continuing up or will be falling back from some still higher intermediate position. In other words, there is not just an immediate continuity to take into account but a progression of continuities throughout the time span under consideration.

Extrapolation procedures have the advantage of focusing attention on these continuities and in doing so make a valid contribution to the forecast. However, discontinuities are only one kind of error, and as the forecast is pushed into the more distant future, the value of the immediate continuity greatly dwindles. The forces making for over-all change may be altered drastically within a year. That is a long enough period for even the most stable segments, like construction or consumption, to change significantly, and sharp reversals may occur in the more variable segments, like government expenditures or inventories. Mere projection of recent changes is, therefore, unsatisfactory over periods long enough to make an over-all forecast really useful.

This conclusion in turn falls short of telling the whole story, since the objections to informal extrapolation as a source of over-all projections do not apply with equal force to projections of specific segments or branches of activity. There are many series that cannot effectively be projected by more formal statistical methods, because they do not conform sufficiently to any of the trends, patterns, or relationships upon which those methods are based. Moreover, most series have at least some elements of erratic or independent movement that cannot be effectively dealt with by statistical techniques. These have to be handled by the simpler, less formal types of projections that take off from where we are at the moment. Hence a question that assumes some importance is: "What is the basis for the valid use of such projections?"

The answer to this question lies in the analysis on which the projections are based. Such analysis may take various forms. It may proceed in terms of plans or programs, established characteristics of behavior, or known special forces or influences affecting the series in question. Only brief remarks on these procedures will be made at this point, as more detailed examples of the forms which such analysis can take will be presented in later chapters.

Plans or programs that indicate the future movements of important series are sometimes known in advance. Government programs are fairly well defined in terms of annual and interim budget estimates, appropriations, and authorizing legislation. Information on planned outlays by business for new plant and equipment are currently collected and published by both government agencies and private organizations. Data of this kind can be used to chart the future course of activity where available, but careful scrutiny of the reported plans in relation to the situation as a whole and to any anticipated changes in it is essential, for plans are subject to rapid change whenever the situation changes. Some plans are never carried through to completion, and others are put into effect quickly even though they were not planned sufficiently in advance to appear in the reported statements.

Knowing the way certain types of variables behave in characteristic situations may also provide an important basis for projecting a series. Stable series, like population, may advance at slower or faster rates but are not likely to reverse direction. Other forms of activity, like construction, tend to be fairly stable in the short run but change drastically in the course of the business cycle. Others, like inventories, are subject to sharp reversals, but these reversals are not entirely arbitrary, so that in specified situations the course of future changes may be charted. To the experienced forecaster, differences in characteristic amplitude of fluctuation alone provide a kind of criteria for making future projections.

There are, finally, any number of special considerations that may provide suitable clues to the action of important segments. The effects of government controls—such as allocations, priorities or materials-use restrictions—are sufficiently well known to provide a fairly dependable basis for certain kinds of projections. The appearance of credit stringency and an increase in interest rates may affect such activity as new-housing construction for a time at least. The existence of a large number of over-age automobiles in operation would tend to indicate a better than normal new-car market for several years. Where any such condition exists or can be foreseen, it may be used as a means of projecting certain affected segments.

All such forms of analysis may be used in the situations where they are appropriate. With sound analysis a reasonable projection may be made. Without it any projection can hardly be more, beyond a limited period, than a guess.

There is another situation in which the methods of simple projection have to be relied upon, that is, in correcting estimates derived from statistical trends or relationships after a large enough deviation has appeared so that the fitted line at least temporarily cannot be accepted as a satisfactory explanation of what is happening. At times, in a period of advance, a deviation of such magnitude may appear that the actual value exceeds the calculated value for the following year or two. In these circumstances it is generally necessary to make some allowance for the fact that the actual value is running ahead of what would have been expected on the basis of the computed line of relationship alone. Then an estimate has to be adopted that departs to some degree from the established relationship—just as the marksman aims off the target in order to hit the bull's-eye in a cross wind.

The necessity for such corrections or adjustments is widely recognized by practical statisticians. It is, in effect, a process of making short-term projections of the deviations from an established trend or relationship. Such a projection might move further away from the original line, or it might be curved back to the original relationship after a period. Again, no general rule can be given. Just what is done is largely a matter of judgment, but it should be judgment backed by research into the causes of the deviation that is being forecast. If the causes of the deviation can be discovered, it may be possible to determine whether those causes will carry future results further away or back into line with past experience.

If no such causes can be discovered, the projection will have to be made in terms of the statistical record itself, and its soundness will depend on how well founded the relationship is and how deviations from it have behaved in the past. If the past deviations have been randomly distributed, so that it was impossible to predict the direction and magnitude of any one from those that went before, and if the existing deviation is not unusually large, the line of relationship may still be taken as the best estimate for the period ahead. If, on the other hand, the deviations have shown positive serial correlation, it may be best to carry along the latest observed deviation for the next year.

In the latter case, the serial correlation calls in question the relationship itself. But the current deviation has already posed the problem for the forecaster, and he may be able to utilize the serial correlation in adjusting the current estimates. For the presence or absence of serial correlation is in part a function of the behavior characteristics of the data. Some series that are relatively stable display a large measure of serial correlation. Others fluctuate more rapidly, and there is not so much opportunity for similarity of deviations to persist. It is partly because both series are stratified in terms of the same time interval, the calendar year, that this difference is obtained.

Almost all series display some continuity of change, depending upon the nature and variability through time of the forces that produce changes in them. From an annual point of view, the deviations from a relationship may appear to be random, but when monthly or quarterly data are considered, successive deviations are highly correlated. When going from a positive residual in one year to a negative in the next, the monthly changes are likely to be quite gradual—a series of descending positives through the late months of one year and of increasing negatives through the early months of the next.

If a series of deviations has built up month by month through the year, reaching a peak at the end, the average deviation would be only half as large as the final term in the series. Carrying forward the annual deviation would then mean bringing the series back into line by the end of the next year. Carrying forward the maximum deviation reached at the year end would introduce a deviation twice as large in the next year, and projecting the same rate of departure from the original curve would produce an average deviation three times as large for the second year as a whole. The logic of these projections is all-important. The first procedure might be appropriate when the causes of the deviation were purely temporary; the last, where they were continuing in full effect. To know what has disturbed the relationship is often to know what should be done about projecting it.

What needs to be clearly understood in making corrections and adjustments, as in the case of simple projection of those segments of the economy to which statistical curves are unsuited, is that the result can only be as good as the analysis and the judgment that underlie it. Without discriminating treatment, the results cannot be dependable. It must be recognized that this is essentially an uncontrolled procedure and, like any other uncontrolled procedure, is subject to abuse.

This is the basis for the statistician's objection: "You can't make arbitrary adjustments!" The answer is: "Of course you can't make *arbitrary* adjustments. But there is no reason you shouldn't make *logical* adjustments!" This does not settle the dispute. It is hardly possible to satisfy both the desire for strict rules of procedure and the desire for the correct answer. The practical forecaster usually has to adhere to the latter criterion, and he finds that the flexible approach gives him definite advantages. The fact is that enough is known about the effects of various kinds of disturbances to take them roughly into account, when they are occurring or can be foreseen, and it is only a mistake to rule out this kind of information because it is not well founded in statistical terms.

There is another danger and another requirement for the forecaster in the use of informal extrapolations. Such projections cannot have the same validity as a statistical trend or relationship derived from the experience of many years. When results do not agree with the projection, there is no reason for thinking they will come back into line with it, as they are likely to do in the case of a relationship that has been used with good results for some time. Hence the forecaster is required to watch the situation more closely and correct his projections whenever it appears that they are not proving adequate. The best way to do this, again, is by finding out why the situation is turning out to be different from what had been conceived at the time the projection was made.

After analyzing or projecting any statistical series, it is a good practice to set up the results on a chart for visual review. Peculiarities in results arising from data or procedures may be apparent when this is done. New seasonal developments in a previously stable seasonal pattern may be clearly revealed. Projections of trends or cycles may show up as completely inconsistent with recent movements of the series. Comparisons of actual and estimated values may reveal the need for revision of a correlation and may even call attention to previously overlooked errors of computation.

This simple type of review chart allows the fullest scope for judgment in the use of statistical tools. It hardly ever pays to use a statistical method mechanically without considering the plausibility of results and without considering their consistency with other information. Emphasis is put on this point, because in working on practical statistical problems the most irksome part of the task may arise from errors or discrepancies of various kinds, but unless they can be dealt with effectively, they may vitiate the entire analysis.

CHAPTER 4

Constructing Over-all Forecasts

These are the elements from which any sound system of forecasting is made: facts that provide an understanding of current developments, techniques of projecting key statistics into the future, and judgment applied in a process of unbiased inquiry to resolve the difficulties encountered. Given these essential working materials, the problem is to put them together into a meaningful pattern of prospective change. It is in the truest sense a research problem, and like any other research problem it must be solved by the formulation and testing of hypotheses.

The over-all forecast is itself a kind of hypothesis in the first instance. The more specific, detailed hypotheses considered in working it out could conceivably relate to anything within the entire range of economic activity, from the most comprehensive over-all measures to the most specific bits and pieces. But no haphazard roving about in the realm of economic and business affairs could lead to a reasonable solution. There has to be an approach that will direct attention to significant points of attack and lead to a synthesis in which all the interrelated facts fit together like the pieces of a puzzle. Only the hypotheses that fit into such an approach need be put to the test.

The testing of the hypotheses must proceed in terms both of facts and of relationships. The facts of the current situation are of obvious importance in this context, but the facts of the future situation, not yet known, are themselves only hypothetical in character. Some can immediately be defined to a substantial degree of probability, and if the segments to which they refer are important enough, they may be decisive enough to determine the whole outcome. More commonly, however, no such certainty is to be found in the collection of hypotheses on

99

which projections have to be made. The only procedure immediately available, therefore, is to test the various hypothetical projections against each other. To the extent that certain relationships between segments are known to exist, any inconsistencies in the initial formulation may be immediately ironed out; and once an over-all forecast is obtained, it provides a kind of "factual" background against which the consistency of each specific hypothesis may be tested.

What this suggests is that the best approach proceeds from the particular to the general and then back to the particular. In this way it is possible to take full advantage of what is known about the important segments that can be effectively projected under the given circumstances. On the basis of relationships to these particular segments, it is possible to project still others, including the broad aggregates. After the preliminary investigation it is necessary to reappraise each of the important segments in the light of what is known about all of them. One or more of the original hypotheses may be clearly inconsistent with the over-all picture developed. Revision of that one may require revision of others to which it in turn is closely related. Out of this process of projection, adjustment, and revision comes an end result that is internally consistent and incorporates all that is known about the special forces affecting each important segment. This is all that can be done at the moment, since the facts that will provide the final test are not yet available.

In speaking of moving from the particular to the general, there is no implication that the particulars are defined indiscriminately. They are, rather, the items that are significant in making the economy move. It follows that they are themselves aggregates important enough in their own right to produce appreciable effects on the economy as a whole. But it is not enough that they are important in themselves. Their movements must to some extent be determined independently of movements of the general economy, so that information about them is of value apart from what is known to be happening elsewhere. And there must be some basis for analyzing their behavior in such a way as to make projection into the future possible. The segments of the economy that conform to these criteria may be appropriately termed the "strategic factors."

The search for strategic factors is in sharp contrast to attempts to amass evidence for projecting as many bits and pieces as possible and then merely to add the separate projections together as a means of getting a forecast of the whole economy. The latter is, nevertheless, a fairly common procedure in forecasting. Many regard it as a way of getting more dependable results than those gained through dealing with broader aggregates. While this may be true in particular instances, it can hardly be considered a sound generalization. Combining a number of detailed projections might be better than making a single total projection in some circumstances, but it might be worse in others, depending partly on how the projections are made and partly on what the course of developments turns out to be. Probably the most common result of using the more detailed method—in the absence of any preconception of the final result—is that it tends to give rather stable projections. The stability is the result of the averaging process involved in combining a number of component series. For this reason alone, the method may sometimes produce a good result, especially if the person who is doing the projecting might make a rather wild projection of any one series taken alone. On the other hand, if the situation should change sharply, the method tends to underestimate the change. Any successes that have been achieved by this method were probably due more to other elements in the procedure than to the mere aggregation of a series of independent projections.

RELIANCE ON JUDGMENT ALONE

At the opposite extreme from dealing with a mass of relatively independent particulars are attempts to move directly to an over-all forecast without consideration of the specific forces operating in various parts of the economy. The philosophy of this approach was succinctly stated by the student who wrote in his examination paper: "The first step is to get in mind a picture of the situation and what direction the economy may be expected to take. Then one can go forward with the analysis and see if the figures bear him out." The person who goes at the problem in this way will always find figures to bear him out, but he will wind up with nothing better than an unsupported judgment, for all the appearance of support it is subsequently given.

Informal methods of judgment have, of course, been the stand-by of the business executive who was forced by practical necessity to make decisions affecting his company's operation. These decisions could be said to imply forecasts even though none were explicitly made. He had to make up his mind, and the only way he could do so was to make the best judgment possible in the light of his knowledge, however limited, of the general economic situation, the outlook for his own industry, and the position of his own company.

Forecasts made in this way, often with no apparent system of analysis and possibly on the spur of the moment, sometimes turn out to be surprisingly accurate. The seasoned and mature veteran of many business situations acquires the knack of playing by ear. He picks up cues from small snatches and isolated details and may be able to piece together a fairly accurate representation of the complete score.

The dangers of playing by ear when there is a high intercorrelation among the things being said are frequently not recognized. The businessman listens to others, who may or may not be doing their own forecasting. He also talks to others, and what he says to them may come back to him in somewhat exaggerated form several rounds later. This concert in the air tends to call the tune. But it does not determine the course of business.

Good judgment is usually considered one of the prime requisites of the efficient executive, though what constitutes good judgment in this sense is seldom defined or tested. The process by which the decision is arrived at may not be remembered, and no explicit attempt is made to check the accuracy of the reasoning that underlay the decision. Partly, of course, it is simply a process of learning through experience. Successes and errors register, perhaps subconsciously, and provide the basis for a correct answer the next time a similar situation arises.

Where the method of judgment is more specifically described and supported, it is possible to distinguish at least two definite procedures. The first involves the use of historical analogy. Such analogies may be explicitly spelled out, or they may lurk in the background of the forecaster's experience without conscious formulation. When a situation is identified as essentially similar to a known previous situation, the analogy is put to work to supply a forecast of future developments.[1]

The difficulty with this procedure lies in the identification of sameness. Certain similarities are bound to appear in each business decline; that much is almost a matter of definition. But superficial likenesses are not enough, for concealed differences may be of overriding importance.

One of the fundamental propositions of logic is that an analogy can at best establish only a probable inference. Even that is valid only to the extent that there has been a fair sampling of similar situations and an essential identity of relations and conditions exists.

In this complex, dynamic world of ours, economic conditions are never exactly the same. Even in two postwar periods, when they might be expected to be most nearly alike, there are important differences. Thus, while the initial postwar inflation of 1946 was correctly forecast by analogy with 1919, serious declines in 1947, 1948, and 1949 were incorrectly forecast by analogy with 1920.

It is true that we rely on the past for an understanding of the processes by which economic change takes place. Analogies often provide hypotheses or clues that prove valid on further analysis. For any of them to be more than a clue, however, it must fit into the unfolding pattern of real events. The future flows not from the past but from the present—

[1] As an example, see the article by W. S. Woytinski, "Postwar Economic Perspectives," Social Security Bulletin, December, 1945.

not from any repetition of previous experiences but from the forces currently making for change. Analogies, therefore, will always have but
limited usefulness in forecasting.

The second procedure consists of striking a balance between the
favorable and unfavorable factors affecting current rates of activity. The
selection of factors on each side may be systematic or unsystematic; it
may cover the whole economy or merely certain parts that are considered
decisive at the moment; and it may take up major segments in their
entirety or consider some of their subsegments only. Appraising the
impact of the factors selected may be equally systematic or haphazard.[2]

In most cases, this approach produces highly indefinite and qualified
forecasts. At its worst, it may leave the analyst right where he started,
without any conclusion about what is likely to happen. At its best, it
may come very close to a sound quantitative analysis of emerging economic developments. The closer it comes to the latter extreme, the more
likely it is to produce sound forecasts.

A balancing of factors has no validity in anything but quantitative
terms. Otherwise, one factor may be sufficient to override all the others
and yet may be played down as relatively unimportant. Or all the important factors may be on one side and yet may be judged in qualitative
terms as less consequential than those on the other side. If consideration
is limited to certain segments only, those omitted may actually be
the decisive elements. There can be no substitute for a complete
accounting in quantitative terms of all important aspects of the economic
picture.

Those who consider sound judgment to be the answer may wish to
quarrel with this statement. Some will argue that judgment in some
informal, mysterious manner accomplishes the same result. They may
point to instances where judgment alone was successful. But all of this
needs something in the way of more logical support. Intuitive processes
cannot be shown to perform the objective recording and comparison
necessary for explicit testing, and any test that omits consideration of
failures cannot demonstrate the validity of processes that produce some
successes. What seems the more likely alternative is that there can be
no consistent judgment in the absence of a quantitative approach.

[2] As an example of this approach, see the pamphlet by Marcus Nadler, *Inflation
or Deflation?* the Hanover Bank, New York, 1951. After an extended review of the
factors making for inflation and those making for deflation, Nadler summarizes his
analysis in 10 conclusions. These are mainly of a long-term rather than a short-term
character and deny that either drastic inflation or major depression is in prospect.
Factual material is used throughout, but the discussion is mainly in nonquantitative
terms. It is therefore difficult to assess the case for or against either inflation or
deflation in the near future, even though a good summary of important considerations is presented.

Consider the bases of sound judgment. The first is experience. But experience is always limited and partial. No matter how mature and well-trained a person may be, he will suffer many elements of doubt if his information is not quantitative in character. The expert begins with superior knowledge and may also have special sources of information from which he can find an answer to the specific question that represents the key to the whole problem. But the extent to which he can be successful depends on knowing what to look for and being able to discriminate between what is important and what is trivial, and these are themselves points of difference that can be significant only as they take account of the quantities involved.

The second basis for sound judgment may be termed the scientific attitude of mind. The scientist solves his problems not by jumping to a conclusion and acting upon it without further ado but by developing and systematically testing hypotheses to explain the observed facts. The attempt is always to explain each situation in terms of the forces that have made it what it is, on the assumption that each kind of force will tend to produce the same effect in every situation in which it is operative. In this kind of analysis of economic events, the only dependable significance of the forces themselves and of the net effect which any combination of them produces is in quantitative terms. There can be no explanation without a statement of the various factors in terms of a common measure that permits their analysis and recombination into a meaningful whole.

The successes of unsupported judgment may perhaps be attributed to the fact that it partially, even though unconsciously, incorporates elements of such a process. This is particularly likely to occur in situations where one decisive factor is dominating the entire trend and some experience with the operation of that factor has previously been recorded. It cannot be expected to produce consistent results, however, in new situations, in situations dominated by factors not previously experienced, or in situations where various factors are operating in conflict so that the outcome is dependent upon the specific balance of the values on one side and the other.

THE SURVEY OR INTERVIEW APPROACH

Another nonanalytical approach sets up an over-all forecast as the consensus, or perhaps the average, of a number of independent forecasts obtained by means of surveys or interviews. Almost all our economic data are compiled by survey methods. Reports are obtained from people who know the answers to the questions asked. Usually the information requested is quantitative in character—relating to such measures of activity as production, sales, prices, or income. Usually, also, it refers to recent past experience rather than future estimates and preferably is taken from actual operating or accounting records. In short, the survey is the basic means by which we know what is going on in the economy.

In recent years, surveys have been made much more efficient and accurate by advances in sampling and interview technique. With the development of improved sampling methods, based on probability theory, the information can generally be obtained with greater assurance of accuracy and at lower cost than before.

Sample improvement cannot, of course, eliminate response errors, but fortunately improvements in questionnaire design and interviewing technique have also been engineered to meet the needs of situations where many interrelated bits of information were required. More numerous and complex questions could be asked—though perhaps only of a subsample—without making the conduct of the survey overly expensive. Thus surveys without practical limit on scope of information could be designed and carried out with limited resources and relatively good prospects of obtaining worthwhile results.

With "results" so easy to obtain, it is perhaps not strange that this device should be turned to forecasting use. Why not move directly to the end product, ask about the outlook, and thus produce a ready-made forecast without the complications involved in other methods? That this idea has been widely embraced is hardly a matter of doubt.

The survey or interview approach can be made as broad or as narrow a forecasting procedure as may be desired, simply because it is possible to ask questions about anything. When used as a general forecasting device, the questions may deal broadly with the movement of the general economy in terms of such basic statistics as gross national product, industrial production, employment, and prices.

What is commonly overlooked by those advocating this approach is that the basic function of a survey is to obtain information, not to create it. Just as the prospector goes around discovering valuable ore deposits, the interviewer can unearth valuable information. He can no more create information that does not exist than the prospector can create mineral deposits. Nevertheless, this fact is frequently lost sight of by enthusiasts of the survey approach.

The basic difficulty with any forecast survey is that the interviewer can usually succeed in obtaining answers from respondents who do not know the answers. The uninformed individual will make unguarded statements when confronted by the interviewer with a question he feels he must answer. The businessman may fill out a questionnaire—perhaps indicating his uncertainty by an entry of "no change"—in order to show his desire to cooperate with a government bureau or other survey agency. No one can give an informed opinion about innovations or other matters beyond his experience. Nevertheless, a skilled interviewer can get many people to "cooperate," and they may dream up answers beyond the scope of their actual knowledge. No matter how many such answers may be obtained, there is still no information worth having. That is why surveys on the future of the general economy, or of the stock market, can contribute little.

The use of the survey as an economic-forecasting device has in large measure grown out of the new "psychological" theories of economic activity. At the extreme, these theories present a form of psychological determinism of economic affairs. What people will do, the theories state, depends upon their attitudes, expectations, or other preconditioning. "If you want to know what people will do in the period ahead," says the survey expert, "let me analyze their attitudes, goals, and intentions for the answer. Since these elements intervene in the processes of action, we have but to tap in at this point to determine what the course of that action will be."

There is, no doubt, good justification for a movement toward socio-psychological analysis. The realistic economics that is needed as a basis for forecasting may properly be regarded as a branch of social psychology, belonging in the general area known as group dynamics. Much of what is currently being said on the subject, however, does not fit into such an approach. It is rather a kind of individualistic psychology, with primary attention being focused on motivations. It barely touches the subject of group action, which, as has frequently been pointed out, cannot be considered as merely the expression of the aggregate of individual motivations.

Discussions of economic problems with advocates of the psychological approach often involve a considerable semantics difficulty. There is a psychological counterpart to every type of human behavior, of course, and it is as appropriate to view economic behavior from the standpoint of the psychologist as from that of the economist. Viewed in this way, there can be no dispute about the role of psychology in analysis of business fluctuations. The difficulty arises when the "psychological factors" are presented as something separable, things existing in their own right and exerting force on the economy, which can be objectively defined and measured by written or verbal reports from a specific sample or group. If the validity of such specific psychological forces is challenged, their proponents may retreat into the concepts of the broader psychological perspective describing essentially the same economic phenomena from another point of view. There is a need, apparently, for a careful definition of concepts and of the research techniques appropriate to each.

From the strictly economic point of view, the psychological approach has its roots in the fact that certain phenomena or processes seemingly cannot take place without decisions by the various persons or groups involved. Thus investment in plant and equipment requires that management make a decision to expand. Such decisions, made in the course of the business cycle, sometimes prove to be "mistakes," because the investments undertaken at the peak of the boom may earn no profit in the depression years that follow. It would seem, therefore, that a realistic theory of economics should explain these mistakes. Obviously, the people who made them did not know they were mistaken at the time. They expected their investments to turn out better. Evidently expectations are at the root of the difficulty, possibly at the root of the cycle itself. From this proposition a whole theory of the cycle may be evolved—in terms of expectations, confidence, fears, and waves of optimism or pessimism.

There is, however, a gap in the logic. Just because actions have a seeming element of foresight does not mean they are determined by that element. It is sometimes said that forecasting is an unavoidable necessity, implicit in the actions of both businessmen and customers. The decision to build a house, for example, is said to imply the anticipation that the house will be needed. What this overlooks is that the need may already exist or that new needs may develop *pari passu* with the building. The decision flows from the situation with which we are confronted. It might just as well be said that we have to decide to *eat*. It may even be said that we *do* decide to eat at certain specific hours. But what is really obvious is that we cannot decide *not* to eat. The decision we make, therefore, is no more than an incident in a more complete pattern of behavior. We find it necessary to adapt ourselves to circumstances, and we do so by eating, by building houses, and by performing all the other acts that make up our way of living.

The patterns of intelligent behavior have displayed elements of foresight through all the ages. The progress of the human race may be said to derive from our ability to plan ahead. But planned action gains its effectiveness by controlling effort in the interest of specified goals and not by predicting possible events that are largely beyond our knowledge and control.

In other words, anticipations or expectations are only one, and a relatively limited, aspect of economic affairs. They play a role in the pattern of ongoing activity without in any significant sense causing it. When the underlying causes change, the pattern of activity changes and expectations change with it. The fact that they may change more quickly, before action itself can be adjusted, in no wise makes them responsible for the shift. On exceptional occasions, expectations may change without a change in the underlying causes, but the movements resulting from such a shift are usually neither large nor prolonged.

One of the biggest fallacies in economics is the notion that just because "everybody" believes something it will happen or will be prevented from happening. Even the most widely accepted forecasts are likely to be disappointed. But it is not the acceptance that results in their disappointment. It is merely that the forces at work were not correctly appraised and could not be overturned by a mistaken view.

There is little evidence to support the theory that expectations are self-fulfilling. On the contrary, the studies that have been made—as contrasted with mere theorizing on the subject—indicate not that expectations cause the turns in activity but rather that the turns come when the popular impression is that there is no end in sight.

The view of the outlook held by important decision makers only partly influences their decisions. And the decisions made by any such group only partly determine the results. Many things happen that nobody decides, wants, or expects.

On the consumer side, many activities take place without thought or question, and many plans or projects go by the board before fruition. Results obtained from follow-up surveys of consumer panels indicate that only about half the people who say they are going to buy specified items actually buy them in the specified period. But the total sales are approximately as high as indicated, because others who did not intend to buy nevertheless step in to fill the gap. The persistent patterns of behavior that are important from an economic point of view are thus only partly revealed by the intentions reported at any given moment.

The operation of business enterprises is not essentially different. The businessman may expect a decline, and he may cut his inventories, but he will produce enough to fill the orders he receives; and as soon as the expectations of a decline prove to be mistaken, he will again rebuild his inventories—to increase his sales and to operate his business most conveniently for himself and his customers. When demands are strong, so that he is operating under pressure with no reserves of capacity, he will add to capacity even though construction costs are high and financial terms are not as attractive as he would like.

In short, what people are intending to do at any given moment will not necessarily be done, and what they believe about the future may be relatively unimportant in determining what they do when the time comes. Plans and anticipations are subject to change without notice. In fact, they are almost sure to change at the critical points in the business cycle.

For all these reasons, hopes, fears, anticipations, and other purely psychological factors have only limited economic effects. There are certain basic patterns of adjustment that constitute the primary determinants of economic behavior; and although waves of pessimism or optimism may produce deviations from the rates of activity determined by these basic economic factors, such deviations are limited in amount and in duration.

Considered from this standpoint, the whole "psychological" theory of the business cycle appears to be hardly more than an inversion of the real causal sequence. Expectations more nearly derive from objective conditions than produce them. The businessman both expands and expects that his expansion will be profitable because the conditions he sees justify the expansion. Moreover, as he goes ahead, he helps to produce a situation that justifies his view, and by his action he helps to justify a similar view on the part of others. It is not the wave of optimism that makes times good. Good times are almost bound to bring a wave of optimism with them.

On the other hand, when the decline comes, it comes not because anyone loses confidence but because the basic economic forces are changing. Once let the real support for the boom collapse, and all the optimism bred through years of prosperity cannot hold the line. Typically, confidence tends to hold up after a downturn has set in. In the spring of 1930, optimism produced an abortive recovery in the stock market, in construction contracts, and in various other phases of economic activity, but it merely concealed for a time what was to follow. By the same token, a decline initiated by lack of confidence will not long continue if it is not reinforced by other factors. In the spring of 1947 the business community was swept by a wave of pessimism, but it failed to overcome the basic strength.

The effects of the temporary bulges resulting from such psychological states are largely limited to the field of speculative buying and selling and related changes in inventory policy. When a speculative boom develops, it gains momentum for a while because the dominant attitude is one of trying to make a quick profit by selling before the boom is over. The price rise stimulates rather than restrains the upsurge. But this kind of movement is self-destructive. Inevitably a point is reached where prices stop going higher. Then they cannot stabilize but have to drop back; for when the prospect of an easy profit is gone, the sole objective is to get out from under. Then the collapse is equally severe and will ordinarily overcarry to the opposite extreme.

It is in this field that changes in expectations can make themselves fully and immediately effective. Hence to forecast how far a speculative movement may go, how far prices might be bid up or slashed, it would seem desirable to know whether businessmen or security holders had a predisposition toward a particular line of action. If it appeared that a definite bias existed, a forecast might properly be slanted one way or the other, but only during the temporary period in which that bias might be expected to persist; for such attitudes are subject to quick reversals.

Any information obtained by the survey method would apparently have to be very current to do any good, and even then it would probably not be suitable for calling the turns but only for modifying the projection of the ensuing movement in its early stages.

Even at best, in other words, the psychological approach leaves the forecaster in a state of uncertainty. It does not solve his problem. It merely changes it from that of determining what will happen to that of determining what will happen to psychological states of mind as the situation changes in the way anticipated.

Surveys supported by so weak a theoretical prop cannot lead to good forecasts. Is there, then, no validity at all to the analysis of intentions, plans, and programs? To answer this question in the affirmative would certainly be going to an extreme that might in specific cases prove as far from the truth as inappropriate surveys would in others. The important distinction here is between indefinite forms of expectations or intentions as reported in a survey and definite measures relating to what people are doing or about to do. The former provide only vague indications of what might be done if future conditions, developments, or circumstances warrant. The latter are in effect measurable early stages of the activities by which things are done. Among the latter are planned expenditures, projects, contracts, and orders. Planning a project and letting the contract are essential portions of the activity that is consummated in the actual building of a structure. Placing orders is a preliminary to getting goods produced. These early stages have a forecasting value because they precede the productive activity to which they relate.

Even intentions may take on this quality if they are closely enough related to the activity that follows. Chart 4–1 uses an example from agriculture to illustrate this. Note that the reports of breeding intentions are timed to coincide with the beginning of the breeding season, just as the farmers are about to make commitments for the spring pig crop.

Similarly, analyses of plans and programs may represent a procedure of real merit when they are definitely stated and mean what they say. In the case of the Federal government, for example, the best clues to probable changes in expenditure and tax programs come from the budget and related discussions in Congress. Here the proposals under discussion are really intended to determine the course of operations, and the apparatus of government usually attempts to perform to the full extent of its authorization. Perhaps part of our ability to utilize this source successfully lies in its public character. Everyone is in on the discussion, can view the pressures for or against the undertaking of any specific program, and can apply reasonable judgments to the question of how those pressures will work out into approved plans. Even here, however, plans and programs are subject to change, and economic developments modify results greatly, so that substantial errors in budget estimates of expenditures or receipts are common.

Surveys of business plans for future operations or capital outlays attempt to provide a similar basis for analysis in this field. Most of these surveys, however, lack the advantages of the budget and its open discus-

Chart 4–1. Breeding Intentions* for Spring Pigs Compared with Sows Farrowed

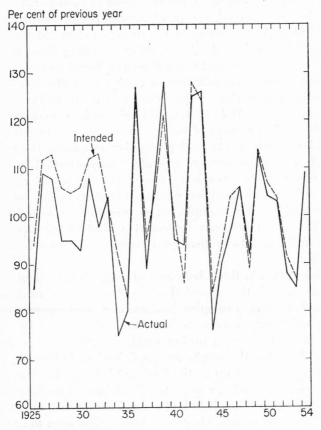

* As reported in December.
SOURCE: U.S. Department of Agriculture, Agricultural Marketing Service.

sion. The plans are subject to quicker changes. The surveys do not provide so comprehensive a statement of what is behind the indicated plans or what will support their completion. The reports received from the companies are usually confined to a bare description of what the programs provide. Sometimes they are not even stated in terms of definite quantities, but merely in terms of general comparisons with a previous base.

A review of postwar surveys of business expectations and plans from the point of view of their forecasting validity indicates that most have not made an impressive record. The best results have been obtained by the capital-expenditures surveys, which hold the greatest theoretical promise because forward commitments and orders for future delivery of equipment provide a definite basis for estimating prospective outlays. The annual forecasts made at the beginning of each year have a rather good performance record, except at turning points. Further experience is needed to judge the ability of the surveys to forecast the turns. Surveys reporting anticipated sales or other operating items have, on the whole, poorer records than the capital-expenditures surveys.

The surveys have generally tended to give low estimates. This reflects a progressive discounting of the future that seems to be characteristic of business surveys. At least it would tend to be confirmed by experience with wartime surveys of various kinds—such as materials requirements, labor requirements, and production schedules. Beyond the immediate future, these surveys typically underestimated, with the degree of underestimate increasing throughout the period covered. This bias was substantially modified whenever contrary policy considerations were involved—as, for example, when priorities for material were desired or it was felt necessary to protect a plant's labor supply. But the general rule seemed to be that what business had not scheduled it did not report.

Experimentation in this whole area of research is unquestionably justified, since an effective appraisal of results cannot be made until data are available through a complete business cycle under normal conditions, meaning, specifically, conditions less drastically affected by war or the threat of war. However, a further word of caution may be inserted at this point. Whether the results are good, bad, or indifferent, there is a tendency to play them up as the final word. Partly because results are often presented in such a way as to attract interest to their most newsworthy features, there tends to be too much rather than too little acceptance of the survey results. They seem to be relied upon to an extent not justified by the performance to date. Until an adequate demonstration of their validity is forthcoming, the forecaster may well continue to look upon these experimental findings with skepticism. As yet they provide no safe substitute for sound analysis.

RELIANCE ON EXPERT OPINION

The use of a panel of experts as a basis for forecasting has been reserved to this point because it may be either a survey or a good judgment method, depending upon the manner in which it operates. It is the former when results are merely tabulated and accepted as given. It is the latter when the reasoning behind the experts' views is examined and an effort to reconcile and synthesize those views is attempted.

In either case, the panel may be selected in various ways. One way is to get together a group who are all, for one reason or another, considered to be good consultants or forecasters in general. Another way is to select a group who are specialists in various branches of economics or represent various functional points of view, such as labor, finance, industry, and agriculture. Selecting the panel in accordance with the first of these criteria presumably involves the difficulty that certain branches of activity or certain functional areas in which important developments originate may be overlooked. In the second case, the difficulty is that the specialists may not be broadly enough informed on general economic conditions to cast their views into the broader perspective needed for successful forecasting. The two kinds of criteria may, of course, be interwoven.

When the survey technique is used as a means of obtaining a composite view, all that can be said for the results is that they represent the average opinion, or consensus, of the particular group of experts canvassed. These experts have qualifications of various kinds, which may or may not be explicitly indicated. As a rule, only a limited number of them make any systematic analysis of the situation. For the most part, they merely put down numbers which seem to be approximately consistent with their general view of the outlook. The conclusion thus tends to portray the unsupported judgment of the group. If some of the experts should happen to work out answers by detailed analytical techniques, they tend to be buried in the process of combination or averaging.

Although there is little in the whole history of forecasting to encourage its use, the procedure is quite commonly adopted. The post–World War II period is literally crammed with instances of forecasts in which the consensus was mistaken. It is probable that a group opinion of this kind will typically express the dominant bias of the day, just as businessmen lean to optimistic ventures in the boom phase of the cycle. Current conditions tend to set the theme, which gains acceptance through the visible evidence of those conditions themselves, and the theme is then repeated and hammered home, day by day, to such an extent that it becomes difficult for anyone to maintain the objectivity which independence of judgment requires. Where independence is lacking, mere numbers add little or nothing to the probability of the answer given.

Review of actual forecasts indicates that there tends to be a good deal of agreement on underlying assumptions. In a given situation, a group of forecasters may all work on the assumption of full employment.

Then the results obtained by each seem to support the others. The construction expert, the auto-industry analyst, the agricultural specialist, and the financial forecaster—each can rest his conclusions in good part on the work of the others, apparently without recognizing that the only result of such a combination is what was assumed in the first place.

The difficulty perhaps arises less from conscious preagreement on assumptions than from subconscious translation of what is into what will be. Economists, like others, often have only a restricted sense of time perspective. In forecasting, the popular attitude summed up in the expression, "Seeing is believing!" commonly takes the form. "We cannot see anything in the current picture to suggest a definite change."

An illustrative set of results is obtained from the work of Joe Livingston, who conducts a forecasting panel for the *Philadelphia Bulletin*. In the report published January 1, 1950, summarizing the returns from "38 of America's top-ranking economists," he points to a swing to the optimistic side and then goes on:

The optimism is a recent development, encouraged by the improvement in business since July. Which proves that economists not only influence business, but are influenced by it. They reflex as well as reflect.

A striking instance of this was 1946. In June, the economists were bullish. But after the September break in the stock market, they turned bearish. When the business collapse didn't come, they gradually became more optimistic.

Again in 1949, events governed opinion, rather than opinion events. At the outset of the year, four out of 10 were moderately pessimistic. By March, after business started to drop, six out of ten were bearish. By June, eight out of ten. Yet, at the height of the bearishness, the inventory recession was over. Production had turned up. Fluctuation in the economists' optimism is shown in the following table:

	Percent expecting business to:	
	Decline	Rise or remain stable
December, 1946	92	8
December, 1947	61	39
December, 1948	41	59
March, 1949	56	44
June, 1949	76	24
December, 1949	36	64

Subsequently, Livingston made an analysis of the forecasts by semi-annual periods. The results are presented in Chart 4–2. Not only are the forecasts rather inaccurate in a general way, but also they display a persistent inaccuracy over extended periods, as in the rise following the

Chart 4–2. Scoreboard on Economists

They are nearly right only once out of three times

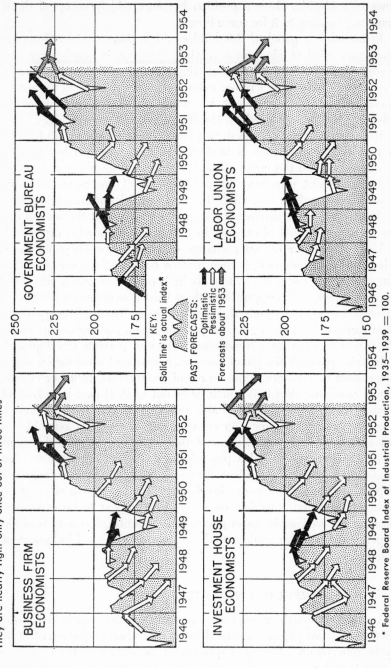

* Federal Reserve Board Index of Industrial Production, 1935–1939 = 100.

SOURCE: Reproduced from The Reporter, May 26, 1953, p. 19. Chart by Starworth.

lows of mid-1949. Once a position becomes widely accepted there is a tendency to cling to it for some time.

Presumably a panel of this kind could be improved by dropping the least successful of its members. This, however, is hardly ever done. It would introduce a problem of getting suitable replacements, and in any case it would require a rather extended period of testing to ensure that those being dropped were not the victims of the particular circumstances affecting the period in which the initial surveys were made.

If any conclusion can be drawn from the results of group forecasts, it is that the best practice is to disregard the consensus but to seek the reasoning behind the views of the various panel members and to test and utilize the most promising ideas by means of the same techniques of quantitative analysis that might be used to work out an original forecast.

At this point, the discussion has in effect arrived at the second method for utilizing a panel of experts. In this case, the panel is organized into a kind of seminar for an exchange of views between panel members. The burden of judgment is then thrown back on the sponsor or the person conducting the seminar. Usually he is presented with a number of divergent views, each supported with at least a semblance of logical argument. Sometimes the facts themselves are in dispute. The sponsor must then sort out from among the facts, hypotheses, and arguments presented those which make up a convincing picture of possible developments.

In this approach the panel becomes a source of information and ideas but cannot be considered the source of the forecast itself—or of any policy or operating decisions which grow out of it. It may be a fruitful approach for the sponsor who is able to use it effectively. It is likely to be a costly procedure, since a group of experts cannot be assembled without considerable expense. Against this must be weighed the sponsor's own time limitations and a possible lack of other opportunities for obtaining information and ideas that may be of overwhelmingly greater importance than the expense involved. With the growth of great organizations, the conditions for the panel's use appear to be expanding, in business as well as in government. The validity of results is obviously dependent upon the quality of the panel and the good judgment of the sponsor.

BUSINESS-CYCLE INDICATORS

Another approach to over-all forecasting which has been frequently used in the past places considerable reliance upon projection of business-cycle movements. The inadequacies of projecting a fixed cycle were recognized by many analysts, who therefore turned to methods of obtaining an indication of variability in the cycle, so that turns in the specific cycle then under way could be freed from the rigidity of the cyclical projection as such. These attempts to appraise the state of the cycle and gauge the approach of important turning points commonly took the form of finding or devising statistical indicators, or "barometers," of business conditions. In the simplest form, such an indicator would be no more than a single series whose movements preceded those of general business in some fairly consistent manner.

For many years the stock market was widely accepted as an outstanding indicator of future business conditions, but with the series of failures recorded by this indicator in the postwar years it has lost many adherents. The logic of the stock market as a barometer of business derives from the fact that it responds quickly to changes in business conditions or sentiment, and then its movement reinforces the sentiment to which it responded. This cumulative process drives the market to extremes, but the sharp variation does not carry over into business generally. Business commitments may be temporarily curtailed, but they are quickly reinstated. Whatever value the market may have once had as an indicator is perhaps gone for good, because government regulation has wrought structural changes in the market that tend to undermine its value as a barometer.

Another illustration is found in the statement that "machine tools are a good bellwether"—meaning that activity in this particular industry leads both other forms of investment and business activity in general. Whatever merit this contention may have had at one time, the close connection of machine tools with tooling for military production and the increasing use of other types of equipment, even in the metal working industries, has severely limited its usefulness since World War II.

Another barometer, one that is still in common use today, is the price of iron and steel scrap, which is very sensitive to changes in conditions in the steel industry. The demand for scrap, which is needed in advance like any other raw material, runs somewhat ahead of production; and the supply of new scrap, that is, scrap originating in production processes, runs somewhat behind production. In addition, demand changes are aggravated by the fact that inventories of scrap tend to be built up to support higher rates of production and to be run off after a decline. Hence, when production is rising, the demand for scrap is very high and its price is bid up. But when the turn comes, demand falls off sharply and its price drops. This very sensitivity involves a handicap, however, because even minor economic turns may produce wide price swings. In the year mid-1948 to mid-1949 the price of heavy melting scrap dropped from $43 to $19 per ton, and this extreme short-run sensitivity could give no indication that the general decline would not be correspondingly severe.

Among the more complex barometers devised was a series of three lines on a chart which a group of Harvard economists worked out from financial data. The crossing of these lines seemed to forecast turns in business activity with remarkable accuracy during the 1920s. With the depression of the 1930s the method broke down and has been abandoned.

There has recently been a revival of interest in statistical indicators of business-cycle movements as a result of work done in this field by the National Bureau of Economic Research. The most comprehensive exposition of the new techniques is Geoffrey Moore's *Statistical Indicators of Cyclical Revivals and Recessions.*[3] In this book are presented the preliminary estimates of forecasting efforts based on years of painstaking and detailed analysis of the business cycle.

The studies of the National Bureau are, of course, far more sophisticated and scientific than earlier work in the field. There is none of that fixed-periodicity, invariable-pattern type of projection so characteristic of earlier business-cycle analysis. Nor is there any seeking for that simple, perfect barometer which will always call the turns sufficiently in advance to make profitable action possible. These ghosts of the past are, in fact, being laid to final rest by the National Bureau's research.

Here, in other words, is the rare spectacle of an approach that is being at one and the same time revived and discredited: the former, because stability of relations can apparently be discovered in statistical compilations of indicators selected from a large number of historical series; the latter, because analyses of the entire collection of statistical series available reveal marked variation and lack of any permanent reliability in the behavior of most indicators.

The essence of the new approach is to select not one but a substantial number of statistical series that have in the past typically led the movements of business at the cyclical turning points. These are compared for purposes of confirmation with the behavior of other series that lag behind or closely conform to the general turns. Many series were examined, and more than two-thirds of them were rejected because their past behavior did not consistently display any regular pattern in relation to the general cycle, as defined by the "reference cycles" which the National Bureau had already established.[4] Thus from among all the available series were selected those that appear to be dependable on the basis of past action, and the turns in these "dependable" series are observed as indicators of approaching turns in general business.

In order to put the method to practical use, a limited list of the most

[3] National Bureau of Economic Research, Inc., New York, 1950. A weekly review of the position of these indicators is available on a subscription basis from Statistical Indicators Associates, Great Barrington, Mass.

[4] See Arthur Burns and Wesley Mitchell, *Measuring Business Cycles,* National Bureau of Economic Research, Inc., New York, 1946.

dependable series was selected as the basis for current observation of business fluctuations. These total 21 in all: 8 are series that typically lead the general business cycle, 8 move coincidentally with it; and 5 lag. The behavior of these 8 leading series from 1936 to 1954 is shown in Chart 4–3.

The indications they provide may be roughly described as follows: After a movement has been in progress for some time, the "leading" series will begin to turn. If this reversal is unanimous and persists for several months, there is a definite indication that a cyclical peak or trough is being approached. Then, as the "coincident" series also begin to reverse direction, the turn is in progress. Only subsequently will the "lagging" series turn; they are less affected by mild disturbances, and as they turn, a movement may be identified as a cyclical reversal of substantial magnitude.

The effort, clearly, is to get away from the average performance of fixed cycles as the guide to changes in the immediate future. The National Bureau's work not only segregated typical cycles but also showed that there was substantial variation from one cycle to another in amplitude, in timing, and in the behavior of specific variables. If these differences could be revealed in the early stages—for example, by a set of indicators —the analysis would be freed from any fixed pattern and possibly provide a more adequate basis of forecasting.

The process of selection of the indicators actually used is indiscriminate in the sense that no logical appraisal of the reasons for observed differences in behavior was attempted. The indicators were selected entirely on the empirical basis that they consistently behaved as indicated. In earlier works, it was sometimes held that knowledge of causal relations is irrelevant, or even that knowledge of what the series represent is irrelevant, because the only important fact is that the observed behavior of any indicator in relation to the cycle is consistent. Such indiscriminate methods have typically been abandoned after a while, because the whole history of such devices shows that at some time or other they explode in the user's face.

Any list of indicators selected without regard to their causal significance must of necessity be partial. It will be partial in the sense that it covers only part of the significant sources of change in the economy. Among the important types of activities not represented in Moore's indicators are government expenditures and exports. Such a list will be partial also in the sense that it will serve some situations well and others badly. When there is coincidence between the forces moving the economy and the series included, the signal obtained from the indicators may be "normal," as defined in terms of the observed past sequences. When those forces are quite different—and new situations are always

Chart 4–3. Behavior of Selected Statistical Indicators: Eight Leading Series*

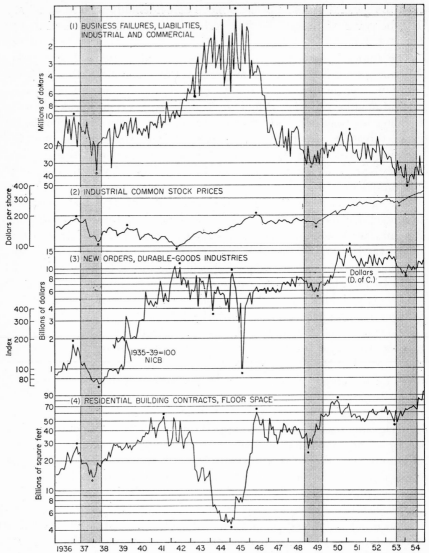

* Shaded areas represent contractions of business cycles; unshaded areas, expansions.
SOURCE: National Bureau of Economic Research, Inc., New York.

Chart 4-3 (continued)

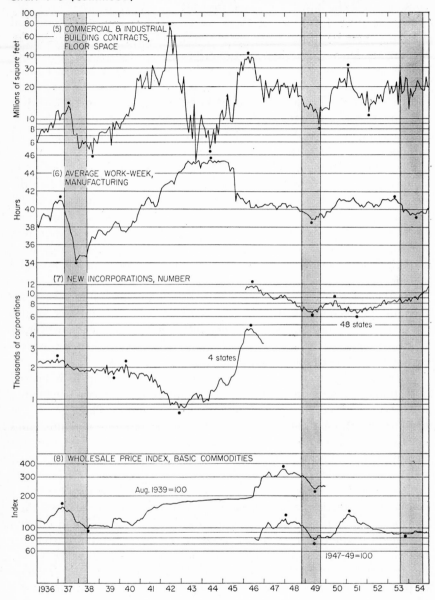

(5) COMMERCIAL & INDUSTRIAL BUILDING CONTRACTS, FLOOR SPACE

Millions of square feet

(6) AVERAGE WORK-WEEK, MANUFACTURING

Hours

(7) NEW INCORPORATIONS, NUMBER

Thousands of corporations

48 states

4 states

(8) WHOLESALE PRICE INDEX, BASIC COMMODITIES

Index

Aug. 1939=100

1947-49=100

1936 37 38 39 40 41 42 43 44 45 46 47 48 49 50 51 52 53 54

121

emerging—there is no reason to think that any specific set of indicators could provide the basis for a sound forecast.

In other words, the use of these indicators, like any other statistical measure, must be justified in logical terms. It is true that the leading or lagging tendencies exhibited by the selected indicators do show considerable stability over a number of cycles, creating a substantial probability that at least some of the relationships are governed by more than pure chance. On looking beneath the surface, reasons can be found to indicate that this is actually the case. A fairly substantial number of indicators involve causal relationships that justify their use in an index designed to anticipate the turns of the cycle.

Thus two of the most dependable of the "leading" series relate to specified kinds of construction contracts. Here are data which by the nature of their relationship to important segments of economic activity are entirely suitable for inclusion in an index of leaders. In any forecasting system, construction contracts should provide one of our best measures of future activity. But to use such a measure merely as a statistical indicator serves only to divert attention from its essential significance.

Another of the leading series is new orders for durable goods. Since the durable-goods industries largely produce on order, this series also has a direct connection with subsequent activity. The lag, however, is relatively shorter than in the case of construction contracts, and the forecasting value is correspondingly reduced.

Average working hours also have a basis for leadership in industrial operations. Changes in hours provide a quick way of adjusting labor inputs, and changes in input precede changes in output. The lag between labor input and output is normally not great, but this measure gains advantage from the fact that business management may be either unable to adjust the working force quickly or reluctant to do so because of policies that call for the stabilization of employment.

The other indicators in this group have relatively less direct and dependable connections with business activity. For various reasons, their movements are erratic and display a time phasing so variable in relation to general business that their usefulness is limited. It is rather farfetched to think that the 1945 peak in business failures or the 1946 peaks in new incorporations and common-stock prices signify anything at all in relation to the 1949 recession. When a movement has been under way for some time as a result of underlying conditions, there is considerable doubt about when its movement should be taken as a signal of an approaching reversal.

The roughly coincident series basically represent the cycle itself—that is, the current movement—and therefore have little forecasting value.

The lagging series require no comment in this respect and can hardly be said to perform the function of indicating the probable extent or duration of a movement. In this group are included two series—consumer installment debt and manufacturers' inventories—which lag for what may be regarded as purely statistical reasons. The adjustments that bring about a turn in these series require time, and while they are being made, the original movement continues.

This brief discussion of the various indicators brings out a number of the problems connected with their use. Where a dependable advance indication is given, the timing is short and the forecasting value is therefore limited. Moreover, the relationships are not constant, and when a reversal is getting under way, it may require a tricky appraisal of the situation to determine whether the observed behavior conforms to the usual cyclical pattern or is merely the consequence of some temporary condition that has disturbed it. Finally, and most important, this approach contributes very little to an understanding of the current situation, which is almost the first requisite of a good forecast. When the indicators signal that something is happening or is about to happen, they do not give, in addition, an indication about why it is happening or how far the move is likely to go.

An alternative procedure derived from the National Bureau's work operates through changes in the percentage of series expanding, which is termed a "diffusion index." The behavior of this measure over a long period is depicted in Chart 4–4. Here no attempt is made to segregate series by the timing of their movements in relation to the cycle as a whole. The result depends, rather, upon having a large number of series that represent all aspects of business activity. Nearly 700 were used in making up the first line on the chart.

In an upward movement, more and more of the series participate in the advance, until the point of most rapid advance is reached, at which point relatively few are declining. As that point is passed, some series begin to turn down, reducing the percentage undergoing expansion. As long as the general movement is still upward, more than half of the series continue to show expansion. After a majority have made the turn, the decline is under way. This pattern of behavior is reversed through the trough of the cycle.

A noteworthy feature of the diffusion index lies in the extent of the movements portrayed on the chart. It may readily be seen that in serious reversals—such as those of 1920, 1932, and 1938—the curve drops far below the 50 percent point, whereas in mild reversals—such as those of 1924 and 1927—it dips only moderately below.

Two points must be made by way of qualification. First, the various series are classified as expanding or contracting with the aid of hindsight; that is, they are considered to be expanding throughout the period from their cyclical lows to their cyclical highs, regardless of what the direction of their actual monthly movements in the interim may have been. Without hindsight, the difficulties of identifying turning points in many series at the time they occur are often well-nigh insurmountable.

Chart 4—4. "Historical" and "Current" Diffusion Indexes*

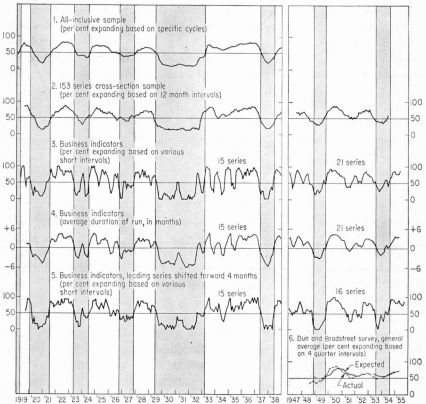

* Shaded areas represent contractions of business cycles; unshaded areas, expansions.

SOURCE: Geoffrey Moore, "Diffusion Indexes: a Comment," The American Statistician, October, 1955, p. 17.

In other words, it is frequently impossible, because of the magnitude of erratic short-term fluctuations, to tell whether a series is still rising or has begun a cyclical decline.

Finally, there are many practical difficulties in the application of this method. The mere inclusion of a large number of indicators, which itself affords a means of protection because no situation is likely to invalidate all of them at once, multiplies the burden of statistical review and adjustment.

This difficulty is reflected in the alternative diffusion indexes shown on the chart below the all-inclusive index. These give similar indications, but when only a small number of series is included, the index becomes much more erratic and at times difficult to interpret from one month to the next. The second line, it may be noted, is always 6 months out of date. The final lines, at the lower right, are based on anticipations surveys rather than on the kind of data used in the other lines.[5]

Moore and his associates at the National Bureau have thoroughly covered the ground and are aware of all these difficulties. In fact, they specifically bring them to the reader's attention and refrain from making specific claims about any practical value of the method in forecasting until further study indicates that such claims may be justified.

In concluding this brief discussion, it may be pointed out that the indicators are still tied to the more comprehensive approach to the problem of business fluctuations—business-cycle analysis—which they modify. By far the most extensive and complete record and description of business fluctuations in this country is to be found in the published works and files of the National Bureau. This work serves many useful purposes of both a theoretical and a statistical character. Everyone doing research in this field at some time or other turns to the National Bureau for source material or the means of testing hypotheses. It cannot give the forecaster everything he wants, because much of the material is basically descriptive in character; and description, no matter how detailed and complete, cannot explain the forces underlying business movements in a significant way.

This does not mean that descriptive analysis of the cycle is wholly lacking in value from the forecaster's point of view. Through the information it provides on the current stage of the cycle, it may very well help to improve the interpretation of current developments. Thus when a movement is once started, it may be expected to continue for some time, the exact period depending on the character of the movement; and after a movement has run for some time, a turn may be looked for. When it is known that a boom condition exists, it may be considered more likely that business will turn down than that it will go up much further.

The validity of any such proposition will, of course, vary with the circumstances. In the boom, the outcome really depends on what factors have made business high and whether or not they will make it still

---

[5] The chart and a discussion of these variants of the basic procedure, some of which are experimental only, may be found in Geoffrey Moore, "Diffusion Indexes: A Comment," *The American Statistician*, October, 1955.

higher. By taking the cyclical approach as an alternative to analysis of those factors, the question becomes: "Is there sufficient regularity in the cyclical movements that they can be depended upon to give practical answers in an emerging situation?"

Similar conditions tend, of course, to call forth similar economic responses—a fact that lies at the heart of the business cycle and at the heart of any effort to forecast. But in each specific situation, there are differences, perhaps new factors appearing from outside the established patterns. What is needed is a way of telling when the differences are becoming more important than the similarities, for example, when new variants of action in such areas as government programs promise to be of overriding importance. Even the most comprehensive recounting of similarities and differences in past situations cannot provide this kind of evaluation.

From this point of view, there is little to be gained from the analysis of cyclical movements as such, regardless of how accurately they are measured or how any group of specific indicators behaves in relation to established reference dates. Although these methods offer an approach that utilizes historical data to the full, it requires expert judgment to interpret the signals the current data provide, and it lacks a framework of analysis capable of integrating the forces actually at work on the economy. It must therefore be considered at best a partial solution to the problem.

ECONOMETRIC MODELS

Another method which may be described as partial, at least for the time being, is the use of econometric models. It is partial not because it lacks a framework of analysis but because it excludes too much in attempting to adhere rigorously to a predetermined framework of analysis.

The term *model building* is not confined to the use of econometric models but is often applied loosely to any kind of systematic analysis in which a series of interrelationships is relied upon as a means of deriving the final result. In forecasting use, these models have most commonly been applied in working out long-range projections. Fitted trends for such key variables as the labor force are the heart of the procedure. The model helps to prevent the trend projections from going astray, by forcing consistency between the variables included.

Both the model and the trend lines are usually constructed in such a way as to apply only under certain special conditions, such as full employment or prosperity otherwise defined. For this reason, and because of the numerous sources of uncertainty affecting long-term forecasts, the models are often held to be not forecasts at all or to be at best only "conditional forecasts." They then become illustrations of the situation that might be expected under presumed conditions more or less explicitly specified by the author. For example, it might be "forecast" that at full employment in some future year production will reach such and such a level—a statement which completely dodges the key question for the forecaster: "Will full employment prevail in that year?"

Building economic models in this way is basically a separate and distinct process from forecasting. The term *model building* suggests the construction of a model, which, like the model airplane in the wind tunnel, could be used to test the working of the actuality itself. In economics, however, there is no such exact replica to make similar use possible. Most model building, therefore, necessarily attempts only a partial representation of economic conditions on the basis of certain stated assumptions. The model represents the situation as it would be if the assumptions were fulfilled. It can have no more validity than the assumptions underlying it.

This is quite different from forecasting. In forecasting, the basic objective is to avoid any assumption that might predetermine the result. It is simply a matter of determining where we are going from where we are. In essence, it attempts to do this without limitation as regards unforeseen contingencies and developments. In actual practice, limitations frequently cannot be avoided, and a forecast has to be made conditional, as, for example, to abstract from the possibility of all-out war. Sometimes actual forecasts are so hedged as to be almost meaningless. But conceptually, at least, a forecast deals with reality in all its complexity and variability.

Pointing up this distinction so sharply is not intended in any way to belittle the value of model building. Setting up models and tracing their consequences is extremely useful as an aid to understanding certain kinds of situations and processes. It is rigorous in defining the relationships that are thought to exist between the various factors under consideration, and it thus represents a valuable tool of theoretical research. It may be decisive in policy discussions by revealing possible consequences if certain proposed courses of action are adopted. Frequently the problems put before the forecaster are of this character, and the answers desired run into the distant future. Then models embodying properly adapted trend lines may be the forecaster's most effective tools.

Depending on what is represented in a model and on the character of the assumptions made, the building of the model may range all the way from an attempt to solve a real problem to mere daydreaming in the form of a highly abstract and unreal explanation of economic structures and processes. In other words, model building can be a working tool of economic analysis at a fairly realistic level, or it can be a way of retreating from reality. Only when it is the former can it be considered a valid approach to forecasting.

The econometric model as such is closely tied up with the recent developments in mathematical statistics that revealed biases in the least-squares method. Since a series of single equations expressing relationships between the variables could lead to error, the way to eliminate this contingency was to set up a system of equations that expressed the relevant relationships and solve them simultaneously to obtain the correct answer. Such a system of simultaneous equations adapted to forecasting use is an econometric model in the sense appropriate to this discussion.[6]

An econometric model could, of course, incorporate an analytical framework to any degree of refinement desired. In practice, it is limited by the availability of statistics that are in suitable form and cover a past period of observation sufficient to make a valid solution possible. In these respects, it is perhaps not essentially different from other approaches. What gives it its specific character is that once certain data are fed into the equations the result is produced automatically and with mathematical precision, on the basis of the "maximum-likelihood" method. There is no room for judgment in making special adjustments or allowing for possible error in key statistical series.

As a rule the econometric-model builders lean toward the latest developments in theoretical framework as well as toward the best statistical techniques. The most ingenious formulations of relationships between variables and of patterns of change through time are utilized. Some of the constructs so devised have indeed been revealing; and although others have sacrificed reality to elegance in the elaboration of the structure, they retain the prospect that further research and data collection may ultimately prove them valid.

After a certain point, abstraction and elaboration tend to confuse rather than enlighten. Yet even where the model as a whole lacks practical applicability, it may contain elements of immediate usefulness. Its equations are in effect no more than statements of the way in which certain variables may be estimated from other variables, and as such they are perfectly proper tools for the forecaster's use. This may be true, however, not because such equations compose a model but because they represent tools of analysis which may be of value apart from the model as well as in it. Some of them may indeed be quite valuable tools, but it may be doubted that any will be so foolproof that it can continue to be used without review or question over an extended period of time.

[6] As an example, see Daniel B. Suits, "A Statistical Model of Economic Activity as Applied to 1957," *Conference on the Economic Outlook,* University of Michigan, Ann Arbor, Mich., November, 1956.

For practical purposes, in other words, it may be necessary to extract and simplify the relations discovered by the model builder before they can be put to immediate use. His work may supplement and facilitate that of the forecaster. But it cannot wholly displace the latter's need for comprehension and judgment in what is of necessity a less theoretical and more factual approach. Experience impresses upon him the lesson that unless he takes account of the limitations of his tools the results cannot be trusted.

There is, no doubt, some validity in efforts to escape the vagaries of human judgment. But in setting up models we do not escape judgments; we merely transfer them to other points in the process of working out a solution. It is a very relevant and important judgment to decide that such and such a mathematical function represents a relationship in the sense appropriate to a solution of the problem at hand. It makes no difference that the econometrician does not assume that the volume of capital expenditures will reach a certain level at a specified time, when such an assumption is in effect built into his system in an equation that will automatically bring it to that level under the conditions projected at that time. The rigor of mathematical language may even force greater rigidity into the solution for such a variable than the econometrician would be willing to advocate on his judgment of the facts. The effort to eliminate judgment merely takes on the character of a kind of quest for certainty—a certainty that can never be found in practical affairs.

Econometric-model building is in this respect similar to economic theory in general, where the main effort has been to establish principles whose validity was by their nature not dependent upon the exigencies and confusions of actual affairs. Study of the theory of equilibrium may be essential to the progress of the student who begins by knowing almost nothing of the workings of the economy, but the whole concept is one that may well be ignored in analyzing actual short-term economic developments. Similarly, the notion of a distributive system that allocates returns to various factors in proportion to their marginal products can contribute little to a portrayal of what lies ahead.

The forecaster must inevitably operate in a world of reality—a world of social beings, of politics, and of sentiment as much as of profits. Many of the factors that affect economic conditions in the actual world are not readily subject to mathematical treatment. The political victory that will sway the balance of power sufficiently to change the distribution of income in favor of farm receipts or wages or profits may be the result of conditions almost wholly unrelated to the economic issues it affects. International disturbances, policies of devaluation or economic aggression, which do not directly involve a given country but nevertheless affect its economy, can hardly be built into a system of equations. Again, judgments have to be made by the econometrician as well as by the forecaster who uses other methods.

It is obviously impossible to make any final appraisal of a method in general terms. Nevertheless, consideration of the conditions under which the method might be expected to hold good may throw some light on its potential application to practical problems. The requirements for satisfactory use of the econometric model in forecasting may be considered under four headings: "Variables," "Equations," "Data," and "Basis for the Solution."

Variables. The variables included must represent all the important forces affecting economy, including those which may at some time or other become important. It would seem practicable to prepare a list of variables that is not unlimited but is nevertheless sufficiently comprehensive to offer a reasonable basis for proceeding. However, the requirement for completeness is much more severe when a mathematical solution is to be derived than when some simpler alternative approach is being followed. At a minimum, a substantial number of variables will have to be dealt with—so many that at times a solution may be impractical by reason of the sheer burden of work alone. This is not to say that a less valid method should be used just to save a little work. The real question concerns the applicability of the method, and until this can be fully demonstrated, economy remains a relevant consideration.

Now that electronic computers are available, the difficulty of solution may be a less serious obstacle than before, but not all the relevant variables will necessarily be suitable for mathematical treatment. New variables which have just been given quantitative form in current statistics may have to be excluded because back data are lacking. Other information that is certainly relevant, and is reliable enough to give a satisfactory approximation or at least to indicate that an error will be positive or negative, will be neglected because it is not subject to more rigorous treatment. In other words, merely being confined to variables that are amenable to treatment by precise mathematical methods may be a serious disadvantage.

Furthermore, factors that could be taken into account by rather simple adjustments and allowances must be explicitly represented in the equations. Those who advocate the use of the econometric method are inclined to consider this a desirable feature of their approach, and from an idealistic point of view there would be no point in debating their position. In practical terms, however, it means that some things must be omitted entirely and others must be treated in a specific manner and with a rigor that is not justified either by what is known about their interrelationships with other variables or by the adequacy of the statistics which constitute the only available measure of their behavior.

Moreover, the effects of disturbances are hardly ever random, and unless specific allowance is made for nonrandom special influences, the character of the interrelationships will be modified by something that occurred once and may never be important again. Thus while it may be theoretically possible to deal with everything in the prescribed manner and the model may be revised from time to time to take newly discovered elements into account, there can never be any assurance that it meets the requirements of what is yet to appear.

The econometricians who have applied the method in practical forecasting make it clear that they have not been able to escape this difficulty. They have from time to time found it necessary to adopt some "arbitrary" procedures to deal with exogeneous or autonomous variables —that is, variables governed by forces not represented in the model. They have also attempted to deal with some problems by creating artificial variables—for example, variables that take the value 0 in some years and 1 in others. If available information is to be used fully, it seems unavoidable that expedients will have to be adopted which are not strictly part of econometric technique.

Equations. A set of equations has to be devised to express correctly the relationships between the variables. The determination of appropriate functions for use in these models is still in the experimental stage. Conceptually, it is possible to take account of almost anything in such functions. There could be dynamic models in which the parameters vary through time, or even models in which the parameters vary as functions of other variables. In practice, however, the forecaster is usually limited to relatively simple relationships, using fixed parameters. Testing such models is difficult at best, and comparing functions on the basis of available tests to select the "best" is well-nigh impossible.

The standard errors of estimate, where such have been computed in the past, are large—in fact, large enough to widen the probable range of a forecast of such a variable as gross national product so much as to make the forecast meaningless to most people who might have a use for it. This does not mean, of course, that the probable error of a forecast will be any less simply by reason of not being computed. Other bases must be relied on to judge the relative merits of results produced by the various techniques, and for this very reason the computation of standard errors tends to lack practical value.

Any lack of correspondence between goodness of fit and forecasting accuracy merely emphasizes the point. As part of his study of consumption functions, Ferber[7] made comparisons of the estimates of consumers'

[7] Robert Ferber, *A Study of Aggregate Consumption Functions*, National Bureau of Economic Research, Inc., New York, 1953.

expenditures obtained from a large number of functions that had previously been developed by research in this field with the actual consumers' expenditures of the postwar years 1947 to 1950. Among the results of his study was a finding that there was little relation between the coefficient of determination of a function and its predictive error. Indeed, when all the functions were considered together, there was a slight negative correlation between goodness of fit and forecasting accuracy.

This seemingly strange result came about partly as the result of the particular time periods involved. During the postwar years, savings were low because of backlogs of demand and accumulated savings carried over from the war period. Maximum variation, on the other hand, occurred during the period 1929 to 1940; this gave not only more extreme results when projected to the postwar years but also a higher coefficient of correlation on the past data. Fitting to the period 1923 to 1940 put a restraint on the variation occurring in the shorter period, 1929 to 1940, and gave a closer projection to the low savings of the early postwar years, but it also lowered the correlation.

Correlations always have to be fitted to the data for specific periods, of course, so that problems of this kind will always be encountered. Even after segregating the various functions by type and period of observation, Ferber found that the decline in forecasting error with improved goodness of fit was slight. Functions of this kind cannot be depended upon to produce wholly accurate results, no matter how well the tests of significance have shown them to fit the past observations.

Furthermore, the available evidence points overwhelmingly to the fact that there are few invariant functions in economic behavior. For example, current emphasis is being placed on private-capital expenditures as a determinant of the level of economic activity, and models like that constructed by Hicks seem to offer improved explanations of the cyclical changes in capital outlays.[8] The essence of this approach lies in the shifting of capital-demand schedules at critical points in the cycle. Yet it may be doubted that even a specified series of cyclically shifting functions can provide an accurate solution in all circumstances. To meet an increase in orders from customers, producers may, when operating near standard one-shift capacity, adopt various expedients. They may (1) increase the number of employees and rearrange work assignments to speed up production; (2) increase working hours, operate bottleneck equipment extra shifts, or even put the entire plant on extra shifts; (3) install additional bottleneck equipment or efficiency mechanisms, such as automatic-control devices or materials-handling

[8] J. R. Hicks, *Contribution to the Theory of the Trade Cycle,* Clarendon Press, Oxford, 1950.

systems, to expedite the flow of work through the plant; (4) undertake major remodeling of facilities, increasing both capacity and operating efficiency; or (5) build a new plant. There are obviously great variations in the investment and time required to make each of these alternatives effective. Which alternative will be adopted depends upon the particular circumstances existing at the time, so that the volume of capital expenditures called forth in any particular situation may vary widely from that derived by means of any preconceived functional relationship.

What must be emphasized is that it is extremely difficult to find equations that consistently turn up the right answers. If any of the relationships is unsuitable, if any of the interrelationships is ignored, or if some variables are neglected, errors exceeding any reasonable limit may appear in the solution and at times in the most unexpected places. Relatively small changes in the values entered at specific points, as, for example, by reason of a change in the time period on which the computations are based, often produce large changes in the values obtained as an end product. The simultaneous-equation method, like the complicated multiple correlation carried out by the least-squares method, may play queer tricks on the user, so that judgment is required in appraising the results.

Data. A third requirement is good data—not necessarily data without error, but at least data with errors nonsystematic and reduced to tolerable proportions. The problem of data is one of the most serious that has to be faced. The kinds of back data needed to establish sound relationships are largely nonexistent. The current data also leave more than a little to be desired. Those available shortly after the fact are usually no more than estimates subject to various kinds of inaccuracy. The substantial revisions necessary in most series from time to time are sufficient evidence of the problem. Even the "bench marks" on which those revisions are based involve indeterminate margins of error.

Suffice it to say that there are no data without errors, and the errors are likely to be greatest in the most recent period—on which the projections have to be based. Recently an attempt to reconstruct a past forecast for illustrative purposes in terms of revised data brought out forcefully the fact that revisions in the data were in many cases larger than the errors of forecast. This is not intended to imply any criticism of the organizations compiling relevant data. On the contrary, theirs is an essential part of the common task, and they deserve profound respect for recognizing the importance of and devoting themselves to this prerequisite for a solution despite the insuperable obstacles to complete accuracy.

In the process of simultaneous solution, the effects of errors in data, like those of inappropriate equations, carry all through the solution and often affect results in curious and unpredictable ways. It is all very well to say that the data are being improved all the time and that each year adds to the historical record. How much it adds is, of course, the important question. To use the consumption function again as an illustration, the entire record of the postwar period through the Korean War added little that would enable an unequivocal choice from among the various formulas supported by one analyst or another. People who want forecasts now for the year or so ahead cannot afford to wait for the unfolding of historical records.

Basis for the Solution. Finally, there must be a basis for solving the equations as applied to the future period to be forecast, involving a basis for estimating at least some of the variables as of that period. The conditions for the solution may therefore be of critical importance in determining the results obtained. Some forecasts based on models rely on the relationships themselves to project the key variables. Among the devices used for this purpose are difference procedures, rate-of-change projections, and lead-lag relationships. The difference equation projects the change during a given period, usually the most recent, into the next period—perhaps with variations, such as taking a fraction or a multiple of the observed change, using some other period judged to be more appropriate than the most recent, or setting up a combination of changes using not just one but several past periods. The rate-of-change projection assumes that the current magnitude is a function of the rate of change in the same or some other appropriate measure at some prior date; the most widely discussed example of this is the acceleration principle, where expansion of capacity is assumed to depend upon the rate of change in the demand for the goods produced by that capacity, with allowance for a suitable lag representing the time needed to produce the new capacity. Lead-lag relationships in econometric models depend on the same assumptions as in the ordinary correlation. These devices, however, can hardly be considered satisfactory for more than brief intervals at best. Most variables are only partly determined by what has gone before, or even by what is currently going on.

Most variables also have some elements of autonomy in them. Erratic movements alone may be of a magnitude that would rule out the use of any fixed formula for their projection. In addition, there are all the special influences that lie outside the system of relationships. These introduce, in the true sense, the autonomy of movement that characterizes the behavior of strategic variables. There is little in the way of past trends or existing economic relationships, for example, that will enable a sound projection of the important government sector.

It is necessary, therefore, to make forward estimates of at least some of the variables by other methods, and the forecast as a whole can have no more validity than the specific estimates of the variables selected for independent projection. Making such estimates is the critical part of the whole forecasting process, and unless there is a technique for working back from the final solution to the initial projections of those variables to test their consistency with each other and with the whole, the entire forecast rests on a very shaky foundation.

In practical applications, models that have used equations representing the whole sweep of the past experience recorded in available data have resulted in substantial forecasting errors. These errors were partly due to the existence of past deviations from the relationships, that is, deviations that were already in evidence in the current data at the time the forecast was made. To avoid this difficulty, econometricians have turned to projecting changes from the most recent observations into the forecast period—a practice referred to as putting the solution on the observation vector.

That this procedure is capable of producing the best results may be doubted. True, it eliminates the past "errors" from the projection. However, it cannot prevent still wider departures from the relationships in the forecast period, and it loses the possibility of forecasting the return to "normal" which may be expected when the established relationships are well founded. In many situations, movements of the latter character are of substantial value to the forecaster. He can experiment in a more flexible type of analysis with a highly advantageous interplay between what is called for by the past relationship and what is called for by the logic of extrapolating from where things stand at the moment. The advantages of discretion in such a process of analysis are not attainable in the mathematical solution.

In short, none of the conditions needed for a satisfactory utilization of the econometric approach is sufficiently fulfilled to make it a satisfactory working tool in and of itself. The attempt to use mathematical procedures rigorously introduces too many inflexibilities into the forecasting process, and these rigidities enhance the possibility that the model will misbehave and produce wholly unrealistic forecasting results, at least in some of the significant variables. It is not strange, therefore, that experiments with this procedure have not produced satisfactory results to date.

For the time being at least, model building is more a branch of theoretical research than a forecasting method. As such it provides a basis for understanding how the economy works—an understanding that is essential to good forecasting. It also resembles forecasting in that it accepts the course of actual events as the test of validity. However, the testing of principles to establish their scientific validity is not the same as forecasting actual developments in all their complexity. As an independent approach to the latter, it is, and perhaps will always remain, impractical.

FLEXIBLE STATISTICAL ANALYSIS

In describing these methods as partial approaches to the forecasting problem, the thought is simply that they lack one or more of the essential elements required for a sound analysis of current and prospective economic developments. This is not to say that they are without values of their own. It has already been pointed out that partial methods will work in some situations, namely, those where special circumstances coincide with the methods' capabilities. They may also be useful in situations where they could not produce a satisfactory forecast by themselves, by directing attention to factors that might otherwise be overlooked.

Forecasting is not an easy task at best, and the forecaster has nothing to lose by drawing upon the best features of other methods or by learning from the valid ideas of his competitors. Account should be taken of the useful information provided by surveys, particularly as they relate to key segments rather than the general economy. Interchange of views with a group of experts is both a source of fruitful hypotheses and a means of checking accepted hypotheses for possible error.

Similarly, understanding of the current phase of the business cycle is a necessary part of the forecaster's equipment. The interpretation of developments relating to any of the strategic factors will depend in large measure on the more general circumstances in which it occurs, because the responses of those factors are themselves sensitive to the course of general business.

The approach to analysis of business fluctuations need not be narrow or rigid. Cycle analysis is at its best when it focuses primarily on getting at the causal relationships behind these business swings, or identifying and measuring the factors responsible for each decline or recovery. This analysis may start with the assumption that there are no business cycles as such but merely that there are various forces operating on the economy, which may be recognized as partly independent and partly interrelated, and that more general movements develop in the direction which the interactions of those forces dictate. Any conjuncture of forces that is sufficient to get a general movement started will in turn bring other forces into play. In each case, the outcome depends not upon any fixed relationships, magnitudes, or sequences in timing but upon the specific nature of the forces that become operative in the specific circumstances.

This does not in any way deny the existence of business fluctuations of the type ordinarily described as cycles. On the contrary, it stipulates that the interrelationships between some of the factors are such as to make these business cycles almost inevitable. Thus whenever a decline occurs, inventory liquidation will set in and lend force to the other factors responsible for initiating the downturn; and whenever a movement to liquidate inventories sets off a decline, the decline gains support from such other factors as reduction in capital expenditures and liquidation of consumer credit. Viewed in this way, inventories are not thought of as lagging one cycle and leading another. In the one case, their movement is responsive to changes initiated by other factors. In the other, the reversal of inventory policy is the decisive factor initiating the whole movement.

In this approach, any number of "specific cycles" may be recognized. Many of the strategic factors have characteristics that make for cyclical behavior, with some regularity in timing, these characteristics being largely tied up with the lengths of their periods of production and consumption. In practically any line of industry, we have the resources to raise production above long-run rates of consumption, and then it is only a matter of time until surpluses accumulate, bringing on the reversal that culminates in a compensating period of liquidation.

In this respect, many of the other "specific cycles" are not unlike the "inventory cycle." In the case of inventories, attention tends to be focused on the stock of goods held and ignores the process of production by which they are accumulated. In the case of houses or capital equipment, attention is usually focused on the activity of production and ignores the stock of goods held. Both perspectives are necessary to a correct viewing of the swings between boom and depression.

The general level of activity around which the shorter cyclical swings occur is primarily determined by the rate of long-run investment established by the construction cycle. In booms construction activity sustains the economy against short-term depressing fluctuations; in depressions it provides little aid to incipient revivals. Construction and related activities that predominate in the long cycle exhibit short-term movements that are much more limited than the swings of such short-run factors as inventories and government expenditures. Hence the turning points of all cycles tend to be determined by the short-run factors, and calling the turns over the short term is primarily a matter of forecasting inventory movements, government programs, and other factors that may be subject to decisive short-term variations. To this extent, the emphasis put upon capital expenditures as a factor in short-term forecasting is almost wholly misplaced.

Everything that can be explained as a phase of the business cycle fits perfectly into forecasting theory, but many things that cannot be cast into the cyclical mold also form integral parts of the forecasting approach. Here analysis of each situation is directed toward the specifics of that situation, toward determining the decisive forces at play and explaining how the manner of operation and effectiveness of those forces differs from that in other situations. The essence of forecasting approach is that propositions are always put to the test of actual events, so that their validity or falsity is soon revealed. Mistakes in forecasting will undoubtedly continue to be made, but such mistakes represent the crucial testing of hypotheses about what makes the economy move.

Anything that helps explain why things are the way they are or how they may be expected to change in the period ahead is potentially a valuable forecasting tool. The basic need, however, is not just collection of valuable clues but synthesis of a significant composite. The forecaster must be able to draw on various sources of information and ideas, to utilize the valid elements in various procedures and techniques, but most of all to put everything together into a meaningful picturization of the future as it flows out of the changes currently taking place.

The only way to do this—to make the specific analyses of the particular segments and put them together into a unified whole—is through a broad-gauge analysis of the economy in quantitative terms. From this it follows that the construction of the over-all forecast must proceed in terms of data that add up to a comprehensive total.

If the forecaster depends chiefly on the national-income and product data, he has an approach that has unique analytical advantages. For these data provide measures of important elements of economic change and also of the success of the economy in realizing desired objectives. The forces making for change are, of course, almost innumerable; they include forces of nature, such as weather, and group actions, such as war, which are not ordinarily regarded as economic. Basically, however, economic activity is expressed in those patterns of human behavior that represent what people do to achieve their goals, to meet their needs, or to protect themselves against possible adverse developments. Underlying these patterns are, of course, the physical needs of the people and the social institutions and living arrangements that have made them what they are. The basic focus for the economist, however,

is on the goals or objectives of human action, and these are defined
most clearly in end results rather than in intermediate forms of production or implementing activities. In economic terms, the end results
are represented by the goods and services flowing to final users.

People want the goods and services that will provide the kind of
living they desire, and they strive for a surplus of income to save as
a measure of future security. Business wants the facilities that will
enable it to function effectively. Government decides upon programs it
will carry out in the light of the circumstances with which it is faced.
Foreign countries cannot realize certain objectives without our exports.
Those needs and activities are the driving forces of the economy. Disturbances of one kind or another may force temporary deviations, but
the response of the community will eventually turn activity back to
the patterns dictated by these basic determinants of economic activity.
Being cast in those terms gives the gross-national-product data special
advantages as a starting point for the forecaster.

The national-income and product data also fit nicely into the theoretical framework that has been developed as a basis for economic
analysis. The structure of dynamic theory today rests on a firm foundation and is being expanded and improved year by year. In this framework, certain factors are identified as strategic and others as mainly
derivative. The analysis begins with provisional forecasts of the strategic factors and works through the various succeeding stages to derive
the complete income and product accounts. This procedure directs the
forecaster's attention toward both the important forces affecting activity
and the derivative changes that the operation of those forces will call
forth.

Working through the various relationships to obtain a complete picture of the economy from the income as well as the expenditures side
of the account forces consistency on the forecaster, just as the double-
entry system forces accuracy on the accountant. The process of ironing
out discrepancies, of adjusting the strategic and derived factors in
relation to each other, produces the only kind of check that is immediately possible. Judgment is evidently needed to revise and correct the
relationships in the specific circumstances in which a forecast is being
made. Yet, by and large, there is sufficient basis for most of the relationships, so that this general technique of analysis provides a sound
approach for the forecaster.

As an alternative procedure, the forecaster might rely on the Federal Reserve Board index of industrial production, another set of data
suitable for broad economic analysis. Before the compilation of the
gross-national-product data, it was the forecaster's stand-by. It is not
so comprehensive as gross national product, since it omits services, both

private and government, and other activities relating to the distribution of commodities. This deficiency is minimized, however, by the fact that it concentrates on the key industrial sector in which the important economic changes are quickly and rather fully reflected.

These production data also have other good qualities. In the 25 to 30 subindexes regularly published, there is sufficient detail to represent a great deal of specialized information about developments in various parts of the economy. They add up to a total against whose movements the preliminary projections on the subindexes may be checked, and there are also interrelationships among the parts that aid in working out a consistent forecast.

The primary difficulty in using them arises from the fact that so many of the segments portray the movements of raw materials or intermediate products and processes. As a rule, the probable demand for materials or components can only be worked out in terms of the end products into which they go. Nobody wants or can use a ton of steel in ingot form. Consumers, business, and government all have very definite needs for the products into which it may be fabricated. An attempt to forecast steel production almost inevitably gets into the needs of these groups for machinery and equipment, construction, containers, and other major items of steel use.

The Federal Reserve index has been used with some success by the Econometric Institute. That organization proceeds, however, by redistributing most components of the index into a kind of end-use classification. Chart 4–5 shows the movements of the index and its major components in this revised form.

Even when used in some such way, to bring end-use information to bear on the projections, the production index is comparable to the gross-national-product side of the picture alone. It does not directly take into account changes originating on the income side, such as taxes, wage rates, or transfer payments, nor does it provide the balancing of the income and product entries as a check for consistency.

Another basis for over-all forecasting is provided by employment data. The Bureau of Labor Statistics reports include enough detail for most purposes, and working in these terms might be of special value where interest centered on labor developments or final estimates were to take the form of total employment or unemployment.

These data are more comprehensive than the production indexes in that they cover such fields as construction, transportation, trade, and services. On the other hand, they are less sensitive, since changes in activity may be reflected first of all in changes in working hours. Moreover, the data are a step further removed from the final demands that represent the basic point of attack, since each industry's needs

Chart 4–5. Federal Reserve Index of Industrial Production: Economic Groups

Index numbers

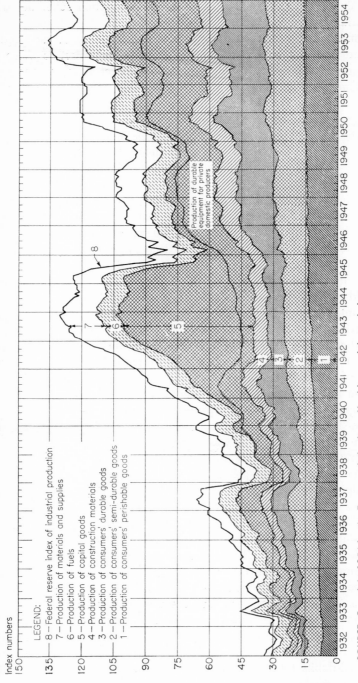

LEGEND:

8 – Federal reserve index of industrial production
7 – Production of materials and supplies
6 – Production of fuels
5 – Production of capital goods
4 – Production of construction materials
3 – Production of consumers' durable goods
2 – Production of consumers' semi-durable goods
1 – Production of consumers' perishable goods

Production of durable equipment for private domestic producers

141

for labor are basically derived from its production schedule, whether material or finished product.

Almost all the disadvantages inherent in the use of the production indexes are also encountered here. As a partial offset to these disadvantages, the employment data provide a direct attack on the problem of changing technology or other factors that change the quantities of labor required per unit of output.

These three sets of data practically exhaust the statistics suitable for the kind of analysis described as the basis of sound forecasting. Price data are also available in great detail, but prices do not represent activity as such, and at times it would be difficult to interpret a forecast carried out in these terms. There is a multiplicity of forces acting on prices; some tend to produce quick and erratic movements, and others tends to make for sluggishness and stability. When prices are moving, they may tell much about the nature of the current situation, but such a movement may show little persistence and have few repercussions in following periods. A comprehensive analysis of prospective price movements might well be very informative. To be realistic it would have to be carried out largely in terms of demands of various consuming groups, rates of production, and the other basic measures of activity that have been discussed. The forecaster is generally better off, therefore, to work out his analysis in these basic terms, treating price movements as by-products that derive from the changes affecting rates of activity as such.

One more approach may be mentioned in this context—the one that attempts to relate activity or prices to the money supply. This approach has a long history in forecasting. It is a holdover from the period when the business cycle was regarded as primarily a monetary phenomenon, but its use is still widely enough advocated that a brief comment appears to be justified.

This approach proceeds in terms of the money value of all transactions taking place in the economy, which means primarily debits to bank accounts. The primary reason why bank debits and related financial data are not informative from the forecaster's point of view is that knowledge of detail is lacking. Since breakdowns are not provided, the movements of the broad aggregates cannot be interpreted. This is all the more of an obstacle because total debits include financial transactions, which, though very important in total dollars changing hands, do not represent productive activity. In an attempt to avoid this obstacle, debits for New York City, where financial transactions are concentrated, are sometimes separated from and compared with the national-debits total, but this provides only the roughest indication of the movement of nonfinancial transactions over the short run.

In the usual application of financial data to forecasting, it is assumed that bank debits should be supplemented with the total of payments made with other forms of money, specifically currency, to obtain the total value of money payments or receipts. This total value of transactions is defined so as to equal either of the two sides of the equation

$$PT = MV$$

where P = price level
T = number of transactions at this average price
M = number of money units
V = their turnover, or velocity of circulation

A number of variants of this equation can be set up, depending on the data used.[9] If PT is taken to represent gross national product, T would presumably be deflated gross product, and P would be the implicit price index used in deflation. However, other measures of production and other price indexes may be used. Since M is rather exactly defined—though again there are variations, such as inclusion of time deposits—V is usually calculated as the factor needed to balance the equation. Then by taking account of whatever can be said about prospective changes in M and by assuming V to be stable or projecting it as seems appropriate under the circumstances, the total value of transactions can be forecast.

Whatever value this procedure may have would seem to lie in long-term rather than short-term forecasting. Over substantial periods, in which major changes in the money supply or in the velocity of circulation have taken place, some rather broad indications of probable changes may be obtained.[10] Such situations are so rare, however, that the procedure could hardly be considered a routine forecasting method.

In the usual short-term forecasting situation, use of this procedure reduces to a problem of projecting two broad measures on a very sketchy basis. On the whole, there is a fair possibility of making a reasonable projection of the money supply, but the probable behavior of velocity is likely to be completely baffling. Trend methods may be used, but the velocity series is rather erratic and cyclical in the short run, so that such methods are not clearly applicable. The alternative is to project the short-term movement on some other basis; but again it is not clearly advantageous to do so as compared with directly making a projection of gross national product or some other general measure of activity on a similar basis. Experience with such projections suggests only

[9] For a more extended recent discussion, see George Garvy, *The Development of Bank Debits,* Federal Reserve Board, 1952.
[10] For an illustration, see the postwar price forecast discussed in Frank D. Newbury, *Business Forecasting Principles and Practice,* McGraw-Hill Book Company, Inc., New York, 1952, pp. 77–80.

skepticism about the possibility of getting sound short-term forecasts through the use of this approach.

This discussion of approaches to over-all forecasting may be concluded by stating that good forecasting is just sound economic analysis. Such analysis must conform with our best understanding of the forces that make the economy move, it must evaluate those forces in quantitative terms, it must take into account sufficient detail to encompass important special knowledge of independent movements or unusual developments in various parts of the economy, and it must systematically fit together and reconcile the diverse hypotheses that arise in the process.

It follows from this that forecasting based on the realities of the situation is no easy task. It requires close attention to detail, sufficient familiarity with methods to discriminate between the valid and invalid, and constant application to the solution of problems that arise in the process of assimilating new information and adapting techniques to new situations. There is no alternative to working through the chores that alone offer a means of keeping abreast of developments in order to put together the structure of quantitative projections that makes up a sound over-all forecast.

Of course, there can be no assurance that a valid conclusion will be reached—or, once reached, that it will not be set aside in a short time by some unpredictable disturbance. Any forecast is subject to error. In any given situation, a soundly based forecast may have only a little higher probability of success than one made by some short-cut procedure without nearly so much hard work. Year in and year out, however, the difference may be all-important. The test of any method that can at best establish only a probability lies not in any single success or failure but in consistent results over an extended period of time.

PART TWO

The Expenditure-Income-Flow Approach

CHAPTER 5

Strategic Points
of Attack

The attempt up to this point has been to set forth the general principles of an approach to forecasting that shuns mysticism and attempts to make as realistic an appraisal of economic prospects as is possible on the basis of known facts and relationships. All through the preceding sections are qualifications and warnings about the information and methods of analysis discussed. Points are made, then often seemingly subjected to destructive criticism, and then partially retrieved. This is necessary because in many cases there is not much that can be established beyond all doubt. Anything that can logically be considered helpful may be used, but no short-cut procedure can be considered consistently valid.

The question that now arises is: "Just how does one go about making a forecast?" Mention of the specific character of the various forces that affect the level of economic activity has been brief, and little or nothing has been said about just how they may be analyzed. It is to this process that attention is now to be turned, with illustrations of its various phases in terms of the expenditure-income-flow approach.

One of the advantages of this approach is that it provides a means of organizing and classifying the various factors tending to affect the pace of economic activity in such a way that their bearing on the situation is clearly developed. Some of those factors fit neatly into the basic theory of cyclical movements. Others appear as forces tending to lift or lower the general level of economic activity over the longer run. Still others appear as temporary disturbances, which possibly cannot be themselves foretold but which call forth predictable actions that are designed to readjust or adapt activity to the situations the disturbance

147

created. All can be oriented and measured in the common terms of expenditures and incomes.

If we look beyond the immediate economic measurements in terms of dollars and cents, the whole process might be approached from the standpoint of social psychology, as an analysis of the dynamics of group action. A particular group will respond to a given situation in rather well-defined ways. Then its actions provide a stimulus to other groups, and these groups respond in ways that react on the behavior of the first group. This is what the social psychologists refer to as the process of interstimulation and response. Such activities have their own momentum or inertia and tend to overcarry points of balance or equilibrium. Developments of this kind may be observed in almost any line of business activity. People who have built a good business and have made a satisfactory profit for many years want to carry on, even though the conditions that made their early success possible no longer exist.

The process may be illustrated in building construction. One family in a community builds a house to provide itself with suitable living arrangements. The members of that family talk to their friends. They work up a lot of interest on the part of others with the same need. Some of these sign up for new homes, too. The builder sees more and more people buying, so he expands his operations. He may even begin to build speculatively, on his own initiative, without specific buyers in view. After a time, the number of houses becomes sufficient to fulfill the needs, but builders and buyers alike are optimistic. They are moving vigorously, and they keep right on going, so that the movement overcarries, and then the surplus has to be liquidated in a period of stagnation.

Another illustration may be found in the stock market. Those who get in early make good profits on the upswing. Their success provides a stimulus to others, and the greater the number that participate, the greater the success of all tends to be. They keep bidding prices up, eventually to a point that is not justified by business prospects. Further increases are then purely speculative in character. Sooner or later, something brings about a break in the speculative fever, and then prices are knocked down in a panic.

This is certainly a way to understand some of the processes that have to be analyzed, and with the aid of hindsight it seems to provide a reasonably good account of what has happened. In practice it tends to fall short of an adequate explanation, because the economy is more than an aggregation of persons, it is also an aggregation of things—goods of all kinds, capital equipment, and the structures in which we live and work. These things also influence the outcome. In fact, the rates of accumulation and disappearance of things ordinarily determine the decisions of persons. Too much may be accumulated for a while, too many houses may be built, and the prices paid for each unit may be too high, but the movement cannot go beyond the point where the excesses become apparent.

The psychological approach also presents difficulties in fitting together the parts of an over-all forecast. Substantial difficulties are encountered in describing, classifying, and organizing the various behavior patterns into a readily understandable whole. From the economist's point of view, it is essential that all such patterns of behavior be put in common quantitative terms suitable for combined analysis. Almost invariably, patterns of what we refer to as economic behavior can be put into such terms by consideration of their monetary aspects, because the economy is so organized that to get anything done requires the use of effort and other resources, and the immediate inducement for the use of those resources is money income. Thus the money flows provide a convenient way of accounting for a diversity of activities.

Today almost all economists agree on the validity of one method for analyzing these flows. This method is based on the theory of income determination that explains the size of the flow by the processes of income adjustment. Imbalances between the factors that increase or maintain the flow and those that reduce or obstruct it call forth reactions that tend to equalize the rates at which the former add to and the latter take away from the aggregate income stream. The additions and withdrawals are ordinarily referred to as investment and saving, following the pattern set by Keynes in his *General Theory of Employment, Interest, and Money*.[1]

There are, of course, conflicting schools of thought, and many who use the method do not consider themselves Keynesians, at least not in the full sense of the term as it is commonly used. From the standpoint of forecasting, any argument of this nature is purely diversionary. Nothing could be gained by refusing to use a technique of analysis that produced good results, and it would be equally futile to refrain from making modifications or improvements when they appeared to be necessary or desirable. The broad outlines of the approach are generally accepted, and since some knowledge of the underlying theory is essential to understanding its use in forecasting, a brief explanation may be worthwhile.

THE CIRCULAR FLOW OF INCOME

The basic theory of income determination proceeds in terms of what is ordinarily referred to as the "circular flow of income." The simplest form of the circular flow is shown in Part A of Chart 5-1. The stream of

[1] Harcourt, Brace and Company, Inc., New York, 1936.

Chart 5–1. Graphic Illustration of Expenditure and Income Flows

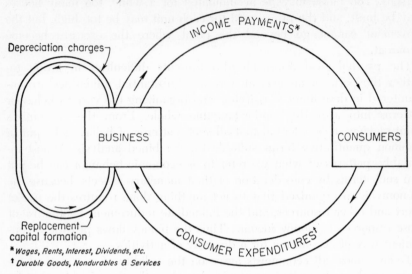

Depreciation charges

INCOME PAYMENTS*

BUSINESS

CONSUMERS

Replacement capital formation

CONSUMER EXPENDITURES†

* *Wages, Rents, Interest, Dividends, etc.*
† *Durable Goods, Nondurables & Services*

(a) Simplified closed economy: No net investment or saving

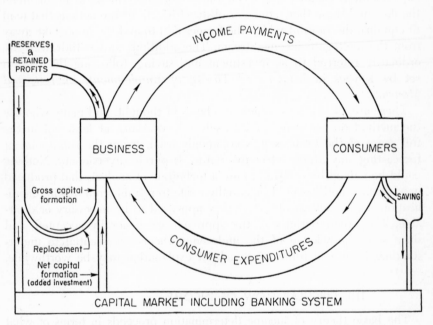

RESERVES & RETAINED PROFITS

INCOME PAYMENTS

BUSINESS

CONSUMERS

Gross capital formation

Replacement

Net capital formation (added investment)

SAVING

CONSUMER EXPENDITURES

CAPITAL MARKET INCLUDING BANKING SYSTEM

(b) Growing private economy: Net savings by both consumers & business

Chart 5–1 (continued)

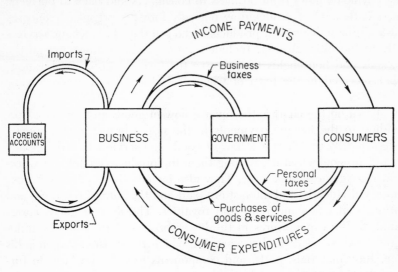

(c) Income flow supported by exports & government expenditures

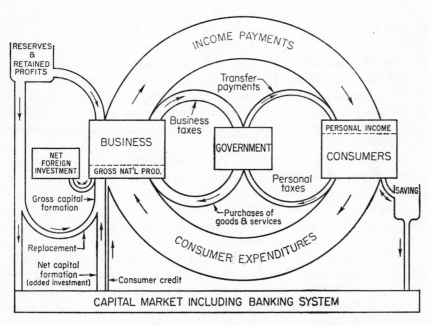

(d) Composite flow to gross national product & national income

money payments flows from business to consumers and back to business. Business is thought of as including not only formally organized concerns but also all the independent producers who sell their products or services directly to the ultimate user. Included among the consumers are all the individuals and households that receive the income earned by business, whether received in the form of wages, salaries, interest, dividends, or rent.

Not shown on the chart is the reverse flow of goods and services. Corresponding to the income payments in the upper branch of the money flow depicted by the chart is a flow of goods and services that the money payments are compensating. Among them the productive efforts of workers and management bulk large. They also include the capital for whose use profits, dividends, and interest are paid and the natural resources and inventions that command rents and royalties. The flow of goods corresponding to the expenditures in the lower branch of the chart includes only the finished goods and services for which the consumer spends his income. Raw materials, parts, and components used by business in further production are retained in the business sector and do not enter the income flow proper.

This first version of the flow chart is termed a "closed economy" in order to exclude changes that might arise from outside. It also assumes no net investment or saving. The only investment shown here is the minor but important flow originating and terminating in the business sector, namely, the flow of business outlays needed to replace productive capital items of various kinds. In this preliminary version, that minor flow is assumed to be uninterrupted. Everything withdrawn in the form of depreciation charges is put back into replacement of facilities, and all new capital outlays are paid for with the amounts withheld to cover depreciation.

The exclusion of saving means that everything business or consumers receive is passed on within the course of a single time period. Business passes on the entire value added by its operations to the factors of production it employs—the workers, proprietors, stockholders, and others who have a claim against it. Consumers pass on the entire income they received in purchasing the goods and services they desire.

Under these conditions, the flow can only remain constant. It is a purely static situation. The specific acts of production and consumption represented in total by the flow are always taking place, but these average out, so that the total remains the same. In the aggregate, production, consumption, income, and employment remain unchanged from period to period.

Suppose now that something happens to change the flow. Assume that a consumer loses a money unit and cannot buy what he otherwise would. Business receipts are then cut, and business cannot provide the same income to the labor or other factors of production it employs. It would, in effect, disemploy some of the factors it had been using. Since their income was reduced, consumers would be able to purchase correspondingly less. In other words, the size of the flow would be reduced. If it had been 100 in the first instance, it would now be 99 and would tend to continue indefinitely at that lower level.

The reverse changes would take place if the money were found and put back into the income stream. Then the flow would be reestablished at the original level. The effects would be the same if the money had not been lost but merely hidden away for a rainy day and then subsequently restored to circulation. Note that these one-time changes have one-time effects, and once the adjustment has been made, the flow is stabilized at the new level.

In the usual analysis, changes in the income stream are thought of not as single increments but as continuing rates. It is important not to be misled in this respect by the static appearance of the statistics reported for any given time period. The expenditures data and the income data are usually recorded as billions of dollars spent or realized in each year and thus take on the character of fixed amounts. Properly speaking, however, they measure rates of flow which, persisting a full year, would produce those amounts. Actually, of course, the rates of flow that may be observed in the economy do not remain constant for anything like a full year but are ever changing. Part of the variation within the year is reflected in the differences between the quarterly totals expressed as seasonally adjusted annual rates. The income earning and spending period relevant to the circular-flow diagram is generally considered to be about a quarter rather than a whole year, but the changes occur continuously and would overlap any system of calendar periods. Monthly data, where available, reveal still more extreme variation in rates within the year, because there is a certain amount of averaging even within 1 quarter. For the moment, however, the multiplicity of changes in the rate of flow that ordinarily take place may be ruled out.

Modify the previous illustration to provide for a constant rate of withdrawal rather than a one-time change. Assume one money unit to be lost each period. Then the decline would be progressive, period by period, to 99, 98, 97, and so on. If one can imagine a situation in which this could go on indefinitely and nothing were done about it, income would go right on down to 0.

This is still a highly simplified example in that only one kind of change is considered. If some consumers attempted to build up their cash balances—either as reserves against future contingencies or as a means of gaining from anticipated lower prices at a later date—the decline would not progress steadily but would be speeded up. Others might restrict their purchases by permitting existing stocks of durable goods and semi-durables like clothing to wear out. The liquidation of these stocks would correspondingly reduce the need for new production, so that the decline would progress by leaps instead of by regular changes period by period. Long before the point of total collapse, the economy would be effectively disorganized.

Consider also the opposite type of movement. Suppose someone discovered a gold mine that added a money unit to the stream each period. The size of the flow would increase to 101, 102, 103, and so on indefinitely. Production and consumption would tend to move up correspondingly. Business might raise its prices, but if it paid out the additional profits and stockholders spent that much more for consumption, the increased demand would call for ever-increasing output.

When the income flow reached a magnitude at which all resources were fully employed, its size would still go on increasing, but only in monetary terms. Prices would tend to rise more rapidly than before because there would no longer be any increase in output to satisfy buyers. This would be the beginning of inflation in the proper sense of the term.

If people then got panicky and all started trying to reduce cash balances in favor of goods, prices would go up even faster. If they then tried to reduce the period in which this exchange took place, in order to get rid of their money income more quickly, the upswing would be aggravated still further. These are the conditions of extreme inflation. At some point in such a movement, the drive for goods would almost surely bring full employment, because anybody who is capable of producing could get a very high return for his efforts. But when it is carried to an extreme, it tends to interfere with production. When people get too interested in running around "cashing" their money income before it can depreciate in value, they lose time from other activities, including production. Also, people then begin hoarding supplies of certain kinds of materials and finished goods, and this too interferes with production processes. So there comes a time when production may actually decline. By then the disorganization of the economy is relatively complete.

The point of these illustrations is that under the conditions assumed there would be no restraint on any movement that got under way. Whenever a stream of additions expanded the income flow at a rate greater than the growth potential of the economy, or a stream of withdrawals reduced it, the movement would tend to progress explosively and ultimately result in a breakdown of the economic processes. As a practical matter, when such conditions develop, they can be remedied only by drastic government intervention to change the terms or conditions under which ordinary transactions take place.

RESTRAINTS ON THE INCOME FLOW

It is recognized, of course, that movements progress to such extremes only rarely. There are restraints that operate effectively as a rule, and for an understanding of these restraints attention is directed to Part B of Chart 5–1. Here little reservoirs have been inserted as repositories for the savings accumulated by consumers and for the reserves and profits retained by business. These little reservoirs can hold or release substantial amounts, and in the ordinary course of affairs both business and consumers do tend to vary the amounts they withdraw from or put back into the income stream.

The amounts they withhold are not necessarily complete withdrawals from the income stream, because they usually deposit them in financial institutions of various kinds, as shown at the bottom of the diagram, and from the capital market they can come back into the income stream at another point. It is the relationship between these withdrawals and additions that regulates the pace of economic activity.

This diagram represents the Keynesian Model in the narrower sense —the one to which Keynes devoted major attention in presenting his theory of how the economy works. He clearly did not intend to rule out other variants. It is merely that the others fall readily into place when the basic relationships of this model are understood.

Here the major source of additions to the income stream derives from increases in the rate of business-capital formation. To proceed from the previous illustration, suppose one concern decided that it needed to expand its capacity somewhat and began to construct a new plant or purchase new equipment. With the money supply fixed, it might be able to draw down its cash balance to make the investment, or, if it could not do that, perhaps it could get a producer of capital goods to extend it credit. The latter, in turn, would then have to draw down on his cash balance or otherwise obtain funds in order to pay the people who assist in producing those goods. But once that extra amount was paid out, it would flow around the circle as an additional income payment and then back into the hands of business as an additional receipt. Thus the process of expansion that has already been considered would get under way.

As soon as the pace of activity began rising, it would provide a stimulus to other producers to expand their investment outlays. A higher rate of investment would be induced by the need for additional capacity and inventories. The increased expenditures for these capital items would quickly expand the income flow and stimulate a still higher rate of investment in productive facilities. This response of business investment to an increase in over-all demand is known as the *acceleration principle,* or simply the *accelerator,* and is regarded as a primary cause of the "business cycle."

If business tried to finance the higher investment outlays by setting higher prices in order to increase the earnings available for financing new investment, it would still have to bid against consumers for the use of productive resources, driving up prices still faster. It is characteristic of the economy that the price increases first made in order to adjust do not stop an expansion. In fact, they may tend temporarily to accentuate it, because they provide an additional stimulus to buy before prices go up still further.

In actual practice, the business that wanted to expand would not have to draw down its cash balances but would go instead to the capital market for the needed funds. The capital markets are well designed to channel savings to the point of need. Long-term capital could be obtained by issuing bonds, stocks, or other securities. Short-term capital could be obtained as credit from suppliers to some extent, but most short-term credit would be supplied by bank loans. The lending process, based on the practice of expanding deposits against limited reserves, enables the banking system to expand the money supply and not just to channel a fixed volume of funds from savers to the business enterprises that need capital. Considered as a whole, the capital market facilitates the process of expansion in various ways and helps make the swings more violent. It should not, however, be regarded as being responsible for causing them.

The small flows in the diagram (Chart 5–1, Part B) reveal that consumers and business do not pass on everything they receive but withdraw part of it to hold as savings or reserves. Because these withdrawals tend to reduce the income flow, they put a brake on the expansion. The expansion goes on to the point where the withdrawals, in the form of savings and reserves, are equal to the flow of gross capital formation. There can be no balance before that point, because the income stream changes in the direction of any existing disparity. As long as the additions are greater than the withdrawals, the income stream increases.

Any increase in the income stream, however, tends to increase the rate of withdrawals. This is particularly true of consumers' savings, which Keynes viewed as governed by "a fundamental psychological law," namely, "that men are disposed, as a rule and on the average, to increase their consumption as their income increases, but not by as much as the increase in income." This law is usually referred to as the "consumption function," and the proportion of any increment of income spent is termed "the marginal propensity to consume." It follows from this principle that, given any reasonable upper limit on new investment, saving will eventually rise as a result of expanding incomes to a point where it comes into balance with investment and brings the movement to a halt.

In this process, the expansion of income might have to be very large before the point of balance was reached. As the funds added by investment run around the circular flow, they expand consumption also, and not just once but through a whole series of succeeding periods. If one-tenth were saved, 90 percent would complete the first round; this 90 percent would in turn increase the flow, with an additional 81 percent completing the second round; and then successive increments, each nine-tenths of the preceding, would be added with the passage of time. Any new addition, therefore, increases the stream not only directly but also by its reaction on consumer spending and not only by an equal amount but also by some multiple of that amount. If the withdrawals are a constant proportion of the added income on each round, the extent of the ultimate expansion may be computed as the reciprocal of the proportion withheld. If one-tenth of each increment of income were saved, the ultimate balance would be reached at a point 10 times the increase in investment. If one-half were saved, the expansion would be twice the increase in investment. That ratio of income change to a change in the flow of investment outlays is termed the *multiplier*.[2]

The multiplier works in reverse, too, and serves to depress income as well as to expand it. Whenever investment is reduced, the reduction in the income stream reacts on consumption, through successive stages, until the whole flow is cut by the same multiple of the original reduction.

Any such reduction in the flow would tend to induce further curtailment of investment. Inventories would be excessive, and production would have to be reduced to liquidate them. Business would have excess capacity and would not have to replace worn-out or inefficient machinery. As incomes and prices fell, there would be a progressive reduction in the profitability of new investment, so that fewer and fewer new investment projects could be contemplated. Under these conditions, the accelerator as well as the multiplier works in reverse. Such a movement might continue to the point where investment and saving both approached zero. At this point, total income might still be substantial, and at least some incomes would still be high enough so that their recipients would be saving, but others would be drawing upon their past savings

[2] The flow shown in Part B of Chart 5–1 has been made wider than in Part A to show the expansionary effects of the investment that is needed to keep the economy growing. In general, the widths of the channels on all parts of the chart are drawn with regard to the amounts of the flow through them, but the smaller channels are progressively exaggerated in width to make them large enough for easy perception.

or otherwise dissaving an equivalent amount. In an economy where investment was normally high, such a decline would be too drastic to contemplate, leading to the breakdown of economic and social order.

It follows that an economy in which net investment is large on the average but tends to vary substantially from time to time will be correspondingly unstable. This instability will be mitigated if the marginal propensity to consume is low and the multiplier correspondingly so. Under conditions like those in most underdeveloped countries—where investment is low and the propensity to consume is very high—relatively limited changes in investment may produce explosive reactions, even though the accelerator effect on investment expenditures is quite limited. An attempt to force progress by means of a "development program" may quickly transform itself into an all-out inflation unless measures to restrict the expansion in consumption are immediately taken. In more highly developed countries also, restraints may have to be imposed at times to check too rapid an expansion, because any increase in income tends to create opportunities for profitable expansion of investment.

The question remaining, therefore, is whether in the ordinary course of affairs there is any reasonable upper limit on new-investment expenditures. On this point the Keynesian Model reveals some shortcomings. Keynes falls back on a monetary type of explanation in which rather heavy emphasis is placed on the interest rate as a regulator of the flow of investment. The effectiveness of the interest rate as a regulator is doubtful. At best it is a mechanism for checking a rise. The model throws little light on the question of why a boom never ends in continuing high prosperity but is promptly followed by a decline. Nor does it answer the question why recovery gets under way after a long decline. To answer these questions, it is necessary to consider not only the flows but also the stocks of goods and facilities in existence at any given time; for the accumulation or liquidation of stocks puts another kind of restraint on the flows. This is the critical restraint at the turning points, but the stock-flow relationships were not explicitly considered by Keynes.

This simple representation of the economy, admittedly incomplete in various respects, is the Keynesian Model in brief. The dominant source of changes in the pace of activity is seen to lie in investment rather than in consumption. Changes in consumer expenditures produce the same kind of effects on the income flow as changes in investment, but, by and large, consumption is income-determined and relatively stable and therefore tends to put limits on movements that originate in the investment sector. In other words, the patterns of economic behavior are such that the level of consumption, and therefore of saving by individuals, is largely determined by the level of income, while the latter in turn is largely determined by the volume of investment. Without net investment the economy would tend to be static at a low level of income. The higher investment rises, the higher will be the level of income.

ALTERNATIVE FORMS OF INVESTMENT AND SAVING

In Part C of Chart 5–1 it will be seen that the income flow can be expanded or supported fully as well by exports and government expenditures as by the investment expenditures of business concerns. This point is important for both forecasting and policy purposes, since investment is dependent upon the need for capacity, and a high rate of investment requires a rapid rate of growth in the economy, whereas neither exports nor government expenditures impose a similar requirement.

This diagram is simplified by omitting the capital market, although both government and foreign borrowers clearly have access to that market for needed funds. The foreign sector is set up in precisely the same way that capital formation was set up in the earlier diagrams. Any expenditure by foreign accounts for export goods, provided that the necessary financing could be obtained, would enter the income stream and expand it round by round in the same way that it would be expanded by an increase in capital outlays by domestic business.[3]

This derived expansion of income and consumption explains what sometimes appears to be a perplexing paradox. It would seem at first sight that the more we exported the less we would have left for our own consumption, but in the usual circumstances the change in the income flow turns this straightforward relationship just the other way about. In other words, the more we export the more we consume. There are temporary periods of inflationary pressure when exports can be made only at the expense of domestic consumption or domestic investment. More commonly, however, resources are available to increase production, and the increase matches not only the expansion in export demand but also the domestic expenditures derived from the incomes produced by the larger export volume.

If there were nothing but foreign-trade items affecting the income flow, the expansion would continue until imports were lifted sufficiently to balance the exports. The imported goods would enter into consumption, either directly or after further processing, and their volume would be governed by the level of consumer expenditures, which in turn would

[3] A more detailed discussion of this process and of some related aspects of foreign economic policy may be found in William Salant, "Foreign Trade Policy in the Business Cycle," in *Public Policy*, vol. II, Harvard University Press, Cambridge, Mass., 1941; reprinted in American Economics Association, *Readings in the Theory of International Trade*, Richard D. Irwin, Inc., Homewood, Ill., 1949.

be governed by the level of income. Thus imports would rise as the flow of income expanded. But the amounts paid for imports no longer flow around the income circle. Instead they are withdrawn into foreign accounts. When income rose sufficiently so that these withdrawals balanced the additions in the form of receipts for exports, the expansion would come to a halt.

In this case, although the imports entered consumption, their effects would be like that of saving by domestic consumers. The extent of the expansion would be controlled by the propensity to import, rather than by the propensity to save, and could be calculated as the reciprocal of the proportion of each increment of income that went to the purchase of imported commodities.

If the propensity to import were low, the expansion of income might have to be very large before the movement came to a halt. If there were other limiting factors, such as domestic saving, it might be halted far short of the point at which imports came into balance with exports. Then, however, another regulator would come into play, namely, the balance of international payments. Since the funds flowing into foreign accounts to pay for imports would reach a fixed upper limit, the amount those accounts could use to purchase exports would be subject to the same limit. This limit would be lifted in the first instance to the extent of any gold and dollar reserves held in those accounts and beyond that to the extent of any financing which foreigners could arrange by way of capital items or transfers, such as loans, gifts, or grants. All these alternatives are subject to definite limitations, so that total exports tend to be kept pretty well in line with imports, no matter how large potential export demands might be.

On the downside, these factors would operate in reverse. A reduction in exports would restrict the income flow, which would restrict consumer purchases, from abroad as well as from domestic producers, and would ultimately reestablish a balance between exports and imports at a lower level.

If consumers wanted to resist the reduction in living standards and had means of payment that foreigners were willing to accept, the reduction in imports could be averted, at least for a while. Consumers would then be dissaving in an amount equal to the reduction in the balance of payments on international account, and foreign accounts would go on accumulating dollar reserves in the same amount, period by period. When the available sources of financing ran out, consumption would have to fall to the lower level engendered by the reduction in export demand.

Flows into and out of foreign reserves tend, on the whole, to have a stabilizing effect on our economy. When our economy is running high, with import demand at a peak, prices of imported goods are bid up and foreigners accumulate dollar exchange. To the extent that they do not immediately use this exchange to expand purchases from our producers, the resulting net withdrawal imposes a corresponding restraint on the over-all expansion. Conversely, on the decline, our imports tend to be curtailed drastically, much more so than domestic production, because of the reduction of inventories of imported materials. Foreigners then try to limit the effects of the movement on their economies, maintaining their purchases from us, at least until lack of dollar exchange forces a curtailment. In the interim, there is a net contribution to the income flow, not sufficient to halt the decline, but at least partially mitigating the effects of the other factors responsible for it.

The effects of government operations are essentially similar. When the government decides to carry out certain programs, it purchases goods and services from domestic producers,[4] and the payments for those goods and services go into the income stream and tend to expand it in multiplied volume. At the same time, the government makes withdrawals in the form of taxes. Once the tax rates are set, whether on business or on personal income, the tax collections would go on increasing with each increase in the income stream. Eventually the tax withdrawals would rise to the point where they balanced the expenditure programs, and under the simplified assumptions of this illustration the expansionary effects would then be counterbalanced.

Like the foreign sector, government programs tend to be stabilizing, except for the tremendous expansions of military spending that take place from time to time. Other types of government spending tend to find a ceiling during boom periods, and taxes mount sharply. Progressive tax rates produce increases in collections more than proportional to the increase in incomes. Capital gains taxes tend to accentuate this process. The higher income goes, the greater the burden of withdrawals with which the expansionary forces must contend.

When a decline sets in, tax receipts are automatically curtailed, and the decline is disproportionate to the decline in income. In addition, tax rates may be cut, further limiting withdrawals. Moreover, government expenditures increase, some automatically and others as the result of programs specifically aimed at checking the decline. Whether they will actually achieve this aim depends upon how large they are in relation to the forces responsible for the decline and how they affect the other activities already being carried on by businessmen and consumers, but the practice of undertaking such programs seems to be well established.

[4] Note that in this context government employees are regarded as at once business enterprises and consumers; the payments they receive are included both in business receipts and in income payments.

With government operations at such a high level as they have been since World War II, these measures are indeed powerful influences on the pace of economic activity, but it cannot yet be said that effective control of the economy has been established.

GROSS NATIONAL PRODUCT AS A MEASURE OF THE FLOW

In Part D of Chart 5–1, the elements separately presented in the other parts are brought together with some minor additions to depict the composite flow under more realistic conditions than those portrayed in the earlier analytical diagrams. One point that immediately becomes apparent is that the various kinds of expenditures for goods and services come together at the point of business receipts to form the total gross national product. The main circular stream has now been widened to represent the combined effect of the various kinds of expenditures in expanding income and production.

Two modifications of the earlier diagrams may be noted at this point. First, the operations of the foreign sector have been changed from a gross-flow basis to the net flow into or out of foreign accounts, which is carried in the gross national product as net foreign investment. It is a net figure because the gross national product is designed to measure production in this country and not foreign production that happens to be consumed by our citizens. When we import more than we export, we are to that extent living off our capital, or disinvesting, and must make a corresponding deduction from the goods taken by purchasers in this country to obtain the correct total of what we actually produced. Conversely, when we provide foreigners with more goods and services than we receive, we transfer part of our production to other countries; and in so far as we retain a claim against foreigners for such amounts, that part of our production is invested rather than consumed.

Exports for which no claim is retained, that is, gifts and grants, are included in consumer expenditures or government purchases rather than in net foreign investment. This item is thus minimized, but it is still needed to complete the accounting for the expenditure flow, and at times it becomes an important influence on the magnitude of that flow.

The second modification adds the stream of funds flowing from the capital market to support consumer expenditures, as measured by the change in consumer credit. When consumers borrow to finance purchases, especially purchases of large, durable items which are paid for in installments, they add to the income stream. The extension of credit may be made by the seller out of his working capital or by a finance company and in either case may require the immediate supplier of funds to obtain loans from the banks. When consumers subsequently pay off their debt, part of their income is withdrawn from the circular flow and returned to the capital market, just as it might be if it were saved in a form to which the consumer retained title. Hence this item also is a net figure that may be either positive or negative in any limited period of time. It is not strictly required in accounting for the flow, since it properly falls within the sphere of consumer spending and saving, but it is significant enough in affecting that flow to merit special attention.

One other new feature appears in this diagram—the flow of transfer payments from government to consumers. These are payments for which there is no corresponding transfer of goods and services in the current period. They consist mainly of social security payments, other relief and assistance expenditures, and veterans' programs of various kinds. They join the stream of income payments, adding to the total flow of income received by consumers, where they appear in the national-income accounts as part of personal income.

As soon as the analysis is cast in this more complex form, it becomes apparent that the various kinds of additions and withdrawals portrayed in the earlier versions do not stand alone but are related in various ways to other kinds. For example, a government project to construct a large hydroelectric dam may require immediate investment in private facilities to carry on the construction, new industries and towns may spring up to take advantage of the new power source, and a recreation industry may be created on the lake above the dam. On the other hand, the dam might displace private power projects and to some extent merely shift industrial and community development from other locations, so that the expenditure cannot be considered a net increase in its entirety.

These interrelationships create no special difficulty for the analyst in dealing with the expenditure side of the account. The total gross national product remains a fairly clear-cut measure, and shifts from one type of program to another are almost automatically taken into account in the review of current developments.

On the income side, and particularly in the analysis of saving and other forms of withdrawal, the problem becomes much more complicated. A withdrawal at any point clearly tends to affect the amounts withheld at other points. When foreigners accumulate reserves, they may withdraw gold, and this could affect the money supply, investment, and saving in various ways. When business retains a larger part of its profits at the expense of dividend payments, consumers have that much less at their disposal and individual saving is reduced to some extent. When business pays higher wages, the increase might come mainly out of taxes and retained profits.

Most taxes affect the ability of business and consumers to spend and save, and this is particularly true of income taxes, which vary directly with the amounts received. Business may maintain its investment expenditures despite higher taxes by drawing on the capital market. Government also draws on the capital market when its receipts are insufficient to cover outlays. Consumers tend to maintain living standards and may curtail their savings somewhat when the after-tax income at their disposal is reduced.

A mere balance between receipts and expenditures in any sector does not mean that it is neutral with respect to the economy as a whole. Even when the government budget is balanced, its operations tend on the whole to have a stimulating effect, because the tax withdrawals are offset in part by reductions of private saving. Large wartime expenditures would probably be inflationary even if they were fully covered by tax receipts; the withdrawals by themselves would be unlikely to curtail private activity to the same extent that the government spending stimulated it.

As a result of these interrelationships, the concept of the multiplier becomes correspondingly complex. The base of the computation is a broad aggregate made up of all the various nonconsumption expenditures, and the extent of the multiplication must be thought of in terms of rather broad tendencies, which may apply on the average, though not necessarily in the specific manner that would be required for an exact computation.

Despite all these qualifications, the general lines of analysis remain the same. The dominant forces in bringing about changes in activity are those determining nonconsumption expenditures. These are sometimes referred to as the "income-producing expenditures that offset savings." They comprise mainly the flows to government, to foreigners, and to the various forms of private domestic investment, including the change in consumer credit, which may properly be regarded as a form of business investment. Through changes in the volume of these expenditures, effect is given to the forces outside the sphere of the established economic system, such as war preparations, geographical expansion, and increases in population. Likewise, through changes in such expenditures, effect is given to shifts in the policies pursued by business units, such as inventory liquidation when prices are declining or underreplacement of facilities when capacity is excessive. Consumption also exhibits some independence of movement and does have repercussions upon these expenditures; but in a first approach to the problem consumption may nevertheless be regarded as income-determined in character, whereas nonconsumption expenditures are income-determining.

THE EQUALITY OF INVESTMENT AND SAVINGS

An important feature of this analysis is that the withdrawals tending to restrict the circular flow always come into equality with the expenditures tending to expand it. The equality is forced in a purely formal sense by the measurement process. Measurements are taken for a given period of time, and in that period of time there will always be a fixed total of production, whether the measurement is made from the income side or from the product side. The make-up of this total may be viewed from either of two perspectives. From the standpoint of income disposition, the primary distinction is between consumption expenditures and the various forms of withdrawals that divert income away from consumption and into savings, taxes, and reserves. From the standpoint of source, the total may again be divided into two parts: (1) the portion moving into consumption and (2) the investment outlays, government programs, and other nonconsumption expenditures. When these two perspectives are brought together, it is apparent that the total withdrawals must always equal the total expenditures that "offset saving": since consumption, as measured from either perspective, remains the same, it follows that the remaining portion of the total value of production must also be the same.

More important, however, is the fact that what is true in a formal sense, because of the nature of the measurement process, also becomes true in an analytical sense as a result of the economic processes that force this kind of equality if they are allowed to operate undisturbed over a period of time. In other words, any condition that represents an effective disruption of the equality brings on adjustments that will restore it at a higher or lower level of income. It is the change in income, with its repercussions on both spending and saving, that effectively restores the balance in the sense that is important to the analyst.

Confusion about the validity of this approach is sometimes encountered among students of business-cycle fluctuations. This confusion arises from two facts: (1) particular acts of saving are largely independent of particular acts of investment and seem to have no observable direct effect upon them, and (2) an initiating change in saving and investment may be either stimulating or depressing, depending upon the direction of the change in income.

This confusion may be avoided if it is recognized that the decision to produce has no direct connection with the decision to consume. The decision to produce includes, of course, the decision to invest. This decision, under modern conditions, has become almost exclusively the function of the business manager, who only to a limited extent provides the capital of the enterprise. Through the purchase of securities or the placing of funds in various types of deposit accounts, the individual saver has come more and more to place even the monetary aspects of the investment function in the hands of banks, insurance companies, and other business enterprises. Thus the manager who is responsible for the current operations of the business is also allowed to determine the total level of output. Government is an important factor with respect to this determination, but aside from government action the restricted management group comprises in a very real sense the producers who decide upon the level of output which seems most advantageous under current and prospective circumstances.

At the same time, consumers decide upon the extent of their purchases, in the light of the income and assets available to them, but without knowledge of the decision taken by the business managers. Since their purchases will not be exactly equal to the quantity produced, something has to be added or withdrawn from inventories to take up the slack. Investment in inventories is then greater or less than expected, to the extent that the anticipated level of sales was overoptimistic or overpessimistic.

The change in inventory investment forces the equality between savings and investment but in itself does not determine the subsequent change in income. Thus an increase in saving at the expense of consumption results in a roughly equivalent amount of investment in the form of unintentional inventory accumulation. Alternatively, a voluntary increase in inventory investment results in an increase in incomes; and until consumption is increased, the additions to income represent additional savings. The two cases are alike in terms of the immediate movements of saving and investment; but when the adjustments are made, the first depresses and the second expands the flow of income. The only immediate difference lies in the movements of the money and income flows. In the first case there is an immediate decrease in the flow of money and, to a lesser extent, income, and a definite depressant is felt upon any subsequent attempt to liquidate inventories, which may in the new situation have become too high relative to the volume of sales. In the second case the flow of money and income is immediately stepped up, and the stimulating effect is felt throughout the economy as the initial increase flows into the markets for other goods and services.

As an additional conclusion of this analysis, then, it may be stated that, in the very short run, the level of income is determined by the decision to produce and that the decision to consume determines what proportion of the total goes into savings or into investment. The decision to produce is not entirely independent of the decision to consume, since, under ordinary circumstances, business knows a lot about consumption

requirements. It is not the decisions designed to meet these requirements, however, that initiate the important changes in aggregate income
and saving. These changes derive more closely, on the whole, from decisions relating to the nonconsumption expenditures.

In speaking of "decisions" in this way, the word is not used in the
narrow sense of what someone consciously decides. It refers, rather, to
the sum total of all the decisions, conscious or otherwise, and all the
other activities, planned or unplanned, that result in the actual production or consumption. The idea that the conscious plans or expectations
of one period determine what is done in the next leads only into frustration. Similarly, the idea that adjustments are made because plans
or expectations are disappointed has yet to be proved fruitful. The overoptimistic businessman who produced more than he could sell does not
reduce his operations because of his disappointment; he cuts back because his sales are low and his inventories are high. What he did in the
last period is water over the dam; what he must do now is dictated by
the conditions he actually faces.

Other points of decision in the circular flow also become critical at
times and provide valuable clues to the future course of developments.
When the government passes legislation that makes substantial changes
in tax rates, the expenditure-income flow is divided anew, and this shift
will probably change its volume to some extent.

The forecaster must provide for constant review of all these sources
of variation, but the primary implication of the analysis is that attention
should be focused first and foremost on those classes of expenditures
which exert leverage in affecting the income flow. These are designated
as a relatively limited group of nonconsumption expenditures. The primary point of attack, therefore, lies in the selection from this group of
the particular items which in the given circumstances are for definite
reasons expected to change and which will undergo changes important
enough to dominate the movement of the total.

The analysis is basically sound when the changes and adjustments it
specifies are thought of as general tendencies that will work out on the
average and in the absence of disturbances. Difficulty arises when one
attempts to specify too closely the period-to-period relationships between the various activities. The total for each period is itself but an
average of the sequence of changes that is continuously taking place.
The consumption of the current period is not a fixed amount, relating to
a fixed amount of income or any other factor; it is a summation of the
changing flow between what it was the last period and what it will be
the next. In periods of disturbance, it may display a good deal of independence of movement, so that the division of consumer income between spending and saving becomes a highly important point of anal-

ysis. More commonly it tends to maintain a certain relation to income which can be turned to good analytical account.

THE STRATEGIC FACTORS

The expenditure-income–flow approach may be utilized not in any fixed pattern of analysis but merely as a background in the search for the important factors affecting the level of incomes and expenditures. The attempt is then to isolate the various influences affecting the incomes and expenditures of various important groups in the economy and subsequently to put them together into a pattern of over-all change. This procedure—based on what is sometimes referred to as the "theory of aggregate demand"—leads to essentially the same conclusions regarding the strategic points of attack on the forecasting problem as the analysis just described.

The point of departure in this case is the setting up of certain criteria of what is strategic. Then the factors that conform to those criteria become subjects for special analysis. What are such criteria? Among the various possibilities at least four would generally be accepted as valid.

The first criterion is importance. There are two senses in which any factor may be important: it may be so large that it forms a substantial portion of total activity, or it may change so rapidly that its changes represent a substantial portion of the changes that take place in the total economy. The latter sense is clearly the more important for forecasting purposes.

The second criterion is autonomy or independence of movement. This refers to variables that are not closely controlled by others in the system and therefore move independently, rather than being governed by their relation to other factors or to the total. These are factors largely ruled by special forces relating to their own behavior or by forces outside the economic system as such, whose changes therefore represent new influences on the economy.

The third criterion is influence. A factor should exert an influence on other parts of the economy to a marked degree. Anything whose movements induce reactions in other factors that in effect reinforce and extend its own movements is of special significance.

The fourth criterion is suitability for forecasting. It must be possible to analyze and project the factor's movements effectively. None of the other criteria will really matter much if this quality is lacking. No matter how significant a factor may be in any other way, if there is no way to tell what is going to happen to it, if there is no way of forecasting its changes, then it cannot be strategic.

The analysis of economic variables from this point of view may also be carried out in terms of the gross-national-product and national-income accounts. Greater detail is available in those accounts, and in other economic statistics, than it would be possible to cover in a brief discussion. The following is therefore intended as no more than a suggestive illustration of the approach.

From the standpoint of importance, most of the classes of nonconsumption expenditures in the gross national product would qualify as strategic. Both government purchases and inventory fluctuations are frequently large enough to dominate the short-term movements of the economy. Construction and other investment expenditures tend to move more slowly but introduce the most drastic variations between the highs and lows of longer cycles. Net foreign investment is ordinarily more limited in its range of movement but at times makes a major contribution, as in mid-1947.

Consumer expenditures make up the largest segment in the total, but the bulk of these expenditures is fairly stable in character. This is true of most of the nondurable goods—the foods items particularly but also many other items like soap and paper products. Stability is also characteristic of the ultimate consumption of the services of durable goods, though not of the purchases of the durable goods as such. The latter show great variation; and since existing stocks can be made to do for limited periods, sales of new durable goods fluctuate with increasing violence as the stock in use expands. If any part of consumption expenditure is important in the relevant sense, it is the durable-goods segment. Purchases on credit, which relate in large part to durable goods, also show substantial variation, and a reversal from expansion to repayment of consumer loans may constitute a large element in a recession. Otherwise, the stability of consumer expenditures tends to put a damper on fluctuations rather than to represent an important source of variation.

Items appearing on the income side of the account also have to be judged in the light of these criteria. Changes in aggregate income must be large enough to match those in expenditures, of course, but the former represent mostly derived changes rather than initiating forces. Income is produced when productive activities are undertaken. Some production changes are induced by changes in income, but except for consumer expenditures the relations are lacking in dependability. Consumption tends in the usual pattern to remain more stable than income, smoothing rather than aggravating its movements; and when it departs from the usual pattern, the changes are not income-derived. Hence most of the changes in items going into the make-up of income—such as employment, wage rates, profits, and taxes—are derived from changes in the pace of activity. Only when there are changes in basic regulators of the income flow, as when new tax rates or social security laws are passed, do the changes on the income side provide a sound independent indication of probable movements in the total.

This lack of autonomy is one of the main reasons why approaching the problem from the income side represents a reversal of the strategic sequence. Taxes and transfer payments are clearly determined factors in the usual situation; given a system of rates, the payments vary automatically with changes in income, unemployment, or other established criteria. Corporate profits and reserves are not ordinarily thought of as closely determined, and yet, by and large, they are. The flow into these accounts is a residual—the difference between total receipts and total costs. The main item in costs is wage payments, which derive from the employment needed to support production, so that as a rule they are closely related to activity. This brings the calculation back to receipts, that is, to the product side of the account.

On that side, it is found that many items behave with a good deal of autonomy, though none is wholly independent of the movements of the total. Net foreign investment is largely determined by outside influences, because neither policies nor developments in other countries coincide with our own; yet our position in world trade is so important that major shifts in the net balance of international payments derive from developments here. The same is true of government programs. They are to a considerable extent determined independently, by political action, but they are also modified to fit the prevailing conditions.

Changes in gross-private-capital formation display a similar mixture of independent and induced elements. Sometimes changes in inventory policy on the part of business occur with a good deal of autonomy; at other times they are merely designed to bring inventories or productive capacity into line with the volume of business being obtained. Investment in plant and equipment tends to be highly responsive to changes in total output, but its movements progress through the stages of the business cycle in such a way as to show at times little regard for short-term developments. Residential construction is even more self-determined, though it too shows definite responsiveness to changes in income and employment.

When consumer expenditures are considered from the point of view of autonomy, dependent elements are found to be preponderant. The largest segment of the total, purchases of nondurable goods, shows little independence of movement as a rule, though even here there may be substantial hoarding of items like soap and sugar in times of stress. Services must be consumed at the time they are produced, so that hoarding is eliminated as an element of variation, and although expenditures in this general class may be postponed or moved up in timing under special conditions, they are on the whole even less subject to independent change.

Only in the durable-goods segment of consumer spending are the independent movements likely to loom large. These expenditures respond to changes in income but are less definitely controlled by it. Durable goods may be accumulated rapidly for considerable periods of time and, once the market is relatively saturated, drop back even though income may still be rising. Their movements are in large measure freed from those of income by consumer credit. Hence there is a large element of variation here that is in no way different from that in some types of private-business investments. One way to handle the problem is to treat the portion that is in effect business investment, that is, the part financed by credit, as the strategic part of the total and let the remainder go with nondurables and services as items whose changes are primarily induced by changes in income.

The various types of nonconsumption expenditures may also be considered significant in their effects on other parts of the economy. All have a leverage in expanding the income flow in terms of the multiplier effect. In addition, they influence each other in various ways, as when military procurement or a construction boom stimulates investment in capacity for aircraft or for building materials.

An extraordinary increment of consumption expenditures would also tend to have a multiplier effect, but consumer expenditures are at the same time a charge against income. In order for an increment of consumption to have the same multiplying effect over an extended period, there would have to be a continuing change in the relationship of spending and saving within the income total. Such structural changes in consumer behavior patterns may occur but as a rule only slowly, over long periods of time.

The more common shifts in durable-goods spending that take place for limited periods while stocks of goods in use are being built up do not represent permanent changes in the structure of income disposition. For example, consumers tend to splurge on new cars when the auto industry introduces major model changes. Such splurges are abortive, however, since spending is likely to be correspondingly depressed the following year. Moreover, this is practically a one-industry phenomenon, as none of the others is important enough to make a significant difference in the over-all situation. High-level spending for other durables is likely to be tied up with such factors as a building boom, which has repercussions on furniture, furnishings, stoves, refrigerators, and other appliances. Such spending is likely to be at the expense of other consumption to some extent, but it does not force any decline in the other items because the over-all level is stepped up by credit expansion.

Other extraordinary shifts in consumer spending result primarily from disturbances, such as wartime curtailments of production, and must be analyzed in terms of the special circumstances imposed by those disturbances. None of these are circumstances that make the volume of consumer expenditures as such strategic. Rather, the key to such changes themselves must be looked for elsewhere.

Changes in the flow of total income and consumption also have repercussions on other factors. These may be clearly observed in the expansion of inventories to match an increase in sales or in the response of investment to growth that demands enlarged capacity. Secondary effects of this kind come into play whenever there is a change in the level of activity and may readily be taken into account. Indeed, it might be said that all factors respond to changes in total income, so that this is a response common to all. What we are seeking, however, is a way to decide what the change in income will be, and this common response does not provide a separate indication of the direction in which the economy will move. It is part of the mechanism by which the extent of any movement must be projected, but the analysis has to proceed first in terms of other specific factors, as the turns will generally be called by the indications of independent changes in those specific factors.

The analytical basis for appraising any such set of factors will necessarily be varied, as attention must be directed to the forces and relationships significant in each specific case. Succeeding chapters will attempt to develop such lines of analysis for the various nonconsumption components of the gross national product, which will be treated as the strategic factors and will illustrate the process of organizing the various parts into a composite for the economy as a whole.

Suffice it to say at this point that procedures which give provisional estimates for each of these factors within a tolerable range of error are available. In the case of government, legislation precedes action and provides a basis for forecasting; in residential construction, changes in demographic data foreshadow construction needs; and so forth. No doubt other factors and relationships than those described can be effectively used. The choice will probably never be final, because procedures are subject to revision with the growth of knowledge. The specific techniques presented here are merely the best the author has been able to bring together up to this time.

In the process of analysis, the movements of aggregate income play an important role. They assist in estimating the extent of the changes in other factors and are essential in evaluating the consistency of the forecast as a whole. They do not, however, provide a good point of departure, because consumer expenditures and most of the items on the income side of the account, which are necessary for the translation of gross product to personal income and then to consumption, cannot be effectively projected without an estimate of the over-all movement itself.

Even when knowledge of probable changes in any of the income items is available and can be taken into account, it is usually by way of modifying the changes that would ordinarily flow from their relationship to the total rather than in setting up an independent projection. In this entire collection of items, there is little in the way of independent clues and indicators to use as the basis for a projection. That is a second main reason for directing attention to the product side as the strategic point of attack.

GENERAL CONSIDERATIONS IN WORKING OUT A FORECAST

An apparent dilemma may be perceived in the fact that over-all income has so much influence on other factors, including even the most autonomous, but cannot itself be independently estimated. If other factors are dependent on income and income is dependent on those other factors, is it possible to break the vicious circle in order to obtain a solution? The answer is: "Yes," because the circle can be broken anywhere a reason can be found for expecting significant variation. Yet, since the whole and all its parts are interrelated, the solution must embody all the effects of the process of mutual determination.

There are two ways around this difficulty. One is the method of simultaneous solution; the other is the method of successive approximations. In the latter method an initial projection is made on the basis of all the special circumstances known to be affecting the strategic factors. Then this provisional estimate of the total becomes a basis for revising and firming up the projections of the separate factors. But the revisions thus made may change the total also, and this second approximation in turn may require still further revision of the parts. In stages a solution is reached that incorporates everything known about the special forces affecting the various segments of the economy and is consistent with everything known about the relationships of the factors to each other and to the total.

In the forecasting of price changes, income as such more nearly assumes strategic importance. An index of prices is basically an expression of the relationship between the total income and other funds seeking goods and the volume of goods available; or, to put this another way, it is an index of the value of purchases divided by an index of the physical volume of goods transferred. Even here the changes in wage rates and other price items that go into the make-up of total income will have to be projected in relation to the changes in volume that constitute the demand for the factors of production. Price changes occur mainly when efforts to obtain or to clear out supplies are otherwise unavailing. Nevertheless, if price changes are to be forecast, the analysis has to take account of the income changes that do not merely represent changes in the flow of goods and services. But then the volume of that flow is also essential to the computation.

There are times when the primary focus of the forecast will be on income and prices. As capacity operation is approached, the changes in volume tend to diminish and the changes in income and the related inflationary price responses become the primary elements of variation. Ordinarily, however, what is most desired is a projection of rates of activity as such, in the sense that physical-volume changes involve the use of manpower and other resources. From projections of this kind estimates of employment derive, and these are usually taken as the basic measure of the health of the economy, as, for example, in deciding public policy aimed at minimizing unemployment.

There are three reasons, then, why the initial analysis should proceed in terms of volume rather than money values. First, the primary objective of the forecast is a measure of changes in rates of activity, employment, and real goods and services produced. Second, analysis of resource use and of possible underutilization of capacity or manpower can be realistic only in such terms. Third, a measure of probable price changes can be derived only in comparison with a volume base, which is itself an important indicator of probable changes in wage rates and other money returns to income recipients.

Profits as well as prices are best arrived at as the result of an extended process of analysis that first forecasts physical volume, then translates that forecast into terms of the money income available to consumers, and finally obtains changes in price levels by comparison of the aggregate income to be spent and the corresponding aggregate of real goods and services available. This order of attack, it may be added, is much the same as that used by the practical man. Tell a steel or railroad executive what his operating rate or traffic load will be, and he will be able to calculate the dollars per share his company will earn. Implicit in his calculations may be a conception of the market conditions and prices which that operating rate implies. But that rate itself, which derives from the over-all level of activity as a whole, may be the one thing he cannot supply.

The only way to arrive at a sound forecast of the level of over-all demand or output is by a broad, quantitative analysis that balances the various forces influencing activity against each other in the light of the over-all situation which those forces are likely to call forth. No mere summation of partial views—whether by industry, commodity, region, or other criteria of selection—will produce the desired result. All such partial views are subject to modification in terms of their relationships to each other and to the whole, and none of the specialists holding them is in a position to make the necessary adjustments.

The forecaster should not be led astray by statements that point out the multitudinous variations in economic events and conditions. Attempts to break down the problem into all the detail that would go into a complete explanation are bound to be self-defeating. No doubt every factor making up a whole economic galaxy is of some significance in determining any important phase of economic behavior, such as consumer spending and saving, but to approach the ideal of analyzing all their individual and specific effects is unsound as well as impractical.

The forecaster, in other words, necessarily operates at a fairly high level of aggregation—meaning that he deals with the economy in terms of broad measures and overlooks a considerable amount of detail. This disregard of detail is in fact a necessity for the forecaster, for he must reduce his job to manageable proportions by sifting out the important facts about the current situation from the welter of "information" that is constantly being forced on his attention.

What is of highest importance to the individual or the particular business concern may be of no significance whatever to the economy as a whole. When one gains at another's expense, the net effect may be nothing at all. The crucial events in the life cycle of the individual may be disregarded in analyzing changes in the group as a whole. When each year's crop of births, marriages, and deaths supplants that of the year before, there is no change, but only stability, in the total pattern of community life. And when millions of units are involved in the process, the laws of probability average out individual differences and produce a high degree of continuity in the over-all results.

In these facts lies the answer to the criticism that an aggregative approach leads to error because it overlooks so much that is important in all the detailed segments making up the aggregate. This is a field in which errors of fragmentation can easily become more important than those of aggregation.

The thought here is not to suggest that oversimplification is desirable. Familiarity with detail can add greatly to the understanding that produces nicety of projection, both in magnitude and in timing. But detail is useful only as it fits into a framework of over-all analysis.

The basic requirement is an approach that utilizes strategic points of attack effectively, whether they inhere in the detail of a fragment or in the gross movement of a broad aggregate. An essential part of such an approach is to open the initial projections of all the parts to reflexive adjustment as the pattern of the new situation begins to emerge. In the framework of the national-income accounts, the nonconsumption items in the gross national product provide a good starting point, and the necessity for balancing the accounts with due regard to known interrelationships makes appropriate adjustment almost inevitable.

CHAPTER 6

Government Programs

It has frequently been pointed out since the Great Depression of the
1930s that the impact of government programs on the economy has been
so important that they have assumed an outstanding role among the
factors determining the business outlook. The vast and varied operations
of government are discussed, for example, by Solomon Fabricant in his
book *The Trend of Government Activity in the United States since 1900*.
He says: "One out of every eight persons employed in the United States
today is a government worker. One out of every five dollars of the
nation's capital assets, even excluding public roads and streets and
most military and naval equipment, is government property. One out
of every twenty dollars in the consolidated net sales of business is made
to government."[1]

This describes the end result of a trend that goes back to the beginnings of our history as a nation. Chart 6–1 shows that total Federal
expenditures in constant dollars have risen at an almost stable rate since
1794, if war peaks are ignored.[2] Each war necessitated a strong
upsurge in spending, and after each war expenditures dropped back,
but not all the way to the prewar level. The result is growth in real
expenditures per capita through a series of major steps, each taken as
the consequence of an emergency.

The growth of government activities over a long period of time is
not the most important aspect of its programs needing emphasis in
forecasting. Transitory changes in government undertakings are more
decisive for short-term movements in either direction. Increases in government programs determine many of the advances in economic activity,

[1] Solomon Fabricant, *The Trend of Government Activity in the United States since
1900*, National Bureau of Economic Research, Inc., New York, 1952, p. 3.
[2] M. Slade Kendrick, *A Century and a Half of Federal Expenditures*, Occasional
Paper 48, National Bureau of Economic Research, Inc., New York, 1955, p. 4.

176

Chart 6–1. Federal Expenditures, Annually, 1794–1952

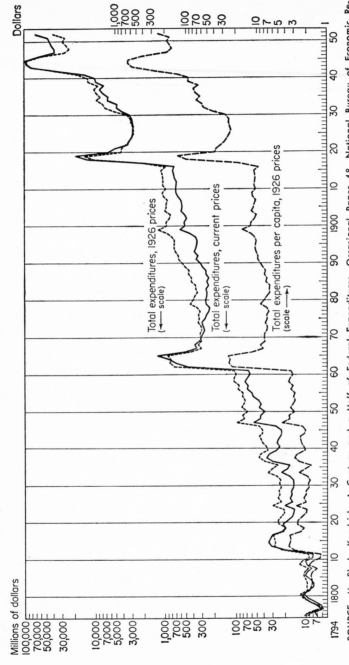

SOURCE: M. Slade Kendrick, A Century and a Half of Federal Expenditures, Occasional Paper 48, National Bureau of Economic Research, Inc., New York, 1955, p. 4.

and curtailments are at times responsible for or at least contribute greatly to the recessions.

Matching the significance of the government sector is the complexity of the analysis required to evaluate its effects on the general economic situation. Any realistic appraisal of the government contribution to the community's income and production involves consideration of a multiplicity of activities, policies, purchases, transfers, and revenue legislation. The economic counterpart of all the government's functions and operations is summarized in its fiscal programs, which are made up of large, complex composites of expenditures and receipts. Everything that affects the spending or revenues of the government to an appreciable extent has to be taken into account. This means, of course, that many things of a noneconomic character—political, social, and other phenomena not subject to precise quantitative measurement—as well as most significant economic developments become part of the field of operation in which the forecaster must work.

All government operations and all the needs of the community for which government assumes responsibility underlie the expenditure side of the government account. They may be considered as made up of two major parts—those of the Federal government, which are most important not only because they are larger but because they change more drastically, and the whole range of state and local government programs in all their variety in size, functions, and other characteristics.

Each of these major parts includes a wide range of activities. The operations of the Federal government alone cover almost the entire field of economic activity, competing for many products that are ordinarily regarded as consumers' goods and services as well as for the many kinds of supplies and equipment needed to carry on operations in which the government or its corporations are engaged. It will readily be seen that the operation of a large government office or the maintenance of a large public building requires a great variety of supplies, equipment, and services, all of which have to be procured from business concerns or individual workers, in competition with other purchasers of the same items.

Within the military programs alone almost the entire range of economic production appears. Military personnel are, of course, also consumers and must be supplied with food, clothing, and equipage. Military operations also require mechanized equipment of various kinds, including not only vehicles, planes, and ships but also many related types of equipment, such as construction and loading machinery, and in addition numerous kinds of industrial equipment to carry on necessary operations in armament manufacturing or repair facilities.

State and local operations also cover the gamut of economic activities.

Here also there are public offices and schools to build, operate, and maintain. Modern police and fire departments are highly mechanized. Hospital, health, and sanitation activities also require a variety of food, supplies, equipment, and facilities. Some state and local units operate their own utilities, transport systems, and repair shops. Many also provide recreational facilities and other direct services to the public. Altogether, data on the activities of non-Federal-government units involve a mass of detail on which only scattered information is available and which would be practically impossible to analyze in detail.

All these various activities are subject to a significant degree of variation in levels of operation and expenditure. In this connection it should be remembered that government agencies operate like private individuals or businesses in anticipating needs and in using what they already have to maintain operations when appropriations or revenues are cut. When shortages are anticipated, they move to protect themselves through forward buying in exactly the same manner as private businesses do, and on other occasions when funds are available—and possibly about to expire, as at the end of a budget period—they may spend considerably in advance of needs to take advantage of funds immediately available.

On the other side of the government account, against all these expenditures which directly and indirectly raise the level of over-all production, are the at least partially offsetting withdrawals in the form of tax collections. The various kinds of taxes collected have widely different impacts, but practically all of them have some effect in reducing the income stream. The magnitude of these withdrawals from the income stream is determined not only by changes in tax rates but also by all the economic changes that affect the bases on which taxes are levied—income, profits, sales, production, or payrolls, as the case may be. On the whole, taxes in the postwar period have amounted to about as large a total as government expenditures, and the effects of changes in the former have to be analyzed in conjunction with expenditure programs to assess the consequences of government action for the economy.

GOVERNMENT AS A STRATEGIC FACTOR

A brief review in terms of the criteria set forth in the last chapter indicates that government programs conform par excellence to the concept of a strategic factor. First, government operations are important from the standpoint of sheer size alone. Purchases of goods and services, as reported by the Department of Commerce, have consistently represented more than 10 percent of the total gross national product since 1931. In the war year of 1944 they rose to a peak of $96.5 billion, or about 45 percent of the total. After the war, they dropped back to their prewar percentage of the total, something under 15 percent, and then rose again under the impact of the Korean War, reaching a high of $85 billion in 1953, or about 23 percent of the total.

This large segment of activity changes rather rapidly, and these large changes greatly influence changes in the economy as a whole, though they are not necessarily decisive in determining its movements. Thus from 1947 to 1948 total government purchases increased from $28.6 billion to $36.6 billion, an advance of $8 billion. Then in 1949 such purchases continued to expand to $43.6 billion, an additional advance of $7 billion. From 1947 to 1948 total gross national product advanced $25 billion, but in 1949 total gross national product remained unchanged as the influence of changes in the private sectors of the economy—particularly a reversal in inventory policy—offset the additional increase in government purchases. Here were changes that had important effects first in pushing the economy ahead and then in supporting it on the decline.

Government expenditures are not confined to purchases of goods and services, of course, but also include transfer payments of one kind or another. A broad summary account of government operations in the early 1950s is provided in Table 6–1. This table shows the sharp expansion in total receipts and expenditures and the comparative stability of transfer payments during this period. These 4 years show both surpluses and deficits in the government accounts and illustrate divergence of movements between Federal and state and local accounts in this respect. During these years of the Korean War, the expansion of government programs was the primary factor pushing the whole economy upward toward the new highs achieved in 1953.

Government programs also measure up to the second criterion for strategic factors, since they constitute one of the most completely autonomous elements in the whole economic picture. Many changes in these programs are planned and put into effect without regard to what is happening elsewhere in the economy. This fact may be deplored by advocates of stabilization, but it gives the government sector a strategic independence of movement.

It is true that some expenditure programs are based on economic need and that most revenue items rise or fall with changes in the general level of economic activity, so that government operations as a whole tend to compensate or offset movements in other parts of the economy. Yet there are many changes in government programs or legislation that are not designed to stabilize the economy, and hence large, erratic movements may originate in the government account. For example, tax reductions are always likely to be made when the government has a surplus, even though they are not justified on economic grounds.

In 1948 both expansion of military and foreign-aid programs and reduction of taxes were undertaken in an inflationary situation in which the labor force was fully employed and bottlenecks prevailed in many industries. Changes of this character must always be expected, and the considerable independence of movement in the government accounts provides a source of economic change that lies wholly outside the influence of other economic developments.

Table 6–1. Government Income and Product Accounts

Calendar years, in millions of dollars

Receipt or expenditure	1950	1951	1952	1953*
Total government:				
Receipts	$ 69,719	$86,778	$ 91,976	$ 99,200
Expenditures	61,445	79,711	94,401	101,200
Surplus or deficit	$ 8,274	$ 7,067	$−2,425	$−2,000
Federal government:				
Receipts	$ 50,534	$65,508	$ 68,829	$ 74,100
Taxes	44,627	58,422	61,370	66,500
Contributions for social insurance	5,907	7,086	7,459	7,600
Expenditures	40,950	58,055	71,189	76,300
Purchases of goods and services	22,139	41,113	54,162	58,100
Other	18,811	16,942	17,027	18,200
Surplus or deficit	$ 9,584	$ 7,453	$−2,360	$−2,200
State and local governments:				
Receipts	$ 21,524	$23,700	$ 25,730	$ 27,900
Taxes	18,222	20,183	21,963	23,800
Contributions for social insurance	963	1,087	1,184	1,300
Federal grants-in-aid	2,339	2,430	2,583	2,800
Expenditures	22,834	24,086	25,795	27,700
Purchases of goods and services	19,899	21,770	23,355	25,200
Other	2,935	2,316	2,440	2,500
Surplus or deficit	$−1,310	$ −386	$ −65	$ 200

* Preliminary estimate by Council of Economic Advisers.
SOURCE: Council of Economic Advisers, *Economic Report of the President*, January, 1954, p. 144.

One reason for this is that definitive criteria for government action have never been established and by the nature of the situation cannot be established. One commonly accepted principle of fiscal policy is the concept of annual balanced budgets supplemented with a policy of debt retirement in prosperity periods. This still has strong political appeal, but in any actual situation it is likely to give way to pressures for tax reduction or large expenditure programs. Each new administration and each new Congress insist on flexibility in deciding what are the best pol-

icies and the best measures to implement those policies in the light of
the current circumstances. Thus program determination is and always will
be a political process. Economic considerations have a place, but they
will ordinarily be given no more weight than they deserve and frequently much less than they deserve.

A third respect in which changes in government programs are important for forecasting lies in the repercussions they have on other factors.
This effect may be observed most clearly, perhaps, in connection with
movements into a war situation in which all kinds of economic activity
will probably be affected. In such a situation, actual or anticipated
changes in government programs have almost infinite repercussions.
Some of these may be directly related, like the capital expenditures to
provide new capacity for filling armament orders. Others may derive
from psychological reactions, such as fear of shortages. From both of
these an almost unlimited number of indirect and secondary adjustments
will flow in waves or ripples. As may be seen in two waves of scare
buying—the first in July, 1950, and the second in the following December and January—the induced effects may have greater immediate consequences than any immediate changes in government programs themselves.

Other examples of changes in government programs that induce
changes in private activity may be cited. The depression measures
establishing the National Recovery Administration in 1933 induced an
inventory boomlet of very considerable magnitude. In 1936 to 1937
a similar boom and decline were induced by building up expenditures
for work relief, in combination with a large one-time shot in the arm
in the form of the 1936 veterans' bonus payments, and subsequently
cutting off those expenditures, in combination with the enactment of
payroll taxes under the social security program. The recovery of 1938
was sparked by the revival of work relief, aided by an expansion of
private-residential-construction activity stimulated in part by the program for insuring mortgages on low-cost houses. Here is an instance
where the movements induced by changes in government programs
dominated a whole cycle.

The effects of government fiscal programs may vary greatly, depending
upon the groups favored or restricted. How any group receiving payments or required to pay taxes modifies its course of action in response
to new legislation determines in part the total effects of the measure.
Nonfiscal measures may be difficult to assess, though almost any important measure is likely to influence private activity to some extent.
Changes in social legislation, such as that regulating labor-management
relations, may have far-reaching effects over a period of time, to which
no definite quantitative values can immediately be assigned.

A mistake commonly made in evaluation of nonfiscal measures is to think that government action is mainly restrictive in its effects, that it merely prevents people from doing things and retards progress. There are such features to some measures, of course, but, on the whole, government action is designed to solve problems and stimulate general activity rather than the reverse. If it does this only indirectly, through the responses of business or other groups, it may be effective nonetheless.

The fourth requirement of a strategic factor is likewise met by the government sector. Many program changes are instituted in such a way that the forecaster is provided with an effective basis for projecting their future course and analyzing their effects. To perform its functions, government necessarily has to do some advance planning, and the plans have to obtain approval in public forum before they are put into effect. The mere fact that legislation precedes action gives an indication of what will occur.

Usually programs are given thorough consideration before being finally adopted, and the process of debate and discussion which precedes decision gives an ample forewarning of what is likely to take place. Sometimes the course of changes in government programs is charted for a fairly long period ahead, and when these changes are entered into a forecast, they may provide a very important basis for it. Anybody who reads the newspapers and takes the trouble to get official statistical reports about what is going on is in a position to make such projections.

In making an analysis of government programs, it is usually essential to consider separately at least the two major segments, Federal and state-local. The movements of the two major parts are often distinct and may even be conflicting. The sources of information available and the techniques of analysis utilized are so clearly different that hardly any point concerning the one can be considered applicable to the other. The more important of the two segments by far as a source of variation in the general economy is the Federal, and it is to the operations of this segment that primary attention must be devoted in working out a forecast.

BASIC DATA ON FEDERAL FISCAL PROGRAMS

For anyone who wants to make an analysis of Federal-government programs, there is a wealth of useful data. The outstanding source of information becomes available in January of each year, in the President's three messages to Congress: the State of the Union message; the Budget message, with summary budget statements; and the *Economic Report* prepared by the Council of Economic Advisers in accordance with the Employment Act of 1946. These documents are all interrelated. They are, in effect, chapters in a single large volume and become a primary basis for the discussions and actions of the next 6 months, by which the program of the coming fiscal year is set.

The kind of information available in these documents may be illustrated by several summary tables from the budget for the fiscal year 1955. In the first part of the President's Budget message appears a brief résumé of the entire budget in its conventional form. After some preliminary discussion of these estimates, a similar summary of receipts and expenditures is provided on a cash basis. These summaries are presented together in Table 6–2, with corresponding data for several earlier years.

Table 6–2.   Federal Receipts and Expenditures

Fiscal years, in millions of dollars

		Actual			Estimate	
Accounting basis	1950	1951	1952	1953	1954	1955
Conventional budget:						
Receipts	$ 36,495	$47,568	$ 61,393	$ 64,593	$ 67,629	$ 62,642
Expenditures	39,606	44,058	65,410	73,982	70,902	65,570
Surplus or deficit	$ −3,111	$ 3,510	$ −4,017	$ −9,389	$ −3,273	$ −2,928
Consolidated cash statement:						
Receipts	$ 40,946	$53,400	$ 68,022	$ 71,283	$ 74,932	$ 70,842
Expenditures	43,160	45,807	67,968	76,554	75,166	70,727
Cash surplus or deficit	$ −2,213	$ 7,593	$ 54	$ −5,272	$ −234	$ 115

SOURCE: Council of Economic Advisers, *Economic Report of the President*, January, 1954, p. 142.

It may be noted that both receipts and expenditures are considerably higher on the cash than on the conventional basis. The differences consist mainly of social security funds. Receipts of the social security payroll taxes are held in trust for the participants, and payments to beneficiaries of the system are made from the trust funds. Since tax receipts under the social security program have been running considerably higher than benefit payments, the cash deficit has been several billion dollars lower than the budget deficit or the cash surplus several billion higher than the budget surplus throughout the postwar period.

Although the consolidated cash statement shows considerably higher figures than the conventional budget, it by no means reveals the total flow of funds through the Federal accounts. The figures shown are net of various deductions applicable to specific kinds of gross receipts or payments. Cash refunds of tax receipts, for example, averaged about $3 billion a year during this period.

At the time this budget message was prepared, near the end of 1953, the latest actual data available were those for fiscal 1953, supplemented by partial data for the last 6 months of 1953 (which are, of course, the first 6 months of fiscal 1954). The fiscal 1954 estimate is therefore based on actual data for a period of one-third to one-half of the fiscal year. Shortly after the budget went to Congress in January, 1954, complete data for the first half of the fiscal year were available and could be used to help translate the budget estimates into a quarterly projection. The fiscal 1955 budget estimates not only had to be completely estimated but also utilized an assumption in arriving at the estimates—namely, that proposed legislation would be enacted. However, the figures corresponding to proposed legislation are shown separately and could be deducted out or subjected to other analytical treatment as desired.

The summary budget tables are usually followed closely by tables showing the major breakdowns of receipts and expenditures. Further detail on the first line of figures given in the initial summary are presented in Table 6–3. It may readily be seen from this table that over $50 billion, or about four-fifths of total budget receipts, were being obtained from income taxes, including taxes on both individual and corporate earnings.

Next in importance among the revenue sources are the excise taxes. These include a wide variety of taxes on production or sale of goods of various kinds. Most important of these are the alcoholic-beverage taxes, which have been producing over $2 billion per year. Tobacco taxes also provide considerable revenue. Other important taxes in this group are the manufacturers' taxes on such products as gasoline, automobiles and parts, and electrical appliances. Of about equal importance to these miscellaneous manufacturers' excise taxes were taxes on telephone service, transportation, and admissions to theater and other recreational performances. Retailers' excise taxes on jewelry, furs, luggage, and toilet preparations were of a distinctly lower order of magnitude in terms of total receipts.

The payroll taxes, which are immediately set aside in trust funds, as the appropriation to the Federal Old-age and Survivors Insurance Trust Fund in the lower portion of Table 6–3 indicates, are also very important cash receipts, but, being those against which future claims are held by workers, they are excluded from budget receipts. Refunds of taxes are also deducted to obtain the latter total.

Most of these receipts fluctuate directly with changes in the level of economic activity. They are based on incomes, profits, production, and employment, all of which represent important measures of general activity or prosperity. Thus, when the general level of activity changes for any reason, government receipts are correspondingly increased or reduced, and for the progressive personal income taxes these changes are more than proportional. In fiscal year 1949, for example, when government payments were rising sharply, receipts fell off because of the economic recession, contributing almost half of the reversal in government finances from a budget surplus of $8½ billion to a deficit of

Table 6–3.   Budget Receipts*

Fiscal years, in millions of dollars

Source	1953 actual	1954 estimated	1955 estimated
Individual income taxes	$32,478	$33,433	$30,908
Corporate income taxes	21,595	22,809	19,694
Excise taxes	9,943	10,038	9,221
Employment taxes:			
Federal Insurance Contributions Act	4,086	4,600	5,369
Federal Unemployment Tax Act	276	290	292
Railroad Retirement Tax Act	626	640	640
Railroad Unemployment Insurance Act	10		
Estate and gift taxes	891	955	955
Customs	613	590	590
Internal revenue not otherwise classified	49		
Miscellaneous receipts	1,827	2,312	2,454
Total receipts	$72,394	$75,668	$70,123
Deduct:			
Appropriation to Federal Old-age and Survivors Insurance Trust Fund	$ 4,086	$ 4,600	$ 5,369
Appropriation to Railroad Retirement Trust Fund	625	640	640
Refunds of receipts	3,120	2,988	2,644
Adjustment to daily-treasury-statement basis	+30		
Budget receipts	$64,593	$67,440	$61,470

* Includes only receipts under existing legislation.
SOURCE: *The Budget of the United States Government for the Fiscal Year Ending June 30, 1955: Budget Message of the President and Summary Budget Statements*, p. M28.

almost $2 billion. The automatic changes in receipts tend to be the most important initial budget changes, in gross quantity at least, whenever shifts in income not initiated by government programs take place.

Changes in receipts are to a considerable extent beyond control. Some types of expenditures are also largely uncontrolled, but the budget generally represents an attempt to control expenditures in great detail. It covers the operations of each agency by function and subfunction in tabulations running to over 1,000 pages. Most of the detail on anticipated expenditures is not included in the summary budget statements, but little of it would be useful to the analyst in any case.

A summary of the expenditure estimates is provided in Table 6–4, including proposed as well as existing legislation, and requests for new appropriations or other authority needed to carry out the proposed programs are also listed. It may be noted that the bulk of budget expenditures were for military and international-security programs and that

Table 6–4. Budget Expenditures by Major Program

Fiscal years, in millions of dollars

Major program	1953 actual	1954 estimated	1955 estimated	Recommended new obligational authority for 1955
National security	$50,274	$48,720	$44,860	$34,859
Veterans' service and benefits	4,298	4,160	4,192	3,959
International affairs and finance	2,216	1,779	1,250	1,547
Social security, welfare, and health	1,910	1,947	1,807	1,857
Housing and community development	549	57	−277	176
Education and general research	277	278	223	185
Agriculture and agricultural resources	2,936	2,654	2,366	2,791
Natural resources	1,358	1,172	1,103	978
Transportation and communication	2,077	1,856	1,418	1,482
Finance, commerce and industry	76	164	162	42
Labor and manpower	281	265	281	314
General government	1,439	1,175	1,160	1,019
Interest	6,583	6,600	6,875	6,875
Reserve for contingencies	......	75	150	200
Adjustment to daily treasury statement basis	−292			
Total	$73,982	$70,902	$65,570	$56,283

SOURCE: *The Budget of the United States Government for the Fiscal Year Ending June 30, 1955: Budget Message of the President and Summary Budget Statements*, p. M33 and *Special Analysis B.*

most of the estimated change in the total during this period was also accounted for by these items.

This table shows the total expenditures for each program regardless of the nature of the items included. Some represent purchases of goods or services; others represent payments of various kinds for which there is no counterpart in the form of real goods and services. Transfer payments are predominant in several important items in the table: All of the interest on the public debt, the bulk of the veterans' payments, and the larger part of expenditures under social security, welfare, and health are of this character. These are types of expenditures that either are stable, as in the case of interest payments, or vary in a fairly predictable fashion, as specified by legislation, in relation to changes in economic activity. Because they partly derive from and run counter to the movements of the economy generally, their inclusion in the budget introduces a complication in relation to the analysis of gross national product, but not a really serious one.

Each of the important programs listed in the table has a supporting section in the President's Budget message, which describes or comments on the programs the President wishes to have implemented. Each section includes a table breaking down the estimated total expenditures into a number of subsidiary parts. Accompanying these estimates is a brief textual statement that indicates the nature of the changes proposed and, by way of justifying those proposals, explains why the various items of expenditure should be neither more nor less than the estimated amounts.

One thing that must be kept in mind in using these data is that the actual economic effects resulting from any program may not coincide with it in point of time. Both expenditures and tax collections tend to lag behind the activities with which they are associated, though there are exceptional cases where they may lead. This is not very troublesome as a rule, but one distinction is very important in this regard—namely, the distinction between expenditures on the one hand and appropriations or authorizations on the other. Funds which are appropriated but which cannot be spent, perhaps because programs cannot be pushed rapidly enough, are important primarily as indicators of what is likely to be the future course of actual expenditures. In the early stages of a rearmament program, many obstacles to increased production have to be overcome and delays of various kinds are inevitably encountered, so that the course of expenditures may have little relationship for a time to appropriations or authorizations. Similar disparities may also occur in other types of programs, and projecting these activities on a valid basis poses the primary problem for the forecaster.

For most of the programs, which operate on annual appropriations, discrepancies between appropriations and expenditures are not likely to be large. Some programs, however, are open-ended, and certain kinds of expenditures may be authorized without definite limit, so that deficiency appropriations may have to be made later to cover expenditures not provided for in the initial appropriations. The military programs typically operate under contract authorizations, and their appropriations carry over from year to year, so that defense expenditures may deviate widely from appropriations. The difference of $10 billion shown in the table indicates that past appropriations or authorizations would provide for the national-security programs to that extent in fiscal 1955.

Another kind of difference appears in housing and community development. Here budget expenditures are negative because expected receipts from such sources as insurance premiums and mortgage sales exceed total new outlays, but new obligational authority is needed for expenditures that would have to be made in carrying on these programs. Still other programs are provided for in trust funds or are operated through government corporations, and these may have access to sources of funds that are effectively independent of current appropriations. For all these reasons, it is the course of actual expenditures that must be followed rather than the changes in appropriations or obligational authority.

A helpful feature of recent budgets is a tabulation segregating various types of expenditures by controllability. Three major classifications are the basis for this tabulation: national security, major programs which are not readily controllable, and all other programs. In the key middle group are the veterans' programs, agricultural programs, grants to states, and interest on the public debt. For most of these programs the basis for expenditures is stipulated in advance, by legislation or administrative regulations in accordance with legislation, and the response of the designated group determines the amount that is actually spent. Forecasts of most of these items are contingent upon general business conditions or upon future rates of activity in specific areas, such as crop production, so that the budget estimates can be considered tentative only. This uncertainty does not greatly affect the initial projection of gross national product, since most of these items do not represent purchases of goods and services.

Criticisms of the budget have been made from time to time. Its failure to segregate transactions in accordance with the economic significance of the activities involved has been a major source of such criticism. One frequent suggestion has called for segregation of capital expenditures from other budget expenditures, on the theory that the acquisition of capital assets, and particularly the types that would be self-liquidating investments, should not be treated as ordinary expenditures. Out of a long period of discussion of such proposals, the budget has in recent years been set up to include a series of "special analyses" that provide some information of this character, and these appear as appendixes to the Budget message and summary statements. Reclassifying the data in this way is not always satisfactory, however, because the details of the cross classification cannot be fully provided within the limited space available.

A limitation on the usefulness of the budget arises from the fact that it appears only once a year, in January. This difficulty is mitigated by the fact that as the new fiscal year opens, roughly 6 months after the budget was originally presented, it is again reviewed. The President usually issues his Mid-year Review of the Budget in August. Data on expenditures and tax collections in the previous fiscal year are then nearly complete, and legislative action has been taken or is fairly well indicated, so that estimates can be worked out with considerably more assurance than before. These revised estimates become a primary basis for making projections through the next calendar year.

No such periodic reports can be entirely satisfactory, however. It is necessary to keep much more nearly up to date on government operations, so that other sources must be utilized. Two important publications available for this purpose are the *Treasury Bulletin,* a monthly publication of the U.S. Treasury Department, and the *Daily Treasury Statement.*

The *Treasury Bulletin* begins with a summary of fiscal operations, giving back data for a number of years and current data by months for the last year. It first presents budget receipts and expenditures and the surplus or deficit. Then it shows adjustments for trust accounts and the clearing account, changes in the public debt and in the general-fund balance, and the level of the general-fund balance and the public debt at the end of each period. This summary is supported by a series of tables giving receipts and expenditures in major sources or classifications, and it then goes on to give a variety of statistics concerning government securities and debt operations.

The *Daily Treasury Statement* is a means of keeping considerably more current with government fiscal operations. It summarizes major items of receipts and expenditures on a day-to-day basis and shows the accumulated total for each month through the designated date. The statement for the end of the month thus provides a relatively complete accounting of the entire month's operations and is available within a few days after the end of the month. Some difficulty in the use of these data will be experienced by most analysts, because they are subject to large, erratic fluctuations on days when large sums happen to be paid out or received, actions that are clearly not coincident with the activity for which payment is made. For example, in portraying military expenditures by months, adjustment has to be made for the number of Tuesdays in the month, because some expenditures accumulate through the week and are paid in total on the following Tuesday. Making these adjustments in timing, and other necessary adjustments to the *Daily Treasury Statement* data, as for financial transactions, requires a great deal of attention to detail and may appeal to only a limited group of specialists regularly engaged in analysis of the government accounts.

These basic general reports on Federal programs will have to be supplemented from time to time by greater detail from other sources. Additional published reports are available from various agencies— among others, the Bureau of Internal Revenue, on taxes; the Social Security Board, on transfer payments; the Commodity Credit Corporation, on farm price supports; and the Departments of Commerce and Labor, on construction. On occasion, published data will be inadequate, but the desired information may be obtainable on direct request from the agencies involved. Articles and news reports from nongovernmental sources may also, of course, be helpful.

ANALYZING FEDERAL PROGRAMS

In analyzing Federal-government programs, either of two approaches may be followed. The analysis may be carried out in either net or gross terms. The result of the former approach is commonly referred to as the net government contribution; it makes its basic evaluation in terms of the cash surplus or deficit. The latter deals initially with government purchases of goods and services and makes subsequent adjustments for other expenditures and for revenue changes; in this approach each item appears in its relation to other factors at the point at which it enters the national-income and product account. Both approaches rely on essentially the same sources of information and methods of analysis.

To consider first the net-contribution approach, both the Department of Commerce and the Council of Economic Advisers make summary comparisons of income and outlay accounts for various sectors of the economy in conformity with this concept. In the annual National Income Number of the *Survey of Current Business,* the Department of Commerce publishes a section for the latest year entitled "National Income and Product Accounts." In addition to accounts for the four major segments of the economy—business, government, foreign, and consumer— there is a gross savings and investment account, which brings together items of savings and investment from all the other accounts.

In the government account, the balancing item, which is the key item from a net-contribution point of view, is the deficit or surplus on income and product transactions. This is the residual obtained after the accounts are adjusted to exclude intergovernmental transfers, debt, and other capital transactions, and the timing of entries is adjusted to correspond to production or delivery rather than to payment dates.

The Council of Economic Advisers, in a section of the *Economic*

Report entitled "The Nation's Economic Budget," attempts a simplified version of the national accounts. These show for each of the same four major groups total receipts, total expenditures, and the excess of receipts or expenditures. The net figure for each sector is computed, indicating its net contribution to or withdrawal from the income stream. On this basis, the government contribution assumes the more usual and readily understood form of the cash deficit or surplus, that is, the difference between gross cash receipts and gross cash payments to the public. It differs from the Department of Commerce deficit or surplus on income and product transactions by removing the timing adjustments, using actual tax payments rather than liabilities, putting social security on a cash rather than an accrual basis, and making other adjustments to a cash basis. What is in effect a fifth sector, entitled "Adjustments," is then necessary in order to convert gross receipts and expenditures of the four major economic sectors to a gross-national-product basis and account for any remaining imbalance in the net contributions.

This approach to forecasting was used effectively by a group of government analysts in the late 1930s. Federal Reserve Board economists had compiled a monthly net-contribution series for the Federal government. It was defined as the excess of cash expenditures over receipts, with some adjustments in the totals on both sides, so that it was on essentially the same basis as the Council's annual and quarterly data.

When a net contribution in this sense was being made, the government was running a cash deficit, which had to be financed through borrowing in so far as cash balances were inadequate to cover it. Prospective changes in various government programs could readily be combined and projected in this form, and since substantial changes sometimes took place in the course of a few months, it represented a valuable tool in the forecaster's kit.

Difficulties in its use arise from both analytical and practical considerations. The analytical difficulty arises from the fact that a single net figure of this kind does not take account of the differential effects of various expenditure and revenue items. Whenever a net figure is used in evaluating the effects of economic changes, it has to be justified in terms of the relative equality of items added or deducted.

Such equality does not appear to exist in the case of government expenditures and receipts. Expenditures for goods and services represent a direct stimulus to production and employment, and transfer payments largely go as income to recipients who have inadequate incomes from other sources and have to use them for current consumption expenditures. On the other hand, taxes merely take something out of increased incomes or leave a little in reduced incomes and are in part withdrawals at the expense of savings, so that their effects on the income flow are quantitatively different from an equal volume of expenditures.

It has become customary to speak of a deficit as inflationary and a surplus as deflationary, but this simple proposition is likely to be misleading at times. Except for war periods, a deficit is likely to be associated with deflation, even though in such periods it is making a contribution, but not one large enough to bring the decline to a halt. Moreover, it is not hard to envisage a set of changes in which a deficit would even be deflationary in an absolute sense—as in a period when expenditure programs were being cut drastically, thus contributing more to speeding recession than a somewhat larger decline in tax receipts could contribute to slowing it. Similarly, a moderate surplus at a time when programs were high and going higher might have no effect in restraining an advance, depending, of course, upon the specific nature of the spending programs and the tax structure in effect at the time.

To remedy this analytical deficiency was the aim of a research project carried out at the University of Illinois.[3] It attempted to set up an analytical budget for the Federal government, as distinct from either the regular or the cash budget. Various items of expenditure or taxation were weighted by factors designed to take account of their indirect effects on activity through personal income and consumption, in order to reduce them to approximate equivalence in terms of reactions on activity in subsequent periods. The general conclusion reached was that in the decade of the 1940s government operations provided a net stimulus to private activity in addition to its own purchases of goods and services, that is, expenditures somewhat overbalanced tax withdrawals in subsequent effects even if direct purchases were left out of account. With the latter included, there was a distinct contribution to total activity throughout the period, even in the postwar years, when military spending had been cut back and a cash surplus was realized by the government.

Unless some agency were to undertake the difficult analysis that goes into the make-up of such a measure, however, the practical problem of detailed analysis remains. Since any net-contribution estimate is determined by expenditures on the one hand and revenues on the other, all the factors affecting expenditures and revenues help to account for the movement of this net balance, and it is necessary to analyze the composition of these broader flows from which the net contribution is obtained.

Looking forward, there is no basis on which a deficit or surplus as such can be projected in its own right. It is merely a residual from two large

[3] John Van Dewater, *The Effects of Federal Fiscal Programs on Economic Activity*, unpublished doctoral dissertation, University of Illinois, Urbana, Ill., 1954.

totals, and its changes derive from numerous changes within those totals. In order to obtain an estimate of the difference between those larger totals in any period, the components of the totals themselves must be considered. Since that is the case, the forecaster might as well begin in the first instance with an analysis in gross terms.

A deficit or surplus appears as a result of the way things happen to come out, after Congress has threshed out expenditure and tax legislation and business developments have run their course in determining the level of income. The net residue that will appear on one side or the other can be estimated in advance only on the basis of assumptions. Among these assumptions are a number concerning the future level of employment and incomes, on which both tax receipts and transfer payments depend but which can be estimated in advance only by means of an over-all forecast.

It is in terms of this consideration that one of the outstanding advantages of the alternative approach may be recognized. Using government expenditures for goods and services as the key total produces a figure that is only to a minor extent derived from the expected level of economic activity. It is true that programs will be set up or expanded in the event of a decline and perhaps that some additional economies will be undertaken in a period of inflation, but these are of secondary importance and can be entered as adjustments at a later stage. The primary effectiveness of government programs in determining future activity lies in those operations which are decided upon before the course of economic developments is clearly revealed.

The logic of utilizing the total purchases of goods and services rather than all expenditures lies in the fact that this procedure deals with items directly affecting production rather than those which affect it only through changes in the level of income. The latter trend to have an effect that is essentially stabilizing, and in the case of government-provided income in the form of transfer payments, including public welfare and assistance, this stabilizing effect is heightened by the fact that they run counter to changes in general activity. In short, the computation in terms of purchases of goods and services tends to segregate the items that are autonomous and predictable from those that depend on the level of activity and therefore must logically be calculated at a later stage after a more general forecast of the level of activity has been compiled.

USE OF THE BUDGET IN FORECASTING

The process by which government programs are established is a process of deciding in advance what is to be done. Program proposals originate, of course, in innumerable ways. Measures may be proposed to meet national needs or to serve the special interests of some limited group. Whatever their origin, they have to be put before Congress and approved, and then funds have to be appropriated to carry them out before they can have significant effects.

The most comprehensive statement of proposed programs is found in the budget, which may therefore be taken as a starting point. The budget may be regarded as the President's proposal for operations during the next fiscal year, but it is in a real sense much more than that. It has behind it the biggest part of a year's work on the part of the Budget Bureau and all the controlling and budgeting units in the various government agencies. Proposals are reviewed to establish general policy and then re-reviewed for conformity with that policy and for consistency between needs and resources. Decisions are made, appeals are taken, and then the programs are reviewed again. Out of this process of discussion, and sometimes controversy, evolves the budget.[4]

One of the most common mistakes regarding the government's operations is the idea that things are decided at some central point and then put into effect. The fact is that the government is anything but a monolithic structure which acts on a unified basis. There is always pushing and hauling to advance one objective or another. The various agencies view the situation in quite different ways, and each is in a position to know and support the needs of the community or of special groups within it for programs under its jurisdiction.

In the preparation of the budget, conflicts occasionally arise that cannot be resolved at the staff level and have to be put before the President. He then has to make the decision, perhaps arbitrarily, in order to get the budget completed, but for the most part the process is a two-way street. He cannot be familiar wih detail and at best decides general policies as guides to the agencies. Their appraisals and judgments of the situation flow upward, to determine his policy decisions in so far as possible and to get them modified when they are adverse. If he is adamant, the issues are likely to be reopened when the budget goes before Congress.

In other words, the budget is a broadly based document, which organizes a mass of detail in convenient form after a process of selection that rules out most of the spending which could not be considered valid. Budget procedures are specifically focused on the objective of achieving economy and efficiency in government. They are supposed to limit funds to what is actually needed and to prevent waste. Things do happen when something or someone effectively demands action, and frequently the actions taken result in programs that might from one

---

[4] See S. M. Cohn, *Managing the Expenditure Side of the Federal Budget*, U.S. Bureau of the Budget, 1952. (Mimeographed.)

standpoint or another be considered ill-advised. Yet underlying practically every program are demands that have at least some reasonable basis, and for the most part there is at least some logical justification for the programs proposed.

At this point it might be asked: "Does the budget as it is sent to Congress represent a satisfactory basis for forecasting?" The answer to this question has to be an unequivocal "No!" It is useful in arriving at a forecast but cannot in itself be considered to present the kind of estimates needed.

There are several qualifications that have to be immediately noted. Legislation will modify existing programs to some extent, and the budget proposals for new legislation may or may not get through. Business developments will modify results through their effects on flexible spending and tax programs and may even induce the undertaking of new programs. Furthermore, there are likely to be biases of one kind or another in the estimates, reflecting the policies of the administration or the attitudes of the agencies involved, since both have to follow arbitrary assumptions to some extent in order to arrive at specific figures.

The expenditures estimates in the budget are likely to be based on an optimistic view of what will be approved and what can be accomplished once approved. In the early stages of building up an emergency program—for war or depression—progress is likely to be more limited than is first expected. Therefore, there is a tendency to overstate expenditures. This was true through most of the first decade after World War II. In contrast, the estimates of receipts are likely to be made on a conservative basis and therefore tend to understate the amount the government will receive. In the early postwar years this was due not only to the natural inclination of the Treasury to avoid criticism by maximizing the difficulties of its financing problem in advance but also to the general prevalence of pessimistic views of the outlook on the part of prominent economists whose estimates of income the Treasury partly utilized in preparing its revenue estimates.

Thus the deficit for fiscal 1952 turned out to be only $4 billion instead of the $16.5 billion estimated in January, 1951. President Truman's initial estimate for fiscal 1954, released with the original Budget message in January, 1953, was $9.9 billion. President Eisenhower, in his mid-year review, with the advantage of knowing that programs had been cut, made a revised estimate of $3.8 billion. The actual was $3.1 billion.

Substantial discrepancies of this kind indicate why the budget estimates have to be adjusted. They have to be corrected for bias or assumptions involved in their preparation, for feasibility of programs included, for unforeseen economic developments, and for political influences of various kinds.

The first step in this process of adjustment is to convert the budget-expenditure estimates to the basis of purchases of goods and services, or at least to an approximation of that basis. This automatically eliminates some of the problems arising from expenditure and revenue items that will be determined by the level of business activity. One way to obtain a provisional estimate on this basis is to deduct changes in the major items that do not represent goods and services from the change in total budget expenditures and then apply the result to the gross-national-product estimate in the most recent period. If only a limited number of major items is considered, a rough conversion can nevertheless be accomplished. Minor elements that should logically be retained will then be subtracted out, and others that should be eliminated will remain, but these minor discrepancies will not ordinarily invalidate the result.

Certain further adjustments can be made in the initial analysis, but others have to wait until the over-all forecast is worked out. Thus, the course of military programs can often be projected effectively from an analysis of the recent rate of over-all progress, at times even more accurately than from a knowledge of all the confidential detail going into the make-up of the production schedules, since the course of such a program must be expected to change sharply following a change in international conditions. Among the adjustments that have to be held over to a later stage are those affecting flexible programs like farm price supports, which depend partly on general trends, and public works, which are usually authorized to a fixed total amount but which can be speeded up or slowed to some extent in the light of current developments. The experienced analyst will be able to tell by inspection of each of the important functions or items, and by the descriptions of what is included in them, which have to be treated in this way. The most difficult of all to forecast, as a rule, are the changes that depend on the passage of new legislation.

The procedure of making a quarterly projection is illustrated in Table 6–5, in terms of a forecast for fiscal 1955. In Part A of the table, budget estimates were adjusted to eliminate major items that do not represent goods and services. Actually, a good part of the veterans' and social security programs, which were deducted in their entirety, do represent goods and services; however, the parts of these items that belong in this category, such as administrative expenses and medical and hospital care, are fairly stable, so that the change from one year to the next is not greatly affected by the conceptual error. The last two items deducted appear in the "special analyses" section of the budget. Loans made a substantial difference over this period, not because operations were being curtailed but because repayments were being made on the outstanding

Table 6–5.   Projection of Federal Purchases of Goods and Services
In billions of dollars

A. Estimating Prospective Changes from Budget Data

	1953 *actual*	1954 *estimated*	1955 *estimated*
Total budget expenditures	$74.0	$70.9	$65.6
Less:			
Veterans' benefits	4.3	4.2	4.2
Social security, etc.	1.9	1.9	1.8
Interest	6.6	6.6	6.9
Government loans (net)	1.8	0.2	0.0
Grants-in-aid (schools, highways, etc.)	0.7	0.8	0.7
Adjusted total	$58.7	$57.2	$52.0
Year-to-year change		−1.5	−5.2

B. Quarterly Estimates at Annual Rates

Quarter	*Actual* (as of *January*, 1954)	*Projected Changes* *(cumulative from* 1953 *IV)*	*Forecast*	*Actual* (as of *August*, 1955)
1952 III	$54.6	......	.....	$56.7
IV	56.4	......	.....	56.5
1953 I	57.4	......	.....	59.0
II	58.9	......	.....	61.0
III	58.4	......	.....	59.3
IV	57.5*	......	.....	58.7
1954 I	......	$−1.8	$55.7	54.7
II	......	−4.1	53.4	48.6
III	......	−5.5	52.0	47.7
IV	......	−6.2	51.3	45.7
1955 I	......	−6.7	50.8	46.4
II	......	−7.0	50.5	45.2†

* Estimated.
† Preliminary.

loans of past periods. The "grants-in-aid" item excludes grants under the social security and welfare programs, since those were already deducted above.

Another category that usually has to be considered is "new legislation." In this instance, new legislation consisted of $700 million for extension of the mutual military program and other items of a more doubtful character. The extension of the mutual military program represented a partial offset to large reductions in direct military expenditures which were proposed in accordance with the "massive-retaliation" concept.

Since the international situation was again threatening, in both the Near East and French Indochina, it seemed logical to assume that the additional military-aid expenditures would be approved. On the other items, some were already excluded under social security and probable changes in the remaining were judged to be largely offsetting. Therefore, no special adjustment was made for new legislative proposals.

The changes derived in this way indicate a decline of $1.5 billion from fiscal 1953 to fiscal 1954 and an additional $5.2 billion decline from fiscal 1954 to fiscal 1955. In making the projection of quarterly estimates from the fourth quarter of 1953, as shown in Part B, it appeared unlikely that a decline of $1.5 billion could materialize in fiscal 1954. Although the first part of the year indicated the beginning of a downturn and the reduction in the armed services was to be accomplished by July 1, 1954, changes of a magnitude that would produce a $5.2 billion decline in the following year would not lower the annual average nearly enough. Moreover, it was not clear that the $5.2 billion decline would be fully realized: In view of the fact that an economic recession was in progress, there appeared to be some probability that new programs would be undertaken to counter the decline, and the disturbed international situation seemed likely to limit the decline in military programs. Nevertheless, a series of changes was set up to give effect to a decline in excess of $5 billion, with most of it occurring in fiscal 1954 and only moderate declines following in fiscal 1955.

The results obtained in this way did not give full effect to the change derived from the budget for fiscal 1954; that year averaged only $½ billion below the then available estimate for fiscal 1953. The extreme decline from the second quarter of 1953 to the second quarter of 1955 was estimated at over $8 billion. But this was only about half of the actual decline for the same period revealed by the revised and subsequent figures shown in the last column of Part B. Any basis of projection that appeared reasonable in January, 1954, would probably have fallen short of this drastic 2-year change.[5]

It is evident that a much more detailed series of adjustments of the budget estimates than those shown in Part A could be worked out, by using the wealth of data provided in the budget documents. Detailed procedures, however, could neither eliminate the need for judgment in interpreting changes in major programs nor guarantee accuracy in the forecasts.

An alternative procedure to that illustrated would start from the cash budget rather than the conventional budget. In this case, additional

[5] A forecast made 2 months earlier, before the budget was available, proved to be more seriously in error. For a discussion of its role in an over-all forecast, see Chap. 13, p. 482.

deductions would have to be made for transfers to individuals or to state and local governments from trust funds as well as from the conventional budget accounts. If the various adjustments were carried out in sufficient detail, the two procedures ought to end with the same results, or at least with differences of negligible proportions relative to the total change projected.

TAKING ACCOUNT OF POLITICAL FACTORS

Despite the extended work of review and refinement that goes into the make-up of the budget, it is in a sense only the proposal of the President when it is put before Congress. As a rule, some of the measures proposed go through and others are rejected. Some programs are expanded and others are cut back.

Congress is never satisfied with the budget as it is. The operations of the Budget Bureau are regarded with suspicion, particularly by the opposition party, because it is a branch of the Executive Office and may merely be formalizing the President's pet policies. Hence Congress insists on its own investigation and analysis. The question for the forecaster is: "Which programs will get through unchanged, which will be thrown out, and which will be substantially modified? Also, which other programs, among those that have not been accepted by the administration, will nevertheless win enough support to obtain passage?"

This is not a simple question to answer, nor is this the place for a detailed discussion of the various factors, tangible and intangible, that would have to go into an answer. What is passed depends not so much on logic, on the total benefit from programs in relation to their cost, as on the pressures that can be brought to bear while each measure is being considered.

There are, of course, a multitude of pressures that bear on congressional action, and the following attempt to classify them is no more than a tentative summary. To begin with, a broad distinction between two kinds of pressures may be drawn. The first kind arises out of specific situations that generate their own pressures; these situations are the result of important developments in international, economic, or political affairs. The second kind arises out of group action of various kinds; any group with special interests may organize a bloc or lobby and in that way get its own specific proposals enacted.

In the first category, the outstanding example is the threat of war. It creates a situation that develops many pressures, direct and indirect, which are effective in getting things through. Direct preparedness programs are only one aspect of its results. Aid to friendly nations may be another. Most of the government subsidies to business operations, such as shipbuilding and air transportation, have some kind of security angle. In a tense situation, a relatively minor incident will sometimes provide a spur to the passage of items that were very much in question up to that point.

Another kind of situation that in and of itself generates pressure for action is a depression. When unemployment is high or rising, many programs may be undertaken as a remedy. Such action was made an explicit objective of national policy in the Employment Act of 1946, and the first Republican administration to take office following the passage of the act demonstrated that it was not a one-party idea.

Some enthusiasts for countercyclical action go so far as to state that effective compensatory action is now assured, that the government can be relied upon to step in and prevent extreme declines in economic activity. This is a dubious proposition at best. Government action is always slow. It is the subject of controversy and endless debate. Economic programs not only are late in acceptance but also are usually a compromise and limited in amount. When it is clear that a situation demands action, it is likely to be too late for the appropriate action to be taken before the movement will progress considerably further. Once a downswing is well under way, it is very doubtful that government programs can effectively be expanded enough to bring it to an end. On the other hand, it is clear that something will be done, and when a forecast indicates a worsening of the economic situation, some allowance must be made for programs that will increase government expenditures or reduce taxes.

Measures to counter inflation will also be undertaken, but, except in a war situation, they are likely to be rather ineffective. Opposition to restraints during a boom is strong. Hardly anybody wants income curtailed in such a period. Most merely want it maintained on the decline. Nevertheless, there are times when controls appear to be essential for the prevention of adverse consequences. In 1950, after the outbreak of the Korean War, when President Truman asked for controls, he did not ask for controls on wages and prices. Congress, however, wrote those controls into the bill because of intense popular demand. Congressmen were flooded with messages from all over the country asking for price controls, and this concerted appeal brought other stabilization measures as well, such as substantial tax increases at a time when tax rates were already high.

As a third category under this heading, any proposal that is regarded as politically popular will obtain substantial support. Popular favor is sometimes referred to as a "ground swell" of public sentiment, and even if the favored proposal cannot command a majority, it may gain a compromise. If several elections in which an issue was raised seem to indicate popular acceptance, a number of Congressmen will attempt to capitalize on it, and those who are inclined to oppose it may become unwilling to make an open fight that might damage their positions. Such movements of public opinion may, however, prove no more than crosscurrents or eddies that temporarily disturb the normal flow.

The second major source of pressures, that originating with special groups, is seen to exist primarily in the organizations that such groups build. Unorganized pressure is ineffective except when it is very widespread. Organized pressure may gain action even when it has very limited backing.

There is nothing strange in the fact that congressmen who are themselves elected by political organizations should decide to organize in order to get their programs through. Most congressmen prefer to team up with others to get their own projects through rather than to fight and kill off one another's projects. Thus blocs come into existence, and such units, although only loosely and informally organized, can be expected to vote in unison, even though specific measures are not in the interests of all their members. Each member is willing to trade his vote on certain measures in which he has only a minor stake or may even mildly dislike for the votes of others on measures in which he is interested. The effectiveness of blocs, such as the farm bloc and the silver bloc, is widely recognized.

The committee organization of Congress facilitates this process. Not only do both houses have their own committees, but there are several joint committees, like the Joint Economic Committee, made up of key men from both houses. The average congressman is a very busy man and relies heavily on the judgment of committee members. He has to spend much of his time seeing other people and carrying out other duties, so that it may be practically impossible for him to familiarize himself with the details of all the issues coming before Congress. He therefore works for a place on the right committee and casts his vote with other committees in order to minimize opposition to the measures sponsored by his committee.

The committee organization also enables outside interests to concentrate their efforts where they can be most effective. The lobbies organized by groups of various kinds who happen to be interested in pushing certain types of measures consistently work with and for the key committees and make every effort to get men who agree with them placed on the committees. These lobbies may be supported by industrial or business groups, such as farm organizations or trade associations. They may represent labor organizations; most of the big unions have now set up offices in Washington. Many large industrial concerns maintain

Washington offices or retain consultants, lawyers, or public relations firms to represent their interests with the government.

The lobbyists may deal only with some specific issue, or they may be permanent agents or organizations. The National Association of Manufacturers and the Chamber of Commerce of the United States recommend detailed programs for enactment by each new Congress. They also send special-purpose groups to Washington to get some measure across or to block action on some measure considered adverse to their interests.

These lobbies work mainly through efforts to persuade government officials and congressmen to support programs in which they are interested. They go to Washington, visit with congressmen who might be in a position to influence the outcome, and request action in their favor. The implication is clear that they in turn are going to support the congressmen if they vote "right" and oppose them if they vote "wrong." In this way considerable pressure is created. In many cases the congressman is sympathetic, so that the pressure is not needed; but even if this is not the case to begin with, it is a hardy congressman who will refuse to pay some attention to the recommendations of a large group of his constituents who come to Washington for the specific purpose of asking his support on some desired measure.

There can be no doubt about the effectiveness of such activities. Their results are readily observable in the votes. The votes of congressmen in states where special-interest groups are strong may be readily matched with the proposals of the lobbies representing such groups. There are exceptions, of course, but the rule generally prevails.

Whenever there is a strong lobby against some measure, there is a serious question whether it can be put through. Moreover, the effects of blocs and lobbies may often be counted not in whole but rather in partial victory. Many of the measures proposed get through only in compromise form. Possibly the compromise will be one that bears little resemblance to the original proposal.

In forming a judgment on these things it is necessary to approach them not in terms of what the forecaster thinks ought to be done but in terms of the positions taken by interested groups. In formulating their positions, politicians are likely to consider not only whether a proposal is reasonable but also whether it will embarrass his opponents. Some appear to operate entirely on the basis of expediency. Sometimes, with a change in party fortunes at the polls, a broad shift on policies may take place on party lines. At other times, policy may remain unchanged. A wisecrack going around Washington in the post–World War II period stated that the Democrats favored the capital budget in the depression, when deficit financing was necessary, and that the Republicans favored it in prosperity, when tax reduction was wanted.

There are times when the general political situation will provide clues to what might get through. In some situations, one side effectively controls the decision, as in the late 1930s, when the Democrats piled up an overwhelming majority under Roosevelt. At other times, however, the administration may have little or no control over Congress. Under Truman, there developed a comparative balance of power between the Administration and the congressional "coalition," consisting primarily of Republicans and Southern Democrats. Out of this developed a comparative stalemate in the government. The Administration could not get anything passed against the wishes of the "coalition," and the "coalition" could not muster enough votes to pass anything over the President's veto. The result was that measures agreed upon by both sides went through easily while those disputed did not get through at all. Except for measures like rearmament, for which both sides tried to claim the credit, there was a deadlock that prevented change.

All the various types of pressure are, of course, interacting. Both the basic underlying pressures that originate in major issues and the personal pressures that originate in political relations determine the decision to some extent. In the long run the underlying pressures are likely to be more important, but in any immediate situation the effectiveness of personal action should not be discounted. When an influential congressman, say, a senator or representative who is chairman of a key committee, takes a public position on some issue, that fact may in itself be of substantial significance, though there are many instances, of course, where such influential men have failed to carry the day.

It is recognized that all this is a difficult field of analysis for someone who is not versed in government operations and in the politics of economics. It is, nevertheless, the only way. All that is intended in this brief summary is to provide some suggestions about where the answers may be sought.

Even if the forecaster cannot forecast how some of the disputed measures will come out, he may still be able to forecast the progress on related programs by waiting until the legislation is passed. The lag between legislation and action is usually sufficient to provide him with at least some indication of the course of future developments in the government sector. It is by following the discussions and enactments that he keeps himself in a position to revise the initial projections based on the budget. By keeping up with the news in this area and observing the actual course of programs in the data reported by government agencies, reasonably good projections can usually be made for a year or more into the future.

STATE AND LOCAL PROGRAMS

In the case of state and local operations, there are no good current data. Not only is there much less current information, but the limited amount available is much less timely. The underlying source material consists of budgetary and accounting reports prepared by the various government units for local use. The data compiled from these reports, particularly for the local governments, which number some 115,000, are incomplete and relatively inaccurate. They are particularly inadequate in the breakdowns of expenditures and receipts by type.[6]

Table 6–6. State-government Finances in 1953

In billions of dollars

Total funds available	$19.3	Total expenditures	$17.3
Borrowing	1.3	Debt redemption	0.4
Intergovernmental transfers*	2.8	Intergovernmental transfers†	5.4
Revenue from own sources	$15.2	Direct expenditures	$11.5
Taxes	$10.6	Current operation	$ 5.6
Sales	6.2	Education	1.3
License	1.6	Highways	0.7
Personal income	1.0	Health and hospitals	1.0
Corporate income	0.8	Liquor stores	0.8
Other	1.0	Other	1.8
Liquor store revenue	1.0	Capital outlays	$ 2.8
Current charges‡	0.8	Highway construction	2.1
Other revenue	0.4	Other	.7
Insurance trust	$ 2.5	Assistance and subsidies	1.5
Employee retirement	0.6	Interest on debt	0.2
Unemployment compensation	1.6	Insurance-trust benefits	$ 1.4
Other	0.3	Employee retirement	0.3
		Unemployment compensation	0.9
		Other	0.2

* Includes $2.6 billion Federal transfers.
† Includes $2.7 billion for education and $0.8 billion for highways.
‡ Education, highways, hospitals, and other services.
SOURCE: *Summary of Governmental Finances in 1953* and *Compendium of State Government Finances in 1953*, U.S. Bureau of the Census.

The Governments Division of the U.S. Bureau of the Census compiles annual data on the expenditures and revenues of government units at all levels. These are reported in the annual *Summary of Governmental Finances*, with a separate summary giving greater detail for each of the various kinds of units. All 48 states are covered by the annual *Com-*

[6] See George W. Mitchell, "Forecasting State and Local Government Expenditures," *Journal of Business*, University of Chicago, Chicago, January, 1954.

pendium of State Government Finances, and the 481 cities of over 25,000 inhabitants are covered by the *Compendium of City Government Finances.* Other kinds of local governments, including county, school-district, and township units, are less adequately represented in the reports, so that only survey estimates of operations are available. The numbers of such governments are reported in the special study *Governments in the United States in 1952,* and their employment and payrolls appear annually in *State Distribution of Public Employment.*

Table 6–7.   Local-government Finances in 1953

In billions of dollars

Total funds available[a]	$24.6	Total expenditures[a]	$23.1
Borrowing	3.7	Debt redemption	1.4
Intergovernmental transfers[b]	5.7	Transfer to states	0.2
Revenue from own sources	$15.2	Direct expenditures	$21.5
Taxes	$10.2	Current operation[c]	$14.5
Property	8.9	Education	6.0
Sales	0.7	Highways	1.4
Other	0.6	Police and fire	1.5
Charges and miscellaneous	2.3	Health and sanitation	1.4
Utility revenue[d]	2.4	Utilities[e]	1.8
Insurance-trust revenue	0.3	General control	0.9
		Other	1.5
		Capital outlays	$ 5.1
		School construction	1.5
		Highway construction	0.7
		Utility construction	0.7
		Other[f]	2.2
		Assistance and subsidies	1.1
		Interest on debt	0.6
		Insurance-trust benefits	0.3

   [a] Partly estimated from sample data. Excludes intergovernmental transfers between local units.

   [b] Includes $309 million direct Federal transfers.

   [c] Breakdown of current operation into subsidiary items was derived by deducting partly estimated capital outlays from corresponding items of general expenditure.

   [d] Includes $160 million liquor-store revenue.

   [e] Includes $133 million liquor-store expenditures and $184 million interest on utility debt.

   [f] Includes $767 million for purchases of land, existing structures, and equipment.

   SOURCE: *Summary of Governmental Finances in 1953,* U.S. Bureau of the Census.

The basic revenue and expenditures data for 1953 are presented in Tables 6–6 and 6–7. Among the most important operating activities of state and local governments are education; police, fire, and other measures of public safety; highway construction and maintenance; and health, hospitals, and sanitation. Expenditures of these governments also include a substantial element of transfer payments, both to each other and to the public in the form of assistance, unemployment compensation, and other programs.

Although state governments tap almost every revenue source, their most important revenue producer by far is the sales tax—one that is highly responsive to changes in the level of economic activity. Expenditure programs, on the other hand, are relatively stable. Education, for example, goes on year by year regardless of business conditions; state expenditures for this purpose, including transfers to local governments, operating costs, and capital outlays, exceeded $4 billion in 1953. Under prosperity conditions, therefore, with revenues increasing faster than expenditures, state governments tend toward a position of financial ease. In 1953 revenue and borrowing exceeded expenditure and debt redemption by $2 billion, or 11 percent.

Property taxes are of relatively minor importance to state government units but provide almost all county tax revenues, and about three-fourths of city tax revenues. Most of the other one-fourth of city tax revenues are derived from sales taxes and license fees of various kinds. The property tax is a most stable kind of revenue producer, because rates cannot be readily adjusted when revenue needs expand or contract. Local-government operating programs are also relatively stable. But costs of operation rise more rapidly than revenue on the advance and, together with capital outlays, create larger financial needs. Difficulty is also encountered on the decline, when operating costs are sticky and expenditures are swollen by relief and other transfer payments. Hence these governments always face a revenue problem.

Borrowing and debt redemption of large-city governments alone are of the same order of magnitude as those of the states. In 1953 borrowing by the large cities was slightly more than double their debt redemptions, producing a net increase of over $600 million in debt outstanding. The total outstanding at the end of fiscal 1953 amounted to $11.3 billion, as compared with $7.8 billion for the state governments.

The *Summary of State Government Finances* is usually released in the spring of the year following that to which the data apply. The *Summary of City Government Finances* is not available until the following summer, so that the national-income and gross-national-product components for state and local governments are in the first instance projections rather than actual data.

Under these conditions, extrapolation procedures are practically the only resort for the forecaster. Fortunately, many phases of state and local operations are dependent on population growth and display great regularity of change. Moreover, program changes take effect over fairly long periods, not only because of their nature but also because of lack of uniform action on the part of the various government units. The over-all results are therefore amenable to projection by these methods.

Current changes in the more stable types of local-government operations may be inferred from changes in employment. Estimates of total government employment as well as of Federal civilian employment are provided by the Department of Labor, and these are adjusted for seasonal variation by the Federal Reserve Board. The wage rates that are needed to translate employment into income also change slowly, with considerable lag, and therefore add no serious difficulty to the projection.

Aside from program changes that are reflected directly in the employment figures, the important changes are likely to take the form of construction activity. Even here there is a great deal of regularity. The really big changes take place over extended periods, and some forewarning of the important short-run changes may be obtained from the reports on public construction activity available from the Departments of Commerce and Labor. If these are used to supplement the indications of the employment data, the current picture is practically complete. For the most part, therefore, changes in payrolls of government units and in their construction activity provide a means of adequately portraying the course of changes in state- and local-expenditure programs.

To a considerable extent, state and local programs run counter to Federal-government programs aimed at stabilizing the economy. The building of highways, schools, and other structures that make up the bulk of state- and local-construction projects are dependent upon community pressures. People want streets and sewage systems when they are building their homes, and they want schools when their children are growing up, not when it might be convenient to build them. These activities typically tend to aggravate the private-construction boom.

After a decline, it is difficult to keep such activity going, not only because the need declines but also because finances are pinched. Even if increased Federal aid is available, such programs face obstacles. When the people feel their needs are met, they reject new projects, and the government units that might wish to go ahead may find themselves blocked at the ballot box to the extent that voter approval is necessary to the authorization of any project or to its financing. As state and local government revenues decline with activity, current services must be maintained from the smaller income. Hence the impact of the decline is focused on new capital outlays, and Federal public-works programs specifically undertaken to support the economy must fight an adverse trend in state and local government as well as in private investment.

CHAPTER 7

Inventory Changes

Next to government programs, inventory changes have been the most important factor in what would ordinarily be referred to as the "cyclical swings" in business since the depression. These two factors, taken together, have almost completely dominated the short-term advances and declines of business for the quarter century beginning in the early 1930s. Before government assumed such an important role in the economic picture, inventory fluctuations alone tended to dominate the short-term movements of business.

Accumulation of inventories represents additions to goods produced but not sold to consumers or other final users. Liquidation represents the reductions in stocks when sales exceed production. The goods sold to consumers are mostly in final form, but those held in inventory are in all stages of processing and fabrication, so that many cannot be sold until they have undergone further processing. These goods embody an almost infinite variety of materials, supplies, parts, components, and scrap, as well as the whole range of finished products.

The decision to produce inevitably involves some accumulation of inventory, if only for a temporary period. Materials have to be procured, work has to be done on such materials in order to convert them into useful goods, and finished products must be put into distribution channels and sales stocks. Until the goods are finished and sold to final users, they are inventory, and their value goes on increasing through each stage of processing and distribution from the original resource to the ultimate consumer. Some accumulation is necessary, therefore, without regard to the type of goods produced. Even in the service industries, some type of inventory is essential, if no more than a minimum of operating supplies. Even the bootblack cannot ply his trade without a can of shoe polish, and when he buys in advance of actual need, he is accumulating an inventory.

In practice, inventories are almost always well above the indispensable minimum. In the case of basic farm crops, with the year's production becoming available in one season, stocks must provide for some carry-over and therefore average more than a half year's supply. Even apart from such seasonal influences, convenience in purchasing and efficiency in production demand that stocks be high at times and gradually dwindle until a new order is placed or a new production run is scheduled. These events may be spaced at fairly long intervals running to weeks or even to months, so that holdings may substantially exceed actual needs during this interval. Beyond the stocks held for such reasons, which may be regarded as necessary accumulations, surpluses accumulate from time to time and may remain in existence for a considerable period if there are obstacles to liquidation.

Inventories may also be accumulated by consumers. Although these are not measured or treated as inventories in the usual sense, there are times when the existence of such inventories creates the same problems of economic adjustment as business inventories. This is particularly the case with respect to durable goods, but on occasion excessive holdings of some foods and other semiperishables may be built up against anticipated shortages and subsequently have to be liquidated.

Whenever inventories are being accumulated—except for such accidental accretions as farm crops resulting from unusually favorable weather—the level of income to producers is raised above what is derived from the current level of consumption alone. The farmers, loggers, and miners who extract the raw material are paid for their efforts. The workers in any of the manufacturing establishments that process the materials, adding to their value through successive stages, receive wages for their work, whether or not the goods are sold to the final users. The trainmen and the stock clerks who handle the goods have their pay added to the flow of income before the goods are finally sold. So, also, managerial salaries and even profits in the earlier stages are realized by producers who have contributed to the additional inventories. All these payments have to be made, and incomes are augmented just as they are in the case of goods actually delivered to the final consumer.

Conversely, when inventories are run off, the incomes of producers are cut, even though consumers are spending as much as ever. Industry saves all the various costs of new production, while it permits existing stocks to take care of the demand. Changes in inventories, in other words, have the same economic effects as any other kind of business investment or any other kind of nonconsumption expenditure, such as that provided by government programs.

THE STRATEGIC ROLE OF INVENTORIES

The basic work in this field is Moses Abramovitz' *Inventories and Business Cycles*.[1] This volume contains a summary of background theory relating to the role of inventories in the business cycle and presents a detailed analysis of the behavior of various kinds of manufacturers' stocks. A condensed version of this larger work appears in a pamphlet by the same author.[2]

To illustrate the importance of inventories in the business cycle, Abramovitz shows that[3]

a very large share of the cyclical changes in gross national product has regularly taken the form of changes in the volume of inventory investment. . . . during the five business cycles identified by the National Bureau between the two World Wars, the average increase in gross national product between the trough and peak years of business expansions was some $12 billion in 1929 prices. The average increase in inventory investment from trough to peak years was nearly $3 billion—about 23 percent of the average expansion in gross national product. The average share of such a variable process as the fabrication of producer durable equipment, on the contrary, was only 14 percent, that of construction only 6 percent, and that of the output of consumer durable goods, 13 percent. During contractions, the average share of inventory investment change in the average change in gross national product was even more impressive—47 percent. The other major elements of investment all cut smaller figures: producer durable equipment 26 percent; construction, 11 percent; consumer durable goods, 19 percent.

These figures tend to overstate the case somewhat, since they deal only with the short cycles in which inventories play so important a part. If longer cycles or trends are considered, inventories will not obtain the same emphasis, because by their nature inventory changes cannot contribute so much to those longer movements. Nevertheless, the importance of inventories is appropriately emphasized, since they do tend to dominate the short-term swings by reason of the speed with which reversals take place. The full swing from accumulation to liquidation usually takes place in the course of a year or so, and during such a reversal the inventory movement is likely to be the most volatile factor in the whole picture.

After the outbreak of the Korean War, there was a major build-up of inventories followed by a reversal. Accumulation reached a peak rate

[1] National Bureau of Economic Research, Inc., New York, 1950.

[2] Moses Abramovitz, *The Role of Inventories in Business Cycles*, Occasional Paper 26, National Bureau of Economic Research, Inc., New York, 1948.

[3] *Ibid.*, p. 1.

of $16 billion in the second quarter of 1951; a year later the reversal re-
sulted in minor liquidation. The net swing on inventory account from
peak to trough therefore amounted to $16 billion—a tremendous de-
flationary force. The economy generally, however, showed no corresponding setback, because other factors, primarily government expenditures,
were holding the line. In an ordinary situation, a deflationary force of
that magnitude would dominate the course of business for considerably
more than a year.

Partly because of their extreme volatility and partly because of other
factors, inventory movements cannot sustain themselves over long periods. Production cannot create its own market, because leakages from
the income stream take their toll of purchasing power. The price of the
product must cover not only the direct costs but also such elements as
taxes, depreciation, and the like, which go into reserves that do not appear in the market as current income available for purchases. These portions are withdrawn, or at least withheld until there is a decision to
invest, with the result that the purchasing power created by the additional production is less than that required to move the goods. Furthermore, part of the funds dispersed as the direct costs of the additional
unsold product go into savings, so that the total returned to the market
is less even than the total of the direct-cost outlays.

The definite stimulus from investment in inventories is felt, therefore,
only while the desire to accumulate remains unchecked, and the accumulation itself cannot indefinitely maintain that desire, because the
increase in stocks is cumulative, whereas the increase in sales that derives
from it approaches an upper limit set by the multiplier. Hence the need
for larger inventories must come to an end after a limited period in the
absence of support for the movement from increasing expenditures of
other types.

Most inventory movements are not initiating in character but come into
action quickly to support other factors. Like other strategic developments,
however, inventory movements do have important autonomous elements.
The inventory runoff that began in the fall of 1948, for example, would
have been difficult to predict from anything happening in the economy.
Inventories were not excessive. The income flows were running at a peak
rate, and many of the basic determinants of activity remained high almost continuously through 1949. Nevertheless, the merchants became
frightened; and when they cut or canceled orders, the decline got under
way. Behind their action were some straws in the wind: Farm prices had
fallen, and farmers were tightening their purse strings. Consumers were
saving more, after the exceedingly low rate of 1947, and unusually warm
November weather cut department-store sales for the month considerably. To this extent the movement was not completely autonomous, but

it certainly had independent elements that did not derive from these minor shifts.

There are special occasions when inventory reversals take on the character of complete autonomy, if not inevitability. Such occasions typically develop at the end of movements that carry inventories out of line with sales. This was the situation approached in the middle of 1949. The preceding rapid liquidating movement made stocks deficient in relation to the flow of goods to final users. Government purchases, residential construction, and automobile purchases remained strong, and consumer buying generally was well sustained. The peak rate of inventory liquidation was reached in the second quarter, and then, even though inventories were being liquidated rapidly, this factor was no longer forcing production down. In any such movement, with the economy generally holding firm, as soon as pressure to increase the rate of liquidation is off, the decline ceases and inventory changes become a potentially favorable force. At this point recovery can be predicted with assurance, because there is nothing to justify the liquidating movement, and it is almost sure to come to a quick halt. Reversals of this character almost always occur at the end of an upswing also.

The analysis of inventory movements for forecasting purposes is necessarily complex, since many factors bearing on the position of inventories and on the desire to expand or reduce them have to be taken into account. Nevertheless, certain governing principles can be clearly defined, and since these principles have wide applicability to all kinds of "cyclical" movements of business, they will be considered in some detail. At this point it may merely be stated by way of summary that each phase of the cycle derives from an imbalance developed during the preceding phase, and the occurrence of a sequence of such imbalances is virtually unavoidable in any economy capable of producing storable goods in excess of current needs.

As a first approach to the problem, it may be said that the analysis of inventory changes proceeds in true perspective when approached from the standpoint of the definition of inventories: goods produced but not sold to final users. Thus inventories are created or used up only through differences between rates of production and consumption. The adjustment of those rates to each other and the way they will have to change in correcting imbalances is the fundamental point of attack for the forecaster.

To illustrate the basic interrelations, reference is made to Charts 7–1 and 7–2, which are reproduced from a study carried out by the author just before World War II.[4] Chart 7–1 shows estimates of production and

[4] *Production Consumption, and Inventories of Consumer Goods* (mimeographed); U.S. Department of Commerce, 1939; revised, U.S. War Production Board, 1942.

consumption of consumer goods in terms of monthly indexes for the period 1929 to 1941. The estimates of inventory changes shown in Chart 7–2 are derived as differences between these indexes of production and consumption, multiplied by a factor to bring them up to an appropriate constant-dollar total.

These changes, whether considered in themselves or as differences between production and consumption, tell only part of the story. The position of aggregate inventories is also important. The index in Chart 7–1,

Chart 7–1. Indexes of Physical Volume of Production, Consumption, and Inventories of Consumer Goods

Adjusted for seasonal variation, 1935–1939 consumption = 100

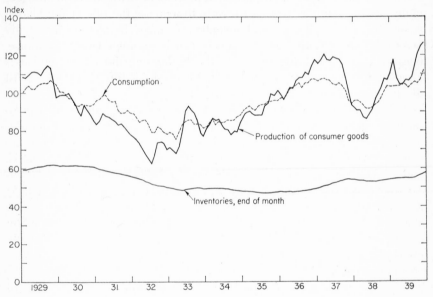

which provides a measure of total inventory holdings in comparison with the flows of goods, was obtained by linking the estimated changes month by month to the value at the beginning of the period and then reconverting the resulting total values to the indicated index base. In other words, the inventory series portrayed in Charts 7–1 and 7–2 show the same changes in two different forms, cumulative and direct. Both are derived from the indexes of production and consumption.

In Chart 7–1 the index of total inventories appears as a relatively stable series. However, that apparent stability conceals highly erratic variations in the rate of inventory investment, as is shown in Chart 7–2. In some years, like 1935, which show little change for the year as a whole, in-

ventory changes were highly important in the over-all economic movements that took place during the year. In the decline of 1937 and 1938,
the reversal from a rate of over $200 million per month accumulation
to $100 million liquidation meant a swing on inventory account of $3.5
billion at an annual rate. The importance of this may be better appreciated if it is considered in relation to the size of the economy: in 1937,
the total gross national product amounted to only $90 billion. As a rule,

Chart 7–2. Estimated Changes in Inventories of Consumer Goods

Adjusted for seasonal variation

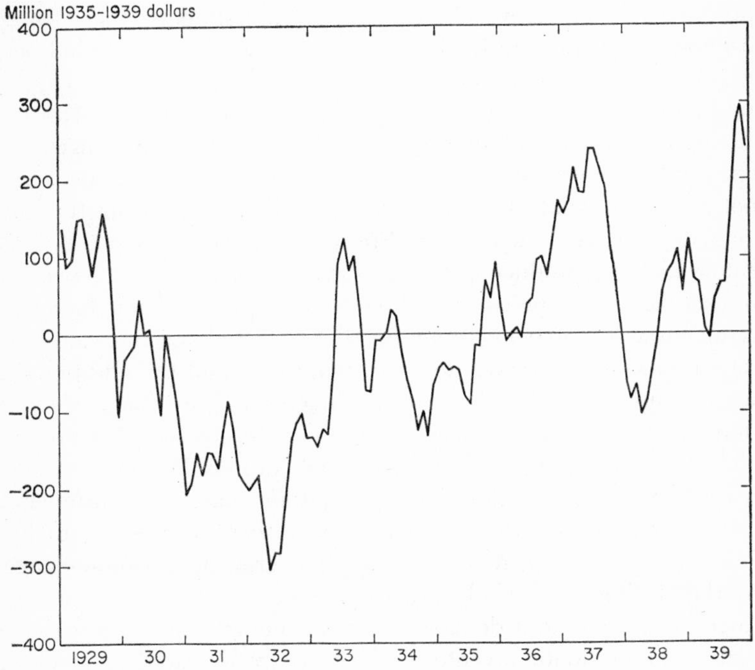

Million 1935–1939 dollars

such an inventory change will dominate the situation for a time and even
carry other factors with it.

THE BEHAVIOR OF INVENTORIES

Inventory changes are a transitory type of income-producing expenditure. They have the same sort of stimulating effect as any other type
of investment while the accumulation is taking place, but this effect disappears as soon as the accumulation ceases, and it becomes negative as
soon as liquidation sets in. Any decline in the rate of accumulation means
that the stimulus provided has been correspondingly reduced, and any
decline in the rate of liquidation means that a stimulus has been pro-

vided. Substantial changes in rate may characterize a period of general advance or decline, such as the movement to the depression lows of 1933 or the recovery from the lows of 1938. When changes alone are considered, as in Chart 7–2, they are seen to shuttle across the zero line with a rather bewildering display of instability. But considering the period as a whole, they remain within a reasonably narrow range, sometimes on the side of accumulation, sometimes on the side of liquidation, without long-sustained contributions in either direction.

In this respect, inventory investment is different from what is ordinarily thought of as investment proper, namely, new construction or installation of producers' equipment. These types of investments, taken in gross terms, always remain positive but fluctuate widely over extended periods of years. Over the long periods in which they make their greatest changes, inventory investment tends to be comparatively neutral. Accumulation reinforces the upswing, and liquidation the downswing; but except for brief intervals at the turning points, these inventory changes do not necessarily make the long-term peaks much higher nor the troughs of long depressions much lower. From this longer-term point of view, inventory changes produce large short-term shifts away from an economic norm established by the combined effects of the more stable factors.

As inventories are being built up, they expand income, and the expansion of income increases demand. Sales rise, and the additional consumer takings retard the increase in inventories, so that the effort to accumulate inventory is at least partially self-defeating. Moreover, the rise in sales appears to justify still larger inventories. Orders are therefore increased further, production is stepped up, income rises, consumers take still more, and the effort to increase inventories again tends to be defeated. The process repeats itself through a series of expanding stages.

On the decline, the whole process works in reverse. At each stage, production, income, and demand are cut, unemployment increases, and the effort to liquidate inventories is partially defeated. The effort to bring stocks down then requires further cuts in production and brings on the next stage of deflation.

This process has been aptly described by Hawtrey as the "vicious spiral."[5] Hawtrey's graphic account tends somewhat to overplay inventories as the exclusive factor in such swings. It is focused too completely on occasions when an inventory movement develops such a pitch of speculative fever that it keeps itself going for a while with little or no support from other factors. The expectation of shortages and of continuing price increases leads to excessive ordering, and until the stocks

[5] R. G. Hawtrey, "The Trade Cycle," in *Trade and Credit*, Longmans, Green & Co., Inc., New York, 1928, chap. 5; reprinted in *Readings in Business Cycle Theory*, Richard D. Irwin, Inc., Homewood, Ill., 1944.

of goods on hand are actually excessive, there is no convincing reason to halt the drive for speculative gains. Similarly, on the decline the expectation of a fall in prices becomes an additional motive for liquidating inventories, and in the extremity of fear this may be sufficient to keep the whole movement going for a while.

These movements are the exceptions, however. In the more usual case, business finds its best advantage in keeping inventories low in relation to sales, a practice that avoids the penalties of excesses. This practice also means high turnover, reducing necessary investment and minimizing losses from such causes as obsolescence, spoilage, or other deterioration. Moreover, business policy tends increasingly to be directed away from short-term speculative gains, which involve the risk of speculative losses, in favor of a long-term basic position. Many large companies prefer allocating output among their regular customers in a period of shortage to realizing the greatest gains by obtaining high prices from temporary new customers.

This is not to say that inventories ordinarily do not rise with an increase in business. They do. The manufacturer who is stepping up output must put more goods in process. He wants more materials to protect his operations against stoppages. He finds it more convenient in filling orders to have larger stocks of the finished product. It is also convenient for the distributor to hold larger stocks when sales increase, because that is what he immediately draws upon to meet temporary surges in demand. By and large, therefore, whenever demand increases, greater inventories are justified, and the effort to build them produces something of a spiraling effect. If, in such a situation, capacity is substantially in excess of current needs, the additional inventories can be accumulated almost as rapidly as desired, and the upward movement may for a time become violent.

During such an upsurge, businessmen who are not inclined to participate may be forced to act in at least a limited way against their wishes. To refuse means that they may incur the penalties of a loss in business volume. If they cannot meet customers' orders or cannot obtain needed supplies, they may suffer a distinct loss of competitive position. Since this is likely to be regarded as more serious than the risk of temporary speculative losses, they go along. On the decline, the incentives shift to the other side, inducing liquidation. The effects of withholding purchases to avoid inventory losses are the same as those of holding off to profit by an anticipated price decline. For all these reasons, rapid shifts in the volume of inventories usually tend to become at least partly speculative in character, though from the standpoint of the individual businessman the accumulation or liquidation may appear merely to be protecting him against possible losses. Anticipations of price or cost changes thus lead to very rapid shifts in the rate of production, in the direction of the expected price or cost change.

The most common business measure of inventory position is the ratio of year-end inventories to sales during the year. When inventories are high relative to sales, efforts are made to bring them down; this is the typical situation after a downturn. When the inventory-sales ratio is low, efforts to bring the level of stocks into line with sales result in greater inventory investment; this characterizes the contribution of inventory changes to recovery movements.

Abramovitz observed that inventory-sales ratios remained low throughout periods of business advance. This may be due in part to the self-defeating character of attempts to accumulate inventories, as stressed by Hawtrey. It is also due in part to the inflation of the sales base, which includes the output going into inventories as well as that going into consumption. When inventories are judged in relation to the latter alone, the deficiency in inventories does not appear so large at any time, and excesses more quickly put in an appearance.

At the end of an upswing, surpluses almost inevitably develop. Holdings are eventually brought into line with sales, even though demand is greatly enlarged by the expansion of income; and once this occurs, production must drop, so that the existing inventories become excessive. What forces the cutback is the fact that goods are in ample supply. When everyone has all he wants, no one wants to keep piling up more. It is necessary to stop accumulating, and that fact is itself of critical importance. For the only way to stop accumulating is to cut production, and when production is cut, stocks that were previously in line with output and sales are too high for the new rate of operations.

Even after the decision is made, accumulation tends to go on for a while. At that time, consumption may itself be falling, so that the period of accumulation is prolonged. When accumulation finally stops, the level of income and demand has been cut not by any switch to liquidation but merely by the stopping of accumulation. With that reduction in income and demand, the stocks that were only in line with demand before the reversal suddenly become excessive.

In other words, the rate of production achieved in building up inventories is too high to be maintained without the special element of demand deriving from the excessive rate of accumulation. Cutting it down to size makes the accumulated stocks excessive and brings on the reversal.

Almost inevitably, at the turn, there is not merely a cessation of the movement that was taking place but also, at least temporarily, a reverse movement. If the rate at which inventories were being accumulated was moderate, not far above general rates of growth, the reversal may be a very minor one. If it was rapid, the reversal will be correspondingly aggravated.

The reversal at the end of a decline is as automatic as the one that terminates the advance. Diligent application to the task of bringing inventories down eventually results in reaching a position where the pressure to liquidate eases, and then the reversal takes place.

The force for recovery begins to exert itself as soon as any move to reduce the rate of liquidation is made. For the moderation or cessation of inventory liquidation is not merely an easing of deflationary pressure but a positive force on the upside. An upward shift from a negative to zero is just as much a gain as an equal increase beginning at a higher level. In practical terms, liquidation can come to an end only when production is brought up into line with consumption. For this to happen, no one has to expect recovery; business merely has to decide that inventories are low enough. Then recovery will be under way. It is almost certain to occur at the end of a strong liquidating movement, and although it is an outgrowth of what went before, it is likely to occur with a good deal of independence of anything else that is going on at the same time.

At the end of a movement in either direction, the shift in policy is as a rule reflected immediately in the rate of inventory accumulation or liquidation but cannot so quickly reverse the movement of total inventories. At the end of an advance, production has to be cut, not just a little but all the way to the level of consumption, before accumulation stops. At the depression low, liquidation continues until production is raised sufficiently to eliminate all of the previous gap below the level of consumption.

From Chart 7–1, it may be seen that in 1932 and 1933 liquidation continued for almost a year after production had made its low. In the 1937 downturn, accumulation continued for more than a half year after the production peak. Occasionally the adjustment can be made quickly, particularly if consumption is maintained for a time by other factors, as in 1929. As a rule, the timing will be intermediate between the longest and shortest of the periods cited in these examples, say, several months. Since there are many differences from one situation to the next—in the role of inventories as well as in other relevant factors—there is no reason to expect any regularity in the observed lags.

If the reversal occurs as a result of shifts in other factors, the original movement of inventories may temporarily be speeded. This kind of involuntary change in inventories is an unavoidable part of the basic processes of an economy in which the current decisions to consume and to produce are largely independent of each other. It interrupts the normal process of adjustment for a time and may lengthen the period in which it is completed, but on those occasions the reversal is all the more certain and usually more violent.

Even when inventory policy is the initiating factor in a reversal, the lag of total inventories must occur. It might almost be said that these lags are a matter of arithmetic, given a period of production of any significant duration. It is therefore hardly meaningful to state that inventories give only a tardy indication of the turn. For the same reason, attempts to explain the lags in terms of confidence or expectations, and the subsequent reactions in terms of the disappointment of those states of mind, are practically sure to miss the point.

The extent of the lag depends at least partly, of course, upon the speed with which adjustments can be made. When there is an increase in consumer demand, it takes the retailer a period of perhaps several weeks to observe that his inventories are running off and orders have to be adjusted. He then increases orders to the wholesaler or branch distributor. Here another period of several weeks may elapse before the increase in demand is passed on to the producer. The latter in turn may find his inventories getting low before he can step up his production schedule and adjust orders to his suppliers. As the process goes through the various stages of fabrication, there are additional time periods required before production is fully stepped up to match the increase in demand. During this period, stocks have to be drawn on to meet orders, and they are in large part merely passed from one stage to the next.

The lag at each stage tends to be aggravated by two factors. First, there is the question of when an initial reversal must be considered a real turn rather than just a temporary or irregular fluctuation. Second, businessmen do not like to disrupt operations or disband a trained working force needlessly and therefore do not make adjustments as promptly as they might. Even aside from these tendencies, however, adjustments could not be instantaneous. In the case of the heavy-durable-goods industries, the very length of the production process implies a long lag of production behind orders, so that months may pass before a shift in demand is reflected in output.

As an adjustment proceeds, its impetus is accelerated by stages. When the retailer steps up his orders, he provides both for the increase in sales and for the replacement and increase of inventories. The shorter the turnover period, the more rapid will be the acceleration of orders resulting from the inventory increment. The same kind of acceleration occurs at each of the succeeding stages. Production and purchases fluctuate more than sales. Manufacturers' inventories fluctuate more widely than distributors', and raw-materials producers' more widely than final-goods producers'. In fact, the materials producer is quite likely to lose all of his finished inventory. As this occurs, the movement may come up against virtual inelasticity of supply, and the whole process of adjustment has to wait until supply in the bottleneck stage can be augmented. During this period, buyers compete strongly for the quantities available, making for extreme flexibility of prices in many of the raw-materials-producing industries. Where these conditions exist, the recovery of inventories may be very gradual; but even where they do not, some lag in inventories can hardly be avoided.

Such lags have been the subject of theoretical discussion and have been empirically verified by students of the business cycle. Metzler[6] set up some ingenious theoretical models based on certain assumptions concerning the mutual responses of inventory investment, other investment, income, and consumption. These models reveal why inventories lag behind the general cycle and why the oscillations of inventories between accumulation and liquidation tend to persist through a succession of cycles. They provide, without statistical verification, an essentially valid account of the role of inventories in the business cycle and of the interactions of inventory changes with other factors in the various phases of the cycle.

AGGREGATE VERSUS SPECIFIC INVENTORIES

Abramovitz utilized the mass of statistical data compiled by the National Bureau of Economic Research to measure the tendency for inventories to lag and result in surpluses or deficiencies. For this purpose, he divided manufacturers' inventories into a number of significant categories and then attempted to explain the lag in terms of the processes of adjustment involved in each case. To quote:[7]

> The cyclical behavior of these categories reflects differences in the motives behind inventory policy and in the ability of businessmen—for reasons of technique, market organization, or contractual arrangements—to implement their policies. The validity of the view is, I think, demonstrated in the case of manufacturers' stocks. Here the observed lag of total inventories behind output is to be explained as the net resultant of the disparate behavior of at least seven classes of stocks: (1) goods in process, which vary together with output; (2) raw materials purchased from domestic manufacturers or dealers, which lag by, say, two or three months; (3) raw materials purchased from distant sources or on long-term contracts, which lag behind output by many months; (4) finished goods made to order which, like goods in process, are closely tied to output; (5) perishable finished goods sold from stock, which probably lag behind output by a few months; (6) staple

[6] Lloyd A. Metzler, "Nature and Stability of Inventory Cycles," *Review of Economic Statistics*, August, 1941. See also "Business Cycles and the Modern Theory of Employment," *American Economic Review*, June, 1946.

[7] Abramovitz, *The Role of Inventories in Business Cycles*, p. 20.

finished goods made to stock, which vary inversely with output in short cycle phases and positively with a long lag in long phases; (7) agricultural raw materials and finished goods made from such materials, which, under certain conditions, inject an irregular element into the movements of manufacturers' stocks.

On the basis of his analysis, Abramovitz concludes:[8]

. . . no simple, general explanation of inventory fluctuations is valid. An adequate theory of inventory cycles must explain the disparate behavior of the several categories of stocks that move in significantly different ways.

It is my conviction that progress toward an understanding of the cyclical behavior of stocks has been blocked chiefly by the fact that inventories have generally been treated as a homogeneous mass within which differences in behavior are not significant and to all parts of which much the same explanation is appropriate. True, one sometimes finds gross and inadequate distinctions, such as between finished and unfinished goods, or categories with nonoperational definitions such as Keynes' "working capital" and "liquid capital." By contrast, I believe that a sound explanation of the behavior of stocks can be reached only when fairly numerous categories are distinguished, and I propose to support this view by analyzing the large block of stocks—about 40 percent of the total—that is held by manufacturers.

The danger in this approach is that concern with specific detail may result in losing sight of the main point. The specific differences in behavior which make up an over-all movement, even though they partly offset each other, are not effective in moving the economy, so that only the broad sweeps of inventory change are of concern to the forecaster. It is distinctly a situation in which the significant focus of attention is the forest and not the trees.

To show how little meaning results may have when obtained from an analysis confined to manufacturers' inventories alone, Chart 7–3 shows Abramovitz data on crude rubber and raw silk. The rubber stocks move inversely to the cycle; the silk stocks show a close correspondence, with perhaps a slight lag. Here are two commodities produced under relatively similar circumstances from natural processes that make for inelastic supply. Why do they behave so differently? The fact is that they do not. When demand falls off, stocks of both pile up. The chart for rubber shows this, but the chart for silk does not. The difference is that in the case of rubber the manufacturers are also the producers and hold practically all the stocks. In the case of silk the manufacturers adjust their buying to operations and force the producers and dealers to hold the stocks, so that manufacturers' stocks fall. Abramovitz makes these facts clear but passes over the conclusion that the two situations are essentially the same from a broad economic standpoint.

[8] *Ibid.*, pp. 21, 6.

As stocks of crude rubber pile up on the decline, the accumulation is largely involuntary. It is the lesser of two evils to let it go on rather than to bring it to a halt. The accumulation of surplus rubber should not be considered an offset to the inventory liquidation that is more generally taking place during such periods. As surpluses pile up, prices drop, adding to the incentives to liquidate. The effect is to depress investment in the producing industry and perhaps also in competitive parts of the economy.

Chart 7–3. Stocks of Raw Materials: Average Cyclical Patterns during Cycles in Manufacturing Activity

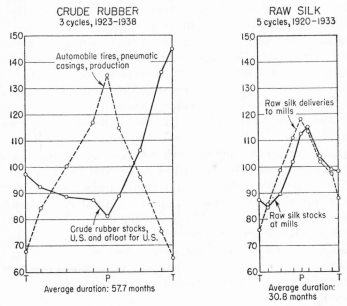

SOURCE: Moses Abramovitz, The Role of Inventories in Business Cycles, Occasional Paper 26, National Bureau of Economic Research, Inc., New York, May, 1948, p. 9.

Conditions of inelastic supply also result in what appears to be an inverted movement of inventory investment on the upswing. If capacity of an industry is inadequate to meet peak demands, inventories are drained off, unfilled orders pile up, and prices are bid up. The inventory decline under these circumstances in no sense indicates any desire to reduce activity. If the shortage persists, new investment will be undertaken, to increase capacity and perhaps to open new resources. If efforts to expand are successful, the opposite kind of situation may ultimately develop. The high rubber prices of the 1920s were partly responsible for the surpluses and extremely depressed prices of the 1930s.

Inventories of natural raw materials like these, whose flow cannot readily be adjusted to variations in demand, comprise a type that is practically irrelevant to over-all analysis, and their changes might well be excluded if possible. Inventories of many farm crops show large unpredictable changes, resulting mainly from favorable or unfavorable weather conditions, so that changes may occur without affecting employment or even subsequent rates of production. The farmer does not put himself out of work because he has inventories. Surplus stocks do have some effect on his income by affecting prices, and he will adjust his spending somewhat if the price changes are substantial. But the inventories have to be held in any case, and up to the time they get into the business stream they do not affect the economy generally except through the anticipatory change in farm expenditures. Fortunately, farm inventories, including those under government loan, are separately reported and can therefore be segregated in working out the forecast. Other commodities, like rubber, cannot be conveniently separated out in the same way, but they are not so important quantitatively as to seriously qualify analysis of the general inventory movement.

Other illustrations of the fallacy of looking at inventories in a specified position only are not difficult to find. The experience of the Office of Price Administration in rationing such commodities as sugar shows that it would be impossible to base effective controls on data concerning stocks in one position only. If only refiners' stocks were considered, a growing emergency in the disappearance of distributors' stocks might be overlooked. The position of holdings was highly important in this kind of situation, because such an emergency usually meant that the stocks were passing into the hands of particular consumers who were reserving them for their own future use and thus preventing others from satisfying their minimum needs. But the position of holdings in other cases may be irrelevant.

The same lesson was learned in making international allocations of fats and oils. If stocks were measured only at one point, say in the hands of processors, disappearance rates would appear at times to be extremely rapid, although final use was going on at a perfectly steady pace. As stocks shifted from one position to another, the partial statistics gathered at the first point could only result in misleading conclusions about the level of over-all consumption.

It makes no real difference for the economy as a whole whether a given finished product is held by the manufacturer or by his distributor. Within manufacturing, it makes no difference whether steel is held by the steel mill as a finished product or by the auto manufacturer as a raw material. Much more important than the question of whose inventories are going up is the question of whether inventories in total are going up. If distributors are rapidly piling up stocks, they will soon pass the accumulation back to the manufacturer by cutting orders, and the piling up will continue until he reduces his production schedule. It is the movement of the aggregate rather than the stages in which changes are taking place that is of primary importance.

One further comment may help to clarify this point: it is well known that inventories may under certain circumstances be a stabilizing factor rather than one that aggravates instability. The experience of a number of companies, like Procter & Gamble, Eastman Kodak, and the integrated oil companies, is sufficient evidence that inventories can be used to iron out seasonal variations in the work load and reduce the total capacity needed by providing for peak-season demand out of stocks. In fact, firms in a seasonal industry often find it more profitable to build stocks against the peak demands than to build capacity for meeting such demands from current production. Such use of inventories is practically confined to the seasonal situation, however. If the variations in demand are not regular enough to be definitely predictable, it is a dangerous practice.

It is true that staple finished commodities are sometimes accumulated by keeping production above sales through short cyclical declines, as Abramovitz points out, but the companies indulging in this form of "stabilizing" activity are essentially speculating. In a prolonged decline, the policy will probably break down, resulting in efforts to liquidate stocks when it is most difficult to do so and aggravating unemployment in the depths of depression when it is impossible to find other work. This results in the empirically established "long lag in long phases."

In commodity and industry forecasting, the details of inventory behavior cannot be overlooked. It is impossible to approach many of the specific problems relating to particular commodities and industries intelligently without considering the movement and position of stocks. In this field, Abramovitz' study is outstanding. But from the standpoint of over-all forecasting it is marred by the insistence that attention to detail is necessary for meaningful results, for only the concerted movements of inventories affect the economic picture significantly. These are determined by differences in over-all rates of production and consumption and, since consumption is comparatively stable, primarily by variations in rates of production. The conditions under which imbalances develop and the means by which a new adjustment will be worked out are the essential lines of investigation. These are questions that must be considered in terms of the broad aggregates.

REAL CHANGES VERSUS VALUE CHANGES

Underlying the discussion of how inventory changes affect the level of economic activity is a concept of inventory investment as additions to the volume of real goods on hand. From the point of view of economic dynamics, only these real changes in inventories affect production and employment and have the same kind of multiplier effect on income that other investments have. Therefore, it is necessary to get at the changes in the physical units on which productive effort is expended and to exclude as far as possible changes that are merely brought about by the revaluation of existing stocks as prices change. In other words, the appropriate concept is the change in the physical volume of inventories valued at current prices. It is this change that represents real production and involves a real change in activity when it occurs.

This is the concept underlying the inventory data presented by the Department of Commerce in the gross-national-product and national-income accounts. Those data, like others in this field, are based upon reports from manufacturers, retailers, and other business concerns. However, these business concerns typically measure their inventories in terms of the value of the total stocks on hand at the end of an accounting period. This total book value changes not only with changes in the number of physical units on hand but also with changes in the prices at which those units are valued. For this reason, the change in book value is not the same as the inventory investment it is desired to measure, and the Department of Commerce makes a series of adjustments in order to arrive at the current rate of inventory investment or disinvestment.

Although this adjusted measure of inventory changes is suitable for use by the forecaster, it becomes available only quarterly and then after a lag of another half quarter, so that it is not entirely adequate for keeping abreast of current developments. In dealing with so highly volatile a factor, it is not desirable to wait something like half a year to get an indication of change. But to operate with more current data requires ability to make adjustments that will at least approximate those included in the gross national product. For this reason, and also because a clear understanding of the problem is essential to effective analysis of inventory movements, it is worthwhile to consider the data and their adjustments at some length.

On the expenditure side of the account, the adjustment is straightforward. It attempts to measure in dollar terms the volume of current production that was not taken by final users and thus complete the measurement of gross national product. Any adjustment on the expenditure or product side must, of course, be carried over to the income side to preserve the balance in the accounts. On the income side, the problem is somewhat more complex, because it involves questions of business accounting and price policy, but the most direct and simple expedient is adopted. It is presumed that the revaluation elements in the inventory account appear in business profits also, and reported profits are therefore adjusted accordingly. This not only accomplishes the objective of presenting a more meaningful estimate of inventory investment on the product side but also improves the relationship of profits to gross national product. On the whole, therefore, it serves the purposes of over-all analysis for which these accounts are set up.

Business firms are not primarily concerned with such analysis, of course, but rather with data and analysis relating to their own operations. Among the purposes their reports are intended to serve is that of presenting their financial positions correctly. Prevailing business practice usually assumes that inventories turn over on a first-in, first-out basis, and in order to avoid overstatement of assets inventories are generally valued on the "conservative" basis known as "cost or market lower." That is to say, inventories are valued at cost in periods of rising prices, when costs are lagging somewhat behind the current market, but they are valued at the current market in periods of falling prices. This procedure introduces substantial elements of revaluation into the book-value figures, which, in the usual accounting procedure, get carried over into the income account as profits or losses. Income is computed as the difference between sales receipts and cost of goods sold. But the goods actually sold are practically never segregated, nor is their specific cost computed. The cost of goods sold is merely computed as purchases less the change in inventory, which means book value of inventory, including any revaluation elements that may be present.

That such revaluation is present in a period of declining prices is clear. Inventories are arbitrarily marked down to the lower market value, and whether or not the physical volume of inventories has changed, the write-off is indirectly added to the cost of goods sold.

What is not so clear is that upward revaluation takes place in a period of rising prices and costs. In this case, the marking-up process takes place automatically, as higher prices are paid for materials and higher wages are paid the workers for bringing the goods in process to the same stage of completion. Then, even though the number of units in inventory remains the same, the stated value will increase. If the number of units increases, the value will increase by the value of the additional units plus the increased value placed on the original number of units; and if the number of units goes down, the increase in value placed on the remaining units may offset, or more than offset, the value of the units taken from stock.

Viewed from the product side, the situation is apparent. Some units are added; others are merely revalued. The former are the counterpart of real production; the latter add nothing to real investment. It is when the approach shifts from the product side of the accounts to the income side that confusion arises about the so-called "expansionary effects" of revaluing the existing units. The fact that costs are income payments creates an illusion that the revaluation involved in replacing inventories at higher prices represents a real element of income. This confusion can be avoided only by keeping in mind that computation of the national income involves the elimination of duplication at various stages of production. Since these revaluation elements of cost are already counted as income at an earlier stage, they do not represent income paid out or received in the same sense as wages or noninventory profits.

Inventory revaluation is just what the term implies—a process of revaluation. It takes effect at the end of the accounting period, through the bookkeeping transaction by which costs are adjusted for the change in inventories. This adjustment affects the statement of assets and through it the computation of profits; but in so far as a profit does result, it is only an unrealized book profit. This is one of the quirks of accounting procedure, which permits inventories, unlike capital equipment or structures, to be revalued each year. The fact that changing costs are the basis of the revaluation, rather than appraised market value or some other "arbitrary" figure, does not change the essential of what is done.

Consider, for example, the simplest case, disregarding complications: A trader holds a bushel of wheat in inventory at the beginning of the year, which cost him $2. He sells this bushel of wheat to the consumer for $3. The farmer produces another bushel of wheat. The trader purchases this bushel from the farmer for $3 and has it in inventory at the end of the year. Now all the cash transactions are in. The gross-product entry is $3 for consumer expenditures on a bushel of wheat. The farmer has received $3 in income, and the accounts balance. The trader has received $3 in receipts and paid $3 in costs, so his cash position is unchanged. However, he now reviews his position. He has a bushel of wheat which (by using the cost basis) he considers to be worth $3 instead of $2. He therefore writes up his assets by $1 and shows $1 profit, making total income (including both the farmer's and his own) $4 instead of $3 and creating the revaluation discrepancy of $1 between income and gross product.

It may be pointed out that he actually paid $3 for the bushel of wheat he holds. But that $3 is already accounted for in the payment received by the farmer; and when the trader writes up his inventory, he in effect takes back the additional cost he previously deducted from his receipts and adds it to his profit. In other words, it is not the $3 actually paid but only the additional $1 originating in the bookkeeping adjustments that is in question. If he held the same bushel of wheat throughout the year and the farmer sold the wheat directly to the consumer, the markup would not be considered a legitimate profit. Yet all actual net payments and receipts would be the same.

These revaluation elements are maximized in a period of rising prices by use of the first-in, first-out basis of inventory accounting, usually referred to as FIFO. This means that the oldest units in stock are considered to be used first, regardless of the actual order of use; and since the lag is longest for the units held at the beginning of the period, the margin of current price over cost is the greatest. Inasmuch as the typical turnover period is less than a year, the bulk of all inventories are revalued each year, to the extent of roughly the year's change in prices. This revaluation is at times very large. It may readily exceed the value of the physical change in stocks; and if it is opposite in sign, it may create a wholly misleading impression of the inventory movement.

In a period of rising prices, revaluation creates the impression that profits are high. It produces no actual cash receipts, though it may require higher tax payments for which cash has to be raised. In a period of falling prices, it creates the impression that inventories are low. Excessive inventories, being valued down, may appear to be no more than in line with sales, since the more sensitive materials prices may drop faster than sales in a period of general recession.

To eliminate revaluation as far as possible, many companies have shifted to the last-in, first-out basis of inventory accounting, termed LIFO. In this case, regardless of the actual order of use, the last units purchased are considered to be the ones used, and the units charged to current production or sale are therefore charged at current prices. Since the units originally purchased at lower prices are still considered to be in inventory, their value is considered to be unchanged. Since they are not revalued, no revaluation element is entered in the accounts, but over a long period the disparity between the prices at which the inventories are carried and their current market values may be very large.

Many business concerns that do not use LIFO—possibly the bulk of them in terms of aggregate receipts and expenditures—make some effort to avoid being misled by inventory-revaluation profits. Reserves against possible price declines are commonly set up, and in some postwar years these reserves amounted to more than one-third of the total value of inventories held. Seldom would a businessman wish to borrow from the banks in order to realize this inventory profit, but if he withdraws such "profits" or pays taxes on them, he may have to borrow to replenish his cash balance. In such exceptional cases, it is the expansion of bank credit rather than the inventory revaluation which should be considered the expansionary factor in the situation.

The point may be further emphasized by pointing out that no deflationary effect is felt when the inventory-revaluation item disappears after prices stop going up. Assume that in the year following the one in the above simplified example the price of wheat remained stable.

Production and real income would remain unchanged, but there would be no basis for the trader to credit himself with the inventory-revaluation profit. However, activity in terms of real production and other actual transactions would be completely unaffected by the leveling-off of prices, and no letdown in the economy other than the elimination of the inventory-revaluation profit would be observed.

In short, inventory revaluation is a bookkeeping adjustment pure and simple. It is not a separable money flow and does not have an expansionary effect on the economy. Workers do not receive from it any funds with which to make consumption purchases, and businesses do not obtain any cash increment to use for ordinary business purposes or for dividend payments. There is no multiplier effect, such as the one that results from real-capital formation.

In contrast, the reverse of these propositions holds when inventory volume changes. When there is an increase in the physical volume of inventories, materials have to be purchased and wage payments have to be made to workers, and these actual expenditures have to be financed either from internal sources or by borrowing. The revaluation involves no such payments. It adds to the asset total without any corresponding expenditure not already accounted for. That it does so in a concealed way, being confused with real additions, does not alter the fact.

ELIMINATING REVALUATION FROM INVENTORY CHANGES

The consequence is that in analyzing inventory changes it is necessary to get away from the reported book values and back to the physical units which represent investment in the true sense. Since the basic data reported are book values, this can only be done by translating those book values into physical equivalents, by deflating them with appropriate price indexes. Then the change is simply computed by taking the difference between the deflated totals for the end and the beginning of the period, and that difference represents the physical volume change—plus or minus as the case may be. The volume change can then be put on a current-value basis by reflating to the average price prevailing during the period.

Even for those concerns using the LIFO basis of inventory accounting, some adjustment is necessary. In periods when inventories are increased in volume, there is no problem, because the added inventories are valued at prices close to the desired current level.

When inventories are run off in volume, however, a difficulty arises, because the units sold are necessarily valued at prices of some previous period. The difficulty is not one of revaluation, because the remaining inventories are still carried on the original basis; it arises because the change shown does not reflect current values, which may differ widely from the original cost base. If current prices are higher, which has usually been the case since the post–World War II inflation, the firms may segregate the extraordinary profits by setting up a reserve for the replacement of the inventories at higher current prices. Then when the inventories are again built up, their valuation in the inventory account is kept at the original level, and the additional cost is charged to the reserve. If current prices are lower, the loss is likely to be accepted and reported as such. If a suitable price index relating to the specific inventories is available, it is still problematical just what base period to use in converting the inventories run off to current values. Fortunately, the price adjustments required for LIFO inventories have been negligible to date.

The Department of Commerce summarizes its procedure for deriving the current value of the change in nonfarm inventories in six principal steps, as follows:[9]

(1) Reported book of values of year-end inventories are raised to complete coverage.

(2) Estimates of the portion of total book value that is reported on a last-in, first-out (LIFO) basis are deducted from the total and separately processed. This step is necessary because the valuation procedure underlying LIFO inventories requires an adjustment procedure which differs from that applicable to the remainder of business inventories.

(3) The estimates of book value of non-LIFO inventories are converted to a constant price basis by means of price deflation procedures.

(4) The change in these inventories at constant prices is obtained by subtracting beginning from ending inventories at constant prices.

(5) The current value of the physical change in inventories is obtained by multiplying the change in inventories at constant prices by the ratio of current prices to the constant price base.

(6) The inventory valuation adjustment is obtained by subtracting the change in the book value of inventories from the current value of the physical change in inventories.

The Department applies this procedure in great detail, making separate computations for some 40 industries and in most cases for noncorporate as well as corporate inventories. In addition, LIFO inventories have to be segregated in various manufacturing industries and in department stores; they currently represent about one-tenth of total book value. There are so many statistical difficulties in carrying out this procedure that the accuracy of results can hardly be guaranteed. The problems involved in compiling a series of suitable price indexes relating to the various blocks of inventories are almost insurmountable, and they

[9] *National Income, 1954 Edition,* supplement to *Survey of Current Business,* U.S. Department of Commerce, p. 136.

frequently have to be solved by the most fragile of expedients. The Department consistently refers to its methods as estimating procedures. It states: "This adjustment of the reported book value data is a quite difficult procedure, involving the revaluation of the entire volume of nonfarm business inventories given only limited knowledge of the prices reflected in them."[10]

It might be added in summary that in this area—one of the most critical for short-term forecasting—the data are among the weakest. Nevertheless, they are far superior to anything available in the past and provide an indication of inventory movements that is generally acceptable.

CURRENT DATA ON INVENTORY CHANGES

The basic book-value data used in compiling the back series on inventory changes are the Bureau of Internal Revenue tabulations of income tax returns and the periodic censuses of business. These provide a very high coverage of all business inventories but are available only after a lag of several years. In the interim, other less reliable data have to be utilized, both in compiling the gross-product estimates and in carrying out current analyses.

Again the Department of Commerce has done its best to fill the gap. It not only compiles monthly data on inventories in the largest single sector, manufacturing, but also brings together data on distributors' inventories from other sources and combines them, with seasonal adjustments where necessary, into a comprehensive series on business inventories. The data are presented monthly in the Survey of Current Business, together with comparable estimates of business sales. The totals are broken into three major segments—manufacturing, wholesaling, and retailing, each subdivided into durable goods and nondurable goods. Since the reports are on a corporate or firm basis and many firms handle both durables and nondurables, the inventories are not clearly segregated between these categories, but there is a preponderance of each type in the indicated group.

Over half of the total value of business inventories is held by manufacturers. Reports on these are received each month by the Office of Business Economics from some 2,000 firms, which account for more than 45 percent of total manufacturing sales. The relatively large proportion of sales from so limited a sample indicates a heavy weighting with large corporations and a relative deficiency of small firms. The data are compiled separately for more than 20 industries, about half of which are durable-goods industries. The samples of reporting firms vary

[10] Ibid., p. 135.

considerably from industry to industry. Actual reports are blown up to levels representing industry totals as derived from Bureau of Internal Revenue tabulations of tax returns.

Manufacturers' inventories are also broken down by stage of fabrication into purchased materials, goods in process, and finished goods. This distinction is not entirely clear-cut, since the reports are based on the firms' own definitions, and the finished products of one firm are the raw materials of another. In order to use this kind of information effectively, it is important to know enough about the company or industry to have some understanding of the character of its inventories; but since the information is not consistently enough reported by cooperating firms to give reliable results by industry, it is presented only in the aggregate, and its usefulness is correspondingly reduced.

Trade inventory statistics also vary considerably in quality. The Department of Commerce series on chain stores and mail-order houses and the Federal Reserve series on department stores are relatively satisfactory. Wholesale-inventory data, though spotty in individual lines of business, are acceptable in the aggregate. The most serious gap in current inventory statistics is the lack of data for independent retail stores. Totals for this group are carried forward from month to month by use of related chain-store data and departmental data from department stores, but these methods are generally unsatisfactory. Since small firms are so important in the retail field, this deficiency presents a real problem. The problem is aggravated by the fact that reported data cover only about one-fifth of total retail stocks, necessitating a much higher blowup than in the case of manufacturing.

In addition to these comprehensive statistics on the dollar values of stocks held by industry or trade groups, there are extensive current statistics on stocks of particular kinds of goods in terms of the measures of physical volume suitable to each. These cover a wide range of commodities, as may be readily observed by inspection of the *Survey of Current Business* statistical pages, with the greatest concentration on minerals, farm products, and other raw or semifabricated materials. Still other series are available from other sources, such as trade publications or trade-association reports. The primary usefulness of this material is in connection with specific problems relating to the commodities reported. Attempts to utilize them for over-all analysis have not been fruitful.

For the latter purpose, attention must be focused primarily on the book value of business inventories reported in seasonally adjusted form by the Department of Commerce. The various surveys underlying this series are conducted with as short a lapse of time as possible, so that the comprehensive reports are received promptly.

Any attempt to utilize book values, however, runs into the immediate difficulty that the movements it is desired to measure, the real changes in inventories, are obscured by changes in the prices at which the inventories are valued. It is necessary, therefore, to adjust out the effects of price changes, in order to obtain preliminary estimates of the gross-national-product type. The rule here, as it was there, is: "Deflate, difference, and reflate."

What is needed is a price index appropriate to deflating the reported book values. The Bureau of Labor Statistics index of wholesale prices is clearly the best source of price data for this purpose. Complications arise because the index not only must have variants representing both cost and current market but also must be time-phased in relation to inventory holdings. There is also a need for conserving effort, which means that a high degree of aggregation cannot be avoided; any attempt to utilize all the price detail would result in a statistical chore of a magnitude that could not be justified merely for obtaining a rather crude approximation of the inventory movement.

A price index meeting these general conditions can be constructed along lines worked out in the author's study of consumer-goods inventories.[11] Only the three major components of the BLS index need be used—farm products, foods, and all other commodities. For each a "market" value is computed by averaging the 2 months adjacent to each end-of-month inventory. This is also taken as "cost" in the case of farm products. For foods, "cost" is estimated by averaging the index for the preceding 3 months. For other commodities, "cost" is the average of the preceding 7 months. In each case, it is necessary to select the lower of the alternatives; frequently the movement of the index itself makes it possible to select the lower figure by inspection, eliminating the necessity for computing the other. The three component indexes are then combined with weights that make the result most nearly represent the Department of Commerce implicit index of inventory values—that is, the index derived by dividing the reported book-value total by the deflated total, which is the sum of all the deflated industry segments.

The procedure is illustrated in Table 7–1, which provides the computations relating to data for the year 1951. Since this is a year in which prices turned down, the table illustrates how the peak is cut off in the index of inventory valuation. The index of current prices reaches its peak of 116.5 in February and March, but the index of inventory valuation does not reach its peak until May, and then at a level of only 115.1. The difference between the two in March does not appear great—only 2½ percent—but it is enough to make a very important difference in the estimated rate of inventory investment.

[11] *Production, Consumption, and Inventories of Consumer Goods.*

Table 7–1. Method of Revaluing Monthly Inventory Book Values

	BLS wholesale prices				Cost or market lower						In millions of dollars			
					Farm	Food		Other			Inventory book value		Month-to-month change	Change reflated¶
	Farm	Food	Other	Weighted average*	Market	Market	Cost†	Market	Cost†	Weighted average‡	End of month	Deflated§		
	1	2	3	4	5	6	7	8	9	10	11	12	13	14
1950:														
December	107.9	106.6	114.1	112.1	110.1	108.4	104.6	115.4	108.0	107.7	64,721	60,094		
1951:														
January	112.3	110.2	116.6	115.0	114.8	111.6	106.8	116.9	110.0	110.1	66,682	60,565	471	542
February	117.2	112.9	117.2	116.5	117.4	112.4	109.9	117.2	112.0	112.4	68,119	60,604	39	45
March	117.6	112.0	117.3	116.5	117.6	111.9	111.7	117.2	113.6	113.8	69,838	61,369	765	891
April	117.5	111.8	117.1	116.3	116.6	112.1	112.2	117.0	114.9	114.7	71,643	62,461	1,092	1,270
May	115.7	112.3	116.8	116.0	114.8	111.8	112.0	116.5	115.8	115.1	73,157	63,560	1,099	1,275
June	113.9	111.3	116.2	115.1	112.5	111.0	111.8	116.0	116.5	114.8	73,481	64,008	448	516
July	111.1	110.7	115.7	114.3	110.8	111.0	111.4	115.3	116.7	114.0	74,162	65,054	1,056	1,196
August	110.4	111.2	114.9	113.7	110.2	111.1	111.1	114.8	116.5	113.6	74,864	65,901	847	963
September	109.9	110.9	114.8	113.6	110.7	111.2	110.9	114.7	116.1	113.6	74,738	65,790	−111	−126
October	111.5	111.6	114.6	113.7	111.8	111.3	111.2	114.6	115.7	113.7	74,904	65,879	89	101
November	112.0	111.0	114.5	113.6	111.6	110.8	111.2	114.5	115.4	113.6	75,008	66,028	149	169
December	111.3	110.7	114.6	113.6	110.6	110.4	111.1	114.4	115.0	113.3	75,179	66,354	326	370

* Weights: Farm products, 13; foods, 15.5; other, 71.5.
† Taken as average of last 3 months for food and of last 7 months for other.
‡ Underlined figures from columns 6 to 9 combined with same weights as in note *.
§ Using index in column 10.
¶ Using index in column 4.

The high correlation of this provisional valuation index with the more exacting Commerce Department series is indicated in Chart 7–4. Although there are significant differences at times, the provisional index may usually be taken as a suitable criterion of inventory-valuation changes for interim use pending publication of the gross-national-product estimates.

Chart 7–4. Relationship of Department of Commerce Inventory Deflator and Computed Deflator

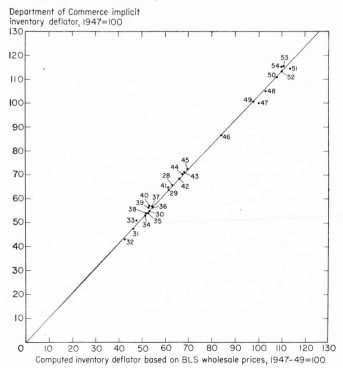

After the business-inventory series is deflated and the difference is computed for the period desired, whether a single month or several months, the result is the current change expressed in the average prices of the base period. It must therefore be reflated to the current level of prices. Note that this reflation never changes the sign; an increase remains positive, and vice versa. The index used for this purpose is not the same as that used for deflation. What is desired is the current value of the increment of goods produced or run off during the period, and the average price prevailing in that period represents the appropriate level. The weights for combining the various component parts must be the same, but such considerations as cost versus market values are no longer relevant.

The monthly series obtained in this way is shown on Chart 7–5 for the period 1939 to 1954. These data are not directly comparable with those shown on Chart 7–2, but the two series display a common feature that immediately commands attention, namely, extremely erratic behavior.

Chart 7–5. Monthly and Quarterly Inventory Changes

In billions of dollars at seasonally adjusted annual rates

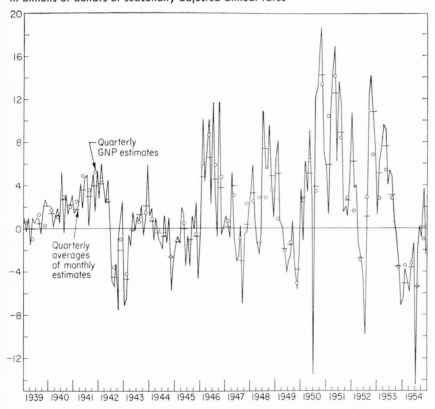

There are patterns of more or less continuous change over definite periods of time—as in the rise from 1939 to 1941, the sharp decline into the war period, and the rapid upsurge after the end of the war— but these tend to be obscured by the large month-to-month fluctuations, which often represent changes of several billion dollars at annual rates.

This range of variation is, of course, partly inherent in inventory movements, which take up the slack when there are temporary dispar- ities between production and consumption. It is also, however, inherent in the process of estimating inventory changes. It is necessary to take the differences between two large aggregates that are subject to various kinds of errors and blow up those monthly differences to annual rates, so that errors appearing at any stage in the process are magnified by a factor of 12. Thus the errors of sampling, of seasonal adjustment, and of price adjustment are all greatly magnified. Even the errors of rounding appear significant, because a difference of less than $100 million may appear as $1 billion on this chart. Shifts in the monthy rate must therefore be interpreted with extreme caution.

When adjacent months are averaged, the month-to-month fluctuation is greatly reduced. The short horizontal bars are averages for the calendar quarters and may be compared with the gross-national-product estimates, which are shown as circles. There is a high degree of correlation between these quarterly data over the period as a whole. The provisional estimates tend consistently to fall short of the gross-national-product estimates in a period like 1946 to 1947, when inventories were rising strongly. The differences are due largely to price discrepancies and to the exclusion of "other" inventories; the gross-national-product data include estimates for construction and other segments of the economy not covered by the series on business inventories.

It is not intended in this discussion to argue that the short-cut procedure outlined is entirely sound. However, nothing is entirely sound in this particular field, not even the gross-national-product estimates. It presents one of the most difficult problems in economic analysis and one that is of greatest importance in short-term forecasting. All that can be said is that anything producing a valid interpretation in most situations is worth using.

Because a considerable margin of error is unavoidable and is likely to persist even through use of the most complicated techniques, certain short cuts may at times be justified. For example, one way to arrive at a quick approximation of the inventory investment indicated by a change in the total book value of inventories is to consider it in relation to the recent change in prices. Suppose book value in a given quarter advances 2 percent. Then if prices had been advancing at 1 percent a quarter, about half the increase in book value may be taken as the rate of inventory accumulation. But if prices had been advancing at 3 percent, there would be a corresponding amount of liquidation.

Whatever the methods followed, there will be periods when it is difficult to interpret the role of inventories in the current economic scene. In those situations, it is desirable to supplement the direct indications provided by inventory data as such with those provided by other data that bear on the problem. What have been the recent movements of production and consumption, and how far can they be explained by special developments in various parts of the economy? The movements of prices may also be enlightening, since price changes may both reflect and induce changes in inventory policy. Financial developments as indicated by bank loans or credit policy may also throw light on developments that at first seem anomalous.

FORECASTING INVENTORY CHANGES

Considerable emphasis is placed upon the various statistics and adjustments that contribute to an understanding of the current inventory movement, because such understanding is one of the most important bases for a forecast. The current movement in many instances provides clues to what the next shift will be. Other important clues are provided by the level of inventories in relation to consumption and by a third kind of consideration, external to inventories—the anticipated behavior of other factors affecting the over-all level of activity. When inventories are out of line, being either excessive or deficient, there is likely to be a move toward eliminating the discrepancy, and any move that would increase it is likely to be restricted. In addition, any movement of inventories will be affected by changes in other factors. It may be prolonged or brought to an end by such changes; and whenever levels of income and consumption are changing under the influence of other factors, inventories will probably move also. These three lines of analysis are the basis of inventory forecasting.

In evaluating the current movement of inventories, several kinds of considerations are important. Mere size is one. A movement of extreme magnitude is not only likely to wear itself out more quickly, but will have more important repercussions when it does.

Next, the origin of the movement is of special significance. Why did it get under way, and are the same causes still at work, or have they been dissipated? Related to this as a special aspect is the question of whether the movement is the result of deliberate policy or of circumstances beyond business control. Is it voluntary in the sense of being intended or desired, or is it involuntary in that it arose out of unforeseen developments or miscalculations of the market? The answers to these questions are key items of information in projecting its future course.

An involuntary movement usually sets off a voluntary movement in the other direction. The former may start from a neutral position, as a result of unforeseen changes in demand, or at the end of a voluntary movement, as an extension or overcarrying of that movement. Producers try to gauge customer demands and set their production schedules accordingly. When they are wrong, they get stuck, either with an unintentional inventory investment or by loss of stocks they have to replace at higher cost. In either case, they react to correct the mistake. An involuntary movement may also occur in situations which, from the business viewpoint, are out of control. These usually result from disturbances—war, labor disputes, and other interruptions of production.

With some exceptions arising out of situations of the latter kind, a large, involuntary change in inventories cannot persist for very long, because business will act quickly to bring it to an end and go on to adjust inventories to the new conditions. It might be impossible to anticipate a sudden change in demand, but once it occurs, the adjustment that will follow can be forecast with considerable accuracy.

A movement of the involuntary type occurred in the early part of 1951. Producers had hardly built their production schedules up to peak rates at that time when consumer demand dropped back sharply, and inventory accumulation then pushed to a rate that could not have been maintained even with the best advance in over-all demand that could be expected in the next year or so. That meant that the movement could not continue, and it was possible to predict an end of the inflation on this basis. A similar reversal had also occurred in 1937. Beginning at the start of the year, for 2 or 3 quarters, business was caught in an involuntary expansion of inventories. The extremely sharp recession to the 1938 lows ensued.

Voluntary changes in inventories sometimes take on the same unstable character as involuntary ones. They may be pushed to an extreme rate that is not justified by underlying conditions, and then a quick reversal of policy must be expected. This happened in the decline of 1949. Business moved to cut inventories because a lower level of demand was generally expected. But the economy was held steady by the action of other factors, primarily by government programs, so that liquidation was not really called for.

Both the 1949 and 1951 situations developed out of miscalculations of the rates of production that would be required by future demand. In early 1949, a recession that had been anticipated ever since the end of the war seemed to be getting under way, and many people said, "This is it!" By summertime, the mistake was clear, and recovery was again the order of the day. In 1951, producers were similarly misled by the surge of consumption that took place following the outbreak in Korea. The upsurge reached an extreme in December, 1950, and January, 1951. It should, perhaps, have been perceived at that point that consumer buying was excessive, with saving reduced to almost negligible proportions, but these facts were lost sight of in the excitement of the war scare.

There was another sort of a miscalculation in the 1951 incident also.

Everyone expected inflation to continue, and price controls were being imposed to prevent it. Costs and prices were expected to rise much higher, and this expectation caused many to buy speculatively against the price rise. Although the sharp rise in prices was projected into the more distant future, it was, in fact, taking place immediately, in part merely as a way of jumping the gun on controls.

In contrast to these miscalculations, there are situations where expectations are more soundly based. In these cases, the result may be a voluntary movement of inventories that has the effect of adjusting business operations to conditions that do materialize after a time. Frequently expectations of future changes are not at all arbitrary but are based on known forces that will be operating for a considerable period. In the Korean episode, part of the difficulty was only in being too extreme. Prices and costs did rise, shortages did develop, and if international tensions had moved on toward all-out war, the extreme rates of accumulation in many lines would have been justified.

An occasion of this kind had developed at the end of World War II, when it was widely expected that demand for durable goods would be high, and there was a scramble for supplies of the materials and other factors needed to produce those goods. The scramble for steel persisted for almost 3 years. The accumulation of inventory that went on in the first year, 1946, was almost wholly justified. It was not until the end of 1946 that scattered excesses began to appear in a few lines, and those lines were rather inconsequential in the picture as a whole.

How long a voluntary movement may run depends on the specific circumstances. The nature of the conditions expected may provide some clues. If drastic changes are necessary to fulfill the expectations, then the situation is obviously different from those in which only moderate adjustment must be made, and the nature of the obstacles to carrying through that process are of great importance. In 1946 it was a question of how long it would take industry to reconvert, how long to build up supplies of parts and materials, how long to recruit and train a labor force, and how long to work off the accumulated demands after production was built up to a peak level. All this was a long-drawn-out process for some industries—for example, the auto industry and the construction industry.

Part of the answer in such situations may be obtained merely by watching how rapidly progress is being made. At the end of 1946 the process of rebuilding was nowhere near completed, and that fact became a key element in forecasting the continuation of prosperity. Not until the recession of 1949 was sufficient steel available to the auto industry to produce enough cars to make a quick reduction of backlogs possible. It was not until the big upsurge of production in 1950 that the wartime accumulation of demand for cars was substantially worked off.

More frequently, voluntary changes of this kind are designed not to adjust to expected changes in conditions but to bring inventory back to the desired level after there has been a movement out of line. This kind of a movement usually follows miscalculations like that of 1949, when expected conditions failed to develop. The movement after the end of World War II was in part a movement of this character. The war had reduced inventories considerably in most civilian industries, and the immediate postwar upswing in production, involving nondurable goods as well as durable goods, was partly an effort to rebuild stocks and bring them back to more normal levels.

How long a movement arising from the need to adjust inventory positions will persist depends partly upon the influence of factors other than the initial imbalance. If inventories alone are involved, the adjustment can usually be made quickly. We ordinarily have capacity to produce at a rate well in excess of current needs, so that the additional demands for stock can be met in a relatively short time. In such a movement, based on inventory policy alone, there would tend to be a prompt reversal when the drive to accumulate ceased. Since such movements typically overcarry, the cutback in production would proceed not just to the starting point but enough lower to liquidate any excess that involuntarily accumulated at the end of the upswing. However, various external factors are almost always operating or are brought into action by the inventory movement itself, and the extent of the movement would depend upon whether the changes in those factors facilitated or prevented the adjustment.

WHEN ARE INVENTORIES EXCESSIVE?

Sometimes inventory movements are complex in nature, having elements of various kinds in them, both voluntary and involuntary. They may be intended both to adjust for changes that have already occurred and to anticipate future changes. The 1946 situation progressed rapidly because stocks were deficient and because higher levels of operation were universally anticipated. As a rule, whenever one of these elements is present, the other tends to come into play at least temporarily. Thus a recession lowers the level of required inventories, so that current holdings appear to be excessive; it also tends to drive prices down and produce an incentive for speculative reduction of inventories.

In judging a movement of this kind, the initial position is important. The role played by inventories in a recession where they were excessive at the outset is likely to be quite different from that where they temporarily become excessive on the way down. Although the extent of the runoff is bound to depend in part on the excess temporarily developed, it may depend even more on the relationship of the original level of inventories to the level of demand that will be established after the recession has ended. In forecasting future changes, therefore, one must analyze the over-all position of inventories at the start and through the succeeding stages of the movement.

Before proceeding to the criteria for appraising the size of inventory holdings, a comment on concepts may be in order. The distinction between levels and changes is important here, just as it was in arriving at the correct measure of rates of inventory investment, but now the focus turns to its other aspect. There the objective was a measure of change, and the total value of inventories was accordingly written out of the picture by taking the difference between the beginning and end of each period. Here the objective is to appraise the size of total inventory holdings, and although the change may be modifying the total, it is of little relevance to the question. Both aspects of the situation are, of course, important to the forecast.

It is said at various times that the rate of inventory accumulation is excessive. This proposition may very well be valid, but it usually lacks definiteness and leads to confusion with the proposition that inventories in total are excessive. From the longer-run point of view, any but the modest rate of accumulation needed for growth is excessive and cannot continue indefinitely. The needs for long-term growth of the economy are not only small but are constantly being reduced in relative terms by the more efficient use of existing inventories. Therefore, almost any accumulation of inventories beyond an annual rate of a billion or two must come to an end eventually.

It can be much more definitely stated, however, that any rate of accumulation, large or small, is likely to be halted soon if the total is excessive. A high rate of accumulation can continue with surplus stocks on hand only through the operation of extraneous factors, like price supports, or in one of those involuntary spurts that calls for a quick reversal. In contrast, when stocks are deficient, a moderate rate of accumulation can go on for some time or even increase. If it is small relative to an existing deficiency in total stocks, there is even a strong probability that it will increase. By and large, these propositions may be inverted, and they hold for liquidation also.

The magnitude of aggregate inventory holdings thus provides an essential part of the analysis. This is particularly true in those situations where inventories have moved out of line, so that the existing excess or deficiency provides a definite indication of the movement to come.

The question is: "What is the normal holding for inventories?" It is easy to answer this question by saying that inventories are governed by the volume of business being done. There is, for example, the important work-in-process category, which bears a direct relation to production. Even beyond that, inventories tend to line up with volume of business, because it is desirable to hold the minimum inventories that will permit maximum sales to be realized. The merchant has to maintain his display stocks and supply all the customers who are likely to come in before the next shipment is received, but he does not want much more than that, because it would entail the costs of an extra investment and the risks of loss on the goods held. Hence when business is good, inventories tend to move up correspondingly, and when it is bad, they are cut back.

Many businesses maintain inventory-control systems to ensure optimum holdings. New orders are placed when inventories fall to a specified point, and then the volume ordered is governed by the recent rate of sales, a purchase budget, or some other appropriate measure of volume. On the other hand, if inventories rise above a certain point, special sales or other inducements may be used to clear them out.

Saying that inventories are tied to sales, however, does not tell the whole story, nor does it indicate just what measure of the relationship should be used. Businessmen's ideas of what constitutes necessary or convenient inventories do change from time to time. When it is easy to get supplies and purchases can be made at special concessions, they hold off. When shortages or interruptions of supply threaten and prices are moving up, they order further ahead. Allowance may have to be made, therefore, for the special characteristics of the situation. Throughout the Korean War, for example, business maintained inventory holdings somewhat in excess of their long-term relationship to sales.

The most common measure for assessing this relationship is the inventory-sales ratio. Frequently this is expressed in terms of number of days' supply, by dividing inventories by the daily average rate of sales during a recent period. Inventories are said to be normal or in balance when they conform to some standard set up in terms of the past behavior of this ratio.

The inventory-sales ratio, however, is subject to distortion by several factors and therefore is not an entirely satisfactory measure of the relationship. Differences in pricing may produce changes that bear no relation to the actual rates at which goods are flowing into consumption. On the one hand, there is the inventory-revaluation item, whose effects are particularly important at the beginning of a downturn. On the other, there are changes in margins and markups, which affect the total value of sales but only partially get into inventory valuations, since inventories are carried at cost. The possibilities of such distortion are magnified by the fact that the inventory total is an unduplicated figure for the economy as a whole, whereas sales contain a good deal of duplication between the various stages of production and distribution.

Moreover, production has to provide for inventories as well as consumption. With sales tabulated at all stages, speculative buying may boost manufacturers' sales with no change in the flow to final users, or liquidation might lower aggregate sales while the flow is maintained. For all these reasons, a constant inventory-sales ratio may not indicate a satisfactory inventory position.

What has consistently been observed in past studies is the tendency for inventory-sales ratios to be low during periods of cyclical advance and high during periods of decline. At the turning points, they tend to move quickly from one position to the other. The lag in inventories and the sharp turn in production required to get the inventory reversal accomplished are the primary factors bringing this about. The inventory-sales ratio may move across the normal value so fast that a state of balance could hardly be said to exist at any point in the movement.

Furthermore, there is no reason why the inventory-sales ratio should remain constant over time. The appropriate level of inventories is influenced by a variety of technical conditions and by patterns in the distribution of final products, so that the ratio should tend to change rather than remain stable. Historically there has been a tendency for the ratio to decline over long periods.

There are two possible explanations for the behavior of the inventory-sales ratio, accounting for both short- and long-term movements. The first views the inventory-sales ratio as essentially stable in the short run, so that actual cyclical movements presumably derive from the appearance of deficiencies or excesses of actual inventories relative to normal. The long-term downward movement of the ratio is then regarded as a true trend, resulting from permanent improvements in production, transportation, warehousing, and marketing techniques, which enable business to utilize a given volume of inventories more efficiently.

The second views inventory volume as being relatively more stable than sales, indicating the ability of business to handle somewhat larger or smaller sales with a given volume of inventories. Then the cyclical swings of the ratio are regarded primarily as normal variations, possibly without any deficiencies or excesses, and the long-term downward trend presumably reflects the long-term upward trend in business operations accompanying the expansion of the economy.

Both explanations are consistent with the data. The fall of the ratio on the advance and its rise on the decline could result either from deficiencies and excesses of holdings or from inventory stability in comparison with sales.

A study that makes use of the second of these approaches is to be

Table 7—2.   Nonfarm Inventories and Flow of Goods

In billions of 1947 dollars

Year	Change in* nonfarm inventories	Nonfarm† inventories, beginning of year	Total flow‡ of goods	Adjusted§ nonfarm inventories, beginning of year
1921	$−0.2	$33.9	$ 62.0	$27.7
1922	0.3	33.7	67.4	27.8
1923	4.3	34.0	75.6	28.4
1924	−1.4	38.3	77.1	32.4
1925	2.5	36.9	80.8	31.6
1926	1.9	39.4	85.3	34.2
1927	0.6	41.3	87.3	36.2
1928	−0.5	41.9	87.9	37.2
1929	2.6	41.4	92.1	37.2
1930	−0.2	44.0	83.6	40.0
1931	−3.0	43.8	78.6	40.3
1932	−5.1	40.8	68.1	38.0
1933	−3.0	35.7	65.7	33.6
1934	0.3	32.8	71.7	31.3
1935	0.7	33.1	77.8	31.9
1936	3.7	33.8	89.2	33.0
1937	3.0	37.4	94.3	37.0
1938	−1.8	40.4	91.4	40.4
1939	0.5	38.5	98.6	39.0
1940	3.1	39.0	106.8	39.9
1941	6.0	42.1	123.7	43.6
1942	0.6	48.1	145.8	50.4
1943	−0.8	48.8	166.2	51.4
1944	−0.8	48.0	169.6	51.6
1945	−0.7	47.2	172.7	51.3
1946	7.7	46.4	141.0	51.0
1947	1.3	54.2	147.6	60.3
1948	2.8	55.5	156.4	62.5
1949	−0.7	58.3	160.7	66.5
1950	6.0	56.6	169.2	65.5
1951	7.1	62.6	176.0	73.1
1952	1.6	69.8	188.2	82.5
1953	1.5	71.4	201.7	85.4
1954	−2.4	72.9	194.4	88.2

* Inventory changes are computed as the difference between beginning-of-year

found in the article "Business Inventories—Recent Trends and Position," by Louise J. Paradiso and Genevieve B. Wimsatt.[12] The authors discuss inventory-sales ratios as a means of judging the current position, but their main reliance is on correlations between inventory book values and total sales. A relatively high correlation is found between inventory holdings at the end of the year and sales for the year, indicating a lag of approximately ½ year. When quarterly data are used, sales are lagged 2 quarters, so that current sales data in effect provide a basis for forecasting the inventory movement of the next 6 months. Separate relationships are presented for durable-goods industries and nondurable-goods industries, and the discussion indicates that similar correlations were worked out for a number of specific industries within these broad groups.

The basic deficiencies of reported book values and gross-sales data

---

and end-of-year inventories shown in column 2.

† Year-end book values of inventories in current and 1947 dollars for 1928 to 1953 were supplied by the U.S. Department of Commerce. For years before 1929, Kuznets' estimates of inventory changes in 1929 dollars were chained to the Department of Commerce figure in 1929 dollars, and the resulting constant-dollar series was adjusted upward to conform to the level of the Department of Commerce series in 1947 dollars. Simon Kuznets, *National Income and Capital Formation, 1919–35; A Preliminary Report*, National Bureau of Economic Research, Inc., New York, 1937, p. 40.

‡ Data for 1929 to 1954 are from *Survey of Current Business*, July, 1955, p. 22. Excluded from the flow of goods were the following components of deflated gross national product: personal services, gross government product, net foreign investment, one-half of new construction, and change in business inventories. The adjustment for government construction utilized data from *Construction and Building Materials: Statistical Supplement*, U.S. Department of Commerce, May, 1954.

Data before 1929 were compiled for each of the remaining components from a variety of sources, as follows:

Consumer expenditures: Simon Kuznets, *National Product since 1869*, National Bureau of Economic Research, Inc., New York, 1946.

Private construction: *Construction and Building Materials: Statistical Supplement*, U.S. Department of Commerce, May, 1954.

Producers' durable equipment: Mary S. Painter, "Estimates of Gross National Product, 1919–1928," *Federal Reserve Bulletin*, September, 1945; deflated by price index from Solomon Fabricant, *Capital Consumption and Adjustment*, National Bureau of Economic Research, Inc., New York, 1938.

Government purchases: estimates derived from data in M. Slade Kendrick, *A Century and a Half of Federal Expenditures*, Occasional Paper 48, National Bureau of Economic Research, Inc., New York, 1955; Solomon Fabricant, *The Trend of Government Activity in the United States since 1900*, National Bureau of Economic Research, Inc., New York, 1952; and *Construction and Building Materials: Statistical Supplement*, U.S. Department of Commerce, May, 1954.

§ Adjusted inventories were obtained from the data in column 2 by correcting for the downward time trend in the ratio of year-end stocks to the year's flow of goods (see lower panel, Chart 7–6). The adjustment in logarithmic terms is equal to $0.00517(T)$, where T = time in years, with 1938 = 0.

[12] *Survey of Current Business*, May, 1953.

are, of course, inherent in this study as in any position analysis making use of them. They may be avoided only by getting back to the concept of the "real norm" underlying such analysis. This concept is one that relates the physical stock of goods on hand to the flow of goods it is intended to support or facilitate. For this purpose deflated data on both inventories and flow of goods to final users are needed. The deflated-inventory data are available from the computation of inventory investment. A similarly deflated measure of the flow of goods to final users is also available in the gross-national-product data.

A study utilizing this alternative approach may be briefly summarized at this point. Most important in the flow of end products is the flow of goods to consumers. Ultimately inventories can be liquidated only through consumption. Inventories specialized for investment use are in a sense already sunk investments; they can be used only by completing the capital goods for which they are intended. But they do change the timing of investment in a way directly relevant to a forecast, and producers of such goods must look to the flow of capital expenditures as the basis for their operations. Hence producers' equipment must also be included in the measure of the flow to final users. Government purchases from business have both consumption and investment aspects and on the whole provide a suitable measure of the flow of goods to the government sector. Construction expenditures, however, include so large a proportion of on-site labor cost that in some respects they are more like consumer services or government payrolls. Perhaps half the total of construction expenditures represents a measure of the flow in the sense relevant to a comparison with business inventories. Inventory accumulation itself must, of course, be excluded. These data for 1921 to 1954 are presented in Table 7–2.

The results of comparing deflated inventories with the total of deflated expenditures in the indicated segments is presented in Chart 7–6. The lower part of the chart shows the ratio of year-end inventories to commodity flow—expressed in terms of the differences in logarithms—as a time series to which a straight-line trend has been fitted. This computed trend was used to adjust the actual inventory values to bring them into line with the flow of goods. The results of adjusting out the downward trend are shown in the upper part of the chart, where both actual and adjusted stocks are superimposed on the flow of goods. Using this comparison as a means of judging the business inventory position assumes, of course, that the flow of goods represents a suitable norm for adjusted inventories, around which they will fluctuate and to which they will tend to return under the usual conditions of operation.

In most years, the adjusted inventories show substantial conformity with the flow of goods. In 1930, inventories moved up into an excessive position. That excess was not entirely eliminated until 1934, after consumption made a noticeable recovery. A still wider departure occurred during World War II, when production was restricted. A final substantial excess occurred during the Korean War; possibly memories of war shortages contributed to the willingness of business to hold larger inventories under the conditions engendered by the cold war. In all three of

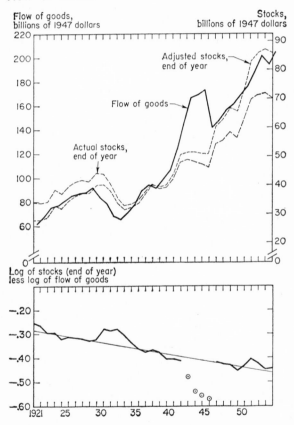

Chart 7–6. Relationship of Stocks on Hand to Flow of Goods

these cases, departures from the norm persisted for some time. In the 1920s and late 1930s, deviations in either direction brought prompt corrective action, and this kind of response must be regarded as typical for short-term forecasting in ordinary circumstances.

When there has been a movement out of line, the extent of the deviation is an important factor in determining the magnitude and timing of a reversal. Once a deviation has been eliminated, the incentive to keep on accumulating or liquidating is gone. But because of the lags and rigidities in the production process, it takes a while just to halt a movement that has gotten under way, then it takes a while longer to build up a rate of change in the opposite direction, and then still an additional interval is required to eliminate the disparity. Moreover, any reversal shifts the norm, at least to the extent of the multiplier effect on consumer expenditures. These circumstances introduce an unavoidable tendency to overcarry. The rate of accumulation or liquidation changes quickly at the end of a corrective movement, but total inventories continue on out of line in the original direction. Since each situation has its own peculiarities, the characteristics of each movement differ, and what is known about them must be merged with data on the current position of inventories to form a valid hypothesis for projecting the next move.

INVENTORIES AS PART OF A COMPLETE FORECAST

Two of the keys to inventory forecasting are thus found in the character of current changes and in the position of inventories relative to the flow of goods into final use. When inventories are changing rapidly or are out of line with consumption, there will have to be an adjustment. One or the other of these imbalances almost always prevails at any given time. There remains the question of how the indicated adjustment fits into the general pattern of the forecast, of whether other changes going on in the economy will assist in its completion or prolong and increase the difficulty of the process.

In almost every short-term swing of business, inventories influence and are influenced by other factors. An inventory movement creates an impression of unusually prosperous or depressed conditions, with the result that the movements of even the most stable segments of the economy tend to be accelerated or retarded. Conversely, the movements of the more stable segments condition, and may even initiate, changes in inventories. The situation as a whole will of course, be the result of all these interacting forces, but the level to which inventories will tend to adjust is determined primarily by the other factors.

There are exceptional periods in which inventories may be relatively neutral, with little or no change taking place and the total on hand roughly in balance with needs. Then if a change in income and consumption can be forecast on the basis of other factors, a whole inventory cycle will probably get under way—first, an involuntary change will take place in inventories, followed by a movement to reestablish an inventory position appropriate to the new conditions, and then the corrective movement will tend to overcarry and bring on the next reversal.

The whole sequence must be superimposed on the pattern of changes produced by the other factors and the two patterns reconciled with each other.

At other times, inventories may be out of line, and efforts to bring them back will initiate a more general movement. When inventories are excessive, the excess might, under rather exceptional circumstances, be eliminated by an upsurge in the rate of use, with stabilizing effects on the economy. More likely there will have to be some liquidation. If the liquidating movement starts when the economy is otherwise strong, it will probably be short-lived. If, however, other factors react in the same direction and help to depress income, the position at which an inventory balance might have been reestablished is dropped, and the movement to liquidate will have to continue, perhaps at an increased rate.

In a downturn, a high rate of liquidation may be reached early in the movement and thereafter inventory changes may represent a series of deviations around that rate as long as the movement as a whole is prolonged. In a major decline, like that of the early 1930s, with everything continuing weak, a higher rate of liquidation may be called for after the decline has been under way for some time, but the additional liquidation brought on by such conditions is likely to be smaller than the primary reversal from accumulation to liquidation. In the primary reversal, inventories are likely to be the most violently unstabilizing element in the whole picture, but thereafter they become a potentially stabilizing element. Once a relatively high rate of liquidation is attained, inventories may contribute little if anything more to the decline. The continuing recession is then dependent almost entirely upon the other factors, and inventories have become a force potentially capable of working against those factors. The same kind of considerations are relevant in reverse on the upswing.

Since inventories are likely to be the most erratic element in the picture, prolonged liquidation or accumulation at a fixed rate is unlikely. At any stage in a prolonged downswing, the excess might temporarily be eliminated, and then the rate of liquidation might be greatly reduced or even cease entirely. The stimulus might for a time offset continuing declines in other factors, creating the impression that the whole movement is at an end. The validity of this impression would depend, again, upon the action of other factors. If they continued downward, despite the temporary stabilization, the easing of inventory liquidation could not hold the line and the over-all decline would be resumed.

Questions of timing and magnitude are closely interwoven. If accumulation or liquidation is rapid, the time consumed in achieving a given position or objective will be less than when the rates are moderate. Also the probability that an inventory movement will accelerate and provide an additional impetus to the general swing of business is low when the rate of accumulation or liquidation is already large. On the other hand, if accumulation or liquidation is only moderate, it might be sharply accelerated whenever it becomes clear that it is not sufficiently rapid to bring about an adjustment within a reasonable time. This is likely to be the outcome when sharp reductions in income and consumption are being forced by other factors.

Chart 7–7. Annual Changes in Nonfarm Inventories

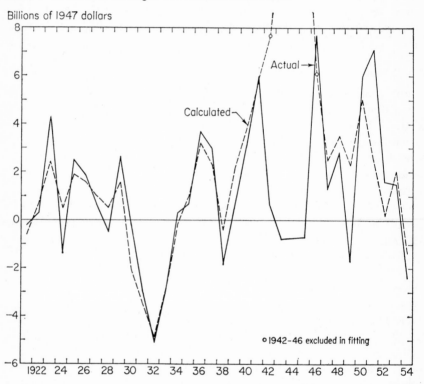

When an inventory movement starts because it is expected that demand or prices will be changing, how far the movement will go depends partly on whether demand or prices are actually going to move as expected. This is a question that can only be answered in terms of an over-all forecast. If demand is actually going to expand or contract, the inventory movement will carry through to complete the adjustment; if it is not, the movement will make an early reversal. In working out the first approximation, the question cannot be answered, except in a very provisional manner. It may be that the size of the inventory movement is itself decisive, or the magnitude of holdings may be such as to suggest a reasonable hypothesis for the first approximation. Subsequently, any such hypothesis will be tested in the light of the over-all pattern developed. When it becomes clear where the economy is headed, a better estimate of the probable inventory movement can be incorporated in the forecast.

In summary, the approach to inventory forecasting is to analyze the inventory situation in terms of the following criteria:

1. Size and character of the current movement
   a. Whether extreme or moderate
   b. Whether voluntary or involuntary, and if voluntary, whether intended to adjust to given conditions or to anticipate future conditions
2. The position of total holdings, whether excessive or deficient relative to the flow of goods into consumption
3. The relation of inventories to other parts of the economy, whether changes in other factors will aggravate or minimize the inventory adjustment

From these ingredients, a hypothetical projection must be formulated. All three can to some extent be taken into account in a simple relationship that expresses the change in inventories as a function of the flow of goods and the beginning-of-year stocks on hand. The forecasts of other factors must, of course, be included in the estimates of the over-all flow of goods. The results of a correlation study following this approach are presented in Chart 7–7, in terms of the actual and calculated changes in nonfarm inventories.[13] For a more detailed discussion, see Appendix B.

In actual forecasting situations, various aspects of inventory movements do not lend themselves to the application of precise quantitative methods, but experience teaches that reasonably adequate judgments can be made on the basis of this approach. Judgments may be slanted in various particulars to take account of existing conditions. Such conditions include imponderables like the state of world politics and the predisposition of business to seek liquidity or to expand commitments. The basic lines of analysis, however, are of overriding importance, and the only rule offered is that they be followed as rigorously as the conditions permit.

---

[13] The estimating equation is

$$\Delta H = -0.598 + 0.251G - 0.562H'_{-1} \qquad (R^2 = .721)$$

where ΔH = change in nonfarm inventories during the year
G = flow of goods as defined above; see Table 7–2
H'_{-1} = total stocks on hand at the beginning of the year, adjusted for relative down trend

CHAPTER 8

The Foreign Sector

Discussions of the economic relations between this country and other countries commonly attempt to summarize them from our point of view in something called the "foreign sector"—or, in Department of Commerce terminology, the "rest-of-the-world sector." It is a term applied as a kind of shorthand to cover all the ramifications of changes and influences arising outside our own territorial limits.

In discussions of this subject a question that frequently arises is: "Why is there a foreign sector of the United States economy?" In the most direct terms, the answer is that part of our economy depends upon foreign transactions for its livelihood. Some of the goods we produce go abroad, and some of the goods we consume are produced abroad. Many things that happen abroad change those flows and in doing so affect our income, employment, and consumption. Some of them occur with a good deal of autonomy and may not be at all to our liking. They cannot be disregarded either in accounting for past changes or in appraising those likely to take place in the future.

Foreign trade is not merely an adjunct of our own economic operations but to some extent determines those operations. The essence of the exchange process lies in the fact that production is made more efficient by producing things that can be produced most easily here and exchanging them for things that others can produce more efficiently. Producing machinery and exchanging it for coffee is in effect just a good way of producing coffee. For the other country the reverse is true, so the exchange produces a mutual benefit.

Once two countries have adjusted to trading with each other, their economies are modified in various ways, and trade tends to continue in the patterns that have become established. The countries are interdependent. Each looks to the other for part of the market its producers enjoy and for part of the goods that make up the way of living of its con-

254

sumers. Each is more efficient in an over-all sense. It finds better ways to use its resources and allocates its labor force accordingly. It distributes the total income produced to lines of production and to localities in a different manner. These are important changes to its people. It can no longer move to eliminate the trade without serious consequences to important groups of both producers and consumers. The same is true in the other country or countries with which it trades.

Even after the broad outlines of these economic interrelations have been established, the level of income in each country is partly determined by shifts in its trade or in the way it is financed. Net imports may make unnecessary an equivalent amount of production and release resources in the same way that any fall in domestic demand reduces the work producers are called upon to do. If there is an alternative use for those resources, other lines of production may be expanded to fill the gap. Sometimes investment can be undertaken only on this basis, and borrowing from abroad, which makes an import surplus possible, facilitates a general expansion of incomes and production. On the other hand, if there is no alternative employment for the released resources, they remain idle and the level of income falls, just as it does when demand is being satisfied by sales from inventories rather than from current production.

Changes of the reverse character occur when there are increased exports. These absorb resources, just as domestic-investment expenditures absorb resources. If resources for producing the additional exports are available, the level of real income is raised, so that lending abroad may stimulate the pace of activity. On the other hand, if resources have to be bid away from other production, their prices tend to rise, so that export or other demands would have to be restricted in order to prevent inflation.

MEASURING THE EFFECTS OF FOREIGN TRANSACTIONS

In order to carry out any detailed analysis of the foreign repercussions of changes in our own economy or of the effects of changes originating abroad on economic activity here, it would be necessary to consider a whole chain of interactions involving many countries and many kinds of transactions. The problem of tracing the channels by which changes are transmitted throughout the world and back again not only is extremely complicated but also is hampered by lack of adequate data. Conclusions are necessarily provisional. All that can be hoped for is an approximation of what is really desired. Hence it is customary to summarize the whole complex in some relatively simple measure that can be taken as an indicator of the combined effects of many things that cannot be treated in detail and to some extent may not even be known to exist in advance of the changes they produce.

In compiling a broad measure of activity like the gross national product, all we can really credit ourselves with producing in the foreign sector is the excess of the goods and services which we export over those which the other nations send to us. The foreign goods consumed by our people or used by business are already included in our consumption- or investment-expenditure totals, so that imports must be deducted in order to avoid double counting. As a convenient expedient, they are usually treated as a direct offset to exports, and only the net balance of exports over imports is included in our total production.

In some periods, the total output of the economy includes a relatively small portion that is going, on balance, to foreigners. In other periods, a relatively small portion of our needs are supplied by net imports which represent a deduction from total output. It is therefore necessary to adjust for these small net balances in order to obtain a measure of the goods produced by our own efforts. The precise method of adjustment used by the Department of Commerce in compiling the net-foreign-investment figure for inclusion in the gross national product deviates somewhat from this straightforward concept of the net balance of goods and services, for reasons that will be indicated shortly, but the basic principle underlying it is the same.

It may be recalled from the discussion of the circular-flow chart (Chart 5-1) that gross exports seemed to be important, and not just the net balance. This would be the case for a country just opening up trade and finding new world markets for part of the total output it was capable of producing. Conversely, if a country's export markets were eliminated while its demand for imports continued high, its prosperity might be seriously affected. Except for wars and similar disturbances, however, trade practically never changes in so drastic and arbitrary a manner. Moreover, the necessity of financing trade in another country's currency tends to bring about equality between exports and imports, so that the broad aggregates tend to move together.

Gross exports may also be important if indirect effects are considered, such as their effects on domestic investment. A concern that expands to meet foreign demands raises income to the same extent as another making a similar investment to produce for domestic markets, and the drying up of foreign trade may help to drive the economy deeper into a depression. But such effects are treated as part of the domestic-investment picture and therefore are not included in the foreign sector.

When following this approach, it would be improper to include gross exports because they tend to reflect movements originating elsewhere in the economy. Thus a movement in gross exports tends to overstate the role of the foreign sector in so far as it derives from a change in imports. If exports decline because declining imports make fewer funds available to other countries, responsibility should be assigned not to exports but rather to the factors bringing on the decline in imports. In fact, if exports are maintained on such a decline, a net advantage is being realized from the foreign sector, in line with the improvement shown by net exports. Similarly, if exports increase because foreigners spend part of the funds obtained from expanded imports, the increase does not represent an additional stimulus. The stimulus derives from the factors pushing up income and imports. To the extent that exports then lag behind imports, they actually put a drag on the movement, so that the foreign sector's contribution is negative, as shown by the shift toward net imports. Thus the net balance provides a reasonably correct index of the effect of changes from an existing trading position.

How serious the effects of a change in the foreign balance will be for any country is determined by how much its economy depends on trade. If trade is large in relation to its own production, if it is dependent upon foreign sources for food, industrial materials, and other essential commodities, important changes in its foreign balance may have highly advantageous or disastrous effects. If, on the other hand, its trade is relatively small in relation to total production and it can get along without almost any imports, even the most drastic changes in its foreign balance may leave it relatively little affected.

In these respects, the United States stands at the latter extreme, a position gained by reason of its tremendous resources and productivity. Although the total volume of our trade is the largest of any nation, it represents only a small portion of the aggregate flow of goods and services available to us. In 1954, for example, our total merchandise imports amounted to $10 billion. This $10 billion represented 13 percent of total exports by all countries outside the Soviet bloc but only 3 percent of our gross national product of $361 billion. Thus a relatively small shift on our part could produce changes in the volume or pattern of trade that might seriously disrupt the economies of other countries heavily dependent on that trade.

In addition, the United States is the most self-sufficient country by far. The extent and diversity of our mineral resources, the range of our agricultural production, and the all-inclusive ability of our industry give us an unrivaled degree of independence from other sources of supply. The trend toward self-sufficiency was greatly accelerated during World War II. Before the war, for example, we were heavily dependent upon rubber imports to keep our autos running and to maintain the efficiency of our industrial operations in both mechanical and chemical processes. Afterward, however, synthetic rubber continued to supply about half of the market and could be counted on to serve most of our needs if necessary. Silk was almost completely displaced by synthetic fibers. Other commodities could also be dispensed with. All the essential commodities that could not be produced in large volume here were stockpiled by the government in quantities sufficient to meet our needs in a future emergency.

On the other hand, there are respects in which our ability to produce has less fortunate results. For the extent to which a country is affected by changes in its foreign balance is also a function of the existence of alternative opportunities for employment in its economy and of the ability of its productive resources to shift into alternative employment. In some of the underdeveloped countries, needs are so far in excess of production that there is an insatiable demand for productive services, and, with exceptions, the possible loss in shifting from an already low level of income is limited. In this country, capacity becomes more than ample almost everywhere in periods of decline, so that opportunities for shifting quickly disappear. Even in ordinary times, shifting may be possible only at a great sacrifice to those who find it necessary—a fact fully emphasized by the proponents of tariffs or other forms of protection for domestic producers.

For this reason, a decline in the net foreign balance at a time when the domestic economy is weak is not a matter to be taken lightly. It puts the export industries in an excess-capacity condition along with the others whose demand has fallen and inevitably affects investment expenditures. From the prosperity of the 1920s to the Great Depression of the early 1930s, net exports dropped by about $1 billion; and although this was only one-fifteenth of the decline in private domestic investment, the collapse in the foreign sector added to the debacle.

Fortunately, in the more usual circumstances, net exports are likely to help support the economy, at least for a while after the beginning of a decline. In the spring of 1947, when the easing of domestic demands made goods more freely available, foreigners who urgently needed supplies expanded their purchases and net foreign investment rose sharply, to a peak second-quarter annual rate of $10 billion, or about twice the level prevailing in 1946. This provided a substantial prop to activity generally and helped bring the incipient recession to a quick end. Then, in the next year and a quarter, it dropped all the way to zero, and this loss of markets contributed to the fears that brought on the recession of 1949. Hence, while the United States is less seriously affected by outside influences than are most foreign countries, such influences are by no means insignificant and may on occasion be quite important.

THE DEFINITION OF NET FOREIGN INVESTMENT

Up to this point the discussion has proceeded as if the item to be considered in appraising changes in the foreign sector were the net balance on current account in our transactions with other countries. This current-account balance includes not only merchandise but also services—shipping, travel, financial, and other services that require payment. The net current balance is a relatively simple concept, and to the person concerned primarily with international trade and finance it usually appears as the item best representing the logical objective of his analysis. There is a difficulty, however, arising out of international gifts, and it is this that leads to substitution of net foreign investment for the net foreign balance in the gross-national-product tabulations.

A net balance on current account is in the course of ordinary business transactions a form of investing abroad. Since the excess of receipts due from foreigners over payments due to them requires a transfer of funds, the existence of a net balance involves a change in our claims against foreign countries; and until these accruing claims are settled, they represent investments. The investment may be of a purely short-term character, such as an increase in bank balances or in accounts receivable or in short-term commercial paper. We could regard the export surplus as, in effect, an accumulation of inventories in foreign locations until they were paid for, but the relevant timing would be the current period in which the inventories were transferred and not when the actual money payment was made.

If the account was settled in gold, our investment would take the form of gold purchases. If, instead of taking the gold in payment for goods already shipped, we merely purchased it to add to our existing stocks, foreigners would receive dollars in payment; and when they spent the dollars, exports would be increased, and the value would appear in our net current balance. Of course, they might not spend the dollars at all but merely hold them as reserves; in that case, the transaction would be purely monetary in character, with foreign countries making an investment here that offset ours.

The balance earned in any period might also be placed in long-term investments, as by purchasing securities, buying properties, or constructing facilities to start new enterprises abroad. It is in the context of building new capacity abroad that foreign investment is usually thought of as a means of developing the resources of other nations. Investment in this sense is likely to be a slow process, taking place steadily over a long period of time. When such an investment is undertaken, funds may be immediately committed for the entire project. If so, the later portions of the project, for which funds are merely earmarked, do not affect activity immediately and only become part of investment in a real sense when the funds are actually spent, at which time they appear in the net current balance. In other words, it is the net current flow of goods and services that measures the investment effect in the significant sense.

The change in claims against foreigners thus seems to represent our net foreign investment. But inspection of the net balance on current account shows that it includes net exports which do not involve any such claim. Substantial portions of our export surplus are financed not in a commercial manner but by gifts or grants. The dominant portion of these in recent years has been government grants, but even private gifts and remittances are significant.

These gifts break the equivalence between net foreign investment and the net balance of goods and services. Unfortunately there is no entirely satisfactory way of handling the statistics under these circumstances. The Department of Commerce, after considering various expedients, adopted that of including the net-foreign-investment item in its rest-of-the-world sector and excluding those transactions for which no claims against foreigners are retained. In this system private remittances are treated as personal-consumption expenditures, and government grants are treated as government purchases of good and services. When individuals or the government make gifts to foreigners, they are in effect considered to be "buying" something from those to whom the gift is made, even though the "commodity" obtained is nothing more tangible than good will.

This treatment involves the analyst in some difficulty. If his analysis proceeds in terms of net exports, he must deduct gifts and grants to obtain net foreign investment. Since net exports have been mostly merchandise and gifts have been mostly government grants, differences in these items show a fairly close correspondence with net foreign investment in the postwar period, as Chart 8-1 shows. The differences between the lower two lines on this chart are accounted for, of course, by the balance on service items and by personal remittances.

The data shown on this chart are especially significant in another way, namely, in keeping up with current developments. The analyst must use the merchandise-trade data, because they are the only part of the balance of payments compiled on a monthly basis; and the data on the mutual-security programs, both military and economic, are available in the monthly-exports release. With these data, he can operate almost a full quarter ahead of the balance of payments as such, though, as the chart shows, the preliminary results will be only rough approximations.

Ever since the war, government grants have been important. They began with lend-lease as a means of assisting the war efforts of our allies and have continued with the Marshall Plan and subsequent foreign-aid programs. They have fluctuated widely and to some extent in an artificial manner, because loans and grants have partly served the same purposes. When government loans were high, as in 1947, aid programs were low and net foreign investment appeared to be high; but when loans were exhausted and aid programs took up the slack, the proportions were reversed.

On the other hand, there are arguments in favor of the Commerce Department's method. The fact is that a large portion of the goods shipped

Chart 8–1. Net Foreign Investment and Related Items

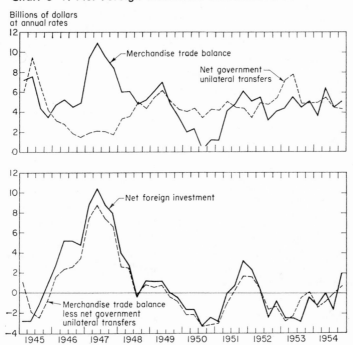

under foreign-aid programs are actually purchased by our government. This is particularly true of military items, contracts for which may not distinguish the part of the output to be turned over to foreign governments from the part held for our own forces, and both may be shipped together under military orders. The decision to exclude all these items from the foreign sector was made just at the close of the war, after lend-lease had dominated our export trade for several years. Subsequently, the military-aid programs of the Korean War period introduced a similar complication. The problem is made more acute by the fact that accounting for the supplies transferred to other countries by our military forces has never been entirely satisfactory.

The alternative to this method would be to consider the gifts and grants as a kind of international-transfer payment and let the net balance of goods and services stand as the gross-national-product entry. From the standpoint of the personal accounts, this would seem to be the better alternative. A goodly part of the remittances are by churches, charitable institutions, and the like rather than by persons; and these expenditures have little resemblance to other consumer purchases.

Anyone interested in reconstituting the gross national product in this way may do so, at least on the annual data. The amounts in the balance of payments for personal remittances and for government grants would then have to be deducted from personal-consumption expenditures and from government purchases, respectively, in order to keep the total the same. The process is complicated in the quarterly data by the adjustment factors used in computing the seasonally adjusted annual rates.

The really important criterion of what should be done would seem to lie in the method of analysis used. Here again questions about the validity of using a net figure arise. Does the net foreign investment really measure what the forecaster wants to know about? And if so, how can it be projected?

ANALYSIS OF THE GROSS FLOWS

Any net figure that is itself a residual from two larger aggregates is likely to incorporate disadvantages like those inherent in the concept of the net government contribution. The first question is: "What are the comparative effects of items on each side of the balance?" Unless it can be shown that the items on each side are of approximately equal effectiveness, the analysis would have to be carried out in gross terms, with a final deduction of payments items to arrive at the gross-national-product total.

In the present instance, the case in favor of such a procedure is not at all clear-cut. Merchandise exports are the largest single item on the receipts side and constitute a fully effective form of stimulus to the flow of income. Even shipments of farm products whose supply is inelastic have definite repercussions on income because of the price response to such shipments: a Department of Commerce study correlating farm income with other factors indicated that for each $1 of farm products exported farmers gained $1.60 as prices rose. On the other side of the balance, the merchandise imports which offset the bulk of our exports go into all kinds of producers' and consumers' goods and generally represent equivalent withdrawals. Possibly they should be weighted down slightly because they include items of a semiluxury character, which are more costly or might not be consumed at all without the special attraction of the foreign label.

On the services side, most items may be considered less directly effective than the merchandise transactions. Transportation charges have been running pretty much in balance, and in any case these expenditures are rather heavily weighted with overhead-type charges, which do not necessarily stimulate additional activity. This country obtains a substantial balance of receipts in the form of income from investments, and these are received in investment accounts, where they may not be immediately reinvested or paid out to consumers. On the other hand, we have a substantial deficit on travel expenditures. These would seem a rather unequivocal form of withdrawal, because the person who is abroad cannot be spending here at the same time; but, again, it is a special category of luxury spending and may in part represent living on accumulated savings rather than redirecting expenditures from current income.

In striking a balance between all forms of receipts and payments, it would appear that the net balance may on the whole be appropriate for purposes of analysis. On the receipts side, there is a combination of some highly active and a smaller amount of relatively inactive items. On the payments side, there is a series of withdrawals which also vary in effectiveness but which seem to conform to an average of the items on the other side rather than to approach any greater extreme. From this point of view, there seems little objection to proceeding in terms of the net balance.

The second question concerns the forecaster's ability to make satisfactory projections of net foreign investment. Here objections to working in net terms are immediately encountered. There is substantial continuity in rates of net foreign investment, and this fact can be used to make short-termed projections. Such projections can be made with a fair degree of accuracy if the analyst has in mind the world conditions responsible for the existing situation and some idea of how those conditions may be changing. It is a hazardous procedure, however, as many important sources of error are likely to be overlooked.

Net foreign investment is, as indicated above, the net current balance adjusted for gifts, and the net current balance is itself the difference between much larger totals of receipts and payments. There is no dependable way of forecasting the net result directly. Autonomous elements in the capital items may be considered separately but cannot depict the over-all behavior of net foreign investment. Only by forecasting the larger totals and from them computing the desired net can the implications of facts and logical relationships be utilized in making the projection.

In brief outline, the method is as follows: Exports depend upon conditions abroad and upon the financial resources at the disposal of other countries. The most important part of the means of financing are provided by imports, which depend upon business activity and national income in this country. Also important are capital movements and gifts. Building up a total of financial resources in this way and then converting it to exports in the light of economic programs and controls established in other countries offer the most valid approach to deriving net foreign investment.

Gifts, particularly government gifts, represent as independent an item as any in the whole constellation making up the foreign sector. It is also an essential item. The forecaster must have it first to forecast exports and then to translate net exports into net foreign investment.

From this point of view, the Commerce Department treatment involves no more difficulty than any alternative that might be devised. It merely forces analysis of an item that should be separately analyzed in any case. Furthermore, the nature of the analysis required becomes clear. It is the same as that appropriate to the analysis of any government program, with the qualification that what the government will do depends in part on the situation faced by other countries. The expert on international affairs can make an important contribution to the forecast, but it behooves him to consult the expert on government fiscal programs, because hardly anything can be taken for granted in this field. The slogan "Trade, Not Aid!" for example, which was taken up in this country and gained so much currency in fiscal 1953, somehow got distorted to aim primarily at reducing the foreign-aid program and only to a minor degree at opening the door to increased imports.

Inasmuch as there are several stages in this process involving estimates of items which have to be derived from the over-all solution—for example, imports from general business conditions—there is something to be said for using the short-cut procedure of projecting net foreign investment itself in order to obtain a first approximation. Later, when the first approximation of the over-all forecast is available, the detailed analysis of the foreign sector can more readily be made.

Until this is done, however, the short-cut projection has to be regarded as wholly provisional and subject to correction in the light of the over-all situation forecast, as that situation is bound to affect action on our part and on the part of other countries.

STATISTICS ON TRADE AND ITS FINANCING

Behind the balance-of-payments data which provide the basic approach to analysis of the foreign sector is a whole complex of statistical series concerning the various items that go into its composition. The basic statistics are those on merchandise trade. These also have the longest history. Governments have typically maintained administrative units for control of trade and collection of customs duties. They have also felt they needed trade information for policy purposes, such policies being represented, for example, by constant attempts to gain advantages through the promotion of trade or through protection of domestic producers against trade. Hence statistics on trade have been compiled continuously over long periods.

The Bureau of the Census compiles monthly data on merchandise imports and exports in sufficient detail to give a practically complete picture of our trade by commodities and areas. These data originate at ports or customs districts and are brought together and tabulated in great detail. Exports are divided first of all into two groups—exports of United States merchandise and reexports of foreign merchandise, which are commonly referred to as "domestic exports" and "reexports," respectively. Imports similarly distinguish between general imports and imports for consumption. Further breakdowns give detail for thousands of commodities and practically all countries of destination or origin. In striking a balance for over-all analysis, the most inclusive totals on each side are used.

The trade statistics are compiled in both value and volume terms. Generally the values stated on the export or import documents are accepted as valid, though some misstatement is known to exist. Volume is compiled in terms of both gross shipping weight, which is of special importance with respect to related data on transportation, and also other units in which each commodity may be measured—number, barrels, and so forth. Ordinarily the analyst who is interested only in the broader questions of trade is confronted with too much detail rather than with too little. However, most of the detail is useful to specialists in various industry or commodity operations.

Statistics on the foreign trade of other countries are also available over long periods. For the more important countries, the record goes back over 100 years and in the case of the United Kingdom for some 350 years. For some areas, these are the only statistics available, and even though not entirely accurate, they may be of some value for special analyses. Again, however, they are frequently difficult to use and are not of great concern to the general business forecaster.

Before inclusion in the balance-of-payments data, the trade statistics are adjusted for omissions and for differences in concept. Among the items omitted from the trade statistics are gold and silver shipments, unrecorded mail exports, and offshore transfers or purchases by government agencies, particularly the military services. For a description of these adjustments and their importance in the postwar years, see *The Balance of Payments of the United States, 1949–51.*[1]

This volume also gives a relatively complete statement of the sources of information and methods used in compiling other items in the balance of payments. It presents a whole series of questionnaires relating to such items as ocean shipping, travel, remittances, and investments, some of which obtain reports covering practically the entire field, and others reports from a sample only. The questionnaire forms are reproduced, and the accompanying text discusses the problems encountered in their use and the nature of the adjustments necessary to obtain the comprehensive totals included in the final reports.

Revised data on the balance of payments in a form consistent with those currently published appear in a supplement to the *Survey of Current Business* entitled *Balance of Payments, 1921–53.* Current balance of payments estimates appear quarterly in the *Survey of Current Business,* accompanied by articles interpreting recent developments. The basic data are given in the detail shown in Table 8–1.

In addition to the summary for all areas, separate columns show the United States balance of payments with specific geographic areas. The selection of areas reflects current interest in particular groups of countries under existing international circumstances, and includes a separate statement for international agencies, such as the United Nations, the International Bank, and the International Monetary Fund.

It may be noted that in 1954 merchandise trade made up almost three-fourths of our total exports and about two-thirds of our total imports. Total exports of goods and services exceeded imports by $5 billion. Since unilateral payments totaled $5.3 billion, net foreign investment amounted to minus $300 million. This was the amount added to foreigners' claims against us. It may also be computed as the net balance on capital account less their gold purchases from us.

The net balance of goods and services was heavily in our favor with respect to Western Europe and in relative terms heavily against us with respect to the dependencies of the Western European countries; but the import surplus from the latter was nowhere near sufficient to offset the export surplus to the former. To the extent that it did provide such an offset, however, it represented the old interwar pattern of world trade, whereby Europe earned dollars by selling its products to colonial and other underdeveloped countries, which in turn earned them by selling to us. This three-way pattern at one time also included the Latin American countries as intermediaries between Europe and the United States, but their trade shifted after World War II and provided us a substantial export balance in 1954.

[1] Supplement to the Survey of Current Business, U.S. Department of Commerce, 1952.

As might be expected in view of the high concentration of unilateral transfers to the countries of Western Europe, reflecting mainly our military-aid program, most of the $1.8 billion increase in foreign gold and dollar reserves accrued to those countries in 1954.

The items following unilateral transfers in Table 8–1 indicate the nature of the net-foreign-investment item for this country in 1954. The continued outflow of United States long-term capital in the form of private direct investments abroad (that is, investments in enterprises controlled by United States business concerns) was supplemented by a large short-term capital movement and substantial portfolio investments in foreign securities. Both long- and short-term government loans were more than offset by repayments of past debt. Transactions almost equaling our private investment abroad came on the side of foreign capital, as foreigners increased their short-term balances by more than $1 billion and also increased their other investments here. Substantial gold purchases swung the over-all balance to their side. After allowance for all these changes, there remained $37 million still not accounted for, which appears as the final item in the table, under the designation "Errors and omissions. . . . "

This item requires special comment. It was originally regarded as a kind of statistical discrepancy, with no particular significance. Year after year, however, it persistently appears on the side of net exports and in some postwar years ran as high as $1 billion. Also, it displays other systematic behavior characteristics, such as regular seasonal movements. For these reasons, it has come to be regarded as a separate element in the picture, probably to be explained in large part as concealed movements of capital to this country. These movements are commonly referred to as "capital flight"; they involve understatement of earnings from shipments to us, overstatement of the value of imports from us, and other unreported transfers that cannot be recorded in the statistics. Thus in the column "All areas" this item may be regarded as an element of foreign investment in this country, like any of the other foreign-capital transactions above it.

In the specific-area columns, however, it has quite a different significance, because interarea payments or receipts in dollars or United States payments in currencies of third countries change the accruals or losses of dollar reserves among those areas. Therefore, the errors or omissions reported in the all-areas column cannot be considered in any sense to originate in the individual areas in the amounts reported for those areas in the last line of the table.[2]

[2] For a more detailed discussion of this item, see the section "Errors and Omissions" in *The Balance of Payments of the United States, 1949–51*, supplement to *Survey of Current Business*, U.S. Department of Commerce, 1952. This volume is practically required reading for anyone who plans to work in the field.

Table 8–1.   Balance of Payments of the United States by Areas, 1954

In millions of dollars

Line		All areas	Western Europe	Western European dependencies	Eastern Europe	Canada	Latin American republics	All other countries	International institutions
1	Exports of goods and services, total	$20,896	$7,269	$702	$30	$3,830	$4,695	$4,295	$75
2	Military transfers under grants, total	3,132	2,312	.....	.....	*	47	773	.....
3	Supplies	2,948	2,167	.....	.....	.....	43	737	.....
4	Services, including freight	185	145	.....	.....	.....	4	36	.....
5	Other goods and services, total	17,764	4,957	702	30	3,830	4,648	3,522	75
6	Merchandise, adjusted, excluding military	12,707	3,483	488	16	2,850	3,312	2,542	16
7	Freight	556	137	43	.....	43	167	166	.....
8	Other transportation	666	382	5	.....	46	144	89	.....
9	Travel	538	48	9	*	311	144	26	.....
	Miscellaneous services:								
10	Private	816	375	13	4	101	163	115	45
11	Government, excluding military	136	72	*	*	2	24	38	.....
12	Military transactions	179	22	*	.....	107	11	39	.....
	Income on investment:								
13	Direct investments	1,665	185	143	.....	236	630	471	14
14	Other private	229	46	.....	.....	133	21	15	.....
15	Government	272	207	1	10	1	32	21	.....
16	Imports of goods and services, total	15,872	4,957	1,063	45	3,034	4,078	2,654	41
17	Merchandise, adjusted, excluding military	10,304	2,024	845	42	2,341	3,434	1,614	4
18	Freight	387	211	23	.....	40	82	54	.....
19	Other transportation	614	284	60	.....	48	161	98	.....
20	Travel	958	344	*	*	284	244	26	.....
	Miscellaneous services:								
21	Private	347	261	7	.....	28	48	10	.....
22	Government, excluding military	248	95	123	2	3	67	46	.....
23	Military expenditures	2,595	1,456		1	192	24	799	28

		C1	C2	C3	C4	C5	C6	C7	C8
	Income on investments:								
24	Private	360	251	4	....	87	13	5	*
25	Government	59	31	1	....	11	5	2	9
26	Balance on goods and services	5,024	2,312	−361	−15	796	617	1,641	34
27	Unilateral transfers, net [to foreign countries (−)]	−5,290	−3,573	−26	−25	7	−138	−1,461	−60
28	Private remittances	−452	−231	−25	−16	2	−47	−135	
	Government:								
29	Military supplies and services	−3,132	−2,312	....	....	*	47	773	
30	Other grants	−1,578	−1,000	*	−9	....	37	472	−60
31	Pensions and other transfers	−128	−30	1	*	9	7	81	
32	United States capital, net [outflow of funds (−)]	−1,528	5	19	4	−423	−535	−435	−163
33	Private, net, total	−1,621	198	12	*	−425	−501	−345	−164
34	Direct investments, net	−761	36	6	....	−469	−102	−160	−88
35	New issues	−309	....	....	....	−167	....	54	7
36	Redemptions	124	11	....	....	89	8	9	....
37	Other long-term, net	−40	67	7	....	145	97	79	83
38	Short-term, net	−635	240	1	*	23	−310	61	....
39	Government, net, total	93	203	7	....	2	−34	90	1
40	Long-term capital, outflow	−306	105	*	4	8	−114	79	....
41	Repayments	−507	335	7	....	11	83	66	1
42	Short-term, net	−108	27	....	*	1	3	77	....
43	Foreign capital, net [outflow of funds (−)]	1,459	1,115	−59	1	51	236	86	201
44	Direct and long-term portfolio investments other than U.S. government securities	225	214	5	*	−40	32	4	10
45	Transactions in U.S. government securities	8	6	2	....	−135	85	2	68
46	Short-term liabilities to foreign banks and agencies	1,234	942	−56	1	230	79	83	121
47	Other short-term liabilities	−8	35	6	....	4	40	5	2
48	Gold sales [purchases (−)]	298	379	*	....	12	69	12	−12
49	Foreign capital and gold, total	1,757	1,494	−59	1	39	167	74	189
50	Errors and omissions and transfer of funds between foreign areas [receipts by foreign areas (−)], net	37	238	427	35	−405	−111	329	

* Less than $500,000. SOURCE: U.S. Department of Commerce, Office of Business Economics.

MEANS OF FINANCING UNITED STATES EXPORTS

Throughout the postwar period, the world economic situation has been dominated by two facts or conditions: the cold war and the superior productive power of the United States. The former is not primarily economic in character but affects economic conditions everywhere. The latter would not be quite so important if it were not for the cold war but is basic to an understanding of international relations.

The cold war determines the current international situation in many ways. Who can trade with whom and on what terms has been largely a political question. What ships can go where for what commodities is a similar question. Every country is affected by the armaments race to some extent, whether that race has opened economic opportunities for it or imposed burdens. Military procurement has added heavy demands in many countries where production was already limited, and the consequence of those additional demands has been inflationary pressure. Everywhere the drive for production has been intensified, not only for war goods but for all kinds of civilian goods and services.

The United States has assumed leadership on one side in the cold war. But even apart from this, important consequences flow from our economic position in the world economy. A broad generalization covering the point would be that this is the one country with a real surplus of capacity over its current needs. We have been able to produce a large military program and a very large investment program based only in part on military requirements and at the same time maintain a very high standard of living. In fact, the military program hardly reached a peak before surplus capacity brought on highly competitive conditions in many civilian industries. These are developments that would not have been possible anywhere else.

In contrast, the over-all needs of other countries have been almost unlimited in relation to their resources. All have aspired to higher living standards. All have sought to increase productive capacity. All have been hampered by shortages and bottlenecks. War burdens have added to economic burdens. Their gold reserves and other external resources have dwindled. Outside help has seemed at times the only means of averting collapse and chaos. The only country they could look to for such help has been the United States. To look beyond all the superficialities of specific programs and transactions, those needs for our goods represent the essence of what has commonly been termed the "dollar shortage" or "dollar gap."

In terms of needs and resources, two groups of countries may be distinguished. First are the industrialized countries, mainly in Western Europe. Second are the underdeveloped countries, mainly in Latin America, Asia, and Africa.

The industrialized countries came out of the war affected by varying degrees of war damage and had to undertake large programs of reconstruction. They faced a situation in which rates of output were generally far below prewar levels and demands were much higher. They attempted to deal with the problem in various ways, maintaining controls and restrictions of various kinds to minimize inflation at home and loss of reserves to other countries. All could clearly improve their productive potentials more quickly with assistance. By 1952, the problem of reconstruction was a thing of the past, though they were still unable to meet the needs of all their programs. In 1953, their growing strength was reflected in a distinct improvement in financial position, as indicated by increased gold and dollar reserves, but the extent of United States government grants still raised a doubt about their ability to meet their needs unaided.

The underdeveloped countries, on the other hand, never had sufficient capacity to meet their needs. Their people always had to get along on the barest essentials, very often on less than a subsistence income. Money incomes in many cases averaged as little as $1 a week, or even less. Few people in this country have any idea of the semistarvation conditions that ordinarily prevail in some of these underdeveloped countries. They sometimes ask: "How can anyone live on an income as low as that?" The answer is: "They cannot. They do not. They die young." That is the main reason why death rates are so high in many of those countries. Conditions are generally being improved, but it will be a long time before satisfactory living standards will be achieved. In the interim, how fast they can be achieved depends partly upon how large a volume of net imports they can obtain.

Thus, even allowing for the fact that this account is greatly oversimplified, there is a pervasive need for our exports. This country is potentially the source of goods that can be obtained nowhere else. The amount bought, however, tends to be limited by the amount of dollars available to foreigners for making purchases here. In these circumstances, the means of financing at the command of other countries is a key factor in analyzing the balance of payments. It is not the whole story, because the outcome depends on their decisions and their business conditions too, but it is a good point at which to make a beginning.

To facilitate this kind of analysis, the balance-of-payments data, with military-aid items omitted, may be rearranged in the form shown in Table 8–2. Forecasting by means of this table utilizes a roundabout approach. The most important item, receipts from foreign countries for goods and services supplied, is placed first, but it is the least predictable and therefore the end result of the whole process. There are so many diverse factors in the international scene which bear on this item that the analyst would be very much adrift in projecting it by itself. In contrast, our payments to foreigners and the funds we otherwise make available to them, as represented by most of the items in the lower portion of the table, are much more predictable. After these have been projected, there is still the problem item, "Liquidation of gold and dollar assets. . . ." The negative sign shown for this item indicates that funds were withheld from current purchases and used to increase foreign holdings of these assets. If the problems involved in estimating these items can be

Table 8–2.   Exports of Goods and Services and Means of Financing, 1954

In millions of dollars

Exports of goods and services (excluding military aid)	$17,764
Means of financing:	
Imports of goods and services, total	$15,872
Merchandise, excluding military	10,304
Transportation	1,001
Travel	958
Military expenditures	2,595
Income on investments	419
Miscellaneous	595
United States government sources	$ 1,613
Grants, excluding military	1,706
Loans, net	−93
United States private sources	$ 2,073
Long-term capital, net	986
Short-term capital, net	635
Remittances	452
Liquidation of gold and dollar assets, including "errors and omissions"	$ −1,794

dealt with successfully, the result is an estimate of the amount of financing that is likely to be used for the purchase of our exports. Once that figure is derived, any of the desired measures relating to the foreign sector can be computed.

FOREIGN EARNINGS FROM UNITED STATES IMPORTS

The largest item by far among payments made by the United States to foreign countries is made up of merchandise imports. The goods imported go in part directly into consumption and in part to industry as materials for further processing or fabrication. The quantities demanded for these purposes are dependent upon consumer income in the first case and industrial activity in the second. Imports can be estimated, therefore, from changes in over-all measures of economic activity.

There are many ways in which this relationship may be set up. Imports in value terms may be correlated with national income or gross national product. Volume of imports may be correlated with deflated national income or the index of industrial production. The import total may be broken into commodity classes, and each of these classes may be correlated with related economic factors, such as consumer expenditures, business-investment outlays, and inventory movements. Similar breakdowns by countries may be utilized. Other factors than income or production may be introduced. The possibilities are almost endless.

A number of studies utilizing such techniques have been made. One of the earliest studies[3] showed that the departure of import values from a simple correlation with national income during the 1930s was the result of the drastic fall in import prices during the depression and the growth of policies and controls which restricted trade. This thesis is supported with data for important commodities, such as tobacco, coffee, sugar, silk, petroleum, and newsprint. Data on income and imports for other countries are utilized to show that imports fell off relative to national income almost everywhere and that imports from the United States were curtailed even more drastically than imports from other nations by the severe trade restrictions imposed in many countries.

A subsequent publication[4] extends the analysis through World War II and the early postwar years. Charts 8-2 and 8-3 from that study reveal how the war disrupted trade in major classes of commodities and how the trade with each continent was affected. The countries directly involved in the war suffered the most serious losses in export markets, and these losses persisted through the postwar years, in which they were unable to attain past rates of output. Studies of important commodities like rubber, petroleum, wool, copper, and newsprint showed that imports tend to be drawn upon primarily to supplement inadequate domestic output.

In still another version of these studies, it was found that results could be improved by excluding a number of key commodities from the correlations and making special analyses of those commodities to add to the computed results for the items remaining in the several commodity classes.

The results obtained from any of these relationships are necessarily subject to adjustment and correction in the light of deviations that have appeared or may be expected. The simplest forms of relationship are inaccurate because the effects of disturbances are so important. Shifts that

[3] Prepared by Hal B. Lary and Associates, International Economics Unit, Bureau of Foreign and Domestic Commerce, *The United States in the World Economy*, U.S. Department of Commerce Economic Series, no. 23, 1943.

[4] Prepared under the direction of Robert L. Sammons, *The Balance of International Payments of the United States*, 1946–48, U.S. Department of Commerce, 1950.

Chart 8–2. United States Imports for Consumption

Actual and calculated by economic classes*

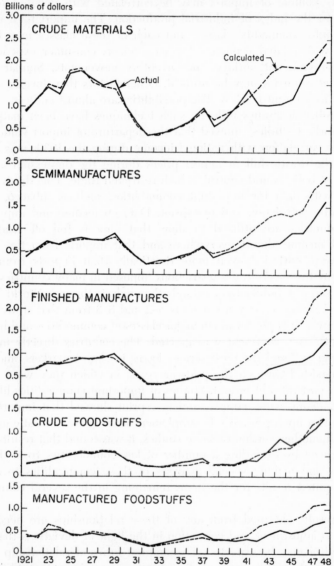

Billions of dollars

CRUDE MATERIALS

Calculated

Actual

SEMIMANUFACTURES

FINISHED MANUFACTURES

CRUDE FOODSTUFFS

MANUFACTURED FOODSTUFFS

1921 23 25 27 29 31 33 35 37 39 41 43 45 47 48

* Calculated imports were derived from the relationship between gross national product and imports for 1921–1938; for crude and manufactured foodstuffs, regressions exclude the years 1934–1937, when drought conditions caused abnormally high imports.

SOURCE: Prepared under the direction of Robert L. Sammons, The Balance of International Payments of the United States, 1946–1948, U.S. Department of Commerce, 1950, p. 50.

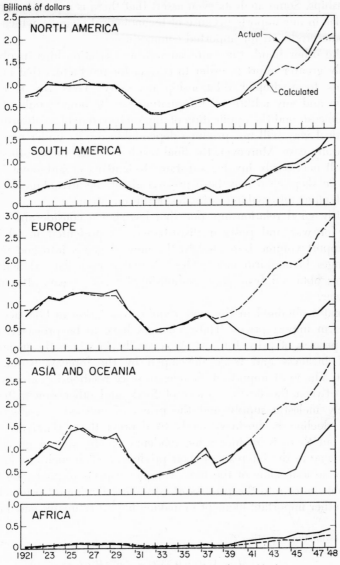

Chart 8–3. United States Imports for Consumption

Actual and calculated, by geographic areas*

Billions of dollars

NORTH AMERICA

Actual

Calculated

SOUTH AMERICA

EUROPE

ASIA AND OCEANIA

AFRICA

1921 '23 '25 '27 '29 '31 '33 '35 '37 '39 '41 '43 '45 '47 '48

* Calculated imports were derived from the relationship between gross national product and imports for 1921–1938.

SOURCE: Prepared under the direction of Robert L. Sammons, The Balance of International Payments of the United States, 1946–1948, U.S. Department of Commerce, 1950, p. 51.

275

last from several years to a decade are produced by wars, abnormal weather conditions, and depression- or boom-induced changes in price relationships. Some analysts even assert that there is a permanent downward bias in our imports because of technological changes which substitute home-produced for imported commodities.

On the other hand, the more complicated relationships involve considerably greater effort in order to correct for the factors that make adjustments to a simpler relationship necessary. Thus any increase in precision and any additional information can be bought only at a considerable cost, and the application of any such system of relationships in a mechanical way will not produce dependable results under new conditions in any case. Moreover, the final result in which these estimates are used will necessarily involve substantial elements of judgment in other places. So skepticism may be expressed about the advantage of putting so much effort into making estimates of this one item.

A fairly good relationship, one that has shown considerable stability except for war and postwar disturbances, is presented in Chart 8–4. Here import volume is related to the flow of goods into end uses and to changes in nonfarm inventories.[5] Actual imports lagged behind the estimates obtained from this relationship for some years after the end of the war.

Estimates obtained in this way require translation to take account of changes in import prices. These changes have to be projected as part of the process of price forecasting generally, in which the general pattern of business and trade developed by the forecast is taken into account. The most important changes in price relationship are, as a rule, those between the flexible prices of foods and other raw materials in relatively inelastic supply and the prices of finished manufactures. A general decline in business tends to depress these relatively flexible prices, but there is an increasing tendency on the part of governments to intervene in the interests of their producers when such circumstances develop, so that some of the more complex aspects of analyzing foreign conditions enter into the process of correcting for import-price changes.

One other important element in making import estimates may be noted

---

[5] The estimating equation is

$$M = 47.3 + 0.533G + 2.67\Delta H$$

where M = import quantity, 1936–38 av. = 100 (*Survey of Current Business*)

G = flow of goods to final users

ΔH = change in nonfarm inventories

Data for the last two items, in billions of 1947 dollars, appear in Table 7–2. Note that the coefficient on inventory changes is approximately five times that on the flow of goods.

at this point—the effect of inventory changes on import demand. When there is an inventory reversal, the rate of liquidation tends to be accelerated as it carries back through the stages of production. At each stage, time is required for the adjustment, so that the imbalance created at

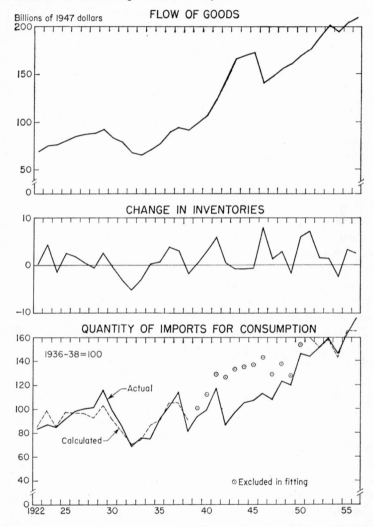

Chart 8–4. Estimating Volume of Imports

that stage is, for a while, at least, greater than in the preceding stage. Then, in order to eliminate that imbalance, a more extreme rate of liquidation becomes necessary. At the raw-material stage, the imbalance tends to become most extreme. If the supply is inelastic, so that surpluses continue to pile up, prices drop sharply. Conversely, during a push to accumulate inventories, prices tend to be bid up sharply. Hence, when an inventory swing occurs in this country, it tends to be exaggerated in terms of our purchases abroad, and special allowance for it has to be made in projecting import volume and prices.

Such movements are perhaps most clearly illustrated by recessions like those of 1938 and 1949, where inventory changes dominated. Even though the 1949 recession was very mild from our point of view, it led to a sharp decline in dollar earnings abroad, particularly in the sterling area, and was one of the factors leading Britain to devalue the pound in September of that year.

Subsequently, as a result of the Korean upsurge, there was a whole cycle that led to another crisis for Britain in the latter part of 1951. After the outbreak of war in mid-1950, the United States immediately began buying up everything it could lay its hands on. It was a general movement, in which consumers, business, and government all participated, to protect against future shortages. The first result of these heavy purchases was to drive prices up and put additional dollar exchange in the hands of other countries. Other importing countries in turn had to pay the higher prices, and they had lagged somewhat in stepping up their own imports. Then, in the spring of 1951, our economy began letting down and the government cut its purchases for strategic stockpiles. The earnings of foreigners were cut by the reversal while they were committed for large imports at peak prices. The initial inflow of dollar reserves quickly turned into a severe drain, and foreign-exchange controls were tightened. Thus the buying wave was reflected not only in our balance of payments but also, after a short lag, in the economic fluctuations experienced by other countries. Again, allowance has to be made in projecting trade patterns when such inventory swings are in prospect.

It may be well to stress in concluding this brief discussion of import estimates that the primary interest is in an over-all forecast, and from this point of view a summary approach may be satisfactory, though it might not be for other purposes. Analysts whose primary interest is in the international balance of payments as such will no doubt wish to make more detailed studies, considering commodity and country developments in the first instance rather than merely utilizing such information for making rough adjustments or corrections. Despite the extreme simplification, errors arising from the summary approach outlined not only are likely to be small but also will be partly offset in the final estimate by matching changes in exports. Before this stage is reached, however, the other items that put funds at the disposal of foreign buyers have to be considered.

SERVICE EXPENDITURES

Transportation charges are closely associated with the movement of goods. Since the importer, not the exporter, pays the freight, these charges relate mainly to our imports. The total paid is relatively stable, tending to rise in relation to total import value on the decline and to fall relatively on the upswing. The reason for this is that transport rates are relatively stable whereas import prices are flexible. Over long periods when basic changes in prices and wage rates are taking place, transport rates move also, and allowance has to be made for this fact, as well as for changes in import prices themselves.

Furthermore, certain long-term trends may be observed in the proportions of our trade carried in foreign ships. The underlying tendency is for a higher proportion to move in foreign bottoms, because their wage scales are lower, and in this occupation their labor is directly competitive with ours. But trends of this character were sharply reversed by two wars, as foreign fleets were sunk, seized, or otherwise made inoperative. The underlying trend is also restrained to some extent by subsidy and other shipping measures designed to keep the United States fleet in condition to meet a future emergency. Immediately after World War II, our payments were only a fraction of our receipts from shipping. By 1954, our receipts had fallen off a little, and our payments had risen almost enough to close the gap. In the light of such considerations as these, our transport payments to other countries may be projected as a time series in relation to import volume with an acceptable degree of accuracy for most purposes.

Another item of importance in the service accounts is travel expenditures. These have been a source of net dollar receipts for other countries for many years, because Americans, having higher incomes and more leisure, can better afford to travel than people of other countries. A considerable travel industry has been built up abroad to take advantage of this fact, and it is rapidly being expanded, in part with United States capital, to provide "luxury" accommodations of a type to which Americans are accustomed but which have not been generally available abroad.

Travel expenditures represent a form of consumer expenditures, though containing some business and other private nonconsumption elements (government travel is excluded), and might be treated in a manner similar to other consumption expenditures. The relationship to income is by all means the decisive consideration, though judgment must be exercised to take account of special factors producing significant deviations. In the late 1930s, for example, well before the outbreak of World War II, travel to Europe fell off sharply as a result of the disturbed conditions abroad. Moreover, there are limitations on the nature of the relationship used, since no satisfactory measure of price changes is available. A simple relationship to gross national product, adjusted in the light of current conditions, produces usable results.

Income paid on foreign investments in this country is a fairly stable item. Miscellaneous private services, which consist in large measure of movie rental receipts, behave in a similar manner. Any error in projecting these by methods of extrapolation, provided available information on relevant changes in the situation is taken into account, is almost sure to be small.

Government purchases of miscellaneous services comprise another item that is usually small and stable. Once the level of our government's nonmilitary operations abroad has been decided, establishments must be maintained and staffs paid year after year.

Government military expenditures abroad include purchases of goods as well as services and include expenditures of military personnel in other countries as well as those of the Armed Forces themselves. The great increase in these expenditures in recent years has resulted in an item that now dominates the entire services group. It, too, promises to be relatively stable after it reaches the planned level. Our military establishments abroad, like the nonmilitary ones, are taking on permanent characteristics. Parts of the program represent aid to our allies. Other parts consist of far-flung bases through which the policy of "massive retaliation" is to be made effective, and they will undoubtedly be maintained as long as the threat of war exists. In other words, military expenditures abroad have to be appraised in relation to the international situation as a whole and to the programs adopted for dealing with it.

GOVERNMENT GRANTS AND LOANS

Government grants and aid to other countries have to be analyzed in the same manner as any other government program. There have never been any definite criteria adopted for use in determining the size of the program. It is related to foreign needs, but we have only rough indications of what those needs amount to, and we do not necessarily allocate supplies to the points of greatest need as defined by any objective standards. The aid program has been almost completely *ad hoc* in character, with no longer-term goals to guide year-to-year variations. It is supposed to be limited in accordance with its effects on the government budget and on potential inflation in this country, but again neither the magnitudes nor the timing can be shown to have been governed by such considerations. What the analysis comes back to is the character of the pressures supporting each year's proposals.

The Marshall Plan was originally set up with the combined support of three primary motivations. The first motivation was the cold war; it was just becoming an important factor in the international situation at the time, but considerable anti-Communist feeling already existed in this country. The second was a group of motives that might be called liberal or altruistic—the desire to help war-torn countries rebuild and to help underdeveloped countries obtain a better standard of living. The third was the self-interest of various exporting groups, who knew that the foreign countries could not buy our products without assistance and therefore that they could sell more if those countries had additional funds. These groups had to contend with a traditional isolationist move- ment and with attempts to minimize the Federal budget and hold down taxation. The opposition was by no means insignificant, and if any one of these three motivations had not supported the Marshall Plan, it prob- ably never would have been instituted.

The history of the program through the next 7 years is that it was cut back on the eve of each new crisis. This was not intended. It merely happened that new war-threatening incidents followed each period of quiet. In these quiet periods, foreign aid, like military programs, were subject to "stretch-outs" and "new looks," which usually reduced expend- itures. This tendency toward drifting along until an emergency prods new action may be fairly typical of both kinds of programs under the comparatively constant pressure to cut government spending.

More and more, the foreign-aid program has taken on a military cast. Almost everything done in the field of international affairs is judged by the government in terms of its effects on the balance of power between East and West. Government grants and loans must perforce be judged in terms of the same considerations that determine military programs generally.

Government loans in part serve the same purposes as grants and may be indistinguishable from them in many respects, though in the case of loans a schedule of repayments is usually made part of the original agreement. The Export-Import Bank is a permanent government agency authorized to make loans for the purpose of financing our foreign trade. Its operations are governed by the general policies of the government as a whole. Credits that would build the economic potential of the enemy are ruled out by the same considerations that ban shipments of stra- tegic materials to the Soviet-bloc countries. Thus, lending has somewhat the same military and political bias as grants, and there is good justifica- tion for treating them in the same way analytically.

World politics also enter into consideration of funds disbursed by the International Bank and the International Monetary Fund. These organi- zations were set up on a fairly large scale. Neither has disbursed any- thing like the potential amounts originally contemplated. There are various reasons for this. Some countries could not have participated satisfactorily, and others perhaps willfully adopted programs that prevented participation. But the operations of these institutions were also immobilized in part by the cold war. It seemed better for them not to act at all than to act discriminately. In the course of time, they might come to play a more important role, but for the time being they were blocked from assuming that role.

In recent years, the International Monetary Fund has been receiving repayments on loans made just after the war. The International Bank has continued to make a moderate number of loans to the underdeveloped countries. By and large, the operations of these agencies are a matter of public record. When they make loans, particularly large loans, announcements are made at the time negotiations are concluded, and these can be used to project subsequent changes in the scale of their operations.

PRIVATE CAPITAL AND GIFTS

Movements of private United States capital provide another important source of funds for foreign use. Immediately after the war, large government loans were more important, but after 1948 such loans dwindled, and private capital dominated the outflow.

Private United States capital flowing to other countries is usually classified as direct investments, other long-term investments, and short-term loans and capital transfers. Direct investments represent the United States equity in foreign enterprises in the management of which our investors have an important voice. Portfolio investments in foreign stocks and bonds are reported in terms of total purchases and sales of such securities during the year. Direct investments, short-term loans, and other long-term loans are reported net, after repayments and redemptions are deducted. This breakdown of the total has definite advantages in making projections, but fairly large shifts sometimes occur and are not easily explained, at least not in the first instance, since preliminary data are subject to considerable error.

The most important and steadiest flow of United States capital is in direct investments. This item has averaged about two-thirds of a billion dollars for the postwar decade. It is a seemingly large amount but is in fact relatively low considering the level of prices and the tremendous expansion that has taken place in domestic investment. It was primarily concentrated in the Western Hemisphere, going at first largely to Latin American countries but later in increasing volume to Canada also. Furthermore, it was highly concentrated industrially; investments in the petroleum industry dominated the total until 1949, and although they subsequently declined while other industries grew in importance, they continued to make up an important part of the total.

Portfolio investments had their heyday in the mid-1920s, just before the great stock-market boom. From a peak of almost $1 billion net, they fell off rapidly during the depression, and in spite of many defaults, redemptions exceeded new issues during most of the 1930s. In the period since World War II, new issues have generally exceeded redemptions, but the margin has been relatively small.

Other long- and short-term investments exhibit somewhat more erratic behavior. On the whole they made funds available during the 1920s, withdrew them during the 1930s, and again made limited amounts available after World War II.[6]

Both the limited amounts of United States capital that have been moving and their distribution close to home bespeak obstacles to international investment. For most countries, the need for capital is actually very large in relation to the amounts received. Most could use more to improve their economies, and the rates of return realized on new investment in many countries are comparatively high. Thus larger capital exports would appear to have advantages for both sides, stimulating economic progress everywhere. Instead, opportunities for foreign investment are passed over. This makes the United States more self-sufficient, circumscribes the dollar earnings of other countries, and magnifies the disparities between income levels here and abroad.

The fears that hamper foreign investment grow out of mistrust on both sides. Each country desires independent control of its own affairs and insists on directing them in what it considers its own interests. Countries needing capital may yet fear that too much outside influence might disrupt their plans and subject their economies to cyclical swings into depression or inflation. We in turn fear that we shall not be able to reap the rewards due the investor who undertakes a risky venture.

Our fears take two forms, which may be described as the theoretical and the practical. The theoretical fears center around the notion that capital exports will be self-defeating, that eventually interest and amortization will rise so high that we shall become net importers and thus suffer unemployment to compensate the added employment which the capital exports initially provide. This is largely a fallacy, though a very persistent one. It overlooks the fact that investment must grow with the economy. It fails to see that the problem is really internal to this country's own economy. The problem is that of maintaining full employment as

---

[6] An extended discussion of our international-investment position, with detailed data by type and by area for the years 1946 to 1953, may be found in the *Survey of Current Business*, May, 1954. See also *Foreign Investments of the United States, Supplement to the Survey of Current Business*, 1953.

new investment and increasing productivity make more goods available with less expenditure of human effort. If that problem is soluble, foreign investment creates no greater difficulty than domestic investment. This theoretical point is not, however, a matter of great concern to the practical man who might be considering a venture abroad.

The practical fears have greater substance. Under present conditions of political instability, the risks of foreign investment are almost prohibitive. The danger of expropriation is serious, as indicated by difficulties in colonial areas all over the world. Even barring outright expropriation, taxes may be made confiscatory or conditions of operation impossibly onerous. Or it may merely be made impossible to realize on the investment, since neither the original capital nor the earnings on that capital may be convertible into dollars. In other words, the investor contemplating a foreign project must consider a complex of economic and political conditions, both favorable and unfavorable. Some investments that were undertaken naïvely were bound to end in failure. The investor, once burned, says, "Never again."

To reduce the risks, proposals have been made for government guarantees against both expropriation and nonconvertibility. Such guarantees cannot succeed without foreign cooperation, and ways around the obstacles to joint action have yet to be discovered. Even if certain governments are friendly, there is no assurance that they will continue in power long enough to justify long-term investments. The threat of world conflict itself bars any such assurance. It is unlikely that any sound basis for confidence in foreign investment can be developed while the cold war continues.

It may seem that this reiteration of references to the cold war places undue emphasis upon a condition that may turn out to be temporary. The point is that such conditions do have a profound influence on our foreign economic relations and cannot be ignored by the analyst. It may be that this particular state of affairs will pass peacefully away and cease to represent a substantial element in toting up the accounts. If so, some other conditions may be equally important. For example, it would be a most elementary mistake to think that satisfactory conditions existed before World War II. The period of the 1930s was merely a different kind of unsatisfactory situation, with a different kind of economic warfare disrupting the world economy. Thinking was dominated then by the problem of unemployment, as it is now by the conflict between capitalism and communism. The fear that the world might return to such a situation in the event of another serious depression in this country is a major handicap to proposals for freeing trade and currency exchanges from the bonds placed upon them in the postwar years.

Disturbed international conditions do not necessarily handicap but rather tend on the whole to augment the other source of private funds flowing to foreign countries, namely, private gifts and remittances. The flow of these payments in large measure derives from the needs created by wartime destruction or other difficulties abroad and from the international movements of people induced by disturbances.

Like any other type of personal expenditure, private remittances are influenced by changes in income. This is true of institutional remittances

Chart 8–5. Private Remittances*

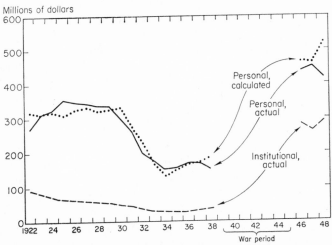

* Calculated personal remittances were derived from the relationship between personal-remittance payments, national income lagged 1 year, and 14-years accumulated net immigration lagged 5 years.

SOURCE: Prepared under the direction of Robert L. Sammons, The Balance of International Payments of the United States, 1946–1948, U.S. Department of Commerce, 1950, p. 109.

as well as personal ones, since these in large part indirectly derive from personal contributions or from earnings on capital assets. Another powerful influence on personal remittances is exerted by immigration. Foreign-born residents of the United States, particularly those who have recently arrived, remit gifts or other payments to relatives or other persons abroad to whom they may be obligated, and these constitute an important part of the total. On the whole, therefore, private remittances constitute a comparatively well-behaved type of payment. Chart 8–5 compares actual remittances with values estimated from their past relationship to national income lagged 1 year and to 14 years' accumulated net immigration lagged 5 years.[7] The downward drift in personal

---

[7] Sammons, *op. cit.*, p. 109.

remittances in the interwar period is thus seen to be accounted for by the decline in immigration.

THE USE OF FOREIGN RESERVES

Even more than in determining gifts or capital movements a broad review of international developments is necessary in appraising prospective changes in foreign holdings of gold and dollar assets. This item is really the key to the forecast of net foreign investment. From the earlier items, prospective changes in the funds placed at the disposal of foreigners through imports, gifts, and investments are obtained. These changes may be taken as an indication of the *derived* changes in our exports, that is, the changes which occur because our own operations affect foreign production, prices, and purchasing power. Our exports will differ from this, however, to the extent that foreign countries may or may not use the funds we make available. If the additional funds are used, exports will rise. If, instead, they are added to reserves, our exports may remain stable or even fall.

The decision lies largely outside the area of our control. It is determined to a major extent by other countries and can be understood only in the light of the conditions those countries face, the policies they adopt, and the actions they take to make those policies effective. Information on these subjects is available from many sources, including the daily press, articles in both popular and specialized periodicals, and official reports of international institutions and agencies of the United States and other governments. Worthy of special mention are *The Economist*, a London weekly, and the United Nations *Economic Reports on Europe*, which include studies made by the Organization for European Economic Cooperation.

The item "liquidation of gold and dollar assets" consists of the foreign-capital items in the balance of payments, both long and short term, including gold movements, with signs reversed, to match the word "liquidation" in the title. The total of these items then has to be adjusted for the transactions of the International Bank and the International Monetary Fund, to take away dollars paid to those institutions but not yet made available by them to other countries and to include the dollars they actually disbursed to foreign countries. The result is the net value of reserves used by other countries in purchasing goods and services here, or if the sign is negative, the amount of dollars otherwise available that was withheld from such purchases.

The possibility that reserves may be used or withheld takes practical shape for the forecaster in two questions: "What level of reserves would foreign countries like to hold? And how much will they be able to build up in the period ahead?" Even though they may wish to build reserves, conditions may force them to run off reserves, at least for a while. This has been the situation of the European countries in about half of the post–World War II years. Reserves are never equally distributed, of course, so that some countries may have adequate reserves, while others are lacking. Yet conditions may prevent even those with adequate reserves from using them or permit them to be used only after a lag, so that the holders keep on accumulating beyond actual needs for a while. This was the situation of many nonbelligerent countries during the war.

The approach used in attempting to answer questions relating to the use of foreign reserves is a combination of the methods used in analyzing government programs and inventories. Changes in reserves are in a real sense the result of government programs, and those programs are determined in much the same way as our own. Also the foreign reserves may be regarded as an inventory, and the considerations bearing on inventory changes are applicable here.

From the latter point of view, the incentive to accumulate will be strong when holdings are inadequate, and liberal spending will be induced when accumulations are large in relation to needs. The needs for reserves vary greatly from country to country. In many countries, they provide the basis for the monetary system, so that their loss would force credit curtailment and deflation, or necessitate changes in the monetary structure. All countries have to obtain goods and services from others in order to maintain essential operations, and without reserves they would be at the mercy of day-to-day fluctuations in receipts. All are faced with the necessity of maintaining production and employment. Without reserves sufficient to carry over a temporary drop in export demand, production in both export industries and industries dependent on imported materials would be adversely affected. Moreover, reserves might be needed to get compensatory domestic activity under way. In short, the reserves required by any country are a function of its own financial and industrial structure and of the degree to which it is dependent on trade. Outside influences are very important to many of them, so that they have to give careful attention to developments the United States ordinarily disregards.

Participation in international finance also affects a country's need for reserves. Great Britain displays a special concern for reserves because of its controlling position in the sterling bloc. If reserves get too low, credit tends to be impaired. In 1949, before the devaluation, there was a wave of speculation against the pound sterling. In such a speculative movement, holders of liquid balances try to convert them to dollars or other "hard" currency, exporters delay receiving payment in dollars on goods shipped, foreign buyers hold off purchases in expectation of lower prices, and domestic importers try to get as much as they possibly can into the country and paid for before the expected change in rates makes foreign purchases more costly. With exchange losses thus occurring on all accounts, what would otherwise be a moderate drain becomes an acute crisis. It is difficult to bring such a movement to a halt unless action is taken to correct the imbalance or until it becomes clear that the reserves will prove adequate after all.

In the early postwar period, needs for goods were so urgent that most countries were willing to let reserves run off in order to get them. In 1947, after our own business situation eased enough so that we could make goods available in quantity, about $4.5 billion of foreign reserves were used up. After the summer of 1949, the movement was mostly the other way. By the end of 1952, with the assistance of the foreign-aid program, the old high was reached, and in each year of the mid-1950s almost $2 billion more was added, raising their total holdings to over $30 billion. This was substantially above the prewar level, but considering the advances in incomes and prices that had taken place over this period, total reserves were still generally regarded as inadequate.

When holdings are inadequate, there are continuous efforts to bring them up, and movements in the opposite direction tend to be sternly resisted. Since rates of accumulation are likely to be moderate as long as demands for imports remain almost universally high, the general tendency to accumulate reserves will persist for some time, probably a decade or more. If and when they can be brought up to the desired level and opportunities to accumulate more still exist, allaying foreign fears, the need to keep on accumulating will disappear and resources will be more fully used in the interest of activities requiring imports.

When reserves are being accumulated, adverse movements that merely bring the accumulation to an end are more likely to be tolerated than those which produce an actual loss. Thus, a $2 billion reduction in the funds the United States was making available in the mid-1950s— whether through imports, investments, or gifts—might have left our exports relatively unaffected, since other countries could then meet the situation by merely foregoing an increase in reserves. But if the total reduction were greater than this, other countries would tend to restrict their imports; and if the drain grew to large proportions, drastic steps would be taken to bring it to a halt.

These are the most likely circumstances to be faced under prevailing world conditions. United States grants and net foreign investment will constantly tend to be offset in part by accumulation of reserves abroad, and situations that cut into those reserves will call forth action to eliminate or minimize the drain. Under other conditions, the other criteria of inventory movements will come into play. Again it is necessary to consider the level of reserves, the rapidity of the change, the reasons for the change, and the effects of other factors that will tend to eliminate the movement or cause it to grow, even though it may not be desired by anyone.

FOREIGN ECONOMIC PROGRAMS AND CONTROLS

What we have to deal with here are the reactions of other peoples to situations created by changes in United States economy or by other international developments in so far as such developments can be foreseen. Foreign countries might react in such a way as to maintain their own plans and programs and thus insulate their economies from outside fluctuations. Or they might modify programs to adjust to changes in the situation and set up or intensify controls to assist them in making the adjustment.

In the event that they hold to a steady course and use reserves to obtain necessary imports, the effect would be stabilizing on the area in which the change originated. Hence any country in effect creates a stabilizing element in its own economy by helping foreigners accumulate reserves of its currency. On the other hand, although economies heavily committed in foreign trade are less likely to be victims of their own instabilities, they become more easily victims of changes coming in from the outside. When such changes are experienced, they may be disregarded if they seem likely to be moderate and short-lived, but not otherwise.

In the event that any country feels it necessary to act, a whole battery of measures is at its disposal. Some of these measures may affect trade directly; others may affect the means of financing it or the terms on which exchanges may be carried out. The tendency today is to avoid the traditional, slow-acting measures, which require changes in price levels, in favor of direct action to accomplish specific changes in the volume of trade or its financing. Even as tariffs are being reduced, quotas or embargoes may be established. Use of foreign exchange may be restricted or exchange rates manipulated. Subsidies or loans may be used to encourage the flow of exports. A combination of such measures must be expected when the circumstances demand extensive action. What has already been done, or is being done, may be taken as an indication of what will be done. So many of these devices have been and are still being used that they need only be reactivated or tightened to produce the desired result.

What any measure will accomplish depends partly on the circumstances. Devaluation, for example, is quite different in a depression period when everybody has excess capacity from what it is in an inflationary period. In the former period, as an attempt to gain an advantage for domestic producers in foreign markets, it may merely make resources idle elsewhere, and such "beggar thy neighbor" policies bring sure retaliation. In a boom period, devaluation may simply pile inflation on inflation. It may then act as a measure of domestic control by helping inflation run its course, squeezing the purchasing power of all whose incomes cannot keep up with rising prices. In this case, no foreign retaliation is called for, since the other countries may merely get more for what they sell to the devaluing country.

In order to judge the course that will be pursued, it is necessary to acquire an understanding of foreign conditions and policies. There are always new problems to be solved, and each situation poses different problems for different groups of countries. Each group responds in a way determined by what it is trying to do and how the change affects its ability to accomplish that objective. Since the impact of any change affects countries in different ways, the reactions from different parts of the world may vary greatly.

One of the major groups to be distinguished in this regard is the underdeveloped countries. They are increasingly aware of the disparities between their living standards and those of the Western world, and their aspiration for improvement provides an unalterable policy goal. To accomplish this, they must engage in special programs of industrialization in addition to public programs carried on in all countries, such as health, housing and public works. The existing state of health, skill and education of their people makes it difficult for these countries to speed progress even when foreign exchange is available. Local resistances to programs of various kinds have to be met. Imports cannot be confined to capital goods, because investment projects require on-site expenditures that raise local incomes; and if domestic supplies of consumer goods are inelastic, the demand for imports may outrun the availability of exchange. Thus, even though progress is strongly desired, it can be achieved only gradually. The earning power of underdeveloped countries is likely to be dependent upon a relatively few commodities; and when demand for these falls, progress may be brought to a standstill, unless reserves of foreign exchange are available or credit can be obtained to keep improvement programs going.

The industrialized countries of Europe have other kinds of problems. Having achieved accumulations of real capital, they are faced with the threat of deflation and unemployment, but their capacity is still limited enough to leave them close to the margin of inflation. They must set their sights on progress, but not too much progress. They must be sensitive to step on the accelerator, to coast along without added power, or to apply the brakes quickly as the situation requires.

Knowledge of what is happening and what is being done about it should, of course, go beyond vague generalizations. There were, for example, important differences in the way various countries of Western Europe attempted to deal with the problem of reconstruction. Great Britain pursued policies of full employment and unimpaired consumption and attempted to maintain real values for the time being through price controls and rationing; not until the devaluation was there a substantial shift away from these policies. Western Germany restricted consumption through a series of deflationary measures in order to get productive facilities rebuilt as quickly as possible. Unemployment, low real wages, heavy taxation, and an extreme of poverty for large segments of the population could be tolerated only because of the special circumstances of a defeated and divided people. France pursued still other policies, with intermediate effects. It attempted to maintain full employment but permitted real wages to decline under the impact of inflation, and this aggravated political instability. Britain and France were handicapped as compared with Germany by the large military budgets they had to maintain. In all countries, the processes of recovery gradually took hold, so that within a decade competition for world markets began to intensify.

As each new situation emerges, it will be necessary to consider how it is affecting important countries or groups of countries. Each is subject to pressures of various kinds. As in the United States, there are pressures growing out of the economic situation, and the difference in circumstances means that the international economy and not just the domestic economy is important. There are also political pressures. Each country has its own warring political groups seeking to gain power, and in the political as well as the economic field external pressures may assume paramount importance.

The approach most likely to ensure understanding of foreign behavior lies in trying to see things from the other fellow's point of view. Our attitudes are often narrow and one-sided. We roundly condemn attempts by other countries to gain special trading advantages for themselves, whereas we merely debate our own use of similar devices in terms of whether or not it represents sound policy.

Foreigners are acutely aware of the fact that we can and do use the devices of trade control to further our own interests. Our financial resources have been so large that certain kinds of exchange control have not been necessary, but quotas, embargoes, and subsidies are in constant use. When we apply such measures against friendly countries

—as through the "escape" clauses and "peril-point" provisions of existing legislation—we violate the free-trade policy for which we officially stand, and we invite retaliation. These protectionist measures, which we are constantly putting into effect despite official utterances against them, inject a substantial element of uncertainty into our foreign relations, but that fact is commonly overlooked.

The forecaster has no need to consider whether one country's policies are better or worse than another's. He does have to know something about what those policies are and what kind of response any change on the one side will bring on the other. The appropriate attitude grows out of recognition that people are much the same everywhere. What happens here happens there also, and like ourselves, they do the best they can under the circumstances.

This in no way denies the existence of differences. The country that suffered major war damage or lived through an extreme inflation is bound to have different attitudes from one that has never experienced those disasters. Reactions to certain kinds of shocks will be correspondingly affected. Understanding the differences as well as the basic similarities that underlie various policies provides insight into the shifts that will be made as the situation changes.

CHAPTER 9

Private Construction

It has become the custom in discussions of construction to begin by pointing out its importance for the prosperity of the economy as a whole. The point is usually made in terms of either the size of the industry in prosperity periods or the wide swings from boom to depression. It is summarized neatly in the following quotation:[1]

> Altogether, the building industry manifests two features that cause it to be the focus of the problem of great depression. The first feature is its huge size, the fact that it is the nation's largest single industry next to agriculture, having a strategic position with regard to the production and employment of almost every other industry in the country. The second is . . . the severity of its fluctuations, the fact that swings in productive activity from valleys to peaks are the widest of any important industry.

The second feature mentioned in this statement implies a qualification on the first: how important the industry is evidently depends in part on the time at which it is measured, whether prosperity or depression. The forecaster soon finds that the time element places a qualification on the second aspect also: how important the swings in construction are to a forecast depends upon the interval to which the forecast applies.

Only in the long-term swings, those corresponding to the peaks and troughs of the long cycle, are the fluctuations in construction extreme. In the short-term movements of business, those running to only a year or two, construction is one of the most stable sectors of the economy or, when it is changing rapidly, one of the most readily predictable. The very idea of a long cycle implies a high degree of continuity from year to year, so that the pattern of change in any year tends to resemble that of adjacent years.

[1] C. D. Long, *Building Cycles and the Theory of Investment,* Princeton University Press, Princeton, N.J., 1940, p. 9.

These facts may be turned to good account by the forecaster, but an understanding of the nature of the construction cycle and its relation to income flows in the economy as a whole is important to dealing with the special situations that constantly arise. The flow of investment in construction is at the heart of the modern theory of business fluctuations. Yet that flow and the long, wavelike patterns it tends to form are governed by the specific characteristics of the product and the industry, so that they assume a good deal of autonomy in the setting of general business developments.

Only the briefest summary of some of those characteristics will be attempted here.[2] The industry has been described as "a service industry undertaking work for others at the time and place desired."[3] The work done is usually to the customer's order, on the basis of drawings and specifications. The great bulk of it, except for speculative home building, is started "only when the buyer appears and places his order."

CHARACTERISTICS OF THE CONSTRUCTION INDUSTRY

The structures created by the industry—whether houses, larger buildings, bridges, dams, fences, sewers, or other objects—are intended to be permanent, at least in terms of the time spans relevant to economic thinking. They are practically never consumed or used up in any particular year, though some are destroyed each year by hazards of one kind or another. As a rule, they are consumed slowly, by providing the services for which they are fitted over a long period of years. The work done in creating them and the services they provide are quite dissimilar, but both are valuable enough to be separately accounted for in current production. That is one reason, in addition to the difficulties of compiling alternative statistics, why the gross national product is gross, why it counts twice the values in these structures and in other capital goods.

Most construction is so durable that, from the standpoint of realistic forecasting intervals, it never wears out. When a building is depreciated at an annual rate of $2\frac{1}{2}$ percent, that does not mean it will wear out in 40 years; it is merely a way of charging the capital value to operations over a long period. Many structures last much longer than that. Century-old houses are fairly common in parts of the country where permanent houses were being built more than a century ago, despite fire and other hazards that have destroyed many houses prematurely. During such a long period, of course, structures tend to become obsolete and may not

[2] A more extended discussion may be found in Miles L. Colean and Robinson Newcomb, *Stabilizing Construction: The Record and Potential*, McGraw-Hill Book Company, Inc., New York, 1952.

[3] *Ibid.*, p. 78.

serve effectively unless renovated. When this happens, it too provides work for the builders.

Once any structure is completed, it remains on hand indefinitely and represents a sunk investment whether or not it is used. If it is left idle for a while, it nonetheless stands ready to serve at any time it may be reactivated. Once a surplus of buildings exists, in other words, it may be used to meet new demands and thus stands as an obstacle to new construction. The surplus cannot be eliminated by consumption, because that process is so slow that there is practically no reduction in the stock of structures available, even when new construction is at a complete standstill.

For practical purposes, the existing stock of buildings is on an escalator that permits no downward movement. Structures may accumulate; they never diminish. Some are destroyed each year as the result of natural or man-made hazards. Others are demolished, mainly to clear sites that are more valuable for other uses. But even in the poorest years, new construction pretty much makes up the current losses. A surplus can be eliminated, therefore, only as the growth in needs is resumed. Demands for structures must come up, because the stock of structures does not come down.

This point must be qualified to some extent by reason of the fact that the structures already built are immobile whereas the demands for them are not. When the need shifts to a new locality, new structures must be built, even though others are standing idle somewhere else. Cities—like civilizations through the longer span of history—grow and die. Ghost towns are reminders that the usefulness of locations may die more quickly than the structures built on them. Conversely, some new needs demand action by builders even in the depths of depression. However, in the great swings of the construction cycle from peak to trough, most localities are pulled along with the tide. Although population movements produce some new building independently of the cycle, mobility itself tends to come with the excitement of prosperity or of war. Migration in the boom creates additional demands in all the favored places, and its waning after the inducement to move is gone helps to deepen the depression.

Even when the pace of construction is fastest, however, the stock of structures in use changes only slowly. Peak rates of building add less than 3 percent a year to the existing stock of structures, and the average over a whole cycle is only about one-half that rate. Following the trough of the depression, several years usually pass before the average rate of increase for the entire cycle is achieved. In the meantime, the stock of structures available for meeting needs remains practically constant. If demand increases by as little as 5 percent, it means several years of expansion for the construction industry. If it increases by 10 percent, it swings the industry all the way from the depth of the depression to the peak of the boom.

The failure of supply to respond quickly to changes in demand is largely a consequence of the fact that so little of the total supply on hand is produced in any one year. It is also, however, a function of the time required to get increased output from an industry that is inadequate to the magnitude of the task imposed.

The processes of production are nowhere near so slow as the processes of consumption in the building industry, but they take a good deal of time nevertheless. In the case of as simple a structure as a custom-built, one-family dwelling, the time involved in planning, contract letting, and actual construction is likely to be about a year. In larger structures, the planning period alone may exceed a year, and the actual work on the site of the project may run over several years.

The fact that the work is local also retards expansion. When a new location is opened, it means building not only the project itself but also living quarters for the construction workers and all the service facilities they need for everyday living. When activity expands in an existing location, it may still be necessary to bring in new workers; some may be transferred from other occupations, but this shift in turn may draw new workers into the community. Expansion of building may even require the organization of new concerns, because existing concerns may feel too much pressed by what they are already doing and refuse to take on new projects. Assembling workers and materials and organizing them to produce the structures ordered, each project being new and different in various ways, is a time-consuming process. Prefabrication and other large-scale operations contribute something to shortening the period of time required, but these developments are a necessary phase of evolution in an industry called upon for successively higher peaks of output.

Getting construction going may be described in economic terms as a problem in moving resources. People who are already employed do not move readily, and even the unemployed may hesitate to move into what looks like both temporary and hazardous employment. Employers as well as workers often find it hazardous employment, for the risks are financial as well as physical. Work and gains may be only temporary, not sufficient to compensate for subsequent periods of idleness. A miscalculation may be ruinous, and when the boom collapses, many are sure to fail. To call forth the necessary efforts, high rewards are essential, and even though high wages and high prices are willingly paid during a period of high demand, it takes not just months but years to get an efficient construction industry organized in any locality after a period of quiescence.

After the industry has been operating at high levels for a while, downward adjustments in production are almost as hard to accomplish as were the increases that brought them to the peak. The builders have just been through a period of practically limitless demand. During this period, instead of there being idle structures to satisfy most buyers, the construction shanties had to compete for labor and materials with the home buyer. Immediately after, it is hard for the builders to believe that the boom is ending; they are reluctant to curtail their operations before the market is clearly saturated. Some have commitments that cannot be canceled. Others who have been building solely on contract may shift their operations to speculative home building. Many will not quit until they have actually been burned. An attitude common among the most aggressively competitive is: "Let the other fellow fold if he can't stand the gaff!" Overbuilding in many localities is inevitable.

The boom usually tends to overcarry in a burst of excessive optimism that aggravates the ensuing surplus. In this respect it differs from the depression, where there is practically no incentive to let a deficiency develop. Yet, in the trough of the depression, there are surpluses of builders as well as structures, and discouraged builders continue to fail or decide voluntarily on closing shop for some time after the nadir of demand has been passed. The crossing of declining industry capacity and reviving demand is so gradual that it is not immediately evident in the early stages of recovery. By the time it is apparent that recovery is under way, the industry is still comparatively inactive, and the unavoidable lags in adjusting to the new situation permit a deficiency to develop. However, even at the low, operations tend to be more than sufficient to keep the total number of structures in existence from declining.

The total stock of structures thus tends to be relatively stable in relation to changing aggregate demand for them. The number holds steady when the pace of building is low; it increases when new building is high but does so only slowly. Hence occupancy at any given time depends upon what exists, not upon what is being built. With the supply of structures so inelastic, their prices are bound to fluctuate widely. Capital values are bid up in the boom as new demands focus on buildings already in use. They fall sharply in the depression, when owners offer buildings at a sacrifice because they would otherwise remain idle or because lenders insist on protecting themselves as far as possible against further declines. Here, again, there are risks and rewards of a magnitude that tend to stifle or overexpand construction activity.

The swings between almost complete idleness and almost intolerable pressure help make the industry what it is. From a long-run point of view, needs change only slowly, but actual demand tends to be concentrated in limited periods of high activity and high incomes until, being finally satiated, its force is spent. The industry then slips back into the doldrums for a period long enough to render it ineffective in promptly meeting the requirements of the next upsurge. High variability of demand combines with the lack of fixed working sites to limit the organization of permanent, efficient working units. Each depression hampers the adjustments needed in the succeeding boom, and each boom in turn lays the ground for the next depression.

THE NATURE OF THE CONSTRUCTION CYCLE

It has for some time been the accepted doctrine that the major fluctuations in construction activity conform to a fairly regular cyclical pattern of almost 18 years' duration. A series of research projects, carried out since the early 1930s, have brought together scattered statistics that go back over long periods—in one case, more than 100 years.[4] These studies agree that there has been a cycle, varying in duration from 15 to 21 years, whose peaks and troughs roughly coincide with major peaks and troughs of general business activity—though shorter swings in general business largely unrelated to construction activity are also recognized. The conclusion frequently drawn from these studies is that the construction cycle is one of the most dependable phenomena in our economic history and therefore one of the most dependable tools for the forecaster.

Practically all discussion of the construction cycle has been confined to the activity of creating new structures, with little or no regard to the over-all supply of structures in existence or to the underlying needs those structures are intended to serve. In contrast, discussions of growth, in which the latter aspects of the situation appear, have usually treated the cycle as something superimposed, which modifies or retards rates of growth from time to time, but have not attempted to explain the cycle in relation to the long-term supply and demand factors under consideration. From the former point of view, it may be concluded that high rates of construction saturate the market after a few years. From the latter, it may appear that the cycle carries various measures out of line with the trend, both in prosperity and in depression. From either, it may be seen why the sharp advances and setbacks of the cycle bring cumulative forces into play. But from neither alone can it be seen why the reversals are unavoidable.

Both points of view are satisfactorily combined by regarding the construction cycle as a special kind of inventory cycle. In this perspective, it is clear not only why the movements are cyclical in character but also

[4] See *ibid.*, appendix N, for a discussion of the data underlying the measurement of construction activity over this period.

why the cycle is long. The movements gain momentum because construction reacts on income, which in turn creates demands for additional construction. In relation to income, a deficiency of structures develops. The rate of construction must be pushed above the rate required by current needs and income in order to eliminate this deficiency. After it has been eliminated, construction must be slowed to halt the accumulation. But the slowing of construction, like the curtailment of production to halt the accumulation of any other kind of inventory, is not merely the cessation of an upward movement; it is the beginning of a decline.

A difference appears because inventories fluctuate between accumulation and liquidation, whereas construction always remains positive. This difference is merely superficial. Output from the lines of production that create inventories cannot fall below zero any more than construction; it merely falls below consumption. Moreover, the process of consuming structures is going on all the time, even though existing structures are not visibly affected in a short time, and there is no reason why construction may not fall below this semiconcealed rate of consumption.

Another difference lies in the way the construction cycle flows through its long span of years in seeming disregard of short-term business movements. Sometimes a business reversal severe enough to affect almost everything else, like that of 1937 and 1938, will produce hardly a ripple in the long sweep of construction. This independence is, however, no more than a result of slowness in making adjustments. Several years may pass before a deficiency of buildings can be met or before growth demands a resumption of building.

The disparities underlying these slow movements carry over the period of most inventory cycles. Construction may be slowed during the adverse movement of an inventory cycle, but work in progress or under contract cannot be stopped before such movement has run its course and the short cycle again turns in conformity to the construction cycle. Specific cycles vary in characteristics throughout the entire realm of industry. In no other industry do adjustments require so much time to work themselves out as in construction.

Considered in this light, construction fits into the theory of money flows in exactly the same way as inventory investment. Construction is, as a matter of fact, the kind of investment that fits the investment-savings models as a determinant of income in the truest sense. It adds to income and consumer spending without at the same time adding to consumption. It is work whose product does not displace workers in other industries competing for current income. It provides an outlet for savings, and it typically consists of such large units that it requires outside financing. Thus it puts past savings to work and draws upon the expansive powers of the banking system. The lenders find opportunity to put their funds to work and are given a voice, with the owners, in initiating and directing activity. Many resources and efforts combine into a surge of activity that lifts the economy from stagnation to prosperity.

As an advance gets under way, expanding demands for floor space are first met by increasing the utilization of existing structures and by bringing idle structures back into use. During this period, construction tends to lag; but total demand in an economy with an appreciable rate of growth must eventually catch up with the existing supply. When relatively full utilization of existing structures has been achieved, the response of construction quickens, but rising demand is by then definitely ahead and is still moving up. Delays in planning and building help prevent construction from making up the deficiency, and for a time demands may even go on increasing faster than the stock of buildings available. As construction is speeded, the effort to remedy the deficiency is for a time self-defeating, because the rise in income stimulates new demands and provides the financial basis for carrying out new projects. The flow of savings is expanded. The prices of existing buildings are bid up, and lenders who see opportunities for loans with improved security make additional commitments. There can be no early stopping point, because the interacting forces mutually support each other, driving the economy and the industry upward as long as the deficiency of structures persists.

The economy does have the resources to provide the needed buildings, however, and in the course of time those resources are organized to meet the need. The greater the deficiency, the further the upswing of construction must progress. It eventually achieves a rate sufficient not only to meet current demands but also to work off the backlog. But once the boom has worked off the backlog, that rate begins to produce surpluses and cannot be maintained.

Even if new construction began to be adjusted downward as soon as the supply of houses was in line with needs, an actual surplus would develop. During the time in which the adjustment was being made, the supply would continue to expand; and since the adjustment would involve a decline in income, needs would tend to fall. Hence, in relation to the new level of income, the total stock of existing structures would be redundant.

Conversely, in the depression, activity having been lowered sufficiently below requirements for growth to bring idle structures back into use, new construction would have to be expanded to keep the supply of structures in balance with needs. But the slowness of the adjustment would let demand get out in front, and since the expansion of construction increases incomes, demand would be pushed up still further. Hence, in relation to the expanded level of income, the stock of structures is bound to be deficient. If these initial adjustments were made quickly, the succeeding phases would be both moderated and shortened, but they could not be eliminated entirely.

Before a boom ends, as a rule, vacancies begin to appear, first in just a few localities but then becoming progressively more prevalent. The stream of new projects dwindles, and the industry begins grinding to a halt. Each time operations are cut back, income falls and the need for building diminishes still further. Since the process of adjustment is slow, the slide may be gradual at first. The implications of that gradual slide may not be immediately apparent. Business in general may even hold up for a while, because equipping the new structures and communities tends to lag behind their construction. Hence, when general business falls, the crucial downturn that ends the boom may appear to result from changes in other factors.

As business declines, the whole interacting process works in reverse. The stock of structures becomes increasingly redundant, and the drop in construction is accelerated. Lenders become fearful of their security and either seek to liquidate existing loans or at least restrict new commitments, forcing construction down still faster. Workers who are laid off sit still for a while, waiting to be called back. With occasional periods of employment, some remain hopeful of improvement through the dreary years. Others seek opportunity elsewhere, but many find it only at somebody else's expense, since the decline in income is creating unemployment in other industries also. The process is the same "vicious spiral" that characterizes the downswing of commodity inventories.

Cycles of varying length in various lines of production may run concurrently, of course. The short inventory cycle may at times reinforce and at times offset or restrain the swings of the construction cycle. Both, moreover, tend to be supported by interrelated changes in other factors. However, most of what has been said applies primarily to private construction, and there is at least the theoretical possibility of offsetting such movements by compensatory adjustments in government spending. Whatever the merits such a policy eventually may prove to have, it is clear that the really sharp swings in business will continue to occur when the various cyclical factors are moving in phase; and although substantial stability may exist when they are moving out of phase, such stability is only temporary and will disintegrate into the next sharp swing as the quickest-turning factor reverses. There can hardly ever be any true stability in an economy governed by forces that change in this manner.

Recently the view that the construction cycle repeats itself with great regularity has been challenged by Colean and Newcomb in their work entitled *Stabilizing Construction*. Chart 9–1 presents their compilation of the best available data from the time of the earliest available records. Superimposed on their data is a long-termed trend line. Note that the

chart is on a semilogarithmic scale. Before 1915, the data represent a
3-year moving average and are adjusted in other ways. The chart clearly
portrays the tremendous swings of the great cycles following the Civil
War and World War I. (A third such cycle appeared to be in progress
at the end of the period shown.) Of the existence of interim cycles—
those ending at the turn of the century and during the period of World
War I—they are doubtful. They point out that in those situations there
were only minor declines in activity. If the term "depression" fits, it is

Chart 9–1. Dollar Volume of New Construction, 1831–1951

1920–29=100

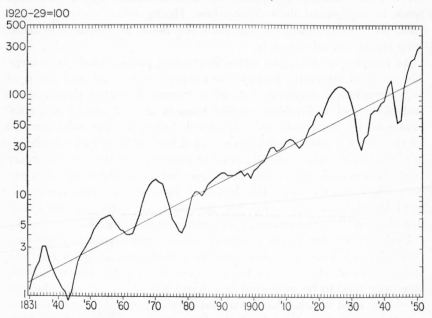

only because activity dipped somewhat below the trend line, and not
because any major decline occurred. On this basis, they conclude:[5]

> The supposed regularity of major construction cycles over a long period
> of time thus does not appear to be proved. Therefore, we may not infer
> that the forces that have caused the spectacular distortions in the flow of
> activity such as we have encountered twice in the 80 years before World
> War II are due to characteristic combinations of influences either in the
> construction industry or in the economy as a whole. They may be phenomena
> brought about by the very special circumstances among which war obviously
> plays a crucial part.

This conclusion appears in some respects rather strained. The authors
ignore the data before 1860 because they regard them as too sketchy to

[5] *Ibid.*, p. 57.

warrant dependable conclusions. They also insist on throwing all kinds of construction together, which smooths the cyclical swings somewhat, as, for example, during World War I, when military and other government construction offset declining private construction. On the other hand, it must be conceded in their favor that the wartime declines in construction were not properly to be considered cyclical declines in the first place, since they are the special result of disturbances and restrictions.

Their case appears to be entirely sound with respect to the lack of regularity in the construction cycle, whether it is regarded from the viewpoint of timing or of amplitude. In the construction cycle, as in any other inventory cycle, the underlying forces and controlling conditions vary with each new situation, so that there could hardly be a sound demonstration of precise regularity. Their case appears weaker with respect to the nonexistence of such cycles. The fact that the most extreme cycles have followed great wars is not evidence that something of the same sort does not occur at other times. The great postwar cycles may, on the contrary, be regarded as merely more revealing than the others. They put the full nature of the beast on display, and although he does not perform with equal ferocity on all occasions, the threat of similar misbehavior is always present.

SHORT-TERM MOVEMENTS OF CONSTRUCTION

Even though the construction cycle is accepted in principle, there are many difficulties in applying it to actual forecasting situations. Applying a fixed pattern mechanically will certainly result in frequent errors. The least precaution that must be observed is to modify the cyclical pattern in accordance with knowledge of any special influences that may be affecting it. For example, when the upward phase of the cycle is interrupted, as it was in 1942 by the war, the whole boom must be shifted across the war years to the postwar period, and in addition the boom has to be increased in amplitude or duration, or both, to take account of the backlog accumulated during the period when activity was artificially restricted. With such adjustments, an approach to realism in the projection of the cycle can be achieved.

In most forecasting situations, however, there is no occasion to apply any extended cyclical pattern. Seldom is a forecast expected to cover a period of as much as 5 years, and seldom could any be considered realistic for as long as that, but this is only enough to include the movement into the next phase of the cycle. For shorter intervals, the cyclical pattern as a whole is largely without significance.

The year-to-year changes in construction activity are usually very limited in comparison with some of the more volatile factors. This is particularly true in the boom and depression phases, when a level tends to be maintained, so that changes in the value of construction activity from one year to the next may be only $1 or $2 billion. But even in a major swing of construction, when potential annual changes could run to $5 billion or so, the construction change in a single year might be only a fraction of the swings in inventories that sometimes occur in the same span. The way construction runs to extremes, passing even the major swings of inventories, is by chaining a series of these relatively limited changes together over a period of several years. That is how some 80 percent of total construction activity was wiped out in the major decline of the early 1930s. But in that decline, less than $3 billion, or only about one-fourth of the peak level, was lost in any one year.

From Chart 9-1 it may be seen how little construction activity was affected by the business setbacks of 1921, 1938, and 1949. This would not be true of other situations to the same extent, because all three of these reversals came when construction was in a relatively strong position, so that they do not reflect the full responsiveness of construction to changes in business activity in general. The most serious of the three declines was that of 1921, but then a wartime backlog as well as the rising phase of the cycle supported construction activity. In 1938, the construction cycle was again entering its strongest upward phase, and the industry received an additional stimulus from the new government mortgage insurance program. In 1949, the backlog was again large, and construction contributed very little to a recession that was for other reasons so moderate as to present no real obstacle to the boom. Even though these specific instances are discounted on the indicated grounds, the industry does tend to display a high degree of short-run stability despite its volatility over the cycle as a whole.

Part of the explanation for this lies in the long-drawn-out processes of adjustment. Another part lies in the fact that the immediate response to changing business conditions appears in new orders, that is, in new contract awards, rather than in construction activity as such. The actual work of building lags behind the letting of the contract, of course, and work based on contracts already let continues through a period when new contracts are being withheld. Then, if the reversal proves temporary, the contracts withheld will be reinstated and new projects will be started before the letdown has fully affected activity in the field of operations.

The relation of activity to contracts is known as a "distributed lag." The portion of the work put in place in each of the months following the letting of a contract tends to follow a typical pattern. The total value of the contract is distributed over the months in accordance with the pattern of construction activity appropriate to the specific kind of project undertaken. Since some projects take 2 or 3 years to complete, current activity may be reflecting contracts awarded 2 or 3 years earlier. When all the contracts awarded over an extended period of months are distributed in this manner and the distributed portions falling in each month are retotaled, the result is a measure of activity for that month.

The effect of redistributing total values in this way is to smooth out the short-term variations in the original contract awards, just as they would be smoothed by a moving average. The result is in effect a weighted moving average of the original awards, centered at a point following the letting of the contracts by roughly half the time it takes to get the average project completed. As a result of this smoothing process, erratic fluctuations in contracts are ironed out and may not show up at all in activity. Contracts may vary all the way from zero in one month to several times the annual average in the next without producing more than a ripple in the course of activity.

Construction contracts awarded have been compiled by the F. W. Dodge Corporation since 1901. They show highly erratic movements, particularly in the nonresidential category, where a single large contract may represent a greater total value than all the other contracts let in the same month, or even in 2 or 3 adjacent months. In order to reduce these erratic movements to manageable proportions, the Federal Reserve has reconstructed the original series by taking a 3-months moving average and adjusting it for seasonal variation. These data are shown in Chart 9–2. The adjusted series still shows erratic tendencies, but it has some usefulness in this form as a "leading" indicator of business.

Because of the inherent relationship between contracts and work put in place, a short-term forecast of construction activity—up to about 6 months ahead—may be derived from current contract awards alone, though judgment is essential in evaluating erratic movements in the awards series. For residential construction, building permits issued by local authorities provide a better indication of work authorized than contract awards. The procedure for using these authorizations in short-term forecasting is basically the same as that used in deriving the activity estimates from them.

There are no systematic reports from projects under way about work actually put in place except for large Federal-government projects and for some projects undertaken by railroad or large public-utility companies. For these, accounting and capital-budget records are utilized, but for the great bulk of construction, including state- and local-government construction, the data rely mainly on contract awards and building permits, adjusted to correct for coverage and undervaluation and distributed with appropriate lags to put the timing of the total value on a "work-put-in-place basis."

The residential-construction series is dependent primarily upon re-

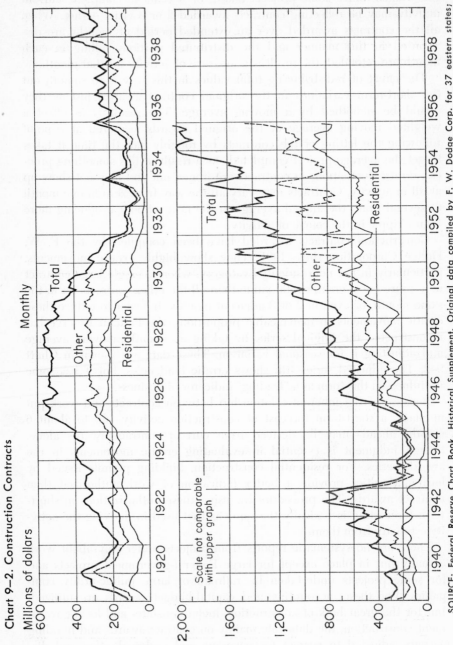

Chart 9–2. Construction Contracts

Millions of dollars

Monthly

Total

Other

Residential

Scale not comparable with upper graph

SOURCE: Federal Reserve Chart Book, Historical Supplement. Original data compiled by F. W. Dodge Corp. for 37 eastern states; 3-months moving average adjusted for seasonal variation by Federal Reserve.

ports of building permits received from local-government units.[6] The permit originates as a device for enforcement of control and regulatory measures enacted by the governing authorities in whose jurisdiction the work is to be done. These laws were designed by the governing units to enforce standards of sanitation and safety and to improve land use and property values by zoning. They also to some extent encourage or enforce monopolistic practices on the part of the builders or building-trades unions, but these unfortunate aspects may be regarded as by-products, as are the building statistics obtained from the permits issued.

Building permits typically understate the value of the work actually to be performed, frequently because of the applicant's assumption that tax assessments may be lower as a result. Before World War II permits were estimated to understate actual costs by about 15 percent. Just after the war the estimate rose to 25 percent, but by 1954 it was back to 15 percent. On the other hand, not all the permits issued actually result in building, and on some projects months may elapse before work is actually initiated. Special surveys are made from time to time to obtain the adjustment factors and starts patterns needed to correct for these deficiencies.[7] A typical pattern for residential building used in the early postwar period was as follows:

Month of start	Percent of units started during specified month	
	Urban	Rural
Never started	1.5	1.2
Permit month	56.8	59.2
1st month following	30.5	29.6
2d month following	6.3	6.0
3d month following	3.7	4.0
4th month following	0.8	
5th month following	0.4	
Total	100.0	100.0

Preliminary tabulations of the permits data are made each month to obtain the number of dwelling units on which work was started, disregarding the ultimate total cost of the work involved. Since average values for such a large number of units do not change much from month to month, the number of units started provides a fairly accurate and quick representation of work to be done. Chart 9–3 shows the seasonally

[6] For a description of methodology, see *Techniques of Preparing Major BLS Statistical Series*, U.S. Bureau of Labor Statistics Bulletin 1168, 1954.

[7] See Kathryn R. Murphy, "Contractors' Use of Home-building Permits Issued," *Monthly Labor Review*, January, 1952.

adjusted monthly starts for more than a decade after the end of World War II.

Work put in place in each month after the start is measured as the percent of total construction cost incurred during that month. To convert starts into activity, therefore, a distribution-of-cost pattern is needed. The distribution used during most of the postwar decade was as follows:

Month	Percent of cost incurred during specified month
Month of start	13.1
1st month following	29.4
2d month following	25.0
3d month following	15.6
4th month following	8.4
5th month following	4.2
6th month following	2.2
7th month following	1.0
8th month following	0.5
9th month following	0.3
10th month following	0.2
11th month following	0.1

(The first four rows, Month of start through 3d month following, are bracketed together and marked 83.1%.)

This distribution assumes a total construction period of 12 months. The actual period might be shortened somewhat without modifying the result, since the last few months contain so little of the total. The percentages in the early months would have to be modified substantially to make any important change in the final result. More important in this respect would be changes in the starts pattern, since starts might be deferred and permits allowed to lapse during a decline. It should be emphasized that both of the patterns shown are appropriate to a situation in which activity is at a high level and would have to be modified in other circumstances.

The series on private nonresidential building is compiled in a similar way. In distributing expenditures made under the contracts awarded, it is assumed that all projects are started in the month following the award. It is recognized that this is a questionable assumption, but starts on nonresidential work are relatively prompt, because contracts usually call for as early completion as possible. Current information on the actual pattern of starts would be the only means of effecting a distinct improvement, and such information has not been available.

Beginning in the month following the award, the values for each type of project, taking into account not only the nature of the structure but also its size and the season of the year, are distributed over an appropriate period of months. For this purpose, a whole series of patterns has been established, on the basis of surveys of thousands of actual projects. Most buildings follow a pattern somewhat like that shown above;

expenditures rise rather quickly, flatten near the peak, and then taper off. Small buildings valued at less than $100,000 might be completed in 6 months or less; work on large buildings, running to values over $2 million, might be extended over 2 years or more. Other types of projects, such as roads or sewers, rise more abruptly toward the peak rate and also fall off sharply, making a relatively flat pattern throughout the construction period. The over-all result is a composite governed primarily by the character of the work undertaken in each period.

Chart 9–3. New Private Nonfarm Dwelling Units Started, 1946–1956

Seasonally adjusted, annual rates

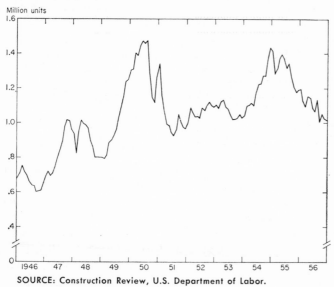

SOURCE: Construction Review, U.S. Department of Labor.

There are a number of arbitrary elements in the procedure of distributing contracts or permits data in this way. For example, various kinds of delays encountered in the construction process are of necessity passed over. During the period just after World War II, when shortages were known to be delaying projects, the patterns were modified accordingly, but ordinarily this cannot be done. However, errors introduced in this way probably do little violence to the construction picture in most periods. On the whole, the procedure gives a good approximation of what is happening in the field. It puts the activity series on a more nearly coordinate basis of timing in relation to employment in construction and to the money flows it is desired to measure.

Other kinds of construction are subject to nontypical influences and in some cases are measured by special procedures. Data on state- and local-government construction are derived in the same way as private nonresidential construction, but the bulk of Federal construction is reported by the agencies under whose supervision the work is done—military by the Department of Defense, highway by the Bureau of Public Roads, and public residential by the Housing Authority. Railroad and utility data are reported in much the same way as public construction, but the reports are made on an annual basis only. The railroads report to the Interstate Commerce Commission, the electric utilities to the Federal Power Commission, and gas utilities to the American Gas Association. Telephone construction is reported by the American Telephone and Telegraph Company. These are the important segments, and the annual data are generally adequate. The problem lies in keeping current between annual reports, which are themselves available only after considerable lags. However, this kind of work has a very long construction period and in the aggregate therefore tends to display a high degree of year-to-year stability.

The weakest segment in the whole construction picture is farm construction. Errors and omissions in this field, however, are not considered to have any considerable effect on the construction picture as a whole. Much of the work is done by the farmers themselves, and it may be charged to current expense or otherwise omitted from capital values. Work of this kind cannot swing the economy in the same way as the major swings of the nonfarm-construction cycle.

These estimates of construction activity are initially obtained in dollar terms, and price changes have important effects in these terms. For this reason, construction-cost indexes have been compiled for the longer period covered by the national estimates, beginning with 1915, and these have been used to deflate the value data in order to obtain estimates of physical volume. The deflated data are available monthly for the postwar years.

The construction-activity data are supplemented by reports of employment in two forms: the numbers of workers employed by construction contractors, by type of contractor, and the estimated labor required for new construction, by type of construction. The data on contractor employment are available annually from 1919 and monthly from 1939. In the postwar period these data are available by states and also by selected metropolitan areas. No differentiation is possible by type of construction on which the workers are employed.

The Departments of Labor and Commerce issue monthly reports bringing the various estimates and indexes up to date. These are supplemented periodically by basic statistical reports containing the back data as far as they are available. Each year the two agencies, jointly and in consultation with other experts in the field, prepare forecasts of activity in the following year. These embody a systematic review of all the information available on various types of construction and are therefore of considerable value to anyone not specialized in this field.

FORECASTING RESIDENTIAL CONSTRUCTION

In forecasting residential construction, two methods have commonly been used: the first consists of projecting the cycle; the second attempts to appraise the various forces or factors influencing the level of housing activity and make forward estimates consistent with anticipated changes

Chart 9–4. Residential-building Cycle, 1830–1937

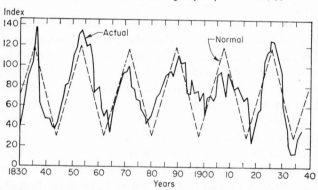

SOURCE: By permission from Business Forecasting: Principles and Practice, by Frank D. Newbury, McGraw-Hill Book Company, Inc., New York, 1952, p. 137.

in those factors. The second method is coming into most general use, but the first may retain some value for the forecaster who is able to use it properly.

The cyclical movement is shown in Chart 9–4 as an index constructed from original data showing deviations from a trend, together with a kind of idealized 18-year cycle computed by Newbury to portray the regularity of cyclical advances and declines. In discussing this cycle, Newbury states:[8]

[8] Frank D. Newbury, *Business Forecasting: Principles and Practice,* McGraw-Hill Book Company, Inc., New York, 1952, p. 137. For a discussion of the original data, which were compiled by John R. Riggleman, see Colean and Newcomb, *op. cit.,* appendix N. As the series is extended backward, the number of cities on which the data are based dwindles continually. At the beginning, in 1830, the sample contained only three cities; by 1875, the sample included 20 cities; from 1900 on, the sample contained 65 cities.

This cycle has a characteristic length of 18 years which has been very regular throughout its recorded history of a full century.

. . . it is responsible, under peacetime conditions, for the long periods of prosperity and also the long serious depressions. Since a long depression in 1840–1843, we have never had a major period of prosperity that was not also a period of boom in residential and other construction, except during three major wars. Since 1840, we have never had a long depression that was not also a period of depression in building.

He goes on to point out that "even this most dependable cycle is not infallible in its movements. . . ." After discussing some necessary modifications of the pattern for a postwar projection, he quotes an end-of-1946 forecast in which he successfully predicted prosperity in the early 1950s, primarily on the basis that the construction cycle was entering its boom phase.[9]

The common practice in computing idealized cycles of this kind is to round the peaks and troughs so that the pattern conforms to a smooth curve. This has some advantages, but any such idealized cycle, whether the turns are sharp or rounded, is of necessity based on the data of a past period, and to the extent that conditions subsequently change, the past pattern no longer continues to fit. Thereafter, it can only be used with adjustments, and the ability to draw valid conclusions from it is not greatly dependent on the curve form used.

The "cycle" is in effect no more than an expression of continuity or serial correlation in the underlying data, and this property can be used in projecting residential construction without the derivation of any fixed cyclical pattern. Just knowing that there are several years in each phase of the cycle gives some basis for extrapolation. Within each of these phases, the projection may be slanted to match the changes in income.

Chart 9–5 shows actual building expenditures compared with a series of 1-year projections derived by this method.[10] It may be noted that these projections tend to be unresponsive at the turns and that they go rather badly off at times—as in the 1950 Korean War upsurge and the following year of restrictions on building. In other words, this approach also requires intelligent application in the light of current conditions. It comes back to a consideration of the specific influences affecting construction activity in any period under consideration.

[9] Newbury, *op. cit.*, pp. 185–189.

[10] The estimating equation is

$$Y = 0.06x_1 + 0.33x_2 - 0.075$$

where Y = the change in construction expenditures, billions of dollars

x_1 = corresponding change in disposable income

x_2 = preceding change in construction expenditures

The years 1942 to 1946 and 1950 to 1951 were excluded from the computations.

Past discussions of the forces influencing construction have ranged over a wide variety of factors. These may be classified into four types: demographic, income, price, and other factors. Among the demographic factors are population, its age distribution, marriages, family formation, births, and size of families. The income factors, in addition to total income, are income distribution, rates of joint occupancy, liquid-asset holdings, and employment or unemployment. Price factors include rents, construction costs, down payments, interest rates, and costs of maintenance and operation. Other factors include the availability of credit, mortgage foreclosures, migration, vacancies, the condition of existing houses, and intensity of utilization as indicated by number of persons per room.

N. B.

Chart 9–5. Residential-construction Expenditures

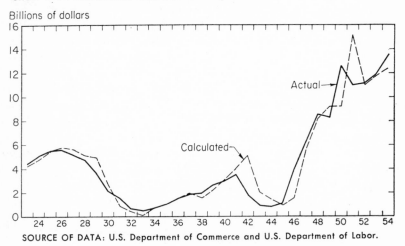

SOURCE OF DATA: U.S. Department of Commerce and U.S. Department of Labor.

Some analysts stress the importance of the demographic factors; others put primary emphasis on such factors as incomes, costs, and credit.

It may readily be seen that all these factors do indeed bear on the problem. However, the degrees of relationship to new construction vary widely. Some are important; others may be comparatively insignificant. Furthermore, the various factors are themselves interrelated. Demographic, price, and financial factors are all influenced by changes in income. Altogether, the list is so imposing and knowledge of the relative weight to be given each item is so limited that the task of analysis in these terms becomes almost insuperable.

There are times, like the immediate post–World War II period, when all the factors are favorable, so that a boom of considerable magnitude may be predicted. These periods are revealing because they show how the combined effects of the various factors are concentrated in a limited period to force the pace of construction to a peak. Subsequently the various factors again operate in combination to deepen the depression.

Immediately after the war, marriage and birth rates surged upward. The demand for dwelling units increased sharply as returning veterans sought separate homes for their families. Many had become acquainted with new places and moved as opportunity seemed to beckon from the more attractive locations. Down payments could be made from wartime savings. Credit was freely available as a result of war financing and of policies for stabilizing interest rates on the government debt. High incomes and employment, together with mortgage insurance, justified the liberal use of credit resources. Prices were quickly bid up and costs were inflated, but low interest rates and long periods of amortization kept monthly payments down. Rents were restricted by controls carried over from the war period, so that many landlords found selling out the best way to realize on their investment. The number of rental units available was greatly diminished by a tremendous shift toward owner occupancy. Almost the only way to get a place to live in many localities was to build. Construction forged ahead.

The specific character of the early postwar boom was largely determined by these conditions. Many of the new families were small. They had a distinct preference for the one-floor homes generally referred to as "ranch type" or "ramblers." Although the income distribution had been considerably equalized during the war, only the smaller units were within the financial reach of many. The builders could put up these small units most quickly, and they put off working on larger units with more exacting specifications while they were engaged in volume building of small units. The movement to the suburbs, where land was readily available at low cost for this type of building, was accelerated by the threat of atomic attack growing out of the cold war.

The upsurge of building in 1950 was partly a rush by those who contemplated building to beat the expected obstacles of the Korean War. In addition, population movements were again stimulated, and the draft and other military-manpower policies helped to stimulate family formation. Marriages continued high, within limits imposed by the dwindling numbers of unmarried adults available, and birth rates rose to a new peak. Growing families demanded more space, so a shift toward larger houses got under way, and many of the original small units were remodeled and enlarged.

In 1950, a substantial backlog of demand for housing still existed as a result of the low rates of construction during the depression and the war. Between 1940 and 1950, the number of households formed exceeded by approximately 3 million the number of new permanent dwelling units built. For the 3 million extra households, an estimated 1.75

million units were obtained by such means as conversion of attics or basements and subdivision of existing units; some 600,000 units had been erected as temporary public housing for war use; and another 700,000 were trailers or other marginal units. In addition the 1950 Census of Housing listed some 2.5 million occupied units as dilapidated and a much larger number as without running water or bathroom. Rates of joint occupancy—"doubling-up," as it is usually called—were down considerably from the postwar peak, but many families still in this situation were seeking separate quarters. In the aggregate, several million families were unsatisfactorily housed, and the number of vacant units available for rent or sale, although up somewhat from the immediate postwar extreme, continued abnormally low. High incomes provided the means of improving housing standards. New units had to be built for this purpose, and they helped keep the rate of construction high after the rate of increase in family formation began to slacken.

By the end of 1952, it began to appear that the forces supporting the boom had largely spent themselves. Marriage rates were down considerably from the peak, doubling-up was being reduced to a minimum, and vacancies, though still low, had risen. After a review of the various factors, the Commerce Department said:[11]

> If the upward trend of income continues, the catching-up still to be done and the continuing availability of financing on comparatively favorable terms may support high activity for another year or so. However, the analysis indicates that once the backlog factors are fully dissipated, new construction for other than replacement purposes will decline from the current volume of roughly 1.1 million new units annually towards the net household formation figure.

Two years later, however, the boom was still very much alive. With the minor letdown of general business in 1954, the Housing Act of 1954 was passed. The flow of investment funds into housing began to increase as soon as it appeared that favorable government policies would be adopted. With interest rates generally low, mortgage loans guaranteed at relatively favorable rates, and other demands for funds restricted, the availability of credit for home building under VA and FHA programs was expanded to support the spurt that took place late in that year. Many buyers found that they could obtain better living quarters, at lower current cost, and with little or no down payment, and they often proceeded in disregard of the long-term obligations they had to assume. A rising level of demolitions—to clear sites for commercial, highway, and other nonresidential projects—augmented the shift of families to new

[11] *Markets after the Defense Expansion,* U.S. Department of Commerce, Office of Business Economics, 1952, p. 48.

homes, and a steady flow of migrants from rural areas where housing was substandard helped to keep vacancies low in the less desirable units remaining in the central cities of the North and West. The negative factors in the picture were thus offset for a time, and construction rebounded toward the earlier peak. In summary, these are the developments of the postwar boom.

Looking backward, it is easy to see how the various factors affected its course. What their effects would be was much more difficult to determine at the time. Near the end of 1948, it was widely feared that the boom would collapse, and both lenders and speculative builders temporarily restricted their commitments. Again in 1953, housing starts dipped as the "hard-money" policy of the Eisenhower administration took effect; and the public was treated to a debate between builders' associations and the Housing Administrator on whether construction would fall 40 to 50 percent or only half that far. There was a clamor for easier financing, and interest-rate policy was reversed during the summer months. Building for the year was fully maintained, but it was not yet apparent that the boom would soon gain a new lease on life. In situations like these, it is no simple matter to judge the relative force of conflicting tendencies.

BASIC FACTORS IN THE DEMAND FOR HOUSES

To reduce the analysis of changes in housing construction to manageable proportions, it is necessary to appraise the relationships between the factors and use them selectively. As a starting point, it may be observed that the underlying need for housing is set by the number of families, quasi families, and individuals who would like living quarters for their sole use. For this reason, it may be said that the demographic factors are the basic ones in determining the demand for houses. This, however, is true only from a long-term point of view; from that point of view, it may be said that the formation of households, as family units are able to move into their own quarters, sets the trend against which the supply of dwellings must be measured.

At any given moment, of course, there may be disparities. In order that all who want quarters may be able to obtain them, the buildings have to be there; in addition, the families wanting houses must have the means to command their use. This means primarily that adequate incomes must be generally available, because those wishing to own homes must be able to carry interest and amortization payments and those wishing to rent must be able to pay rents that cover all costs. At times, until new houses are actually built, the supply may be inadequate. At other times, the level of income may be too low, so that many who would like separate quarters cannot afford them. Because the number of households varies with these nondemographic factors, the number of family units rather than the number of households must be taken as the basic measure of need.

The difference between families and households is a measure of the amount of doubling-up. In periods when the supply of houses becomes excessive, most of the doubling-up is due to existing economic conditions. This is clearly an income effect, or perhaps it is better to say an employment effect, because the complete loss of income forces doubling-up much more quickly than a partial reduction of income. When employment is low, some family units cannot make ends meet, and they economize by joining others in a single dwelling unit. If they resist this solution, they may be forced to it anyway, because they are subject to eviction when they can no longer pay the rent or meet the mortgage payments. In a decline, therefore, the existing stock of houses shows a growing surplus in the form of vacant units.

These unoccupied dwelling units, or vacancies, make up the difference between households and total houses available. When vacancies are low and doubling-up is high, the basic long-term factors are favorable for an increase in home building. If employment is depressed, however, construction may respond only slowly. This was the situation in the late 1930s. New construction moved up against the business decline of 1938 with the assistance of government programs, but it remained comparatively sluggish until after the stimulus of war expenditures began to lift employment in mid-1940. Then the annual rate of starts increased by roughly 50 percent in the year before wartime restrictions took effect.

In the construction cycle, the variations in the rate of building are considerably greater than those in the rate of family formation. The latter may be taken as an appropriate norm for the former. What happens is that in periods of boom new construction rises above the increase in families. At first this mainly facilitates undoubling, both because more units are available and because rising employment provides the means for action on the part of families that desire separate quarters. Eventually it creates an inventory of houses in excess of the number of families desiring them. When there are just enough units, construction must be slowed to prevent a surplus, but the consequent decline in incomes reduces the number of families wanting houses. Construction must then fall, not just to the level of new family formation, but below that level. After such a decline, construction must remain low until the number of families wanting separate quarters again catches up with the stock of houses in existence and available for use.

In the basic relationship, families wanting houses serve as the norm for housing units, and the distinction between levels and changes is important. What counts in boom and trough is the gap between the total number of families and the entire supply of existing houses. As long as a disparity in these over-all totals exists, it is not inconsistent for year-to-year changes in family formation to run counter to changes in construction. When there is a surplus of houses, construction is likely to fall even though the number of families is rising. In a boom, construction may continue strong for a while after the rate of family formation has turned down. If the rate of family formation accelerates or drops off a bit in any year and if new construction does just the opposite, those changes are likely to have such moderate effects on the position of the larger aggregates—that is, the total families and the total houses—as to be neither stimulus to nor drag on new construction, because the relationship of those basic aggregates remains almost unchanged. The nature of the influence of the over-all excess or deficit cannot be appreciated in terms of any analysis of current rates of family formation and construction alone.

What counts in declines and recoveries, on the other hand, is the reaction of the change in construction activity on incomes and employment, and thus on the number of families wanting houses. This reaction produces the opposite kind of imbalance from that which existed prior to the turn.

Testing these relationships is difficult, because back data are not available in suitable form. A simplified version of the relationships is presented in Chart 9–6. In the upper panel of this chart, the trend in the total number of married couples is compared with the trend in available housing units.[12] Both lines on this chart are oversimplified. Not all families consist of the basic, married-couple type, and not all married couples maintain households of their own. Similarly, the housing-unit series is based on new permanent construction, with an allowance for destruction and demolition, and does not give effect to conversion, temporary, or other marginal units. Nevertheless, the two series may be taken as a generally sound illustration of what happens during the housing cycle.

The lower panel of the chart shows the changes that occurred in these broad, stable aggregates during the course of each year. The data for the decades following World War I and World War II illustrate how construction rises above family formation to eat into the accumulated deficiency of dwelling units and ultimately produce a surplus. Through most of the decade of the 1930s and the subsequent war years, construction was depressed and the opposite kind of movement occurred. After the number of married couples came into balance with housing units in 1937, construction received an important stimulus, but family formation was also stimulated by rising incomes and by military-service policies, so

[12] The data for this chart are described in Appendix C.

Chart 9–6. Married Couples and Nonfarm Housing Units Available

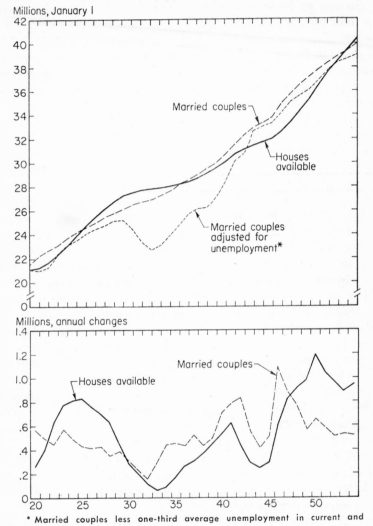

Millions, January 1

Married couples

Houses available

Married couples adjusted for unemployment*

Millions, annual changes

Married couples

Houses available

* Married couples less one-third average unemployment in current and previous year.

that the deficiency in dwellings kept growing through 1941, and then right on through the war.

The rate of family formation itself is not immune from income effects, as the depression decline and the recovery of 1940 and 1941 indicate. Marriages are restricted when the means of support are lacking, and deferred marriages are speeded when the expansion of activity again offers opportunity for satisfactory family living. For family formation, as for household formation, employment rather than income as such appears to be the meaningful measure, but, whatever the measure used, it is clear that changes in business conditions pull the rate of family formation away from the long-term trend it would follow in a constantly growing economy.

In so far as family formation is pulled away from such a trend by the fluctuations in income and employment, the resulting waves are in essence business-cycle effects. Even the so-called "echo effect," in which a concentrated change in families tends to be repeated 2 decades later, when the new generation reaches maturity, might be regarded as a long-delayed cyclical reaction to the extent that it could be identified with an original wave of this character.

Reasons have already been cited why employment rather than income represents the best measure of the economic factor in the housing cycle. Employment is a more direct indicator than income of the opportunity for separate living. It is also more nearly coordinate with the family in terms of the basic unit of measurement. There is, however, an unduly high correlation between trends in employment and in families over long periods of time. To avoid this difficulty, a substitute means of gauging short-term movements may be utilized, namely, unemployment, which in this context provides a measure of the deviations from the employment trend. In other words, most of the potential demand for home building is reflected in family formation, including much of the part created by the growth of incomes, and most of the cyclical loss in opportunity for families to maintain separate households is indicated by the lack of jobs for workers who are seeking employment.

The results of a correlation that relates new construction to married couples, unemployment, and available dwelling units are shown in Chart 9–7.[13] Unemployment may be regarded either as a separate factor that pulls construction away from the norm set by the number of families or as a factor that establishes, in combination with the number of families, the basic demand against which the supply of houses must be gauged. The latter measure appears in Chart 9–6 as the line labeled "Married couples adjusted for unemployment."

During recovery, rising employment and household formation keep demand moving ahead of supply, right into the boom phase. After construction catches up with the increase in families, employment is still rising and continues to advance for a while as construction moves out ahead. This is the full-boom phase of the cycle. If other factors then keep employment advancing after the rate of family formation has leveled and begun to decline, the boom is prolonged, as it was in the late 1920s. After a time an adequate supply of houses accumulates. Vacancies begin

[13] See Appendix C for explanation of data and methods.

to increase, but the movement is slow until building has passed the peak. Eventually new construction has to be cut back. For a while the surplus continues to mount. Referring back to Chart 9–6, it may be seen that in the late 1920s construction had to fall by more than half before increases in the surplus were eliminated. The decline in construction reduces employment, both directly and indirectly, and the slump gains momentum.

In the depression, rising unemployment combines with a reduced rate of family formation to put a drag on recovery. The situation is not

Chart 9–7. Nonfarm-housing Starts, 1920–1956

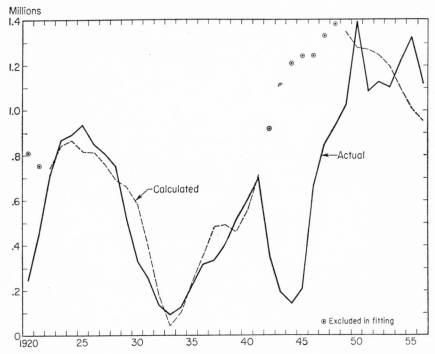

symmetrical with the boom as it is in inventory cycles, because the surplus of existing houses retards new construction after normal rates of family formation are resumed. Hence the rebound from the lows is not so automatic as the decline from the peak. Nevertheless, after a period of low construction, the continuing advance in family formation effectively liquidates the surplus, and construction moves up toward the level of current need. But the advance in construction reacts upon demand, and a new upward spiral gets under way.

The construction cycle is thus on a par with other cycles but has its own drawn-out period, which gives its major swings substantial independence from other developments. Shorter-term movements originate more completely in general business considerations, and special government programs or policies may for a time produce important deviations of their own.

EFFECTS OF OTHER FACTORS ON RESIDENTIAL CONSTRUCTION

The basic factors in the analysis of residential construction may thus be regarded as only three. All the other factors mentioned above—such as formation of households by quasi families or individuals, rates of doubling-up, intensity of utilization, prices, and migration—are intercorrelated with these and vary with them through the cycle in a fairly consistent manner, except as military policies or other special conditions aggravate or interfere. As a partial exception, migration tends to increase in depressions as well as in booms, but the kind of migration that takes place when unemployment is high involves people who lack the means to undertake new-home construction.

Other factors, such as vacancies, are also intercorrelated and might be independently useful if current estimates were available. Not only have current data on vacancies been lacking until recently, but also past data are scattered and almost hopelessly confused by constant changes in concepts and in methods of enumeration. During the Depression a number of surveys were made year after year in a large number of cities.[14] The results are presented in Chart 9–8 in terms of the average rates in cities where at least several surveys were made during the period shown. These data cannot be considered highly dependable. They appear somewhat low on the average in the light of the 1940 census and other scattered surveys. To take them as they are, however, it may be inferred that vacancies began rising in the mid-1920s, definitely depressing construction by 1929, when unemployment was making a low for the decade. They continued up sharply to 1932 and 1933 and then fell sharply to 1937. In 1937, they were less than half as high as in 1930, whereas unemployment remained almost twice as high. Lack of such data in the early 1950s hampered analysis aimed at gauging the potential duration of the building boom.

Financial factors appear to be of some importance in determining the pace of construction. Most units require financing, and this fact gives lenders an important role in determining what will be done. At times their decisions may have a significant effect on housing starts, particularly when they are unwilling to extend commitments. This factor played an important part in the declines of early 1949 and 1953. In both cases, not

[14] See S. B. Barber, "Urban Residential Vacancies," *Survey of Current Business,* August, 1938.

only were terms on mortgage loans tightened but also loans were less readily available. Both times, after a period of months, the restrictions were eased, and building forged ahead. Under some conditions, such restrictions might have more lasting effects. It is difficult to assign definite quantitative importance to financial restriction as a separate factor, but at least some adjustment has to be made when it is known to be operating.

Chart 9–8. Vacancy Rates and Unemployment

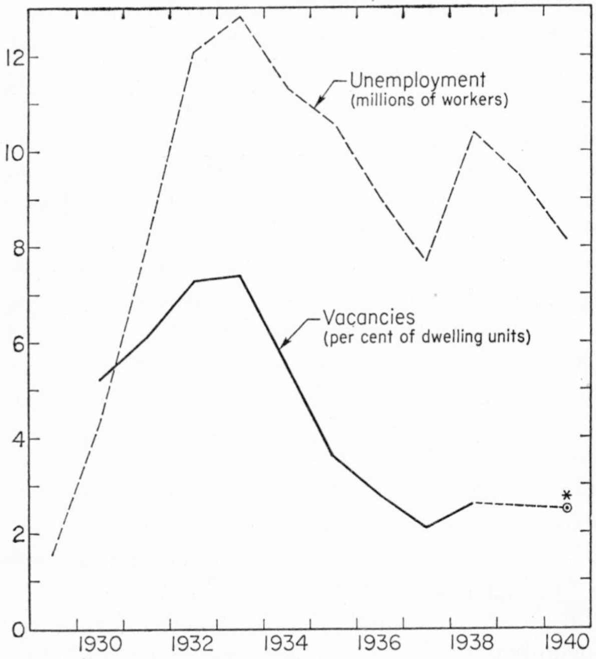

* From 1940 Census of Housing, not strictly comparable with earlier data.

Price factors, in contrast, appear to play only the most limited role in determining the level of new construction. This may be due partly to the fact that in the past quarter of a century changes in cost items have tended to offset each other. Although construction has become more costly, monthly payments have been held down by lower interest rates and longer periods of amortization. Developments in financing technique, accomplished partly with the aid of the government-mortgage-insurance program, have made homeownership possible for a much wider group of families. It seems clear, nevertheless, that a major postwar boom would have taken place even in the absence of these changes.

In the past, neat theoretical models have been formulated to show how the relation of rents to building costs or other items of the kind establish a profit incentive to expand or retard construction. However, all these factors reduce in the end to aspects of the availability of dwelling units. When there is a shortage of units in relation to the number of families who can afford them, rents can be raised and ordinarily will be raised enough to make building profitable. Then the effort to remedy the building shortage forces construction costs up. Higher costs in turn justify higher rents, and higher incomes make it possible to obtain higher rents from tenants. These conditions persist as long as the shortage persists.

In the early stages of a boom, costs usually surge upward, but the rising costs are seldom a deterrent to building. The increases result from rising demand; that is, costs are high because activity is high. The cost of construction is at a low before the boom, and the main volume of building takes place during the period of highest costs.

Prices of houses are even more inflated in the early stages of an upswing than the building-cost indexes show. Those indexes are mostly based on wage rates and building-materials prices and include neither profit margins nor overhead. Some do incorporate an hours-of-work or productivity factor, but some loss of productivity is tolerated by contractors on the upswing. They are then being offered special inducements to undertake new work, their margins are fully adequate, and their primary desire is to get the work done. After the sharp early upsurge, costs as measured by the indexes tend to level out, and prices may actually decline, even though wage rates and materials prices continue at the peak. Builders become familiar with new materials and techniques. They learn how to increase efficiency. They can improve on the houses just built at lower cost and are willing to accept lower margins. This helps keep the boom going. Buyers are attracted by the better values now available. They see that they can get better houses at lower costs than their neighbors did in preceding years. The whole picture adds up to a persistent failure to adjust activity before the saturation of the market is completed. It is aggravated by efforts to prevail upon government to make financing for home building progressively easier.

After a surplus of housing has been created, further concessions to buyers can attract little new business. Rents may still be high enough to cover costs, and some speculative building may continue to add to the surplus. After a time, in order not to have houses vacant, landlords may lower rentals somewhat, but this tends to be a purely competitive move which cannot eliminate the surplus. Almost any rent is too much to be paid by the workers who become unemployed, since they in effect drop out of their normal position in the income distribution. For the most part, therefore, the aim is to get as much as possible out of those who are still able to pay. The same policy is followed by contractors and labor unions, so that costs are notoriously sticky. Builders and workers attempt to protect themselves in a recession by maintaining wage rates and prices but have to take an unavoidable loss in income through enforced idleness. Recovery waits, with the industry, until the surplus has been worked off.

The picture that emerges is one of making the most of the opportunities that present themselves, by charging all that the traffic will bear. What it will bear depends, on the one hand, on the availability of houses and, on the other, on the number and incomes of the families desiring them. When the supply is short and incomes are high, it is not necessary to seek higher prices; they are freely offered. The boom is not restrained, because the high prices are merely one aspect of it. In contrast, when houses are redundant and incomes are low, there is nobody in the market with whom to discuss price concessions. The few who wish to build rather than to buy a marked-down existing house may be able to drive a reasonably good bargain, but it has little effect on other buyers, who prefer the still better bargains available in existing houses. Any building that adds to the surplus can only drive the prices of existing units still lower. Each of these situations succeeds the other in the course of time, as the basic factors slowly shift in relation to each other.

NONRESIDENTIAL CONSTRUCTION

The situation in nonresidential construction is generally similar to that in home building. When nonresidential activity is considered as a whole, it may be said to follow a long cycle, like that of housing, but not coincident with it. It shows some tendency to lag behind the housing cycle, and this lag can only in part be accounted for by the fact that the construction period is longer for most nonresidential buildings than for houses. It occurs in part because the construction of related facilities necessarily follows the growth of residential developments and suburban communities. As shown in Chart 9–2, nonresidential contract awards remained on a high plateau from 1926 to 1930, showing no letdown for more than 2 years after the decline of residential building had begun.

Nonresidential construction is more responsive than residential construction to changes in economic activity generally. Industrial building is much more closely tied to over-all business conditions than is home building. A serial correlation, like that used for housing (Chart 9–5), would here add little to a relationship that includes a measure of general activity, such as gross national product. What can be obtained from such a relationship is obtained by the correlation with activity alone. It is not a high enough correlation to give dependable results, but it is of some use in adjusting the early approximations.

Many of the observed differences in behavior from that of residential construction originate in the fact that the nonresidential total includes a number of dissimilar items. It represents a conglomeration of different types of work, each of which has its own specific determinants. In the Commerce Department–Labor Department data, nonresidential building is broken down into some eight categories exclusive of farm, utility, railroad, and industrial construction in the narrower sense. If public construction is included, it is still more of a conglomeration, because certain types of public works, like highway construction, which are not building at all in the narrower sense, may be a relatively large portion of the total.

Although the general principles of cyclical development apply to the various nonresidential types of construction, just as they do in the case of housing, there are different inventory and use factors affecting each type. Each has its own characteristics, or, it may be better to say, its own cycle. Hotels may be taken as an illustration. In the 1920s there was a tremendous surge of hotel building, reaching a peak value of about one-third of a billion dollars in 1926. There was a lot of travel then, little competition from motels, and a high demand for luxury-type accommodations. After that boom came to an end, there was a very extreme decline. Hotel construction fell from that high to a low of $8 million, a decline of 98 percent, and there was practically no revival during the 1930s. In 1937 it got back to only $22 million, and in 1941 back to only $37 million, little more than one-tenth of the earlier peak. Even in the decade following World War II there was no substantial revival. Most of the construction in this field in the postwar period has been in the form of tourist courts, motels, and other accommodations catering to automobile traffic. Construction of the old-type, large hotel in the crowded area has not revived. The downtown hotels are often so seriously affected by the parking problem that they cannot capture the patronage of automobile travelers. What they require is a larger number of travelers without private cars, and the shift from commercial transportation has restricted growth in this area. A limited revival has occurred in some rapidly expanding localities, but the conditions bringing this about have not yet been general enough for another large wave of hotel building.

Dissimilarity in the components does not mean that it is necessary to analyze a large number of specific cycles in order to project nonresidential construction. A large part of the total is closely enough connected with residential construction to be regarded as practically a joint demand with new home building. This part consists of stores, garages, schools, churches, hospitals, and other commercial and institutional structures that may be classified under the general heading of community facilities. The same is true of a good deal of local public construction, such as streets, sewers, water systems, social and recreational structures, and buildings for public protection and administration. People need and demand these facilities when they are building their homes. If they are not immediately available, individuals make their own arrangements for a while but at the same time keep the pressure on public officials to make better arrangements. A situation in which home building is high practically forces a large volume of such work, although some lag is unavoidable.

Chart 9–9. Major Components of New Private Construction

Billions of 1947-1949 dollars

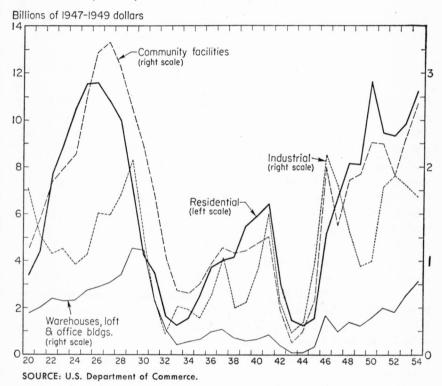

SOURCE: U.S. Department of Commerce.

The relation of private work of this kind to home building is shown in Chart 9–9. The close similarity of cyclical patterns, with only a moderate lag in community facilities, is apparent from this chart. Differences exist within the total of community facilities, of course, but these tend to offset each other in various periods. The relationship of this segment to residential construction is therefore a fairly satisfactory way of projecting it.

An alternative approach to forecasting institutional construction—social and recreational, educational, medical, and religious—was developed by the Department of Commerce.[15] This approach set up a rough criterion of needs as a basis for projection, namely, the physical volume of new construction actually put in place during the period 1920 to 1941 for each additional person in the population or for each new student enrolled in private schools. When this criterion was applied to the period 1942 to 1952, it indicated that a substantial volume of deferred building needs had accumulated. The conclusion was drawn that activity would rise from the 1952 level and remain high for several years. The pattern of the movement is difficult to outline in these terms, but the method does provide a basis for projecting a substantial portion of the nonresidential-construction total. The principle involved is not essentially different from that underlying Chart 9–9, since the housing cycle also bears a fairly definite relation to the needs of a growing population.

Also shown on the chart is industrial construction. This segment shows greater short-term variation than other types of construction. As a rule it represents only a fraction of the nonresidential total, but in bursts it rises to as much as one-half. Industry moves more quickly on its construction work when the situation demands, as is indicated by the peaks reached in the years immediately following the two world wars. Industrial construction also accelerates sharply in other years of economic advance, and it is this variation in industrial construction that makes the whole total of nonresidential construction appear to be responsive to changes in general economic activity, as already noted. Its changes are subject to the same factors that influence business capital expenditures (to be taken up in Chapter 10) and must be analyzed in the same terms.

A third segment of private nonresidential construction shown in the chart consists of warehouse, loft, and office buildings. It displays considerably more stability than industrial construction and more responsiveness to changes in general activity than community facilities. It tends to follow with a long lag, but, like the hotel cycle, this may largely be explained by special developments in transportation and communication that affect ways of transacting business and handling goods.

In appraising the outlook for nonresidential construction, the expert can bring various kinds of information to bear. This specialized knowledge may at times require primary emphasis on noncyclical factors. In those special situations, ignoring the cyclical pattern may result in substantial improvement of the results otherwise obtainable. On the whole, however, the errors that occur from short-term projections made in accordance with the principles outlined above will seldom be large—practically never large enough to invalidate a general forecast covering only 1 or 2 years ahead.

[15] *Markets after the Defense Expansion,* pp. 44–46.

CHAPTER 10

Producers' Plant and Equipment

During the last half century, the theory of business fluctuations has become increasingly focused on the problem of business investment in fixed capital. Earlier it had been perceived that outlays for plant and equipment fluctuated much more widely than those for consumers' goods, but it was only with the conversion of the West from a primarily commercial to a heavily industrial type of economy that responsibility for business movements began to be assigned to business investment in new productive facilities. Since then, this kind of investment has come to play an almost dominating role in theories of the cycle.

The concentration of attention on the important role of business investment in "the cycle," while contributing much to our knowledge of what makes the economy move, has had some unfortunate consequences. It commonly resulted in a jumbling together of diverse factors and influences that do not conform to a single pattern into what purports to be a description of a unified cyclical structure. Approached in this way, the roles of factors other than fixed investment—each of which is governed by different conditions relating to response, amplitude, timing, and adjustment—tend to be overlooked or confused. This is particularly unfortunate for forecasting, because actual developments make it necessary to recognize elements of irregularity or nonconformity as well as those that fit the dominant pattern. Nevertheless, there can be no question that business investment must play a major role in the analysis of economic changes.

The features of fixed investment that contribute to its specific behavior were recognized long before they came to be incorporated in cycle theory. Its role in the production process was widely discussed. Before the emergence of cycle theory, it was recognized that producers' durable equipment constitutes a large class of products that go into consumption only indirectly, through the production of consumer goods, and that such equipment increases goods available for consumption by making production more efficient. Its use made the production process as a whole indirect, by requiring prior production of machinery; and discussions of the advantages of "mass production" shifted from the "division of labor" to the "roundaboutness" of the production process.

The earliest discussions of the role of capital formation were theories of economic progress rather than of cycles in which surges of rapid advance were partially retracted in recurring setbacks. The growth of income and consumption was seen to depend on the use of ever more complex and powerful equipment. At the same time, it was understood that the broadening of the market required more widespread use of the best equipment available. In other words, economic growth both resulted from and was responsible for continuous expansion of industrial capacity.

Notwithstanding the relatively steady growth of the market, it became apparent that there were irregularities in rates of investment. These were partly dependent, for example, upon the sporadic character of discoveries and inventions. Innovations in the form of new products or processes, commonly involving use of large amounts of fixed capital, were not put into operation at a regular pace, but in spurts. Great new industries, like the railroad or the automobile industry, forged ahead from time to time and lifted the whole economy in spreading waves of expansion. Such developments were in large measure independent of the course of activity elsewhere in the economy, but when they occurred, they tended to stimulate activity everywhere.

The durability of capital goods was also seen to be a factor determining the pace of investment. Equipment once installed was to a lesser degree like permanent structures. It provided valuable services over an extended period of time, and the investment incorporated in it could be recovered only gradually as its products were sold. Once an investment was embodied in structures and equipment, it was "sunk" and could be recovered only as the income realized from the goods and services it helped to produce exceeded the direct costs of production.

Growth was not so all-pervasive as to ensure the success of any particular investment. Individual concerns and industries declined and passed out of existence, and even well-established businesses had to struggle along in the doldrums for considerable periods. When demand dropped back, the existing plant and equipment were made idle, but they remained on the scene, ready for use when additional output was again called for. If demand did not resume its growth shortly, new investment might be retarded for a long time, because it would be profitable to put the existing idle equipment back into use before incurring unnecessary expenditures for new equipment. The capital-goods industries, therefore, feasted on high prosperity when the economy was growing rapidly but had to endure prolonged famines during periods of inactive demand.

It was recognized, furthermore, that the financing of fixed investment was largely independent of current earnings. Large projects typically required capital outlays beyond the funds immediately available to those undertaking them, and it was necessary to go to the capital markets to obtain the finances needed. These the capital markets provided, by drawing together the accumulated savings of individuals and by expanding the money supply on the basis of limited reserves held in the banking system. There was a financial counterpart, therefore, to the experienced expansions and contractions in business investment.

THEORY OF INVESTMENT'S ROLE IN THE BUSINESS CYCLE[1]

Early theories of the cycle, taking financial aspects as a point of departure, regarded its mitigation as a problem of monetary reform. The boom usually collapsed in a financial panic, and real values had to be sacrificed to meet financial commitments. Subsequently a new expansion of credit began to lay the ground for the next crisis. Efforts were therefore directed mainly toward maintaining the soundness of the monetary structure, let the business operations that provided the background go where they would.

The dramatic growth of heavy industry in the latter part of the nineteenth century brought attention back to real investment. Railroad and steel expansion supported each other, and the increasing availability of steel facilitated development of improved structures and equipment for other industries. The products of the steel industry were going predominantly into fixed investment, so that fluctuations in its operations were tied to investment demands. By the turn of the century, it could be seen that the periodic expansion of business capital formation represented a genuine prime mover for the economy as a whole.

Not only transportation and steel but any kind of expansion temporarily created opportunities for other expansion, because the various parts of the economy were mutually interdependent. Once a concerted movement to expand got under way, it tended to proceed until a condition of general overproduction developed. This saturation of the

[1] Many valuable contributions to this theory have been made by a long list of authors in various countries. It would hardly be appropriate to review the development of such theory in detail here. The reader who is interested will find a good summary in A. H. Hansen, *Business Cycles and National Income*, W. W. Norton & Company, Inc., New York, 1951, part 3. References to the works of all the writers mentioned in this section may be found in this source.

capital-goods market led in turn to the collapse. Tugan-Baranowsky's early account of the cycle in these terms (1901) remains essentially correct today, though the mechanisms relating the various forces involved were by no means clearly defined at that time.

The interplay of real and financial aspects of the cycle were also developed in early accounts, in terms of the inducement to invest. As early as 1898, Wicksell showed that investment would be profitable whenever the net earnings obtainable from it exceeded its cost, which in simplest terms is the going rate of interest on investment funds. When prospective earnings are high relative to the interest rate, investment would tend to expand, and vice versa.

In the early stages of an upswing, the interest rate tends to be held low for a while, because bank reserves and other loanable funds have accumulated and the improvement in conditions encourages holders of liquid capital to bring their funds into the market. Conversion of these funds into fixed capital is the driving force of the upswing. Investment thus is induced to proceed to a point beyond the continuing availability of funds. Eventually the interest rate must be raised to match the relative scarcity of loanable funds, and this tends to choke off new investment. The investments just made begin to look insecure. Panic ensues, and funds are hardly available at any rate of interest. New investment falls not just to the point of reestablishing balance but to a considerably lower level. Then surplus funds again begin accumulating, the interest rate is lowered, and another upswing gets under way.

Theories of this kind, which rested heavily upon the monetary aspects, left much to be explained. Both the shift in the profitability of new investment and the penalty imposed by rising interest rates are factors that should work gradually to restrain rather than to reverse the movement. Any cyclical movement derived from such changes would be at best a greatly damped affair that would tend toward equilibrium rather than sustained or ever-increasing variation. Financial developments indeed serve to aggravate some of the movements that occur in course of the cycle; they cannot be regarded as sufficient causes of those wavelike movements.

Reason for the violence of cyclical movements could more readily be found on the side of real investment. The kind of investment that occurs when innovations are introduced, involving more efficient processes and usually more capital per unit of output or of labor, is only one kind of investment. It is the kind usually referred to as "autonomous investment." The other kind consists in the expansion of known processes to get increased output of goods for which demand has expanded. The demand for the latter kind of investment was seen to be derived from the demand for the end products to be produced. It is called "induced investment," because its changes are brought about by changes in final demand. The larger the increase in final demand, the larger the volume of the investment that increase would induce. Moreover, the increase in investment would be more than proportionate to the increase in demand, because it is derived from the change in rate of growth of demand and not from the absolute or relative increase as such. This "principle of acceleration" was explained by J. M. Clark in an early article entitled "Business Acceleration and the Law of Demand."[2]

The main difficulty with the principle of acceleration has been that it does not wholly accord with the facts revealed by the study of actual cyclical movements. Actual investment generally showed neither the amplitude of fluctuation nor the quarter-cycle lead called for by the theory, except perhaps in some rather specific and limited areas. Even when the lag between the decision to invest and the actual building of capacity is allowed for, the lead could not be adequately established. Nevertheless, the concept of investment's responding to changes in consumption did provide an explanation of how business advances or declines gathered force as they progressed. Induced investment has therefore come to be looked upon as a primary force in the business cycle.

The rapidity with which investment expands during the upswing was sometimes held to be the cause of the collapse. Output of producers' goods was viewed as getting out of balance with output of consumers' goods, creating a situation that could not continue. Just what there was about the imbalance that forced the downturn was never well defined. Some reached the logical conclusion that markets for producers' goods became saturated, but they had no way of making a factual demonstration of this point. The illustrations that could be offered related mainly to autonomous investment: a new industry reached maturity, and investment in it came to a halt; but its beginning was in the nature of a disturbance or shock, and the termination of investment could be regarded in the same light. The market-saturation thesis was not integrated into the mechanism of the cycle as such. Tugan-Baranowsky's great contribution was commonly overlooked in subsequent theoretical discussions.

A great forward stride was made in Keynes's *General Theory of Employment, Interest, and Money.* Investment there became explicitly the active and volatile force in the cycle. Its movements were reinforced by the response of consumption through the mechanism of the multiplier. At the same time, the movement was ultimately restrained by the growth of savings. On the decline, these mechanisms effectively worked in

[2] *Journal of Political Economy*, March, 1917; reprinted in American Economics Association, *Readings in Business Cycle Theory*, Richard D. Irwin, Inc., Homewood, Ill., 1944.

reverse. The whole cycle could proceed in step with the variations in investment.

In presenting the theory of investment and saving as determining the course of cyclical movements through their reactions on the income flow, Keynes dodged the problem of induced investment. In his formulation, the economy goes where investment goes, whether it is autonomous or induced.

He perceived that difficulties with his theory would arise at the turning points. Investment might increase beyond the bounds of full employment. Or, income might fall too low, even though it could not go all the way to zero. To deal with these problems, Keynes fell back on the monetary factors.

Keynes felt that a limit on the upswing was imposed by two factors, which he called the declining "marginal efficiency of capital" and "liquidity preference." The marginal efficiency of capital refers to the profit that can be made on additional increment of investment. As the best investment opportunities were used up, those remaining would produce ever lower rates of return; and since new investment would not pay if it returned less than the market rate of interest, a point would be reached at which it would be unprofitable to expand investment further.

At the same time, the interest rate would tend to rise. This rate Keynes regarded as the payment necessary to induce holders of cash to give up the advantages of having the cash, to use when and as they pleased, and to accept securities or other nonliquid assets instead. Those who made this shift would, of course, be subject to the risk that the prices of such assets might decline. In his theory of liquidity preference, as an expansion proceeds and prices rise, the risks of illiquidity would increase, and more and more people would prefer to hold cash. In addition, the increase in activity would require larger cash reserves to finance the higher volume of day-to-day transactions. The result of all these demands for cash would be a sharp tightening of the money supply, to such an extent that the rise in interest rates would rule out many projects and bring the expansion in investment to a halt.

On the decline, most of these effects would be reversed. However, Keynes saw that the monetary factors would be ineffective in stopping a serious decline. The interest rate would fall, but only to a minimum at which it became insensitive to further increases in the money supply. He concluded, therefore, that other measures of control would be needed. It was a situation calling for action from outside the economic process itself. It would be particularly effective, Keynes felt, for the government to take over the role of investor, undertaking a public-works program sufficiently large to turn the tide. This argument proved so persuasive that the principle of government action to stem a decline is now generally accepted. In the context of cycle theory, it is an admission that the automatic restraints on a decline do not effectively operate at any point short of the almost complete cessation of gross investment.

The adequacy of the restraints at the upper turning point also remains in doubt. The difficulty was made clear by the addition of the mechanisms of induced investment to the Keynesian Model. When an initial increase in investment puts income up, it also brings about an advance in induced investment. The initial movement of investment gains the support of induced investment, directly through the immediate advance in output and indirectly through the multiplier. As the accelerator and the multiplier interact, the combined effect is a sort of supermultiplier, and the primary restraint imposed by the advance in saving may no longer be effective in bringing the movement to a halt.

The possible outcomes have been explored by Paul Samuelson in an article entitled "Interactions between the Multiplier and the Principle of Acceleration."[3] Defining the accelerator in terms of the investment induced by a unit change in consumption from the preceding to the current period, Samuelson shows that certain typical situations can be defined: Only when the accelerator is small relative to the marginal propensity to consume does the kind of change specified by the multiplier theory occur. If the accelerator were larger, but less than the reciprocal of the marginal propensity to consume, the oscillations resulting from an initiating impulse would be damped, with income gradually moving toward stability. If the accelerator exactly equaled that reciprocal, a regularly recurring cycle of constant amplitude would result. If the accelerator exceeded that critical value, the situation would disintegrate either into cycles of ever-increasing amplitude or into a continuous, explosive expansion beyond any definite upper limit. In other words, these two factors alone are capable of producing cycles that recur automatically, without regard to the appearance of any kind of outside impulses or shocks.

A dilemma arises from this analysis.[4] It would seem to be a most extraordinary coincidence if the accelerator were precisely the reciprocal of the marginal propensity to consume. If it were less, the cycles would die out, so that the observed variations would have to be ex-

[3] *Review of Economic Statistics*, May, 1939; reprinted in American Economics Association, *Readings in Business Cycle Theory*, Richard D. Irwin, Inc., Homewood, Ill., 1944.
[4] A highly informative and stimulating discussion of the problem may be found in J. R. Hicks, *Trade Cycle*, Oxford University Press, New York, 1950.

plained in terms of recurring forces that appear from outside the economic system. If it were greater, the cycles would explosively overreach the observed limits, so that some other type of unexplained restraint would have to be effectively operating.

Various writers have chosen one or the other of these alternatives. If the values of the multiplier and the accelerator combine at a point not too far from the critical value, either might serve as an explanation that would not be grossly inconsistent with the available data. Ragnar Frisch, on the one hand, chooses the damped alternative, insisting that the sources of energy which maintain the economic cycles are erratic shocks; this is commonly referred to as "the rocking-horse theory." Hicks, on the other hand, chooses the unstable alternative but places the cycle under an additional restraint—that of full employment. When output reaches this ceiling, it can no longer continue its violent expansion but is more or less stabilized. The decrease in the rate of growth then moves the accelerator into reverse, and the decline gets under way. This hypothesis presents an interesting possibility, but it is hardly more convincing than some of those which Hicks rejects.

CAPACITY AS AN INVENTORY

Many of the obscure points in the analysis of capital expenditures may be clarified by thinking of the investment cycle as another kind of inventory cycle. Capacity is the inventory of productive facilities. Net investment in plant and equipment is the current addition to this inventory. The current rate of over-all industrial output is a measure of the flow of goods by which the adequacy of the inventory may be judged. Then the whole cyclical movement falls into line with the pattern of the stock-flow relationship inherent in any inventory cycle.

The dominant aim of business concerns with respect to fixed investment is to acquire the capacity that will enable them to maximize potential sales, but no more than that amount. Few are willing to incur the loss of markets to competitors which may occur if they cannot supply goods of suitable quality at the time purchasers are ready to buy them. Few wish to be burdened with unnecessary overhead costs. This implies, for the economy as a whole, that some excess or reserve capacity, tending to be strictly limited in amount, will be the normal condition.

The actual extent of excess capacity on hand will, of course, vary widely in the course of the business cycle. In slack times, the excess will greatly surpass the desired level, so that there is no need for expansion or even for maintaining existing facilities fully. On the other hand, when sales and consequently output are high, capacity is almost fully utilized, and the realization of higher sales potentials must come from expansion.

The need for additions thus varies widely, and investment shows correspondingly extreme fluctuations, because new investment is inversely
related to the gap between capacity and output, or, what comes to much
the same thing, it is dependent primarily upon the rate at which capacity
is utilized.

Perhaps this is just another way of saying that induced investment is
the important kind in analysis of the business cycle. It does not, however, confine the analyst to any particular kind of investment. All forms
of investment are considered to have full play in moving the economy
between its booms and depressions, but in addition the approach to
investment that regards capacity as an inventory explains why the downturn follows as an unavoidable outgrowth of the boom. Whether the
expansion was autonomous or induced, as capacity accumulates the
point is ultimately reached at which it becomes adequate. Then investment must be curtailed to prevent an excess from developing. But the
very attempt to prevent that undesirable condition brings it about. The
decline in employment and income that results from cutting investment
back to the level of replacement changes part of the capacity that was
no more than adequate under conditions of full employment to an excess.
For a while, new-equipment installations continue, because programs
already under way have to be carried through to completion. Such
completions, of course, merely add to the surplus. The decline cumulates.

The restraint on investment at the peak of the boom develops not
from the full-employment ceiling on total output but from the building
of capacity to the point of saturation. Behind the superficial appearance
of unending progress during the boom, the economy has been in a real
sense growing at a slower rate all the time. The boom developed as a
temporary deviation from the underlying trend, because capacity was
being built not just to meet the needs of growth but also to make up
the deficiency that developed when the flow of goods moved ahead in
the upswing. Finally, the economy loses, not the ability to expand, but
the desire to expand. It is not the decline in over-all growth but the
overaccumulation of capacity that makes it neecssary to halt the expansion. But the process of "catching up" cannot be stopped without bringing on the decline.

The difficulty arises because the economy can produce too much
rather than because production cannot be increased without limit. Success breeds instability in two ways. First, the larger over-all capacity is,
the more quickly any deficiency can be made up and the sharper will be
the cutback after the deficiency is eliminated. Second, the greater the
stockpile of productive instruments on hand, the longer can necessary
services be provided from existing facilities and the longer and deeper
will be the following period of liquidation. It is because we are able to

create excess capacity that we get both the sharp, almost automatic reversals at the upper turning point and the long-drawn-out periods of unemployment in the trough of depression.

In other words, the stability of an economy tends to be inversely related to its productive potential. High capacity makes possible great surges in output and correspondingly more rapid accumulation of goods, including producers' durable goods. Accumulation of these durable goods increases capacity, making possible still more rapid rates of accumulation. The availability of resources thus builds on itself, and excesses are bound to develop. The greater the progress of the boom, the greater will be the surplus when it ends and the lower will be the need for continuing investment after the decline.

The ability of an economy to maintain full employment is thus seen to depend in part on how productive it is. If it is capable of providing little more than current needs, a limited volume of investment will be enough to keep it at the ceiling indefinitely, and efforts to force growth at even a little faster rate may result in inflation. On the other hand, if it is capable of producing greatly in excess of current needs, a high volume of investment or other nonconsumption expenditures will be required to keep it operating at high levels.

The latter is peculiarly the problem of the United States. The Korean War period gave a clear demonstration of our tremendous productive potential. A large war program and a major investment boom, including facilities for both war and civilian production, were piled on ordinary civilian demands, the latter being left almost unrestricted. The implication of productivity like this is ever-increasing instability.

The imbalances that develop industrywise in boom and depression also may be effectively analyzed in terms of capacity as an inventory. Whenever rates of capital-goods production are above the requirements for long-term growth, an imbalance between output of producers' goods and consumers' goods may be said to exist. However, there is no way of knowing just when that condition appears or what its immediate significance may be. The critical imbalance arises on another level, the level of accumulated stock of facilities, and consists in the relation of capacity to output. When expansion is only moderately above the rate that can be maintained indefinitely, so that moderate lack of balance in favor of producers' goods exists in the current rates of output, the imbalance may continue, or even increase, as long as capacity remains deficient. Situations like this are passed through as intermediate stages in every upswing.

An underdeveloped economy, in which the ceiling on total output places a severe limit on capital formation, may go along at a relatively slow pace for extended periods without bringing capacity up to the desired level. It will seemingly be capable of maintaining a slow rate of growth indefinitely. A more highly productive economy will achieve its capacity goals more quickly but cannot so effectively maintain a steady rate of growth. As a rule, its spurts will overcarry. But the saturation effect is felt even before capacity becomes truly excessive, since the attempt to prevent this critical imbalance from developing is itself the beginning of the downturn.

In the late stages of a boom, capacity gets built up to the desired level over wide segments of industry. The movement does not, of course, affect all segments of industry equally. Some reach the point of saturation while the bulk are still moving up. If the advance goes far enough, some of those reaching the saturation point first may again be open to expansion. The others, however, no longer contribute to the advance, and after a while the number still favorably situated dwindles to a distinct minority. Some industries that find themselves with excess capacity attempt to retrieve their profit position by cost cutting and may, as wages advance, replace part of their existing equipment with more efficient types. In lines where relatively short-lived equipment is important, gross investment may continue high for a while, even though over-all capacity is sufficient. The auto industry, for example, makes heavy outlays in tooling up for its new models. Such demands in industries that no longer require over-all expansion help keep the movement going while other industries are expanding to the desired level. In time, facilities are not only adequate generally but also for the most part fresh and new. Industry is then capable of getting along with what it has for quite a while.

Earlier the boom created investment opportunities more rapidly than the current rate of expansion was using them up. At the peak, however, although income is still rising, it is no longer capable of creating investment opportunities on balance, because there are so few segments of demand still to be satisfied. The market is blanketed by producers with adequate capacity, and it is increasingly difficult for those still expanding to win shares away from those already established in the market. The need for additional capacity dries up, and there is nothing to justify the continuation of investment at the same rate. Once the decline gets under way, as it must when widespread expansion plans are brought to completion, the situation can no longer be rationalized as one requiring piecemeal adjustments in specific industries. For each industry, the fault lies not with itself, but elsewhere, and it can no longer be expected to work out its own salvation. That is why, to put it in Keynesian terms, the marginal efficiency of capital more than just declines, it collapses.

As soon as over-all sales decline from the peak, capacity becomes excessive practically everywhere. The disparities between industrial segments, which made for considerable unevenness on the advance, do not persist on the decline. To most firms, it is evident almost immediately that demand has been overestimated. With capacity already excessive, the only way to deal with the situation is to curtail commitments for new capacity as quickly as possible. The decline is almost inevitably sharper than the advance.

SPECIAL FEATURES OF THE INVESTMENT CYCLE

Although capacity exerts controlling force on new investment at certain stages in the cycle in the same way that existing commodity inventories do on further accumulation, the analogy is not complete. Some aspects of capacity building represent peculiarities that have to be dealt with in their own terms. One important point of difference lies in the speed of recovery from the depression lows.

In the depths of the depression, practically no production facilities are strained, and the existence of excess capacity is widespread. Some machinery wears out. Other parts of the total stock deteriorate in idleness, perhaps to the point where they must finally be replaced. Some unnecessary maintenance may be undertaken to keep key staff at least partially employed. But the expenditures that result from these causes are only a fraction of normal maintenance and replacement. When a breakdown occurs, production may be shifted from the broken-down machines to others still in good operating condition, or repair parts may be transferred from idle machines to keep the others running.

In addition to a minimum of continuing expenditures for replacement, some investment still goes on, mostly in the category of autonomous investment. There are local situations that require new installations, even though similar capacity is idle elsewhere. There are some exceptional lines of business that do not conform to the general pattern. New products and industries, sometimes referred to as "growth" industries, may continue to develop. Some expansion may be undertaken to provide depression goods and services, which are not particularly desired when people are prosperous but become all they can afford in a depression. A few farsighted and financially strong concerns may decide to buy future expansion when it is cheap. Others who are in danger of losing their market position to competitors may be forced to install new equipment to improve quality or cut costs. For all these reasons, there is a floor for gross investment. It continues at a rate somewhat over zero but well below the level of normal replacement or current write-offs.

Unfortunately, part of the autonomous investment that goes on in the depression is not a fully effective force for recovery. The laborsaving equipment that is installed displaces workers as soon as it comes into operation and adds an increment of technological unemployment to that which results from lower output. To put this another way, there is an employment multiplier as well as an income multiplier, and the installation of laborsaving equipment interferes with its operation. From the income point of view, the laborsaving devices have two effects: they transfer some income from wages to interest or other capital charges, and they make it possible for producers to realize a saving in costs that becomes profit or is passed on to consumers in lower prices. The shift to these other forms of "real income" is more likely to reduce the dissaving that would otherwise occur than to increase consumption.

In the boom such shifts seem to be of little consequence, and over the long run, the adjustments have to be made in any case. But at the end of the boom both the decline and the depression are intensified. On the decline the new technology that accumulated during the boom is given full effect, because the least efficient units are retired from service first. Later, extension of that technology to additional areas hampers the recovery.

The primary reason for the delay of recovery, however, is that the durability of fixed capital keeps idle facilities on hand, waiting for new orders to put them to work. When the first beginnings of recovery are experienced, there is little need for new investment. Some of the existing excess capacity is merely brought into use. In this respect producers' durable equipment behaves more like construction than like commodity inventories.

Some liquidation of the stock does occur, mostly of obsolete or inefficient types of equipment, but the turn at the depression low is not automatic after the peak rate of liquidation is reached. The liquidation does not take place quickly enough to permit any such rebound. Reduced production does not use up capacity, as it does commodity inventories, but makes capacity still more redundant. Hence capacity remains above demand for some time, so that there must be a growth of demand resulting from other factors before the surplus of existing capacity is so reduced as to permit new investment to be resumed. Recovery in the investment cycle is almost inevitably slower than the decline.

At the very bottom of the depression, recovery in over-all activity is likely to begin with an initial spurt as liquidation of commodity inventories ceases. This is unlikely by itself to raise production from the low of a major decline to a point where excess capacity is substantially reduced. Nevertheless, it helps put some industries in a better position, so that limited opportunities for new investment may appear. Others gradually appear for reasons unrelated to the cyclical mechanisms. These may be only local situations at first, in scattered areas or industries, but the investments undertaken in those areas give the whole economy a lift.

As the pace of activity quickens, the need for capacity is first met by reactivating idle equipment. Investment is thus held through the early stages of recovery below the level of long-term needs for growth and replacement. When the point is reached at which the combination of slow liquidation of facilities and growth in activity has reestablished a balance between capacity and output, the rate of investment has to be stepped up to preserve that balance. But stepping up the rate of investment to bring it into line with needs that are now apparent pushes up income and makes capacity deficient. Recovery then enters its most rapid phase.

As income and demand move ahead, business has several alternatives to building new capacity. Relatively inefficient equipment may be brought out of retirement and put back into operation. Bottleneck types of equipment may be expanded and semiobsolete facilities refurbished. Various kinds of existing facilities may be operated extra shifts and overtime hours. These alternatives involve heavy penalties in the form of high labor costs but are widely used in the early stages of the boom when it is feared that recovery may be only temporary. Later these alternatives are completely used up. Then increasing numbers of firms find their capacity inadequate and are forced to make new installations.

The shortcomings of the acceleration principle become clear when viewed from this standpoint. That principle may still be used to explain the upper turning point. There its deficiencies may be rationalized in terms of the complexity of a situation where cycles of varying length intermingle, where alternatives to new investment may be widely used for a while, and where production delays and excess capacities exert differential effects by industries. Interferences are set up by too many claims on a given labor force and on existing capacities. Hence, what might happen in the individual line cannot hold for the economy generally. As a result, the lead of investment in the downturn might be small, as it is seen to be when the governing principle is accumulation of capacity.

In the depression, on the other hand, the observed disparities in investment behavior cannot be explained in terms of changing rates of production, because investment does not lead at all, but lags. Interferences are then of little consequence, since idle labor and facilities are available for any work desired. Similarly, attempts to rationalize the failure of investment response in terms of the lack of symmetry in its relationship to current production appear plausible only in relation to the existence of accumulated capital stocks. In the latter terms, however, the entire sequence follows as a natural consequence of capacity accumulation. The fact that capacity keeps going up through the early years of a decline and then remains relatively stable until recovery gets under way explains both the lag in the trough of the depression and the failure of investment to recover fully by the time output again reaches its previous high.

It appears as a corollary of this that the influence of the accelerator is low, or at least concealed in the depression. When activity first flattens, the acceleration is offset, because the excess of capacity is still growing; then for a while the contribution of gradually reviving demand remains small in relation to the depressing effect of the excess. Only as production comes back up into line with capacity does the accelerator gain in effectiveness. Particular industries where shortages first develop may then be expanded sharply, while others in which capacity is still excessive are lagging.

In the early stages of the boom, more and more industries find expansion necessary, and it is then that the accelerator exerts its maximum force. Its action is supplemented, furthermore, by the development of a backlog as deficiencies in capacity are encountered. Expansion plans begin to look beyond the current level of output and attempt to provide for growth into the more distant future. After a while, investment is built up to the point where it begins to eliminate the deficiencies in capacity, industry by industry; and even though some industries come back for another round of expansion, the ceiling is fixed. Unfortunately it is fixed at a level that cannot be maintained.

During the period when the economy is forging ahead most rapidly, prices rise faster than costs, and profits mount. In contrast to the depression, when practically nothing is profitable, almost any venture promises to produce a high return. As losses turn to profits and profits soar, internal sources of funds provide a large part of the financing needed for the expansion, making the firm largely independent of the capital market. Moreover, profits and costs can no longer be considered entirely controlling. Investments are frequently made to gain or preserve a strategic position, which is measured not by profits but by market shares or by such intangibles as prestige and reputation. The mail-order executive who stubbornly resisted the expansion needed to keep his firm in line with competition despite all criticism provides the horrible example by which the importance of emulation is impressed on other executives.

Under these circumstances, the interest rate can no more limit the boom than it could prevent the depression. In so far as industry is cost-conscious, it is likely to be thinking in terms of profits that will pay off an investment in 2 or 3 years. In the early post–World War II years, it was not uncommon for a new plant to achieve an annual return of over 100 percent on the assets invested in it. Furthermore, interest is a charge on earnings before taxes, so that its impact on after-tax profits is correspondingly reduced. In the case of utilities, to whom long-term interest charges are an important cost consideration, the effectiveness of higher rates is minimized by the rate-making process, which provides earnings net of all charges. Hence the most drastic interest-rate action possible in the light of institutional factors, which are soundly grounded in the history of modern monetary systems, could at best only moderate the cyclical swings of business investment a little.

Even credit restriction as such tends to be ineffective as a restraint on enthusiastic business expansion. The economic system always forces an amount of savings that corresponds to the investment undertaken. Ordinarily the banking system facilitates this process through the expansion of the money supply. It is not alone, however, in doing the job. The price system, through the high profits it generates, is the really effective means of accomplishing this result, and it would continue to operate with a stable money supply, though somewhat less forcefully. This is not to argue that the contribution of monetary policy to economic stability should be rejected because it is limited. The point simply is that the financial aspects are not at the heart of the business cycle. The real problem lies in the maladjustments between stocks and flows that continually, and indeed quickly, arise in a highly productive economy.

INTERACTIONS OF SPECIFIC CYCLES

This description of "the cycle" has been largely cast in terms of a structural unity that never actually exists. The business cycle as a whole is made up of a combination of elements that tend to differ significantly in respect to the characteristics that affect the adjustment between the processes of production and consumption in each case. Both directly, by industry, and indirectly, through their effects on income, residential-construction cycles and inventory cycles interact with the business-investment cycle.

The latter is itself a complex containing practically all the shades of variation that can be found in both of the former. Capital requirements vary, for example, by the nature of the consuming industry; they are fairly low in some cases, as in the construction industry, and high in others, as in the steel industry. The ability of individual industries to adjust operations to customers' demands varies greatly, and the availability of capacity is only one element of variation. In some industries, where capital requirements are readily met, imbalances may be corrected quickly; in others, the process of adjustment is long-drawn-out. These differences smooth the cycle in its prosperity and depression phases. They may also shift the timing of changes somewhat but do not appear to moderate substantially the drastic swings from the highs to the lows.

Producers' durable equipment includes many semistandard items whose production period is no longer than that of consumers' durables; thus a variety of hand tools and other small items are produced to stock, just as consumer items are. But this class of goods also includes an important volume of heavy equipment, such as generating equipment or large, special-purpose machines for which the production period may be several years. Between these extremes lies a continuum of machinery designed to provide power, shape materials, move or preserve goods, package finished products, or perform other kinds of work. These may be obtained in some cases quickly and in others only after an extended period of waiting; they may remain in service many years or be retired within several years. Investment in most types is fully variable in the swings of a major cycle, but some are pulled only a little off their own self-determined courses by the more moderate fluctuations of a minor cycle. Yet differences tend to average out, and when the averaging takes place over so large a number of elements, the result is fairly dependable behavior in the aggregate.

The primary responsiveness of investment to changes in over-all demand is in equipment, because that is where adjustments can more readily be made. However, there are limits to which equipment can be crowded into existing plant, and there are also limits on the adaptability of existing plants to new, improved techniques. Seldom is there a straightforward replacement of an existing machine by another of the same type, and often new processes differ widely from those previously used. In the recent trend toward automation, buildings and machinery have to be designed for each other, so that the special features of each are well matched. The long planning period needed for such units would seem to slow the building of new capacity, but industrial research readies the plans in advance of need, so that the whole project can go forward quickly when the time is ripe. Thus, even plant construction tends to be somewhat responsive to changes in production.

From the short-term point of view, the interactions between producers' equipment and inventories are of particular significance. It is not at all strange that two such segments, both of which are responsive to changes in income and demand, should tend for the most part to move in unison. When producers' equipment initiates a movement, the change in income and sales brings about a quick adjustment of inventories. When inventories move, investment responds to the change in output, which includes both the change in sales and the change in inventories. In this short cycle, there is a kind of super-supermultiplier at work, with acceleration in both inventories and equipment pushing them quickly past any theoretical points of long-term stability.

Consumers' durables are also responsive to such movements and show correspondingly wide fluctuations. In the boom, both consumers and business increase and improve their holdings of durable equipment. In the depression, consumers cannot improve their durable-goods standards because they lack the necessary means of financing purchases. Many businesses still have sufficient cash balances or satisfactory credit standing to upgrade their capital-goods inventory, but they neither need nor want to do so. Thus policy aims at liquidating stocks of durable goods in the hands of consumers and business users along with business inventories as such. Together these three segments are capable of swinging the economy widely in the course of a single year, as in 1921 or in 1938.

The movements of these factors are not, of course, always in accord. In early 1947, investment continued strong while the accumulation of nondurable goods inventories came to a halt. However, the situations in which such offsetting occurs will always be exceptions to the basic tendency toward coordinate response.

Investment in new equipment responds, also, over the longer term, to changes in construction. Part of the equipment is needed in new structures, and there are also the induced-investment effects that result from changes in construction activity. It has been suggested that equipment should be analyzed in two parts—the part tied up with new construction and the part tied up with other factors. Even if this were possible, it would probably be an unnecessary refinement, because construction affects the over-all situation indirectly through changes in industrial production, which includes output of both building materials and consumers' goods.

Investment in equipment is thus tied to both the inventory cycle and the construction cycle. These two cycles vary so greatly in amplitude and timing that they may be rather clearly distinguished. The specific cycles within the producers' equipment aggregate are largely indistinguishable from each other and to some extent also from these other important cycles. For this reason, it is appropriate to think of "the short cycle" as the inventory cycle and "the long cycle" as the construction cycle and to recognize that each of these cycles both induces and gives effect to changes in equipment building.

Reference to these movements as cycles is justified, because induced investment gives them such cumulative force on the upswings and downswings and the reversals so consistently follow the termination of accumulation or liquidation at the ends of those movements. The use of this terminology is in no way intended to contradict the point that what actually happens in any specific period is the result of a variety of rather diverse forces which are in part noncyclical, or are even counter-cyclical, in nature.

In analyzing actual "cycles," it must be kept in mind that the precise points of reversal will reflect the behavior of the more volatile elements in the current situation. Even though the ground for a recession is laid by an overexpansion of investment, the precise timing of the actual downturn may in effect be determined by inventories or some other factor that moves more sharply over the short term. The immediate occasion for the reversal may be an entirely unexpected news report or a shift in speculative psychology that has little if any relation to the current position of investment requirements.

BASIC DETERMINANTS OF INVESTMENT

The conclusion to be drawn, stated in most general terms, is that business investment depends primarily on the rate at which capacity is being utilized but that this primary relationship is modified by the intrusion of other cyclical and autonomous factors. To abstract from all the latter, another way to formulate the basic relationship is to state that the change in capacity is a function of existing capacity and of the aggregate production which that capacity is currently called upon to turn out. The level of output or sales expresses the need for capacity. The level of capacity expresses the ability of the economy to meet that need. When the need increases relative to the ability for meeting it, investment tends to expand, and vice versa.

To leave this as merely another theoretical formulation would accomplish little. Several statistical tests have therefore been applied in various industrial areas to establish its validity. Statistics available for this purpose are limited, for despite the importance assigned to business investment in the theory of business cycles, no direct current data on this subject were compiled before World War II.

Such data as are available—the Department of Commerce estimates of producers' durables included as part of the gross national product, as well as the ground-breaking estimates prepared by Simon Kuznets and the National Bureau of Economic Research for earlier years—were built up by the commodity-flow method. The essence of this method is to begin with data on the production of various kinds of materials and equipment and from these production data to build up the flows to final users, adding estimates for transportation costs and distributors' margins at the various stages through which they pass and allocating the totals arrived at in this way to business, consumers, government, and exports. Although the errors produced by this method may be relatively limited, it is not a method that can be used to produce satisfactory current statistics of investment and therefore is not a satisfactory tool for the short-term forecaster.

At the end of World War II, the Department of Commerce and the

Securities and Exchange Commission started a new quarterly survey of planned capital outlays. In addition to the information on plans for the future, this survey obtains actual expenditures during the most recent quarter. So much attention has been given to the forward estimates that the basic value of the actual data which it provided has been obscured. These data are very useful for current purposes, but do not afford a good basis for statistical analysis because they do not extend far enough into the past. For this purpose, the older data have to be relied on. There are, in addition, physical-volume data for a number of important industrial segments that may be used to supplement the findings based on available statistics of producers' investment outlays as such.

Manufacturing and Mining. The results of a study relating deflated capital outlays in manufacturing and mining to industrial production and to capacity for such production are shown in Chart 10-1. The study from which this chart was obtained is summarized in Appendix D. The upper panel of Chart 10-1 shows the relationship of capacity to production for over 3 decades beginning with 1920. The capacity index has been adjusted to conform to the base used for the production index. The war years have little meaning for this relationship for three reasons: first, the production line includes output from government facilities as well as from private producers; second, both private and government facilities were worked under abnormal pressure during the war through the use of multiple shifts and extensive overtime hours; and third, military items not ordinarily produced in large volume are heavily weighted in the production index. In the other years, the relationship of capacity to output fits the theory.

Immediate postwar years, such as 1920 and 1923 or 1947 and 1948, show an unusually high utilization of capacity. Capacity is subsequently kept pretty well in line with rising production through the boom. Considerable underutilization develops in years of decline, such as 1930, 1938, and 1949, but capacity continues up for a while after the decline has begun. The expansion comes to a complete halt only in a period of extended depression, as in the early 1930s, or as a result of wartime restrictions, as in 1942 to 1945.

Use of these two series as the independent variables in a correlation aimed at estimating industrial-investment expenditures reveals a high degree of relationship, as shown by the actual and calculated values in the lower panel of Chart 10-1. In most peacetime years, the error of estimate was considerably less than $0.5 billion of investment expenditures in terms of 1947 prices. The correlation is positive with respect to production and negative with respect to capacity. In other words, investment tends to move up or down with output, allowing for a moderate lag, but rising capacity puts a constant drag on investment during the advance and combines with declining output to produce a sharp drop in the early stages of a decline.

Investment has to drop far, however, before any actual liquidation of capacity occurs. With gross expenditures falling about two-thirds from 1929 to 1932, to a low of less than $2 billion, net investment became neg-

Chart 10–1. Industrial Production, Capacity, and Gross Investment in Manufacturing and Mining Facilities

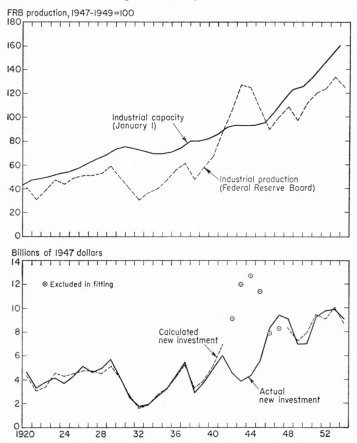

ative by only about $1 billion. Actual liquidation was confined to the years 1931 to 1934 and amounted to only 8 percent of the capacity in existence at the beginning of that period. Furthermore, these figures may overstate the actual liquidation, because the deductions from gross investment are based on depreciation charges, which tend to be stable because they in turn are based on accumulated past investment, whereas actual retirements are not governed by the accounting write-offs. The picture presented by these estimates, however, is probably not far from the mark.

Capacity remained relatively stable from 1931 to the revival of investment in 1936 and 1937. This period of catching up was a little shorter than that in which the housing surplus was liquidated. The reversal of government policy and inventories in 1937 temporarily brought the upswing to a halt, but recovery was gaining momentum at the end of the decade. The restrictions on investment demand during the war served, of course, to carry over needs for additional capacity into the postwar years and heightened the postwar boom.

Electric Power. Another illustration is provided by the expansion of electric-power capacity. The underlying data are shown in the upper panel of Chart 10–2. Here all the basic units of measurement are expressed in physical terms. Capacity is stated in kilowatts. The effective utilization of capacity is theoretically measured by the peak load, also in kilowatts, which this capacity is called upon to produce. Unfortunately, peak-load data are available only back to 1938, and the seasonal-peak output in kilowatthours had to be substituted as the only suitable measure of utilization available throughout the period covered.

Peak monthly output is in some respects a less satisfactory measure of utilization than peak load, not only because of the difference in units but also because there has been a constant trend toward greater power output with given capacity or given peak load. Changes in both market demand and methods of production and distribution have brought this about. On the one hand, new power uses have not coincided in timing with previous demands, and markets with varying peaks have been integrated. On the other hand, power systems have been consolidated and interconnected, so that surplus power in one system could be drawn upon to meet peak demands in neighboring systems. Both peak load and peak output are measures of actual production, however, rather than of demand; and in periods of power shortage, such as the war years, peak load tends to understate demands more than peak monthly output, because some consumers shift their power demands off the peak. In these years, peak output may provide the better measure. If it is assumed for the other years of the period that the trend toward greater output in relation to peak load has been a gradual one, the correlation with investment should not be too adversely affected by switching to what is at first glance an inferior measure of utilization.

The gross installations of new capacity during the year were taken as the dependent variable. Data available from the Federal Power Commission back to 1941 had to be partially estimated for earlier years; the estimates converted available data on net installations to gross by splicing depreciation to retirements at the earliest date possible and adding the resulting estimates. Of course, installations and completions lag considerably behind contracts and commitments and to a lesser degree behind actual building of capacity.

Chart 10–2. Electric-power Production, Capacity, and Gross Changes in Capacity

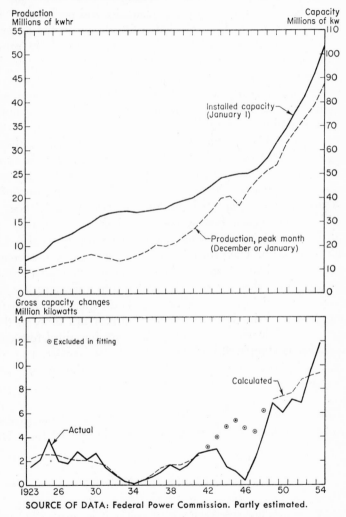

SOURCE OF DATA: Federal Power Commission. Partly estimated.

During the depression, capacity continued to increase through 1933, long after output turned down, and only one year, 1934, showed an excess of retirements over new installations. The strong upward trend in electric-power use, being dependent upon ever more widespread use of electrically operated machines and appliances, created a relatively favorable situation for renewed expansion, but it was probably retarded in the late 1930s by the rise in public power and the Holding Companies Act and other power policies.

Since electric-power projects usually take several years to complete, the capacity and utilization of several previous years are relevant to the installations in any given year. In setting up the relationship, therefore, the averages of the three previous capacity and peak output figures were used. The results of this correlation are shown in the lower panel of Chart 10–2.[5] Again the relationship is close enough to provide a basis for forecasts, especially if used in conjunction with data on planned installations. In the early postwar years, actual installations were below the estimates, probably as a result of the inability of the equipment producers to fill heavy orders quickly. In some of the following boom years, installations tended to exceed the estimates.

Railway Freight Cars. Another illustration is provided by the building of railway freight cars. The upper panel of Chart 10–3 shows capacity as represented by the number of cars owned, average weekly carloadings in the fiscal year ended September 30 as the utilization of those cars, and the maximum reported shortage to indicate deficiences of car supplies in specific years. During the period as a whole, there was a moderate downtrend in carloadings modified by the cyclical pattern of the Great Depression. The growth of the economy was more than offset by increasing car capacities and by the shifting of traffic to the highways. The downtrend in carloadings was translated into a more or less equivalent downward trend in the need for cars. Train speeds were increased, and other changes helped reduce average turnaround time, so that the same number of carloads could he handled with one-third fewer cars in the early 1950s as compared with a quarter century earlier. To complete the picture of needs, car shortages are shown for the specific years in which they were reported; they were important only in the two postwar periods.

The results of a correlation utilizing these three factors to estimate new-car construction is shown in the lower panel of Chart 10–3. The dis-

[5] The estimating equation is

$$G = 2.591 + 0.5990\overline{O_{B_0+2B_{-1}}} - 0.196\overline{K_{2B_{-1}+B_{-2}}} \qquad (R^2 = .93)$$

where G = gross installations, kw

$\overline{O_{B_0+2B_{-1}}}$ = weighted average of the seasonal peak production (the higher of December or January) for the current and previous year, with the latter weighted double, millions of kwh

$\overline{K_{2B_{-1}+B_{-2}}}$ = weighted average of installed capacity at the beginning of the previous year and the year before, with the former weighted double, millions of kw

Chart 10–3. Freight-car Loadings, Car Ownership, and New Cars Delivered

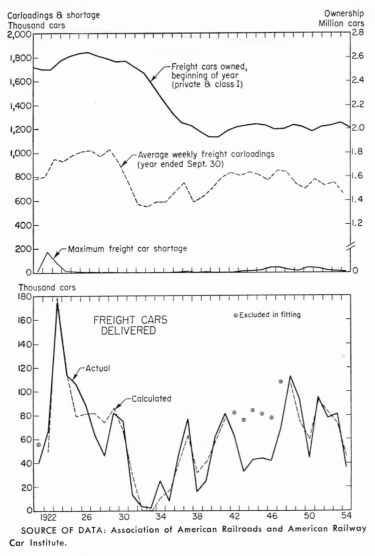

Carloadings & shortage
Thousand cars

Ownership
Million cars

Freight cars owned, beginning of year (private & class I)

Average weekly freight carloadings (year ended Sept. 30)

Maximum freight car shortage

Thousand cars

FREIGHT CARS DELIVERED

⊚ Excluded in fitting

Actual

Calculated

SOURCE OF DATA: Association of American Railroads and American Railway Car Institute.

turbing effects of the war are clearly apparent on this chart but are less important than for many other types of equipment. New-car building was restricted during the war, but only to a level that approximately offset current losses. Carloadings were restricted by the limitations on car supply, but the traffic handled was greatly increased by a series of rules and regulations designed to maximize the traffic that could be handled with the available cars. When these rules and regulations were relaxed after the war, demand for cars moved up, creating new shortages in the immediate postwar years. At that time, insufficient steel was available to car builders to fill railroad orders promptly, so that car building in 1947 did not fully reflect demand. In 1949, when steel became more readily available, cars were for a time built more rapidly than the situation warranted. In general, however, the estimating relationship is satisfactory.[6]

Shortages of cars, which mean that shipments are being delayed because cars cannot be supplied for loading, result in extreme bursts of car building. This kind of situation disturbs customer relations and results in diversion of business to competitors or to alternative forms of transportation. These are regarded as the most serious eventualities to be faced, and the railroads act quickly to correct the situation. A sharp upsurge in demand may thus bring a rapid acceleration of investment, and if demand then levels off, eliminating the shortage, investment tends to fall back. To the extent that extreme movements result from the carry-over of wartime backlogs, however, they cannot be considered to fit any normal peacetime relationship.

Farm Investment. There is one area of the economy in which capital investment cannot be estimated in terms of the relationship of output to capacity, and that is agriculture. Here the concepts of output and capacity do not apply in the same way as in manufacturing or utilities. The variation of output is irregular with respect to anything that might be termed capacity. Weather differences make it irregular even with respect to the combination of all inputs, including labor, seed, fertilizer, and other noncapital items. If there is a need to step up output in the short term, increases in some of these other inputs are likely to produce the surest results, though the addition of laborsaving machinery has represented a steady long-term trend and tends to be accelerated in periods of high industrial activity, when labor is placed in short supply by being bid away from farm work.

The existing stock of capital does place a restraint on new investment when output is generally adequate to meet the community's needs. But an increase in output under these conditions does not necessarily put

---

[6] The estimating equation is

$$D = 33.33 + 0.2049L_F - 61.03K_b + 0.5829M_{-1} \qquad (R^2 = .89)$$

where D = freight cars delivered, thousands

L_F = average weekly carloadings in the fiscal year ended September 30, thousands

K = private and class I cars owned at the beginning of the year, millions

and M_{-1} = the maximum car shortage reported in the preceding year, thousands

Data are from the Association of American Railroads, Car Service Division, and the American Railway Car Institute.

any pressure on capacity at all. More likely it puts downward pressure on prices, and far from calling for further increases, the situation may call for downward adjustment in investment. The situations that call forth the greatest amount of investment are those in which prices are high, in which high demands are calling for increased output and high returns make financing of new investment easy. Under prosperous farm conditions it would only be after an extended period of high farm income that the stock of farm capital could effectively restrain new investment, and then the decisive change might come from the decline in prices and income rather than from the additional increment to capacity.

Farm investment, therefore, varies not with output but with income. In this respect it is more like consumers' durable goods than like other producers' goods. A number of studies have revealed the close correlation between farm-capital outlays and farm operators' net cash income.[7] Simple correlations of this type give good results for the interwar period because of the relative stability of the stock of farm capital from the mid-1920s to the beginning of World War II and for a number of postwar years because of the surge of equipment buying that resulted from the accumulated backlog of demand and high wartime and early postwar incomes.

The results of an alternative formulation, in line with the others in this section, are shown in Chart 10–4.[8] This study utilizes deflated data for capital outlays and for income and includes the capital stock as a second independent variable. The effects of rising stocks are apparent in the latest years, after the succession of major postwar increases. After the Korean War farm income was relatively steady, but equipment purchases drifted downward.

The point developed by these examples is that investment is dependent upon the intensity of capacity utilization. In each case, the basis for estimating is provided by a measure of the flow of product and a measure of the capacity used in producing it. These are much the same factors, it may be noted, that were found in earlier chapters to be decisive

---

[7] See J. W. Kendrick and C. E. Jones, "Farm Capital Outlays and Stock," *Survey of Current Business*, August, 1953.

[8] The estimating equation is

$$F = -1.033 + 0.2713Y - 0.00667K \qquad (R^2 = .98)$$

where F = farm-capital expenditures, billions of 1935–1939 dollars (unpublished estimates prepared by E. W. Grove, U.S. Department of Agriculture, Farm Income Branch)

$\qquad Y$ = gross farm income, billions of 1910–1914 dollars (deflated by index of prices paid, U.S. Department of Agriculture)

$\qquad K$ = index of farm capital stock, 1947 = 100 (unpublished estimates prepared by L. McHugh, U.S. Department of Commerce, National Income Division) in gauging inventory changes and new residential construction.[9] The general principle governing the relationships is that increases in the flow tend to stimulate investment and increases in the stock tend to depress it. However, in all cases the coefficients reflecting the influence of the

Chart 10–4. Farm Income, Capital Stock, and Gross Investment

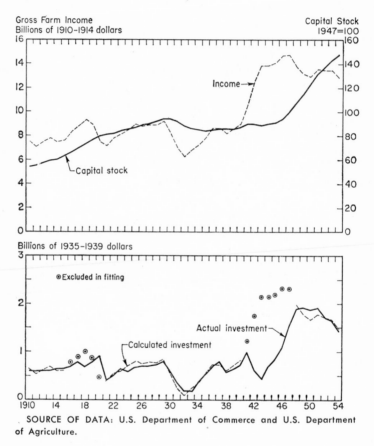

SOURCE OF DATA: U.S. Department of Commerce and U.S. Department of Agriculture.

output or need factors are considerably larger than those reflecting the influence of capacity or stock factors, so that changes in output exert a greater leverage on investment than do changes in capacity.

Not only are the changes in capacity a generally less effective influence on new investment than changes in output, but changes in capacity

[9] For a more general discussion of the nature of the relationships involved, see Appendix B.

tend to be relatively small over the short term. Hence, the year-to-year changes in investment are dominated by the changes in operating requirements, as measured by the output that the facilities are called upon to produce.

These facts may be utilized in a still simpler relationship between investment and activity—the simple correlation of changes in aggregate

Chart 10–5. Relation of Change in New Fixed Investment to Change in Gross National Product

In billions of 1947 dollars

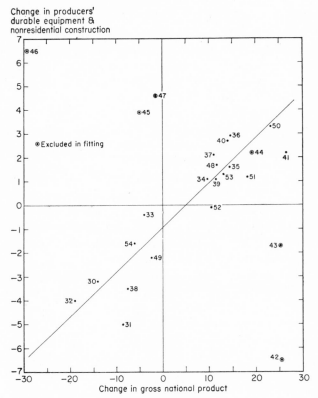

Change in producers' durable equipment & nonresidential construction

producers' investment and changes in over-all activity. Both investment and production must here be thought of in the physical-volume sense. Such a relationship between annual changes in deflated investment expenditures and deflated gross national product is shown in Chart 10–5. The relationship accounts for the bulk of the variation in expenditures for new industrial facilities. This statement holds for both plant and equipment expenditures, but plant construction, with its longer periods of production and consumption, shows somewhat greater independence of movement.

The changes in investment and over-all production are almost invariably in the same direction, except for the large departures from the relationships in years of disturbance. Note that the line of regression passes below the origin. This may be interpreted as the effect of rising capacity. When output is steady, rising capacity causes investment to fall. Only when a critical, minimum increase in output is exceeded does new investment tend to increase. (Taking $5 billion as the critical point on Chart 10–5, investment tends to rise by 19 percent of any further increase in gross product.)

An inference to be drawn from Chart 10–5, as well as from the earlier examples in specific areas, is that the changes in plant and equipment expenditures derive primarily from changes in production. This seemingly contradicts the theory that investment is the primary determinant of economic activity. The question arises: "How is it possible for investment to be both derived and determining?" The contradiction is, however, more apparent than real. All that is needed to give investment this dual quality is a chain of interaction, whereby what is determined may react on what is determining. Here the chain exists in the circular flow of income, with the multiplier working in one direction and the accelerator in the other. The determination is mutual rather than unilateral. It would be as accurate to reverse the scales of Chart 10–5 and portray the relationship the other way. No one factor is controlling.

In practice, it is important to approach the problem of estimation from both directions, because the situation as a whole reacts on all the segments. In short, it helps to know that any factor is substantially determined, since it may be possible through this knowledge to avoid large errors that could result from regarding it as free to go where it would. At the same time, it is essential to look for the changes that are not strictly determined, because these may produce important differences in the outcome.

AUTONOMOUS FACTORS DETERMINING INVESTMENT

To deal with the investment picture in true perspective, it must be kept in mind that the procedures discussed above embody a certain amount of oversimplification. Many factors are at work, some almost entirely noneconomic in character, and these affect various segments, or even the total, in ways not contemplated by the relationship. The fact that such influences are diverse in character probably helps make the relationships appear so dependable over the whole span of years covered by the existing records. But it would not be proper to conclude on this basis that the special influences affecting any future period under consideration could safely be ignored.

In other words, the relationships discussed above may be used as a basis for projecting future changes, provided that autonomous elements are separately estimated as deviations from the average relationship. For example, when a war production program is started, there will have to be additional installations above those that would ordinarily be required by the movement of the economy. To stimulate mobilization during the Korean War, the government granted certificates of necessity which authorized the amortization of defense facilities over a 5-year period. In some cases the certificate holders were also assisted by loans or purchase agreements covering the amortization period. It was recognized, of course, that the facilities had civilian as well as military usefulness, and for this reason the special amortization privilege was not applied to the entire cost of the capacity but was restricted to a specified portion of the total cost, depending upon the nature of the facility to be built. Other kinds of disturbances than those relating to a war effort are not likely to produce such drastic changes, but whenever there is an indication of special influences at work, they may be allowed for by separate estimates.

In the case of new-plant outlays, there is a kind of long-cycle effect, which kept such expenditures low in relation both to equipment outlays and to general economic activity after World War II, right through the Korean War years. Equipment outlays move more nearly in a fixed relation to output, and this does not appear to have been greatly disturbed by shifts between either replacement and expansion or portions installed in old plants and portions required for new plants. Replacement is not a stable item, remaining in year-to-year conformity with a long-term projection, but fluctuates with current activity; and expansion requirements, whether going into new plants or old, show a similar pattern of behavior. There are autonomous elements that affect equipment outlays, of course, producing such deviations as the bulge in 1947 and 1948, when large reconversion backlogs were being met, but the basic pattern of the relationship is only temporarily affected by such conditions.

Another type of autonomous change that tends to produce only temporary deviations is that deriving from innovations. Schumpeter's comprehensive study of this subject showed that, although discovery and invention laid the ground for steady progress, the actual introduction of new products and processes occurred in waves. Innovations thus became essential ingredients of the cycle as well as of long-term growth. Nevertheless, some developments of this nature may be significant enough to result in appreciable deviations of their own.

In the recent literature, the products of scientific and engineering research are often cited as the primary form of autonomous change in the economy. In so far as they contribute to the underlying trend, this is a correct view. What is often overlooked, however, is that most changes of this kind come rather quickly under the control of the stock-flow relationships. Many new products or industries displace existing operations, and from the very start the investment necessary to introduce them is partly offset by declines in other industries. Others are new or different enough that their effects may for a while be almost entirely additive. But in all these cases, after a preliminary period of progress toward maturity, the importance of newness dwindles and the demands of the market for current output become the controlling factor. In some cases, like that of the antibiotic drugs, the initial surge of enthusiasm in use and of "pipeline" requirements may lead to overexpansion of investment in a few years. An industry like air conditioning may build its capacity to the level required by the rate of current installations in only a fraction of a cycle, and thereafter investment must proceed in accordance with the usual determinants.

Another aspect of the situation that tends to preserve the validity of the basic relationships is the fact that, in a complex situation of this kind, all the various factors that bear on the problem are likely to be inter-correlated. Prices, profits, and costs all fluctuate together, with irregularities and lags imposed by institutional or other conditions. Many other factors, such as income or the state of financial markets, also fit into the general structure of influences affecting investment. No doubt many of these have a bearing on the problem, but they are best regarded as supplementary rather than as alternatives to the basic relations of demand and production to existing capacity.

Since there is no way to take account of all the special influences that may affect the outcome, a certain amount of oversimplification is inherent in any practical approach. All that can be done is to reduce the difficulty to a minimum. What is suggested is that the kind of simplification which proceeds in terms of the basic determinants is likely to be least damaging to the final results. The situation calling for new investment is that in which the economy is operating near to capacity, and it brings all the other factors into play. If there is anything special about current conditions, such as the Federal-power policies of the late 1930s in relation to electric-utility investment, it is likely to produce only a temporary discrepancy rather than to modify the relationship throughout.

Many attempts have been made to utilize other factors in forecasting investment, but in so far as such methods have been made public, none has been outstandingly successful. Perhaps the most commonly used is profits. The rationale of this approach is easy to understand: business expands when it is profitable; at that time it has part if not all of the financing with which to expand investment, and high earnings create optimism in the stock market, making it easier to obtain any additional financing needed. This line of thinking is incontrovertible if one does not look beyond profits to the underlying conditions on which they depend.

As already indicated, the approach in terms of profit possibilities has played a prominent role in business-cycle theory. It has been summarized in the following terms.[10]

> Complex as the ultimate forces underlying the formation of capital may be, they strike investors as a comparatively simple calculus. . . . All forces affecting the inducement to invest . . . operate through three, partially distinct, channels: marginal cost of producing and owning the investment good; rate of discount or interest at which expected values of the uses of the durable agent are translated into present values; and expectations concerning what the values of those uses will be.

This calculus may be explained in terms of the following equation:

$$C_{-2}(1 + r)^2 + C_{-1}(1 + r) + C_o = \frac{E_1}{(1 + r)} + \frac{E_2}{(1 + r)^2} + \cdots + \frac{E_n}{(1 + r)^n}$$

The Cs are annual costs of bringing the project into operation. The subscripts designate years, o referring to the year in which the project is completed and the negative subscripts to earlier years. The Es are the earnings obtained from the project over the n successive years of its service life. Both the costs and the earnings are brought to a present-value basis in the year o by means of the interest rate, r, adding interest to past costs and discounting future returns. The rate r does not represent any actual rate but is a purely conceptual rate that can be computed from the equation, assuming that all the costs and earnings are known. There is always a rate, positive or negative, that will bring the two sides of the equation into balance. This rate, considered as a typical rate for new investment projects in general is equivalent to what the Swedish school called the "natural rate" of interest and Keynes called the "marginal efficiency of capital." When this rate is high in comparison with the rate at which funds are available in the capital market, there is an inducement to expand investment; when it is low, investment tends to dry up.

In practice, of course, the costs and earnings underlying such a calculation are never known in advance. The costs may be fixed by contract at some point, but the earnings are dependent upon future sales volume, prices, and operating costs, which can in no sense be considered fixed. In other words, the approach is far from a simple calculus. It presents

[10] Clarence D. Long, Jr., *Building Cycles and the Theory of Investment*, Princeton University Press, Princeton, N.J., 1940, p. 11.

an exceedingly complex forecasting problem, one that is, indeed, insoluble.

Modern versions of this theory, including that of the author quoted, point out that it is the expected earnings rather than the actual earnings on the investment which represent the determining factor. An advantage of this formulation in terms of expectations is that it presumably takes into account the autonomous as well as the induced factors affecting investment expenditures. Both kinds of factors must operate through the decisions of business management, and each can do so only to the extent that it is known to be a factor and is so enabled to produce an expectation of favorable or unfavorable results. From a practical point of view, however, this just leads into another blind alley, because there is no way of knowing precisely when business expectations will change.

Most analysts recognize that expectations are more volatile than investment as such. Business sentiment makes sharp reversals, suddenly passing from an extreme of optimism to an extreme of pessimism. Actual business appraisals of prospects, in other words, have been known, after the fact, to make extreme swings between gross overestimates and correspondingly exaggerated underestimates of what investments will return. For the most part, the effects of such changes are washed out by the lapse of time between the formation of the mistaken expectation and the actual completion of the capital goods involved. This period is long enough so that corrections may be made in time to prevent capital formation from reaching the extremes that might otherwise be engendered by optimistic or pessimistic expectations. The effects of such states of mind tend to be limited, therefore, to relatively brief intervals. The evidence suggests that they are of greatest duration at the end of long periods of prosperity, when speculative fervor in general is running high, and then tend to be most marked in the "growth" industries. Management, having been impressed with the resurgence of growth after a series of letdowns, each of which was itself minor, begins to feel that all its mistakes have been on the low side and presses ahead with projects beyond the bounds of what would have been undertaken on the basis of earlier, more conservative practices. The effect is, of course, to make the situation reached at the end of the boom more extreme than it otherwise would be.

Before going on to the use of the survey approach in forecasting investment expenditures, one other method which attempts to put the profit-incentive approach on a practical basis may be mentioned. This variant recognizes that there is no way of accurately forecasting future earnings over the life of the investment and assumes that business implicitly projects current profit levels into the future. On this basis a high degree of relationship was found when current profits, capitalized by the interest rate on high-grade bonds and adjusted by the relationship of finished-product prices to equipment prices were correlated with investment outlays 6 months later.[11] This method has a high degree of theoretical appeal and resulted in a good fit to the data in the interwar years. It tended to understate investment in the postwar period, when profits fell short of their former relationship to economic activity. An adjustment therefore had to be made to raise the estimates for years in which the economy was operating near capacity.

Just what the price adjustments contribute in this relationship is hard to determine. The effect of rising product prices is largely reflected in profits. Higher prices for industrial equipment may have some tendency to restrict investment, but they also increase it, by increasing the cost of projects undertaken. Despite any theoretical appeal such adjustments may have, the real test is whether they help to produce the correct answers. The data available do not permit an evaluation of the past performance of this method in detail. Although it may have given results within a tolerable margin of error, the procedure outlined above appears to be preferable.

THE SURVEY APPROACH

The attempt to forecast in terms of capitalized-use values fails to satisfy the theorists who believe that profit expectations rather than past or even present profits are the determining factor. Generally speaking, business must expect to be able to sell the products of the new facilities at a reasonable profit. Since the service life is usually long, this means that business must have confidence in some kind of trend projection into the distant future.

Such expectations are not purely arbitrary, of course, but develop with the situation. To most businessmen and analysts, nothing could be more convincing evidence that a future trend position will be realized than to exceed the trend in the present. When the need for capacity is immediately felt, in terms of the problem of filling customers' orders promptly

[11] Charles F. Roos, "The Demand for Investment Goods," *American Economics Review*, May, 1948. Subsequent brochures of the Index Number Institute, directed by Roos, indicate revisions of the procedure, but full details are not available. The basic equation used is

$$y = 0.0210x + 2,500$$

where y = producers' durable equipment, millions of dollars, after a lag of 6 months

$$x = \frac{\text{corporate profits}}{\text{AAA bond yields}} \times \frac{\text{nonfarm prices}}{\text{prices of metal products}}$$

Since prices were not available in the form strictly desired, nonfarm wholesale prices were used to indicate product prices in general, and prices of metals and metal products were used to represent prices of producers' equipment.

and efficiently, not much in the way of growth prospects would ordinarily be needed as an additional incentive.

In recent years, a number of attempts have been made to measure the state of business confidence or intentions. The most common of these efforts have been surveys of business firms or executives to find out what they have thought was going to happen in the economy generally or in their own line of business. They have been asked about future sales, profits, plans, or other variables. Many of these surveys have since been abandoned. Some were not well conceived. Others may have been casualties of the disturbed conditions of the early post–World War II and Korean War years. A number that showed promise have survived.

Of the survivors, the most successful by far is the quarterly survey of planned capital outlays conducted by the Department of Commerce and the Securities and Exchange Commission, which now commands a wide following. An annual survey conducted by McGraw-Hill Publishing Company, Inc., presents similar forward estimates, with some significant differences, among them the attempt to operate over a much longer period of years into the future.

These surveys of planned capital outlays are not to be taken simply as compilations of information about expectations or intentions. The "planned" expenditures under consideration are in various stages of realization. In some cases, contracts or other fixed commitments ensure their completion, though not necessarily within the time contemplated. In other cases, projects have been authorized, and perhaps funds have been appropriated for them, though work has not yet been started or contracts let. In addition to these relatively solid bases for making advance estimates, which may be almost complete for a year ahead in some industries where projects are of a long-term character, the survey estimates include a variety of other probable capital outlays which management feels justified in reporting. Some of these, too, may be good estimates based on knowledge of approved programs. Others are hardly more than guesses. Finally, the data include some more or less arbitrary adjustments for underreporting. The last two categories, which are the least certain, represent only a fraction of the totals reported.

The Commerce Department–SEC survey goes back to 1945. The regular quarterly sample includes reports from about 2,500 firms, of which roughly 1,000 are registered corporations reporting to SEC and the remainder are nonregistered corporations reporting to the Commerce Department's Office of Business Economics. The quarterly reports cover the last quarter's actual outlays and estimates of outlays for the current quarter and for the quarter immediately ahead. Once a year, in the first quarter, the sample is expanded to about 3,500 firms, and forward estimates for the entire year ahead are obtained, providing a comparison with the actual outlays in the year just ended.

The data are regularly presented for seven major industry groups—manufacturing (subdivided between durable and nondurable goods), mining, railroads, other transportation, public utilities, and "commercial and other." More detailed breakdowns of the manufacturing total are reported from time to time. Agriculture is omitted, and no attempt is made to estimate capital outlays charged to current account.

The coverage in the sample varies considerably by industry but is relatively complete for large firms. It is blown up to represent over-all totals in terms of the proportion of assets of reporting firms in each industry group to total assets in the same industries, as reported on tax returns to the Bureau of Internal Revenue. In such industries as railroads and utilities, over 90 percent of total assets are covered by the sample. About two-thirds of total assets are covered in manufacturing and smaller portions in other industries, ranging down to about 10 percent in such industries as service, finance, and construction, which are included in the "commerical and other" category. Special adjustments and estimating procedures are used in certain minor groups where bench-mark data as well as samples are relatively incomplete.

The McGraw-Hill survey has a fairly extensive sample in which large firms predominate. It omits the commercial group as well as agriculture, but reports a fairly detailed breakdown of manufacturing, with the petroleum industry separated from both manufacturing and mining. It accepts the Commerce Department–SEC actual totals and adjusts its forward estimates to the latest government estimates available. Preliminary reports are obtained in the fall of each year, and since they are made available in advance of the beginning of the year, they are of special use to the forecaster who must forecast the whole year in advance. On the other hand, this early reporting weakens the estimates somewhat, because capital plans and budgets are not complete by the reporting date. A more detailed survey is therefore undertaken early the following year, after plans have largely jelled.

A special feature of the McGraw-Hill survey is its attempt to obtain data on capacity and the changes in capacity that are expected to result from the planned investment. No attempt is made to define "capacity," each firm being allowed to use whatever definition is meaningful to it. Since these data have been available for only a limited period, it is difficult to evaluate them as yet.

The performance record of the Commerce Department–SEC survey is shown in Chart 10–6. The preliminary quarterly estimates are designated by the small circles; these show the estimates made 1 quarter in advance of the survey and 2 quarters in advance of actual data. The preliminary annual estimates are indicated by the heavy horizontal lines spanning the 4 quarters to which they refer. The actual data shown by the solid and dotted lines are those first reported, which are most nearly comparable with the forward estimates. Scale breaks shown in 1951 and 1952 are the result of data revisions. As a result of the substantial revision made in 1952, there are no actual figures comparable with the anticipated figures for the year as a whole and for the second and third quarters. If the 1952 anticipated estimate were raised by the adjustment

Chart 10–6. Actual and Anticipated Capital Outlays
In billions of dollars

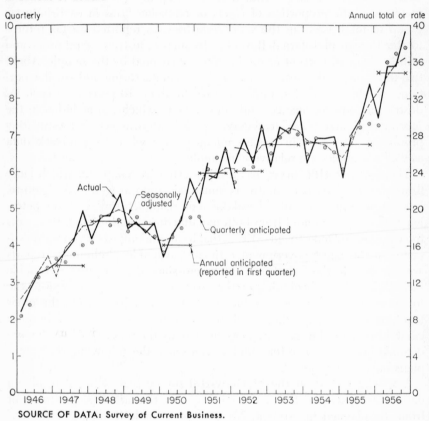

SOURCE OF DATA: Survey of Current Business.

made in the first-quarter actual, it would approximately equal the revised actual figure for the year. The actual annual data for all earlier years were revised upward substantially, but the revised estimates are not shown on the chart.[12]

There is a marked seasonal pattern in the actual data but very little in the forward estimates. The seasonal pattern in the actual appears

[12] Lawrence Bridge, "Business Investment and Sales in 1952," *Survey of Current Business,* April, 1952.

to result partly from the business practice of making year-end adjustments in the capital accounts. These adjustments are partly arbitrary: they include items not allocated by quarters and may thus give effect to work done earlier in the year; they may also anticipate completions actually effected in the first quarter of the following year. The reported seasonal has been fairly dependable, and the data are now being reported in seasonally adjusted form. Independent seasonal adjustments for the years before 1952 have been included on the chart. There is some tendency for the preliminary forward estimates to misbehave seasonally. This appears to arise in large part from the fact that a large block of companies report "no change" from the last actual, so that variation in the actual to some extent appears in the anticipated figure two quarters later.

Over the period as a whole, there has been a definite tendency for the forward estimates to be too low. Many small outlays are made without forward planning, and some larger items whose acquisition is uncertain also fail to get into the reports. The underestimation is so consistent, especially in the "commercial and other" group, that the Commerce Department has undertaken to adjust it out. The new seasonally adjusted series makes allowance for this bias as well as for seasonal variation as such. Whether this will give better quarterly estimates henceforth depends on whether the bias remains the same.

Considered purely as forecasts, the preliminary quarterly estimates have been of little value. Errors in them have been substantial, in view of the fact that one quarter is in any case a relatively short period over which to project a statistical series of this kind. They have correctly indicated the direction of change in about three out of four quarters. In this respect the preliminary estimates are about as good as the second estimates, a seemingly paradoxial result, since so much more ought to be known about what is actually going on at the time the reports are sent in. In any case, this percentage of correct indications is not highly encouraging, because the test is not a severe one.

Short projections of this kind typically rely on continuity, and the seasonally adjusted series does display a high degree of continuity in this instance. A naïve model relying on that fact would also give correct indications of direction in most cases. If the forecaster could bring to bear other information about what is happening, he could improve the results still more, for example, by taking account of the effects of the steel strike in 1952. It is not at all clear, therefore, that the results obtained so far are any better than would be obtained by merely projecting seasonally adjusted lines on a chart in the light of what is known about the business situation.

Although these quarterly estimates may be discounted as forecasts, they do have a real value in providing a periodic interim review of the situation. It is important to keep up with actual developments within the course of the year, since this volatile segment of activity can change greatly in a whole year. In some years, like 1950, this is more important than in others, but in most years such review is highly desirable.

Of greater interest as forecasts are the preliminary annual estimates taken in the first quarter of each year. These are often mistakenly referred to as forecasts for a "year ahead." Actually they forecast only about six months ahead of the last actual data and not much more than a quarter ahead of the March reporting date. However, when the annual estimates are taken in conjunction with the estimates for the first two quarters, they imply a forecast for the last half of the year, and, used in this way, they may be of considerable assistance in making projections through the remainder of the year.

On the whole, the record of the annual estimates has been better than that of the quarterly estimates. The direction of change was correctly indicated in all years but 1950, and despite a tendency for the estimates to run somewhat low in all years of advance, in about two out of three years the magnitude of the change was closely approximated. The large error in 1950 was partly due to the outbreak of war in Korea, but it was apparent that the estimate was too low even before that event. Bearish expectations were widely prevalent in the early months of 1947 as well as in early 1950 and may be assumed to account at least in part for the large deviations in those years. The only serious misinterpretation of the results occurred in 1947, before the seasonal variation in the actual was understood.

The forecasts show a consistent tendency to approximate the seasonally adjusted annual rate for the fourth quarter of the previous year. This is especially noticeable on the upswing, though departures from this pattern in the mid-1950s represented outstanding successes for the survey. In the moderate reversals of 1949 and 1954, anticipations were adjusted downward from the fourth-quarter rates, in line with the reversals of sentiment that occurred in those years. Whether a similar result would be obtained in years of more serious decline remains to be seen. Other studies indicate a reluctance on the part of businessmen making forecasts of this kind to strike out into new high ground on the upswing or down to new lows on the decline.[13]

The Department of Commerce undertook an analysis of the survey results in 1950, by company and by industry. The individual company's returns were analyzed, and a special questionnaire was sent to a sample of companies whose actual results in 1949 did not conform to reported

[13] See Robert Ferber, *Railroad Shippers' Forecasts*, University of Illinois, Bureau of Economic and Business Research, Urbana, Ill., 1951.

plans, asking them to indicate reasons for the discrepancy.[14] In general, the higher the degree of aggregation, the more accurate were the results. Individual-company data showed wide dispersion, but overestimates were largely offset by underestimates. The industry estimates therefore showed greater accuracy than the company estimates, and the total the best result of all. The largest firms showed the greatest accuracy; the smallest firms, the least. Firms undertaking large investment programs and firms whose equipment was relatively old curtailed their planned outlays less frequently than others. These are differences that arise from differences in the ways firms operate, in the ways they have to operate to get things done, and in the degree of flexibility permitted by their own organizations or by the conditions of operation.

The reasons given for the failure of 1949 outlays to conform to plans have to be distinguished by whether actual expenditures exceeded or fell short of the planned level. Where there was an excess of outlays over expectations, no single reason explained as much as one-fifth of the cases. The most important reasons given were changes in the plant and equipment supply situation, in plant and equipment costs, in the sales outlook, in competitive conditions, in new products, in routine underestimates, and in miscellaneous influences resulting in the initiation of substantial new projects.

In contrast, factors deriving from the inventory recession of 1949 accounted for over half of the reasons why firms curtailed their capital outlays in that year. The largest number by far attributed the adjustment to changes in the sales outlook; they amounted to over a third of the total. Next in importance was the decline in net earnings. These two combined with a third, working capital requirements, to make up a distinct majority. Another substantial group apparently had not wanted to cut programs below plans but, through changes in the plant and equipment supply situation, in costs of those items, in the availability of labor or materials, and in time lags of various kinds, found themselves spending less. It is quite likely that some of the firms reporting increased outlays for reasons of this kind would have preferred to cut their programs back but could not do so because of prior commitments. Even without this segment, the data indicate that, in a decline, reduction of capital programs is likely to be widespread.

The timing of a survey in relation to such a movement is evidently of importance. The survey can give the plans as of the moment, and those plans may be very realistic as of that moment. However, if something happens to activity, plans will be revised, and they may be revised drastically. Some projects may be canceled. Or, if the stimulus is on the

[14] Irwin Friend and Jean Bronfenbrenner, "Business Investment Programs and Their Realization," *Survey of Current Business,* December, 1950.

other side, new plans may be set up as additional projects, so that the movement as shown by any particular survey is subject to qualification. In the two months from December, 1950, to February, 1951, the anticipated outlays were revised upward by $2 billion, or almost 10 percent. Any particular survey may give a very good forecast if it is taken just after the adjustments to a change have been made. However, if a change in conditions takes place after the survey but before the results are tabulated, the survey might be wrong even at the first moment it was available. The forecaster is not relieved of the necessity for checking the projection of investment in the light of the expected over-all situation just because it has been obtained from a survey.

The results obtained by the surveys of capital expenditures have been good enough to indicate that they have more than experimental value. Investment requires forward planning, and it may be assumed that the firms undertaking it know what their plans call for. When brought together by these surveys, the reported plans represent a new element of intelligence about the situation. They provide an independent estimate, neither derived completely from other factors nor tied completely to the expectations of the moment. Some early errors based on survey results are not likely to be repeated. When they give an indication at odds with what might be expected in other grounds, the situation at least merits further investigation. If the discrepancy is based on what appears to be widespread acceptance of a mistaken forecast, the results may be discounted. Alternatively, they may be reflecting some important semi-autonomous influence that could not safely be ignored.

CHAPTER 11

Consumers' Durable Goods and Consumer Credit

In the theory of business fluctuations, the role of consumers' durable goods has been a matter of considerable controversy. Expenditures for such goods are sometimes classified with investment and savings, instead of with consumption, as they are in the national-income accounts. Both theoretical considerations and empirical evidence may be used to show that expenditures for consumers' durables are in some respects similar to outlays for producers' equipment and in other respects similar to consumer spending in general. Hence, there is room for considerable differences in individual judgment about the best analytical treatment of this category of expenditures.

Some of the differences may arise from the particular items on which attention is focused. Consumers' durables include a wide variety of commodities. There is a group of items that may be regarded as consumers' capital equipment in the narrower sense; these include automobiles and other mechanical or electrical appliances, such as washing machines, refrigerators, vacuum cleaners, and dishwashers. Another large group consists of home furnishings—furniture, floor coverings, china, glassware, and utensils. A third group is associated with recreation—radios, phonographs, television sets, musical instruments, books, toys, sporting goods, photographic equipment, boats, and motors. In addition, there is a miscellany of utilitarian or decorative articles like timepieces, luggage, writing equipment, and jewelry.

Not only is there a great diversity of such goods in use at any one time but new products are continually appearing. The automobile rose to its preeminent position after World War I. Radios, electric sewing machines, and vacuum cleaners gained widespread use during the 1920s.

371

Electric refrigerators replaced iceboxes in volume during the 1930s. After World War II, television sets, automatic washing machines, air-conditioning units, and dishwashers began to forge ahead. No doubt other items will be developed, in turn displacing some that are now popular. The group as a whole has displayed and no doubt will continue to display greater stability than the individual items which at any given moment enter its make-up.

The common characteristic of all these products is that they last through many income or production periods. Some are once-in-a-lifetime purchases. Most remain in service through several short cycles, and, except for mechanical obsolescence or style considerations, many could be kept in service much longer than they actually are.

Since the existing stock can be "made to do" for any limited period, new purchases can be deferred during any period when they may not be convenient. The result is a high degree of sensitivity to changes in income. In the course of a cycle, these goods display a variability in demand and production that sets them apart from the general run of consumers' goods and services. In this respect they are more like producers' durable goods than like other consumers' goods.

Another similarity to producers' goods arises from the fact that people to some extent regard durable goods as assets and can therefore justify purchases as investments. The extreme example of this occurs in periods of inflation, when people with surplus funds acquire diamonds, or almost any kind of durable goods, as a way of protecting capital values. More commonly, even though these goods may be regarded as capital assets, they much less effectively serve the requirements of a capital reserve. They can be sold in an emergency to obtain cash, but adverse trading margins put a substantial penalty on such conversion. Hence only a portion of the savings embodied in this form can be considered an investment.

Consumers' durable goods are also like producers' equipment or business inventories in that they lend themselves to speculative or protective buying. Accumulation is heavy when incomes and prices are rising or when shortages threaten. In contrast, liquidation produces a violent reduction of purchases, because intensification of use of existing durables, through such means as doubling-up and postponed retirement, facilitates deferral of purchases over extended periods. Similar elements of a speculative character may be observed in nondurable-goods buying at times, but they usually appear only under disturbed conditions, as at the beginning or end of wartime rationing.

Furthermore, for the larger items at least, purchases may be financed from sources other than current income. Past accumulations of liquid assets may be used to effect a cash purchase, which may be regarded as an equivalent dissaving. Or past savings may be used to make a down payment only, with borrowed funds making up the difference.

Independence from current income is not nearly so complete, however, as in the case of producers' goods. A large slice of depreciation in the value of consumers' durables occurs almost immediately on purchase and can logically be charged only to the current period's income. If debt financing is used, short-term repayment of the indebtedness is ordinarily required. Part is ordinarily repaid within the same income period, and to the extent that last period's purchasers are paying off debt from income earned in the current period, the aggregate effect tends to be the same as if this period's purchase had been made entirely from income.

Except for the limited situations discussed, moreover, the consumer's attitude when making a purchase is usually that he is spending money, not saving it. The person who buys most small items—a kitchen utensil, a fountain pen, a new tire for his car, and so on—normally expects them to last a good while, but he certainly does not think he is saving anything. Rather, he is making a purchase, and at least part of the funds would be spent on other things if this purchase were not made. Even most large items are purchased in this attitude of mind. A common expression of the same attitude, one that applies most widely to the large items, is, "I couldn't afford it this year."

The automobile may be considered the primary exception to the view that funds are being spent and not saved, because the market for used cars is so well established and so many people keep about the same capital value tied up in cars year after year. They keep up with the new-model cars even though they may live in the same house all their lives and use refrigerators or washing machines somewhat beyond their reasonable service life.

For this very reason, however, the automobile is one of the prime examples of the responsiveness of consumers' durables to social pressure, a fact that helps distinguish them from producers' durables. The new model is the embodiment of conspicious consumption. It is the way a show of affluence can be made by anyone who feels he can afford the outlay, even by the handy man who does odd jobs and gardening on the week end in order to get enough money to meet the monthly payments.

The same kind of invidious living to some extent affects other durables. The family that sold the children's encyclopedia to get the latest-model television set was doing its best to keep in step with the times. Many people would not consider a home complete without all the latest appliances, and this attitude may force friends and neighbors into purchases they would not otherwise make. Only to a limited extent are business purchases made on this basis. Some executives pride themselves on using the latest electronic computers or control gadgets, but usually there is a real economic justification for the use of such devices.

The point of this introductory discussion is that, in terms of the characteristics and behavior of consumers' durables, they may be fitted into any of the perspectives in which expenditures and saving are ordinarily considered. They fit into the theory of money flows as either investment or consumption. There is a difference from other kinds of consumer saving in that any savings incorporated in them are always matched by equivalent investments. This does not disturb the theory; "investments" of this kind may have the same income-producing effects as any other nonconsumption expenditures. Nowhere can a clear line of distinction be drawn between these and other types of investment expenditures, nor can any clear line be drawn between these and other expenditures for consumption.

FLUCTUATIONS IN CONSUMER DURABLES

There is, however, one clear reason why changes in consumer durables should not be omitted from an analysis of business fluctuations, and that derives from the relationship of new purchases to the existing stock. The goods themselves are desired, ultimately, for the services they produce. At any particular time, with the condition of the economy then prevailing, there may be said to exist a service goal, or desired stock of durable goods for current use. Given such a goal, the situation becomes one where new production is designed to bring the stock on hand up to a specific level and then to keep it at that level. Production will ordinarily be speeded when stocks in use are deficient. There will be a slowing of production when the market reaches the point commonly referred to as the "saturation point." Movements toward the norm tend to be comparatively independent of short-term changes in income.

As in the case of housing and other investment goods, the saturation point may rise with the level of income and with other factors, but it is something that has to be taken into consideration in each boom. For when the requirements for operating inventories are made up, when capacity to produce the desired services is available, production must be cut back to the level of maintenance. But when it does drop back to that level, it induces a decline in incomes, and after the decline in incomes the required stock is lower and the actual stock is excessive, leading to a further drop in production.

When such a reversal occurs, production need not drop all the way back to zero, because there are still replacement demands to be met. The process of wearing out is relatively even and continuous. But replacement can usually be postponed for some time, except perhaps when some units are put out of service by accidents, fire, or other destructive causes beyond the user's control. As a rule, repairs are possible. The question the owner faces is: "Will it be better to incur this repair bill than to junk the whole unit and get a new one?" When a repair bill is higher than the value remaining after the repairs are made, they will hardly ever be undertaken. To put this another way, the old units, well depreciated and perhaps obsolete, are candidates for the scrap heap whenever repairs become necessary.[1] However, the bulk of the existing stock does not reach this condition even in an extended decline, and since supplies are redundant after a decline in income, it is not necessary to replace all the units that are currently destroyed or retired in depressed periods.

Looked at from this point of view, consumers' durable goods represent another situation in which new production is subject to regulation by inventory as well as by income. Their fluctuations therefore take on the same characteristics as inventory cycles in any other kind of equipment.

In the specific case of consumer durables, there is the possibility that shifts to other types of expenditures might make the process of reversal at the peak of the boom less automatic than is true of investment goods more generally. This is only a possibility, however, and must be considered more or less on a par with the possibility that there will be a shift from one type of investment to another. Perhaps an answer may be sought in the character of the situation during which the stock of durable goods was being built up. If accumulation of durables was rapid because there was a corresponding restriction of other expenditures, the total might be maintained by a shift to nondurable goods and services. On the other hand, if total expenditures were overexpanded at the expense of saving, the reaction might be unusually severe. The evidence reveals no consistent tendency for either of these conditions to hold during the upswing, and the automatic reversal following the saturation of the market must typically be expected.

It is important, therefore, to take account of the stocks of goods in use in analyzing any kind of major consumer durable, such as autos. This particular case is especially informative because various kinds of data on autos have been compiled over a long period. Here the underlying need is for transportation services. The availability of those services depends not only upon the number of cars in existence but also upon their condition. With exceptions, however, such as the immediate post–World War II years, the number alone may be taken as a measure of the service level available. As the number in use mounts, as the families

[1] See George Hitchings, "Automotive Transportation," in Herbert V. Prochnow, *Determining the Business Outlook,* Harper & Brothers, New York, pp. 254–258.

and individuals who desire cars increasingly have them at their disposal, an increasingly effective restraint is placed on new production. At some point during the boom, this restraint renders advancing incomes impotent as a force for higher production. But at that point, output is usually in excess of the level needed to meet the growth of service requirements, and as long as it remains above that level, the greater the restrictive force of accumulating stocks becomes and the weaker the expansive force of rising incomes becomes. The decline is then just in the offing.

These two factors—income and stocks—account for the major fluctuations in new-car purchases. Additional short-term influences on car sales are the new-model stimulus and the availability of means of financing in addition to current income. When both of these additional influences are strong, as they were in 1955, the deviation from the basic relationship is likely to be large.

Sales are stimulated in years when major changes in car design are incorporated in new models. Whether this results from improved consumer desire or from a more enthusiastic sales effort is immaterial. It contributes to what is sometimes thought of as a "2-year cycle" in auto demand. Unfortunately, it is very difficult to quantify the new-model stimulus for statistical analysis. In most years, it appears to be small as compared to changes in income as a determinant of new-car purchases. The largest exception was experienced in 1955, when a number of innovations were embodied in the new models. Of these, the bright new colors were the most striking change; they probably stimulated an extraordinary emulative response from the public. Once a new feature has gained general acceptance, however, it loses its power as a special influence on the market. Moreover, it cannot be taken for granted that just any kind of design change will have significant over-all effects. In the usual situation, where changes are moderate though more obvious in some makes than in others, the effects are likely to be more important in shifting sales among competitive lines than in increasing the aggregate for all combined.

Three sources of nonincome financing are available in support of any unusual change in sales—borrowing, capital gains, and existing financial assets. Borrowing is the most common resort, and the specific contribution of changes in credit terms will be considered shortly. Realized capital gains or losses are probably a small factor in the market, but unrealized gains or losses tend to affect purchases also, through psychological reactions in which feelings of affluence or impoverishment make for freer or more restricted spending of funds otherwise available. The use of existing financial assets for expanding purchases is closely tied to capital gains, since the total value of assets available changes more rapidly through price increases than through saving from current income.

Perhaps the best available measure of over-all changes in financial position, including both gains and total-value aspects, is provided by the stock market. Movements in the stock prices may readily be included in a statistical analysis of passenger-car demand. When security prices move up, car sales increase with only a short lag; when prices fall, sales are depressed. This relationship effects a definite improvement in correlations aimed at estimating new-car sales and meets all the usual tests of significance.

The results obtained from a correlation that explains new-car sales in terms of income, the stock of cars in use, and stock-market prices are generally satisfactory. As Chart 11–1 shows, such a correlation based on data for the periods 1925 to 1940 and 1949 to 1955 gave a good fit in most years.[2] The largest deviations occurred in 1950, 1952, and 1955, all of which deviations were subject to special influences on car production or purchases.

The relationship could have been worked out in terms of the same factors used in the housing study—married couples and unemployment —or in terms of total employment rather than deflated income, since all of these are closely enough interrelated to be fairly effective substitutes for each other. Income is preferred in this instance because expenditures for new cars must ultimately be tied in with other consumer spending. The discussion of this point will be resumed in Chapter 12.

A major objection to this kind of relationship as a forecasting device arises from the fact that it requires a forecast of income before it can be applied in deriving the forecast of the durable goods.

SURVEYS OF CONSUMER INTENTIONS

An alternative approach which avoids this difficulty was developed in the period after World War II, its point of departure being the new theories of the role of expectations and planning in economic affairs. It operates through data on consumer intentions to buy, as revealed, for

[2] The estimating equation is

$$X_1 = 0.065X_2 - 0.205X_3 + 0.0064X_4 - 0.104 \qquad (R^2 = .95)$$

where X_1 = new-car registrations, millions

X_2 = disposable income, billions of 1947 dollars

X_3 = total registrations less new registrations, which is the stock of cars in use at beginning of year, millions

X_4 = change in Dow-Jones Industrial Stock Price Average for fiscal year ended September 30

Chart 11–1. Passenger-car Registrations, Disposable Income, and Stock-market Changes

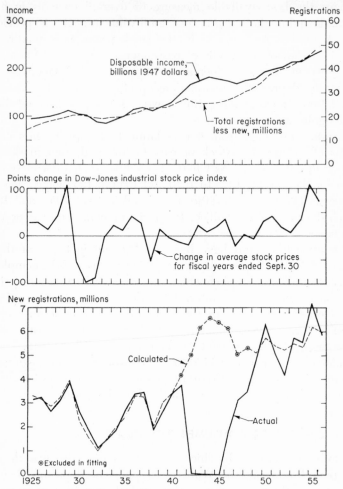

SOURCES OF DATA: Automobile Facts and Figures, Automobile Manufacturers Association; Dow Jones and Co.; U.S. Bureau of Public Roads.

example, by the annual "Survey of Consumer Finances," conducted by the Survey Research Center of the University of Michigan for the Federal Reserve Board. The results of these surveys are reported in the *Federal Reserve Bulletin*, with preliminary data on key points being released in March or April. Again, it may be pointed out that these planned-purchases data do not give forecasts for a year ahead but rather for something less than 6 months on the average. This point is mentioned merely because it is frequently misstated by the advocates of this approach.

The latter are also somewhat inclined toward rather extravagant claims for the forecasting success of the past surveys. Actually it is very difficult to evaluate past results, since a good measure of judgment is required in interpreting the data the surveys have produced. A straightforward comparison of actual and expected results is not possible, because the data on actual purchases of various types of durable goods, as indicated by the surveys, are generally not comparable with the planned-purchases data turned out by the preceding surveys. An attempt to appraise the past performance of the surveys led to the following conclusions:[3]

The correspondence between actual and intended purchases is clearly not very close. Not only is the correspondence not close, but the direction of change appears to have been missed almost as often as not.

Even when the direction of movement was correctly predicted, little correspondence between the figures is apparent, as is shown by the following comparison of relative change in the proportions of spending units intending to buy and actually buying the two big items in this list, new cars and houses:

Period	New cars		All houses	
	Intended, %	Bought, %	Intended, %	Bought, %
1946–1947	2.4	75.8	−15.7	−23.1
1947–1948	−10.6	5.2	−22.0	4.0
1948–1949	11.8	41.0	8.7	−32.7
1949–1950	2.4	17.4	14.0	31.4
1950–1951	−54.0	−18.8	−28.1	6.5
1951–1952	7.5	−18.3	7.3	−26.5
1952–1953	34.9	35.8	27.3	19.4

Furthermore, in the disturbed conditions of the postwar period, results have been determined not only by consumers' decisions but by supply conditions. Outstanding among the successes of the surveys was their indication of an advance in automobile sales in 1949 and a decline in 1951. However, the actual changes in production in both those years were determined primarily on the supply side. With steel freely available in 1949 for the first time, output of cars expanded sharply; with production quotas imposed on automobile producers in 1951, a moderate decline in output had to be expected. In 1952, supply conditions were still decisive, producing a considerable error; production was restricted in the

[3] Robert Ferber, "Sales Forecasting by Sample Surveys," *Journal of Marketing*, July, 1955.

early part of the year by quotas and later by the shortage of steel resulting from a prolonged strike.

Clearly the validity of this approach has not yet been established. Its
value is experimental only, and whether it can ever attain practical validity is doubtful. The basis on which it rests is distinctly less favorable
than that of the surveys of planned capital outlays of business. Advance
planning is ordinarily not required for making purchases of any kind of
consumer durables, and although some such planning does take place,
it seldom reaches the point of a firm commitment, such as a construction
contract or a noncancelable order for heavy machinery. Consumer plans
are more volatile and reach fruition much less frequently. The actual
purchases are much more often the result of impulse buying or irrational decisions. The limitations on the sample and the difficulties of
the interviewing situation introduce much larger margins of potential
error. In short, the rationale for this method is weak, and until better
evidence than its performance to date is offered, it can hardly be considered a sound approach for practical forecasting use.

This does not mean that the survey results have to be dismissed
entirely. The surveys produce a good deal of information on what consumers are doing and thinking and in this way throw interesting side-
lights on various aspects of the current situation, particularly from the
financial point of view. They seem likely to serve the forecaster best as
an aid to judgment in carrying through an analysis by other methods.
In this supplementary role, they may still make a significant contribution to his performance.

THE ROLE OF CONSUMER CREDIT

The forecast of consumer durables will ultimately be needed in
putting together a forecast for the economy as a whole. In working out
the forecast of that item, its place in the over-all forecast must be considered as well as the specific method to be used. Will it simply be
derived from the general forecast, or will it be treated as one of the
determining elements in the situation as a whole?

The foregoing discussion suggests that some kind of compromise may
be in order. Consumer expenditures for durable goods are largely
determined by the level of income but make their own contribution to
changes in income, particularly at the turning points. Some purchases
are made at the expense of other goods and services, some at the expense
of savings. Some are really transfers of assets rather than expenditures.
The part that is a charge against income which would be spent anyway
can appropriately be treated like any other expenditure. The part that
is financed by borrowing or represents the return of past savings

to the income stream would more appropriately be treated like other investment. The total cannot be considered to go all one way or all the other.

A way around this difficulty may be found by treating only a portion of the total—the portion which is financed out of business rather than consumer funds—as a strategic type of income-producing expenditure. This is done not by segregating any particular type of durables for special treatment but by shifting to changes in consumer credit. When business extends credit to finance a sale, it holds a claim against the purchaser for the value of the loan, and whether or not there is a specific claim against the goods, it in effect retains title to that portion of them. The most clear-cut illustration of this type of investment is provided by drive-yourself cars and other items purchased by business concerns for rental to consumers. There are similar elements in other credit purchases, which are in effect business investments initiated by consumers.

A question that must be answered when this shift is made immediately arises: "Why bring in financial measures at this point?" or, conversely: "Why not study bank loans and other credits to business instead of the new facilities and inventories they finance?" This is a natural question in view of the fact that consumer credit is not a part of the gross product, and up to this point the analysis has been confined to items that do appear in the gross product. In this approach, the main line of attack is the distinction between consumer expenditures and non-consumption expenditures in terms of the extent to which they come out of current income. Although consumer credit itself does not enter the gross-product account directly, the activities and goods that it finances do. Since this is a part of consumer spending that clearly does not come out of income, it may be considered as significantly different from other consumer expenditures.

The situation with respect to business loans is quite different from consumer credit. Business credit cannot be used as a measure of activity, because the entire amount of the investment in plant, equipment, and other real business capital is already counted as such and the financing would duplicate these direct measures. Furthermore, business credit does not provide a satisfactory measure of what business is doing but merely of how it is financing what it wants to do. If business borrows solely because it wants to increase its current cash balance, there is no economic effect. If what it wants to do is invest in new real capital, then borrowing provides only part of the resources used, and it may be a highly variable part. For long periods, business may be able to finance its investment with no net borrowing. The financial data would be useful in the absence of the gross-investment data; but as long as the latter are available there is little point in going about the question indirectly.

In the case of consumer durables, the data on total expenditures are also available; but since that total is not properly an investment or offset to saving in its entirety, the financial alternative is adopted.

This use of consumer credit is generally consistent with the theory of consumer behavior as it relates to saving and dissaving. Credit is used to meet the same kind of needs as past savings, assuming that such savings happen to be available. It makes possible the purchase of capital assets or other expenditure items too large to be paid out of current income. It helps to meet temporary deficits brought on by special family needs or ambitions, such as the education of maturing children; or, to put this another way, it adjusts differences between current income and desired consumption patterns. It may be the only means of meeting an emergency, perhaps connected with an accident or ill-health, which involves heavy costs and perhaps loss of income as well. Expenditures like these are ordinarily thought of as the motives for saving. The primary omission from the list of those motives is the creation of an estate, but purchases of durable goods are seldom made for this purpose.

There are not many families who have ready funds to use for these special expenditures. For most, borrowing eliminates the necessity for deferring the expenditure until the necessary funds can be raised from income by saving. This anticipation of income may be regarded as essential, as in the case of major illness, or as unnecessary and wasteful, as when used to finance a gay occasion. In either case, the expenditure immediately increases the value of goods and services "consumed" and produces the same effect as any other type of income-producing expenditure. Later, of course, saving is necessary to finance the amortization of the loan, with the opposite effect. The timing of expenditures relative to income is shifted in the same way it would be by the purchase of a durable good of equal value.

If the loan was incurred for the purchase of a durable good, it in effect puts payment for the good on a pay-as-you-use basis, and this may certainly be considered an appropriate way to pay. The man who pays for his car on the installment plan is timing his payment for transportation in somewhat the same manner he would in paying for the trolley car by handing over daily fares. The private car may cost him more, but he can rationalize the extra cost in terms of convenience, recreation, or other values.

It is evident that the movements of consumers' expenditures for durable goods and changes in consumer credit are closely tied together. These are the highly variable items in the consumer-spending picture. They move with seeming autonomy at times and affect other items in the consumer account. The level of income itself, the proportion of income spent, and the distribution of expenditures by type all shift with changes in the rate of durable-goods expenditures or in the rate of expansion or contraction of consumer credit.[4]

Some writers insist that one or the other of these two factors is causal, implying that the other is passive and therefore not a contributor to economic instability. The facts do not lend strong support to either of these arguments. Essentially the same conclusions may be reached by attacking the problem in terms of either the durable-goods expenditures or the changes in consumer credit. The cyclical mechanisms are virtually the same in both cases. They operate to some extent on stocks of durables purchased with cash; but the recent trend toward the use of credit to finance sales of nondurables gives credit wider applicability in another direction.

GENERAL CONSIDERATIONS ABOUT CONSUMER CREDIT

The difficulty of saving in advance has no doubt contributed much to the spreading use of credit. Many families cannot save except by committing themselves to a series of payments which become a prior claim on income. The idea that it is easy to save this way is, of course, nonsense. It is a hard and expensive way to save, because the interest has to be paid, too, and rates ranging from 1 to 3 percent a month—commonly the maximum permitted by law—are by no means inconsequential to the buyer. Making the payments may strain the family's peace of mind as well as sacrifice many of its current needs. It must be agreed that "easy payments" are a myth, that the best rule to follow is, "Pay down as much as possible and pay up as fast as possible."[5] But it must also be recognized that this is a way of getting things done and will no doubt continue to be used as such.

In recent years, the use of consumer credit has been very widespread. According to the Federal Reserve "Survey of Consumer Finances," about half of all families or individual spending units had incurred some consumer debt other than on charge accounts. Many of these families tend to be in debt almost continuously because they borrow again shortly after, or even before, they have completed the previous payments. A substantial majority of certain kinds of sales, such as automobiles and large appliances, are made on credit, and most of these call for payment in monthly installments. The monthly payments to which some families

[4] For a more detailed, general discussion of how credit influences and is influenced by other economic developments, see Gottfried Haberler, *Consumer Instalment Credit and Economic Fluctuations,* National Bureau of Economic Research, Inc., New York, 1942.

[5] See *Using Consumer Credit,* National Association of Secondary-School Principals, Consumer Education Study, Washington, 1947.

are committed, including not only installment purchases but also mort-gages and insurance, amount to more than half their income.

In good times, almost all consumer debt is paid off in routine fashion. In depression periods, when many who have contracted debt become unemployed, the number who fall behind in their payments rises some-what but remains small relative to the total number of borrowers. Typ-ically the people who default do not repudiate their debts completely but resume payments when they can. In 1936, with the payment of the veterans' bonus, the small-loan companies received a windfall in the form of repayments of loans they had already written off as bad debts. The average losses on consumer credit were an exceedingly small proportion of the total debt contracted even during the depression years.

Discussion of this subject tends to get confused in its moralistic aspects. Negative attitudes go back to the experience of earlier centuries with usury and the debtor's prison. In modern times, the menace of the loan shark has been paramount. Loan sharks have generally charged 10 to 25 percent a month, and in some cases rates ranged up to 40 percent a month, or about 500 percent a year. These exorbitant charges were enforced by the threat of garnishment of wages and loss of employ-ment.

Abuses are still common, and they are difficult to eliminate because the market is highly stratified. Lenders confine their operations to spe-cific localities and also to certain kinds of loans. Borrowers know little of the alternative sources of funds available to them. Most accept the contract offered by the seller to avoid the inconvenience of seeking a more favorable one. The interest rates and carrying charges on such contracts are often complex and concealed, or even misstated. The high-pressure salesman uses the attraction of "easy terms" to weaken sales resistance and move goods without regard to the welfare of the buyer. The holder of the installment paper may in turn adopt high-pressure col-lection policies and even, in some instances, make a practice of stealthy repossession and resale in such a way as to wipe out the original buyer's equity.

The adverse attitudes engendered by unfortunate borrowing experi-ences help make credit controls politically acceptable, but arguments based on the social or personal evils of borrowing contribute nothing to the discussion of economic effects. The answer to such arguments must be sought on the same level, namely, in terms of the borrower's position, his freedom of choice, and his right to time purchases to suit his own need or convenience. But this, too, is irrelevant to the present discussion. These matters are mentioned merely by way of indicating that, in focusing attention on economic effects, the personal and social aspects of the problem have been ruled out rather than overlooked.

Changes in the rate of consumer borrowing are the result of changes in the desired level of purchases and in the ability of buyers to obtain credit. The underlying needs for goods are in a sense always there, though they cannot become active demand unless income or other financing ensures the ability to pay. The consumer's standing as a credit risk also depends upon his ability to pay, and since borrowing generally implies lack of ready funds, this means that it depends upon his current and prospective income. Hence consumer credit varies with income, rising when income rises and dropping back when income falls. The movements of credit, however, are not restricted in the same way. They conform in general with the movements of income but are more violent on both the advances and the declines.

Resort to consumer credit is sometimes thought of as borrowing for the purpose of increasing consumption. In limited special periods, such as the first decade following World War II, the contribution to higher consumption may be the dominant effect of steadily mounting consumer debt. Consumer credit may even have some effect in this direction over the longer run, since the volume of durable goods in use is in an upward trend and the more such goods are being used the faster they wear out. Thus consumer credit, by accelerating the building of stocks, may accelerate consumption somewhat, but, special circumstances aside, it has only a minor effect of this kind on the average. Its effects are rather to change the timing of consumption, and somewhat also the pattern of consumption, but it cannot very much change the total, because the debt contracted in one period has to be repaid in another out of income that is on the whole hardly any higher than it would otherwise be.

The change in living patterns induced by credit expansion is in the direction of greater use of durable goods, because installment selling has largely been focused on items that could be repossessed in good condition if the borrower defaulted on his payments. This shift toward durables is seen most clearly in the years after World War II, when the proportion of total consumer expenditures going into durable goods increased sharply. Of course, this drastic shift was partly the result of disturbed conditions and not one that could be expected to continue indefinitely. When credit has been built up to peak volume, its power to affect the pattern of living will almost completely disappear, particularly since credit can now be obtained much more readily for the purchase of nondurables and services as well as durables.

CYCLICAL NATURE OF CREDIT CHANGES

It is from the shift in timing of purchases that the really important economic aspects of consumer credit derive. When production and employment are rising, credit makes it possible to anticipate the income that will derive from the higher level of activity, and purchases are correspondingly speeded up. When a decline gets under way, payment for past purchases of durables on the installment plan produces a constant charge against income and correspondingly reduces the funds available for current spending. Hence, when income is rising and prospects are good, an acceleration is provided by the expansion of consumer purchases on borrowed funds. Conversely, borrowing falls off on the downswing, and the liquidation of credit intensifies the violence of the decline. What credit does, in other words, is to help the variable portion of consumer expenditures vary.

This tendency is aggravated by lenders' efforts to minimize their risks. During the boom, when jobs are easy to find and buyers have established a record of steady income, credit is rather freely available to all. When conditions turn unfavorable, the specter of unemployment looms large in the minds of lenders, and they become much more cautious about making funds available to anyone who might prove to be a poor risk. The situation is not unlike that of business borrowing. On the decline, the credit base is curtailed by unemployment and loss of income, and those whose credit remains good prefer to postpone purchases and limit their commitments. On the upswing, consumers who want to expand and modernize the stock of goods they own are both made better credit risks and encouraged to go ahead by the improvement in incomes. The swings are correspondingly increased in amplitude.

As the peak of the boom is approached, increasing stocks of durables bring the expansion of output to a halt. Then the expansion of credit also is brought to a halt, and the stimulus from consumer credit is lost.

The volume of credit outstanding, like stocks of durable goods, expands to the point of saturation. This point is itself a variable. It varies from time to time or from community to community with the level and distribution of income and with other factors, just as the target stocks or desired service goals for various kinds of durable goods vary. When the families who buy on credit approach the limits of indebtedness which their income is capable of supporting, the expansion is restrained. Immediately at this point, and well before the total outstanding turns down, an element of deflation enters the picture. Losing part of the increment of sales derived from credit expansion tends to reduce the level of income, and the total debt supportable declines, even though the volume of credit outstanding is still going up. Ultimately the total debt is excessive in relation to income, and efforts to bring it back into line increase the deflationary pressure. This assists in making the downturn sharp.

Conversely, at the depression lows, when the decline in sales of durables is halted, the depressing effect of credit liquidation quickly disappears. As soon as the drive to liquidate outstanding debt ceases, income is freed from an obligatory deduction and can be used to expand purchases. Although the goods for which the debt was incurred are themselves durable enough to outlast the period of debt liquidation, an equivalent liquidation has in effect been forced on the economy by reduced production in other industries, and the initial upsurge may take the form of a release of production in those industries. Hence the mere cessation of credit liquidation, like the mere cessation of inventory liquidation, becomes a positive force on the upside. At this point, therefore, credit also contributes to an actual reversal rather than a mere leveling-off. It hastens recovery.

The effects of credit changes are like those of inventory investment. When it changes, it tends to expand or contract consumer spending. When it is stable, it has no effect in one direction or the other. At that point, the new credit being granted is offset by repayments on debt contracted earlier. Thus the change, which is the moving force, may be measured either as the difference between credit granted and credit repaid during the period or as the difference between the totals outstanding at the end and at the beginning of the period.

Looking at the net credit change as the difference between grants and repayments makes its similarity to inventory investment more apparent, the analogy is carried through by putting new grants in the position of production, repayments in the position of consumption, and the total outstanding in the position of aggregate inventories. Then the relationships between the total outstanding, the new credit granted, and the amount repaid are seen to result in certain semiautomatic patterns of behavior that make for instability in the same way that business inventories do.

Repayments, being based upon the new credit extended over a period of preceding months, continue to advance at a fairly even rate after the advance in extensions begins to slow. If credit extensions remained stable at a high or low rate, repayments would tend to catch up, and the force of the movement would be progressively reduced to the point where it ceased entirely. The action would then be an almost perfect illustration of the acceleration principle. However, such movements do not progress smoothly in accordance with this principle. The advance in credit expands income with multiplier effect, and the advance in income justifies further expansion of credit. The unutilized opportunities for credit expansion after a movement has progressed for a while tend to keep it going beyond the point where the accelerator alone would turn it down; then, after the supporting base for credit becomes strained, the first sign of a downturn imposes a need for liquidation, which combines with the accelerator in making the reversal sharp.

The actual pattern of credit behavior shows great irregularity and conforms more nearly to that of inventory movements than to any strict rate-of-change formula. A movement in durable-goods purchases gets under way, accompanied by a movement of credit, and proceeds along something like a straight line for a while, with minor fluctuations around this "trend." After a turn occurs, there is likely to be a period of relatively uniform movement in the other direction. At the end of any such movement, there may be a final spurt, as in 1929, maintaining the level of credit creation until the very end. Then the "trend" of durable-goods purchases quickly reverses, and the change in credit tends to shift from plus to minus, or vice versa, in just a few months. The cessation of such a movement itself tends to mark the end of the "cycle." At the turn, consumer durables, producer durables, and inventories all tend to move in coordination, with sufficient force to swing the whole economy. The result is that net new consumer credit, like inventories, tends to fluctuate around a zero line, consistently above the line on the upswing and consistently below the line on the downswing, but with considerable short-term irregularity all the time.

Credit is also like inventories in that when a reversal takes place the total swing from accumulation to liquidation represents the appropriate measure of its effect. Large increases in the total outstanding are possible, because repayments may extend over several years and the accumulation of stocks is not subject to as close control as are business inventories. Contraction in a downswing may be correspondingly large, particularly in the future, because credit utilization is reaching a state of maturity not previously attained. Postwar rates of increase have run to $5 billion a year. Past experience indicates that, after a reversal, a similar rate of liquidation may be reached, in which case the total swing might be in the range of $10 billion. Although these changes are more limited than the potential swings in inventories, such a reversal would contribute substantially to the force of a decline. Since a reversal could take place in the course of a single year, credit must be considered a volatile factor of substantial magnitude.

In appraising the effects of such movements, consumer credit may be looked at from either of two points of view—as an element of dissaving by consumers or as an element of investment by the business firms providing the funds. Considered as a segment of business investment, credit is viewed as similar to investment in business inventories. Business in effect invests in durable goods which it places in the hands of consumers, who are responsible over a period of time for overseeing their consumption and paying off the loans. Immediately the goods are transferred from dealers' inventories; but as the dealer reorders, the pace of activity is stepped up. At the same time, a contractual obligation to liquidate the indebtedness through saving is set up; when the withdrawal of these funds occurs, production is correspondingly depressed.

Considered as an element of consumer dissaving, the credit facilitates the purchases through which consumers' decisions to expand their stocks of durables are given effect and to some extent frees those purchases from dependence on current income. While purchases are being expanded, the increase in credit contributes to the pace of activity. The saving that matches this dissaving follows instead of preceding it. When purchases have been cut back sufficiently to bring about a liquidation of credit, the effect on activity is the same as a liquidation of inventories, because the withdrawals from income to liquidate the debt depress activity in the same way as withdrawals from business stocks to meet current demands.

From either point of view, the conclusion is the same. Consumer credit is seen as a significant source of potential change, one that can play an important part in the business situation and therefore something to be taken into account in a forecast. This conclusion would have to be qualified to the extent that there were offsetting changes in expenditures on the part of lenders. If lenders would ordinarily use the funds for something else in the event that the loans were not made, the extension of credit would be without effect. There is no indication, however, that this is what happens. The holders of the debt are mainly retailers and financial institutions. The retailers, who hold the smaller portion, are probably encouraged by high sales on credit to adjust their own inventory and borrowing policies in the same direction.

The bulk of the debt is held by financial institutions. Roughly 40 percent of the total at the end of 1953 was held by commercial banks, and their operations in this field would appear to have the same effect in expanding the money supply as lending to business concerns. Other financial institutions are sales-finance companies, credit unions, and miscellaneous small-loan companies. Of these, the first is by far the most important, with holdings amounting to about 30 percent of the total. They may borrow from the banks, issue securities, or otherwise draw upon the capital markets when consumer borrowing is high. Most of the funds provided by these financial institutions come from other sources than current income and past savings that would be released through other channels. Some small offsets to consumer spending from borrowed funds no doubt occur through the diversion of funds from expenditures on other objects or through the diversion of lenders' earnings from dividends to new loans. It does not appear to be stretching the case significantly, however, to treat the entire change in consumer credit as the basis for appraising its current effects on the economy.

In carrying through an analysis, the consumer point of view would seem to provide the better perspective, because it focuses more directly on the actual point of decision. The consumer has the initiative, and his decisions are largely determined by other elements in the situation than the availability of credit. Various studies of the demand for credit indicate that it is predictable from the movements of income or expenditures and does not basically determine them.[6] Independence of movement is found to occur mainly as the result of changes in down payments and in the size of monthly installments, the latter varying inversely with the length of the repayment period.

This conclusion does not deny that credit has the same effect on the income flow as any other offset to saving. It merely stipulates that the main effect of credit expansion or contraction is to lend impetus to movements of income that are otherwise decided. At one and the same time, credit is determined by and determines income. In this respect it is like induced investment by business, but it is an even more direct and perfect case of the interaction and mutual determination that intensifies each move. What is commonly overlooked is the critical effect of any such form of investment in switching a movement into reverse after it has run its course.

MEASURING CHANGES IN CONSUMER CREDIT

Current data on consumer credit are regularly compiled by the Federal Reserve Board. In addition to making available the monthly data, the Board from time to time publishes special articles analyzing recent developments in this field. Similar material prepared by other financial institutions or specialists appears in financial periodicals and in pamphlets published by lending agencies or their associations.

The monthly reports obtained by the Federal Reserve Board from lending agencies cover credit extended during the month and the total outstanding at the end of the month. Reporting samples for most types of lenders are satisfactory but are somewhat less so for retailers than for financial institutions. The most serious weakness is lack of a reporting sample for the miscellaneous retail group—other than department stores, mail-order houses, and furniture and appliance stores—but this group holds less than 5 percent of the total outstanding.[7] The current series are revised from time to time as more complete bench-mark data become available from such sources as bank reports to supervisory agencies, registration statements of lenders subject to regulation, and the Census of Retail Trade.

[6] See A. Kisselgoff, *Factors Affecting the Demand for Consumer Instalment Credit*, National Bureau of Economic Research, Inc., New York, 1950.
[7] *Federal Reserve Bulletin*, January, 1954, p. 17.

Although these data have certain admitted deficiencies, they must be regarded as one of the better statistical series. A major source of difficulty arises from the inability of lenders to make a definite separation of loans for business and consumer purposes. Thus, although an attempt is made to exclude credit for financing the purchase of commercial vehicles, all credit for the purchase of cars used for both consumption and business purposes is included. Inaccuracies of classification work in both directions, of course, so that some consumer credit is classified as business loans. Other kinds of consumer loans are also excluded. Insurance-policy loans are excluded because a large proportion of such loans are for business purposes. In addition, certain kinds of consumer loans are not reported at all, such as loans between individuals and loans by business concerns to their employees. In summarizing the discussion of this point, the Division of Research and Statistics of the Federal Reserve System states, "The amount of consumer credit omitted from the series far exceeds the amount of nonconsumer credit that still remains in the series."[8]

The implication of this statement is that the estimates tend to minimize rather than exaggerate the use of credit in financing consumption. Any measure of credit would also of necessity omit the cash expenditures that represent pure dissaving—whether financed from accumulated past savings, capital gains, or other sources. However, the use of credit as a measure of expenditures that are not financed from current income is a compromise in any case; and since it is difficult if not impossible to determine the level at which the compromise should be drawn, moderate error in the general level would not seriously affect the results, particularly if the portions omitted or improperly classified are consistently intercorrelated with those included. The series as it stands appears to deal with the bulk of spending from borrowed funds in a satisfactory manner, and its use therefore seems fully justified.

When the past movements of total credit outstanding are viewed in broad perspective, it may be said that the interwar years represented a period of growth and development in the use of credit preliminary to the strong upsurge in the decade following World War II. Credit changes contributed to the cyclical swings of the 1930s, and credit expansion contributed to the sustained prosperity of the first postwar decade.

The large changes that have taken place in the postwar years are reflected in the strong rise in total credit outstanding, as shown in Chart 11–2. A minor interruption to the trend occurred in 1951, when wartime controls were temporarily reimposed, but otherwise there was a steady expansion from $5 billion at the end of 1944 to over $40 billion at the end

[8] "Revision of Consumer Credit Statistics," *Federal Reserve Bulletin*, April, 1953, p. 340.

of 1956. Reference to the earlier years indicates that more serious interruptions to the upward trend occurred during the depression and again during World War II. Before the period shown on the chart, the decade of the 1920s was another period of strong growth associated with rising incomes and the mass production of automobiles.

It may readily be seen from the chart that the bulk of the increase occurred in installment credit. The increase in noninstallment credit was relatively limited over the period as a whole, and this segment has remained substantially stable in the last few years. Charge accounts fluctuate with sales of retail stores that sell on this basis, but they represent

Chart 11–2. Short- and Intermediate-term Consumer Credit Outstanding

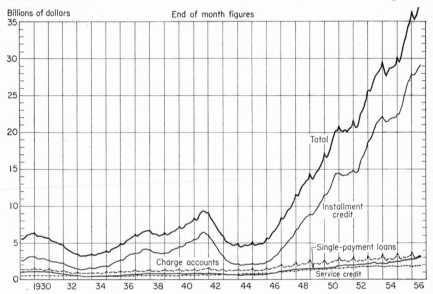

SOURCE: Federal Reserve Chart Book, Historical Supplement, September, 1956.

a convenient form of payment rather than any actual need for financing. Service credit—credit granted by doctors and other professional practitioners, by public utilities, and by such service establishments as dry cleaners and laundries—is similar in character. All of this credit is normally repaid within a short time after bills for the goods or services are rendered, so that large additions to consumer buying power do not originate in this segment.

Single-payment loans are made to individuals for a variety of consumer purposes and are scheduled to be repaid in one payment. Such loans have gone out of fashion, because experience has shown that the consumer who has to pay a large amount all at one time is more likely to get into difficulty than one who has to make small payments month by month. They are still made by various institutions, mainly banks, on various kinds of security and also by such agencies as pawnbrokers and savings-and-loan associations. Like other noninstallment credit, they do not represent a major factor in the economic picture.

The important installment-credit series is shown in Chart 11–3, broken down into its major components, installment-sales credit and installment loans. Well over half of the total consists of credit extended for the purpose of purchasing automobiles and other consumer goods. As a rule,

Chart 11–3. Consumer Installment Credit Outstanding by Major Parts

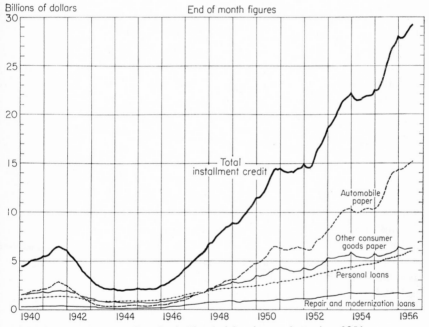

SOURCE: Federal Reserve Chart Book, Historical Supplement, September, 1956.

this debt is secured by the item purchased. "Automobile paper" alone accounted for almost 50 percent of all installment credit at the end of 1955. "Other consumer-goods paper" amounted to about half again as much, so that total sales credit comprised almost three-fourths of all installment credit. This is the highly cyclical segment of consumer credit. It surges up when business activity advances and falls sharply when activity declines.

Installment loans include repair and modernization loans as well as personal loans of a more general kind. Repair and modernization loans —commonly FHA-insured—are used to finance alterations and additions to owner-occupied houses and to purchase furnaces, water heaters, and kitchen and other household equipment needed for home improvement. Some personal loans are also used for purchases of durable goods but, not being secured by the goods in question, are not classified as sales credit. The larger portion of personal loans are made for a variety of personal reasons, such as medical payments, education, travel expenses, payment of taxes or insurance premiums, and consolidation or refinancing of previously contracted debt.

Installment-loan credit is less directly connected with the cyclical movements of business than installment-sales credit, but it has expanded rapidly and is likely to show increasing fluctuations in the future. Consumers are becoming increasingly aware of the financial resources available to them and will utilize such resources as it suits their convenience. There is some evidence that personal installment loans have already been used as a substitute for other credit, such as security loans or installment-sales credit, when the type that would ordinarily be used is restricted or otherwise less readily available.

The fact that total credit outstanding has attained a level over $40 billion—more than 13 percent of disposable personal income—is in itself of little importance. The magnitude of the total as such is neither a force for inflation nor one for deflation, since it is the net change alone that moves the economy. Its significance lies primarily in the fact that the larger the total outstanding, the greater future liquidation might be; but the likelihood of liquidation, or of further expansion, is the issue of immediate concern.

To appraise the economic effects of credit, it is necessary to pass from the total outstanding to the changes within each period. The maximum effect occurs when the total is changing most rapidly and diminishes when the rate of change diminishes even though the movement is continuing. The peak in the total tends to lag behind the peak in business activity, and the trough similarly is reached after business has turned up. In this respect, outstanding credit is like total inventory holdings. To understand this lag and to evaluate the effects of credit on activity, it is necessary, as it was in the case of inventories, to turn to the processes by which credit is expanded or liquidated.

Most consumer credit originates in retail-store or service transactions where the buyer cannot immediately pay because the bill is too large relative to his cash resources. Unless the buyer wishes to make his own arrangements, the seller usually writes the contract for credit, which may be provided from his own resources or through channels prearranged with a financial institution. In 1953, retail stores and dealers originated 58 percent of the installment credit granted and sold 43 percent to financial institutions, retaining only 15 percent. Banks and other institutions originated the other 42 percent and altogether held 85 percent.[9]

When the contract is written, its effect is to charge expenditures not to current or past income but to future income. Later, while the contracted amounts are being repaid, they represent withdrawals from income whose effects must be measured in terms of the extent to which they depress other expenditures.

Repayments ordinarily begin during the month following the granting of the credit and run for a period established by the contract, usually 12 to 36 months. The pattern of repayments, therefore, represents a distributed lag covering the period from the first month to the maturity of the contract. The repayments made in any particular month are the sum of payments required by contracts written in previous months, the earliest corresponding to the longest maturity provided. There are some defaults, of course, and also some prepayments, but ordinarily these do not disturb the pattern of repayments greatly.

In the ordinary course of events, repayments lag behind extensions in the same way that a moving average centered on the last term included lags behind the original series—by approximately half the average repayment period. Since they represent an average of extensions over a considerable period of months, they similarly cut off the extreme tops at the peak and the extreme bottoms in the trough. Minor reversals in new extensions do not fall all the way to repayments and are therefore not sufficient to turn the total outstanding around, and repayments also continue on a steady course for a while after the reversal in extensions has begun. If extensions happened to stabilize at any level, repayments would approach that level as a limit, and the total outstanding would also stabilize at the end of the average repayment period. The amounts extended and repaid each month would then be approximately equal to the total outstanding divided by half the average repayment period.

The amount of new credit granted and the amount repaid during each month of the period for which such data are available are shown in Chart 11–4. The actual reports received from the lenders generally do not include repayments data, but these can readily be computed as the difference between new extensions and the change in the total outstanding. The repayments series therefore logically reflects the net effects of prepayments and defaults as well as payments actually made on schedule.

Unfortunately, the period covered by this chart is not long enough to illustrate the cyclical interrelationships adequately. Extensions continued above repayments throughout the postwar period, except for the brief

[9] "Extension and Repayment of Consumer Instalment Credit," *Federal Reserve Bulletin*, January, 1954, p. 10.

interval following the Korean outbreak when credit terms were tightened and durable-goods production was restricted. The 1941 data illustrate the typical pattern in a reversal, though this was not a downturn of the cyclical variety. In that year extensions dropped while repayments were still moving up. Both elements contributed to making the reversal sharp.

Chart 11–4. Consumer Installment Credit Extended and Repaid

Adjusted for seasonal variation

SOURCE: Federal Reserve Chart Book, Historical Supplement, September, 1956.

FORECASTING CHANGES IN CONSUMER CREDIT

Because of the automatic lag in repayments, the force of consumer credit tends to vary with the change in rate of extensions over the average maturity period, which is roughly half the contract repayment period. Hence credit provides the greatest stimulus in periods when the advance in installment purchases is most rapid, and it has the greatest deflationary effect when the decline is most rapid. The maximum during any given advance is reached when the move has gone far enough to get repayments moving up at the same pace as credit granted. Repayments are furthest behind new extensions at that point, but they maintain a steady upward course for a while after the advance in new credit granted slows or reverses.

The most effective way of forecasting the movements of credit, therefore, is in terms of credit granted and credit repaid. The level of repayments is readily computed from the rates at which credit has been granted in recent periods. The primary focus of attention, therefore, must be the rate of durable-goods purchases, which largely determines the extension of new credit. The forecasting of this item has been discussed earlier in this chapter and will be taken up again in the following chapter. At the heart of it is the forecast of income—the primary objective

Chart 11–5. Relation of Changes in Consumer Credit to Changes in Consumer Expenditures for Durable Goods*

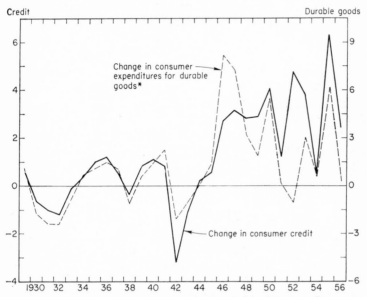

* Current-year expenditures less weighted average of two previous years, with the immediately preceding year weighted double.

SOURCE OF DATA: U.S. Department of Commerce and Federal Reserve Board.

of the forecasting process as a whole. Initially, only a tentative projection can be made, giving effect to any special considerations affecting credit and the durable-goods position as well as to any major changes in the over-all situation that can be anticipated on the basis of other factors.

So strong is the influence of durable-goods expenditures on changes in credit that a preliminary projection of the latter can be based on this factor alone. Chart 11–5 compares the changes in consumer credit with the differences between the current year's expenditures on durables and a weighted average of the two previous years, weighting the more recent year twice as heavily as the more remote. As may readily be seen from this chart, the change in consumer credit tends to be about two-thirds of the change in durable-goods expenditures from the earlier level. This crude correlation, which is hardly more than a naïve model, correctly indicates the direction of credit movement in all years except 1952 and in most years closely approximates the magnitude of the change.

At the end of a boom, after durable-goods purchases and credit granted have made the turn, total credit outstanding continues to rise for a while. The rise comes to an end only when new credit granted falls to the level of repayments. This phase of the movement usually covers a period of several months, and during this period credit is a negative influence even though the total outstanding is still going up. It is not necessary for credit to be actually liquidated before it begins to depress the economy.

Hence the lag in total credit outstanding is an unavoidable consequence of the relationship between extensions and repayments and in itself tells nothing about the causes of a reversal. It is not sound to conclude on the basis of this lag that "the change in trend of consumer credit [after 1929] does not appear to have had any share in the initiation of the decline of incomes. Like the cessation of investments for the purpose of expanding productive capacities, the contraction of consumer credit was a consequence rather than a cause of the decline in income payments."[10]

Conclusions of this kind may or may not be warranted, depending upon the circumstances. Consumer credit may make precisely the same kind of contribution to an automatic reversal as inventories. At the end of an upswing, the expansion of durable-goods purchases cannot halt without changing the contribution from consumer credit. As soon as it halts, the contribution of credit declines, and then income cannot by itself support the level of durable-goods purchases. The tendency is, therefore, for durable-goods purchases to make a well-marked reversal at the end of a movement. At the peak, the effect is very unfortunate, the more so as the volume of installment payments required by the outstanding contracts forces the curtailment of expenditures not directly involved in the credit transactions. In the trough of the cycle, on the other hand, the reversal of credit provides a welcome stimulus to activity, as may be seen from the data for 1933.

It follows that changes in consumer purchases on credit may be an initiating factor in the same sense as any other form of investment. There is every reason to believe that markets for consumer durables had been saturated by 1929 to the same extent as those for housing and producers'

[10] Rolf Nugent, *Consumer Credit and Economic Stability,* Russell Sage Foundation, New York, 1939, p. 207.

durable equipment. Given unusual support from the stock market, they probably reached an unusually high degree of saturation. This extreme accumulation of durable goods helped to hold up the economy in 1929, but it could not be maintained indefinitely and no doubt contributed to the severity of the ensuing liquidation.

Placing the emphasis on consumers' behavior in purchasing durable goods is appropriate, both because that is the dynamic element and because it truly designates where the ultimate responsibility lies. But this neither denies that consumer credit makes a contribution to the movement nor prevents the use of credit as a measure of the effect. The forecaster cannot complete his analysis without working both ways to a consistent result—from durable goods to credit and from credit in its autonomous aspects to consumer income and durable-goods purchases.

Where consumer credit makes its own specific contribution to economic developments is in periods when contract terms are changing. In several postwar situations, changes in terms played a distinct part in determining the course of credit changes and, presumably, the purchases that might have been based on credit. The reimposition of controls in the Korean War upsurge of late 1950 helped to keep total credit outstanding stable through 1951; there were other influences at work, too, such as the quotas on automobile production, but it can hardly be doubted that the credit restrictions had some restraining effect.

The 1952 movements are still more revealing. When controls were eased early in the year, credit outstanding began an immediate sharp expansion, even though auto production and durable-goods expenditures were held down for several months as an aftermath of the steel strike. This was largely responsible for the divergent movements of durable goods and credit shown for that year and for 1953 in Chart 11–5. Finally, the progressive easing of terms after the summer of 1953 contributed to the recovery in auto purchases that began in the fall of 1954 and progressed to the all-time peak of 1955. This, too, is reflected in the high rates of credit expansion in 1955 and 1956.

The effects of prospective changes in terms can be estimated to an approximate order of accuracy by relatively simple computations. Changes in down payments affect credit granted by a corresponding percentage of the value of purchases financed. Changes in the period of repayment affect the size of monthly payments in inverse proportion. With smaller down payments and longer maturities, outstanding credit will tend to rise, and vice versa. Suppose that sales on credit were stable at $3 billion a month, with down payments averaging one-third and the repayment period 24 months; this would produce about $25 billion in outstanding credit over a 2-year period. Now suppose that terms were changed so that down payments were reduced to one-fourth and the repayment period increased to 30 months. This would raise the total outstanding over the 30-month period to about $35 billion, or an annual rate of increase of $4 billion. Conversely, an increase in down payments to three-eighths and a reduction in repayment period to 18 months would reduce the total outstanding to $18 billion, again representing an annual rate of change of $4 billion for 1½ years. These patterns of change are

Chart 11–6. Effects of Changes in Credit Terms on Total Consumer Credit Outstanding*

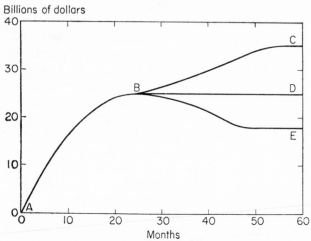

Billions of dollars

Months

* Assumes credit sales stable at $3 billion per month.
Line ABD: Down payment one-third, 24 monthly payments.
Line ABC: Terms changed at point B to down payment one-fourth, 30 monthly payments.
Line ABE: Terms changed at point B to down payment three-eighths, 18 monthly payments.

portrayed in Chart 11–6, no account being taken of the effect of interest charges in modifying the rate at which principal is paid off.

In commenting on a similar chart, Rolf Nugent states:[11]

> It will be noted that even if there were no change in the total volume of credit sales, changes in terms would exert a powerful influence upon the trend of consumers' capital financing. . . .
>
> The most substantial effects of changes in credit terms, however, are likely to result from their influence upon the volume of sales of consumers' durable goods. It is characteristic of the distribution of incomes in the United States that the number of families in each progressively lower income class increases rapidly until very low incomes are reached. . . .
>
> For the upper section of this pyramid, changes in credit terms are likely

[11] *Ibid.*, p. 240.

to have comparatively little influence upon the volume of sales of consumers' durable goods. . . . But for a considerable part of the far larger number of potential buyers in the lower section of the pyramid, access to the market at any given time is determined by the credit terms upon which durable goods may be purchased.

Although it is generally conceded that changes in contract terms are important, there is no conclusive indication of how terms change during the business cycle. One commonly held theory is that terms are eased in the period of competitive selling toward the end of a boom and subsequently tightened in the general drive for liquidity. This sounds logical but is not supported by the relationship of consumer credit to credit and interest rates in general. In the "hard-money" period of mid-1953, terms were tightened with respect to both down payments and maturities; after monetary policy was eased, terms were relaxed progressively, until by mid-1954 down payments were lower and maturities longer than in early 1953. On the other hand, the tie between rates on consumer loans and business loans is ordinarily not very close. The salesmen need a standard contract that will be ready for use whenever a customer is ready to sign. The specialized financial institutions which handle most of the consumer paper are strong enough financially to maintain operations through any temporary period of tightness, and there is reason to believe that they now apply quality standards more consistently than they did during the major cycle following World War I, which offers practically the only basis for comparison.

The times when anything definite can be said about prospective changes in terms are limited. Such changes do take time to work themselves out, however, so that they can be taken into account after the changes are known to have been instated by the lenders. To the extent that they occur in comparative independence of other economic developments, they introduce an element of autonomy into the picture.

Other elements of this kind are introduced by factors directly affecting purchases of durable goods, such as the position of consumer stocks and the rate of introduction of important new items. The concerted postwar introduction of a number of important items, like television sets, dishwashers, and air conditioners, combined with the spreading rise of credit to make the boom stronger and longer-lasting than might have been expected from the backlogs of demand for older products like automobiles and from the credit practices of the prewar period. However, "trends" toward maximum accumulation of durables and toward prearranged saving in contractual form have unfavorable implications for the period after the downturn. Knowledge of these factors can contribute more to a forecast than might at first be thought possible.

CHAPTER 12

Consumers' Expenditures and Saving

Consumers' goods and services ordinarily make up by far the largest portion of gross national product. This is not at all strange, since such goods and services are usually thought of as the end result of all economic activity, to which the creation of productive facilities is auxiliary. Even military expenditures, which assume preeminence at times, may be rationalized as necessary for the protection of the individual in his enjoyment of the things he is able to acquire or create.

The flow of goods and services to consumers consists of an immense conglomeration of products and activities. The variety of objects available has frequently been emphasized by reference to the mail-order catalogue, whose thousand-odd pages of illustrated descriptions do indeed make the point in an impressive way. The fact is, though, that the mail-order catalogue just makes a beginning. Even in the fields it covers, it gives only a limited sampling of the full range of products available. Other kinds of products, perishable or specialized in varying degree, are omitted entirely. Outside the realm of goods, there is the entirety of consumer services—whether for personal care, convenience, protection, education, or amusement.

Any attempt to analyze changes in this vast field must proceed by classification and summary of the infinite detail it encompasses. The most common basis for such a classification is durability. At the one extreme are durable goods; and at the other are services, which are commonly considered to be consumed instantaneously, at the time they are produced and in the presence of the persons or objects providing them. In between is the largest segment of all, comprising what is usually termed "nondurable goods."

The lines of distinction between these groups are by no means so clear as they might at first appear. Durable goods are generally defined as those which last over 3 years in regular use. But some nondurables ordinarily remain in partial use for much more than 3 years and may to some extent behave like durables: The man who wears the same overcoat for something like 10 years may readily be able to postpone its replacement for another 2 years in the event that he finds it inconvenient to buy a new one. Services also tend to merge with nondurables from the point of view of durability. The services of the cleaning woman are consumed over the entire week that passes until her next workday. Similarly, the doctor's advice may govern the patient's behavior over a long period and far outlast the drugs that first accompanied that advice. Nevertheless, the differences are generally important enough to make durability a useful distinction.

Within these durability groups, and particularly within the services and nondurable-goods groups, there are differences in conditions of supply and in consumer response that make for differences in the behavior of the various items included. As one way to take partial account of these differences, attempts have been made in the past to segregate perishable commodities from semidurables in the nondurable goods group. However, as refrigeration and other means for storing perishables came into general availability, the validity of this distinction tended to break down. Both here and in the services, durability by itself fails to provide the most significant distinction, and other differences with an analytical orientation have to be investigated.

In the annual reports of the gross national product a detailed breakdown of consumption expenditures by type of product is provided. There are 12 major product groupings defined in terms of broad objectives of expenditure, as shown in Table 12–1, and each of these in turn is broken down into a number of subsidiary items. Included in these totals, and also carried over into the income totals as income in kind, are the value of food, clothing, and housing for which no actual payment is made, either because it is produced by the consumer himself or because it is furnished by the employer as one aspect of the conditions of employment.

This classification cuts across the simpler classification by durability. The proportion of expenditures in each major product group that falls in each of the three durability classes is indicated in the last three columns of the table. Service items appear in all the groups except food; in that group, tips might be considered pure service expenditures, though this would subject them to different treatment from the much larger wage payments received by the employees of restaurants and other establishments selling food for consumption on the premises. In the case of housing, only the services of existing houses are included, since new-home construction is classified as private-capital formation rather than current consumption expenditures. Personal business relates mainly to the handling of cash, insurance, investment, and debt transactions and includes the value of services rendered without payment by banks and other financial institutions; it also includes costs of legal services, employment-agency fees, union dues, and other charges connected with employment. Religious and welfare activities include contributions to political organizations and to museums and libraries as well as to religious and social-welfare organizations proper.

Table 12-1.   Breakdown of Consumer Expenditures by Type of Product

Major group	Total expenditures in 1954 (In billions of dollars)	Percent of total in—		
		Durable goods	Nondurable goods	Services
I Food, beverages, and tobacco	$ 78.6	...	100	
II Clothing, accessories, and jewelry	24.5	7	80	13
III Personal care	2.8	...	53	47
IV Housing	29.8	...	...	100
V Household operation	30.8	35	24	41
VI Medical and death expenses	11.8	5	14	81
VII Personal business	11.4	...	...	100
VIII Transportation	26.9	46	27	27
IX Recreation	12.2	32	30	38
X Private education and research	2.6	...	...	100
XI Religious and welfare activities	3.2	...	...	100
XII Foreign travel and remittances—net	2.0	...	57	43
Total	$236.5	12	51	37

SOURCE: *Survey of Current Business*, National Income Number, July 1955, Table 30, p. 19.

The full details from which these summary statistics are derived evidently offer a broad field for analysis and investigation. The importance of the classification by major objects lies partly in the fact that it brings together items which serve the same general purpose and calls attention to certain kinds of interrelated variation which may well affect items falling in different durability groups. Thus the expenditure for the automobile or the television set appears in conjunction with the purchased transportation or the amusements which they displace. Shifts occur between groups as well as within them, of course, and no system of classification could relate adequately all the offsetting and complementary changes in expenditures for different goods and services.

DATA ON CONSUMER EXPENDITURES AND SAVING

Making a complete accounting for consumer expenditures of all kinds is a painstaking task, involving a tremendous amount of detail work in compilation and adjustment. In the case of commodities, the provisional estimates reported quarterly are obtained by the National Income Division of the Department of Commerce mainly through the retail-sales method, which consists in obtaining reports on sales from various kinds of retail outlets. These estimates are subsequently firmed up by two other methods, which utilize annual or periodic data of a basic character—the commodity-flow method and the retail-valuation method. The commodity-flow method consists in obtaining estimates of total production of each type of commodity and adjusting them for diversions and additions as they flow through the various channels of processing and distribution into the hands of the final consumer. The retail-valuation method is applied to four types of products—passenger cars, gasoline and oil, household fuels and ice, and tobacco products. It consists in multiplying by an appropriate average retail price the estimated quantities of these commodities purchased by consumers.

For the current data, based primarily on the retail-sales method, the Department of Commerce regularly brings together a variety of monthly-retail-sales data. This comprehensive tabulation gives separate reports for some 20 kinds of stores, segregated into durable-goods and nondurable-goods stores. With some lag, the reports by the stores are adjusted to sales tax reports from state agencies and other data of a more comprehensive character.

The current reports are of necessity on an establishment basis, so that the break between durable goods and nondurable goods is not clean, inasmuch as stores in each group sell commodities belonging in the other group. There are also sampling weaknesses that affect the reliability of reports from certain kinds of stores. But ordinarily neither of these problems represents a serious limitation on the usefulness of the data.

The main over-all difference between the retail-sales and the consumer-expenditures data consists of commodities that flow to consumers through other channels than retail stores. A portion of these commodities moves to consumers without charge, as income in kind, which is withdrawn from consumption by the producer himself or by the distributor from the supplies flowing through his establishment. Other portions also flow directly from the producer to the consumer, as through farmers' markets or manufacturers' house-to-house salesmen. Consumer buying at wholesale also diverts a portion of the total flow from retail outlets. In addition, some sales made by retail stores are not sales to consumers and have to be excluded from the consumer-expenditures total.

All these portions of the total flow must be accounted for in the gross-national-product data. Such an accounting can be made only periodically, however, when comprehensive data on production are available. Between periods when such bench-mark data are compiled, the retail-sales reports must be relied upon. Data for the current period are most affected; the longer the interval since the last bench-mark report, the wider the deviation is liable to be. However, the flow moving through retail outlets tends to be comparatively stable in relation to the total, so that indications of current changes are usually satisfactory.

For most commodities, periodic bench marks are established in years like 1929, 1939, and 1947 by the commodity-flow method. This method starts with the detailed data from the censuses of manufactures taken in those years, supplemented by the censuses of retail and wholesale trade and by the reports on distribution of manufacturers' sales by class of purchaser, in years for which such data are available. The translation of these original data into flows to consumers, at consumer prices, is admittedly roundabout and complex. Its advantages lie in the completeness and great detail of the original data, which make possible not only an accounting for aggregate flows but also a reasonably adequate basis for allocating portions of those flows to durability classes and to different kinds of final users.

All the evidence points to the fact that these procedures give fairly reliable results in the aggregate. A comparison of the provisional estimates for 1947 obtained by the retail-sales method with the final bench-mark estimates for that year showed a divergence of only 3 percent in the totals for all commodity groups. Wider discrepancies appeared in individual commodities, so that the analyst who is interested in particular commodities must exercise care in interpreting the current data. Plus and minus deviations were well distributed between the durable and nondurable segments, leaving the totals for those segments well in line with the final estimates.

A similar conclusion may be drawn with respect to services. The following paragraph begins the Department of Commerce discussion of this point:[1]

> In descriptions of national income methodology, resort is sometimes had to the phrase, "constructed from a great variety of source materials." This easy generalization is probably nowhere so apt as in the case of personal consumption expenditures for services. The 55 service items for which expenditures are shown in table 30 of Part V are comprised of several hundred separate series of estimates; and these represent the incorporation of numerous types of data from many government and private sources, proc-

[1] *National Income,* 1954 edition, supplement to *Survey of Current Business,* U.S. Department of Commerce, p. 117.

essed by procedures virtually running the gamut of those used in national income estimation.

The further discussion reveals that popular notions regarding the inadequacy and inaccuracy of data on services are largely without foundation. One advantage of these data as compared with commodity data is that they involve a much smaller problem of allocation, since so much of the total consists of services purchased by persons only; if purchased by both persons and business, separate reports are available for the two classes of purchasers, as, for example, in the case of electric and gas utilities. On the other hand, there is a more serious problem of extrapolating from the latest bench mark, because there are no current reports for a number of services and the only indicators available may be partial, indirect, or otherwise of doubtful quality.

For the most part, the forecaster can accept these data, at least in the broader aggregates, as a reliable base to which to tie his analysis. The Department of Commerce cites two checks on its over-all accuracy. The first of these is the small size of the statistical discrepancy between the income and the expenditure sides of the national-income and product account. Considerable reliability is placed on certain large components on the income side—such as wages and salaries, corporate profits, and government purchases—and any large errors in consumer expenditures could not easily be offset in the remaining components on the expenditure side.

The second over-all check is obtained from a comparison with the estimates of personal saving of the Securities and Exchange Commission. The Commerce Department estimates of saving are computed as the residual after consumer expenditures are subtracted from disposable personal income. This difference between income and expenditures presumably gets into the balance sheet as net worth. The Securities and Exchange Commission follows the alternative approach of making the measurement from balance-sheet data. Its liquid-savings estimates are derived mainly from changes in personal-asset holdings and debt, such as currency, bank deposits, securities, mortgages, and installment credit outstanding. These statistics are obtained from reports by banks, insurance companies, and other sources in a very large degree independent of those utilized in compiling the national-income and product data.[1a]

Adjusted for differences in concept—relating mainly to farms, other unincorporated enterprises, and nonprofit institutions—the two estimates

---

[1a] The most comprehensive work in this field is Raymond W. Goldsmith, *A Study of Saving in the United States*, Princeton University Press, Vol. 1–2, 1955. It gives detailed estimates of savings by types and by groups of savers and discusses concepts and problems in measuring savings and in relating them to income and balance sheet items.

of savings show a close correspondence, even during the World War II period. In some years, the differences in movement are large enough to create difficulties of interpretation, but the correspondence is so close as to leave little room for doubt about the general validity of the estimates.

The analyst who is primarily interested in savings and related financial data may well find the Securities and Exchange Commission data more useful for his purposes. If he wants to study the components of saving separately or to rearrange them in aggregates alternative to those now being published by the two government agencies, he may find that these data are the only resort, because the broad residual obtained by the Commerce Department method provides no detail with which to work. On the other hand, the forecaster who will be forced to balance the over-all accounts may find it more convenient to work with the Commerce Department estimates, which automatically balance the best available measures of income and expenditures. Most over-all studies will obtain much the same results from either series, since both provide reasonably satisfactory indications of changes in aggregate savings. Neither can guarantee the best results on all occasions.

An alternative source of data on consumer expenditures and savings is found in sample surveys of families and other spending units. Such surveys are very expensive undertakings, and before World War II the number for which results are available is practically confined to a handful undertaken by various government agencies at irregular intervals. The most comprehensive of these was the consumer-purchases study carried out in 1935 and 1936 by the Department of Labor, the Department of Agriculture, and the National Resources Planning Board.[2] Since the war, the surveys of consumer finances conducted under Federal Reserve sponsorship have provided annual data of this kind, though from relatively small samples.

The value of these consumer surveys lies largely in the fact that certain kinds of information can be obtained in no other way. They define the characteristics of the earning and spending units in each income class and reveal not only the average behavior of the units in various classes or groups but also a good deal about the dispersion within each. This permits analysis of income and spending behavior in relation to several other variables, such as asset holdings, family type, and position in social or occupational groups.

Unfortunately, these data have not provided a satisfactory measure of changes in expenditures and saving, and this is only partly due to the few observations available. Sampling errors are large, and response

[2] *Family Expenditures in the United States,* National Resources Planning Board, 1941.

errors may be even more serious. Respondents are reluctant to disclose their asset position, so that the surveys typically understate total holdings as revealed by SEC or other data concerning the universe as a whole. Moreover, such sample data have the inherent deficiency that random or other uncontrolled differences between one observation and the next disturb the dependability of movement which is characteristic of any good time series. Projections will ordinarily be made in terms of the other series, therefore, though not without regard to any insights provided by the consumer surveys.

THE CONSUMPTION FUNCTION

Attempts to project consumer expenditures have commonly proceeded in terms of the relation of expenditures to income—usually termed "the consumption function." This still remains the basic approach to the problem, but it should be recognized that the procedure logically implies a method of forecasting income. In the absence of such a method, the techniques of projection might better be applied to expenditures as such, because expenditures are basically more stable than income and, at least in part, display lag effects that simplify the problem.

The logic of the consumption function is simple: The spending of most families is limited by income, and many spend up to the limit. Some may even exceed this limit, to the extent that credit can be obtained, but even credit is restricted by the prospects for income. There are, of course, a number of wealthy families who always have funds available, regardless of their current income, and a much larger number who have some savings they can draw upon in an emergency. To some extent such funds are always being drawn upon, and dissaving from such funds tends to offset, in part at least, the saving achieved by those whose incomes are sufficient to permit it. Even such dissaving tends to bear a fairly stable relation to income, however. It is greatest in depression years, when loss of incomes creates the greatest need, and this inverse behavior tends to be consistent enough to fit the concept of a functional relationship between income and spending. All the important elements in the situation suggest that expenditures follow the movements of income closely but, being held more steady, approach or even exceed it on the decline and fall behind on the advance.

All this was known long before Keynes formulated the "law of behavior" which he termed the "propensity to consume." A new note was introduced into the discussion at that point, however, because in Keynes's formulation the rise of savings with increased income became part of the fundamental mechanism of income determination. Saving assumed the role of restricting the changes in income that derived from changes in investment, making it important to know how much investment would be needed to support activity at any given level. It therefore became important to measure the propensity to save in quantitative terms, and a number of correlation studies were undertaken in order to establish this relationship.

Since data on saving as such were not available over a long period and saving was in any case the complement of expenditures in making up total income, these studies usually took the form of relating expenditures to income. It was assumed, in other words, that, if the propensity to spend could be determined, the propensity to save could be obtained by subtracting expenditures from the total. The relationship of expenditures to income could be statistically derived and was termed the "consumption function."

As a rule, disposable income, rather than personal income or some other variant of aggregate income, was assumed to be the relevant measure. Thus taxes were excluded in setting up the relationship. This appeared realistic for current analysis in view of the fact that, under present pay-as-you-go tax laws, the bulk of income taxes never enter into take-home pay, and it also appropriately segregated questions of government spending and saving for special treatment.

Utilizing the body of historical data in this way resulted in correlations that could be regarded as highly satisfactory. Coefficients of correlation were usually in the high 90s and in a number of cases exceeded 99. Moreover, departures from the lines of relationship could often be "explained" plausibly in terms of the special circumstances of the years in which they occurred. The results of these studies were therefore applied with enthusiasm, if not always with good judgment, to a variety of forecasting and policy problems.

One criticism sometimes made was that the correlations were bound to obtain good fits to the past data, because they amounted to correlating income with some 90 percent of itself. This criticism might seem to imply that the connection is so close and immediate as to prevent errors, but actual experience in applying the relationships did not encourage any such idea. In practice, the objection could justifiably be put aside, since the sources and methods used in compiling the two series were almost completely independent and introduced no inherent tie other than that which exists in fact.

As an alternative to the correlation approach, the derivation of consumption expenditures from income may be worked out by means of any method of dividing total disposable income between the portion spent and the portion saved. Some forecasters prefer to handle the problem in this way, projecting the percentage saved, rather than total savings, and then applying this percentage to the forecast of income. An example of this approach may be found in Gerhard Colm's *The American*

Economy in 1960.[3] One of the most important questions with which he had to deal in setting up his model for 1960 was whether, in a period of rising income like that required to maintain full employment, the proportion of income saved could be expected to fall as low as 5½ percent of disposable income. This approach has some advantages as an expository device, but the proportion of income saved tends to vary with income, so that a correlation technique would appear to be more appropriate to the problem.

The most comprehensive analysis of the correlations developed in investigating this question is to be found in Robert Ferber's *A Study of Aggregate Consumption Functions.*[4] He examined these correlations from the standpoint of the theoretical considerations underlying them and then proceeded to test them statistically. In carrying out the statistical tests, he recomputed all the functions in terms of revised data, to put them on a comparable basis, and then utilized both goodness of fit and predictive accuracy as criteria of validity.

Altogether, some 60 functions were tested in this way, though most were variants of a smaller number of basic types. The variants were designed in part to test the stability of the functions over time, since any condition other than stability of the relationship would seriously limit the usefulness of such a function. The test of ability to predict actual postwar results was also aimed at this point.

The correlations on the revised data were generally carried out with savings rather than expenditures as the dependent variable. The correlations with the latter were almost uniformly so high as to offer little basis for discrimination in terms of the usual statistical tests. Much greater variation appeared when savings were used in the relationships, and large differences between the various functions became apparent.

The general pattern of relationship established by most of the studies —to ignore other variables than income for the moment—is that savings rise more rapidly than income during a period of advance. In all the acceptable relationships, the coefficients of the income factor were well above the average rate of saving, indicating a marginal propensity to consume well below the average. Thus the results have been generally consistent with Keynes's formulation of the "propensity to consume." The main exceptions appeared in relationships utilizing current price aggregates fitted to data omitting the depression years 1931 to 1934. However, the case for omitting these years, in which the greatest variation occurred, was never convincing, so that there was little need to take the exceptions seriously.

The results were also consistent in a general way with the relationships derived from studies of family behavior showing the proportion of in-

[3] Planning Pamphlet 81, National Planning Association, Washington, 1952.
[4] Technical Paper 8, National Bureau of Economic Research, New York, 1953.

come spent by various income groups. Such studies showed that families in the higher-income brackets do most of the saving. This fact seemed to imply that in periods of advance, when there was an upward shifting in the income distribution as many families realized higher incomes, the proportion of income saved would increase.

On the other hand, long-term studies, covering nearly a century of past experience, revealed no tendency for a progressive increase in the proportion of income saved, as would be suggested by this kind of income-saving relationship. These long-term studies clearly indicated that advances in income have been utilized to increase standards of living rather than to accumulate wealth at the rate indicated by the marginal propensity to save.

The distinction between the short and the long run is evidently important. In the short run, saving rises rapidly and exerts its influence as a moderator of business fluctuations. Over long periods, saving is itself restrained by the desire for higher living standards, permitting the growth of the economy to proceed unhampered.

The long-term shift in the consumption function presents no serious problem for the practical analyst. All that is needed to adjust for it is to introduce a long-term restraint on saving. The nature of this restraint is a question of some debate, but for practical purposes there are a number of alternatives capable of making the adjustment within a tolerable margin of error.

The most common solution was accomplished by inserting as a second independent variable some factor that changes little in the short run but introduces a substantial deduction from savings over long periods. Almost anything that represents a long-term trend is capable of handling the difficulty. The author's own solution was to use population as such a variable.[5] Other analysts used time as an alternative. Two used income itself as a trend measure, by stipulating that, whenever a decline occurred, the highest previous income recorded would be taken as the value of the "trend" variable.[6]

[5] V Lewis Bassie, "Consumers' Expenditures in War and Transition," *Review of Economic Statistics*, vol. 28, August, 1946.

[6] Franco Modigliani, "Fluctuations in the Saving-Income Ratio: A Problem in Economic Forecasting," in *Studies in Income and Wealth*, National Bureau of Economic Research, Inc., New York, vol. 11, pp. 371–443; and James Dusenberry, *Income, Saving and the Theory of Consumer Behavior*, Harvard University Press, Cambridge, Mass., 1952. Both of these authors set up their relationships in terms of the proportion of income saved rather than aggregate savings. The trend factor was also expressed as a percentage of current income. In the second of these studies this factor was inverted, and the reversal of trend resulting from the shift to the reciprocal of this measure was compensated by a reversal in sign of the computed parameter.

All such trend factors show substantial intercorrelation over a long period of time and therefore tend to give similar results. Population may be preferred to time, because its deviations from the straight line have generally been in a direction that improved the results. It increased more slowly in the 1930s than in the 1920s and accelerated rapidly in the 1940s, with peak progress continuing throughout the postwar boom. The income trend with maximum previous values substituted for depressed years had the disadvantage of going to extremes in deviating from the straight line. It was stable too long during the major Depression of the 1930s and followed income too closely in the advance into new high ground after the war.

There were still other relationships, worked out in current dollar terms, that revealed no significant time trend during the entire period 1923 to 1940. A major point of difference, therefore, concerned the importance of price deflation. A half-dozen studies were carried out in terms of current price aggregates without discussion of the validity of this procedure. The analysts who used deflated data, on the other hand, usually presented some kind of justification for this procedure. Their arguments were mainly of two kinds: first, a showing that concern with real quantities rather than money values would represent rational behavior on the part of consumers; and, second, a showing that inconsistencies in the relationship or in rates of consumption would develop under conditions when certain kinds of changes in incomes and prices were assumed to occur.

These arguments may be summarized in the statement that consumers tend to maintain their real living standards when confronted with price or income changes. When prices rise faster than income, real income falls and consumers must spend a larger proportion to maintain their consumption. But this does not mean that savings tend to fall because of rising income; actually, real income would be falling. Similarly, when prices fall faster than incomes, savings may rise, but not because money income is falling. When both move together, real income remains stable, and the proportion spent may remain the same without implying either that it is independent of income or that the marginal propensity to save is as low as the average propensity to save. In all these cases, the logical results would appear to be obtained from the deflated data.

Another important point of difference occurred in connection with attempts to take into account the tendency for consumption to lag behind income. A number of studies used the preceding year's income or the change in income from the previous year as a measure of this effect. The usual rationalization for this treatment is that consumers are slow to adjust their spending to a change in income. Although the additional variable usually improved goodness of fit, the results were not altogether encouraging; the parameters of the lagged income variables were mostly below the level of significance or just over the border line.

The fact that the greatest improvement from this procedure occurred in functions using current price aggregates suggests that the lag is largely a price effect. As such, it would conform to the converse of the examples just cited in the discussion of price deflation, representing a series of situations in which prices changed less rapidly than income. When incomes run ahead of prices, dollar expenditures need not change so fast to provide the goods and services desired. In these terms, the lag in expenditures may be accounted for largely by the lag in contractual or regulated prices for some of the important service items, notably housing and household utilities. Aside from this, the lag appears to be the net result of a complex mixture of leads and lags in various parts of the expenditure total, as will be shown shortly.

THE ACCURACY OF CONSUMPTION FUNCTIONS

This brief discussion of what has been done and of some of the issues involved may suffice as a warning that there are questions that can be answered only tentatively, leaving a good deal of uncertainty to be resolved in the future. Various types of functions are almost equally possible on the basis of the historical data available for the period before World War II, particularly if selection of years is permitted. Some of the functions may be excluded as a result of the experience accumulated in the first decade after the war, but with respect to a number of others that experience still does not permit any conclusive demonstration of superiority.

The practical question is: "Can any of these consumption functions turn up reliable forecasts of consumer expenditures?" If this question implies a strict application of the mathematical formula, the answer has to be: "No." Ferber's analysis shows how serious the errors can be when the formulas are applied mechanically in a new situation. In 1947, a year when savings were very low, errors in the estimate of savings ran as high as several hundred percent. In other years through 1950, errors were also large.

Subsequently Ferber made an additional test using data for 1951 and 1952.[7] In this test errors were generally more limited, and quite a different set of functions gave the best results.

The trouble with any such demonstration is that there are "errors" in the actual data, too. These generally take the form of deviations introduced by special circumstances. From the standpoint of the functions,

[7] "The Accuracy of Aggregate Savings Functions in the Postwar Years," *Review of Economics and Statistics,* May, 1955.

the early postwar years were all seriously in error. The entire period was one of disturbance, so that all the changes recorded were the result of special post–World War II or Korean War conditions. Hence the actual results for those years were bound to deviate from any projection that might be regarded as "normal" on the basis of prewar experience. The fact that these "errors" were themselves predictable to a substantial degree is the best kind of evidence that the relationships were not breaking down but were merely recording the abnormalities of the situation.

It is no serious qualification on the approach, therefore, to admit that no version of the consumption function can provide accurate results in all situations. In practical terms, what this admission means is either that any version which may be used has to be limited in its application to the situations it effectively fits or that the results it gives have to be adjusted to fit the situation in which it is being used. The latter procedure, using the function derived by the author, has consistently given good results over the postwar period.[8] A number of other functions could also have been used effectively in the same way, because the factors at work in the changed circumstances were definitive enough to indicate not only the direction but also something about the magnitude of probable deviations.

Much is known about the character of the adjustments needed in various kinds of situations. By the end of World War II, consumers had accumulated what was by prewar standards a tremendous volume of liquid assets. These could be, and were, used to satisfy backlogs of demand, to finance education or training, and to maintain living standards during temporary periods of unemployment, such as the strikes of early 1946. Other adjustments could not be made in terms of demand factors alone. Allowance had to be made for feasible rates of recovery in industries where production had been restricted—mainly those producing durable goods and services. In these industries output was dependent on the ability of business to organize production—to increase its capacity, to train a working force, and to procure materials. Thus some things had to be determined in relation to demand factors and others in relation to supply factors. With respect to both, the results obtained from the consumption functions by direct calculation could readily be improved.

Another type of adjustment, the need for which has shown some tendency to recur, is that deriving from a special increment to income payments, such as the veteran's bonus payments and insurance refunds. Several such windfall payments have been recorded within the period of the official national-income data, notably the loans on Adjusted Serv-

---

[8] For an illustration, see Bassie, *op. cit.* This article was largely devoted to a discussion of such adjustments.

ice Certificates in 1931, the payment of the certificates in 1936, the Armed Forces leave bonds in 1947, and the National Life Insurance dividend in 1950. The experience in all these cases indicates that a far smaller proportion of such windfall receipts goes into consumption than is true of ordinary income. With allowance for some variation in the lag, something less than half appeared to go into purchases of goods and services within a year or so after the payment was received. The remainder went into liquid-asset holdings or debt repayment. The nature of the payment and the circumstances at the time no doubt affect the use of such funds, and allowance has to be made for specific differences in each case.

The adjustments that can be made in dealing with unusual circumstances are of necessity rough; but even if they are subject to a substantial margin of error, they may be helpful. Situations will inevitably emerge from time to time with circumstances so new that there is little basis in past experience for dealing with them. It may or may not then be possible to work out suitable adjustments on the basis of some reasonable hypothesis. But even if this is not possible in the first instance, a subsequent advantage may be obtained after the fact, because the reaction from a temporary condition may sometimes provide a fairly accurate basis for a new forecast after the development of a situation that could not itself be anticipated.

Such expedients are, of course, anathema to some analysts. Thus the critic with a nihilistic turn of mind, who has already disposed of the consumption function by asserting the importance and autonomy of changes in consumer expenditures and by pointing out its weaknesses in the postwar period, is likely to object to the adjusted estimates also. "You can't have it both ways," he says. "You can't say that the consumption function works and also that it doesn't work!" The argument is not very convincing when put to the test; the consumption function does provide a good basic indicator, and the departures from it can be estimated from the behavior of current and probable deviations interpreted in terms of the special factors that are producing them.

ADAPTABILITY OF CONSUMER BEHAVIOR

The process of devising adjustments to a statistical consumption function is on a par with the selection of the function itself. Neither is possible in a precise, quantitative way from the available data alone. Both are founded upon hypotheses of how consumers behave in various circumstances—these usually being referred to as the "theory of consumer behavior."

To be complete, such a theory should account for occasional deviations as well as for the regular patterns. A generalization that seems to fit both with a minimum of exceptions is that consumer behavior is adaptive. The usual form of adaptation is to live pretty well up to income while perhaps setting some small portion aside as a reserve. Whenever anything happens to disturb this normal adjustment, people react in such a way as to gain the best advantage they can from any change for the better or to salvage as much as possible from a disaster that forces reduced living standards upon them.

When their income is augmented, if only by a temporary windfall, they are in a position both to live better and to improve their future security. Increased expenditures are then likely to be slanted toward desires that could not be satisfied before, toward luxuries or important durable goods that could not previously be financed. In the late 1920s, when the stock market was providing not just a little but a lot of easy money, sales of such products increased tremendously.

On the other hand, when income is curtailed, consumers adjust by eliminating the objects of expenditure that can most easily be dispensed with. Certain kinds of current needs must be met, and new outlays are focused on these to the exclusion of "extravagances" that might be enjoyed at other times. Certain kinds of saving are forced by existing contracts, but these payments may be met in part at the expense of other savings. The first shift tends to curtail or halt the accumulation of liquid assets. As existing contracts are paid off or canceled, saving in general is curtailed. Finally, dissaving by the families with reduced incomes results in net dissaving in the aggregate. In a decline, these are the normal patterns through which the propensity to consume maintains the economy.

Disturbances, too, fit into this pattern of analysis. When a shortage threatens, consumers rush to buy. In 1950, they stocked up on nondurables as well as durables, though the buying was concentrated on the latter. There is a certain logic in the attitude of the man who was buying everything he could because he "merely wanted to get what he needed before the hoarders grabbed it all." He was intent on taking care of himself and his family and did not accept responsibility for the rest of the community.

Fortunately, not all consumers are equally willing to incur the price and quality penalties of buying under emergency conditions. After the shortage has taken full effect, most hold off for better times. They stop trying to buy and save for the future. There are still exceptions, of course, and this group of irresponsibles helps to create the illegal markets that inevitably spring up. A few others, whose need is especially great, may also help to bid up black-market prices to an extreme. The large majority are content to do without some things for a while and wait until they are available on more reasonable terms. The result is that savings rise; during World War II they rose very rapidly. After the emergency, they may be used to expand purchases, but there is enough intelligence about the process to stretch it out over a period of several years.

The proposition that behavior is adaptive thus represents a source of useful hypotheses about both normal and abnormal situations. It provides a basis for judging both current changes and probable developments. It may seem somewhat vague, but the alternatives are either equally so or even more impractical. Neither the maxims of the businessman who must advertise and sell his products nor the abstruse theories of the economist who seeks to explain actual experience through a series of theoretical constructs in the form of rules of optimal behavior offer effective tools for the forecaster.

Most of the consumer actions that concern the salesman or the advertiser are not highly relevant to the question of changes in aggregate consumption. They are primarily concerned with means of appealing to the consumer's sense of values or of trapping him into an impulse purchase which he may or may not enjoy as much as he hoped when he made it. These devices may be effective in diverting purchases from one product to another, or from one time interval to another, but they have little effect on the total over extended periods.

Adaptive behavior includes both rational behavior and habitual or impulse behavior. Certain problems must be solved rationally if they are to be solved at all. Others, which may be thought to have reached a past solution, will be handled habitually unless there is some circumstance that breaks the routine. Thus medical treatment is ordinarily obtained from the family doctor, but in case of serious injury treatment is accepted at the scene of the accident from any doctor. Both the habit and its interruption are intelligent, adaptive reactions.

It might seem that a splurge of buying on the part of consumers or a splurge of special offerings by merchants could have a considerable effect on the market. No doubt a certain amount of transitory instability arises in this way. However, when only a few make such a splurge, it creates only a ripple on the stream of activity. The rest of the group usually lets the few go their way and refuses to be convinced unless there are changes in the situation that justify such action. Even the larger group may mistakenly move in concerted fashion on occasion, but such mistakes are bound to be corrected quickly. More commonly the group is pulled along by changes in the situation, which seem to demand action when they are experienced; and the actions taken, which might appear anomalous in other circumstances, become no more than efforts to adapt to the changes that called them forth. The upsurge of the

Korean War period through the first quarter of 1951 and the letdown through the rest of that year illustrate how such movements are determined by actual developments, including those that are an outgrowth of the mistaken expectations of the recent past.

Perhaps more important than the efforts of the salesmen and advertisers are those of the inventors and industrial designers. Unusually rapid advances in consumer buying are commonly thought to be associated with innovations, with the development of new products that involve large outlays for their introduction into the pattern of consumer living. This is particularly supposed to be true in the case of major durable goods like autos and television sets. What is sometimes overlooked in discussions of this question is that the purchases raise incomes as well as add to expenditures.

From the short-run point of view, as the consumption function shows, expenditures do not tend to rise relative to income on the advance but rather to drop back. This appears to hold without regard to the proportion of expenditures on new products. For a splurge of spending on such products to represent an abnormal stimulus on a continuing basis, it would have to change the relationship of spending to income, and this it appears powerless to do. Although some of the deviations that appear from time to time may be considered of this character, they only temporarily raise expenditures from the level that would otherwise have been expected.

Over the longer run, the effects of innovation and technology appear to be much more important. Measuring from the peak of one major cycle to the next and thus abstracting from cyclical effects, one may see that savings have not risen more than proportionally to income and that the products available to consumers have increased in variety as well as in volume. In view of the progress of research and the steady improvement in industrial know-how, it would be paradoxical indeed if new products were not developed and put into widespread use in a period of as much as 2 decades. So much of the whole organized effort of the economy is devoted to this end as to make it almost inevitable. The question which this fact fails to settle is whether or not the new products contribute to the restriction of saving by confronting the consumer with an inducement to spend.

Frequently tied up with innovations and technology in discussions of this point are changes in habits of living. The profound changes in modern life wrought by the development and almost universal use of the automobile may be pointed to as the best illustration of this lesson. Modern man can flee the congestion of the cities which he created, because he has a second home, a mobile home that takes him easily where he wishes to go. This second home may be cleaner, warmer, and in some ways more comfortable than the house he lives in. The car makes necessary less clothing, or at least less heavy clothing, because it shelters him so much of the time when he is out of doors. But it also provides a stimulus for doing other things. He moves around and sees the way other people live and thus acquires an urge to do the things they do and have the things they have. The car not only becomes a necessity itself but also creates other necessities that fit into the pattern of mobility and suburban living. The transformation in ways of life since the introduction of the auto are striking enough to lend plausibility to the idea that more expensive habits of living have forced larger expenditures than would be called for by the propensity to consume.

These changes offer no conflict with the idea that consumer behavior is adaptive. In any society there are patterns of change, and these may be described in such varied terms as "evolutionary" or "revolutionary." Where ingenuity and enterprise are relatively unrestricted, it is more likely that the latter type of description would apply, but in all cases a diversity of influences is at work to change ways of living and the objects that make new ways of living possible. The people generally participate by seeking some changes and by accepting others over which they have little if any control.

The manufacturer who seeks by invention and design to guide changes to his advantage can generally do so only as he facilitates the adaptation of consumers to the patterns of living that are emerging. His success may certainly derive in part from intelligence and ingenuity; it may also depend upon accidental or other unpredictable developments that are independent of his efforts. Among the criteria that would seem to offer some guarantee of acceptability in our society, foremost rank has consistently been held by material progress, either in reducing human effort or in adding to real income.

INDUCEMENT TO SPEND VERSUS ABILITY TO SPEND

The facts of progress are plain enough, but they do not in themselves tell whether the higher propensity to consume is the result or the cause of the more affluent way of life. Nevertheless, causal significance is frequently assigned to the spending habits of the consumer and to the goods and services that give his expenditures form. The most fully developed theory of this kind is that presented by James Dusenberry.[9] He lays stress on two factors: the interdependence of choices and the relative position of the consumer in the income distribution. The spending decisions of each family or individual consuming unit are viewed as being

[9] *Op. cit.*

determined in part by what others are doing. Each attempts to keep up with others of approximately the same economic status or rank in the social order; and since most families look to the groups above them for the standards they would like to match, there is pressure for continual increases in expenditures at all income levels. This thesis that the proportion of income spent is a function of the relative position of the spending unit in the income distribution as a whole is known as the "relative-income" hypothesis.

It is easy to accept the idea that choices are interdependent. Man grows up in a social environment, which imposes its standards upon him. He lives out his life as a social being who gets along best by adapting his actions to those of the other members of the community in which he works and lives. He can be independent, uncooperative, or even socially destructive at times, but he must expect to pay penalties for the liberties taken. On the whole, it is much easier to conform. All the findings of social psychology indicate that in any society most of the members live on the socially accepted terms. In a relatively free society, these terms are flexible enough to permit much variation, but they can hardly be so flexible as to permit anything like complete freedom of choice. What constitutes the best in modern living tends to be a matter of fairly general agreement.

What is not so easy to accept is the idea that social pressure forces a fixed rate of spending at any given position in the income distribution. The same kind of upward shift in spending would occur if for any other reason the propensity to consume was increasing over time at all levels of income. To put this another way, the family that has moved to a higher level of income as the entire distribution moved upward with an increase in aggregate income might be spending at a rate which corresponded to a lower level in the earlier period because its relative position in the distribution had not changed, or it might be doing so for other reasons. The shift as such is not in dispute. Why this happens is the important question, and there is little if anything to indicate that consumers are forced into it by what others are doing.

It is evidently one of those situations in which interacting forces make assignment of causal significance difficult. Moreover, the answer cannot be found in averages alone but must take account of differences within groups. During an advance, not all the families in the same community or social group move up together as incomes rise. Some families are left behind; others move up faster than the average. Those that gain might be expected to reach for the level of living of those who had already achieved the higher level of income. But if they reach higher still, there is nothing to indicate that their decision is based on their relationships to others rather than on the natural inclination of men with freedom of choice and increased spending ability to go as far as possible in improving their lot.

Confusion arises because it is difficult to disentangle changes in living standards or habits from the increase in income itself. Technological advance is embodied in the concept of "mass production," which means production in sufficient volume and at high enough efficiency to permit sale of the product at a price that the mass of consumers can afford. The ingenuity that focuses on making production more efficient carries over into the sphere of consumer products also. It has resulted not only in the laborsaving devices of the modern home but in the prepared mixes, the ready-to-cook or ready-to-eat frozen foods, and the baby's formula that permits the mother to be elsewhere at feeding time. Even services are affected: the TV set is another way of bringing the antics of the vaudeville performer to the consumer of his services. All these changes, in industry and in the home, result in higher real income, part of which may be realized in increased leisure. They produce, represent, or permit advances in income for the community as a whole and, by reason of that fact, a higher standard of living for its members.

The increase in average income by itself implies a higher standard of living. The higher standard of living by itself implies some change in the manner of living. In earlier days, the high-income groups had a battery of servants to do the many chores that a person of status would not wish to perform for himself. Today the average family has the same chores performed for it by a battery of mechanical devices. Without this technical advance, the higher income could not have been achieved. If all the work had to be performed by the old hand methods, most everyone would still have to do it himself. A community would indeed be lifting itself by its bootstraps if it could advance by letting all its members be each other's servants. The only way consumers can cash in on the increase in income is by adapting themselves to the conditions of operation that make it possible.

The improvement of efficiency that makes the higher standard of living possible of necessity changes ways of living, and in light of this fact the distinction between wholly new objects of expenditure and those which merely displace previous objects appears to be both artificial and inconsequential. Consumption patterns change. They have to change if living standards are to increase, but the qualitative differences are not the essence of what is taking place. The most convenient summary of the complex of changes involved is in terms of the increase in real income.

Such a complex of changes would be experienced in any economy capable of raising its real per capita income, whether or not the propensity to consume was shifting upward through time. An upward shift in the propensity to consume helps a growing economy keep closely in step with the capabilities of its resources and its technology. Its absence would not prevent growth, but without it savings would tend to put a more severe brake on expansion and recurring setbacks and unemployment would be more long-drawn-out.

By the nature of the factors usually cited in explaining the long-term upward shift, there is no reason to think that they cease to operate during depression periods—though their effects are then definitely obscured by the more violent changes taking place for other reasons. The aspiration for higher living standards does not die with a recession. It is if anything intensified by its temporary frustration. In it are elements of longing for a return to prosperity, but the prosperity desired is not that reached during the last boom but the bigger and better prosperity which will be reached in the next.

What appears to happen on the decline is that abnormally high savings on the part of those whose real incomes have been maintained are more than offset by dissavings on the part of those whose incomes have fallen more than prices and particularly on the part of those who become unemployed. Anyone who can find a means of dissaving under the latter circumstances, whether by using his own accumulated assets or by obtaining funds from others, is not responding to social pressures. He is merely displaying the normal swim-or-sink reactions that have characterized the behavior of organisms since life began.

Looked at in this way, the theory of consumer behavior is entirely consistent with a consumption function that specifies a high short-term marginal propensity to consume and provides a long-term adjustment to account for the advance in living standards. It may be agreed that tastes are determined by social value standards and by technology. But it cannot be shown that these factors also determine the proportion of income spent.

For present purposes, it is not necessary to disprove the relative-income hypothesis in favor of an absolute-income hypothesis. All that needs to be shown is that the theoretical reasons in favor of the more cumbersome relative-income approach are not compelling. Both hypotheses may be accepted as describing forms of adaptive behavior: The former describes the adaptation of the spender to the community in which he lives; in belonging to the group he at least partially accepts the inducements to spend which its standards of living impose. The latter describes his adaptation to the economic means at his disposal; in a community whose real income and wealth are growing, he may well find that his best way of life requires some reduction in the rate at which he accumulates savings. If his income is curtailed during recurrent setbacks, the past accumulations make it possible for him to live on his capital. Sacrificing past savings may not permit him to maintain the best standards he achieved in the past, but it is bound to make for a definite shift in the ratio between current income and consumption.[10]

What this line of reasoning suggests is that an explanation of the long-term downtrend in saving may be found in the accumulation of wealth, which provides an alternative to income as a claim against goods and services. The accumulation of wealth puts a restraint on additional saving, because after a point people would rather consume more currently than build up additional claims against future production. The effect over a long period is to keep saving near the same average level—say, in the range of 5 to 10 percent of income—without affecting the much greater variation that occurs in the course of a single cycle. Various writers have suggested this possibility.[11]

The character of this restraint on current savings is perhaps best understood in the present context by viewing personal wealth as an inventory to which new savings make year-to-year additions. Then stock-flow relationships of the type discussed earlier in this volume become operative. The norm for such an inventory would in a general way be the current standard of living. As it does in business operations, this norm calls for cash to maintain the level of current operations, for reserves against contingencies, and for surpluses to build a better future.

Keeping the "savings inventory" in line with the norm over long periods requires a relatively constant rate of saving determined by the

[10] A new version of the theory of consumer behavior that appeared after this passage was written is Milton Friedman's *A Theory of the Consumption Function*, National Bureau of Economic Research, Inc., New York, 1956. It offers a new hypothesis, termed the "permanent-income" hypothesis, as an alternative to those discussed in the text. Consumption expenditures—defined to exclude not only savings but also durable-goods purchases—are held to be determined by the stable, or permanent, component of income, which relegates temporary elements of income gained or lost in any specific year to a "transitory component" that is excluded from the computation. This hypothesis explains certain aspects of consumer behavior very well. Although it may prove in some respects to be theoretically more satisfactory than the absolute-income approach offered in the following pages, it is clearly not a practical working tool for the forecaster. Since there is no way of distinguishing between permanent and transitory components of income for purposes of current analysis, its usefulness is limited. Moreover, by treating expenditures for durable goods as savings rather than as consumption, it leaves unsolved the crucial problem for the forecaster, namely, to explain the fluctuations in the highly variable durable-goods sector.

[11] The suggestion was explicitly made, for example, by James Tobin, "Relative Income, Absolute Income, and Savings," in *Money, Trade, and Economic Growth: In Honor of John Henry Williams,* The Macmillan Company, New York, 1951. It became a central feature of a highly theoretical formulation in Franco Modigliani and Richard Blumberg, "Utility Analysis and the Consumption Function," in Kenneth Kurihara (ed.), *The Post-Keynesian System: Essays in Honor of John Maynard Keynes,* Rutgers University Press, New Brunswick, N.J., 1954.

rate of over-all economic growth. When a more rapid advance occurs, the savings inventory temporarily falls below the desired level and a higher rate of saving is called for; but the over-all advance tends to remain unchecked, because consumers find the need to rebuild stocks of durable goods even more urgent than the need to rebuild capital positions. Late in the boom, the accumulation of assets becomes adequate and savings tend to fall, so that the proportion of income spent does not move up in accordance with the short-term propensity to consume. Also, the flow of savings is chaneled more definitely into financial assets. Security prices are belatedly bid up, perhaps to excessively high levels, and the extraordinary rise in "wealth" also tends to restrain savings and keep the boom alive.

On the decline, those whose wealth has increased in real value join with those whose incomes have become inadequate in restricting the rate of current savings. The liquidation of accumulated savings through their use to sustain current consumption helps to support the economy through the period when liquidation of business inventories is most acute. Security prices are then likely to be unduly depressed, and the loss of "wealth" tends further to depress spending; but for the time being, this only partially offsets the dissaving that the situation makes necessary. After the upturn from the low, the proportion of income saved tends to rebound toward the expected level. It may be inferred that the earliest stages of recovery are characterized by crosscurrents in which some consumers are still dissaving rapidly while others are saving at an abnormally high rate.

The available data are inadequate to give any clear picture of all these developments. As far as can be determined, the short-term changes are generally consistent with an absolute-income approach modified by stock-flow considerations. Over the longer term, the effects tend to be all in one direction, because the accumulation of real wealth tends to go on and on, ever rising like the stocks of durable capital which do not wear out in short periods of liquidation. Under these conditions, the philosophy that "you can't take it with you" operates effectively to limit accumulation.

On the other hand, the analogy between the stock-flow relationships in consumers' savings and in business inventories cannot be too closely drawn. There is lacking the direct connection between an inventory and the operations it is intended to serve. No loss is incurred if asset holdings temporarily fall behind purchases, and there is no penalty in the form of carrying costs when asset holdings rise too high. Furthermore, an adequate test would require data on various kinds of existing assets valued in both current and constant prices, and the difficulties of preparing meaningful price indexes for purposes of deflation are insuperable.

The principles governing the size of inventories are evidently at work here in a general way only and do not produce the direct short-term adjustments that control business investment. Perhaps a more nearly exact counterpart in business operations is to be found in the accumulation of retained profits in liquid form. Most businesses try to limit the accumulation of liquid assets that bring them no significant return. When cash piles up, it presents a problem, and they may attempt to solve the problem by paying higher dividends, by expanding existing operations, or by branching out into new lines. In the same way, consumers who acquire means also tend gradually to expand and diversify their way of life. If the improvement in status is widely distributed through the population, spending tends to rise at all levels of income. The proportion of income spent then tends to rise, and the average propensity to save is held to a relatively stable level over extended periods of time.

THE INCOME DISTRIBUTION

In the post–World War II period, as the failure of prewar consumption functions to forecast accurately was observed year by year, a number of proposals were made to remedy the deficiencies of over-all consumption functions by investigating the influence of specific factors affecting portions of the all-inclusive totals of consumer expenditures and savings. These pleas were usually introduced by statements of postwar experience showing that little was known about consumer behavior except that the simplification embodied in the consumption function was unwarranted. They proposed to solve the problem from either or both of two possible points of view: the specific groups of consumers who were contributing to the aggregate or the specific goods and services going into its make-up. Although the eventual importance of this work for an understanding of consumer behavior cannot be denied, it has contributed little of practical value for the forecaster up to this point.

Some of the proposals for analysis of the problem by segments went to such extremes that they would have been ruled out by requirements for data collection alone. For this reason, it is not only impractical, but also futile to try to deal with all the various expenditures and savings of all kinds of consuming units stratified by all the characteristics that might be considered relevant—such as asset holdings, family type, race, occupation, age, education, or anything else that might be expected to make a difference in individual expenditures. Frequently overlooked in such proposals is the fact that the individual differences tend to average out in the aggregate. For example, older people spend in different ways from young people. But the young are always getting older and being replaced in the position they occupied by others still younger. The age distribution of the entire population changes only gradually. As it shifts, a shift in expenditures might occur; but any measure of such a change would be in the nature of a trend factor whose effects were mixed up with and obscured by larger changes deriving from other causes.

The difficulty of isolating the effects of various factors cannot be entirely avoided even in studies that are realistic enough to proceed with data of feasible scope and to avoid getting lost in masses of detail. Such studies typically utilize existing data or rework the data compiled earlier to bring out their bearing on the specific hypotheses to be tested. To approach the problem first in terms of specific groups of consumers, two kinds of studies may be mentioned: those analyzing changes in specific types of income and those analyzing changes in the income distribution as a whole.

The most common form of study utilizing type of income is that which segregates wage income for special treatment. Over the period for which reliable time series on income and consumption are available, there has been an upward trend in the proportion of wages and salaries to total personal income. It might be concluded, therefore, that the upward shifting of the propensity to consume is due to this factor. This, however, is a difficult conclusion to test. Labor income and other income are interrelated in various ways, and the conditions responsible for shifts in any given period may not be typical. Inasmuch as there are other trend factors at work, reversals in labor income or in other variables over a period long enough to provide reliable new measurements would be necessary to delineate their special effects. Since no conclusive test is likely to be obtained for some time, about all that can be said is that other explanations for the upward shift in the propensity to consume appear to be more plausible.

The same difficulty is encountered by studies utilizing the income distribution, since it tends to change slowly and for reasons that affect other things at the same time. On the surface, the income distribution is a rather simple concept: it is a statement of the number of income recipients and the income accruing to them at various levels of income, and as such it may be taken as a measure of differences in the economic status of various portions of the population. On looking beneath the surface, however, the appearance of simplicity disappears. There are complications that render it ineffective as a working tool.

The best data available, together with an extended description of how they were compiled and of the problems underlying them, are to be found in the Department of Commerce publication *Income Distribution in the United States, by Size, 1944–1950*. It shows that definitions are highly important in determining the results obtained, and this statement applies to definitions of both income and families. At both income extremes, the distribution is subject to considerable error. The soundest part, comprising most of the middle-income brackets, is based on the distribution of wages and salaries subject to withholding taxes. The lowest-income recipients are largely special types, including part-time workers; pensioners, often with other unreported sources of income; single individuals and other small family units; well-to-do families reporting temporary losses; and others who are not particularly depressed from a realistic economic point of view. The highest groups are generally even better off than indicated, since no account is taken of retained corporate profits, expenditures covered by expense accounts or other business costs, and capital gains, which are frequently ordinary income converted for the purpose of avoiding taxes. In general, farm families are not on a comparable basis with nonfarm families, and unattached individuals are not comparable with either. Throughout the distribution, the skill of income recipients in concealing income is given full play, and various forms of hidden income have to be estimated without benefit of actual data. It is necessary at all times, therefore, to use caution in drawing conclusions from the income distribution.

Despite these qualifications, the income distribution has tended to hold a distinct attraction for analysts of consumer expenditures. This has partly been due to the long history of theory relating to the inequality of income and its modification through taxation or other policies. It has also been due to the observed fact that high-income families spend a lower proportion and save a higher proportion of their incomes than low-income families. Moreover, various kinds of expenditures shift in relation to income as families move up the income distribution. The proportions spent on food and housing decline steadily as family income increases from the lowest-income groups, but spending for many other items tends to increase.[12] The increases in specific items provide an inducement for those interested in products which few people can afford, like yachts and mansions, to carry out their analysis in terms of the shifting of families into the relevant income brackets.

Changes in the income distribution are, of course, related to changes in total income produced, though the relationship is not apparently one that varies directly with the different phases of the business cycle. During the quarter century beginning in 1929, there was a fairly steady trend toward greater equality. This fact is brought out by indexes of inequality based on the entire income distribution and by studies of the declining share of total income received by the upper-income groups.[13] This long movement toward equality, mostly through 3 dec-

[12] *Family Expenditures in the United States.*

[13] Simon Kuznets, *Shares of Upper Income Groups in Income and Savings,* National Bureau of Economic Research, Inc., New York, 1953.

ades of recovery, reversed an earlier trend toward inequality that persisted throughout the 1920s.

The steady shift toward equality into the period following World War II has been triumphantly seized upon as a sign of progress and accepted as an explanation of the upward shifting of the propensity to consume over this period. Neither this conclusion nor the hopeful optimism deriving from it is really warranted except as one is also willing to assume that the economy is now depression-proof. Among the reasons for the quarter-century decline in inequality from 1929 to the early 1950s are the following: first, and most important, the virtual elimination of unemployment; second, the shift to higher-paying occupations, mostly in the durable-goods industries, and the relative increase in wage rates in the lowest-paid occupations under the impact of wartime labor shortages;.and, third, the relative decline in property income, deriving in part from relative downtrends in interest rates and rents. On the collapse of the boom, all these "trends" are likely to be reversed. Moreover, the propensity to consume was apparently moving upward just as fast in the 1920s, when the movement of the income distribution was toward greater inequality.

All that measures of a shift in the income distribution can give is a kind of broad indication of change in one direction or the other. Indexes of changes in relative equality are at best rather imprecise measures. If a shift persists for some time, it represents in effect just another indication of a "trend," which may or may not continue and which may or may not be significant for consumption. Under the circumstances, it is easy to agree with Dorothy Brady when she says: "We know little more than that the data are deficient in both quantity and quality, that income is very unequally distributed, and that a high standard of living cannot be attained on the average income."[14]

There is, furthermore, one additional fact that limits the value of the income distribution to the forecaster, and that is the lack of any dependable means of projecting it. The most up-to-date data on the actual distribution in any year become available only after a much longer lag than is true of aggregate income itself. Projections must be made from a position that is already a year, or perhaps several years, old. If they are made as a continuation of the recent "trend," they not only give little assurance of accuracy but also involve "adjustments" in income and expenditures that could be made much more effectively in the process of estimating the expenditures by other methods.

There are, of course, certain kinds of questions relating to public policy and economic structure that can only be answered in terms of the income distribution, and for these the Commerce Department data

[14] *Studies in Income and Wealth,* National Bureau of Economic Research, Inc., New York, 1951, vol. 13, pp. 3–4.

may be considered good practical estimates, in the same sense as the national-income aggregates themselves. It may be conceded that some government policies adopted as a means of modifying the position of various groups of income earners could affect the aggregates to some extent. In actual practice, however, decisions on taxes or other questions of that kind tend toward compromises rather than toward drastic redistribution of income between groups, and any changes in expenditures deriving from this source will probably become apparent in the spending series long before their precise impact on various income groups is revealed. Hence the forecaster who leaves the income distribution to the specialists will seldom if ever be led into significant error by reason of that fact, and he will avoid the frustration that arises from attempts to deal with the complications and imponderables of the income distribution.

THE DEMAND FOR SPECIFIC COMMODITIES

The other line of analysis which attempts to solve the problem of forecasting expenditures by breaking down the consumption aggregate proceeds in terms of its commodity composition. Even brief study of the markets for individual commodities offers convincing evidence that diverse factors are at work influencing the sales of various kinds of goods and services. The same point holds good with reference to various forms of saving. Hence a study of the factors affecting various expenditure items or various outlets for savings would appear likely to contribute much to efforts at predicting aggregate spending or saving.

There is undoubtedly a degree of validity to this approach, but it also contains a major pitfall. Thus a new product, whether or not it displaces another already on the market, typically enjoys a period of growth in which it is free from the influence of changes in income and of some of the other factors that will affect its movements after it has come into widespread use. But to look at such a commodity by itself, without regard to its effects in restricting other purchases—ultimately, perhaps, just through its claim on a portion of total income—may be to learn nothing at all about the aggregate. In terms of the latter, only the net effect is at issue. If the new commodity gains its place entirely at the expense of other commodities, there is no net gain, and the aggregate consumption is unaffected by the changes resulting from the factors influencing the growth of that particular commodity.

An illustration of how selection of a group of rapidly growing products can bolster a generally optimistic point of view is provided by Chapter 7 of the Commerce Department pamphlet *Markets after the Defense Expansion.* This chapter, entitled "Growth of the American Economy," discusses the "dynamics of rapidly-growing markets" in terms of a list of some 50 commodities and services that grew at least half again as fast as the average from 1940 to 1951. Although a warning is inserted, indicating that the growth shown is not "in all cases a net addition to total activity," the general effect is to imply its continuation. The discussion is perhaps best summarized in the following statement: "In every period of our history, the emergence of new industries and products and the continued momentum of the fast-growing industries have been sources of considerable strength in the economy."[15]

This statement may indeed be indisputable. Yet there is little difficulty in challenging many items on the list as either being near the end of their growth or for other reasons being unable to continue growing at anywhere near the same rate. When the question is asked: "Just what does such a list tell about what is likely to happen in the months or years just ahead?" hardly any definite answer can be given.

Studies of individual commodities for special purposes related to their production, storage, distribution, or prices are common. In particular, highly detailed investigations of primary commodities subject to futures trading on organized exchanges have been undertaken, frequently with very revealing and perhaps profitable results, but their bearing on aggregate consumption has never been developed.

A systematic analysis of commodity purchases in relation to changes in income was undertaken by the Commerce Department. Correlation methods were utilized to relate changes in various kinds of consumption expenditure to changes in aggregate disposable income in current dollars, while eliminating trend effects by including time as a second independent variable. The results were reported in terms of a measure of the income sensitivity, or responsiveness to changes in income, of expenditures for each type of product.[16]

Durable goods consistently showed high sensitivity—that is, the percentage changes in expenditures for a given percentage change in income were typically well above average. Nondurable goods and services were more evenly distributed across the whole range of sensitivity. Among the nondurables, clothing was above average, food average, and drugs, tobacco, and paper products below average. Among the services, the above-average group included legitimate-theater admissions, railway fares, taxicab fares, domestic service, and cleaning and storage of garments; the average group included admissions to movies and to a variety of other sports and entertainments, the services of dentists and physi-

---

[15] *Markets after the Defense Expansion,* U.S. Department of Commerce, 1952, p. 67.

[16] Clement Winston and Mabel Smith, "Income Sensitivity of Consumption Expenditures," *Survey of Current Business,* January, 1950.

cians, and beauty-parlor and barbershop services; and the below-average group included streetcar and bus fares, funeral and burial services, interest on personal debt, rents, telephone, and religious and legal services. At the bottom of the list in responsiveness to income changes were water, life-insurance expense, gas, and electricity.

These results are evidently determined in part by price effects. Much of the average sensitivity of food reflects price sensitivity rather than changes in rates of food consumption. The lack of sensitivity of service items at the bottom of the list derives from the fact that their prices are fixed by contract or by law as well as by the relatively constant rates of use of such services. On the other hand, the high sensitivity of durable goods is primarily a physical-volume phenomenon, since their prices also tend to be relatively stable.

The authors of the income-sensitivity study recognized that other factors than time should be taken into account but found that doing so was beyond the scope of their assignment. Also no attempt was made to determine the interacting effects of changes in one item upon changes in other items, whether competing or complementary. Both of these types of considerations are essential to a sound analysis of expenditures for specific goods and services.

Some of the factors other than income affecting expenditures for various products can be indicated with a good deal of assurance. Like income itself, they may have negative as well as positive implications. The case of passenger cars has already been discussed. There the main factor besides income is the inventory of cars in use, and its effect is to restrict sales. Secondary factors, like the stock market or the new-model stimulus, tend to raise sales in some years and lower it in others.

Durable goods in general may be assumed to behave in accordance with similar principles. Important appliances like refrigerators and luxury items like jewelry receive an effective stimulus from rising income and asset values. All are subject to the restraint imposed by rising stocks of the appliances or other durable items. A set of jewelry, once acquired, may last a lifetime and make subsequent purchases unnecessary by continuing to provide the desired decorative services indefinitely. Because of the great diversity of items included, this negative factor operates more smoothly than in the case of any particular item, such as passenger cars, but over a period of time it introduces a fairly continuous tendency toward restricting new purchases, that is, toward limiting additions to the stock in use to those consistent with underlying rates of growth.

The effect of rising stocks of durables and houses is not entirely a minus in the consumption picture, however, because such products tend to require expenditures for other items. The car must have gasoline and oil to run, and repairs become necessary at fairly regular intervals. The house must be furnished, lighted, heated, and redecorated from time to time. Hence the depressing effects of rising stocks on expenditures for new durables tend to be offset in part by the requirements for increased operating supplies of fuel and electricity, for expanded use of furnishings and accessories, and for repair and maintenance services. At one point the stocks in use introduce a downward trend in current expenditures; at another, an upward trend.

The volume of food consumed, like other operating supplies, tends to bear a definite relationship to the number of consuming units, which in this case is made up of the consumers themselves, that is, the total population. Other items, like soap and drugs, behave in much the same way. These day-to-day necessities, including the auto and home-heating fuel mentioned in the paragraph above, display a great deal of independence of income, and in some cases the variation with the number of consuming units or other trend factors is distinctly more important than that deriving from the changes in income.

Some of these necessaries even show movements inverse to income. In part this is due to the fact that there are elements of the inferior good—the resort of the consumer when his income is inadequate—in their consumption. For example, since it is cheaper to stay at home and read or listen to the radio or watch TV than to go to the movies, electric-power consumption may tend to increase as income declines. Or a drive in the country may be substituted for watching the ball game on Sunday; and through the rest of the week, more gasoline may be consumed driving around looking for work than would ever have been used driving to work. Food is too important a part of the consumers' budget not to be rather directly affected by changes in income, but, given the means for obtaining assistance that exist in this country, almost everyone finds a way to continue eating, even when unemployed. After a downturn, expenditures may be so completely focused on necessities that the volume of food consumed moves inversely to real income, as in the short decline of 1938. In all these cases, the movements of relevant factors other than income must be taken into account.

Some of the influences affecting the behavior of particular items are in the nature of disturbances or other autonomous factors. In 1929, consumers spent $1.7 billion for brokerage fees and related investment services, and the hoped-for capital gains that were the objective of these expenditures are by definition excluded from personal income. Within a few years after the boom collapsed, most of this expenditure disappeared from consumers' budgets. On the other hand, the official figures do not show any expenditures for alcoholic beverages in 1929, but after the repeal of prohibition in 1933 those expenditures grew to substantial proportions within several years. Perhaps the shift in expenditures is exaggerated, because the spending on bootleg liquor before 1933 was not insignificant, but in analyzing the measurable areas of activity, this shift can hardly be ignored. Still another example is provided by the decline of foreign travel in the late 1930s, as the threat of war began to dominate the European scene. All these are indeed relevant considerations for the commodity analyst; but if he is interested in the aggregate, he must ask: "Where do the funds go if disturbances depress an important item, and where do they come from if spending on something new is greatly expanded?"

Another fertile field for detailed investigation concerns the effects of one kind of commodity expenditure on those for another. In the postwar period, the growth of TV had a markedly depressing effect on the movies, and the shift of the listening audience from radio to TV was revolutionary. Admissions to spectator amusements were also depressed by the changed conditions of family living. Married couples who were establishing homes and raising small children could not get around as they had before. These factors also helped to depress clothing expenditures, especially for dress clothes. Together with the more widespread use of automobiles, which make lighter clothes suitable for winter use, they brought about a major redirection of the clothing and apparel industries.

Items like clothing and many luxury services may be regarded as parts of the dispensable portion of the consumers' budget. They respond rather quickly and sharply to changes in income, and their fluctuations help to balance out short-term changes in income against stable spending for necessities and fixed contract commitments. Some services can readily be dispensed with in an emergency, and the existing stock of clothing can carry the consumer along for a while without hampering his activity. In addition, the inventory effect in the case of clothing is quite marked at times—as in the tremendous upsurge in clothing expenditures in 1946, following the end of the war, and the persistent letdown in purchases during the next 2 or 3 years. It seems clear that throughout the business cycle there is an almost continuous shifting and adjustment of these discretionary items as income changes and as other uses of funds, for savings as well as expenditures, make demands on the income available under the changed circumstances.

Another illustration of the shifting of expenditures among commodities is found in the displacement of purchased transportation by user-operated transportation. The upper panel of Chart 12–1 shows the effects of this shift in both the prewar and the postwar periods. Of course, the war brought about a substantial reversal of trend by restricting gasoline consumption and auto production over a period in which income was growing rapidly. So strong are the trends in the two series that their movements seem to display little relationship to income. But the com-

Chart 12–1. Consumer Expenditures for Purchased Transportation and Gasoline and Oil

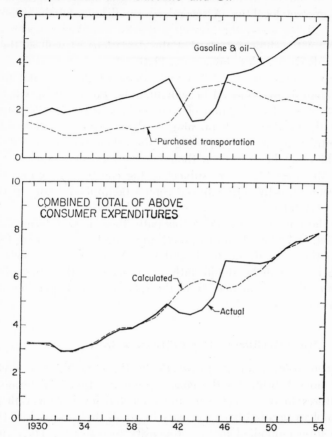

bined total may be estimated closely for the period before 1942 and after 1950 by correlations utilizing income and a suitable trend factor such as the number of passenger cars in use.[17]

The immediate postwar peak in purchased transportation was associ-

[17] In Chart 12–1 an alternative formulation was used, but results are much the same. The calculated values shown in the lower part of the chart are the sums of values computed separately from the following equations, fitted in both cases to the data for 1929 to 1940:

$$G = -429 + 109.78A + 58.50T$$
$$R = 18 + 16.89Y - 0.2727G$$

where G = gasoline expenditures, millions of 1947 dollars
   A = millions of autos in use, mid-year
   T = time, years (1929 = 0)
   R = purchased transportation, millions of 1947 dollars
   Y = disposable income, billions of 1947 dollars

ated with the release of millions of men from the armed services and their subsequent moving about, often with families, before they settled down in their present localities. A secondary, small bulge of the same kind is evident in 1951, under the impact of the Korean War. Inspection of the separate relationships reveals that the deviations as well as the underlying trends show a close inverse correlation.

These examples appear sufficient to demonstrate the point that commodity analysis may indeed be enlightening. But knowing what is happening to any selected group of commodities or services is not enough. For the things that are happening to them may mean that something of a contrary nature is happening to the others not specifically considered. This may be true even though no direct interconnection can be shown. All expenditures are subject to the constraint imposed by available income, and this ultimate test cannot be applied to any specific portion of the total.

Once the analyst starts along this path, there is no intermediate stopping point. He must go on to a practically complete accounting for all the items in the expenditure total, and then he can achieve no assurance that the result will be significantly more accurate than that obtainable in a more summary manner from the relationship of spending and saving to income.

THE CONSUMPTION FUNCTION AGAIN

This conclusion amounts to practically the same thing as saying that there is no substitute for the consumption function in determining the expenditures to be expected at any projected level of over-all activity. This is not to say that it is necessary to go all the way back to the oversimplification embodied in the propensity to consume. There are other factors than income to be considered; these include credit and various forms of asset holdings, both financial and real.

In analyzing the consumption total, durable goods definitely have to be separated out for special consideration. Whether it is necessary to consider separately a number of other subclasses of expenditures is a major point for decision. It is important not only in terms of the relationships themselves but also in terms of the number of residuals and special adjustments to be considered. Although no final determination on this point is here attempted, it may be suggested that good results can be obtained by considering only the four major items: savings, durable goods, nondurable goods, and services. Differentiating the last two is relatively less important in the estimating process, but for other reasons, such as inventory analysis, it is useful to separate services from the flow of goods.

Chart 12—2. Trend Factors Relating to Consumer Expenditures and Saving

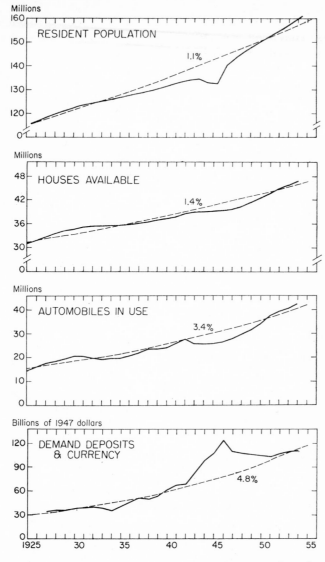

As a starting point, a brief review of the factors other than income that have to be incorporated in the relationships may be helpful. First, current savings are influenced by the growth of asset holdings, or, if the alternative formulation is preferred, total expenditures are influenced by the long-term upward trend in living standards. Second, expenditures for durable goods are influenced by the existing stocks in use; a measure of such stocks is available for the most important item, automobiles, and others bear a fairly direct relationship to the number of households in which they are installed. Third, some of the most important items among the nondurable goods and services are strongly affected by the number of consumers. Thus food consumption and personal care are tied to population. These nonincome variables also have a host of effects on other portions of the expenditure total: rents and other housing expenditures are related to the number of houses, household-operation expenditures are related to the number of houses or to the power-using equipment they contain, and transportation expenditures other than equipment purchases are related to the number of cars in use. Still other items tend to be displaced by these items or for other reasons are affected in a similar manner. Hence such factors, reinforcing each other at some points and offsetting at others, tend to dominate the entire list. Their effects are very important in the aggregate.

Inspection reveals that all these factors are in the nature of irreversible trend variables. As Chart 12–2 shows, some of them tend to level off under the impact of depression or war, but the declines in any, under even the most adverse circumstances, are minor. Moreover, their broad movements show a substantial degree of interrelation. Even population growth slows in depression and accelerates with prosperity. The chart shows how well each conforms to a constant rate of growth curve; the annual percentage increase represented by each dotted line is indicated. The rates of growth differ, but since all constant rate of growth curves are perfectly correlated, it is apparent that the factors to which they are fitted are highly intercorrelated also.

The implication of this is that similar results will be obtained by using any of these factors as a trend variable in a consumption function that relates total saving or major segments of the expenditure total to income and trend. Experiments were carried out to test various alternatives, using data for prewar years separately as well as in combination with postwar data. These indicated that better results are obtained by using the more smoothly changing population factor than any of the others. This held true for savings and durables as well as for nondurables and services. The results in terms of actual and calculated values are shown in Chart 12–3.[18]

---

[18] The fitted lines of regression are as follows:

$$S = 26.3 + 0.228Y - 0.372N$$
$$C = -26.3 + 0.772Y + 0.372N$$
$$D = 10.6 + 0.207Y - 0.177N$$
$$E = -15.5 + 0.357Y + 0.285N$$
$$R = -21.4 + 0.208Y + 0.264N$$

The use of population to represent the other trend factors—which is convenient as well as justified by the past data—must be regarded as an expedient. If the trends do not continue in conformity but turn away from each other, the relationships will have to be reconsidered.

It proved impossible to reconcile the prewar and postwar data in separate relationships for nondurable goods and services. In the years 1929 to 1940, nondurables showed a marked upward trend and services a marked downward trend, in both cases so strong as to be inconsistent with the postwar experience. Important changes underlying this shift during the prewar period have already been indicated: alcoholic beverages helped to expand nondurables, services were depressed by the curtailment of brokerage fees and foreign travel, and expenditures for gasoline displaced purchased transportation in large measure. These shifts represent, of course, a qualification on the relationships. In recent years they have been moderate enough to permit reasonably accurate projections. Future experience will dictate the kind of modifications that will undoubtedly prove necessary in these or other relationships used to project consumer expenditures.

It may be noted that the introduction of the trend factor in these equations is all that is needed to change the pattern of fluctuations in the economic system described by them to one incorporating growth as well as cyclical variation. This follows not simply because of the contribution of population to consumption but because of the reactions of rising consumption on various forms of investment. However, it does not necessarily mean that growth is dependent upon continuing increases in population. The forces making for growth are more complex, incorporating discovery, invention, and all the other elements that go into long-term expansion of real incomes and living standards. It is entirely possible that an economy with a declining population might experience economic growth. Under such conditions, it would be necessary to reconsider the possible trend variables that might be employed, seeking

---

where S = savings, billions of 1947 dollars
  C = total consumption expenditures, billions of 1947 dollars
  D = expenditures for durable goods, billions of 1947 dollars
  E = expenditures for nondurable goods, billions of 1947 dollars
  R = expenditures for services, billions of 1947 dollars
  Y = disposable income, billions of 1947 dollars
  N = population, millions

Savings and income were deflated by the implicit price index for total expenditures. The basic equations for savings and total consumption were fitted to the years 1923 to 1940 and 1951 to 1954; the equations for durable goods, nondurable goods, and services were fitted to the years 1929 to 1940 and 1951 to 1954 and adjusted to the equation for total expenditures fitted to the longer periods.

to determine which, alone or in combination, would produce the "best" results.

The patterns of consumer behavior may be interpreted broadly in the light of the foregoing, as follows: Durable goods and savings display

Chart 12–3. Personal Consumption Expenditures and Saving

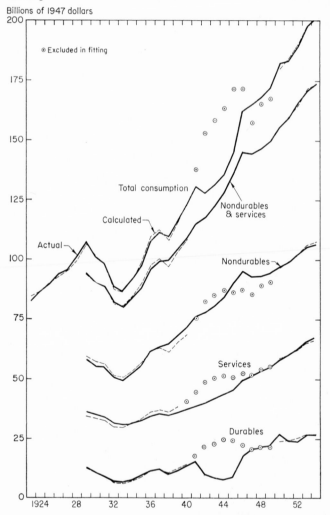

a high variability with income. On the advance, they take larger shares of the income total, running ahead as recovery progresses. In the boom phase, the highly variable durable goods hesitate and develop irregularities as rising stocks in use offset further advances in income. Nondurables and services continue to advance, gaining assistance from trend factors similar to those that are hampering durables and savings. After the downturn, the latter fall off rapidly, but the former are relatively well sustained. Then the trend factors and falling income combine to depress durables and savings, whereas the trend factors help to sustain nondurables and services against the decline in income, so that the shares of nondurables and services in the total are enlarged. As the trough of the depression is approached, saving swings all the way to the

Chart 12–3 (continued). Personal Saving

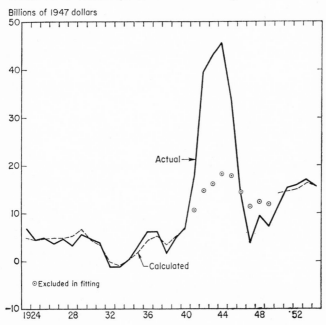

negative side, and new production of durables falls so low that inventories are being liquidated on balance. Then the ground is laid for a rapid recovery in durables; with the first suggestion of recovery, rising incomes and falling stocks work together for a rapid expansion of purchases, and consumer credit may swing from liquidation to expansion in the course of a few months. Savings recover with a short lag and begin to increase vigorously for similar reasons.

The similarity of movements in durables and savings may be pointed up in behavioristic as well as statistical terms. People with high incomes and high stocks of durables are in a position either to expand or to reduce expenditures for such commodities. People with high incomes and high asset holdings have a similar opportunity to expand or reduce expenditures in general, or looking at it from the standpoint of the flow that affects asset holdings directly, to contract or increase their current savings. The wide variations deriving from these facts tend to show a substantial degree of periodicity and may be regarded as the consumer's contribution to the business cycle. On the basis of this view of consumer behavior, it may be seen again why economic instability tends to increase with the standard of living and the wealth of the community.

If the relation of durable goods to income alone is considered, sales tend to run in excess of the average relationship on the upswing, when stocks are still comparatively low, and below on the downswing, when at any given level of income stocks are higher. The sharp shifting across the line of relationship to income alone, which occurs at the turning points, helps to define the peaks and troughs of the cycle.

The special behavior of durable-goods purchases is determined in part by the fact that they may be financed by other means than current income. Credit purchases introduce an immediate increment of demand that is reflected in income only after production is adjusted. In the first instance, these purchases represent dissaving in the same sense as expenditures from existing funds by the wealthy consumers who are able to buy practically without regard to changes in income. Capital gains may also be an important source of durable-goods purchases and of home construction. Omitting them from consideration may produce no important error most of the time, because speculative gains bear a close relationship to the movements of income, but it is precisely at the end of major movements, when income tends to level off, that they may exert their most distinctive and important effects. These special means of financing accelerate the movements of durables, but they do not necessarily determine the basic pattern.

Because of the rapid acceleration of durable-goods expenditures in the early stages of a sharp recovery or downturn, total consumer expenditures tend for a short time, perhaps just for a few months, to outrun income. Thus durables may be expanded at the expense of saving in the initial upsurge—or, to put this another way, the use of credit to expand purchases of durable goods restrains the recovery of saving. Conversely, when durables are cut back, savings tend to rise with the swing of credit from expansion to liquidation, and this tends for a time to stabilize saving against the depressing effect of the income reversal. Except for these brief intervals, however, the factors affecting durables and savings work in the same direction, so that the two move together, in complemental relationship to nondurables and services. Exceptions are found primarily in abnormal situations, like the immediate postwar years, when stocks of durables were low and liquid-asset holdings were unusually high.

The movements of durables may be viewed, of course, in relation to nondurables and services as well as to savings. In the expenditure total, the volatility of durables is offset by the stability of expenditures for a wide range of other products, including such important goods and services as food, housing, utilities, soap, paper, and gasoline. When a change in direction occurs, consumption of these continues on a relatively steady trend for a while, counterbalancing part of the reversal in durables. The total therefore remains in fairly stable relation to income.

Within the savings total also, there are offsetting differences of this kind. Recent studies have shown an enormous increase in contractual savings, that is, savings with a steady flow based on contracts for such items as mortgage payments, installments on other consumer debt, payroll deductions for old-age pensions, other insurance premiums, and regular purchases of government bonds.[19] The contracts for such savings cannot be terminated quickly. They represent fixed commitments that continue in force after the turn in income is made and therefore continue at peak rates for a time. In contrast, other kinds of savings are increasingly volatile. New debt creation falls drastically with the contraction of durable-goods purchases and of new housing starts. Cash balances are used to meet existing commitments in so far as they are available, and the accumulation of money in the bank or in secret hiding places at home quickly shifts to liquidation. The combined effect of these disparate changes is to keep the total current savings more or less in line with income.

Thus the modified consumption function holds good whether approached from the standpoint of expenditures or of savings. Discussions of this point in terms of the inertia of consumer behavior sometimes overlook the role of stocks of durable and semidurable goods in making adjustments possible without an immediate change in the over-all relationship of expenditures to income. The necessary services are built into the high inventory accumulated during the boom, and the consumer inertia that operates against any change in ways of living is satisfied without the necessity of making current purchases in anything like the same volume as before. Inertia in current spending therefore applies mainly to food, gasoline, utilities, and other current necessities, which are insensitive to changes in income, and the real insensitivity of all these current necessities in physical volume consumed may be either moderated or aggravated in terms of dollar expenditures by the sensitivity or insensitivity of prices.

This is not to say that consumer expenditures do not lag behind activity in general. Two obvious sources of such a lag may be observed in the

[19] Raymond Goldsmith, "Trends and Structural Changes in Saving in the 20th Century," *Conference on Savings, Inflation and Economic Progress*, University of Minnesota, Minneapolis, May, 1951.

income flow: Payment of income customarily lags behind the productive operations by which it is earned, and the spending of income in cash purchases lags behind its receipt. Only if the circular flow were instantaneous would there be no lag. However, the former of these lags appears to be more significant than the latter, and neither can be said to operate at all times in a mechanical way.

The second of these lags, furthermore, tends to be reduced to negligible proportions by the speculative elements in consumption. It is commonly stated that past income as well as present income influences consumption, but it is perhaps almost equally true that future income influences consumption. The person who anticipates higher future income can bring it into the present by borrowing. The person who knows that his income is going to be lower in the future is likely to curtail his purchases at once. He may not know it for sure, and if he is confident of his ability to get along under any circumstances, he may enjoy a last fling after being laid off; but as the prospect of no income approaches a certainty, the adjustment to a lower level of living is likely to be made with startling rapidity. Hence no significant error is ordinarily introduced into a quarterly analysis in physical-volume terms by ignoring any potential lag between income and over-all expenditures.

It is recognized that this point, like many others that went before, is merely stated and not proved. In large part, what has been said is not susceptible of proof at this time. All that may be done under the present circumstances is to express certain hypotheses whose validity cannot be completely established.

Reliance on any form of the consumption function is itself a preference based on past experience. The preferred forms of the function are comparatively simple and direct. They express the relationship in deflated aggregates, utilizing a trend factor as a separate variable rather than as an additional deflator. Complications arising from such factors as the income distribution, patterns or habits of consumption, and high-powered equations are best avoided. Deviations and disturbances may be handled on the assumption that consumer reactions are adaptive in character. These preferences provide a satisfactory working basis for the time being. They may be modified whenever new evidence demonstrates the superiority of alternatives.

CHAPTER 13

Integration and Consistency Checks

When the various segments of gross national product have been separately analyzed, there remains the problem of organizing the separate projections into an over-all forecast. An essential part of this organizing process consists of integrating the estimates of the various components, not only in the sense of fitting them together as parts of a complete picture, but also in that of making them consistent with each other and with the derived movement of the total. This implies that the initial estimates have to be modified in the light of what is discovered in putting the complete forecast together. At this point, there is added to the analysis of independent information and autonomous forces relating to each segment the very important series of effects that result from their interrelations, and particularly from the relations of the parts to the total flow of income.

It has been suggested that the strategic elements in the analysis consist of those diverse and partially independent segments that represent nonconsumption expenditures. This suggestion was provisional at best and was to be disregarded, for example, at such times as any special influences affecting consumption expenditures could be expected to have important effects. Now it will be shown that income, too, must be analyzed as a separate entity or as a whole series of entities, each capable of contributing something new to what has already been worked out. The forecast cannot be considered complete until it has incorporated changes arising on the income side and has achieved balance and consistency between the expenditure and the income accounts. These aspects of the problem are the primary concern of this chapter.

There are many ways of proceeding in putting together the various parts of the complete forecast. The discussion here will be confined to a single procedure, but it is not intended to imply that this is the only way to obtain good results. On the contrary, modifications may be introduced whenever they appear to be appropriate under the specific circumstances.

The process of working out the complete forecast must be carried out in at least two stages. There is one inescapable difference between these stages in that at first no estimate of over-all production or income is available. Subsequently, in the second or later stages, such an estimate having been derived, it can be applied to test the validity of projections already made and to derive estimates of other items dependent upon it.

In the first stage, primary emphasis must be placed on autonomous or semiautonomous elements in the picture, that is, upon the special influences affecting various important segments without regard to changes in the level of activity as a whole. About all that can be done with cyclical interrelationships is to take account of the general distinction between phases of the major cycle, which means basically the construction cycle. The momentary influences making for changes in fixed investment —such as the availability of financing or unduly optimistic planning by industrial concerns—usually have less influence than the basic forces that bring about the large changes between the peak and the trough of the major cycle. In contrast, a variety of special influences on such rapidly shifting segments as government programs and inventory changes may be important at any time, and their effects must be superimposed on the cyclical pattern set by the slower-changing types of fixed investment. In the prosperity or depression phases, when fixed investment tends to remain at a high or a low level for some years, the emphasis is primarily on the short-term factors. On the other hand, in the phases when fixed investment is in process of rapid recovery or decline, the question becomes whether or not any influences operating through the volatile short-term factors can reverse the trend. Although there is a bias toward cyclical continuity, it is not conclusive. Since no estimate of the over-all movement is yet available, little can be done to take account of the responsiveness of either the short- or the long-term factors to changes in total income. Any attempt to introduce such considerations tends at this stage to bias the entire forecast. It becomes the primary concern, however, in the second and in subsequent stages of deriving the final forecast.

In addition, the forecaster may be confronted at the outset with difficulties arising from the fact that the data on the recent past are only tentative and sometimes subject to considerable error. When there is something wrong with the preliminary estimates for the current month or quarter, taking them at face value might set the whole forecast on the wrong track. Frequently all that can be determined is that some error or inconsistency exists, and it is impossible to clear up certain areas of uncertainty. This is a handicap, but not an insuperable one, since it merely makes necessary forecasting over a more extended period, partly past, rather than ahead only. It becomes necessary, in effect, to forecast what has been happening as well as what will be happening. Various aspects of the current situation must be judged just like the final forecast, in an effort to determine their true character by appraising them in terms of everything else known about the situation. In these circumstances, some experimentation with various alternatives that appear to be most probable may prove distinctly helpful in indicating the best basis on which to proceed.

For reviewing current developments as well as the projections into the future, it is desirable to depict all the data on a set of simple charts. These charts should show the various components of the forecast as time series, covering a period appropriate to the forecast and including as much of the back data as may be needed to put the projections in perspective. For most short-term forecasts, a period of 10 quarters may be sufficient, showing the movements of each component in terms of seasonally adjusted rates for something over a year past and an equal distance into the future. An illustration may be found in Charts 13–1 to 13–3, which will be discussed shortly. Such charts provide much the easiest way to judge the reasonableness of the projections in the light of each component's past behavior and its role in the current situation.

At this point, a brief summary of the general procedure to be followed in deriving the over-all forecast may be in order. The first step consists merely in adding together the preliminary estimates for the strategic factors. From the combined total of those factors an estimate of the gross national product is derived; this amounts to making a preliminary projection of consumer expenditures in relation to the projected movement of nonconsumption expenditures.

After this preliminary estimate of gross national product is obtained, it is translated on the income side of the accounts into national income, then personal income, and then disposable income; and from the estimate of disposable income, another estimate of consumer expenditures is derived. To this second estimate of consumer expenditures is added the total of nonconsumption expenditures, with the result that a second approximation of the gross national product is obtained.

Any discrepancy between this and the first approximation must then be adjusted out. In addition, all the original estimates must be checked for consistency with the over-all pattern developed, and they are modified as necessary to bring them into line. Finally the process is repeated through successive approximations, until a set of estimates is obtained that meets all the tests of special information and of known interrelationships. At various points in the process, compromises may have to be worked out to give effect to conflicting influences.

All these steps should be carried through first, as far as possible, in terms of changes that involve real changes in income and consumption rather than in current dollar values. There are several reasons why this is desirable. Foremost is the objective of obtaining a measure of changes in activity; the projections in real terms give such a measure directly, uncomplicated by changes in valuation. Second, there are certain derivative measures and tests—such as judging stock-flow relationships for inventories and fixed investment or determining the feasibility of achieving an indicated level of production—that require estimates of activity in real terms. Moreover, many aspects of price change are dependent upon the pressure of demand upon available supplies or, to phrase this another way, upon the availability of resources for meeting real demand. Furthermore, there is little basis for forecasting prices independently, so that the better procedure is to work out the prospective changes in activity first and then obtain the probable price changes as a dependent variable. More will be said about this in the next chapter; for the time being, changes in physical volume are the main concern.

This injunction against incorporating value changes is of strictest application in the field of consumer goods. Qualifications on adhering rigorously to volume terms have to be introduced in certain other areas of the economy. In some cases volume and price changes are so intermingled as to be practically inseparable. In construction projects, for example, the interactions of project specifications, contract price, contractors' margin, and wage rates, including overtime and other premiums, are often such that it may be impossible to tell whether an increase in contract value represents additional volume or merely enhanced income for the producers. Similarly, in the special field of government employment, where expenditures measure the contribution to gross product as well as the personal income received, additions to volume may be indistinguishable from additions to income. In both these cases, furthermore, financing may be from nonincome sources, so that the full amount of the expenditure increases the income flow. Consideration of these special areas suggests a rule to govern the inclusion of valuation elements in the nonconsumption expenditures. They may be included where their only effect on consumer prices is indirect, through the change in the volume of consumer goods demanded, but not when they directly enter into changes in the prices of consumer goods.

There are difficulties in the application of this rule, but it conforms to a substantive point of analysis, namely, that some price and money changes do modify the income flow, with multiplier effect but without necessarily affecting the real value of the income received by consumers from other sources. On the income side, similar effects may be introduced by changes in tax rates or in transfer payments that are not offset by price changes. For the most part, it is not important just where such changes are taken into account, provided only that a consistent form of multiplier is used with a view to obtaining consumption expenditures in real terms.

There would be some point in excluding all valuation changes from the expenditure side and making all necessary adjustments for them on the income side, but this is hardly possible in the first instance. Not only are there the difficulties, already mentioned, of distinguishing and measuring the contribution of changing values to some expenditure items, but the quarterly data are not reported in deflated form, and for items like government services no clear-cut deflator may exist even for the annual data. The initial forecast may therefore be somewhat of a hybrid with respect to valuation changes. This need not seriously affect the results in ordinary circumstances. It does require special care in periods of inflationary pressure, when any kind of increase in income or expenditure is likely to affect the pace at which prices rise.

One further word of warning may be appropriate before the details of procedure are considered. It should be recognized both that not all situations are equally difficult or easy to forecast and that the forecast is almost sure to be judged on the outcome without regard to the complications of the situation. There are times when only a low degree of confidence can be placed in a forecast, and in these situations special care must be exercised not only in considering the various alternatives but also in presenting the results of the analysis. Unless the uncertainties are spelled out, the user of the forecast may be misled, and the forecaster will be held responsible for the error.

THE FIRST APPROXIMATION

The process of putting together the over-all forecast will now be considered in detail. For this purpose, the charts and tables from an actual forecast for the year 1954 will be used to illustrate the various steps in the procedure followed.[1] By the close of 1953, a recession had been under way for some months. The question to be answered at the time was: "How far will the recession go?"

Charts 13–1 to 13–3 illustrate the results of the preliminary analysis;

---

[1] This forecast was prepared in December, 1953, and the results were discussed in the January, 1954, issue of the *Illinois Business Review*. Minor modifications have been made in order to utilize revised relationships, such as a new version of the consumption function, but all the essentials of the original forecast, including its major deficiencies, were retained.

the dotted lines are the original projections form the third quarter of 1953, the latest data available at the time the forecast was made. The actual data are in current dollars, since deflated quarterly estimates were not available and price changes over the recent past had been so small as to involve no serious error in projecting from the current dollar values.

Chart 13–1. Government Purchases of Goods and Services

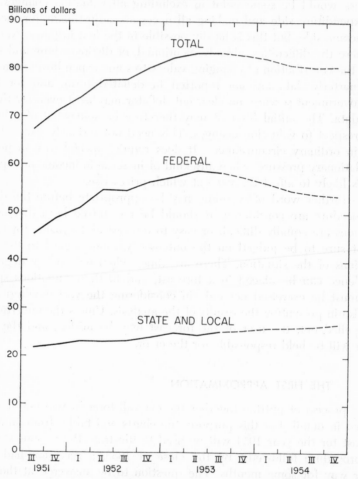

On other occasions, when deflation is necessary, the computations are simplified if the prices of the most recent quarterly data are used as the base, with earlier figures adjusted to the current level.

The projections shown on these charts are in constant dollars, subject to the qualifications already noted. Some of the considerations underlying the initial projections were as follows:

National-security programs had been cut by the Eisenhower administration and were expected to decline throughout 1954. As a result, Federal expenditures had already turned down and were projected to continue down, strongly at first but less rapidly toward the end of the year, since most of the reduction was supposed to be made effective by mid-year.

State and local expenditures were projected upward at roughly the same rate as in preceding periods. They partly offset the decline in Federal expenditures. In addition, income taxes were to be cut and transfer payments were rising, so that changes originating in the government sector showed a net increase on balance despite the large cuts in military expenditures.

The short-term forecast was therefore thrown back upon the appraisal of inventory changes. It was clear that an inventory reversal was under way, and since inventories appeared to be high in relation to sales, the movement would have to progress to the point of substantial liquidation. The precise extent of the liquidation, however, was seen to depend in large measure upon the stability or instability of fixed investment.

Nonresidential construction was continuing at peak rates. Residential construction appeared to be leveling out after a decline, as a result of the easing of the market for mortgage money; and while the decline might be resumed late in 1954, the year as a whole would be fairly stable. Thus construction as a whole had to be counted a relatively stable factor.

Business outlays for new productive equipment were in process of turning down, partly as a result of the cutbacks of military procurement. This decline was projected as continuing throughout 1954. However, even a decline of somewhat more than 10 percent in this item would not greatly reduce the total flow of goods.

It appeared, therefore, that the inventory reversal would be taking place under conditions of relative stability and would be held to correspondingly moderate proportions. The peak rate of liquidation was expected to be reached in the second quarter of 1954, at a rate about equivalent to the average rate of accumulation in the year ended September 30, 1953, and this peak was expected to be followed by a moderate easing of liquidation later in the year.

Consumer durable goods were also declining at the time the forecast was made. This decline was carried to the point where consumer credit would be liquidated moderately. Otherwise consumer income and expenditures appeared likely to be fairly stable.

A partial offset to the declining tendencies would be obtained from net foreign investment, which had declined sharply on the earlier rise. With gold and dollar reserves again available to foreign countries and our imports curtailed by the inventory liquidation, this item was expected to move from a minus to a plus position in 1954.

By working from Charts 13–1 to 13–3, the upper part of Table 13–1 was set up. Note that the table is set up to show annual data, recent quarterly data, and the entire forecast period annually as well as quarterly. Annual and quarterly estimates may be used to check each other. For convenience, certain relationships may be used to make projections

Chart 13–2. Producers' Durable Equipment and Construction

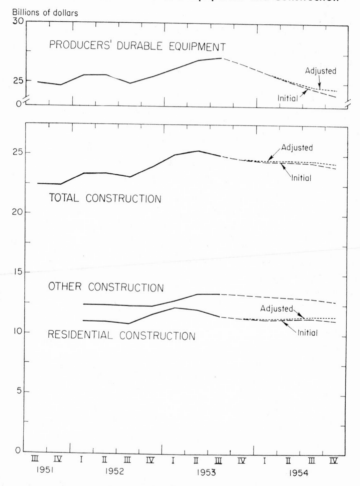

in annual terms. These have to be reconciled with the quarterly estimates, and the reasonable ranges of movement in each series may be used to determine appropriate adjustments in the other. The interplay of annual and quarterly projections makes for explicit consideration of certain aspects of the projections that might be overlooked if they were carried out in quarterly terms alone.

Very often the process of bringing the preliminary estimates of the strategic factors together, either in the table or by comparison of the charts, immediately reveals the character of the prospective situation. Some changes are large, and others are small. The large tend to dom-

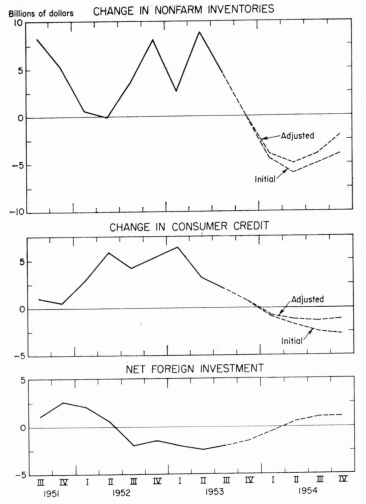

Chart 13–3. Changes in Nonfarm Inventories and Consumer Credit and Net Foreign Investment

inate, and the general movement tends to conform. The exact balance between the various factors must in any case be found by adding all of them together to obtain totals like those shown in the first line in the lower part of Table 13–1.

Table 13–1. 1954 Forecast: First Approximation

In billions of dollars

Strategic factor and derivation of growth national product	1952 actual	1953*	1954 forecast	1953 Actual				1954 Forecast			
				I	II	III	IV	I	II	III	IV
Strategic factors:											
Government purchases	$ 77.5	$ 83.1	$ 81.1	$ 82.4	$ 83.5	$ 83.6	$ 83.1	$ 82.2	$ 81.0	$ 80.6	$ 80.7
Federal	54.2	58.0	54.7	57.4	58.9	58.4	57.5	56.2	54.8	54.1	53.7
State and local	23.4	25.1	26.4	24.9	24.6	25.2	25.6	26.0	26.2	26.5	27.0
Nonfarm inventory change	3.1	3.9	-4.9	2.6	8.7	4.4	0.0	-4.5	-6.0	-5.0	-4.0
Net foreign investment	-0.2	-2.0	0.5	-2.1	-2.5	-2.1	-1.5	-0.5	0.5	1.0	1.0
Consumer credit change	4.4	3.1	-2.0	6.3	3.2	2.0	0.7	-0.9	-1.8	-2.5	-2.8
Construction	23.4	25.0	24.3	25.0	25.3	24.9	24.6	24.4	24.4	24.3	24.0
Residential	11.1	11.8	11.2	12.2	12.0	11.5	11.3	11.2	11.3	11.3	11.2
Other	12.3	13.2	13.0	12.8	13.4	13.4	13.3	13.2	13.1	13.0	12.8
Producers, equipment	25.4	26.7	24.9	26.2	26.9	27.1	26.5	25.8	25.1	24.5	24.0
Computation of G:											
Total (ΣS)	133.7	139.8	123.9	140.4	145.1	139.9	133.4	126.5	123.2	122.9	122.9
ΔS				1.2	4.7	-5.2	-6.5	-6.9	-3.3	-0.3	0.0
$0.22\,\Delta S$				0.3	1.1	-1.2	-1.5	-1.5	-0.7	-0.1	0.0
$0.22\,\Delta S_{-1}$				2.3	0.2	1.0	-1.1	-1.4	-1.5	-0.8	-0.1
Calculated ΔG ($\Sigma\Delta S$)				3.8	6.0	-5.4	-9.1	-9.8	-5.5	-1.1	-0.1
Actual ΔG				0.9	10.4	-3.4	-9.1				
Calculated G	348.0	365.8	345.4	362.0	372.4	369.0	359.9	350.1	344.6	343.5	343.4
Change in farm inventory	0.6	0.1	0.0	0.3	0.1	0.1	0.0	0.0	0.0	0.0	0.0
Nonconsumption G	129.9	136.8	125.9	134.4	142.0	138.0	132.7	127.4	125.0	125.4	125.7
Calculated C	218.1	229.0	219.5	227.7	230.4	231.0	227.2	222.7	219.6	218.1	217.7
Calculated ΔC				3.3	2.7	0.6	-3.8	-4.5	-3.1	-1.5	-0.4
Adjustments:											
Trend							0.3	0.2	0.3	0.2	0.3
Current							2.0	0.0	0.0	0.0	0.0
Tax							0.0	1.0	0.5	0.0	0.0
Adjusted ΔC							-1.5	-3.3	-2.3	-1.3	-0.1
Estimated C	218.1	229.6	223.8	227.7	230.4	231.0	229.5	226.2	223.9	222.6	222.5
G, 1st approximation	348.0	366.4	349.7	362.0	372.4	369.0	362.2	353.6	348.9	348.0	348.2

* Partly estimated.

At this point the first indication of the direction and size of the general change is obtained. With this indication two preliminary checks may be made. First, if the projection indicates a rise in a generally tight situation, the question of feasibility arises. Can the economy provide an over-all rate of increase as fast as that called for? If not, an inflationary situation will develop, and at least some of the volume increases projected will have to be reduced.

Second, some initial checks for consistency are possible, and provisional adjustments in some of the original projections can be made. If some of the factors were projected on rather pessimistic assumptions but the over-all result has turned out to be distinctly less so, then the projections in which the unwarranted pessimism was incorporated should be revised upward. A full revision should not be attempted at this point, however. A forecast can never be correct in all details, and the force of the initial analysis should be at least partly preserved until further tests have been made. The basic check, which is the circular check on consumers' income and expenditures, cannot yet be made; and since the first approximation is sometimes reversed by that test alone, not too much can be done in correcting the projections of the strategic factors at this point. In the present illustration, the declining pattern for the total appeared generally consistent with the projections already made.

The next step is to derive estimates for total gross national product. This may be done in either of two ways. First, gross national product may be estimated directly from the strategic factors by application of a multiplier or other appropriate correlation device, in which case consumption is estimated as a residual, by subtracting the other items from the gross national product. Second, consumer expenditures may be projected directly, having regard to the implications of the strategic factors for changes in personal income; then the gross national product is obtained as the sum of all its components. Both methods are capable of producing satisfactory results for the first approximation, which is not expected to be highly accurate anyway. The experienced analyst may prefer the second approach. For the purposes of exposition, however, the first will be illustrated, but in a manner that incorporates elements of the second so as to utilize knowledge of any special influences affecting consumption itself.

Whichever of the two approaches is used, it should be clear that the result is dependent upon the behavior of consumption expenditures in relation to nonconsumption expenditures. The characteristics of consumption have already been indicated. It is the more stable portion of the total. During periods of relatively continuous advance or decline, it is steadier, less easily interrupted by erratic or temporary setbacks. At the turns, it is slower to respond. Considered as a segment of the total, consumption has a steadying effect on the movement when the level is changing, and it lags at the turns when the direction of movement is reversing. These aspects of its behavior are mutually consistent, and they are also consistent with the theory of the multiplier. On this point, observation confirms theory in specifying the behavior of the important consumer segment of the gross national product.

In application to the point at hand—ignoring shifts in population or other trend factors for the moment—consumption must be projected to conform fairly closely to the movements of the strategic factors. It follows with a slight lag but maintains sufficient stability to smooth out many of the irregular movements in the other factors. In other words, consumption must be projected to take full account of the income effects of changes in other factors in a relatively short period and to turn when a reversal in the other factors is distinct, but not to reflect fractional reversals interrupting a more or less continuous movement toward a higher or lower level. This means, statistically speaking, that changes in consumption represent a kind of lagged moving average of changes in the nonconsumption expenditures. This proposition may, of course, be regarded as a purely empirical description of the multiplier, but the lack of precision is not entirely undesirable, because the relationship is not very close in any case and becomes practically nonexistent in some periods, such as the post–World War II years, when various disturbing factors distorted the consumption function.

In the usual theory of the multiplier, an infinite series of past investment expenditures enters into the determination of current income and consumption. However, when the multiplier is low, as it is in our economy, any change in income-producing expenditures tends to become effective in a very short time. The total effect is still that of a distributed lag, but the contributions from terms in the more distant past dwindle rapidly. The earlier terms are weighted lower, period by period in a geometric progression, so that in comparison with the very recent terms, or with autonomous or erratic elements, they become of very little significance in determining current income. The important changes, therefore, are those that have occurred in the last 2 or 3 quarters. Any residual effects from earlier periods tend to be stabilizing in comparison with these recent changes; they in effect merely help smooth the total and induce a lag.

A rather crude computation of the multiplier may be obtained from annual data by correlating changes in gross national product with changes in the total of the strategic factors. The annual data are averages of the results for several income-flow periods and therefore smooth out some short-term variation; on the other hand, over a period as long as a year most of the secondary and subsequent effects have had time to show up in the data. Two versions of this kind of crude multiplier are shown in the scatter diagrams of Chart 13–4.[2] The panel at the left uses the deflated gross-national-product data as published; that at the right includes the change in consumer credit as part of the base which is multiplied. The slopes of these lines indicate in the first case a multiplier of 1.60 and in the second a multiplier of 1.44. These results imply leakages from the

Chart 13–4. Two Versions of the Multiplier*
In billions of 1947 dollars

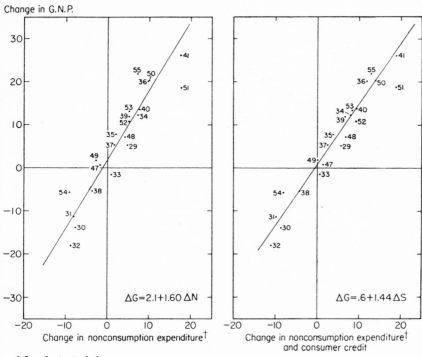

* See footnote below.
† Excluding change in farm inventories.

income stream totaling five-eighths in the former relationship and seven-tenths in the latter.

The conclusion that the leakages are so high and the multiplier so low

[2] The gross multiplier obtained from these correlations is not conceptually the same as that of the generally accepted theory of income flows, since it includes sources of variation not taken into account there and excludes or averages out others that should theoretically be considered. The superimposed lines of relationship were fitted graphically to data for 1929 to 1941 and 1947 to 1955, using a "median" criterion of best fit rather than the more usual "least-squares" or "minimum-absolute-deviation" criteria.

in our economy may seem rather startling. One reason for this is that the relationships are set up in terms of deflated data. In current dollars the ratios would be considerably higher, since consumer prices tend to be considerably more flexible than the prices of investment goods or government purchases.

Including the change in consumer credit in the computation reduces the multiplier by maximizing the base multiplied. This in effect shifts another portion of the total out of consumption and into business investment. Since it at the same time satisfies consumer demands, the secondary effects of the investment-saving total in expanding the total flow are lowered. The theoretical justification for this has already been discussed. Comparison of the two parts of Chart 13–4 reveals that inclusion of credit effects a distinct improvement in the correlation.

The positive intercepts of the lines of relationship may be taken as a measure of the growth components in consumer expenditures. In the right-hand panel, the $0.6 billion constant is about equivalent to the average contribution of population growth to consumption during the period of observation. In the left-hand panel, this basic growth component is increased by the $1.5 billion average change in consumer credit experienced during this period. Since the underlying sources of growth vary within the period and may vary still more in the future, the growth components may be separately analyzed and adjusted to the particular circumstances of the forecast period rather than held constant in all cases.

Repeated use of any relationship of this kind would seem to imply that the derived ratio used as the multiplier remains constant through time. Substantial qualification on this point is necessary, as will be shown in the subsequent discussion. In this "first-approximation" stage of the analysis, no harm is done by applying this rather inaccurate assumption, since any error arising from its use should be corrected in subsequent approximations.

In applying this multiplier to the current changes in the strategic factors, account must be taken of the smoother movement of the total and its lag behind the factor changes. Table 13–1 indicates a method for accomplishing this by using quarterly data. The aggregate change in the strategic factors is itself carried into the change in gross product because they are parts of the total. For the derived part of gross national product —the additional 44 percent of the strategic base called for by the multiplier—half is based on the change into the current period, and the other half is based on the preceding change.[3]

---

[3] In theory, a weighted average of several preceding changes would be better than the immediately preceding change alone, but this kind of variant usually makes little difference in the final results.

This oversimplified procedure implies that, when the current change is in line with the preceding change, the continuation of the entire movement at the same rate will be projected. When it differs from that change, the change in gross product is smoothed by the averaging of the two changes. When the direction of change in the strategic total is first reversed, possibly just by an erratic movement, the derived part of gross product will tend only to level; it will actually turn only if the most recent change in the new direction exceeds that of the movement previously in progress. This criterion for a reversal appears to be more or less in the correct order of magnitude and provides for lag as well as smoothing effects. It is no more than a compromise, however, as any such simplified procedure can give only rough approximations of the related changes in gross product.

The initial estimate of gross product is obtained by linking the changes thus computed to the last reported quarterly figure. Once this initial estimate is available, it may be found that some additional adjustments are desirable. Revisions in the strategic factors may or may not appear to be in order, but in any case the validity of the estimates of consumption implicit in this estimate of gross product should be considered. Although it is still not possible to make final estimates of consumer expenditures, the process of taking successive approximations will be shortened and simplified by adjustments that can be made in the initial estimates.

For this purpose, consumer expenditures must be separated out and their changes analyzed and adjusted. To do this, the projected changes in consumer credit must be taken out of the strategic total and the change in farm inventories added to the result, in order to translate the initial totals into the total of nonconsumption expenditures actually included in gross product. Then the adjusted total for each period is subtracted from gross product to obtain the initial estimates of consumer expenditures, and these initial estimates are differenced to obtain the projected quarterly changes in consumption.

The first adjustment necessary is the adjustment for population growth —labeled "Trend" in the illustration provided by Table 13–1. During 1954, this item was estimated to contribute to higher consumption at an annual rate of $1 billion. So this amount was distributed in quarterly increases over the forecast period.

Any further adjustments to the changes in consumer expenditures at this point are almost entirely a matter of judgment. At least two kinds are usually worth considering. First, an adjustment may be made to bring the estimates for the initial quarter of the forecast period into line with what is known to be happening on the basis of monthly and weekly data. In the present illustration (Table 13–1), it was clear that very little decline was actually taking place, and the large decline originally projected in the fourth quarter of 1953 was therefore reduced by $2 billion, as indicated by the line labeled "Current." It is possible, of course, that such an adjustment will introduce error into the later estimates of consumer expenditures, particularly if the current influences holding up consumption are only temporary. On the other hand, consumption does show a high degree of continuity; furthermore, it is easier to make adjustments in the succeeding approximations if the error appears in the estimates for the more distant periods rather than as a break or discontinuity in an early period. So the risk involved in this kind of adjustment is usually worth taking.

Second, the changes in consumer expenditures may be modified to take account of any special factors known to be affecting consumption during the forecast period. In the case at hand, income taxes were about to be lowered, and this reduction was to be only partially offset by scheduled increases in payroll taxes under the social security system. The net additional tax reduction was estimated at about $2 billion annually. An addition to the rate of consumer expenditures of $1.5 billion a year was therefore introduced by cutting the projected declines in consumption during the early part of 1954. This is the basis for the adjustments to the projected changes in consumer expenditures for the first 2 quarters of that year.

With these adjustments, the changes in consumer expenditures were again chained to the last reported actual figure. The effect of these adjustments was to reduce the maximum decline projected in consumer expenditures by approximately one-third. The estimates thus derived were then combined with nonconsumption expenditures to obtain the first approximation of gross product. The result, appearing as the last line in Table 13–1, shows a sharp decline through the first half of 1954, with a leveling off at the year end. It is consistent with the general consensus on the outlook which was current at the end of 1953. But since it could be considered only a first approximation, further analysis was necessary to affirm agreement with the consensus or to introduce necessary modifications.

THE SECOND APPROXIMATION

Experience teaches that if the analysis is stopped at this point satisfactory results cannot be expected. This statement applies with equal force in the event that consumer expenditures were projected independently, by some other procedure, instead of being derived from a multiplier formula supplemented by a series of sketchy adjustments. Serious errors may have been incorporated at various points. Important sources of variation have not yet been considered. There is no assurance even that the results so far obtained are mutually consistent in important respects. Very often the forecast is drastically changed by further operations.

The preliminary estimate of gross national product obtained in the first approximation presents the second opportunity for making preliminary adjustments to the projections of the nonconsumption expenditures if they appear to lack consistency with the over-all result obtained. Making such adjustments at the earliest possible point, when they are clearly indicated, is advantageous because they are more likely to save work at later stages than to produce irremediable error. On the other hand, this advantage is small because it is subject to the qualification that the basis for such adjustments is still inadequate, so that they may again have to be revised or even reversed. Since no important inconsistency was apparent in the illustrative forecast, no such adjustments were made. This has some merit in the present context, since the logic of the entire procedure may be more simply spelled out if short cuts are deferred in the first instance.

Whether or not it is decided to undertake adjustments in the nonconsumption expenditures at this point, it is necessary to check the over-all expenditure estimate on the income side of the account. To accomplish this, estimates of all the items needed to translate gross national product into personal income must be made. Table 13–2 is therefore set up to include the same set of items as the Department of Commerce regularly includes in its table entitled "Relation of Gross National Product, National Income, and Personal Income."

Most of the items making up the difference between the broad measures of production and income are fairly well behaved. They either are relatively stable in character or move in a fairly dependable manner in relation to the larger aggregates. It is possible to arrive at reasonable estimates for them in most cases by the methods of simple extrapolation. Such methods must be applied in any case to the projection of the one really erratic item, the statistical discrepancy, whose movements specifically require a great deal of judgment to project. By utilizing this procedure, any prospective changes arising from the over-all volume of business or from known special influences affecting any of these items, such as changes in tax rates, may readily be taken into account in making the projections. To indicate the kind of considerations important in estimating the movements of these items, the more important will be discussed at some length.

First, capital-consumption allowances, or "depreciation charges," to use the more common business term, depend upon the level of output and the capital stock in use at the beginning of the year. Thus the steel

Table 13–2. 1954 Forecast: Second Approximation

In billions of dollars

Income-product relations	1952 actual	1953*	1954 forecast	1953 Actual				1954 Forecast			
				I	II	III	IV	I	II	III	IV
G, 1st approximation	$348.0	$366.4	$349.7	$362.0	$372.4	$369.0	$362.2	$353.6	$348.9	$348.0	$348.2
Less:											
Capital-consumption allowance	27.0	29.2	30.3	28.2	29.2	29.6	29.8	30.0	30.2	30.4	30.7
Indirect business taxes	28.1	29.9	29.8	29.3	30.1	30.0	29.9	29.9	29.8	29.7	29.7
Business transfer payments	0.9	0.9	0.9	0.9	0.9	0.9	0.9	0.9	0.9	0.9	0.9
Subsidies, etc. (−)	−0.1	0.0	0.0	0.0	−0.2	0.3	0.0	0.0	0.0	0.0	0.0
Statistical discrepancy	0.5	−1.4	−2.5	−3.1	1.7	−1.5†	−2.5	−2.5	−2.5	−2.5	−2.5
Subtotal	$ 56.4	$ 58.6	$ 58.5	$ 55.3	$ 61.7	$ 59.3	$ 58.1	$ 58.3	$ 58.4	$ 58.5	$ 58.8
National income	$291.6	$307.8	$291.2	$306.7	$310.7	$309.7†	$304.1	$295.3	$290.5	$289.5	$289.4
Less:											
Corporate profits and IVA	40.2	42.8	36.8	43.8	45.2	42.3†	39.8	38.7	36.6	36.0	35.7
Social security contributions	8.6	8.9	9.4	9.0	9.0	8.8	8.7	9.5	9.4	9.3	9.3
Wage accruals	−0.1	0.0	0.0	0.0	0.0	0.0	0.0	0.0	0.0	0.0	0.0
Subtotal	$ 48.7	$ 51.7	$46.2	$ 52.8	$ 54.2	$ 51.1	$48.5	$ 48.2	$ 46.0	$ 45.3	$ 45.0
Plus:											
Government transfer payments	$ 12.0	$ 12.8	$ 14.4	$ 12.6	$ 12.6	$ 12.6	$ 13.2	$ 13.7	$ 14.3	$ 14.7	$ 15.0
Government interest	4.9	5.0	5.3	4.9	5.0	5.1	5.2	5.2	5.3	5.3	5.4
Dividends	9.1	9.5	9.3	9.2	9.4	9.6	9.6	9.4	9.3	9.2	9.2
Business transfer payments	0.9	0.9	0.9	0.9	0.9	0.9	0.9	0.9	0.9	0.9	0.9
Subtotal	$ 26.9	$ 28.2	$ 29.9	$ 27.6	$ 27.9	$ 28.2	$ 28.9	$ 29.2	$ 29.8	$ 30.1	$ 30.5
Personal income	$269.7	$284.3	$274.9	$281.6	$284.4	$286.8	$284.5	$276.3	$274.3	$274.3	$274.9
Personal tax	34.6	36.6	32.3	36.2	36.7	37.0	36.6	32.6	32.2	32.1	32.2
Disposable income	235.0	247.7	242.6	245.4	247.7	249.8	247.9	243.7	242.1	242.2	242.7
Consumption expenditure‡	218.1	229.6	226.0	227.7	230.4	231.0	229.6	226.6	225.4	225.6	226.4
Nonconsumption expenditure	129.9	136.8	125.9	134.4	142.0	138.0	132.7	127.4	125.0	125.4	125.7
G, 2d approximation	348.0	366.4	351.9	362.0	372.4	369.0	362.3	354.0	350.4	351.0	352.1

* Partly estimated.   † Estimated; not available in initial publication.   ‡ See Table 13–3.

industry knows that its furnaces wear out faster when they are working under forced draft than when they are standing idle. But there are also grounds for thinking that facilities deteriorate through time whether or not they are used. Write-offs are therefore geared both to the current rate of production and to the total capital stock against which depreciation is charged.

Chart 13–5. Gross National Product, Capital Stock, and Capital-consumption Allowances

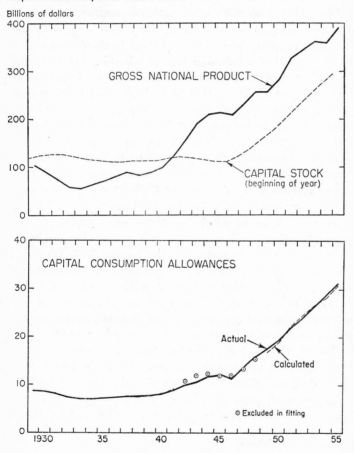

The data used in a study of this relationship are shown in the upper panel of Chart 13–5. Gross national product and capital-consumption allowances are the published Commerce Department series. The capital-stock series was estimated by chaining from an initial estimate for 1929 by adding each year's investment in new construction and equipment and deducting that year's capital-consumption allowances. The results of the correlation are shown in the lower panel of the chart in terms of the comparison of actual and calculated values.[4]

Recent changes in tax laws applicable to amortization of facilities threaten to disturb this relationship, so that it may have to be modified to take account of the practices now permitted. By the nature of the case, however, deviations as well as the underlying series tend to be regular in character, and satisfactory results may ordinarily be obtained by carrying the same deviation through the next year.

Indirect business taxes comprise another deduction that is rather stable in character. They vary with gross national product, because they consist largely of sales and excise taxes. They also vary with the capital stock, because property taxes are important in their composition. However, there are rather substantial lags in adjusting tax rates and assessments, and there is a good deal of resistance to lowering either after they have been put into effect, so that these taxes tend to be very sticky or unresponsive on the decline. One way to project them is by the same kind of correlation technique used in the case of capital-consumption allowances; the results are shown in the upper panel of Chart 13–6.[5] Another way is to increase them proportionally to gross national product on the advance and hold them fairly steady on the decline. In either case, the projection of this item is not likely to involve any large error.

The next important item is the statistical discrepancy. This item is in a sense no more than an admission of the shortcomings of our knowledge. It is a residual, which appears as a practical necessity, and does not measure any definable portion of the income flow. There is no theoretical basis for dealing with it, but dropping it would introduce an arbitrary source of variation and might produce substantial error in the forecast. Hence the statistical discrepancy must be projected through the forecast period just as if it were an actual item of income or expenditure.

Projection of the statistical discrepancy may be troublesome at times, but, by forcing the analyst's attention toward possible sources of error, it may also serve a constructive purpose. Its basic role is to keep the accounts in balance. Since the gross national product is highly variable in comparison with personal income, this item may share with other residuals, such as deviations from the various lines of relationship, par-

---

[4] The estimating equation is

$$D = -3.205 + 0.0356G + 0.0680K \qquad (R^2 = .998)$$

where D = capital consumption allowances, billions of dollars
G = gross national product, billions of dollars
K = capital stock, billions of dollars

[5] The estimating equation is

$$B = 0.686 + 0.0698G + 0.0151K \qquad (R^2 = .988)$$

ticularly the consumption function, in reconciling short-term differences in movement that cannot be readily accounted for. It also serves to absorb biases in the indexes on which the current estimates of gross national product and personal income depend. Were it not for this residual catchall, errors and biases would have to be assigned to other items,

Chart 13–6. Indirect Business Taxes and Corporate Profits

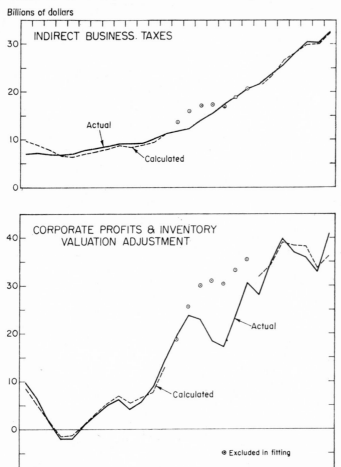

making it necessary on occasion to show movements in some of these items which would appear highly improbable in the light of current statistics.

Since index biases show persistent "trends," continuing for anywhere from several months to several years, there tends to be a fair degree of consistency in the behavior of the statistical discrepancy, especially if there is no reversal in the general movement in the economy as a whole. Periodically these "trends" are eliminated by revision of the data; new bench marks reveal errors that could not previously be assigned to individual series. In the interim, a certain amount of erratic or systematic variation that would otherwise be troublesome may be assigned to the statistical discrepancy.

Considered in this light, the statistical discrepancy performs a useful function in working out a forecast. Nevertheless, it is desirable to keep any of its projected movements within the bounds indicated by reasonable hypotheses concerning the differences between gross product and personal income and to eliminate movements of this item from consideration by carrying forward a constant, if it is possible to obtain a consistent picture in this way.

The latter action was taken in the illustrative forecast for 1954. No estimate for the third quarter was available at the time the forecast was made. In the earlier quarters shown, the statistical discrepancy had been displaying a high correlation with inventory changes. Since the pace of inventory accumulation had slackened in the third quarter, it was logical to reduce the statistical discrepancy. Bringing it down to zero was not sufficient to produce a reasonable estimate for corporate profits, given the published data on gross product and personal income, so it had to be swung all the way over to the negative side, continuing the pattern of the preceding year.

This estimate was provisionally accepted for the forecast period as well as for the third quarter of 1953. However, in the subsequent analysis of personal income, at least a small further adjustment for the next quarter appeared to be necessary. Thereafter, the statistical discrepancy was held constant through 1954. Larger adjustments could have been justified in view of the continuation of the movement started in the third quarter, with the inventory reversal accelerating. However, this limited adjustment produced a reasonable reconciliation of the income and product accounts for the second approximation. Later, when the final projection indicated early stabilization anyway, the decision to exclude further variation from this source appeared to be entirely appropriate.

Corporate profits are also commonly thought of as an erratic element in the picture. There is a good deal of validity to this view, inasmuch as profits make sharp reversals at the turning points and swing widely with changes in business conditions. This is particularly true of reported profits, which incorporate erratic elements of inventory profit resulting from price changes. These inventory-revaluation elements are excluded from the profits item as it appears in this table, but profits nonetheless show marked variation.

It is clear that there has to be something on the income side to coun-
terbalance the high variability on the expenditure side. Corporate profits
assume this role. Just as some expenditure items drop sharply while
others remain stable or continue to advance because of lag effects, so
corporate profits drop sharply while other kinds of income, or other
items in the translation from expenditures to income, continue high or
even rise further. In each case, the stability or lagging rise in the one
segment makes necessary the sharper variation in the other.

The explanation of this analogous behavior of profits and certain expenditure items is found in the relation of profits to volume of business
and to fixed charges. For the purpose of deriving such a relationship,
the capital stock may be taken as a measure of fixed charges. Actual total
fixed costs in the sense relevant to this study include more than the
depreciation charged against the capital stock. They include a wide
range of salaries, repair and maintenance, and other necessary services
that cannot be adjusted to variations in output. Like the capital stock,
these costs tend to grow through time and remain relatively unaffected
by setbacks. The results of a correlation like that used for estimating
capital-consumption charges are shown in the lower panel of Chart
13–6.[6]

Essentially the same results would be obtained from a relationship
using capital-consumption allowances instead of capital stock as an independent variable. In this alternative formulation, the constant term is
very small—practically zero for the interwar period and the early postwar years. Beginning in the middle 1950s, this alternative relationship
began to produce underestimates of profits; the extent to which this may
have resulted from changed practices relating to depreciation charges
could not immediately be determined. Considering the relationship for the
earlier period alone, its implication is that profits plus a multiple of
capital-consumption charges (roughly 2½ times) command a constant
proportion of gross national product (roughly 29½ percent). This formulation may be regarded as stipulating that business pricing practice results in a stable division of consolidated business receipts between operating costs on the one hand and profits plus fixed charges on the other.

From these relationships it may readily be seen why the fluctuations in
profits resemble those of certain kinds of investment or durable-goods
expenditures. They vary with total output but are subject to the constraint imposed by relatively stable fixed charges that continue to ad-

[6] The estimating equation is

$$E = 7.640 + 0.196G - 0.162K \qquad (R^2 = .982)$$

Note that this and the two preceding relationships utilize the same independent
variables, so that they may readily be combined if desired.

vance after the turn. The drop in profits is sharp, not only because the declines in receipts tend to be more abrupt than the advances but because rising overhead works in the same direction. It combines with falling receipts to depress profits on the downswing; it becomes a fairly passive factor in the trough of the depression; and it restrains the advance in profits on the recovery.

The influence of rising overhead also explains the behavior of aggregate profits when considered in relation to gross product alone. A single line of relationship which ignores this additional variable cannot give a good fit, because profits tend to shift downward continually in relation to gross product. This downward shift results from the advance of fixed charges engendered by the more or less continuous expansion of the stock of fixed capital in use.

Next in the table is another important deduction from income—contributions for social insurance. For extended periods during which rates and coverage remain unchanged, these contributions vary directly with payrolls in the covered occupations. They rise and fall with changes in the pace of activity.

One of the exceptional situations occurred at the beginning of 1954. The law had been changed in 1953 to extend coverage, and an increase in rates also took effect at that time. A sharp increase therefore had to be provided for. It was clearly of a magnitude far in excess of any decrease that might be expected from the decline in payrolls then under way. For many workers, the increase in social security deductions more than offset the decrease in withholding taxes that took effect at the same time. The amount of the change in the first quarter of 1954 had to be specially estimated on the basis of information provided in the discussion of the legislation enacted. Thereafter changes could again be calculated on the regular basis.

Also tied up in large measure with the social security system are government transfer payments. These are of four major types. Two types, old-age pensions and unemployment compensation, are the benefits social security is specifically designed to provide. The third type, other relief and assistance programs, supplements the social security system and also makes other kinds of payments to designated limited groups who are unable to provide for their own needs. The fourth major type consists of the veterans' benefits, involving payments under several different programs set up to assist this important segment of the population. Unusual movements, like the bonus payments of 1936 and the insurance refunds of early 1950, frequently occur, and their effects have to be specially accounted for. All four of these types of transfer payments are alike in adding to the income earned in the production of goods and services.

During periods when enacted programs remain unchanged, transfer payments in the aggregate, if not in all the parts, tend to move inversely to other income payments and therefore partially stabilize personal income in relation to gross national product. The most accurate way of obtaining a projection of over-all transfer payments is to project the major components separately. However, the analyst who wishes to conserve time via the short cut of a single projection can generally get acceptable results, provided he keeps in mind the differences in behavior of the components in the various phases of the business cycle.

Direct offsets to changes in labor income derive from unemployment compensation and relief. Whenever there is a decline in activity, both rise with some lag. The extent of the rise is associated directly with the increase in unemployment. However, no measure of unemployment is yet available, and the increase must therefore be estimated in relation to the decline in other income. At this stage in the estimating process, the movements of national income other than corporate profits may be taken as the best available guide for projecting transfer payments.

On the decline, it is necessary to distinguish several stages. First, a lag of several months must be allowed for, because the payments begin only after a "waiting period." Then, for the remainder of the initial year, the maximum effect of the increase in unemployment compensation builds payments to a peak. Finally, unemployment compensation tends to peter out, and although it is replaced at least in part by relief, the offsetting of further wage declines tends to be less complete.

During the middle stage, the total offsets provided by transfer payments may be tentatively estimated at one-sixth of the decline in national income excluding corporate profits. It is estimated that unemployment compensation replaces wage income in the covered occupations to the extent of a little less than one-fourth. It is a much smaller proportion of the total wage loss, because some workers are not covered and the wages of those remaining employed are lowered by reductions in working hours. Other forms of transfer payments also rise, increasing the proportion of the wage loss covered. On the other hand, the income base is raised by the inclusion of proprietors' income, which tends to fall at least as fast as wages. As a rough measure, therefore, the suggested one-sixth of the decline in all income other than corporate profits may not be too wide of the mark. In the later stages of a long decline special estimates have to be worked out along the lines used to analyze other government programs, since work relief and other programs may be used in preference to further expansion of transfer payments.

On recoveries, the offset is not so large, because some forms of transfer payments do not decline. Little if any decline in the total may occur in a minor recession. The effect would be most pronounced, on the other hand, after an extended recession had built up unemployment compensation to a peak. Old-age pensions rise rather steadily, on a long-term upward trend, and tend to maintain the total in recovery periods. Veterans' benefits vary in a less dependable manner and must be analyzed as a special kind of government program. When conditions are prosperous, there is no great incentive to change established programs for veterans. With some lag, they are more likely to be increased than reduced under adverse conditions. In addition, there are lag elements in the directly countercyclical programs, so that transfer payments may continue up through the initial phase of a recovery movement. Through the recovery as a whole, the offset to increases in other income is considerably less than during the downswing—perhaps not even half so large in the most extreme circumstances.

Government interest is a stable item, depending primarily upon the over-all magnitude of the Federal debt and the current rates of interest on government securities. In most peacetime years the change in the debt is small, so the change in interest charges tends to be correspondingly limited. Changes in interest rates are also of importance, but even the most drastic changes are built into the payments total slowly, through piecemeal refunding of maturing portions of the debt. As a rule, enough is known about the conditions that will be affecting interest payments to make errors in the projection of this item negligible.

Dividends constitute another relatively stable item. They are governed in a general way by the movements of corporate profits, but management is slow to adjust dividend rates and may draw upon cash or other liquid reserves to maintain payments for a time when earnings are insufficient to cover them fully. It is necessary, therefore, to allow a considerable lag in the adjustment of dividends to earnings. Relative to gross business receipts, or to gross national product, dividends tend to be adjusted downward in a decline more quickly than they are increased during a recovery. Firms whose income drops sharply are under pressure to protect their liquid position; they may have to meet heavy commitments on capital account, and they often feel that "conservative" policy requires prompt action in conserving cash. On the other hand, total cash flow—including depreciation charges—is restricted on the upswing by the lag in capital-consumption allowances, so that available funds tend to be utilized for working capital and fixed-investment purposes in preference to immediate increases in dividends. A problem arises under the latter circumstances because of the tendency toward payment of substantial year-end extras, but any errors arising from this source are seldom of serious proportions for the forecast as a whole.

Given the projections of these items, the computation of personal income is a matter of simple arithmetic. When this arithmetic is completed, however, a pause must be taken to consider the validity of the computed estimates. A good idea of the immediate future of personal income is available from its recent behavior and current tendencies, as revealed by the monthly data. It is a series that can itself be projected a few months ahead with a fair degree of accuracy. However, if prices are not stable, the effects of price movements have to be adjusted out of the recent income data, since the entire projection is being made primarily in deflated terms. In making the expenditures estimates, the income estimates have to be deflated for use in the consumption function, and the forward estimates must be carried in the same terms.

After the independent projection of personal income in real terms has been made, the question is: "Are the computed estimates in line with this alternative projection?" If not, the source of the deviation must be sought. It may be that no adequate explanation can be found, in which case the deviation may have to be assigned to the statistical discrepancy. However, no real solution is to be found in doing this. Taking the easy way out has to be recognized as a form of temporizing, and the objective must be to abandon it as soon as a satisfactory hypothesis can be developed to reconcile the movements of the larger aggregates.

In the present illustration, the decline in personal income obtained through the translation from gross product was clearly too sharp and had to be partly compensated by a further adjustment of the statistical discrepancy in the first quarter of 1954. The trend of personal income was affected by rising wage rates, of course; but even allowing for the effects of wages on prices, too large a decline would have been projected. Hence part of it had to be shifted to the statistical discrepancy; beyond the first quarter, however, there were no indications definite enough to justify any further adjustment of this kind.

This decision implies that the total near-term influences on consumption, when viewed from the income side, had to be considered stronger than the first approximation estimates of gross national product had provided for, despite the special first-quarter adjustment already made at that point. The alternative would have been to reduce the personal-income projection, which would probably have made it more consistent with the initial estimates, but this would have tended unduly to minimize the evidence of current "trends" in personal income and consumer expenditures.

Finally, estimates of personal taxes have to be prepared in order to convert personal income to disposable income. The correct procedure for doing this involves the translation of personal income to income as defined for tax purposes. Some forms of personal income, mainly transfer payments, are not taxable; other items not included in personal income, mainly capital gains, are part of the tax base. This translation would require a complicated series of adjustments, but here again short-cut procedures usually produce estimates that are not too far off for practical purposes. Probably the best base for the calculation is personal income less transfer payments. If desired, rough adjustments for capital gains can be made on the basis of stock-market price indexes; in this case, substantial lags have to be allowed for, partly because the gains are not immediately realized and partly because taxes are not as quickly adjusted to capital gains as to other income. For ordinary income, the lag is very short under present pay-as-you-go regulations.

Under the progressive income tax system, personal taxes move considerably faster than income and so tend to moderate the effects of income changes on consumption. In periods when tax rates are maintained at the prevailing level and capital gains or losses are not large, taxes may tentatively be computed by either of two methods that usually give closely similar results: The tax may be taken as one-sixth of the change in personal income excluding transfer payments, or the percentage change in the tax may be taken as one-third larger than the percentage change in the income base. Both of these methods are rule-of-thumb procedures that give approximations for the given conditions only; neither can be expected to hold good over long periods in which changes in income and taxes are large.

In the first quarter of 1954 the computation posed a special problem because of the reductions in tax rates that were scheduled to take effect at the beginning of that year. The rate reduction was estimated at somewhat less than 10 percent. In addition, income was declining by several percent. So the combined reduction in the first quarter was set at a little over 10 percent. Thereafter changes were kept fairly well in line with changes in income, though proportionately larger.

The process of estimating consumer expenditures once the estimate of disposable income has been obtained is shown in detail in Table 13–3. This is merely an application of the consumption function discussed in Chapter 12. The price index underlying the computation is the Department of Commerce implicit deflator for consumer expenditures, extrapolated from the last annual estimate published by means of the BLS index of consumer prices. Since separate indexes are not available for the subsidiary parts of the consumer-expenditures total, the BLS index is also used to extrapolate the price indexes needed to reflate the estimates of deflated expenditures for durable goods, nondurable goods, and services. Over short periods, this lack of specific indexes ordinarily does no great violence to the estimates, which have to be adjusted in any case.

The adjustments to the major items of consumers' expenditures and savings, which in the past period are merely observed deviations, represent an alternative to the statistical discrepancy as a means of balancing

Table 13–3. 1954 Forecast: Consumer Expenditures and Savings

In billions of dollars

Factors used in estimating consumption	1952 actual	1953*	1954 forecast	1953 Actual				1954 Forecast			
				I	II	III	IV	I	II	III	IV
Disposable income	$235.0	$247.7	$242.6	$245.4	$247.7	$249.8	$247.9	$243.7	$242.1	$242.2	$242.7
Implicit prices	115.5	117.0	117.6	116.2	116.7	117.6	117.6	117.6	117.6	117.6	117.6
Deflated disposable income (Y)	203.5	211.7	206.4	211.2	212.3	212.4	210.8	207.2	205.9	206.0	206.4
Population (N)	155.8	158.3	161.2	157.3	158.0	158.7	159.4	160.1	160.8	161.5	162.2
Savings (+26.3):											
0.228Y	46.4	48.3	47.1	48.2	48.4	48.4	48.1	47.2	46.9	47.0	47.1
−0.372N	58.0	58.9	60.0	58.5	58.8	59.0	59.3	59.6	59.8	60.1	60.3
Calculated	14.7	15.7	13.4	16.0	15.9	15.7	15.1	13.9	13.4	13.2	13.1
Deflated	17.0	18.4	15.7	18.6	18.6	18.5	17.8	16.3	15.8	15.5	15.4
Adjustment	−0.1	−0.4	0.9	−0.9	−1.4	0.3	0.5	0.8	0.9	0.9	0.9
Estimated	16.9	18.0	16.6	17.7	17.2	18.8	18.3	17.1	16.7	16.4	16.3
Durables (+10.6):											
0.207Y	42.1	43.8	42.7	43.7	43.9	44.0	43.6	42.9	42.6	42.6	42.7
−0.177N	27.6	28.0	28.5	27.8	28.0	28.1	28.2	28.3	28.5	28.6	28.7
Calculated	25.1	26.4	24.8	26.5	26.5	26.5	26.0	25.2	24.7	24.6	24.6
Implicit prices	112.6	112.2	112.8	111.4	111.9	112.8	112.8	112.8	112.8	112.8	112.8
Deflated	28.3	29.6	28.0	29.5	29.7	29.9	29.3	28.4	27.9	27.7	27.7
Adjusted	−1.6	0.6	−0.6	0.7	1.0	0.5	0.2	−0.2	−0.5	−0.7	−0.8
Estimated	26.7	30.2	27.4	30.2	30.7	30.4	29.5	28.2	27.4	27.0	26.9
Nondurables (−15.5):											
0.357Y	72.6	75.6	73.7	75.4	75.8	75.8	75.3	74.0	73.5	73.5	73.7
0.285N	44.4	45.1	45.9	44.8	45.0	45.2	45.4	45.6	45.8	46.0	46.2
Calculated	101.5	105.2	104.1	104.7	105.2	105.5	105.2	104.1	103.8	104.0	104.4
Implicit prices	113.3	113.1	113.7	112.3	112.8	113.7	113.7	113.7	113.7	113.7	113.7
Deflated	115.0	119.0	118.3	117.8	118.4	120.0	119.6	118.4	118.0	118.2	118.7
Adjustment	3.8	−2.2	0.1	3.4	3.4	−1.3	0.6	0.3	0.0	0.0	0.0
Estimated	118.8	121.2	118.4	121.2	122.1	121.3	120.2	118.7	118.0	118.2	118.7
Services (−21.4):											
0.208Y	42.3	44.0	42.9	43.9	44.2	44.2	43.8	43.1	42.8	42.8	42.9
0.264N	41.1	41.8	42.6	41.5	41.7	41.9	42.1	42.3	42.5	42.6	42.8
Calculated	62.0	64.4	64.1	64.0	64.1	64.7	64.5	64.0	63.9	64.0	64.3
Implicit prices	120.0	125.2	125.9	124.3	124.9	125.9	125.9	125.9	125.9	125.9	125.9
Deflated	74.4	80.7	80.6	79.6	80.6	81.5	81.2	80.6	80.4	80.5	81.0
Adjusted	−1.7	−2.5	−0.4	−3.3	−3.0	−2.3	−1.3	−0.9	−0.4	−0.2	−0.2
Estimated	72.7	78.2	80.2	76.3	77.6	79.2	79.9	79.7	80.0	80.4	80.8
Total consumption	218.1	229.6	226.0	227.7	230.4	231.0	229.6	226.6	225.4	225.6	226.4

* Partly estimated.

out the accounts. These deviations are far less erratic than the statistical discrepancy and much more frequently assignable to specific causes, such as liquid-asset holdings, increased use of credit, or shortages of consumer goods. Nevertheless, they do display some similar characteristics —for example, by consistently moving in a given direction over a period of time, as if reflecting bias in the indexes of income and expenditures.

Where the cause is known, it can be used as a basis for the projection. Where it is not known, the deviation may be carried constant through the forecast period or adjusted in accordance with the best available hypothesis. In the latter circumstances, one would seldom be justified in making the adjustments an important source of variation in the forecast as a whole. An exception might arise when expenditures had moved widely out of line, so that a near-term resumption of normal patterns appeared probable.

The latest figures at the time of the 1954 forecast indicated that the adjustments were on the whole tending toward zero. The nondurables and services were, therefore, brought closely into line with the calculated values, though at different rates. The upward movement of the adjustment on savings was extended a little further in view of the reversal in consumer credit that appeared to be in prospect. This was largely offset by a contrary movement in expenditures for durable goods.

The resulting estimates of savings and durable-goods expenditures were not consistent with the original projections of consumer credit. The consumer-credit projections were judged to be unrealistic in requiring overly drastic adjustments in savings and durable goods. The anticipated consumer-credit reversal was therefore moderated to the point where it became roughly consistent; the revised data are shown in Chart 13–3. Subsequent analysis indicated that this modified position was still too extreme, but since this item did not enter further into the computations, no additional revisions were made. This illustration reveals the danger in projecting a sharp credit reversal: It tends to hang the whole forecast too much on the implied change in consumer behavior, and there is ordinarily little to justify forecasting such a change.

The new estimate of consumer expenditures obtained in this way was higher than the original, indicating that the forecast needed to be revised upward. After the initial forecast quarter, there was an increasing disparity, quarter by quarter, between the first and second approximations. In the last quarter of 1954, the disparity amounted to $3.9 billion. The subsequent analysis assumes that the new estimate is more accurate and therefore must displace the original in the forecast.

Adding the new estimates of consumer expenditures to the estimated nonconsumption expenditures gives a second approximation to the forecast of gross national product. Ordinarily the new estimates differ from the original projections—a fact that is not at all strange in view of the different methods of analysis by which the two versions were arrived at. The existence of such differences indicates a lack of consistency in the forecast, and further analysis must be devoted to eliminating it. The means of accomplishing this lie in the construction of further approximations until one is worked out in which the end result conforms to the point of departure. Perhaps several additional stages of analysis will be necessary before final estimates are obtained.

THE THIRD APPROXIMATION

The first discrepancy to be eliminated is that between the first and second approximations of consumer expenditures. A little thought will make clear that this cannot be done merely by taking the second approximation as a starting point. This estimate is higher than the first, but when the increase is carried through the translation process, part of it will again appear as an increase in consumption and a new, though smaller, discrepancy will be encountered in the final estimate. Then, if the new increase is merely added in, part of it will again appear as a still smaller discrepancy. This would continue, theoretically through an infinite number of stages. What is needed is a multiplier to adjust the original discrepancy so that the full adjustment necessary will be completed in a single stage. In other words, the discrepancy in consumer expenditures must be treated as an additional item of "investment" expenditure and blown up to allow for multiplier effects when added to the first approximation.

In making this adjustment, the forecaster has a choice of procedures. As one approach, he may apply the standard multiplier of 1.6 shown in Chart 13–4. The higher of the two multipliers shown on the chart is applicable here, since the adjustment for consumer credit, if any, is handled in estimating consumer expenditures by means of the consumption function.

It is now possible, however, to choose a different multiplier from that obtained in the original correlation. Since the process of making the translation from gross product to consumer expenditures involves an analysis of the leakages from the income stream at various points, it is equivalent in effect to the computation of a new multiplier. In the present illustration, only $5 billion of an initial $21 billion decline in gross national product showed up in consumer expenditures. The gross total of offsets to declining expenditures thus amounted to $16 billion, or 76 percent. However, some $2 billion of the total offsets were provided by changes in tax rates—a type of offset which by its special character could not be expected to play the same role as others that are continuously operative. Allowance must also be made for the items that are invariant with respect to gross national product: The estimate of capital stock does not change, removing almost $2 billion more; and if the billion adjustment to the statistical discrepancy remains unchanged, another billion is eliminated from further consideration. The leakages that vary with gross national product are thus reduced to almost $11 billion, or 56 percent of the initial decline; this implies a multiplier of 1.8. This new estimate was actually applied in proceeding to the third approximation, shown in Table 13–4.

It is evident from this discussion that the multiplier changes from one occasion to another. Further consideration of the nature of the offsets, or leakages, in progressing from changes in gross national product to changes in consumer expenditures indicates the kinds of changes to be expected. They are partly of a long-term character, resulting, for example, from changes in tax legislation; these may often be isolated and adjusted out. But they are also of a cyclical character. The behavior of the offsets indicates that the multiplier varies between declines and recoveries and also between stages of the movements in either direction.

There are wide differences in some cases between the contributions made by specific forms of offset in the various stages of the cycle. Thus corporate profits show a direct relationship with gross product of almost 20 percent, but this is modified by the effects of changes in the capital stock, which must be deducted to the extent of over 16 percent. In the late stages of recovery and in the early stages of decline, the capital stock is advancing and depresses profits; in the late stages of decline and early stages of recovery, it remains comparatively stable. Taking the changes in capital stock to be about the same as those of gross national product in the latter part of an upswing, the maximum offset provided by corporate profits would shift from 3 percent in the late stages of recovery to 36 percent in the early stages of recession. Actually the withdrawal into corporate savings is modified by dividend payments, which generally move in the same direction but with a variable and sometimes considerable lag.

There are also some other partial offsets to these shifts in the contribution of corporate profits. The contributions of capital-consumption allowances and indirect business taxes have inverse elements from those of profits, because the influence of capital stock enters in the opposite direction. Capital-consumption allowances may continue to advance early in a decline. Indirect business taxes exert a strong one-sided effect in restraining advances and permitting declines to progress comparatively unchecked.

Table 13–4. 1954 Forecast: Third Approximation
In billions of dollars

Income-product relations	1952 actual	1953*	1954 forecast	1953 Actual I	II	III	IV	1954 Forecast I	II	III	IV
G, 2d approximation	$348.0	$366.4	$351.9	$362.0	$372.4	$369.0	$362.3	$354.0	$350.4	$351.0	$352.1
Adjustment for consumption	......	......		......	......	......	0.0	0.5	1.5	2.8	3.6
Adjustment for nonconsumption			......				0.0	1.1	.2	2.5	5.0
Adjusted G	348.0	366.4	356.7	362.0	372.4	369.0	362.3	355.6	354.1	356.3	360.7
Less:											
Capital-consumption allowances	27.0	29.2	30.5	28.2	29.2	29.6	29.8	30.0	30.3	30.6	31.1
Indirect business taxes	28.1	29.9	30.2	29.3	30.1	30.0	30.0	30.0	30.1	30.2	30.5
Business transfer payments	0.9	0.9	0.9	0.9	0.9	0.9	0.9	0.9	0.9	0.9	0.9
Subsidies, etc. (−)	−0.1	0.0	0.0	0.0	−0.9	0.3	0.0	0.0	0.0	0.0	0.0
Statistical discrepancy	0.5	−1.4	−2.5	−3.1	1.7	−1.5†	−2.5	−2.5	−2.5	−2.5	−2.5
Subtotal	$ 56.4	$ 58.6	$ 59.1	$ 55.3	$ 61.7	$ 59.3	$ 58.2	$ 58.4	$ 58.8	$ 59.2	$ 60.0
National income	$291.6	$307.8	$297.6	$306.7	$310.7	$309.7	$304.1	$297.2	$295.3	$297.1	$300.7
Less:											
Corporate profits and IVA	40.2	42.8	38.2	43.8	45.2	42.3†	39.8	39.2	37.7	37.8	38.3
Social security contributions	8.6	8.9	9.5	9.0	9.0	8.8	8.7	9.5	9.4	9.4	9.6
Wage accruals	−0.1	0.0	0.0	0.0	0.0	0.0	0.0	0.0	0.0	0.0	0.0
Subtotal	48.7	51.7	47.7	52.8	54.2	51.1	48.5	48.7	47.1	47.2	47.9
Plus:											
Government transfer payments	12.0	12.8	13.6	12.6	12.6	12.6	13.2	13.4	13.6	13.7	13.6
Government interest	4.9	5.0	5.3	4.9	5.0	5.1	5.2	5.2	5.3	5.3	5.4
Dividends	9.1	9.5	9.6	9.2	9.4	9.6	9.6	9.5	9.5	9.6	9.9
Business transfer payments	0.9	0.9	0.9	0.9	0.9	0.9	0.9	0.9	0.9	0.9	0.9
Subtotal	$ 26.9	$ 28.2	$ 29.4	$ 27.6	$ 27.9	$ 28.2	$ 28.9	$ 29.0	$ 29.3	$ 29.5	$ 29.8
Personal income	$269.7	$284.3	$279.3	$281.6	$284.4	$286.8	$284.5	$277.5	$277.5	$279.4	$282.6
Personal tax	34.6	36.6	32.8	36.2	36.7	37.0	36.6	32.7	32.5	32.7	33.3
Disposable income	235.0	247.7	246.5	245.4	247.7	249.8	247.9	244.8	245.0	246.7	249.3
Consumption	218.1	229.6	229.4	227.7	230.4	231.0	229.6	227.5	227.9	229.3	232.0
Nonconsumption	129.9	136.8	127.4	134.4	142.0	138.0	132.7	128.3	126.2	126.8	128.5
G, 3d approximation	348.0	366.4	356.8	362.0	372.4	369.0	362.3	355.8	354.1	356.1	360.5
G, final	348.0	366.4	356.6	362.0	372.4	369.0	362.3	355.9	354.1	356.0	360.3

* Partly estimated.
† Estimated; not available in initial publication.

On the other hand, the large increase in the offset provided by retained corporate profits immediately after a downturn is reinforced by changes in the built-in stabilizers. Thus government transfer payments are built up to a peak in the first year of a decline, but later their contribution tends to diminish as workers pass the limits of unemployment-compensation periods. So they join corporate profits, first, in checking a decline and then, later, in permitting it to progress unchecked. These dominate the combined effects of all the items taken together. The multiplier is at its maximum, so that the economy is least stabilized, near the end of a long upswing. The boom therefore proceeds unchecked. The multiplier is reduced to a minimum, so that the greatest stabilizing effect is obtained, shortly after the beginning of a decline. The stabilizing effects are relatively low in the late stages of a long decline, when the economy is most in need of support, thus contributing to the depths reached in major depressions.

The changes in the multiplier from one forecasting situation to another are, of course, automatically taken into account in the translation from gross product to personal income to consumers' expenditures. This translation process possesses a degree of flexibility and validity not attainable by any simple multiplier. Nevertheless, if its limitations are recognized, the multiplier is a convenient device to use in arriving at a first approximation and in working out subsequent adjustments, and the correlations indicate that it has been stable enough over a long period of time to justify such use.

Whatever the method by which the adjustment in consumer expenditures is made, the result is likely to reveal a situation significantly different from that portrayed in the first approximation. The second estimate of consumer expenditures in the fourth quarter of 1954 exceeded the original by almost $4 billion. To this had to be added another $3.1 billion to allow for the multiplier effect. In addition, the adjustments to consumer expenditures had to be reconsidered. Personal savings had been adjusted upward largely on account of a projected reversal in consumer credit. In the improved circumstances now envisaged, liquidation of credit at the rate projected would be unlikely. So another $½ billion was added back into consumer expenditures to adjust for this shift.

The upward adjustment of consumer expenditures by $7.5 billion from the first approximation made two points clear. First, the over-all decline was to be considerably smaller than the initial projections suggested; gross national product at the low would be down less than $20 billion, or 5 percent from the peak, which is hardly a distressing setback. Second, and more important, there would be a definite tendency toward recovery at the end of the period. These indications of a stronger situation had implications for everything that had been done in making the original projections of the strategic factors. They made necessary the review of those projections in the light of what had now been developed.

Most serious of the implications for other factors were those affecting inventory changes. It was apparent that the stability of the economy was important not only in its own right but also because it offered assurance that the inventory reversal would be held to modest proportions. A situation in which it is easy to liquidate inventories minimizes the incentive to do so. Moreover, the recovery suggested a lessening of liquidation toward the end of the period. The revisions shown in Chart 13–3 were made on this basis.

The improvement in the general situation also indicated that any incipient weakness in new residential construction was likely to be postponed beyond the end of the year. Construction activity was therefore lifted slightly and then held steady through the remainder of the year. This made home building for the year as a whole a little lower than 1953, but the fourth-quarter level was projected higher than the fourth quarter of 1953 (see Chart 13–2).

These changes were expected to affect producers' outlays for new equipment to some extent, so that investment in equipment was also lifted slightly. This adjustment was held to a minimum, however, because capacity had been expanded greatly, with emphasis on equipment rather than on construction. Moreover, two specific developments supported the negative view; military programs were being cut back, eliminating the need for expansion in some industries, and weakness in the agricultural situation made for lower purchases of farm machinery.

Revisions in the other kinds of nonconsumption expenditures were not considered necessary. The combined revisions in these three items totaled $2.8 billion in the fourth quarter of 1954. When raised by the multiplier, the adjustment amounted to $5 billion at that time. The adjustments were progressively smaller in the earlier quarters of 1954. Both these and the adjustments for consumption were added to the second approximation of gross national product to obtain the starting point for the new translation to consumer income and expenditures. They lifted the second-approximation estimates of gross national product by $3.7 billion at the second-quarter low and by $8.6 billion at the end of the forecast period.

As may be seen from a comparison of the fourth and next-to-last lines in Table 13–4, there were only minor discrepancies between these estimates and the final results of the third approximation. In lieu of a fourth approximation, the small adjustments called for by the multiplier were made, establishing the final estimate. Greater precision could contribute little to a process that is necessarily subject to a rather wide margin of error.

Chart 13–7. Government Purchases of Goods and Services

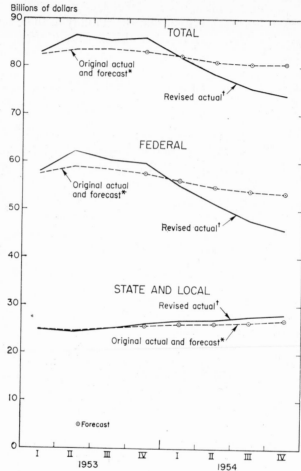

Billions of dollars

* Original actual, Survey of Current Business, November, 1953;
forecast, Tables 13–1 to 13–4.
† Revised actual, Survey of Current Business, February, 1955.

The nature of these final estimates was described as follows in the original publication summarizing the results of this forecast:[7]

The movement as a whole represents what has previously been referred to as a minor fluctuation in a period of general prosperity. Unemployment may continue to increase through most of 1954—to a level of, say, 3½ million workers, which could still be regarded as within the range of a full employment economy. We repeat that the situation justifies the maintenance of policies consistently geared to prosperity conditions.

[7] *Illinois Business Review,* January, 1954, p. 6.

Chart 13–8. Producers' Durable Equipment and Construction*

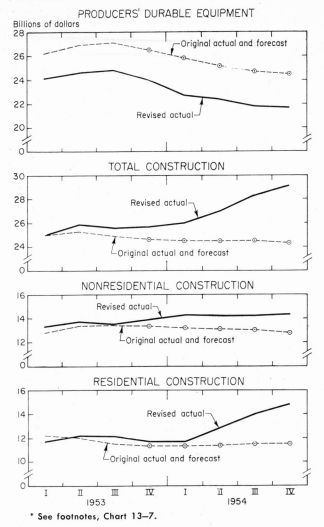

PRODUCERS' DURABLE EQUIPMENT

Billions of dollars

Original actual and forecast

Revised actual

TOTAL CONSTRUCTION

Revised actual

Original actual and forecast

NONRESIDENTIAL CONSTRUCTION

Revised actual

Original actual and forecast

RESIDENTIAL CONSTRUCTION

Revised actual

Original actual and forecast

I II III IV I II III IV
1953   1954

* See footnotes, Chart 13–7.

Comparisons of the forecasts with the actual results subsequently published by the Department of Commerce are shown in Charts 13–7 to 13–10. These comparisons are marred in some cases, particularly producers' durable equipment, by revisions of the data. In these cases, the pattern of change may be regarded as more important than the absolute levels.

Inspection of these charts and comparison of the forecast tables with actual data reveal numerous errors of detail. Two major errors are ap-

Chart 13–9. Changes in Nonfarm Inventories and Consumer Credit and Net Foreign Investment*

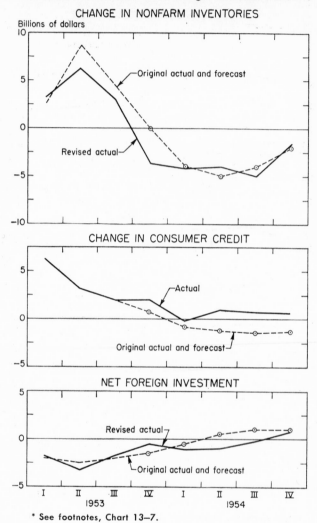

CHANGE IN NONFARM INVENTORIES

Billions of dollars

—Original actual and forecast

Revised actual—

CHANGE IN CONSUMER CREDIT

—Actual

Original actual and forecast—

NET FOREIGN INVESTMENT

Revised actual—

—Original actual and forecast

I   II   III   IV   I   II   III   IV
1953   1954

* See footnotes, Chart 13–7.

parent on the charts: Government expenditures declined much more rapidly than expected, and residential construction forged ahead in a wholly unexpected manner. Fortunately, the effects of these substantial errors were offsetting in the forecast as a whole. In looking backward on the situation, it may be seen that they were not entirely independent. The government passed the Housing Act of 1954, easing the terms of financing new homes, partly because the cutbacks in its own programs had brought on a decline in activity and a substantial increase in un-employment.

Such a coincidence of offsetting errors and compensating changes in expenditure patterns could hardly be expected on other occasions. As a rule, any substantial error of this kind will be reflected in the forecast.

Chart 13–10. Gross National Product*

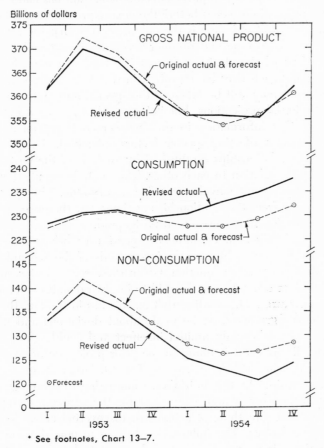

Billions of dollars

GROSS NATIONAL PRODUCT

Original actual & forecast

Revised actual

CONSUMPTION

Revised actual

Original actual & forecast

NON-CONSUMPTION

Original actual & forecast

Revised actual

⊙ Forecast

I   II   III   IV   I   II   III   IV
   1953   1954

* See footnotes, Chart 13–7.

But only if a series of errors are interrelated and reinforcing will they result in a wholly invalid forecast.

CONSISTENCY CHECKS

This forecast provides an illustration not only of the procedure employed but also of the importance of the process of successive approximations. The forecast finally constructed by this process is in definite contrast with that first arrived at. The initial portrayal of a substantial decline continuing throughout the period was displaced by the more realistic one of a moderate decline followed by partial recovery.

One of the most important aspects of this process of working through successive approximations lies in the fact that it reopens initial forecasts of the various factors for reflexive adjustment. Once a result is obtained, the validity of all the initial judgments and computations can be checked for consistency and corrected before the next approximation is taken.

Such a process of checking is the only assurance that the relationships embodied in the income and product accounts are not violated. It puts the projections of the strategic factors in broader perspective, so that forces affecting each may be appraised in the light of the situation as a whole. Account may still be taken of the specific information utilized in making the initial projections, but it is possible to make a better interpretation of that information in this broader context than as a set of isolated influences affecting specific factors only. Both the specific influences and the relationships established by analysis of the past data may be evaluated in relation to each other. They may be conflicting or reinforcing, and the result may be modified accordingly. The specifics pull the result away from the relationships at times, but the movement called for by the relationships can seldom be ignored.

The circular check on consumers' expenditures brings into play the whole series of relationships on the income side of the account, winding up with the consumption function. Given these relationships, any gross-national-product estimate may be said to imply a definite volume of consumer expenditures. The qualification on this lies in the fact that certain unavoidable judgments must be made about deviations and discrepancies, but these are usually limited in effect and could seldom be decisive. Hence if any error is found in the prior projection of consumer expenditures, this implies the existence of a still larger error—that is, the original error raised by the multiplier. Eliminating this error gives a new value for gross product and a new test for the strategic factors, which provides at least something of a basis for discovering errors in the forecasts of those factors. The influences affecting income determination in the immediate circumstances are thus brought to bear on all the initial projections of expenditures.

There is a possibility, of course, that the initial projections of aggregate expenditures, both consumption and nonconsumption, will be in line with the relationships, so that no error will be indicated. This is, in fact, the position arrived at after all checks and adjustments have been made. In it lies the basic hazard of forecasting. The forecast still depends upon the projections worked out and on the judgments that must be made. Consistency alone does not eliminate the possibility of error at various points and does not preclude the appearance of new sources of variation that were wholly unforeseen at the time the forecast was made. In most situations, however, the application of consistency checks through a series of approximations will uncover a number of inadequacies and result in a much sounder forecast.

The consistency checks applicable to each of the strategic factors derive from the fundamentals of analysis for those factors, as outlined in earlier chapters. Many of them represent relationships of the segments to the total, others of specific segments to each other. The process of applying them is in each case a process of reconciling appropriate elements of analysis, of understanding why each factor is behaving as it is currently and how the prospective changes in the situation are likely to modify its behavior in the period ahead.

Considerations of this kind are particularly important in the case of inventories, since their movements are closely tied to the aggregate flow of goods and are often so large as to determine the whole forecast over a short period. For this reason, the effects of prospective movements of other factors on inventories were made part of the initial discussion of forecasting inventory changes, comprising the last section of the chapter on that subject. Since a more adequate judgment about the total flow of goods into consumption is now available, there is clearly a better basis for projecting the probable course of inventory movements.

There are occasions when a shift in inventory investment can definitely be forecast. If inventories are being liquidated rapidly at a time when they are already low in relation to consumption, an early reversal would be probable. That reversal would be distinctly accelerated if consumption were otherwise being sustained and perhaps only moderated somewhat if consumption promised to decline further.

On other occasions, no such definite probability exists. If inventories are being liquidated moderately when the total is somewhat higher than normal, there would be little basis for deciding on any definite pattern of change. If the flow of goods were then to turn distinctly upward or downward, inventory investment would probably turn in conformity; but if consumption were comparatively stable, so that inventories would merely come back into line after a while, the situation would remain indecisive. Either a turn or an acceleration might get under way in these circumstances and might progress for a time without violating the rules of consistency. Hence care must be exercised not to allow a poorly grounded hypothesis about inventory investment to set the whole forecast on a fallacious course.

Consumer credit is perhaps the most closely determined of all the strategic factors. Its changes derive primarily from the movements of durable-goods purchases and must reflect the effects of those movements on credit granted and credit repaid. Only in exceptional circumstances would credit extension change in an adverse manner, and many of the exceptions would involve changes in terms, as in 1952, when the release of credit from government regulation brought on an expansion well in advance of any significant increase in sales of durable goods. At times when no special influences were known to be at work, such independent movements of credit would have to be ruled out and adjustments made to bring the credit change into line. Let it be noted, however, that this statement is in no sense a qualification on the role of credit at the cyclical turning points, when a mere leveling of durable-goods purchases implies a reversal of the credit movement.

Government programs, too, respond to changes in the total and must be adjusted with respect to the movements of activity in general. The built-in stabilizers come into immediate action, but the effects of changing business conditions on government programs are not confined to these built-in stabilizers. Since the Great Depression, the direct expenditures of the government for goods and services have become clearly responsive to changes in total activity. The Council of Economic Advisers has been set up to watch economic progress and to make proposals for action to maintain the economy in a healthy state of activity. There is a distinct probability that special countercyclical action will be taken.

Such action can hardly be fully effective on all occasions, but it ordinarily will make a difference, and in some situations it might make a decisive difference. Declining activity not only affects government programs specially proposed to counter the decline but also makes it easier to get other programs approved or expanded. The Housing Act of 1954 included elements of both kinds. Similarly, on the revenue side, changes in tax rates to restrain inflation or to moderate a deflationary movement must be assigned a substantial probability of approval. In this field, there is a whole series of check-backs against the original projections. Many probable changes could not be clearly formulated until the over-all pattern of change in the economy had been fairly well worked out.

The last of the short-term factors, net foreign investment, displays its own patterns of adjustment to changes in economic activity, as was indicated in Chapter 8. The primary effects are compensatory: The relation of imports to inventory changes and the use or accumulation of gold and dollar reserves by foreign countries tend to stabilize activity in this country.

Expenditures for producers' equipment are in an intermediate position. They are definitely responsive to changes in rates of production, as has already been pointed out, but in variable degree, depending upon the industrial incidence of the changes foreseen. Shifts in demand call forth the greatest response when they are concentrated on industries already operating near capacity.

Even the more stable kinds of long-term investment are affected to a degree. Over short periods, modifications in construction activity will probably be relatively small, because of the short-term stability of that series. Any adjustments must first enter into the contract awards, and only with a substantial lag into activity itself. Nevertheless, the adjustments of any kind of capital formation to changes in the level of activity are large enough so that they cannot be ignored.

Sometimes this process of checking and modification turns up surprising results. A decline may be wiped out, or promising signs of recovery may be turned into a new setback. In a 1948 forecast, made at the beginning of that year, the original projections indicated a continuing advance, but the translation process indicated they were too high. After being modified in various respects, the projections depicted a decline as the point of departure for the third approximation, but the translation process indicated the result was too low. The final forecast was entitled "Plateau of Prosperity in 1948." The situation was shortly thereafter transformed by trouble in Europe, leading to the Berlin airlift and to a larger military program and an expanded foreign-aid program. The point here, however, is not that the forecast was either a good or a bad one but merely that the process of checking for consistency and modifying the forecast through successive approximations is capable of making important contributions to the final result. Although the process varies considerably from one occasion to the next, its results have usually proved to be constructive.

The procedure as a whole is flexible enough to allow maximum scope for imagination and judgment and yet ties the forecaster to the necessity for balancing the over-all accounts and observing all the known interrelationships. The end result is a forecast internally consistent and incorporating all that is known about the special forces affecting each important segment.

In the procedure as it has been described, the process of successive approximations performs the same function as the mathematical solution when the econometric-model method is used. The solution must in either case take account of the known relationships. The successive approximations introduce the same effects in a different manner from the simultaneous equations. The question is sometimes asked: "Why carry out the solution through stages when it can be done all at once, and more accurately, through the mathematical approach?" The basic reason for preferring the nonmathematical approach is its greater flexibility. The forecaster is in a position to know what is being done with each variable in each stage of the solution. He can introduce specific judgments or bits of special information at various points without recasting the process as a whole.

In contrast, when the mathematical solution is utilized, everything that goes into it must be spelled out in advance. Then follows a long series of computations, of little or no informative value in themselves, until the solution is arrived at. Even the forecaster who thoroughly understands the data and what the relationships will do to them tends to be very much in the dark until the machines grind out the answer.

Many of the elements go into and come out of a mathematical solution in a purely mechanical fashion. Greater accuracy in each is obtained in the light of the assumptions underlying the formulation of the model and its solution, but not necessarily in fact. Small changes in relatively minor respects, such as including an additional year of data, often make important differences in the results—how important can only be judged by carrying out the computations both ways, after which still a third alternative may be indicated. Judgment is still necessary to evaluate the results. Unless the results closely approximate what the forecaster would have worked out by other methods, they may have to be rejected anyway.

Any appearance that the method of successive approximations is more cumbersome and involves more work is also superficial. The solution of a complicated set of equations is likely to be very laborious, and it is a kind of work many forecasters are not trained to perform. Most, however, have little difficulty with the successive approximations described above —and seldom will more than three be required.

Ultimately, the merits of any approach must meet the test of actual practice. The procedure described has met this test satisfactorily in a limited number of trials, though not without error on all occasions. It also provides a basis for explaining past business fluctuations. All the records of past business cycles, the regularities and the differences, appear to be capable of explanation in terms of the coincidental or interrelated effects of the variables included in the income and product accounts. These facts offer some hope, though no guarantee, that the tests of the future may be met even more effectively.

PART THREE

Frequently
Encountered
Problems

CHAPTER 14

Broad Questions
of Public Policy

The application of forecasting techniques to specific problems is un-avoidably conditioned by the nature of the problem and its practical setting. Whether it relates to a narrow aspect of business operation or to the broadest question of government policy, the need is immediate and specific. The forecaster is typically asked to indicate the nature of the situation that will prevail, in terms of the alternatives relevant to the im-mediate decision. The question is: "What should be done now to deal with prospective developments effectively?"

The timing of the forecast, as well as its content, is usually determined in response to this question. The range of a forecast aimed at determin-ing whether a commodity should be sold now rather than next month is quite different from one aimed at determining whether a public-works program should be undertaken to reduce unemployment a year or two hence. In either case, the decision is likely to be wanted quickly, before the opportunity disappears—whether it is merely a chance to take a profit or a strategic occasion on which to get agreement on necessary legislation.

The difficulty of the assignment also varies with the problem. A short-range forecast that turns upon erratic factors, perhaps upon the mere whim of speculative sentiment, may hold as much possibility of error as the more distant projection that depends in part upon disturbances or other causes beyond anyone's ability to predict. Error may be readily forgiven when it is perceived as originating in unique and unforeseeable events. Less often will it be excused because the forecast had to be made under pressure, without the aid of adequate research. These are the exigencies of the practical-forecasting situation. The forecaster has to adapt himself to them, and his burden may be heavy or light, depending upon the specific area in which he operates.

The variety of problems which forecasts may be called upon to solve, or help solve, is practically unlimited. Each has its own peculiarities, and the variations in approach needed to deal with them are of corresponding magnitude. All that can be attempted, therefore, is to outline some of the principles involved and to illustrate their application to some problems frequently encountered. This is the objective of Part 3 of this book.

As a starting point, it will be assumed in most cases that a forecast of activity for the economy as a whole is available. Most of the specific segments of economic activity are directly affected by the over-all movement. For many, it is decisive. For others, it is merely important, along with other causes. There are exceptions, of course, and some of them will be noted, but even in these exceptional cases a conception of what the over-all situation will be often proves very helpful in defining the effects of the specific forces that dominate the item in question. For the most part, the discussion will proceed in terms of the kind of over-all forecast developed in Part 2. For many problems any acceptable alternative to national-income and product estimates—for example, a forecast of the index of industrial production—will serve as well. The index of industrial production may in fact be the better starting point for some problems; its relationship to gross national product is shown in Chart 3–7. Generally the most appropriate over-all measure—whether gross product, industrial production, personal income, or employment—should be applied in each case.

In this chapter two difficult forecasting problems connected with public policy will be considered. These are unemployment and prices. In attempting to stabilize the economy, the government is usually concerned either with reducing unemployment or with preventing inflation, and to do either effectively it must have some idea of how far the current movements are likely to carry and how much they are likely to be modified by the actions proposed.

The movements of unemployment and prices are, of course, rather closely related. Rising unemployment is the symbol of deflation; ordinarily it is associated with falling prices. In times of decline, unemployment becomes the most important statistic compiled. On the other hand, minimum unemployment is one of the conditions for inflation. But when unemployment approaches a low of, say, 2 percent of the labor force, it cannot readily be reduced further and therefore no longer serves as an indicator of the extent of inflationary pressure. Attention must then turn to the rate of price advance as a guide to policy.

Unfortunately, these two key variables are among the most difficult to forecast. The following discussion will in each case reveal why this is true. As an introductory generalization, it may be pointed out that both are measures of the differences between broad aggregates, and relatively small errors in those broad aggregates may be translated into much larger errors in the measure that equates them.

Unemployment is the residual after total employment is subtracted from the labor force. An error of 2 million workers would be only about 3 percent of a labor force of 65 million, but it would be 67 percent of unemployment of 3 million. If this error reduced prospective unemployment to 1 million, it would indicate a very tight labor market and call for restrictive action. If it increased unemployment to 5 million, it would indicate a substantial labor surplus and call for efforts to stimulate activity. Thus what looks like a relatively trivial error in either or both of the broad aggregates in which it first appeared could lead to fallacious conclusions in either direction.

Price indexes express the relationship between the flow of money and the flow of goods. They are calculated as the ratio of the total value of goods purchased to the total physical volume of goods for which payment is made. Aggregate physical volume is itself measured in terms of constant dollar values, the prices of a base period being used to convert noncomparable physical units to a form in which they may be combined. Both of these broad aggregates tend to move together, but they diverge as prices change. The price index measures the extent of the divergence. If value tilts up relative to output, then prices are rising; if the tilting is in the other direction, then prices are falling. Comparatively small relative changes in the totals of value and volume might produce important differences in the movement of prices and in the conclusions to be drawn from them. In periods of rapid advance, the possibilities of error are at their height. A comparatively moderate rate of price increase, which would in itself be regarded as tolerable, might be shifted by errors in the projection of current and constant-dollar aggregates all the way across the range from no advance at all to an advance so rapid as to pose a real threat to stability.

A third item that involves a similar problem is corporate profits. It, too, is a residual—the difference between total business receipts and total charges against those receipts. It, too, enters into questions of public policy, particularly those relating to prices, wages, and taxes. The procedure for forecasting this item has been dealt with in part in Chapter 13; further discussion of it will be postponed to Chapter 17.

UNEMPLOYMENT

The logic of forecasting unemployment may be briefly outlined as follows: The working force employed at any time depends upon the volume of goods and services being produced. It fluctuates with output. The total labor force, on the other hand, tends to grow at a fairly steady rate. Subtracting total employment from the labor force leaves unemployment. The key to the whole process apparently lies in working out estimates of the total output required. Since such estimates are available in the forecast of gross product, they need merely to be applied to obtaining the related estimates of employment, and the job is done.

Application of this simple logic, however, encounters a number of important obstacles. The relation of employment to output is not so straightforward as it seems. Agricultural output, for example, may change without any change in employment. In nonagricultural pursuits, a growing proportion of the labor force is engaged in nonproduction activities like administration, research, and selling. In production some lines require more labor than others, so that output might change with a shift of employment to other industries or occupations, without any change in aggregate employment. Or a change in output might be compensated by a change in average working hours. Account must be taken, furthermore, of changes in productivity, which over periods of time make possible a larger volume of production with a given working force. Finally, the size of the labor force itself changes with the availability of jobs and with the pressure for output. Thus all the elements involved in the calculation of unemployment are variables whose movements have to be separately projected.

Each of these variables—the pattern of production, the average working hours, productivity, and the labor force—may normally be projected with a degree of accuracy that appears satisfactory in its own terms. But the errors in any of them, let alone any combination of reinforcing errors, may produce unacceptable results in the end product, unemployment. It was a combination of such errors, particularly errors in projecting the labor force, that made most of the postwar forecasts of unemployment in 1946 unrealistic.

In analyzing the pattern of production and employment, the amount of detail to be considered depends upon the purpose of the forecast and the resources that can be applied to the task. At least two important segments may be identified as groups whose movements are not closely tied to changes in aggregate production—government and agriculture. These have to be separately projected in any case. Within the large remaining portions, representing all private nonagricultural employment, the BLS data on employees in nonagricultural establishments provide more than adequate detail for most purposes. Again, certain segments—such as construction, finance, and service—display a considerable amount of independence relative to the movements of general business, at least for short periods. The largest segment of employment in the private nonagricultural sector, however, representing the industries engaged in commodity production and distribution, must be projected in relation to the forecast of activity in the economy as a whole.

The output forecasts to be used in projecting various segments of total employment have for the most part already been derived. In the translation from output to employment, however, certain difficulties are encountered. To obtain a division of the manufacturing total between durable- and nondurable-goods industries, for example, it is necessary to allocate inventory changes and government purchases (excluding services) by type of product. Current data are satisfactory for a provisional allocation of this kind, but it is difficult to test the relationships that have to be used, because such data are not available over a long enough period. Construction and foreign trade also bear on this alloca-

Chart 14–1. Real Output per Man-hour

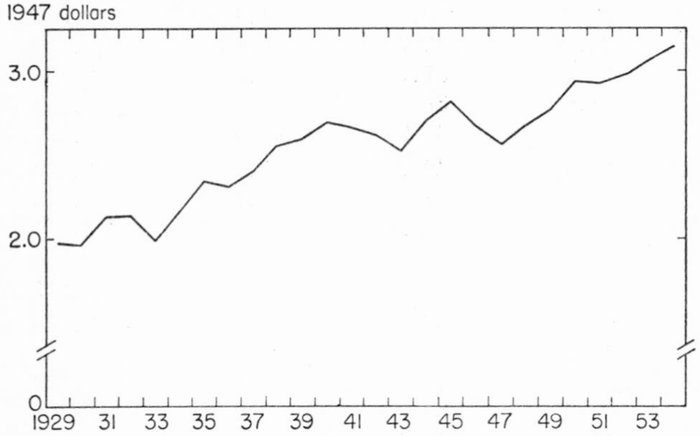

tion, and they are even more important with reference to employment in transportation. Few of these problems are beyond solution, but no attempt will be made here to deal with the many complications that arise in a detailed translation.

To illustrate the fundamentals of the method in broad outline, a comparatively simple technique of estimating total employment in nonagricultural industries may be described. For this purpose, indexes of average weekly working hours and of productivity were compiled (see Table 14–1). The average weekly-hours series was multiplied by employment and raised to an annual basis on the assumption of a 50-week year to obtain aggregate annual man-hours. This series is taken as the basic measure of labor input required for the production realized each year.

To obtain a measure of productivity, deflated private gross national product was divided by the computed aggregate annual man-hours. The trend of output per man-hour is shown in Chart 14–1. Projecting this

Table 14–1.   Nonagricultural Employment, Man-hours, and Productivity

	Employees in private non-agricultural establishments* (in millions)	Average hours per week†	Estimated aggregate man-hours‡ (in billions)	Output per man-hour§ (in 1947 dollars)
1929	23.4	45.9	53.7	$1.974
1930	21.5	43.9	47.2	1.961
1931	18.9	42.3	39.9	2.134
1932	16.2	39.8	32.2	2.137
1933	16.5	39.6	32.6	1.988
1934	18.4	36.5	33.5	2.163
1935	19.2	37.8	36.2	2.349
1936	20.8	39.9	41.4	2.317
1937	22.4	39.7	44.4	2.400
1938	20.5	37.7	38.6	2.556
1939	21.6	39.0	42.1	2.588
1940	22.9	39.2	45.0	2.695
1941	26.4	40.7	53.7	2.660
1942	29.0	41.9	60.7	2.613
1943	30.7	43.2	66.3	2.521
1944	30.1	43.8	66.0	2.700
1945	28.7	42.8	61.3	2.811
1946	29.6	40.9	60.5	2.666
1947	31.5	40.8	64.3	2.554
1948	32.1	40.5	65.1	2.672
1949	30.7	39.7	61.0	2.768
1950	31.8	40.3	64.1	2.936
1951	33.8	40.4	68.3	2.922
1952	34.3	40.3	69.1	2.972
1953	35.5	39.9	70.7	3.060
1954	33.8	39.4	66.6	3.140

* U.S. Bureau of Labor Statistics. Employees in finance, services, and government are excluded.

† U.S. Bureau of Labor Statistics supplemented by National Industrial Conference Board and other sources. Component series for which no direct data are available were extrapolated back to 1929 on the basis of manufacturing or of most nearly comparable industry. Data for all recent years are averages of manufacturing and non-manufacturing. Nonmanufacturing is the weighted average of the following components: trade, 5; transportation and utilities combined, 3; construction, 1; and bituminous coal, petroleum, natural gas combined, 1.

‡ Employment times average hours times 50 weeks.

§ Gross national product in 1947 dollars, excluding consumer services and gross government product, divided by estimated aggregate man-hours.

series is the first step in translating the forecast of gross product into labor requirements.

Detailed discussion of the concept of productivity in general or the procedures suitable for measuring it under various possible concepts would not be appropriate here. It should be noted, however, that the present series represents a gross-productivity concept, which gives effect to all changes in output, however realized, and to all man-hours used, regardless of whether they are used in production, training, preparation, maintenance, or selling. Increases in productivity, as thus measured, may occur in the absence of specific changes in industrial technique or efficiency, through shifts of workers from marginal occupations into industries where wages and product per man-hour are higher, mainly the durable-goods industries. The results obtained in this way are therefore not comparable to the detailed, industry-by-industry estimates compiled by the Bureau of Labor Statistics. This fact does not, however, affect their usefulness in the present context as a statistical means of moving from output to employment.

The behavior of this gross-productivity measure in the short run is somewhat erratic, since it is affected by diverse influences whose combined effects are not readily predictable. Shifts in the pattern of employment should be taken into account, for the reason already indicated. Another important factor is turnover, which to some extent is necessary in accomplishing industrial shifts; turnover tends to make production less efficient and therefore to reduce productivity, regardless of whether employment is growing, falling, or merely holding steady with an unusual amount of shifting from job to job. The lag of output behind inputs and the slowness of industry to adjust the working force to changes in demand also influence the ratio of output to man-hours for considerable periods. Furthermore, short-term changes in production that push the rate of capacity utilization away from the optimum have the opposite effect from those that bring it back toward the norm.

Underlying all these factors, of course, is the continuing advance of technology, which results in relatively steady improvement in efficiency over long periods. Data going back into the nineteenth century show that output per man-hour has been advancing on a compound-interest curve in all major branches of industry at rates averaging about 2 percent a year for the economy as a whole. Even technology, however, tends to work in a rather undependable manner for short periods. As new facilities are brought into operation, they ordinarily increase the efficiency of production; but while they are being installed and brought up to the levels of output for which they are designed, efficiency may be lower than in the older facilities.

Attempts to set general rules for the behavior of productivity in specific situations are risky. Perhaps the most that can be said is that productivity tends to fall during the early stages of any substantial change in the level of output. On the upswing, inputs must precede output. This makes for a decline in productivity despite the better utilization of fixed personnel. In addition, new workers must be trained, and they are not for a while highly efficient. After a time, output begins to catch up with rising inputs and then at a later stage rises more rapidly, so that productivity regains the lost ground.

As new investment is stimulated, diverse tendencies are again experienced; hours invested in installing equipment and making ready for production do not immediately contribute to output. But these hours, like those in the capital-goods industries generally, command a high return, and the advance in gross productivity is in the course of time accelerated by the shift into capital expansion. Finally, peak efficiency is approached as more and more of the new facilities achieve optimum rates of output, but at the same time a certain amount of slackness may be tolerated, since the labor market is tight and workers generally cannot be replaced except with less efficient workers.

On the downswing, fixed elements of labor tend to keep man-hours high in relation to production, so that productivity declines, or at least is kept from advancing. Subsequently, economy drives are put into effect, and the weeding-out of unnecessary and inefficient labor makes for some improvement. Also, laborsaving equipment is introduced by many concerns, and this also tends to promote a recovery in productive efficiency. But increasing efficiency tends to be offset in the aggregate by the shifting of workers out of the more productive durable-goods industries, which are most seriously depressed. The net effect is to keep gross productivity from advancing as the economy sinks deeper into depression.

In each specific situation, there are variations in circumstances that make for differences in the impact of the various factors. The upward trend of productivity is, therefore, no more than a general guide. In making any short-run projection, the forecaster may be more concerned with the probable deviation from the trend than with the trend itself.

Assuming that a satisfactory projection of output per man-hour can be worked out, the total number of man-hours required for the forecast period is readily computed. It then becomes necessary to distinguish the changes in man-hours attributable to changes in working hours from those attributable to changes in employment. For this purpose average hours of work must be projected.

Average working hours tend to be positively correlated with changes in output but tend to move ahead of any change in production, in accordance with their well-known role as a sensitive, "leading" series

in the business cycle. They are, at least temporarily, much more responsive to projected changes in rates of production than is over-all employment. When the demand for labor rises, part of the initial adjustment
to higher rates of output is made by increasing hours of work. Plants in
localities where labor is scarce may have to go on overtime, at least in
some departments or operations. If the rise continues, labor shortages
spread and intensify, and some plants schedule 9-hour days or 6-day
weeks or both. This is a highly expensive expedient, since the extra hours
not only must be paid for at premium rates but do not produce a proportional increase in product. As soon as the situation eases, therefore,
industry moves to eliminate overtime operations, and many plants may
accomplish something in this direction while the level of over-all production is still high. New workers may be recruited and trained, new
plants may be opened in localities where labor is available, new equipment may reduce man-hour requirements, and other means of shifting
the work load or of making production more efficient may be adopted.
Hence working hours tend to ease off in advance of production.

The state of the labor market obviously affects the relation of working
hours to any given rate of production. A tight market makes for higher
hours. On the other hand, if a labor surplus exists, it puts a definite restraint on increases in working hours above the standard 40-hour work
week.

When industry is operating on the standard 40-hour work week, the
actual work week ordinarily tends to average out in the range of 38 to 39
hours. Part of the loss is due to turnover; when one worker replaces another, the average for the two is 20 hours. Part is also due to unavoidable
loss of time through sickness or other personal causes. In recessions, many
plants tend to share the loss of hours by scheduling a shorter work week,
so that the average goes well under the standard. Between prosperity
and depression, the average may vary from 42 to 35 hours, or about 10
percent either way from the standard work week. At times, of course, it
may go outside these limits—above in conditions of emergency production and below in an extended depression. The long-term trend in working hours has been downward, and the general tendency in this direction will probably continue, with large reductions during declines only
partly retracted by increases during subsequent recoveries.

Dividing aggregate man-hours by average working hours gives the
desired estimates of employment. It is usually desirable to reconcile the
current and near-future estimates thus obtained with the actual BLS
data on employees in nonagricultural establishments extended by means
of a simple extrapolation. Not only does this provide a rough check on
the over-all estimates, but the movements of the various components

may throw light on various aspects of the situation, especially if they are considered in relation to the production estimates in the same or related industries.

The estimates of employees in nonagricultural establishments must be supplemented by estimates for three additional groups of workers in order to obtain total employment. These are government, agriculture, and the group representing the difference between the Census Bureau estimates of "nonagricultural employment" and the Bureau of Labor Statistics estimates of "employees in nonagricultural establishments." Government employment is tied to the expenditure programs already analyzed. Farm employment tends on the whole to change slowly, except for seasonal movements. There is a long-term downward trend, which tends to reverse in periods of adversity. Some workers who move off farms to improve themselves under prosperity conditions move back again when suitable opportunities for nonfarm employment are not available.

The third of these groups can hardly be considered a specific group of workers at all. The difference between these two broad measures of employment consists mainly of workers in domestic service, unpaid family workers, and self-employed persons in various lines of trade, service operations, or the professions. Part of the difference, however, is purely statistical in character; it arises from differences in definition and concept and in methods of measurement. For example, the Census Bureau estimate includes workers who are sick, on strike, vacationing, and otherwise have jobs at which they did not work, whereas the Bureau of Labor Statistics estimate excludes these but is swollen by dual employment and by turnover, since all workers are included, regardless of how little they actually worked or how many jobs they actually filled. Nevertheless, the difference may be projected in its entirety as if it were an altogether separate and distinct part of the labor force. It, too, tends to change rather slowly, though in a less dependable manner than farm employment.

The labor force with which the estimates of employment are to be compared is a more stable series but one that may vary significantly in the course of a year. The dominant trend is set by increasing rates of labor-force participation by persons of both sexes in practically every age group. Successive censuses reveal steady increases in the numbers availing themselves of opportunities for renumerative employment. Excluding the war years, annual increases during the last 3 decades have generally been in the range of ½ to 1 million. During the war years, much larger increases occurred year by year. In the first year following the end of World War II, the labor force fell sharply, because many of those who had held civilian jobs dropped out of the labor force and many veterans did not immediately enter it after their discharge. In the first year after V-J Day, the "not-in-the-labor-force" group rose by some 5 million persons.

In recent years there has been a good deal of controversy about the nature of shifts into and out of the labor force. As a rule, the workers who have moved out are still on hand, still available if conditions had not changed. Hence it is commonly contended that the variations in the labor force are as much the result of the method of measurement as they are of real changes in the supply of labor available. When a person is employed, there is only one way to count him; when he is unemployed, he might be considered to be studying or doing housework rather than looking for a job. However, conditions typically are different after any significant movement has occurred, and the question of what the labor force is under the new conditions is the point at issue. Without attempting to resolve this issue, it may be pointed out that the Census Bureau measure of unemployment is now almost universally accepted, and it is toward getting results in terms of this measure that the forecaster must direct his efforts.

The typical short-term movements of the labor force, as depicted by the Census Bureau survey, represent adjustments to the number of jobs available. The labor force expands when jobs are available, especially in the more attractive occupations. When there is pressure to expand production, individuals who were not considered part of the labor force can readily be drawn into the labor market. Conversely, the labor force tends to contract when jobs are lost, especially the better jobs. Many workers will not accept inferior employment but prefer to remain unemployed; and if they are not essential family breadwinners, they eventually stop looking for work and are counted out of the labor force. These movements should be regarded as tendencies only and not as dependable relationships. The gross movements into and out of the labor force during any period are made up of a number of diverse, subsidiary flows, whose character varies with the circumstances. Here again is a context in which the hypothesis that behavior tends to be adaptive is generally helpful.

This brief summary of the considerations involved in forecasting unemployment should serve as a warning against any undue confidence in the accuracy of the results obtained. Since the estimate of unemployment derived in this way depends upon so many projections which have to be made with inadequate bases, it is easy to see why it is subject to a wide margin of error. About all that can be done is to rely on the basic logic of the relationship of employment to production and ensure that each element in the situation is considered as carefully as possible.

Aside from being a point on which he can easily go wrong, unemployment is of relatively little importance to the forecaster. It is not a good indicator of what is likely to happen next, except perhaps in relation to government programing. It tends to lag rather than lead and to be especially sluggish during recoveries. If the forecast of unemployment is good, it gains little; if it is poor, the error may cost a lot. The fiasco of 1946 may well be kept in mind when forecasts of unemployment are hazarded.

PRICES

Forecasting prices also involves a number of complications. Most of these complications can be dealt with satisfactorily by treating prices entirely as a derived measure. The price level thus becomes a dependent variable, determined by other elements in the situation, the resultant rather than the initiator of changes in activity.

This approach is somewhat at variance with the usual formulation of the role of prices in economic theory. In that formulation, the responses of producers and consumers to changing prices constitute the mechanism by which supply and demand are brought into balance and an equilibrium is finally established. There can be no quarrel with this as an abstract exposition of how certain tendencies work themselves out, assuming that the conditions for equilibrium exist. Whether such conditions ever actually exist in the real world is a moot point. Certain basic facts of the real world are, however, clear enough—among them the fact that, in the broad swings of the business cycle, prices and production move together.

In each case, the price changes that appear to be called for can be made quickly, much more quickly than the economy can correct the real deficiencies or surpluses that call them forth. The price changes may therefore call attention to the existence of the deficiency or surplus— they may even be its most striking symptom—but they can hardly be said to have produced it. No doubt prices may be instrumental in bringing about the readjustments that follow when imbalances are encountered, but the correction is ordinarily not completed until it has worked itself out in real terms.

This overstates the case, of course, to the extent that there are situations in which the very rapidity of price change aggravates the condition upon which the price change depends. A special stimulus of this kind typically occurs in speculative booms and in the panics that succeed them. The great all-out inflations of history invariably have moved into such a phase, with fears of price rises forcing the rapid expenditure of available cash before its value depreciates. In an inflationary situation, when resources are fully utilized, activity is in a sense fixed, and the question becomes: "How much will prices rise?" Usually the answer must be sought in the role of the money supply.

In these special situations, the usual relationship is seemingly inverted. But even then, there is no basis for going directly to a forecast of prices. The future course of the price movement must be gauged in terms of the underlying conditions that make its continuation likely or unlikely. It is not illogical, therefore, to operate consistently on the assumption that prices are merely symptomatic, that they adjust to what the real determinants of the situation permit or dictate, without modifying its essential character.

The most decisive influence on prices of most commodities is the pace of activity. Almost all the incentives to raise prices, or to bid them up, are correlated with increases in real demand. The opposite pressure develops when business is declining. From the forecasts of activity that have already been made, the forecast of prices can, and must, be derived.

This thesis may seemingly be called in question by the behavior of farm prices. Farm prices move with a great deal of independence. When output is high, prices are not boosted but depressed. However, the independence of movement is not independence in truth but rather dependence upon a special area of production, which shows erratic movements in relation to output as a whole. In this area, too, the best approach is from volume to prices. The consumption of farm products is typically stable, or inelastic, and when output varies greatly, the surpluses or deficiencies that develop are reflected in wide price movements. Changes in output are seen to have important effects, and they are inverse. But changing levels of over-all production and income also have important effects, and they are not inverse. Movements in general business tend to call forth farm-price movements in the same direction. Nonagricultural income was long ago described as the best measure of demand for farm products.[1] The fact that farm production does not readily respond to changes in income over short periods means that a deficiency or surplus can appear without a change in output, merely as a result of changing demand. Then prices move with the economy as a whole. These are the "normal" results, which the forecaster automatically includes when he is using a projection of over-all activity that makes no special provision for unusual and unrelated changes in farm output.

Realistic appraisals of the price-making process in industry and trade indicate that there are two dominant influences—costs and the competitive state of the market. In some industries, the response of prices to changes in over-all demand is not unlike that of farm prices. In others, where "administered prices" prevail, it is much slower and tends to be more closely tied to changes in costs. This introduces a lag in prices behind other aspects of activity, but this lag need not be separately taken

[1] See L. H. Bean, P. H. Bollinger, and O. V. Wells, *Nonagricultural Income as a Measure of Domestic Demand*, U.S. Department of Agriculture, 1937.

into account, because it gets built into the structure of costs by lagging wage rates and depreciation charges.

The most common formula for pricing on the basis of cost involves the application of a fixed profit margin to average total cost computed by averaging "overhead" at a designated volume referred to as "standard volume." This formula expresses the desire of business for a "satisfactory" profit on a volume of sales that is high but still well within the limits of capacity. If sales rise higher, realized profit margins are lifted by the spreading of overhead; if they fall, profits suffer from both the loss of volume and the reduction of margins. Over long periods, in which capacity may be adjusted, both capacity and standard volume tend to bear a "normal" relationship to market demand, but in any particular situation standard volume may be defined without regard to expected sales.

What constitutes a satisfactory profit for pricing purposes varies with the industry, depending, for example, on the ease of entry into the industry or on the fear that markets might be lost to competitive products. Where competition becomes severe, whether from other firms in the same industry or from other industries whose products are effective substitutes, the desired margin of profit may be sacrificed in part, or even entirely for limited periods, in the hope that the situation will again change in such a way as to permit reestablishing it. Ordinarily the latter kind of opportunity occurs only when the market as a whole expands.

In industries where price leadership prevails, the leading concern sets the price in terms of its costs at standard volume; but since its discretion is not complete, the margin it aims to realize is governed to some extent by what that price implies not only for itself but also for the other concerns in the industry. If the leader's costs are exceptionally low, it may command an unusually high margin of profit, and this may make the industry's profits high even though the average profit for the rest of the industry is no more than that obtained by industry in general. The other firms by necessity set their prices in relation to those of the leader, to enable them to retain a reasonable share of the market, and their profits then vary in inverse relationship to their costs. Efforts to gain larger shares by price cutting are usually not attractive, since they will be countered by retaliation from the rest of the industry.

This kind of pricing implies a high degree of profit variability with changes in volume. Even with "standard" prices, low volume may mean losses for most concerns; and in the depths of depression, the concept of "standard pricing" can hardly be said to exist. At such times, nobody knows what cost or volume will be. Materials prices melt away as surpluses are dumped. Efforts to gain any possible advantage in terms of a price in excess of outlay costs may result in the breakdown of the mechanisms of price administration. Then any tie between over-all costs and prices may temporarily be lost.

When demand recovers, not only are margins reestablished but costs advance. Many materials are produced under conditions of inelastic supply, and their prices are bid up sharply, increasing the costs of all products in which they are used. However, the main item in costs in industry as a whole is wages. Wage rates tend to be bid up, and overtime premiums may be incurred. The loss of productivity that occurs at the beginning of such a move also increases costs. In the early stages of a boom, prices are likely to make their most rapid advances. Later the rate of price advance is likely to slow in comparison with wages. New facilities are brought into operation, and the working force is trained to a peak of efficiency, so that unit labor costs may hold steady despite a distinct upward trend in wage rates. Moreover, in an extended period of prosperity, industry tends to lift its sights on standard volume, and "spreading the overhead" lowers the unit costs charged into prices. Finally, the growth of capacity tends to intensify competitive pressure, so that prices and margins, which had been distinctly high, may be forced down, possibly to a point somewhat below the desired levels. There is little incentive for substantial price cutting as long as demand continues at prosperity levels, but competition for larger shares of the market tends to get stiffer right up to the breaking point.

No doubt this brief summary of how prices are actually set contains some sweeping generalizations that cannot be fully sustained. Its intent is not to provide an account accurate in all details but to suggest a theory of the pricing process that can serve as a working tool for the forecaster in a dynamic situation. The level of activity, in its dual aspects of aggregate income and aggregate cost, is the key to price forecasting.

Real income is ordinarily defined as income deflated by an appropriate index of prices. In this instance, the starting point is the estimate of real income, and the direct approach to the price index is to divide money income by real income. Following this approach evidently involves translating the constant-dollar estimates of income already worked out into current-dollar terms. A forecaster who made his initial projections in current dollars would, of course, be faced with the reverse problem.

The most important segment of personal income by far consists of wages and salaries. To recompute this segment in current-dollar terms involves making a projection of wage rates. Although this is not always easy, the basic hourly-wage series lags and in general displays a highly dependable pattern of variation, so that it is far easier to project than commodity prices as such.

The course of activity gives the primary clue to whether the trend of wage rates will slow down or accelerate. It regulates the demand for labor and the level of unemployment. These are key indicators, but other information may be brought to bear in charting the course of wage rates. The militancy of labor unions makes some difference. Government policy or the character of legislation before Congress may also

Chart 14–2. Comparison of Actual and Estimated Wages and Salaries

In billions of dollars

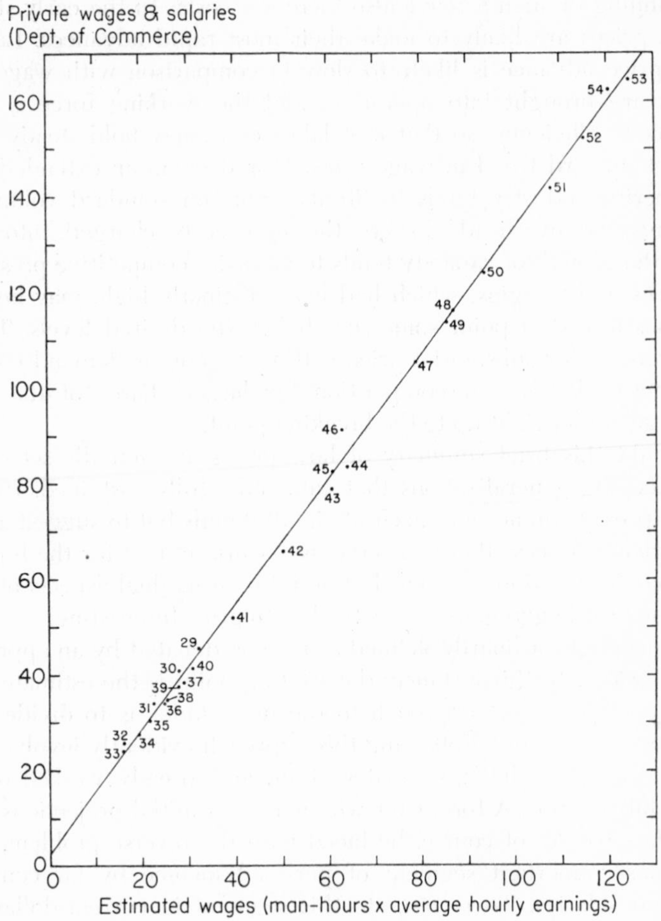

Private wages & salaries
(Dept. of Commerce)

Estimated wages (man-hours x average hourly earnings)

affect the outcome. These and other aspects of the current situation, which affect the willingness of employers to grant increases, may be made part of the analysis. Such supplementary factors, however, ordinarily are capable of producing only minor deviations from the trend within limited forecasting periods.

One source of variation that definitely has to be accounted for arises from the difference between basic wage rates and gross wage rates, including overtime. For short periods, when average working hours are increasing, overtime premiums may raise the level of gross average hourly earnings faster than the increase in basic rates. Subsequently, when hours are cut, gross average hourly earnings are correspondingly depressed. They may temporarily stabilize or even decline a little, while basic rates continue right on up. Basic rates themselves are inflexible and hardly ever decline; only after a serious depression has developed, accompanied by heavy unemployment, are basic rates likely to be cut.

These characteristic patterns of behavior afford an independent basis for projecting wage rates that is not available in the case of prices. Table 14–2 presents back data on wage rates comparable to the average-hours estimates presented in Table 14–1. Multiplying the aggregate man-hours series by average hourly earnings provides a measure of total wage and salary payments. In Chart 14–2, this measure is correlated with the corresponding estimates of wage and salary income compiled by the National Income Division of the Department of Commerce. The approximation to the more detailed estimates is evidently very close and may be taken as a check on the general adequacy of the procedures followed. When combined with estimates of other kinds of personal income, these estimates of money payments become the current-dollar aggregates from which the price index is computed.

Since wages are the decisive factor in the movements of personal income, a simplified calculation of the price level is possible at this point. To ignore other items for the moment, the basic income-product equation may be taken to state that wage income equals the value of product, or output times price. This implies that the price level equals wage income divided by output. But total wages are man-hours times the wage rate, and total output is man-hours times output per man-hour. Hence it follows from canceling out man-hours that prices should be derivable from wage rates and productivity alone. The results of a correlation utilizing these three variables are shown in Chart 14–3 in terms of actual and calculated values.[2]

This relationship indicates a direct relation between prices and wage rates and an inverse relation between prices and productivity. Alternatively, the effect of productivity may be regarded as partially offsetting

[2] The estimating equation is

$$P = 15.85 + 172.3 \frac{R}{E} \qquad (r^2 = .986)$$

where P = the consumer price index (1947–1949 = 100)
R = average hourly earnings, dollars
E = output per man-hour, 1947 dollars

wage cost increases, so that only the net, or adjusted, wage increase is effective in moving prices. The direct relationship of prices to wages has gained widespread acceptance. The inverse relationship of prices to productivity has commonly been ignored. Yet it, too, is important, and it helps explain the pattern of price movements in various phases of the business cycle.

Table 14–2. Estimated Aggregate Wages

	Average hourly earnings*	Estimated aggregate wages† in billions
1929	$0.599	$ 32.2
1930	0.592	28.0
1931	0.564	22.5
1932	0.499	16.1
1933	0.492	16.0
1934	0.573	19.2
1935	0.595	21.6
1936	0.601	24.9
1937	0.654	29.1
1938	0.658	25.4
1939	0.663	27.9
1940	0.689	31.0
1941	0.735	39.4
1942	0.829	50.3
1943	0.916	60.7
1944	0.971	64.1
1945	0.994	61.0
1946	1.087	62.8
1947	1.223	78.7
1948	1.337	87.0
1949	1.398	85.3
1950	1.462	93.7
1951	1.583	108.1
1952	1.664	115.1
1953	1.764	124.8
1954	1.812	120.6

* See footnote (†) to Table 14–1.
† Average hourly earnings times estimated aggregate man-hours from Table 14–1.

This simplified version of the price relationship is a special case of the general approach being followed here, in which the movement of prices is regarded as primarily an adjustment not to costs—whether or not productivity is allowed for—but rather to over-all activity or income.

From this more general point of view, price movements are not resolvable in terms of wages alone but must also take account of changes in other kinds of income. Although there may be special situations in which the distribution of income by kind is important, the precise division of the total between wages and other income is not of primary significance in the usual circumstances. Proceeding with the more detailed approach, it is readily perceived that some forms of personal income, such as dividends, are not price-flexible and may be included on the basis of the previous calculations. The same is true of transfer payments, though a better projection can be made now that unemployment estimates are

Chart 14–3. Consumer Price Index

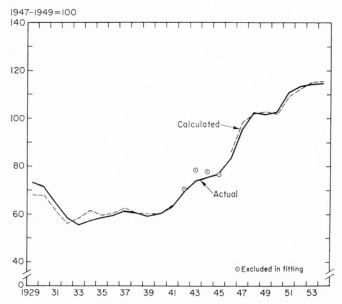

available. The main item requiring further attention is entrepreneurial income. Changes in this form of income are closely related to changes in total wages and salaries and may be estimated from their relationship to this segment. Total personal income computed in this way runs very close to the actual data compiled by the Department of Commerce This high correlation largely derives, of course, from the identity of original source material going into the make-up of the two series.

If the current and constant-dollar personal-income estimates are divided out to obtain the consumer price index, the results will be much the same as those obtained by carrying the personal-income estimates through disposable income to consumer expenditures before the computation is made. The latter procedure, however, is somewhat more closely in accord with strict logic. Carrying it through by utilizing actual tax data and actual ratios of disposable income to expenditures results in an index almost perfectly correlated with the published implicit price index. That some spurious elements of correlation are embodied in this comparison cannot be denied. This is a necessary qualification, to subdue unjustified claims of accuracy for this procedure as a forecasting method. It does not, however, negate the essential validity of the method.

In making a forecast by months or quarters over a period for which the general tendency may be considered established by a forecast worked out in this way, it is necessary to take account of any price movements that happen to be in progress at the beginning of the forecast period. Some price components are very sticky and lag behind the general movement. This is particularly true of rents and such service items as medical care and transportation and utility charges. To the extent that the influences responsible for the prior movements have not worked themselves out, the continuity will carry over into the forecast period, and the projection has to be modified accordingly.

The new estimate of consumer expenditures in current dollars may be carried back into gross national product and included as part of an over-all estimate in current dollars. The price indexes appropriate to reflating the other segments of gross product are not the same as the consumer price index. In general, the prices of investment goods and government services are more stable than consumer prices. Investment-goods prices are more like the administered prices in the consumer-goods field. Construction costs display a pattern of their own and for long periods may respond little, if at all, to the movements of consumer prices. The prices of government services are in reality wage rates; they do show a fairly direct relation to consumer prices, with some lag, but the methods of projecting wage rates are more directly appropriate, supplemented by knowledge of legislation affecting the compensation of government employees. Knowledge of the basic price and wage trends in the economy is helpful in adjusting all these segments.

The wholesale price index may also be projected in relation to the consumer price index. Its movements are somewhat more volatile, for several reasons: First, the consumer price index accumulates wage and overhead elements as the commodities pass through successive stages of processing and distribution; second, the wholesale index is rather heavily weighted with primary raw materials, which are subject to inelastic supply and correspondingly exaggerated price flexibility; and, third, it excludes service items. Much of the relative volatility of wholesale prices is contributed by farm products and foods, so that accuracy in forecasting wholesale prices depends on taking some account of the farm situation.

The index for commodities other than farm products and foods moves in much the same way as the consumer price index under ordinary circumstances but may deviate sharply for short periods. Inventory movements are important in producing such deviations. A drive to accumulate inventories tends to push prices up, and a drive to liquidate depresses them. Some of the most aggravated effects of this kind are inverted, however. They are experienced at the turns, when involuntary accumulation is piling up surpluses or involuntary liquidation is making shortages relatively more acute. To make fullest use of these suggestions, the price analyst must carry them into the field of specific commodities. Although this field is not under consideration in this discussion, it may be noted that the wholesale price indexes are of considerable analytical value because of the great detail they present.

DISTURBANCES

The forecaster must ordinarily proceed in terms of established relationships between variables. On occasion, however, forces that originate outside the realm of economic activity tear the relationships apart. The course of activity as a whole may be modified, sometimes seriously. These extraordinary forces are variously referred to as disturbance factors, shock phenomena, or exogenous forces. A forecast made in the usual way, before such forces are actually in operation, may be qualified so as to abstract from their effects; but when the existence of such forces nears a certainty, there is no alternative to modifying the forecast to take account of them.

Disturbances appear in many forms. Often it is impossible to anticipate them, and even if they are not wholly unexpected, the precise timing of their appearance may be difficult to predict. Obviously, there is not much to be said about events that are unique or almost wholly new. More often the developments that belong in this category fit into certain typical patterns, about which existing knowledge of the kind of effects produced is sufficient to permit the formulation of satisfactory modifications in a forecast.

Some of the more important types of disturbances may readily be classified. They may result from natural causes, such as disastrous storms, or, less spectacularly, from protracted spells of unusual weather. They may be political in character; major wars have been responsible for the most serious economic disruptions on record and have kept the economy in an imbalanced state over a span of 2 decades. They may represent the clash of interests among important social or economic groups, as in widespread strikes and lockouts. Other causes, such as important inventions or extreme shifts in speculative psychology, may also be significant.

Analysis of the past effects of such developments is a good source of clues as to what will happen if and when they recur in the future.

In analyzing disturbances, there are two important questions to consider: "How much?" and "How long?" If the disturbance is significant, it distorts normal relationships, and it may be important to estimate the extent of the distortion. But once the distortion is perceived, it may be equally important to know whether it will be merely temporary or will persist over a substantial period. Both aspects of the problem are usually complicated by the fact that the current data are distorted. How much of the observed changes are due to the disturbance and how much to other causes? The attempt to appraise such a situation while the disturbance is in progress is complicated. Reliance has to be placed largely on knowledge of past situations of the same kind.

As a rule, the direct effects of a disturbance are temporary. While turning activity from its regular course, it also creates the need for subsequent readjustments. As soon as the direct effect is eliminated, the economy moves to reestablish operations on a more normal basis. Very often this reaction can be predicted. The aftermath of a disturbance can often be worked out to a much higher degree of precision than was possible for the disturbance itself.

In the simplest case, that of destruction resulting from hurricanes, floods, fires, and other natural disasters, there is an immediate loss, but the result is a stimulus to business. The destruction creates a need and an opportunity. Enterprise takes advantage of the opportunity by filling the need. Some new investment is invariably required, even though it is no more than reconstructing the facilities that existed before. The people who have incurred the loss ordinarily find means of financing the reconstruction. Possibly much of the financing is available from insurance reserves. The government may rush aid to the stricken area and make loans available for rebuilding. All these expenditures provide a stimulus to activity. They may set a minor inventory cycle in motion. But it is basically a one-time shot in the arm. When the reconstruction is completed and any induced cyclical effects have been worked out, the stimulus disappears and activity tends to drop back. Both the reconstruction and the letdown are predictable, though in this country such movements are usually no more than a ripple in over-all terms.

The other important manifestation of weather disturbances appears in the harvests of farm products. Unusually good or bad weather, resulting in food surpluses or shortages, affects not only the farm community but the rest of the economy as well. In times past, such developments were highly significant, but they have become progressively less so as the importance of agriculture in the total economy has dwindled.

The most acute farm situations developed from the coincidence of unfavorable developments in agriculture and in industry. In the early 1930s, farmers were impoverished as surplus production continued in the face of the most severe decline in consumer income on record. In contrast, farmers realized their greatest prosperity in 1947, and inflationary pressure was intensified as peak consumption at home and famine conditions abroad drove up food and feed prices despite very large harvests. Apart from such special situations, the over-all effects of unusual crops are generally limited, although there may be considerable price distortion and great changes in the status of producing groups.

The old bogey of the farm community was surplus production and correspondingly depressed prices. Under the price-support program—even though the flexible features make it less favorable than in earlier years —surpluses are no longer so greatly feared. In fact, the program has tended to encourage surpluses and to spread them from crop to crop, as yields per acre continue to rise and restricted acreage is diverted to other crops. Even in a business slump, declines in farm prices may now be held to the more modest proportions of price movements in general.

Over a fairly wide range, the mechanism of price change and income shifting has a leveling effect. When farm·prices and incomes are high, consumer budgets are pinched by high food costs and they have less to spend on other products. The farm prosperity means heavier purchases by farmers, but these are offset by lower nonfarm purchases. On the other hand, when farm prices and incomes are low, consumer expenditures for food may be reduced without sacrificing per capita consumption, but this leaves a larger proportion of consumer income available for other products, counterbalancing the decline in farm spending. In either case, the net over-all effect is small. In short, fears that good or bad crops may have serious inflationary or deflationary effects have little real foundation. Only if farm income moved to extraordinary extremes in either direction could the over-all effects be substantial, and the support program, including sales from government stocks, goes a long way toward preventing such extremes from being reached.

Fears that labor disputes may have "crippling" effects are as a rule equally unwarranted. Shutdowns do have some deflationary effects. These are apparent in the over-all indicators of activity. During the prolonged strike in the steel industry in the spring of 1952,·for example, the index of industrial production dipped, inventories were run off, and durable-goods expenditures were depressed. Yet the effects were not serious enough to interrupt the advances in such broad measures as gross national product and personal income. By the end of the year, the economy was pushing into new high ground.

Sometimes strikes may be substitutes for other adjustments that would require loss of employment in any case. When the end of a coal-mining contract is approaching, consumers usually try to build up inventories against the possibility of a strike. Accumulations will then have to be worked off in any case, and a rather complete cessation of production may be the only way to get them down quickly enough to create a market situation that will justify the wage and price increases resulting from the negotiation of a new contract.

The income of the workers involved in a strike, either directly or indirectly, is reduced during the stoppage, and their consumption is also reduced, though not to the same extent. The workers usually have some supplementary income of a temporary nature and also maintain purchases from asset holdings or borrowed funds. Such spending helps to limit any tendency for the deflation to spread. But more important is the fact that the deflationary effects are entirely confined to the period of the work stoppage.

After a settlement is reached, rates of activity are usually reestablished very quickly. With wages restored, often at a higher level, the workers return to normal patterns of living. The real dissaving that occurred during the strike is largely compensated by reduced saving from income after work is resumed. When the period is considered as a whole, the loss in consumption is nowhere near what might be expected from the loss in income during the strike.

Furthermore, the level of activity tends to be at least temporarily higher after the strike. Needs accumulate as a result of the production loss. If the strike affects capital-goods industries, projects are merely deferred for later completion. If the strike affects consumer-goods industries, inventories are drawn down, and production must be stepped up later to restore working stocks. The moderate backlogs of demand that accumulate are sufficient to ensure that recovery will be more than complete. The old stock-market maxim, "Never sell a strike short!" is generally good advice.

The most serious disturbances by far are those resulting from wars. They may begin in advance of actual conflict, as the threat of war begins to be perceived. They may extend for a decade or two after the war is ended, and some for a time are likely to become the subject of controversy centering on the question of whether or not they have resulted in permanent changes in the structure of the economy.

In the past century, war has come to be known as "total war." Everything is involved. The maximum effort requires that all resources be utilized. Certain critical materials and industrial facilities are preempted first, but the orbit of war needs grows wider and wider, and ultimately the allocation of man power becomes the primary determinant of what gets done. Many civilian activities go by the board, and shortages spring up everywhere. Price control and rationing must be established. These controls attempt to ensure civilian distribution that will meet minimum needs, to protect the savings that have to be forced on income earners, and to prevent the diversion of resources into illegal or unessential channels. The regimentation of the economy has to be complete.

Almost as soon as an emergency condition developing at any point in the economy can be anticipated, the emergency tends to become acute. Hoarders and profiteers rush in to take advantage of the situation, and almost everyone is a potential hoarder or profiteer. Most people who operate in a small way cannot be expected to do otherwise than try to protect themselves and their families from discomfort or inconvenience by acting in advance of official prohibition. Many will even do so afterward. The mere rumor of contemplated action is therefore sufficient to set in motion a run on existing supplies. The control agencies have to keep their plans as secret as possible until they are actually ready to issue orders. The controllers themselves may get panicky at times and engage in intemperate or irrational action.

These are characteristics of behavior that will inevitably be encountered in circumstances which hold the threat of a future emergency. Many of them could be observed as recently as late 1950 and early 1951, when fears of World War III rather than the actualities of the Korean War were moving the economy.

The character of the deviations brought about by World War II may be observed in any of the relationships discussed in earlier chapters. Most are of the kind that could readily be anticipated. Consumption and private investment—whether in inventories, construction, or equipment— are bound to be sacrificed to war production. Savings must rise to extraordinary heights unless specific action is taken to keep them low. The possibilities of such action are limited because cooperation is needed: one way to buy it is to give the people claims against the future as part of the promise of better times after victory. The records of World War II are so complete that the probable character of future wartime changes can be inferred by analyzing the recorded experience.

One thing should be kept in mind, however. World War III, if it should come, is likely to be different in at least one important respect. Never in the past has our economy been harmed by war destruction. It was untouched by World War II. Even casualties on the fighting fronts were comparatively minor. But future wars will be tremendously more destructive. Not only are the new atomic weapons incomparably more powerful, but there is no wholly effective defense against them. One popular theory holds that the war will be over with the first devastating blow. Another holds that both sides will be so seriously crippled in the opening stages as to be unable to carry on effective operations thereafter. If such severe damage is sustained or if the war is prolonged to two or three times the duration of World War II, beyond a doubt there will be important differences from anything so far experienced. After a war that imposes severe damage, for example, the chances of all-out inflation in the postwar economy will be multiplied.

The past records of business cycles indicate that every major war has been followed by a major boom, which in turn ended in a major depression. It seems reasonable to conclude on the basis of the earlier analysis that these developments are not coincidental. The war sets the stage by creating the conditions that bring on the boom, and each phase of the cycle then follows as the logical consequence of that which preceded it. The war leaves the economy with large backlogs of unfilled demand. It leaves the people with large accumulations of liquid assets to make their demands effective. Business rushes in to take advantage of the unusual opportunity. Production, employment, and incomes are pushed up to new peaks. Production must be raised above the level of sustainable demand in order to work off the backlogs. In the course of time, the backlogs are worked off, and then production has to be cut back. But cutting production puts the forces of deflation to work. Income and demand are reduced. The stocks accumulated earlier become excessive, and production must be cut still further to liquidate them. Thus the decline gathers cumulative force.

The Great Depression of the 1930s may well be regarded as one of the results of World War I. When the depression is looked at in real terms—the specific monetary and debt features of the late 1920s being disregarded for the moment—it is seen to have developed out of the saturation of markets for durable consumer and capital goods of all kinds. Those goods were being produced in the 1920s at rates that represented substantial overproduction from the point of view of long-term needs. But the overproduction and market saturation of the 1920s was itself the result of the deficiencies that had accumulated during the war years; backlogs of demand stood at a peak at the beginning of the decade. The economy had to overproduce to remedy the deficiencies, and it then had to suffer the depression to work off the surpluses inherited from the boom.

This account of the cycle is no more than a restatement in more general terms of the stock-flow relationships described in earlier chapters. At the beginning of the cycle, there was a serious deficiency of inventories and facilities—almost all kinds desired by consumers, business, and government, particularly state and local government. At the peak of the boom, the deficiencies had been made up, but production was running too high. At the trough of the depression, stocks were seriously excessive. The severity of the entire cycle was an outgrowth of the disturbed state in which the economy was left by the war.

In the future as in the past, developments of this kind may be experienced. The pattern will probably tend to be the same, but if the destruction of resources is great, the deviations from it may be important. Possibly much can be learned about such conditions from the experience of the war-torn countries of Europe. Inflationary pressure in those countries has usually been handled in either of two ways: By letting the inflation run its course or by instituting a battery of deflationary measures to depress consumption while capital is being restored.

If future war damage should seriously curtail facilities and man power, the economy would in effect be thrown back toward an underindustrialized state. The principles of the rationed economy would then tend to be controlling. Restricted consumption would produce constant pressure for higher standards of living. Restricted production potentials would keep the boom from progressing to desired heights. The lower the rate at which deficiencies of durable goods and structures could be made up, the more prolonged would be the years of reconstruction. Whether planning would by then have progressed to the point of effecting a transition at the end of the period from high investment to high consumption without a serious letdown in over-all activity remains to be seen. However, the mere fact that years of prosperity had been experienced would not in itself be conclusive evidence that such a millennium had been achieved.

CHAPTER 15

Commodity, Industry,
and Area Forecasts

Many forecasting problems are not directly concerned with the movements of the economy as a whole. Their primary concern is with the fluctuations in prices and output of a particular commodity, with the operations of a specific industry, or with the welfare of a local community. Prospective movements of the economy as a whole are incidental to the problem of direct and immediate concern and are of interest mainly for the assistance they may offer in the solution of that problem.

Each such problem must be dealt with in the terms and by the methods appropriate to its solution. There is no single method suitable for all. What is useful or significant for one may have little or no validity for another. The first requirement, therefore, is a certain amount of research to determine how the relevant variables behave under different circumstances, what influences appear to be controlling in the current situation, and what analytical procedures promise to result in a satisfactory forecast.

If any generalization is possible about methods for solving such problems, it is that there are two basic approaches. The first is to treat the item being forecast as an independent entity not subject to close control by other parts of the economy, and then any of the methods applicable to forecasting in general may be used. The second is to consider the specific item as a segment of the total economy, and then the methods applicable to translating the total forecast into specific subsidiary parts may be used. Combinations of the two approaches are, of course, possible and may in fact be essential in some cases. Nevertheless, the first requirement in most problems of this kind is to decide whether the item can validly be considered an autonomous variable, governed by

518

its own laws of behavior, or whether it is substantially affected by the movements of the economy as a whole.

There is nothing mysterious about the nature of the research required as the first approach. It consists in getting thoroughly acquainted with the facts of the industry, commodity, or locality and in systematically investigating various possible explanations in the light of those facts. Out of this process of investigation and testing, which may at first resemble a kind of haphazard trial and error, will come an understanding of the forces at work. It will both clarify the relevant procedures and develop a rationale for the method used.

Such research is frequently of considerable value apart from any contribution it may make to forecasting. It may even eliminate the need for forecasts, by leading to the adoption of principles of action that circumvent the uncertainty which the forecast had intended to dispel. Inventory-control procedures, for example, typically have something of this effect.

If forecasts are still needed, the research will help not only in determining the appropriate method but in putting it to use under the new conditions that arise in each forecasting period. Whatever the method of forecasting used, accuracy of projection, both in magnitude and in timing, will be enhanced by familiarity with relevant data and by knowledge of how the data change and what chains of interaction tend to be induced by those changes. Mere details of past behavior may throw light on what to expect in a new situation. Some aspects of this kind of familiarity, especially those relating to underlying principles and interrelationships, might not be acquired in a lifetime of ineffectively organized experience. That is why research specifically directed to these points is essential.

If it is decided to treat the item under consideration as autonomous with respect to items derived as parts of the over-all forecast, the forecaster is on his mettle to discover and invent means of solving the problem. He may rely on judgment, expert opinion, analysis of plans or programs, surveys, statistical projections of trends or cycles, relationships to other available variables, and any other devices his imagination may conceive.

If it is decided to rely mainly on the item's relation to other parts of the economy, there are two basic procedures. The first is the percentage-distribution method, which proceeds in terms of the ratio of the specific item to the total or to an appropriate subtotal. The second consists in the application of correlation techniques relating the item to the total or to any appropriate subtotal or even to dissimilar variables that may be considered significant for indicating its probable behavior. The latter is the more flexible, both because it facilitates taking diverse influences into account and because it more readily permits analysis in terms of leads and lags or other adjustments in time phasing.

These basic methods may be applied in either of two ways: To the commodity or industry as a whole or to separate parts or components of the whole which are subject to different patterns of behavior. This implies a basic fourfold classification of methods, but various combinations and modifications are possible, so that there is practically unlimited room for ingenuity in devising the best solution.

In a real sense, the process of determining the best approach is the working out of the forecasting method to be used. By the time all the promising alternatives have been explored, it is usually clear what can be done. The result may be a compromise embodying features of several methods. Many professional forecasters recommend the use of multiple methods on the ground that they not only check each other but also keep a variety of significant considerations constantly in view. There can be no objection to this, provided it does not reduce the process to a mechanical routine. The really important point is that making forecasts in new circumstances, like determining the forecasting method itself, is a process of solving research problems. It can work well only when each new problem is approached without preconceptions, to develop the implications of what is new in relation to what has already been established.

AUTONOMOUS ELEMENTS IN COMMODITY FORECASTING

Industry and commodity problems are similar in that the main requirement is to estimate future output and sales. The specific orientation, however, is usually different, since the important sources of variation and the elements subject to control tend to differ widely. In commodity problems, like those involving agricultural commodities traded on organized exchanges, interest tends to center on prices, because prices are highly variable, and the physical volume is regarded as inelastic, a known quantity, or a variable of interest mainly because of its effect on the price at which the given supplies will be sold. In most industry problems, especially durable-goods and other industries in which administered prices prevail, attention is focused on market demand; prices and margins are more closely controlled, so that the variable element which determines operations and profit is the physical volume that can be sold. There are numerous exceptions to this statement, of course, since there are wide ranges of output variability and price flexibility in industry as well as in nonindustrial commodities, but it is convenient to distinguish the typical situations in this way.

In both commodity and industry forecasting, the physical volume of production is important. In the former, the quantity produced has an important influence on price and total sales value; in the latter, with price relatively constant, the market determines the quantity purchased. The characteristic behavior of quantity produced thus provides a primary distinction between commodity and industry problems. In the former, quantity is determined by influences largely independent of the current state of business. In the latter, quantity is basically determined by business activity and fluctuates with it through the various stages of the business cycle. It is largely in problems concerning the former, commodities whose supply is independently determined, that autonomous or exogenous elements become of critical importance for the forecaster. Whether or not a commodity falls in this class is, of course, one of the first points to be decided.

It may not be easy to determine the degree of independence to be assigned in any given case. A simple comparison of its movements with those of the broader economic aggregates is not enough. Many relationships are complex, with a variety of forces affecting the dependent variable. For limited periods of time the effects of such forces may be offsetting, indicating an apparent lack of response to any of them; then in another period they may be reinforcing, with results that appear to be astounding as well as inexplicable. Some of the interactions of income and stock in use are of this character; the fact that construction may be stable in a boom period, while income is still rising, does not mean that it is independent of income, but merely that something else has to be considered. The hidden influences must be sought out and analyzed along with these that are apparent from the outset.

Very often it is necessary to rely on a priori reasoning as a basis for the decision. There are a number of items that by their very nature or origin belong in the autonomous category. These are largely associated with government programs, technological changes, demographic factors, and social or religious movements. A firm making military aircraft, for example, would have to consider the international situation and the progress of appropriations for plane procurement in making an appraisal of industry prospects, and it might be justified in ignoring everything of direct importance to most other lines of business. Items of this kind comprise a group apart, one that obviously requires special treatment.

Another type of problem requiring a substantial degree of autonomous treatment concerns items which have a very low sensitivity to income changes. Among the extreme cases are water, electricity, and gas. Demand for these depends upon the number of consuming units—persons, homes, or appliances. In actual practice, the forecasting problem is usually one of community development. It is thus twice-removed from the usual relationship to income—once because the number of consuming units does not vary with income and again because the progress of the community does not necessarily correspond with that of the whole economy.

Utility companies and others interested in the development of a community commonly deal with these problems by projection of trends. The trend may be fitted directly to the item itself, or it may be fitted to related variables for the community, such as population, number of homes wired for electricity, or number of major appliances installed.[1] Very often much the same results are obtained by either the direct or the indirect method, though a good analysis of the components (assuming information to be available) is generally to be preferred. Any special information, such as announced plans for new building or for abandonment of an existing plant, can, of course, be used to modify the trend.

It should be recognized that whenever trends are used reliance is placed on autonomous or unspecified exogenous variables. Time itself is not a variable or a cause of the movements in other variables. It is a means of dividing the flows into segments, thus converting them into quantities higher or lower than those previously observed. There are no economic forces that display the same regularity as time intervals. If the changes show a stable pattern, the regularity observed may be projected, but there can never be any guarantee that its promise will be fulfilled.

The danger in projecting trends lies in the possibility of shifts in the factors producing them. A component may grow at an accelerating rate right up to the point of saturation and then flatten abruptly. For example, the number of wired homes may increase very rapidly up to the point where all are wired, and then it can continue to grow only with the construction of new homes. Or installation of television sets may be very rapid up to the point where almost every family has one and then cease. The impact of such changes tends to be softened by the fact that a slower rate of growth in one item may be compensated by a more rapid growth in another. But during periods of general business decline, many items tend to be retarded at the same time. It is therefore wise to consider whether the trend observed in the current data can be expected to continue indefinitely or whether the point at which it might come up against a ceiling can be anticipated.

Where the records of experience are insufficient to permit statistical analysis, the only possible basis for a forecast may lie in a survey or in such considerations as the nature of the product, its performance characteristics as compared with competing products, its advantages in terms of cost, the magnitude of the total market, and the extent to which the market is already preempted by competing products. Before any record

[1] For an illustration, see G. Clark Thompson, *Forecasting Sales*, National Industrial Conference Board, Studies in Business Policy, no. 25, New York, 1947, p. 21.

of experience has been built up, knowledge of uses, specifications, design, style, and price provides the only clues available. Reliance on such clues cannot be complete, since something may be overlooked, or some unpredictable change may occur to upset entirely reasonable expectations. The failure of the FM radio to displace AM shows the inability of a superior product to contend with the resistance of a well-established rival with which the public is generally satisfied. Nevertheless, the introduction of a new product usually depends upon precisely the kind of considerations that failed to provide success in this instance.

One of the most important fields in which treatment in substantial independence of the general economy is justified is that of new products and "growth" industries. The latter are industries in which a succession of new products or continual expansion of existing products into new uses makes for a high rate of expansion relative to industry in general. In many cases, the growth elements are decisive enough, at least for a time, to prevent any decline during a period of general recession in incomes and employment. Rayon deliveries, for example, maintained a fairly steady uptrend through the great decline from 1929 to 1933. The chemical industry, in which research discoveries continually open new vistas of development, is more commonly cited as the prime illustration of the growth principle.

There are two situations in which the growth of a new product is assured, provided only that it can gain market acceptance. The first is an entirely new product of wide usefulness; the air conditioner is commonly cited as an example. The second is a superior product that can displace an inferior competitor which is already in wide use, as the electric refrigerator displaced the icebox. To clear up the uncertainties of market acceptance, firms commonly use either or both of two alternatives: They make consumer surveys, or they introduce the product on a small scale in some limited local market. If these indicate probable success, they go into mass production.

A very limited record of experience may combine with a priori considerations to provide the basis for a projection that need take little account of over-all business prospects. In the early stages of growth, progress of a commodity that has a practically unlimited market ahead of it may be self-governed to such a degree that its own pattern of development affords the best basis for a forecast. Fitting a trend, perhaps an accelerating curve, may then give the best results. Such a procedure, with minor adjustments from time to time, would have given good results in the case of rayon right into the post–World War II period (see Chart 15–1).

Later, as the product approaches market maturity, the upward trend tends to level out, and then the cyclical factors may become of dominant importance. Such a shift must always be looked for when trend projections have been kept in use for an extended period of years. The break may seem to come completely without warning. Unless the change in competitive relations is anticipated, the forecaster may suddenly find himself in a serious error. Again, the rayon chart (Chart 15–1) illustrates the point with the breakaway in 1951.

The growth curves of new products vary greatly, depending on how rapidly production can be built up, how large the ultimate market will be, and how successful various kinds of competing products, including

Chart 15–1. Domestic Rayon-Acetate Shipments

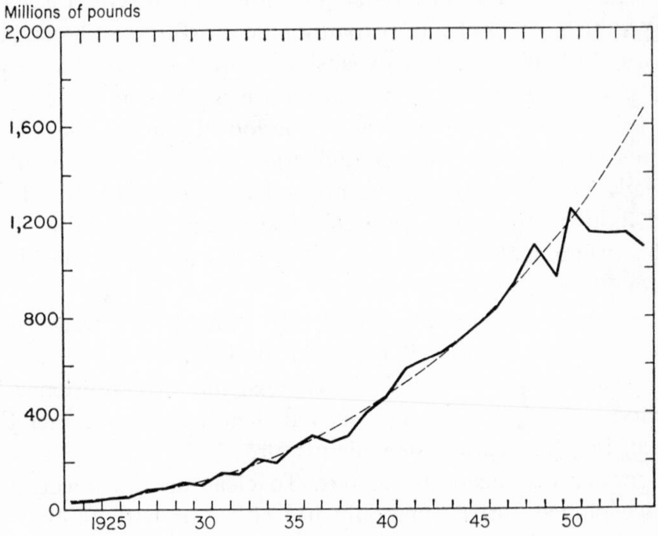

SOURCE OF DATA: Textile Organon, Textile Economics Bureau, Inc., New York.

other new products, will be in establishing shares of the market. Sometimes growth continues over a period of many years. In the case of automobiles, it continued half a century, being maintained in part by changes in the community commonly described as the "trend toward suburban living." On the other hand, full growth may be accomplished in a year or so. In the case of a new drug, it may capture its share of the market in a matter of months. Some of the antibiotics enjoyed only a brief soaring to popularity and then were thrust back into a comparatively minor position; they may have a permanent place in medicine, but nothing like what was expected in the first flush of enthusiasm. Until a record of experience has been built up, projecting a suitable trend may be largely a matter of judgment, and every effort should be made to rule out bias.

What usually happens in the case of a new product is that it is introduced at a relatively high price. At that price, it may prove superior to other products in certain limited uses only. As facilities are increased and efficiency improved, the price is gradually brought down. Then it is substituted in other uses, and its market grows to match the expansion in output. The extent of substitution thus depends upon the price at which the producers of the new product are willing to continue expansion of facilities and output. This is a situation in which "inside" knowledge—that is, knowledge of the producer's own plans and policies—can be of great importance in laying out the course of future developments. Such knowledge may indicate not only a general expansion but also the specific uses into which the additional output will flow. If trends are being used, separate trends for various uses may be set up and the total market estimated as a composite for all uses.

The producer's expectations may, of course, prove to be in error. One reason for this is that the competition may take action to retain its position in the market. It, too, may find ways of improving its product or efficiency, and with the prices of competitive products being forced down, the advantage of the new product may for a time be greatly reduced if not altogether eliminated. In the rayon decline of 1951, competitive price changes played a significant part. The great upsurge in rayon in 1947 and 1948 occurred at a time when the price of cotton had risen above the more stable price of rayon. With greatly increased cotton production in 1951, however, the price of cotton fell sharply, and textile producers found that a substantial consumer preference for cotton existed in many uses where rayon had previously been substituted. Although such movements may have little net effect on the economy as a whole, they are of crucial importance to the forecaster in the special field where they are experienced.

If some products may rise at the expense of others, it follows that some products may fall without regard to developments in the economy as a whole. In the declining industry, the loss of markets may be considered as much an autonomous influence as the rise of the competing product, though it is usually better to use the knowledge of the rising competitor in charting the downward course of the displaced product. In the postwar period, purchased transportation declined from the immediate postwar peak, despite rising incomes, as gasoline and autos became generally available, and railroad travel dropped much more sharply as the airlines took over an increasing share of the common-carrier market. Segregating the diverse influences at work in this field was difficult, even though the nature of the forces at work was known and the existing deviations could be estimated. Trends were subject to severe limitations, not only because of the break from prewar experience but also because of the great irregularities that developed in the early postwar years. What looked after several years like "postwar trends" were in fact slow changes in the direction of correcting existing deviations from new "normal" patterns. In this sense, they were temporary in character and not true trends at all. The question still to be answered at the end of a decade was whether the division of market shares between the various forms of transportation had progressed to the point of relative stability. If it had, the income relationships could be expected to take over; if not, the "permanent" components of the "trends" would have to be projected further. The very existence of such "permanent components" represented a point on which judgments might differ.

FORECASTING PRICES OF FARM PRODUCTS

Agricultural commodities constitute another group in which supply is not readily adjusted to variations in income or aggregate demand. Under ordinary conditions, if weather is more or less average, output tends to be much the same from one year to the next. Unusual weather may affect output greatly, sometimes in a most perverse manner. When output runs ahead of demand, excess stocks accumulate and have to be carried over from one year to the next. The total supply which must be taken into account includes the carry-over as well as the new production.

When production of any commodity is running high in relation to demand, there may be no automatic downward adjustment, because farmers whose land and equipment are specialized to a given crop are reluctant to shift to others, unless price differentials become so large as to offset the disadvantages of shifting. Since prices of various commodities tend to move together, as in the broad sweeps of the business cycle, such differentials do not necessarily develop. Furthermore, since no one farm is large enough to affect the market, there is no incentive for any individual farmer to cut back his output.

Demand for farm products also tends to be inflexible. Consumers do not step up their food consumption much when prices fall, and large declines in the farm prices of raw foodstuffs are translated into relatively small changes in retail-food prices as they pass through the various stages of processing and distribution.

Hence a surplus tends to remain a surplus for some time. Once harvested, the crop is there. It must be held by somebody, and the costs of storage are high. Forcing a commodity on the market is a costly policy for farmers. Traders and speculators will take the goods, but only at an extremely low price, so that their risks are minimized.

To alleviate the unfavorable effects of these conditions and promote an adjustment of supply to demand, the government has intervened with price-support and acreage-restriction programs. Under these programs, it assumes responsibility for the redundant supplies. Keeping prices from falling below the levels established by the support programs necessitated a government investment of more than $8 billion in inventories of grain, butter, cheese, cotton, and other designated commodities by the end of 1954.

The acceptance of government intervention and control in this field indicates how little dispute there is about the basic theory of output and price determination for agricultural commodities. To leave complications aside for the moment, this theory, as applied in price forecasting, calls for determining aggregate demand for any commodity or group of commodities from consumer income; forecasting supply independently; and deriving price from the value and quantity estimates. Very often the whole procedure is embodied in a correlation relating income, supply, and price. Such an equation usually shows the inverse relationship of price and quantity as a demand curve, which can be adjusted by means of the income term to different levels of expected consumer income. Then, by use of the independent estimate of the future supply expected to be available, the price corresponding to the anticipated quantity may be read off the curve.

This is the one place in forecasting where the traditional demand curve of the economist comes into its own. A whole series of studies relating to various commodities and widely different periods of time has established the general validity of this relationship.[2] To illustrate, Chart 15–2 shows a sequence of demand curves for meat at three different levels of aggregate demand—"at 70 percent, 100 percent, and 130 percent of its 1935–39 average level. These levels of demand are approximately those which prevailed in 1923, 1932, and 1941, respectively."[3] The author also shows the same results in the form of regressions of price on per capita quantity consumed and price on aggregate demand, with the other independent variable held constant in each case.

To utilize such a demand curve, it is necessary to have forecasts both of disposable income and of the supply available. Further comment will

---

[2] A comprehensive discussion of the approach may be found in Henry Schultz, *Theory and Measurement of Demand*, University of Chicago Press, Chicago, 1938.

[3] Elmer J. Working, *The Demand for Meat*, University of Chicago Press, Chicago, 1954, p. 12. The equation used in deriving these curves is

$$\log P = 3.4148 - 1.2927 \log Q + 0.6477 \log A \qquad (R^2 = .985)$$

where P = index of price
  Q = quantity consumed
  A = demand index; this index is per capita disposable income deflated not by all consumer prices but by the slow-moving components of the consumer price index

not be made on the former at this point. Substantial resources have been and are being devoted to forecasting supplies of agricultural commodities. To place everyone on a comparatively equal footing, the Department of Agriculture carries on extensive forecasting activities and publishes the results at regular intervals. In November of each year, an "outlook conference" is held to discuss prospects for the coming year. As background material for this conference, a chart book entitled *Agricultural Outlook Charts* is prepared. Into these charts and the other material presented at the conference goes the work of a whole corps of commodity experts. Prospects for output, prices, and income to be realized from crops and animal products are appraised in the light of the best information available.[4]

Chart 15–2. Demand Curves for Meat at Different Levels of Demand

Deflated price

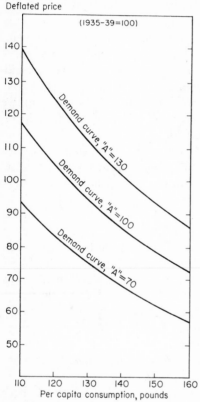

Per capita consumption, pounds

SOURCE: E. J. Working, The Demand for Meat, University of Chicago Press, Chicago, 1954, p. 12. C 1954 by the American Meat Institute.

For many years, the Department of Agriculture has also been making regular forecasts of crop production as a service to those interested in various important commodities.[5] Usually there are three estimates. The first, taken near planting time, is based on a survey of intentions to plant, in terms of acreage, and utilizes such additional information as ground moisture to indicate whether normal yields may be expected. The second, early in the growing season, is a report on acreages planted and attempts to take account of the condition of the crop on the acreage farmers plan to harvest, using such additional information as rainfall during the growing season and damage from storm or insects. The third, near harvest time, is a sort of preliminary

[4] For a brief summary of the Department's methods, see James Cavin, "Forecasting the Demand for Agricultural Products," *Agricultural Economics Research*, vol. 4, July, 1952.

[5] See *The Agricultural Estimating and Reporting Services of the U.S. Department of Agriculture*, Miscellaneous Publication 730, December, 1949.

report on the actual harvest; it is based on returns from a large sample of farmers and embodies estimates of yields as well as of acreage to be harvested. The timing of the forecasts varies, depending upon the conditions under which each commodity is produced.

The forecasts are awaited with great interest by traders, dealers, speculators, and processors, whose profits depend upon the prices at which they buy and sell. When the estimates change substantially from one forecast to the next, they may create a furor in the market, with prices changing drastically overnight. The forecasts are therefore prepared in great secrecy and released simultaneously to the news services and to representatives of other interested organizations.

Collecting and analyzing the necessary reports is a costly operation, which could hardly be undertaken by any but the largest private concerns. Every effort is directed to making the forecasts as accurate as possible, but disconcerting errors sometimes appear even in the final forecast. A few of the large trading organizations make their own forecasts, using analytical techniques of their own and field surveys based on small samples. They try to anticipate both what the official forecast will show and what the crop will actually be in the event that the official forecast is in error. In this way they have a chance to make a double killing—first on the market reaction to the official forecast and again on the rebound to the actual harvest and market. However, it is not easy to exceed the accuracy of the official forecasts. Most analysts rely on the official forecasts, and since most take the state of demand more or less for granted, the market price usually adjusts quickly to the position called for by the indicated supply.

In actual practice, the problem of commodity-price forecasting is much more complex than this simple explanation makes it appear. To do an effective job, it is necessary to know total production; how production compares with probable demand, including exports; the rate at which supplies are flowing to consumers; and the amount that is accumulating as inventory in each of the various stages through which the commodity passes. The results for one commodity often cannot be estimated without taking account of competing products. For example, beef and pork are fairly direct substitutes for each other; the demand for one is partly determined by the supply and price of the other. Moreover, during a general decline in income, potatoes may be temporarily substituted for both. The latter shift should be reflected in the income relationship, but the movements may be irregular, and it is difficult to determine the causes of deviations or errors.

The price-support program also disrupts the normal procedure. The prices of supported commodities cannot fall to the level specified by the demand curve, and the experience in support years cannot be used in deriving or adjusting the curve. Surpluses are not readily eliminated by acreage control, because yields can be increased by keeping the best acres in cultivation and by cultivating them more intensively. The surpluses tend to spread to other commodities as the restricted acres are shifted to other production. Furthermore, if world prices decline while domestic prices are kept up by price supports, the loss of export markets may be severe.

Other countries also undertake programs to deal with their own internal problems, and those programs may have repercussions on world markets of a kind that cannot be explained solely in economic terms. The conditions faced in each country are only partly of an economic character, and the opportunities for profitable exchange with other countries are only partly the basis for undertaking the programs which each country views as offering it a solution. The loss of world markets for American farmers during the 1930s was not originally due to United States price-support programs; rather, those programs were initiated as a reaction to the loss of markets, international as well as domestic. Such far-ranging considerations make it clear that no mechanical approach to commodity forecasting can be entirely satisfactory.

The forecaster who is not specialized in this field may find it difficult to keep abreast of developments because of the great mass of detail involved. One thing he can do is consult the commodity experts at the Department of Agriculture. These men are constantly engaged in making estimates of future supplies and expected disappearance into various channels of use, and their estimates are intended for public use. When one inquires about the kind of nonsystematic or exogenous considerations taken into account in their work, the answers indicate that there is little uniformity, that the relevant considerations change with each change in the situation. This is as it should be, and on the whole it appears to be highly advantageous, though perhaps it tends to lead to thinking in fashions, with some overemphasis on the considerations related to the moment's most pressing policy issues.

Forecasts of imported commodities, farm and nonfarm, must take account of conditions in the producing countries as well as in other consuming areas. No attempt will be made here to classify solutions for these problems. Each must take account of what is relevant for it. Some, such as coffee, are not unlike domestic foodstuffs. Others are classified as strategic materials and are strongly affected by military production and stockpiling programs. Most industrial materials, like rubber and the nonferrous metals, have multiple facets that must be analyzed and defined. A forecast of any of the important industrial materials can hardly be realistic except in terms of its relation to total economic activity or to some important segments which in turn derive from broader measures of general activity. Yet the relationship to activity alone may leave so much out of account that on occasion it will be as unrealistic as the forecast which ignores the relationship. How heavily the one kind of consideration should be weighted in relation to the other is a question that has to be left to the forecaster's judgment of the complete position of the commodity as revealed by the best statistics he is able to compile.

In addition to these various commodities, which display so much autonomy in behavior, there are many industry forecasting problems of a very short-term character which demand *ad hoc* treatment. Forecasts of a month or of several months depend upon what is going on currently plus knowledge of any special influences that may be important just ahead, if only temporarily.

The question may be asked: "Will next month's output be larger or smaller than this month's?" The times when this question could be answered by any complex forecasting procedure are practically negligible. The times when a satisfactory answer can be found in special considerations relating to either the current level or the immediate prospects may be a fairly high proportion of all such comparisons: A strike that has depressed the current month's output may have just been settled; bad weather may have had similarly distorting effects; slow deliveries of materials may threaten next month's output; or an expanded government program may have been announced. There are any number of special bits of information that may be used to modify the pattern of change indicated by current and recent operations. Whether this sort of thing should be called forecasting at all is a question, but much that passes under the name is no more profound.

INDUSTRIES IN RELATION TO THE TOTAL

Most commodities and industries show a high degree of related variation during the swings of the business cycle. Farm commodities *in toto* are more nearly dominated by cyclical movements than are particular farm commodities, because the uncontrolled variation in production of particular commodities tends to average out in farm production as a whole. Specific nonfarm products also show the influence of a variety of forces, but total activity is usually so important among those forces that it provides a good starting point for the analysis. Movements of some nonfarm commodities, such as operating supplies, are controlled almost completely by the pace of industrial operations or by consumer income. Hence the forecaster who has already worked out a satisfactory forecast for the general economy can apply it in numerous industry problems to advantage.

Here again the procedure followed must be adapted to the circumstances. Sometimes it is best to proceed by stages from the over-all forecast to the detailed segments. Sometimes the latter may be approached directly, by methods similar to those used in deriving the larger total of which it is a part. Or, assuming that the forecaster has separately analyzed a number of important segments, the best procedure may be to consider the specific industry in relation to one or more of the subsidiary parts of the total already derived. The various procedures may be classified in the following major types, which in practice are multiplied in number by variants and combinations.

1. **Percentage-distribution Method.** The simplest procedure is to compute the ratio of the specific item to a broad total of which it is a part and to assume that the same ratio, or percentage, will hold in the forecast period. Thus, savings may be taken as a percentage of disposable income; a specific kind of expenditure may be taken as a percentage of disposable income, or of total expenditures; or a certain kind of food, like canned fruits and vegetables, may be taken as a percentage of all food expenditures. If the item is 5 percent in the base period, it is assumed to be 5 percent in the future. When the procedure is broadened to include percentages for all portions of the total or subtotal used as the base of the computation, the entire pattern of the distribution of subsidiary items may be analyzed. If appropriate, adjustments may be made in some of the items, and in the total itself, to allow for special distortions known to have occurred in the period from whose data the percentages were computed.

This method has the advantage that it can be used where time series are not available, perhaps on the basis of a single observation. There is a danger in this, of course. If the 5 percent item should actually fall to 4 percent, an error of 25 percent would occur by reason of the percentage change alone; and if the projection of the total should also be over the actual, the error would be further *magnified. The method is primarily suitable, therefore, where the risk of error has to be taken because no better alternative is available or where the item is relatively homogeneous with respect to others in the same grouping and there is no reason to expect a shift in the percentages. It is used more commonly to project the volume of particular firms producing the same item than to project the volume of various commodities or industries in a broad grouping.

The method is sometimes called the *ratio* or *index method*. The ratio of the item to some other known measure—not necessarily a total of items of the same kind—is made the basis of the projection into the future. Or the item may be converted into a kind of index number, and then its movements may be controlled in relation to another index. The same result may be accomplished graphically by adjusting scales of the related series from a given zero line in such a way as to make the charted movements comparable. If the amplitude of variation is not the same, the scales may be further adjusted by shifting the zero line of one series relative to the other, but this in effect is a shift to the correlation approach. To omit this last possibility for the moment, in all these cases it is the ratio of the item to another variable, which can be more readily projected, that governs its movements.

When one is using such a procedure, it is not necessary to hold the percentages or ratios constant if a reasonable basis for modifying them can be found. If data for more than 1 year are available, say for several scattered years, it may be possible to project shifts in the percentages. Even nonquantitative information may be utilized on occasion. If it is known that a particular segment is exceptionally active, or for some reason is growing relative to the total, the percentage may be adjusted accordingly. Any indicator of shifts in the percentage may be used as a guide. Attention must again be called to the dangers involved; such modification of percentages is a tricky business, as seemingly small adjustments in percentages may represent large absolute differences.

Where a complete series of data is available, the percentages are likely to show a distinct cyclical behavior, rising or falling with changes in the total. It is known, for example, that many foods behave in this manner. When income rises, meat consumption increases, partly at the expense of potatoes and other starchy foods. If the percentage varies directly, as in the case of meat, a positive correlation is indicated. If it varies inversely, however, it may indicate only a lack of correlation, since a constant in relation to a changing total will show such behavior. In either case, a shift in approach is indicated, first, to a correlation analysis, and then to exploration of other techniques in the light of what that analysis reveals.

2. **Correlation Methods.** A number of problems arise in setting up a correlation for forecasting use. The most critical by far are two: First, determining the most appropriate independent variables to represent the forces affecting the dependent variable, and, second, setting up the equation in the best form. These key problems have to be solved in large measure by nonquantitative means, that is, by logical analysis of the forces affecting the dependent variable and of the type of relationship involved, rather than by the statistical results themselves. A little better fit to the past data is ordinarily inconsequential in comparison with a more dependable relationship for future use. Often, when the reason for certain past distortions is known, it is best deliberately to miss a good fit in those years. In other words, it is better to get a relationship that can be expected to hold good in general, even though for special reasons it fitted some of the past data poorly, than to get one that fitted well for a given past period but by the lack of a logical relationship cannot necessarily be expected to fit under other conditions.

Other problems, such as the method of fitting the equation and the period of observation to be used in fitting, are usually of secondary importance. The various methods of fitting ordinarily give closely similar results, though there are extreme cases in which this is not true. In judging whether one method of fitting or another is best, the statistical tests cannot be considered entirely adequate. Ultimately the pragmatic test will apply, and whatever method of fitting is used, the results should be analyzed in this light. If the analysis reveals a "best" fit, the relationship may be adjusted to the indicated form. Changing the period of observation, as by excluding certain years, is one way of making such an adjustment. Other ways—seemingly more "arbitrary" but based on a broader range of considerations—may be fully justified. The forecaster has to maintain flexibility in applying the relationship in future situations, and he may validly exercise the same flexibility in working it out.

At various points in previous chapters, correlations have been presented to illustrate or demonstrate propositions relating to the behavior of economic variables, and these may be regarded as examples of the use of the method. Several additional examples will be taken up here, together with a few summary comments and generalizations relating to its application to industry problems.

The use of the correlation technique in breaking down total expenditures is illustrated by the Department of Commerce studies of consumption expenditures and retail trade discussed in Chapter 12. The assumption made there is that a form of relationship similar to that suitable for estimating over-all expenditures or sales may appropriately be applied to the individual parts of the total for which data are available. The essence of the approach is to correlate everything with income. Since some items are sensitive and others are insensitive to income changes, the ratio of any one to income or to total expenditures may change considerably in the course of the business cycle. Such shifts are built into the method, in contrast to the percentage-distribution method, where they have to be introduced as a special supplementary feature.

In the analysis of the various expenditure items, it was apparent that many of them displayed movements which could not be accounted for by income alone. It is important, therefore, to determine more specifically the other variable or variables which are appropriate and this is something that has to be specially decided each time.

An illustration of how decisive a particular set of variables may be is provided by the analysis of the furniture market reported in *Markets after the Defense Expansion*.[6] Chart 15–3 shows the actual and calculated

[6] U.S. Department of Commerce, 1952, p. 56. This summary was based on an earlier analysis by Walter Jacobs and Clement Winston, "The Postwar Furniture Market and the Factors Determining Demand," *Survey of Current Business*, May, 1950.

values of deflated furniture expenditures from 1923 to 1952. The independent variables used in this formulation were real disposable income, residential construction, and the ratio of furniture prices to consumer prices in general.[7] In the analysis, alternative relationships were tested, using current instead of constant dollars, aggregates instead of per-household expenditures, and linear instead of logarithmic regressions. Correlations were very high in all cases for the period used in fitting (1923 to 1940). The linear regression yielded higher calculated

Chart 15–3. Consumer Expenditures for Furniture

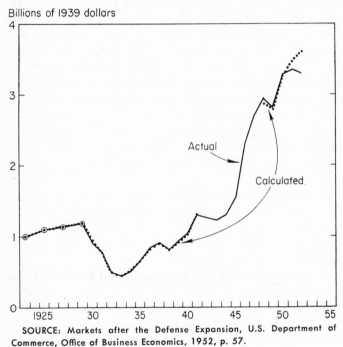

Billions of 1939 dollars

SOURCE: Markets after the Defense Expansion, U.S. Department of Commerce, Office of Business Economics, 1952, p. 57.

values for the war years, and the regressions of aggregates rather than per household data gave somewhat higher values in the postwar years. In other words, there was a high degree of consistency in results despite changes in the units of measurement and in the form of equation.

[7] The equation on which the calculated expenditures are based is

$$Y = 0.0002 X_1^{1.469} X_2^{0.137} X_3^{-0.948} \qquad (R = .99)$$

where Y = expenditures for furniture, 1939 dollars per household
  X_1 = disposable personal income, 1939 dollars per household
  X_2 = new private residential construction, 1939 dollars per household
  X_3 = ratio of furniture prices to prices of all consumer goods and services

That such consistency of results was obtained in this instance does not mean that the problems of equation form and measurement units can be ignored. It was partly due in this case to intercorrelations among the independent variables, with differences in sign producing offsetting movements in their partial contributions. Ordinarily, the shift from linear to logarithmic form alone could be expected to make an important difference when projecting expenditures to a level over three times as high as the average in the base period. Just how much difference such a shift in form of regression will make can be determined only by trying out the various alternatives, as was done in this instance.

A questionable feature of this correlation from a forecasting view is the inclusion of furniture prices as an independent variable. This variable was included primarily on theoretical grounds. It contributes little to the correlation and could be omitted with little loss in goodness of fit. To make a valid contribution, the price variable should correctly reflect the prices actually charged consumers and not nominal or list prices. Even then, an objection to including the price variable in a correlation of this kind is that it creates an additional forecasting problem, one that may be very difficult to solve. Hence, unless a highly satisfactory basis for forecasting furniture prices is available—apart from the demand for furniture itself—the validity of the correlation as a forecasting device is reduced.

Another correlation reported in the same volume concerns new-automobile purchases. It is shown in the central portion of Chart 15–4.[8] Since this relationship employs a similar price variable, the same objection holds; it might be added in this case that the price index used is not a very reliable indicator of actual prices.

The forecasting problem is further complicated by the inclusion in this correlation of a rather vague variable—scrappage age—which even on the past data represents no more than a series of rough estimates. Moreover, there is no real basis for making a projection of this factor. One kind of relevant consideration is shown in the lowest section of the chart—the age distribution of cars—but this provides only a very indefinite kind of clue. Forecasting scrappage is a complicated and difficult affair, involving such variables as the quality of cars on the road, the

---

[8] The equation on which the calculated new car registrations are based is

$$Y = 0.3239X_1^{2.536}X_2^{2.291}X_3^{-1.359}0.932^{X_4} \qquad (R = .98)$$

where Y = new private passenger car registrations per household
X_1 = disposable personal income, 1939 dollars per household
X_2 = ratio of current to preceding year's real income per household
X_3 = ratio of average retail price of cars to consumer prices
X_4 = average scrappage age

Chart 15–4. The Automobile Market

The TOTAL number of passenger cars is nearly in line with income and population

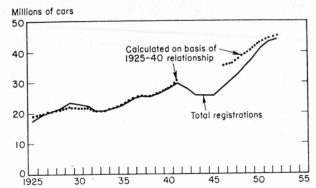

NEW passenger car buying is now roughly consistent with prewar relationship

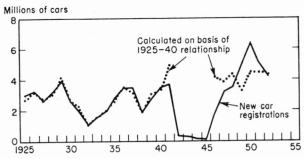

The proportion of OVER-AGE cars in use is about the same as in 1941, although the number is now 2 million higher

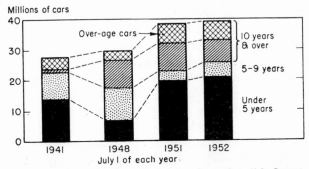

SOURCE: Markets after the Defense Expansion, U.S. Department of Commerce, Office of Business Economics, 1952, p. 55. See also the earlier study by J. L. Atkinson, "The Demand for Consumers' Durable Goods," Survey of Current Business, June, 1950.

price structure for used cars, and the cost of repairs.[9] Certain broad tendencies or trends may be described, but these may be of little help over the short term. About all the inclusion of this factor does is substitute a judgment for a time trend.

Correlations based on income alone have the deficiency that they do not allow for market-saturation effects. In practically all problems relating to durable goods, stocks of such goods in use are an important consideration. Correlations with income in a cyclical situation give a level of durable-goods purchases that could not be maintained through an indefinite period of prosperity. The growth of stocks toward the point of market saturation places a restraint on new production.

One way of approaching this problem is referred to as the *target-stock method*, which is illustrated in the upper section of Chart 15–4. This chart indicates that the desired stock of cars in use may be calculated from two factors: The number of households and disposable income. Alternative target levels could have been based on employment or on adult population adjusted for a percentage of the unemployed with very similar results. The implication of such a target is that, when it is approached, the rate of accumulating stocks must be cut, with the consequence that the new production drops back toward the replacement rate. The target may temporarily be surpassed rather than just approached, but that merely implies a still more drastic letdown later.

One consequence of this target-stock relationship is that purchases run above the income relationship on the upswing and drop below it on the decline. The relationship utilized in the middle section of Chart 15–4 attempts to account for this effect in terms of the change in income: When income is rising, an increment of purchases is added; when it is falling, a corresponding number is subtracted. This is a fairly satisfactory expedient for dealing with this problem, as indicated by the results obtained. It does not in itself, however, indicate the contribution of market saturation toward a downturn, and it is therefore appropriately supplemented by the target analysis.

The method of using lagged variables is useful in a variety of situations. Some of them involve true lags, such as the lag of construction activity behind contract awards or the lag of installation of electric generating equipment behind the placing of orders with the manufacturer. Others merely depend upon characteristics in the timing of movements of different variables when stimulated by common causes, such as the rapid rise in prices as compared with wages or the quick response of profits as compared with outlays for new plant and equipment. Unfor-

[9] For a discussion of this problem, see George P. Hitchings, "Automotive Transportation," in Herbert V. Prochnow (ed.), *Determining the Business Outlook*, Harper & Brothers, New York, 1954.

tunately the situations in which lags can be depended upon are relatively rare.

Some variables display a very high degree of continuity or serial correlation, and in these cases the previous observation may be included as an independent variable. An alternative commonly used is to set up the relationship in terms of year-to-year changes, so that change rather than the absolute quantity is estimated as the dependent variable. In this case the previous change may sometimes be included in the relationship as an independent variable. The danger in such methods is the likelihood that the estimates will overcarry at the turns, with the result that very bad forecasts may be obtained in the most critical situations. A few bad forecasts on such occasions will often discredit a forecasting method despite a whole series of successes at other times.

3. The Component Method. Demand for many products may be regarded as consisting of a number of parts or components which exhibit important differences in behavior. Tire output, for example, may be regarded as being made up of a new-equipment component and a replacement component. Since each new car is ordinarily equipped with five tires, the former may be estimated at five times the number of cars produced. Since each car wears out a set of tires in several years of driving, the latter may be estimated in relation to the number of cars in use, allowing for some lag. The movements of the two are at times quite dissimilar. In any such analysis, all the parts are projected separately, usually by ratios to the controlling end uses into which the product goes, and then they may be combined into the total demand for the industry.

When the components are estimated by the ratio or percentage-distribution method, the advantages and disadvantages of that method by and large carry over into the more detailed computation by parts. A long historical record is not essential. On the other hand, the ratios do not remain constant but change with technology and with the level of activity.

However, the component method does tend to minimize errors from changing ratios. Variations in the over-all ratio for the industry are partly due to changes in "product mix," that is, changes in the composition of the total as between its various parts or components. Thus shifts in the importance of the parts could make for significant changes in the over-all ratio, even though the ratios for all the components remained constant. Returning to tires for an illustration, the new-equipment component varies widely in the course of a cycle because car production varies, but the replacement component remains relatively stable. In other words, the component method does eliminate one possible source of error. By substituting a weighted average of ratios, with changing weights, for a constant ratio, it introduces variation that is likely to be in the right direction. Even when correlation procedures are used, this separate weighting of the components may make an important difference.

Many industry problems can be dealt with by means of relatively simple applications of the component method. Great detail is not necessary, because subsidiary items with similar behavior characteristics may be grouped together. The industry ordinarily knows a good deal about the final uses to which its products and its customers' products are put. If a few major uses or final demands are analyzed, the bulk of the problem is solved, provided only that a direct statistical relationship can be set up to measure the output which will be demanded in each of those uses. If there are small, residual uses that cannot be classified, errors in them probably will not affect the total result greatly, and the unclassified uses may often be estimated *in toto* by any of several expedients.

The component method is not confined to industrial products and their uses. Population, for example, might be broken into component parts by relevant characteristics, such as age, sex, or race, and the parts analyzed separately; or income might be broken into parts by size or by occupation of recipient, as a basis for making a detailed projection of components that behave in different ways.

The method may be applied to changes as well as to absolute quantities. If the change in the total is made up of a set of subsidiary changes —related to different parts of the total or to different causes or origins— a separate type of analysis for each component of the change may be desirable. A great deal of flexibility may be introduced into the analysis in this way.

In the industry problem as such, there is no need to depend upon the ratio method in estimating the components. Correlation methods may be used instead, or a combination of both may give the best results. To recall the tire illustration for further consideration, the new-equipment component may be directly estimated from new-car production, but the replacement component is known to depend not only on the number of cars in use but also on the average miles of travel per car and on the substitution of retreads for new tires. Both distance traveled and preference for new tires to some extent depend upon income. The income effect on average travel may well be of relatively greater importance in the future, after the automobile captures its peak share of the total transportation market. Hence, although the ratio method is appropriate for the new-equipment component of tire demand, a correlation method is better for the replacement component.[10]

Even if the ratio method is consistently applied, it is not necessary to assume that the ratios remain constant. Chart 15–5 illustrates the var-

[10] For an alternative approach to this problem, see Thompson, *op. cit.*, pp. 23–26.

iable-ratio method as applied to bituminous coal. Each of the first five sections of this chart shows a curve fitted to the ratio of coal consumption in one of its major uses to a measure of activity in the indicated use. In fitting it was assumed that the indicated trends were temporarily interrupted by the war, and the war years 1942 to 1945 were therefore deleted from all consideration, as if they had never occurred. The final panel of the chart shows the combined estimates of over-all coal consumption in comparison with the actual.

There are clearly arbitrary elements in the fitting procedures used in this study. However, the trend lines used are essentially the kind called for by developments known to be affecting the various components. Electric utilities and the steel industry have become increasingly efficient in the use of coal. Diesel locomotives have replaced steam locomotives. Oil and gas have been replacing coal in home heating. These are continuing trends, deriving from technical changes and dependent upon the installation of new equipment. During the war, when production of the necessary equipment was restricted, the trends were interrupted. The general character of the changes in the ratios over the period as a whole can hardly be questioned.

To obtain an estimate of total coal demand by this method, it is necessary to forecast all five of the independent variables. The results shown in the final panel of the chart are based on the assumption that they could have been forecast perfectly. However, even substituting calculated values of the controlling variables for the actual data gives good estimates of coal consumption. Methods of forecasting some of them have already been described; others will be discussed in following sections.

The analysis of components is not confined to estimating total demand for a product. It may also be applied in determining the quantities of materials and other resources required to produce any commodity. Each unit must be made of so much steel, glass, fabric, and so forth. Then the total requirements for each material may be calculated by multiplying the unit requirements by the number of units to be produced. This is usually referred to as the *bill of materials method.* It has been used in programing military procurement and in scheduling production of industrial products to ensure that all necessary materials and parts will be available when needed.

INPUT-OUTPUT ANALYSIS

The requirement of one industry is, of course, the demand component of the industry from which it procures needed supplies. It is another case of "for every seller a buyer." If the process of segregating such com-

Chart 15–5. Ratios of Bituminous-coal Consumption in Major Uses to Output or Consuming Units

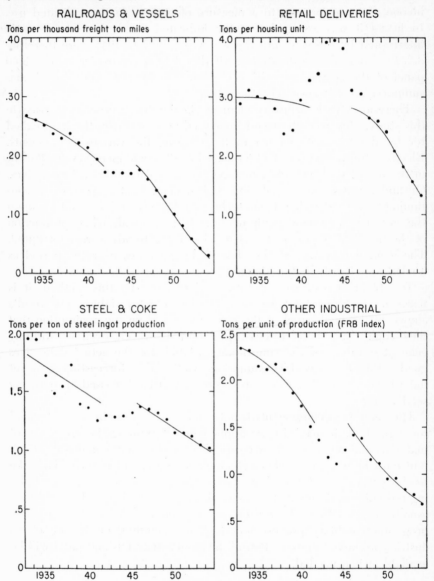

ponents two ways—by producing industry and by consuming industry—is generalized for all industries, the result is an input-output matrix, that is, a large square tabulation of items, each of which represents both the output of one industry and the input of another.

Such a matrix is shown in Table 15–1, with omissions to condense the original sufficiently to fit the page. It is a statement of "Inter-Industry Relations in 1947," prepared by the Bureau of Labor Statistics. This is a minimum matrix; much more detail would generally be needed for analytical purposes. As released by the Bureau, this basic table is supplemented by two others: One shows direct purchases from each pro-

Chart 15–5. (Cont'd) Bituminous-coal Consumption

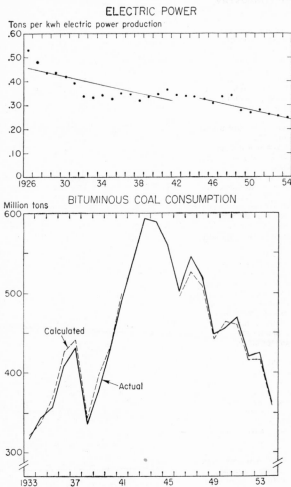

ducing industry per million dollars of output of each purchasing industry; the other shows direct and indirect requirements from each purchasing industry per million dollars of deliveries to final demand by each producing industry. The tables are based primarily on the Census of Manufactures, but various other source materials are incorporated in them, in-

Table 15–1.   Interindustry Relations, 1947†

PRODUCING INDUSTRY	1 AGRICULTURE & FISHERIES	2 FOOD & KINDRED PRODUCTS	3 TOBACCO MANUFACTURES	4 TEXTILE MILL PRODUCTS	5 APPAREL	6 LUMBER & WOOD PRODUCTS	7 FURNITURE & FIXTURES	8 PAPER & ALLIED PRODUCTS	9 PRINTING & PUBLISHING	10 CHEMICALS	11 PRODUCTS OF PETROLEUM & COAL
1 AGRICULTURE & FISHERIES	10,856	15,048	783	2,079	19	192	–	9	–	1,211	
2 FOOD & KINDRED PRODUCTS	2,378	4,910	15	60	9	*	*	30	*	685	
3 TOBACCO MANUFACTURES	–	–	828	–	–	–	–	–	–	1	
4 TEXTILE MILL PRODUCTS	64	2	–	1,303	3,882	3	285	43	25	13	
5 APPAREL	44	204	–	–	1,963	–	5	20	–	30	
6 LUMBER & WOOD PRODUCTS	148	81	18	18	2	1,094	385	267	1	45	
7 FURNITURE & FIXTURES	–	–	–	–	12	–	–	7	5	–	
8 PAPER & ALLIED PRODUCTS	2	453	65	78	25	5	15	2,597	1,081	331	
9 PRINTING & PUBLISHING	–	39	–	2	–	–	–	–	767	16	
10 CHEMICALS	830	1,451	25	800	142	26	63	183	97	2,655	
11 PRODUCTS OF PETROLEUM & COAL	457	58	*	30	5	74	1	63	3	325	
12 RUBBER PRODUCTS	122	9	–	13	18	9	6	9	3	1	
13 LEATHER & LEATHER PRODUCTS	–	–	–	2	53	4	7	–	4	–	
14 STONE, CLAY & GLASS PRODUCTS	65	253	1	1	*	14	34	28	–	258	
15 IRON & STEEL	6	2	–	–	1	10	97	–	–	5	
16 NONFERROUS METALS	–	–	–	–	–	2	16	–	14	189	
17 PLUMBING & HEATING SUPPLIES	–	–	–	–	–	–	–	–	–	–	
18 FABRICATED STRUCTURAL METAL PRODUCTS	–	–	–	–	–	–	5	–	–	–	
19 OTHER FABRICATED METAL PRODUCTS	83	543	15	*	6	35	132	17	1	130	
20 AGRIC'L, MINING & CONST. MACHINERY	59	–	–	–	–	–	–	–	–	–	
21 METALWORKING MACHINERY	–	–	–	–	–	–	–	–	–	–	
22 OTHER MACHINERY (except electric)	–	13	–	35	21	14	11	14	35	1	
23 MOTORS & GENERATORS	–	–	–	–	–	–	–	–	–	–	
24 RADIOS	–	–	–	–	–	–	–	–	–	–	
25 OTHER ELECTRICAL MACHINERY	–	–	–	–	–	–	–	–	–	1	
26 MOTOR VEHICLES	111	3	–	–	–	1	–	–	–	–	
27 OTHER TRANSPORTATION EQUIPMENT	10	–	–	–	–	–	–	*	–	1	
28 PROFESSIONAL & SCIENTIFIC EQUIPMENT	–	–	–	–	–	–	2	6	32	13	
29 MISCELLANEOUS MANUFACTURING	4	11	–	4	256	1	16	15	–	29	
30 COAL, GAS & ELECTRIC POWER	61	193	4	105	36	24	18	123	29	186	
31 RAILROAD TRANSPORTATION	440	548	21	94	60	143	54	224	68	287	
32 OCEAN TRANSPORTATION	73	126	3	13	11	9	*	16	*	44	
33 OTHER TRANSPORTATION	553	367	16	79	25	138	40	117	25	95	
34 TRADE	1,360	418	38	228	369	60	60	176	31	173	
35 COMMUNICATIONS	2	41	1	9	19	10	6	8	39	23	
36 FINANCE & INSURANCE	238	145	1	20	24	77	18	18	23	18	
37 RENTAL	2,393	91	2	25	96	19	17	26	61	34	
38 BUSINESS SERVICES	8	533	98	71	97	19	57	22	58	424	
39 PERSONAL & REPAIR SERVICES	368	119	*	3	3	42	4	4	20	11	
40 MEDICAL, EDUC. & NONPROFIT ORG'S	–	–	–	–	–	–	–	–	–	–	
41 AMUSEMENTS	–	–	–	–	–	–	–	–	–	–	
42 SCRAP & MISCELLANEOUS INDUSTRIES	–	–	–	24	–	–	–	250	–	110	
43 UNDISTRIBUTED	–	2,059	132	438	1,310	880	329	201	610	1,740	
44 EATING & DRINKING PLACES	–	–	–	–	–	–	–	–	2	–	
45 NEW CONSTRUCTION & MAINTENANCE	199	*117	1	39	16	12	7	42	15	36	
46 INVENTORY CHANGE (depletions)	2,660	402	1	120	185	*	14	87	26	140	
47 FOREIGN COUNTRIES (imports from)	690	2,001	104	208	279	183	6	621	8	594	
48 GOVERNMENT	813	1,134	104	639	376	338	112	497	335	762	
49 GROSS PRIVATE CAPITAL FORMATION	DEPRECIATION AND OTHER CAPITAL CONSUMPTION ALLOWANCES										
50 HOUSEHOLDS	19,166	6,262	387	3,286	4,013	2,564	1,063	2,161	3,034	3,431	
TOTAL GROSS OUTLAYS	44,263	37,636	2,663	9,838	13,321	6,002	2,892	7,899	6,447	14,050	

† Each row shows distribution of output of producing industry named at left. Each column shows input distribution for purchasing industry named at top. All figures in millions of dollars. Asterisk denotes entry of less than $0.5 million.

544

Column headings (diagonal labels, left to right):

38 TRADE · 39 COMMUNICATIONS · 40 FINANCE & INSURANCE · 41 RENTAL · 42 BUSINESS SERVICES · 43 PERSONAL & REPAIR SERVICES · 44 MEDICAL, EDUC. & NONPROFIT ORG'S · 45 AMUSEMENTS · 46 SCRAP & MISCELLANEOUS INDUSTRIES · 47 UNDISTRIBUTED · 48 EATING & DRINKING PLACES · 49 NEW CONSTRUCTION & MAINTENANCE · 50 INVENTORY CHANGE (additions) · FOREIGN COUNTRIES (exports to) · GOVERNMENT · GROSS PRIVATE CAPITAL FORMATION · HOUSEHOLDS · TOTAL GROSS OUTPUT

38	39	40	41	42	43	44	45	46	47	48	49	50	Foreign countries (exports to)	Government	Gross private capital formation	Households	Total final demand	Total gross output
8	-	2	-	-	-	-	116	-	-	250	865	92	1,008	1,276	569	21	9,785	44,263
34	71	9	-	-	-	2	251	*	9	134	3,469	2	608	1,528	728	-	22,141	37,636
*	-	-	-	-	-	-	-	-	7	45	-	-	77	217	3	-	1,485	2,663
7	27	*	-	-	*	29	4	-	15	580	-	47	61	919	101	21	1,469	9,838
3	15	1	-	-	-	20	16	*	12	150	21	1	214	301	193	1	9,987	13,321
1	28	*	-	135	1	*	1	-	17	444	5	2,330	174	170	14	36	67	6,002
*	-	*	41	78	-	-	4	-	-	199	-	198	78	35	52	569	1,459	2,892
4	568	2	1	-	2	62	26	-	145	836	57	170	44	154	59	-	344	7,899
20	98	33	213	-	2,234	27	173	13	321	585	30	-	*	72	156	89	1,491	6,447
20	73	3	*	-	7	198	222	2	30	1,181	42	635	305	812	186	-	1,964	14,050
448	200	2	15	780	*	57	56	1	8	357	15	617	56	680	177	*	2,437	13,670
130	63	1	7	*	-	71	4	-	5	468	4	56	94	168	21	8	709	2,825
2	2	-	-	-	-	34	6	-	14	283	-	1	108	84	30	17	2,065	3,810
2	37	*	-	-	-	25	6	-	3	363	59	1,741	99	205	17	15	341	4,844
6	-	1	-	-	-	-	-	-	130	719	-	876	57	605	13	-	-	12,338
2	-	*	-	-	-	-	*	-	21	524	2	315	98	167	5	-	19	6,387
-	-	-	-	-	-	-	-	-	7	106	-	878	64	42	7	60	397	1,745
1	-	-	-	-	-	-	-	-	9	248	-	1,564	15	67	4	145	13	2,316
7	59	1	-	-	1	32	6	-	46	1,138	24	652	127	280	38	74	537	6,445
*	-	-	-	-	-	57	*	-	11	261	-	116	105	566	82	1,640	66	3,292
1	-	-	-	-	-	-	-	-	6	264	-	-	17	205	11	734	31	1,833
12	8	-	16	-	-	146	1	-	53	1,717	-	338	288	990	84	3,450	1,080	10,312
4	-	-	-	-	-	3	-	-	10	257	-	3	33	85	11	128	-	1,095
-	3	1	-	-	*	23	-	-	2	74	-	-	56	113	83	296	639	1,692
8	6	49	-	-	5	62	4	-	25	608	-	716	161	244	76	1,331	673	5,723
131	20	*	-	*	-	1,054	*	-	70	671	1	36	401	1,020	151	2,982	3,128	14,265
132	-	-	-	-	-	2	-	-	14	456	-	1	18	324	1,245	1,203	171	4,001
2	-	*	-	-	7	52	176	-	6	229	-	22	32	184	79	260	630	2,119
4	10	*	-	-	149	164	46	53	112	638	21	32	43	187	85	511	1,934	4,756
91	493	10	63	3,016	5	307	163	54	-	23	219	30	27	355	195	-	133	9,205
58	75	5	6	422	27	29	52	2	10	798	253	706	74	590	332	266	2,061	9,952
-	-	-	-	-	-	-	-	-	5	2	-	-	-	1,340	126	-	102	2,292
253	311	3	4	125	29	14	190	2	6	1,102	97	572	38	314	186	103	3,860	9,855
423	202	7	43	747	135	386	292	7	80	808	1,061	2,506	149	987	45	2,336	27,107	41,657
42	326	66	85	62	429	123	66	11	-	83	11	44	-	38	148	-	1,269	3,173
298	1,002	5	1,851	555	22	118	93	26	-	-	72	400	-	135	32	-	6,993	12,814
147	1,961	52	211	208	58	710	402	180	-	-	386	84	-	-	223	804	20,289	28,855
33	1,706	86	143	37	64	121	17	95	-	421	55	134	-	3	38	-	179	5,097
264	1,415	16	113	25	68	559	76	22	30	2,294	228	819	-	-	83	271	7,333	14,301
*	-	-	16	-	-	-	85	-	-	350	-	-	-	-	5,078	-	7,856	13,385
-	-	-	-	-	-	-	7	392	-	14	-	-	-	128	-	-	2,403	2,944
35	386	10	106	34	20	1	1	13	-	12	-	1	-	30	1	-	-	2,233
73	2,320	88	617	547	575	1,303	960	269	-	-	536	-	-	-	-	-	12,075	24,711
11	-	-	-	-	-	-	152	-	-	1,030	-	-	-	-	-	-	13,270	13,270
134	182	178	32	4,084	3	56	342	25	-	-	73	7	-	-	5,464	5,709	154	28,704
-	-	-	-	-	-	-	-	851	-	-	-	-	-	22	-	-	-	4,887
33	-	33	105	-	-	-	3	69	12	-	-	-	-	1,313	-	-	1,325	9,275
766	3,750	344	1,111	3,997	212	503	170	318	74	2,176	1,410	470	73	831	3,458	216	31,308	63,685
- INCLUDED IN HOUSEHOLD ROW -																		
6,205	26,240	2,165	8,015	14,003	1,044	7,951	9,199	1,456	-	1,801	4,254	11,492	-	847	30,058	218	2,116	220,474
9,855	41,657	3,173	12,814	28,855	5,097	14,301	13,385	2,944	2,233	24,711	13,270	28,704	4,802	17,320	51,060	33,514	191,625	769,248

SOURCE: U.S. Bureau of Labor Statistics, Division of Interindustry Economics.

545

cluding the results of field studies specially conducted for this purpose. They portray the operations of the economy in 1947, and to the extent that results in that year were abnormal or otherwise unique, they cannot be considered representative of operations in other years.

Among purchasers of the products of various industries are final users, such as consumers and government. Their purchases are the expenditures that go into the make-up of gross national product. Table 15–1 thus shows, in the columns headed "Final demand," what is in effect a breakdown of gross product by industry of immediate origin. These direct contributions to gross product are in some cases, such as steel, a small portion of the industry's total gross output; in others, such as food and apparel, they are the bulk of the industry's gross output.

Among those from whom the various industries make purchases are labor, the suppliers of capital, and others who contribute to production; they are included in the row near the bottom of the table entitled "Households." The payments to the various factors of production are shown, together with taxes paid to government, in the final rows of the table as charges against gross output. The table thus shows what is in effect a breakdown of national income by industrial origin. Again, in some cases, such as food, total purchases of the output of other industries are large in comparison with income originating, whereas in others, such as trade, they are small. (Trade is regarded not as purchaser of the products of industry but merely as the provider of services necessary for getting those products to their users; industry is regarded as purchasing these distributive services from trade, whose "output" represents margins earned on the products of the various industries.)

The primary contribution of the input-output matrix lies in the manner in which it defines the structure of transactions between industries in terms of the flows of goods and services between them. This interindustry structure is largely ignored in the national-income and product accounts, which include only summaries of its end results, taken at the indicated points. For many industry problems, the details of relations with other industries are of highest immediate importance, and this is exactly the kind of information which the input-output matrix provides.[11]

It should be understood—despite frequent claims to the contrary—that input-output analysis is not a method of over-all forecasting but rather requires a general forecast as a basis for working out the details of relationships. Nothing in the way of a general forecast can be got out of the matrix that is not put into it at the appropriate points. No matter how complete a statement of interindustry relationships may be, it cannot

[11] For a detailed discussion of the method, its uses, and relations to other data systems, see *Input-Output Analysis: An Appraisal*. Studies in Income and Wealth, vol. 18, National Bureau of Economic Research, Inc., New York, 1955.

segregate the strategic elements on which a forecast must be based. In fact, greater detail may hamper the process rather than facilitate it. Conclusions about the future state of the economy are only in limited degree dependent upon the relations between industries in any given time period. The matrix is so universal, so inflexible, and in itself so undiscriminating that it does not facilitate developing the implications of significant developments which in one way or another may be usefully projected.

When used in connection with general forecasting, input-output analysis is useful in forcing a set of consistency checks that might not otherwise be made. Activity cannot be high in certain lines unless it is supported by correspondingly high activity in others; the durable-goods industries, for example, cannot in the aggregate operate at a level beyond the capacity of the steel industry. Again, high-level operations in the armaments and machinery industries imply high incomes and therefore high-level operations in the consumer-goods industries unless consumer demand is restricted. The input-output matrix is in some respects similar to the econometric-model method of forecasting by means of simultaneous equations. Its solution requires that certain kinds of relationships be observed. The solution may differ somewhat from that obtained by other methods. That it will be in any sense the "best" solution, however, or even that it will be a unique solution, cannot be demonstrated.

The primary use of the input-output analysis consists in translating an over-all forecast into the specifics of industrial segments. It is a method for distributing the totals into subsidiary parts. In doing this from the standpoint of industries, it extends the analysis of the national-income and product accounts into the area of intermediate and primary products which are otherwise given but limited consideration. By setting up bills of materials for any product or program, such as public works or military procurement, it enables tracing the stimulus of such programs to various parts of the economy. By setting up the demands for any industry's output to be derived from planned programs or other foreseeable developments, it calls attention to the consequences of general economic change for that industry and may lead, for example, to the detection of bottlenecks requiring installation of new capacity. It has a wide field of potential usefulness.

In practice, however, a dilemma is encountered in the use of the inter-industry relations. The forecaster's problem is specific. Broad industry groups are too inclusive to meet the needs of the problem. The matrix can, of course, be expanded. The Bureau of Labor Statistics has constructed a 200-industry table. Many of the 40,000 potential entries are zeros, but even so, the number is very large. As the number of entries increases, the solution becomes less manageable and the probability of error increases. As is true of other complicated procedures, the chances that specific elements will misbehave expand geometrically with the number of coefficients, each of which is inevitably subject to error. Just where the expansion of such a matrix passes the point of diminishing returns is a question that cannot be definitely answered.

Another practical difficulty arises from changes in the coefficients relating inputs to outputs which appear in the various cells of the matrix. Data are not available for analyzing those changes in a systematic manner. Some arise from irregularities; for example, the ratios may temporarily depart from the norm as a result of accumulation or liquidation of inventories in a given year. Others represent shifts of a continuing character, like those in which a new product displaces one previously in wide use. Unless these changes in the coefficients can be taken into account, the results will be correspondingly in error. The coal study shown in Chart 15–5 is a case in point. It is admittedly an extreme case, with all the ratios changing and all the changes in the same direction. Nevertheless, such changes play havoc with any general-matrix solution based on an assumption of constant ratios.

Hence, the interindustry-relations approach tends to remain impractical and idealistic. A great amount of research has gone into the construction of the input-output tables now available, and much of this was worthwhile in its own right, but their present usefulness is confined to a limited range of problems for which they may be specially adapted.

COMBINATION METHODS

Even the simpler versions of the component method may get rather complicated as the number of components is increased and the techniques of estimating each are elaborated. Correlation techniques are frequently applied to the latter aspect of the problem, so that the over-all result may combine the effects of a diversity of variables operating through nonlinear as well as linear relationships.

One illustrative study analyzed electric-power demand by components, utilizing a combination of trends and correlations.[12] Four consumption components were separately analyzed—industrial, household, commercial, and public service. It was found in each type of use that the deviations of power consumption from long-term trends were correlated with deviations from similar trends fitted to related economic factors, such as industrial production, disposable personal income, or gross national product. Alternative trend and activity relationships might have been used with advantage to obtain better results in the later

[12] Joseph B. Epstein, "Electric Power Output and Investment," *Survey of Current Business*, May, 1949.

Table 15–2.   Distribution of Finished Steel to Consuming Industries*

In thousands of net tons

Year	Con-tainers	Mach-inery and tools	Oil, gas, water, and mining	Con-struc-tion	Rail-roads	Agri-culture	Auto-motive	Ex-ports	All other	Total
1923	1,350	1,168	3,923	5,527	9,435	1,506	4,684	1,901	7,776	37,270
1924	1,355	1,127	2,880	5,376	8,059	988	3,339	1,703	6,630	31,457
1925	1,598	1,514	3,192	6,203	8,746	1,264	5,472	1,672	7,732	37,393
1926	1,509	1,273	3,973	7,027	8,574	2,020	6,144	2,108	7,107	39,755
1927	1,577	1,170	3,256	7,781	6,980	1,987	5,482	1,953	6,635	36,825
1928	1,813	1,806	3,191	7,907	6,853	2,978	7,799	2,311	7,524	42,182
1929	1,912	2,028	4,117	8,643	8,163	3,061	7,353	2,477	8,247	45,998
1930	1,871	1,342	3,240	7,355	5,241	1,709	4,935	1,582	5,780	33,055
1931	1,585	791	1,722	4,589	3,035	1,349	3,527	810	4,069	21,477
1932	1,161	441	718	2,693	1,176	605	2,088	359	2,464	11,705
1933	1,805	716	1,045	2,713	1,351	1,016	3,621	568	4,336	17,171
1934	1,602	758	1,320	3,266	2,337	1,133	4,219	993	3,887	19,515
1935	2,107	1,007	1,484	3,981	1,809	1,823	6,217	970	5,365	24,763
1936	2,537	1,550	2,476	5,967	3,766	2,065	6,936	1,237	8,394	34,927
1937	2,998	1,680	2,825	5,623	4,364	2,174	7,276	2,745	8,660	38,345
1938	1,936	753	1,649	3,985	1,308	1,006	3,672	1,703	5,344	21,356
1939	2,664	1,306	1,648	5,458	2,908	1,271	5,284	2,354	12,102	34,955
1940	2,915	2,201	1,795	6,552	3,796	1,540	7,524	7,617	12,056	45,996
1941	4,510	3,291	2,864	9,995	5,850	1,646	9,629	6,112	17,046	60,943
1942	3,950	2,767	1,539	10,397	4,269	1,131	3,491*	6,763	26,284	60,591
1943	4,220	3,214	1,867	6,515	5,075	1,435	3,395*	6,622	29,867	62,210
1944	3,916	3,274	2,503	6,291	6,163	1,990	4,750*	5,449	28,915	63,251
1945	4,350	4,751	2,690	8,415	5,266	2,462	5,553*	4,354	18,761	56,602
1946	4,749	4,438	2,480	8,130	4,764	2,100	7,379	4,375	10,361	48,776
1947	5,596	5,648	3,833	10,039	5,999	2,422	10,292	5,919	13,309	63,057
1948	5,844	5,337	5,080	10,157	5,866	2,743	11,330	3,950	15,666	65,973
1949	5,026	4,274	5,455	10,020	4,038	2,644	11,880	4,344	10,423	58,104
1950	6,409	5,812	6,619	12,363	4,796	3,094	15,746	2,639	14,754	72,232
1951	7,242	7,033	6,735	14,184	6,558	3,281	14,488	3,051	16,357	78,929
1952	6,218	6,131	5,973	11,749	4,575	2,764	12,232	3,918	14,444	68,004
1953	6,769	7,307	7,211	14,225	5,454	2,547	16,506	2,907	17,226	80,152
1954	6,427	5,802	6,097	12,906	2,780	2,417	12,959	2,659	11,106	63,153

* Includes aircraft, which in other years is included in the column headed "All other."
SOURCE: Unpublished data adjusted by U.S. Department of Commerce, Business and Defense Services Administration, Iron and Steel Division, from figures supplied by annual numbers of the *Iron Age*, *American Iron and Steel Institute Statistical Reports*, and U.S. Bureau of the Census.

postwar years, but that fact could not have been readily determined at the time. The full sweep of the post–World War II expansion actually realized has been so extreme that a completely accurate forecast might then have been regarded as somewhat unrealistic.

Another illustration of the same general approach is provided by the method of estimating steel demand shown in Chart 15–6.[13] Total steel consumption is estimated by means of nine subsidiary relationships. The

[13] This study was originally carried out under the author's direction in the fall of 1940 by Harold Wein, economist for the National Defense Advisory Commission. It

Chart 15–6. Finished Steel Takings by Major Industries, 1923–1954

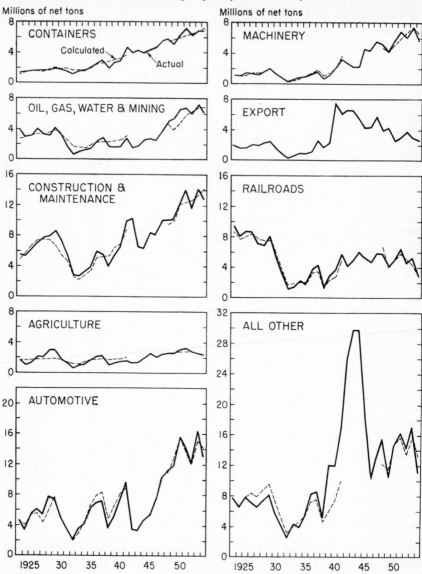

first seven of these are linear correlations, using activity in important
steel-consuming industries as independent variables; in some cases, time
was introduced as a second independent variable to take account of

---

was designed to portray the impact of the military-production effort on the demand
for steel and thus assist in planning for needed capacity. It was subsequently revised
and brought up to date at the University of Illinois with the assistance of Donald C.
Streever, Jr.

Chart 15–6. (Cont'd) Finished Steel Takings

DISCREPANCY IN INDUSTRY STEEL TAKINGS
RELATED TO CHANGES
IN NONFARM INVENTORIES

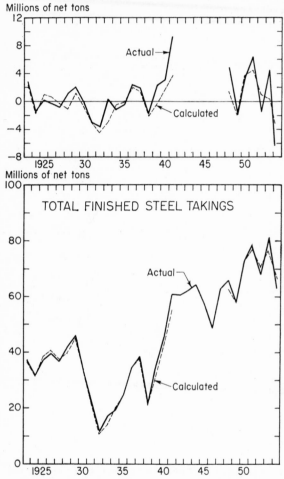

marked disparities of trend between activity and steel consumed. The eighth is a catchall for other uses estimated in the same way, using the combined total of the calculated values for the first seven as the independent variable. The ninth correlates the combined deviations from the first eight relationships with changes in nonfarm inventories. Exports could not be estimated satisfactorily by the kind of statistical procedure used for the rest of the study; the actual exports were therefore simply added in to obtain a calculated total comparable with the actual total reported. The data used in this study appear in Tables 15–2 and 15–3. The equations for the nine relationships are listed in Table 15–4.

Table 15–3.   Measures of Activity in Major Steel-using Industries and Inventory Changes

	Food consumption[a] (in billions of 1947 dollars)	Machinery production[b] (1947–1949 = 100)	Petroleum refining[b] (1947–1949 = 100)	Construction expenditures[c] (in billions of 1947–1949 dollars)	Traffic miles[d] (in billions)	Farm capital expenditures[a] (in millions of 1947 dollars)	Auto and truck production[e] (in thousands of vehicles)	Change in non-farm inventories[a] (in billions of 1947 dollars)
1923	$25.5	32	26	$17.9	534	$ 909	4,034	$4.3
1924	26.6	30	30	20.1	502	823	3,603	−1.4
1925	26.8	33	35	22.5	528	927	4,266	2.5
1926	26.9	38	39	23.8	560	996	4,301	1.9
1927	27.3	37	41	23.8	542	1,042	3,401	0.6
1928	28.4	40	46	23.0	540	1,040	4,359	−0.5
1929	28.6	49	51	20.9	555	1,134	5,337	−2.6
1930	27.6	37	48	17.4	476	852	3,363	−0.2
1931	27.5	25	46	14.0	384	469	2,380	−3.0
1932	25.5	16	41	8.9	293	248	1,332	−5.1
1933	25.0	19	43	6.6	308	263	1,890	−3.0
1934	25.2	26	45	7.7	334	468	2,737	−0.3
1935	26.3	31	49	9.1	349	743	3,971	0.7
1936	29.2	39	54	13.5	418	982	4,661	3.7
1937	30.2	47	60	13.6	442	1,138	4,820	3.0
1938	30.9	31	59	13.5	361	878	2,508	−1.8
1939	32.1	39	63	16.1	410	977	3,589	0.5
1940	33.6	51	66	16.8	453	1,055	4,472	3.1
1941	35.8	82	74	21.7	573	1,379	4,841	6.0
1942	37.1	127		22.9	789	1,113	1,042	−0.6
1943	39.1	165		12.8	948	1,018	700	−0.8
1944	43.6	164		8.2	977	1,167	738	−0.8
1945	47.5	128		8.4	909	1,122	725	−0.7
1946	49.1	90		15.5	762	1,367	3,090	7.7
1947	45.6	103	95	17.8	789	2,336	4,798	1.3
1948	45.5	104	104	20.8	760	2,823	5,286	2.8
1949	46.7	93	101	22.2	631	2,846	6,254	−1.7
1950	48.3	114	111	26.6	686	2,966	8,003	6.0
1951	49.7	130	125	27.0	748	2,995	6,765	7.1
1952	51.3	147	128	27.6	713	2,824	5,539	1.6
1953	53.6	160	135	28.9	697	2,536	7,323	1.5
1954	54.9	142	133	30.9	629	2,236	6,601	−2.4

[a] U.S. Department of Commerce, National Income Division. Both expenditures and deflators partly estimated.
[b] Federal Reserve Board index of industrial production.
[c] Construction Review, U.S. Departments of Commerce and Labor.
[d] Interstate Commerce Commission.
[e] Automobile Facts and Figures, 35th ed., Automobile Manufacturers Association, 1955.

Table 15–4. Equations Used in Estimating Steel Takings*

Industry estimating equation:

1. Containers:

$$y_1 = -2.56 + 0.147X_1 + 0.054t$$

where X_1 = consumer expenditures for food, excluding alcoholic beverages, millions of 1947 dollars

2. Machinery:

$$y_2 = -0.407 + 0.0497X_2$$

where X_2 = Federal Reserve Board index of machinery production (1947 to 1949 = 100)

3. Oil, gas, water, and mining:

$$y_3 = -0.442 + 0.119X_3 - 0.290t$$

where X_3 = Federal Reserve Board index of petroleum refining (1947 to 1949 = 100)

4. Construction and maintenance:

$$y_4 = -1.73 + 0.366X_y + 0.149t$$

where X_4 = value of total new construction, billions of 1947-to-1949 dollars

5. Railroads:

$$y_5 = -1.55 + 0.0193X_5 - 0.2475t$$

where X_5 = weighted total of freight ton miles and revenue passenger miles, with passenger miles receiving double weight, billions of traffic miles

6. Agriculture:

$$y_6 = 0.955 + 0.65X_6$$

where X_6 = capital expenditures for farm equipment and nonresidential construction, in billions of 1947 dollars

7. Automotive:

$$y_7 = -1.72 + 1.58X_7 + 0.172t$$

where X_7 = automobile and truck production, millions of vehicles

8. All other:

$$y_8 = 1.23 + 0.266X_8$$

where y_8 = steel takings by industries other than above, millions of net tons (excludes exports)

X_8 = subtotal of steel taken by the above seven major industries, millions of net tons

9. Inventory change:

$$y_9 = -0.79 + 0.74X_9$$

where y_9 = sum of the differences between actual and calculated values estimated from the above equations

X_9 = change in nonfarm inventories, billions of 1947 dollars

* The ys in the equations represent steel takings in millions of net tons by the industry designated at the left. Where a trend line was used as a second independent variable, t = time in years with 1923 = 0. The years 1942 to 1947 were excluded in fitting. Actual exports are included to complete total.

The over-all result shown in the largest segment of Chart 15–6 is a summation of all the subsidiary parts, including exports. The fit to the total is considerably better than to any of the parts. Errors that are substantial in the smaller segments either average out or are reduced to modest proportions in the total. This is not the primary advantage of the method, however. Its validity derives mainly from the fact that it relates the components of steel demand to a series of factors relevant to steel consumption, each appropriately weighted, and thus gives effect to the various forces and restraints that influence the movements of all those factors. This complex of relevant considerations could not be taken into account in any single relationship based on total steel consumed in all uses.

Another complex procedure, which may be regarded as a variant of either the percentage distribution or the component method, consists in forecasting personal-consumption items by means of the income distribution. The essence of the approach is to project the distribution of income by income classes. The main components are the expenditures in each income class. The pattern of expenditures and savings in each class is applied to the projections of income in all or specified income classes at some future date. This method is most commonly utilized in forecasting large-expenditure items, especially those whose use involves a high original or operating cost. Houses, cars, yachts, and airplanes are items to which it has frequently been applied. However, it can be utilized for other items as well and has been used successfully, for example, in forecasting clothing expenditures.

In using this method, it is usually assumed that both the income distribution and the proportion of income spent for any given item in each of the various income classes remains constant. This does not mean that expenditures for that item remain a constant proportion of income. Since the percentages of income spent in the various income classes are reweighted as the amount of income in each class is reallocated, the average percentage varies. The shifts in the distribution tend to be most pronounced in the extreme income classes—often those of most direct concern—and the projected over-all percentage spent on specific items, such as luxury goods which only the highest-income classes can afford, may therefore change drastically.

A procedure for adjusting the income distribution to a projected level of income is shown in Chart 15–7.[14] The upper part of the chart shows the cumulative percentage distribution of income in 1950. Aggregate

[14] The procedure should properly be applied to specific subgroups of the population rather than to the income distribution as a whole. For an alternative description of the method, see *Income Distribution in the United States, 1953 Edition,* supplement to *Survey of Current Business,* U.S. Department of Commerce, p. 38, note 12.

Chart 15–7. Projecting the Income Distribution

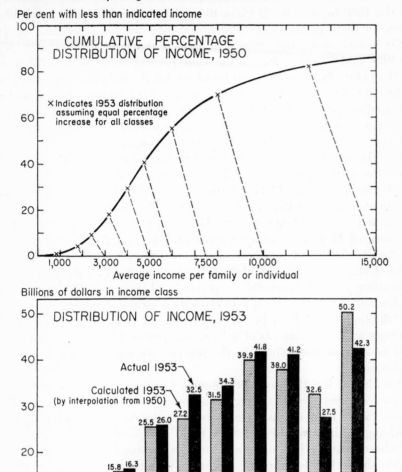

Per cent with less than indicated income

CUMULATIVE PERCENTAGE
DISTRIBUTION OF INCOME, 1950

× Indicates 1953 distribution
assuming equal percentage
increase for all classes

Average income per family or individual

Billions of dollars in income class

DISTRIBUTION OF INCOME, 1953

Actual 1953

Calculated 1953
(by interpolation from 1950)

Income class	Calculated 1953	Actual 1953
Under 1,000	1.9	1.4
1,000–1,999	9.0	8.2
2,000–2,999	15.8	16.3
3,000–3,999	25.5	26.0
4,000–4,999	27.2	32.5
5,000–5,999	31.5	34.3
6,000–7,499	39.9	41.8
7,500–9,999	38.0	41.2
10,000–14,999	32.6	27.5
15,000 & over	50.2	42.3

Income classes

income increased from $217 billion in 1950 to $271 billion in 1953, or 25 percent. If all families obtained the same percentage increase, then the percent of the families with less than $1,000 each in 1950 would become the percent with less than $1,250 each in 1953. Or, to put this in 1953 terms, the percent with less than $1,000 each would be the percent that had less than $800 each in 1950. Taking one-fifth from each of the 1950 income levels gives the points marked by X's on the line. Some of these points correspond to lower-income-class divisions on the 1950 income scale; thus $5,000 in 1953 is the same percent as $4,000 in 1950, and $7,500 in 1953 is the same percent as $6,000 in 1950. Most of the points, however, have to be interpolated within the 1950 intervals. When this is done, giving the full series of X's shown, the calculated cumulative percentage distribution for 1953 is obtained. These percentages may then be differenced and applied to the aggregate 1953 income to obtain the estimated aggregate income in each income class in 1953. The result is shown in the lower portion of the chart in comparison with the actual data compiled by the Department of Commerce.[15]

The income in the highest bracket goes up considerably faster than the over-all total. In 1950, there was $29.3 billion in the $15,000-and-over class, and in 1953 there was $42.3 billion in that class. This is an actual increase of 44 percent, compared with the average 25 percent increase. If the distribution of income had remained the same, there would have been $50.2 billion in the highest bracket, an increase of 71 percent. The discrepancy between this 71 percent and the actual 44 percent is an indication of how difficult it is to estimate what the change in the income distribution is going to be. It is possible to base judgments of such changes on the movements of wages, entrepreneurial income, and profits, but here again small shifts in the percentages represent large absolute differences.

Looking at the 1953 and 1950 figures in reverse, it is seen that when income declines the percentage of income in the highest class goes down much faster than the average. Assuming that spending habits remain unchanged, there would be a very rapid shift in expenditures for items purchased mainly by this group, such as the most expensive makes of automobiles. This is in accord, of course, with the well-known sensitivity of expenditures for high-priced luxury goods.

At the other end of the income scale, shifts take place in the reverse manner. Depression goods—like the jig-saw puzzle and the miniature-golf course—come into being when incomes are low and pass out of the picture when they recover.

In the intermediate-income classes, shifts are not nearly so large as at the extremes. The families shifting out of any middle-income bracket

[15] Selma F. Goldsmith, "Income Distribution in the United States, 1950–53," *Survey of Current Business*, March, 1955. The actual data for 1953 are preliminary estimates, since income tax returns for that year were not yet available. These preliminary estimates were obtained by extrapolating the 1951 distribution on the assumption of unchanged relative-income differences, a procedure similar to that described above but carried out in greater detail.

tend to be replaced by those shifting in from the adjacent bracket. The manufacturer whose product lines are confined in the middle zone of price and quality need not expect the same degree of volatility in sales as his "competitors" at the higher and lower extremes.

The weakness of this approach lies in its inability to take account of factors other than income, such as capital gains and stocks in use. It shows what the level of purchases would be, given conditions like those in the earlier period, when family budgets were studied to determine the relation of family income and expenditures in each class. It cannot guarantee that purchases will remain at that level, given a long period of stable income in which stocks in use are approaching the saturation point or the stock market is making a major reversal. Many more studies would be needed, at regular intervals, to indicate the character of the shifts that take place. In the meantime, it is taking a shot in the dark to assume that the proportions of income spent by each income class are constant throughout the cycle.

Other evidence suggests that the shifts in buying of expensive durable goods are more drastic than would be called for by the shifting of families in the income distribution. After a decline, large houses, yachts, and similar items are a drug on the market. There are no longer enough families in the income brackets high enough to justify ownership of the existing stock of such items. The loss in values on sale of those units is extreme, and the widening gap between the prices of the new models and the old tends to depress production still further. The larger and more expensive the unit, the greater the sacrifice necessary to dispose of it. Declines in other capital values as well as in income force such sacrifices. It seems highly likely that the proportions of income spent change from time to time; and if they change for some items, they probably change for others also.

In analyzing prospects for any industry, the forecaster need not confine himself to one approach or to one kind of evidence. Various methods may be tried, and the effort spent in reconciling the results obtained in different ways may prove to be a good form of insurance.

LOCAL-COMMUNITY FORECASTS

Forecasting for a local community is like commodity forecasting in that the first requirement is research to define the problem and to determine what methods offer promise of success in the particular circumstances. The diversity of conditions is so great that all techniques may apply at times, but those which have proved successful in one situation may be worthless in another.

About all that can be said with assurance is that community differences set the problem. From this it follows that methods must be adapted to the requirements of the specific local situation. Beyond that, generalization ceases, and the ingenuity of the local forecaster takes up the burden. The following discussion will attempt little more than to point up the implications of some important differences and to give several illustrations of the techniques used by analysts who have worked in this field.

From the outset, it should be clear that local conditions may depend upon specific developments or events that are of negligible national significance. The removal of a single large industrial concern may severely depress a community, creating substantial unemployment, without involving any significant change in the national economy. On the other hand, local opportunities may keep the income of an individual community growing through a period of general recession.

The parts of the economy are interdependent, of course, so that the great swings of the business cycle do carry into most local situations. Nevertheless, there are great differences among communities in the degree of their independence from general economic conditions. The local builder, for example, may find himself in quite a different situation from the building-materials manufacturer producing for the national market. Prosperity for the one is not inconsistent with depression for the other.

There are likely to be conditions of both local labor shortages and local labor surpluses in existence at the same time, and these differences in status may be maintained over long periods. Migration of workers should theoretically adjust labor supplies in such a way as to eliminate the disparities, and it does work slowly in that direction. However, knowledge of better opportunities gets to the surplus areas only slowly, and those opportunities must appear to be relatively permanent rather than merely temporary to justify a move. Even when the facts are known, there are various obstacles to the actual movement of workers. After the flow does get under way, it cannot quickly close the gap. The underlying conditions that produced the disparity in the first place may develop further, requiring a still greater movement, and the flow itself tends to aggravate the contrast of prosperity and depression that initiated it, through its reactions on the need for trade and service activities of various kinds. The differences may therefore be preserved despite the corrective forces working to eliminate them.

Superficial definition of the differences between communities, in terms of such broad aggregates as population, income, and location, may be inadequate to the solution of the forecaster's problem. A study of air-traffic potentials, for example, showed the extent to which travel by air varies with the character of communities. This study[16] presents an ingenious characterization of communities in terms of a two-way classification based on deviations from the averages for all communities in two measures available for all, namely, wholesale sales per capita and percentage of total employment in mining and manufacturing. Communities high in wholesale sales and low in industrial employment were designated "marketing centers." Those high in industrial employment and low in wholesale sales were "industrials." Those low in both were "institutionals," such as state capitals and university towns. Those near the averages were "balanced communities." (No cities appeared in the high-high portion of the distribution.) It was found that the amount of air traffic developed by any city varied greatly by size of population, depending upon the group in which it appeared. The marketing centers and institutionals developed far more traffic than either the balanced communities or the industrials. The need to adapt forecasting techniques to the particular circumstances is clearly evident in this study.

In general, the procedures used in attacking area problems are the same as those used in industry and commodity forecasting. The two basic approaches are: first, to consider the area as part of the broader community and deal with it indirectly by forecasting the general economy and then breaking the forecast into subsidiary parts; and, second, to treat the area as an independent entity and deal with it in terms of any of the procedures suitable for forecasting a separate economy in its entirety.

Both of these approaches are illustrated by Census Bureau forecasts of population. The population experts have used three methods to make projections of the populations of political subdivisions.[17] The first, a purely "autonomous" method, is the extrapolation of trend lines fitted to past Census reports. Ordinarily, such projections are not soundly based as only a few observations, those for the most recent decades, are significant for the extrapolation. The deviations from the fitted trends have been so serious that this method has come into disfavor.

The second is the *ratio method,* similar to that described for relating industries to the total economy. The *ratio* of the locality to the state— which in turn may be taken as a ratio of the national total—is extrapolated into the future. Whether the ratios display a higher degree of continuity than the trend as such is a question. Other available evidence indicates, for example, that the movement of population from farms to cities is a prosperity phenomenon, at least partially reversible in a de-

---

[16] *Economic Character of Communities,* Civil Aeronautics Administration, 1948.

[17] See A. J. Jaffe, *Handbook of Statistical Methods for Demographers,* U.S. Bureau of the Census, 1951, p. 222.

pression. If this cyclical correlation were dependable, it might be taken into account in projecting the ratios that are applied to the larger totals. In any case, an important point to be noted is that the ratios themselves may be subject to considerable variation of a noncontinuous character.

The third method is the *component method*. The primary components of the change in population are the natural increase and net migration. The natural-increase component is estimated from births and deaths. This tends to be the more dependable element in most cases. The net-migration component is the difference between new arrivals and those moving away. Ordinarily, current data on migration are not available. It has to be estimated at intervals, partly by taking differences in the total head count. Very often no total head count is available, so that an adjustment has to be worked out from some such substitute as school enrollment. Again, however, when one is projecting into the future, some assumption has to be made about future patterns of migration.

The importance of the assumption made about migration is shown by the recent data. During the decade of war and prosperity from 1940 to 1950, there was heavy migration of both population and the labor force. The censuses showed that, although the population of the country as a whole advanced almost 15 percent, half of the counties actually showed declines. There were important crosscurrents making for the diversity of results. Throughout the country, there was a movement from farms to metropolitan areas and from central cities to the suburbs. In addition, there was a major flow from the Northeast to the Far West and the Southwest, and there was another major movement from the Southeast to the industrial centers of the North and the West. California's population grew the fastest, but in California some counties declined. Mississippi, Arkansas, Oklahoma, and North Dakota lost population, but in these states some counties showed substantial gains. It is with differences like these that community forecasting is primarily concerned.

The forces responsible for the shifts in population among localities were varied. Some were an outgrowth of the war, others of the postwar boom. Some communities lost ground not because of any deficiency of their own but merely because of the greater opportunities that developed elsewhere. Other changes were the result of purely local developments. Until the factors responsible for the movements affecting any community are determined, there is little basis for telling whether those movements are likely to continue or reverse. Hence no past rate of migration may be suitable for application in the future. One possibility is to adapt the projection to what past data show to be the rate in the particular past period judged to be most nearly comparable to that anticipated in the future.

Another method that may be used in moving from a forecast of the general economy to one for a local area is the correlation method. One study of this kind, relating state income payments to the national total, was made by the Department of Commerce.[18] The method used was similar to that used in estimating the sensitivity of consumer expenditures for various items to changes in consumer income. Logarithmic regression equations were worked out for all states, with time used as a second independent variable to supplement the basic relationship to the national aggregate. In presenting the results, the authors suggest the desirability of a more detailed analysis by the major components of income.

In the income data, too, the variation among communities is striking. In 1954 per capita personal income for the country as a whole amounted to $1,770, but the individual states ranged all the way from $979 in Arkansas to $2,414 in California. The aggregate income realized in some states, like Illinois and Ohio, generally moves in conformity with the national total. Some, mainly in the West and South, have shown steady relative gains in incomes. Others, mainly in New England and the Middle Atlantic regions, have lost ground relative to the average. The most extreme movements occur in unusual periods, as in wartime, but important divergences may occur at other times when specific developments have concentrated effects on limited areas.[19]

Part of the reason for these differences in income flows may be found by analysis of the composition of the industrial sources from which the income is derived. A major difference lies in the proportions of income received from agriculture and from manufacturing. More than 10 percent of the income of the Southern and Great Plains regions comes from agriculture; less than 2 percent of income in the Northeast comes from agriculture. In contrast, the Central and New England regions receive almost 30 percent from manufacturing; and the Northwest and Southwest obtain only 10 percent from this source. Income from trade and service is highest in New York and California, amounting to about 30 percent in each. Income from government is highest in Virginia, again about 30 percent. Since these industrial sources show distinctive patterns of behavior, the divergent changes that occur from time are reflected in differences in state positions relative to the total.

Analysis of the industrial composition of a community's sources of income is important both in determining the degree of autonomous movement to be expected and in defining the components to be projected. Analysts following both the separate-entity and the relation-to-

---

[18] C. Winston and M. A. Smith, "Sensitivity of State Income Payments to Nation's Total," *Survey of Current Business*, January, 1946.

[19] Revised data appear in an article by Charles F. Schwartz and Robert E. Graham, Jr., "Personal Income by States, 1929–54," *Survey of Current Business*, September, 1955.

total approaches are on common ground in seeking this kind of information. If it is not available in the desired form, the closest substitute, such as employment by industry, may become the central focus of attention. Facts of this kind are likely to be essential to a solution; in many cases they may be the only kind that bear directly on the problem.

The nature of the problems most commonly encountered in community forecasting involve the analysis of local "resources" (this term being used broadly to include human and financial as well as material resources). The problems do not necessarily first appear in this form, but any attempt to appraise the future of the community comes back to the question of whether resources adequate to justify any contemplated course of action will be available.

Consideration of a few of the problems faced by community forecasters clearly indicates why this is so. From within the community, forecasts may be needed in connection with programs of development and improvement. Local administrations and planning agencies know that certain changes are desirable and should be made at once. But the precise character of such changes should be modified if the community is likely to experience major expansion in the decades ahead. If much more than immediate needs are to be provided for, the future situation must warrant the proposed installations, and the economic base of the community must promise to provide the necessary finances.

From outside, forecasts are called for because it is desired to know whether the community is a good place to locate proposed facilities and operations. An industry faced with this problem sets up the criteria important to it, in terms of its own products, the materials and labor it needs, and the markets it plans to serve. From its point of view, future developments may be fully as important as present advantages. The community must retain the ability to grow beyond the limits of the immediate expansion if future difficulties are to be avoided.

Emphasis on the industry point of view by local administrators is justified, because opportunities to earn a satisfactory income are requisite to attracting and holding workers. But since industry itself has to be attracted to the community, the community must provide something that will enable industry to operate efficiently, or no basis for progress may exist.

The term "industry" in this context refers primarily to productive operations whose markets lie outside the community and not to the commercial and service establishments that serve the local inhabitants. No local community is self-sufficient. Most of each community's needs must be imported from other producing areas, and, like countries in international trade, the community must balance the flow of funds spent for the products of other areas by the sale of its own goods and services outside the area. Over a period of time, the community adjusts to a level commensurate to the income it obtains from "outside" markets.

The trade and service functions more or less automatically adjust to the size of the community itself. When expansion takes place in its "export" industries and in the population supported by those industries, the trade, service, recreation, and other opportunities created by the expansion attract enterprise to meet the local needs. When there is a decline in incomes and employment in those industries, the opportunities for profitable operations in auxiliary trade and service lines are curtailed, and over a period of time those operations are adjusted downward to the lower level of industrial income.[20]

The various aspects of the community, its surrounding area, and its inhabitants which afford opportunities for efficient industrial operations are its economic resources. Among the important kinds of resources that attract industry are the following:

1. Materials. Dependable supplies from mines or farms require processing, particularly if a large portion of the original extraction must be disposed of locally, as in beneficiation of ores or separation of soybean oil and meal.

2. Transport costs. Minimum total cost of assembling materials and distributing products may be decisive for a transport-oriented industry like steel.

3. Water. Water is necessary for waste disposal as well as for processing.

4. Power and fuel. Adequate supplies of cheap power decide the location of some industries, such as aluminum. Atomic sources of power may open opportunities in new areas.

5. Community facilities, housing, stores, and service establishments. Such facilities are necessary to meet the needs of workers and their families.

6. Population and its growth. The age composition and factors determining the trend are important considerations.

7. Labor. The level of training and education of the labor force must be considered in relation to prevailing rates of remuneration.

8. Finances. Sometimes other resources lack only financial support to make them productive.

The list might be greatly expanded to include climate, communications, taxes, recreation, and other conditions of operation or living. Social and political institutions may assist or hamper the utilization of resources, and obstacles to growth, natural or institutional, may or may not

[20] For a more extended discussion of this distinction, see C. Rapkin, L. Winnick, and D. M. Blank, *Housing Market Analysis*, Housing and Home Finance Agency, 1953, chap. 5.

be easily overcome. Each of these factors may be important from the standpoint of the future even if they impose no present problems. Locating in proximity to a market may imply a long-term forecast of the future of that market. To accept the present water supply as adequate may be mistaken if the margin of availability is so slender that it will become inadequate as the community grows or as other communities drawing from the same source develop. Conclusions correctly drawn at the moment may be invalidated by changes in technology that takes advantages away by opening new possibilities or eliminating existing obstacles to progress in other areas.

The forecasting problems involved in such analysis are formidable. Even determining the present status of many important factors may be difficult. It is sometimes possible to send teams into the field to remedy this deficiency. Surveys by engineers, demographers, and market analysts may be used to fill in the current picture. Some pioneering studies of this kind have been made, usually in problem areas or in large cities for which comparatively good data are available.[21] One deficiency with the survey approach is that it cannot bring back the past in the form of data comparable with the present, and without such data it may be of only minor help in delineating the future. Frequently, where budgets for necessary research are not available, there may be no alternative to assembling the informed guesses of the limited number of people in the best position to throw light on critical aspects of the situation.

What can be done is likely to be as narrowly specific as the circumstances of the community itself. Much depends on the availability of information. In the past, there may have been nothing beyond the basic Census Bureau reports. Recent Censuses of Agriculture and Business provide much greater detail by counties and by cities. In addition, the social security system has greatly increased the chances of getting reasonably satisfactory current data on such important matters as employment, unemployment, and payrolls. State agencies are working with the Department of Labor to extend this information. All the states are covered by the basic statistics on employment, payrolls, hours of work, and average earnings, and similar tabulations are available for about 100 areas. For roughly the same number of areas, local labor-market conditions are analyzed, and the Bureau of Employment Security issues reports of existing labor shortages or labor surpluses.

Additional data beyond those published may be obtained from the agencies involved under certain conditions. Furthermore, the Depart-

[21] One such study is *Southern Illinois*, University of Illinois Press, Urbana, Ill., 1949; another is summarized in the booklet *Puerto Rico, U.S.A.: Facts for Businessmen*, prepared by Arthur D. Little, Inc., for the Puerto Rico Industrial Development Company, New York, 1950.

ment of Commerce data on state income payments may be allocated to counties or other areas by means of the social security data and other available information.[22] These are indications of the progress being made to extend statistics to the local level, partly on an established, partly on an experimental basis.

All that has been done, however, leaves much to be desired by the mass of local communities. The broader-area tabulations exclude, or conceal by averaging out, much of the variation with which the smaller communities are most directly concerned. Some of those communities are almost completely specialized; others are dominated by a few lines of activity. Few are sufficiently balanced with broader areas to obtain a satisfactory indication of change from available reports. In restricted areas, without diversification, much greater variation is experienced than in the larger areas—including quick reversals that are not necessarily part of the broader picture.

The data needs for community analysis may be designated as roughly the same as those for national economic analysis—namely, the entire range of data included in the national economic accounts. If something resembling the national-income and product accounts could be compiled, they would by themselves be less satisfactory than they are for national analysis. Income, for example, may tell far less about consumption in a local community; consumers may prefer to shop somewhere else for all but a limited range of day-to-day necessities. Even the largest communities lack the self-sufficiency and the diversity of resources and industry of the national economy. What flows into or out of a community is therefore much more important to local than to national analysis.

Both real and financial flows are important. The products and purchases of local industry are likely to be materials or intermediate parts and components; the analyst therefore finds a need for interindustry relations or input-output data to give him clues to prospects for local industry. The community also has to balance its payments with the rest of the economy; the analyst therefore seeks to develop "foreign-trade models" and "flow-of-funds accounts" to determine the validity of proposed solutions. None of these data are available for communities to the same extent as for the nation.

The solution of such a complex problem requires trained judgment. Methods must be selected, critically evaluated, and adapted to the circumstances of the community and the data that can be compiled concerning it. Many of the processes involved require the work of a trained

[22] See Lewis C. Copeland, *Methods for Estimating Income Payments in Counties*, University of Virginia, Bureau of Population and Economic Research, Charlottesville, Va., 1952.

research analyst. Sometimes an analyst of quality may be discovered locally, in a government administrative office, in the school system, or in the research departments of stores, utilities, or newspapers. More commonly, such a person must be specially brought in, perhaps on a consulting basis.

Forecasting techniques from the whole gamut of those used in other kinds of forecasting may be considered applicable to community problems. Choice of method is theoretically unrestricted, but in most cases the limitations of data make the use of few methods practicable. Each problem must be dealt with in its own terms, by methods which the course of research indicates to be most nearly applicable.

CHAPTER 16

Problems of the Individual Firm

Most discussions of business forecasting focus on techniques or procedures for working out forecasts. The reasons for this are apparent, but taking forecasting out of the context of business operations in this way may produce two fallacies for the concern that attempts to apply forecasts to the solution of its problems. On the one hand, this approach leads to overemphasis on the role of forecasts. On the other, it confuses managerial responsibilities, because the firm has problems of organizing and using forecasts as well as making them, and ordinarily no basis for solving these related problems is provided. For either of these reasons, an attempt to employ forecasts may be harmful rather than helpful.

It is common among writers on forecasting to assert that forecasting is inevitable, since every action implicitly involves a forecast, whether it is consciously worked out or not. Thus, "There is no escape from forecasting . . . for every decision rests upon some assumption or forecast of what lies ahead."[1] Again, "Forecasting, by some method or other, is necessary and is as inescapable in business life as breathing and digestion are in physical life."[2] To make the point more graphic, it has been said, "Every businessman needs a witch!"[3] Other references of the same character may be found in almost any work on the subject.

This theme at best represents a considerable overstatement of the importance of forecasting. Only when forecasting is defined in such a way

[1] Walter E. Hoadley, Jr., "The Importance and Problems of Business Forecasting," in H. V. Prochnow (ed.), *Determining the Business Outlook*, Harper & Brothers, New York, 1954, p. 8.

[2] Frank D. Newbury, *Business Forecasting: Principles and Practice*, McGraw-Hill Book Company, Inc., New York, 1952, p. 2.

[3] *Business Week*, Sept. 24, 1955.

as to give it an identity with processes of living, doing, planning, and the like is there any reason to regard it as a necessary part of such processes. In this sense, it might be said that the caterpillar instinctively creeping toward the light is "forecasting" that he will reach a source of food by doing so. Such a definition, however, is hardly meaningful. The term properly applies to conscious predictions that certain developments largely beyond the predicter's control will occur at some future time. Actions not based on such predictions, including planned actions, involve no forecasting.

It follows that most business activities, as well as those of persons or other organisms, may proceed without forecasting. In the past most business was actually carried on in that way. Today the bulk of business is carried on with the aid of at least some forecasting, though much of it represents a rather elementary or petty type of forecasting that could be dispensed with entirely if desired.

Business is, of course, faced with the necessity of coordinating the various phases of its operations. To hold steadfastly to an unrealistic course can at best result in imbalances of one kind or another, perhaps involving heavy penalties, and at worst it may be disastrous. The latter frequently is the outcome for small businesses that push operations and commitments beyond the limits imposed by financial resources. Imbalances of other kinds arise whenever one of a series of related operations progresses at a rate not matched by others. Accumulation of excess inventories is costly, and acceptance of orders that cannot be filled on schedule may involve permanent loss of customers. The task of management is to avoid such unfavorable developments as far as possible.

What should usually be sought as a means of dealing with imbalances is not accuracy in forecasting but flexibility in control. Since forecasts can never be wholly accurate, they may actually contribute to imbalances at times. On the other hand, suitable controls can usually prevent imbalances from reaching unmanageable proportions if they are promptly applied. The penalties resulting from inadequate adjustment of operations to each other or to the broader business environment can be minimized by intelligence and flexibility in dealing with problems as they arise. Anticipating the changes that may produce such problems can help to some extent, but it can also create problems, and it may be just as important to avoid the artificial problems as to solve the real ones.

Whatever the basis on which action is taken, its results may, of course, be quite different from what was expected. Occasionally a person may be so well satisfied as to admit that he "planned better than he knew." More often it is clear with the aid of hindsight that results could have been better still. It seems evident from this backward look that accurate forecasting can offer considerable rewards. The backward look represents one of the greatest inducements to looking ahead. It leads to a state of mind in which flexibility and intelligence in dealing with day-to-day problems tend to be confused with success in forecasting.

One difficulty with undue emphasis on forecasting is that it tends to introduce a certain amount of inflexibility into management decisions. The department executive who is basing decisions relating to his own jurisdiction on a forecast accepted by top management may to some extent feel relieved of responsibility. Therefore, he may not only be less alert for changes in the situation but loath to take the initiative in deciding upon adjustments in advance of a new decision from above. As a result, emerging problems may sometimes develop into real emergencies before action is taken.

Another difficulty is that forecasting tends to lead into activities that are essentially speculative in character, and it may, again, induce inflexibility in the pursuit of such activities. The mail-order executive who took a bearish view of the outlook and refused to expand operations was speculating on a depression. He stubbornly held to his position through the years after World War II and prevented adjustments that the current level of business clearly called for, with the result that his competitors moved in and improved their position at his expense.

Most businessmen agree in discussions of policy that business should not speculate. They also agree that forecasts should not be used as a firm basis for action, as if the future were actually known. These precepts are more than a recognition that forecasts can never be wholly accurate; they are an acknowledgment that forecasting is largely unnecessary.

There are exceptions, of course, like those encountered by the new firm with an untried product. Then the whole venture may be speculative in character. In these circumstances, the result may be disastrous even though the forecast of an active market proves correct, as in the case of the two new companies that entered the auto industry at the end of World War II.

Most businesses do well enough by avoiding speculative commitments, the penalties for which may prove unduly severe. Action based on a wrong forecast might indeed be "fatal" under certain conditions, and it is precisely such action that should be ruled out if possible. A prayer for salvation may well be made on behalf of the businessman who stakes everything on prognostications obtained by witchcraft.

To conclude this introduction, a brief summary of the approach described in the remainder of this chapter may be in order: The first thing to be determined is the role of forecasting in the general framework of management activities. The second step is to define the forecasting problem or problems in terms of the activities the forecasts are to serve.

Then the forecasting work can be organized effectively, and the staff assigned to it can proceed with the actual development and testing of forecasting procedures. Elements of uncertainty are inherent in all phases of this process, and a substantial amount of experimentation may be necessary before satisfactory arrangements can be developed.

FORECASTING AS A MANAGEMENT AID

As soon as a firm grows beyond the "one-man" size, it is usually forced to institute procedures for coordinating the various aspects of its operations. When such diverse activities as production, selling, purchasing, and finance have to be separated for specialized handling, the need for such procedures becomes acute. In the smaller concern, the necessary coordination may often be obtained on an informal basis by personal contacts between those responsible for the various activities. A single top executive supported by an intelligent team of subordinates may accomplish this effectively. In large concerns more formal procedures for planning and control are usually required. Such procedures do not, however, eliminate the need for intelligence on the part of the individual executives involved.

The desired coordination of activities may be obtained without resort to any forecasting as the term is used here. All that is needed is preagreement on some interim level of over-all operations. That level may be decided upon entirely as a matter at the company's control. As time passes, the results may be appraised in the light of what is happening and a new decision made for the next period. Operations carried on in this manner, with more or less continuous adaptation to the situation produced by previous decisions, may produce results about as good as any that could be obtained by the use of forecasts as such.

Ordinarily, the coordination has to take place at the level determined by the factor that imposes the lowest limit under the circumstances. The reason for this is that controls must operate on the factors subject to control; they cannot determine the others. Control may be restricted by lack of capacity, shortages of materials or parts, insufficient financing, inability to obtain orders, or any of a number of other conditions that cannot be immediately corrected. Ordinarily the limiting factors are not fixed, either in the sense that nothing can be done about them or in the sense that they will not change of themselves in the course of time.

The postwar experience of the auto industry provides good illustrations of the diversity of problems encountered. At first the industry was not set up to produce cars in large numbers. Tucker spent more than $25 million without getting beyond this initial stage. The prolonged strikes of early 1946 made for delays in reconversion and in getting productive operations organized. After these problems were solved, materials became the critical bottleneck for most companies. Kaiser-Frazer rose in 1948 into fourth position in the industry by applying the expediting techniques utilized during the war period to the solution of this problem. That company was not able, however, to match quality to the prices charged, and the market subsequently shifted back to the older firms, who were able to bring their production up after the materials situation eased in the recession of 1949. Ford began its drive for leadership in that year by emphasis on quality and style. It had no problem in financing the engineering and equipment outlays needed for this kind of competition. General Motors also kept pace in the competitive drive for market shares, but all the others in the industry lost part of their markets. The closing years of the decade following the war showed these diverse influences. Ford and General Motors were continuing to expand and improve facilities, while some of the smaller firms were forced into mergers to combine resources and reduce unit costs by spreading overheads over combined market shares that were sharply lower than in earlier postwar years.

This experience indicates that success depends upon effective policies, sound operating decisions, and favorable conditions throughout the diversity of fields significant for that type of business. Among the requirements are ingenuity in product development and design, efficiency in manufacturing, sound facilities planning, standards of price and quality capable of holding the market, effective sales and service organizations, and adequate financial resources. All the companies correctly forecast, in a general way, the greatly enlarged postwar markets. Few were able to supply all the other elements needed to translate that forecast into continuing success. It is futile to think that success in an auxiliary activity like forecasting can automatically render effective all the functions of management.

As an auxiliary activity, forecasting can be useful to the extent that accuracy is attainable. Conscious forecasting can be helpful at various points by substituting facts and analysis for unsupported judgments. It may be desirable to make exploratory forecasts of conditions in all the markets relevant to the firm's operations—the market for its products, the markets for the materials it uses, the local labor market, and the money market. If difficulties are anticipated in any of these areas, early action may make it possible to find solutions which will no longer be available after the difficulty is actually experienced.

Anticipating problems often makes easier the planning needed to deal with them. The values of forecasting can be realized, however, only in the context of actual use, and in this context it must be considered in relation to the other techniques developed by business through the years for planning, coordinating, and controlling operations.

Most widely used of these techniques is budgeting. Others are commonly supplemental to budgeting rather than alternative to it. "Scientific management" was the key word for all these activities in the early twentieth century. More recently, such titles as "rationalization," "program planning," "linear programing," "development research," and "operations research" have come into vogue as designations for similar or related activities. All these activities, like forecasting itself, are properly auxiliary, staff functions in no way intended to take over the functions of operating management as a whole.

BUDGETING

Budgeting is a process of setting up an explicit plan of operations designed to coordinate all the detailed activities of the business and to provide a basis for evaluating the performance of each operating unit. Its point of departure is a program for future over-all rates of operation, stated in terms of some such comprehensive measure of activity as shipments or production. Then detailed plans for all the specific interrelated activities of the various divisions or operating units are prepared in such a way as to meet the requirements of the over-all program or schedule. Ordinarily these detailed plans specify both rates of activity and the resources to be used in carrying on each activity.

Projections of the over-all rate of operation may sometimes be pushed a year or more into the future. As a rule, the detailed operating schedules are confined to a much shorter period, covering perhaps several months, the precise number being determined by the character of the business and the requirements of related industries from which supplies must be obtained. At the end of the period the actual results achieved by each unit can be checked against its budget, and this provides a basis for evaluating performance and discovering explanations for inadequacies.

In view of the great amount of detail work involved and of the need for a common denominator in comparing diverse activities, the accounting mechanism of the concern is appropriately utilized for this activity. Therefore, it is usually placed under the direction of the controller, who also has responsibility for the routine accounting functions of the firm.

Determining the over-all level of operations is, however, the function of top management as a whole and in large concerns is seldom left to the determination of any single executive. The most common practice is to have each period's program worked out by a committee, called the budget committee or the scheduling committee, and presented to top management for review and approval. This committee typically consists of the various departmental vice-presidents or their representatives, so that all important aspects of the concern's activities are represented at its meetings.

The sales department can provide estimates of sales prospects; the purchasing department can outline materials shortages or other bottle-necks in procurement; the production department can define output pos-sibilities, given the existing facilities and labor supply; and the finance department can indicate financial limitations. A whole series of special-ized judgments is thus brought to bear on the determination, and atten-tion is almost automatically focused on the limiting factor.

In this way, management is enabled to accept limitations that are unavoidable or desirable and to concentrate on the solution of the most critical problems whose solutions give promise of improvement. Com-plete coordination of operations need not be contemplated. Risk of a cer-tain amount of imbalance may be assumed in the hope of eliminating a critical bottleneck.

The value of budgeting procedures may go far beyond their specific ac-complishments. The mere fact that they involve a periodic, critical re-view of operations opens the door to improvements that would not other-wise be made. Difficulties or inefficiencies are brought to light. Key ex-ecutives are forced to recognize shortcomings, and knowledge that these are recognized by others provides an added incentive to overcome them. New ideas or other kinds of assistance obtained from joint efforts may provide remedies that would not be found by the individual executive left to himself. The gains realized in this way cannot readily be ex-pressed in quantitative terms but may represent a substantial contribu-tion to the over-all success of the organization.

On the other hand, all the values of budgeting may be lost if it is not kept within proper bounds. If, for example, it is made a means of bu-reaucratic maneuvering, it may well degenerate into bickering and re-crimination and perhaps become inoperative as a result. This tends to be the case when budgeting is pursued so enthusiastically as to restrict the scope for intelligent decision on the part of line executives. Budgeting is an aid to management, not an alternative to it.

Along with other planning procedures, budgeting has a close relation to forecasting in that it involves elements of looking ahead. A fairly com-mon limitation on operations for the firm that has adequate capacity is lack of orders, and forecasting efforts in the budgeting process are there-fore commonly concentrated on sales. Nevertheless, it may be far from true in any particular period or in any particular concern that: "The sales forecast is the keystone in the arch of the structure of planning in a manufacturing or trading corporation. The sales forecast is the support of a corporation's budgetary program, of its financial controls, of its planning for production and its inventory stocks."[4]

What should be emphasized is that the purpose of the budget is not to predetermine operations but to coordinate them. To hold to a fixed schedule through a period when conditions are changing is only to aggravate the problems that will ultimately have to be dealt with.

Not all aspects of operations can be adjusted with equal speed, of course, but there is no need to hold off the adjustments that can be made after it has become clear that the original schedule is in error. Ordinarily, the changes occurring within the budget period will not be so drastic as to make interim rescheduling necessary. On the rare occasions when such changes are experienced, the original budget and any forecasts that went into it should be scrapped promptly in order to gain the best possible adjustment to the new situation. Under these circumstances, the various activities may have to be rescheduled piecemeal, each according to its own determining conditions and, therefore, to some extent out of phase with each other, though still within the scope of the broader readjustment decided upon.

This kind of "controlled" adjustment of related activities to changing circumstances is a primary management objective. Many questions that come up have to be decided on grounds that have little if any relation to the current budget. The solution that is valid from an immediate economic point of view may not be valid from a long-term appraisal of business or public relations. All the broader policies governing the firm's operations usually have to be decided on a different basis from the detailed planning of activities in current scheduling periods.

Forecasting, although it may contribute something, cannot consistently provide the best means of realizing this objective. Adjustments made after the preliminary indications of difficulty have already put in an appearance can frequently give better results than any forecasting technique available. This is particularly true if the penalty for an incorrect forecast is large. The alternative, "after-the-fact" adjustments may be made in the usual way, by specific managerial decisions, or they may be made in accordance with certain preestablished policies or rules of operation that are activated whenever certain developments occur.

FORECASTING VERSUS OPERATIONS RESEARCH

The search for policies or rules that will permit the organization to function most effectively has come to be known as "operations research." This high-sounding title reflects the increasing complexity of business

[4] Newbury, *op. cit.*, p. 237.

operations. Common sense is no longer sufficient unto itself in management. Just as there is little place in industry for the individual inventor —since inventing today consists in solving a series of research problems in materials of high specification and in design to close tolerances—so the complexity of the operation as a whole may render the individual manager ineffective. At this point, calling in a team of specialized analysts capable of breaking down the over-all operation into its essential components and rearranging them for maximum efficiency may be the only way to solve certain problems.

The operations-research team brings a fresh point of view to the consideration of the firm's problems. It sets up operations in their entirety as a system of flows and stocks, preferably as a model or system of equations in suitable form for quantitative analysis. In solving a problem, it attempts to define accurately all returns and all costs, including the costs of idleness, or waiting time. It also attempts to specify optimum results under various circumstances, even though these are sometimes only the least disadvantageous of a number of unfavorable possibilities. It then explores interrelationships and attempts to determine the best of various courses of action. Since many business operations are of a character that can be accurately represented by this kind of system or model, startling results are often obtained from this abstract approach.

Some of the techniques of operations research have particular applicability to the problems of business management, which are largely problems in controlling variation in related flows and stocks. Products flow out to customers, materials and parts flow in, and work progresses from stage to stage. There are important elements of variation throughout. Control cannot be perfect, of course, so the flows must be adjusted to each other by accumulating or running off stocks at various points. Since it is generally desirable that these stocks be kept within limits, they may provide indications of the need for adjustment of the flows at various points in the complete chain or system.

Considering the firm's operations as a whole, and thus bringing elements from distant positions into close relationship with each other, may be requisite to a solution. In a complex system, this may be the only way to effect an adequate adjustment of the flows ordinarily thought of in terms of such functions as procurement, processing, and distribution. The factors important to a decision may not even be recognized if these functions are independent of each other.

When a variation occurs at any point, it has implications for both earlier and later stages. Only as those implications are conveyed can adjustments be effected at other points in the system. The purchasing agent should know as quickly as possible that the flow of orders obtained by the sales force has changed. Hence the prompt transmission of this information is necessary, and the theory of communication assumes an important role in the process of establishing controls. This, too, has been a primary focus of attention for the operations-research team.

Long before operations research came into the picture, business concerns had been attempting to improve efficiency by analyzing their operations through the use of scientific management procedures. The special contribution of operations research, which distinguishes it from earlier versions of research on business problems, is its introduction of recently developed mathematical and statistical techniques. These techniques utilize abstruse probability theory, and in certain kinds of models they are suitable for dealing with causes or sources of variation that do not produce definite results but only a probability of such results. They also put a good deal of emphasis on the early detection of uncontrolled variation through the analysis of irregularities that may provide an indication of coming change. A number of other problems, some relating to external sources of variation over which no control is possible, may also be dealt with effectively by these methods, since they offer a logical basis for selecting policies or lines of action to be adopted in some situations of this kind.

It would hardly be appropriate to consider this topic in further detail here, as the object of the present discussion is merely to compare and contrast the solutions provided by operations research with those provided by forecasting. The latter seeks to circumvent difficulties by anticipating them. The former seeks to eliminate costs or other disadvantages by establishing a controlled system capable of responding effectively and promptly to prevent perceived difficulties from growing to large proportions. If it is possible in the latter way to eliminate 80 percent of the costs imposed by certain kinds of changes, the net result may be better than forecasting those changes correctly four times out of five, since the costs of acting on a wrong forecast may be greater than average. In other words, there may be good justification for business to adopt the rule, "Don't make unnecessary forecasts!"

Looked at in this way, operations research may be regarded as the best alternative to forecasting. Its goal is to achieve a controlled system that will, within limits, make forecasts unnecessary. This goal is perhaps somewhat idealistic, since there are always contingencies that cannot be taken into account and breakdowns that cannot be prevented. There are, moreover, other reasons why operations research may be unable to solve important problems. The models it sets up usually have the same limitations and deficiencies as other models. They are usually partial abstractions, and if they are progressively expanded in complexity to the point of almost complete representation of the actuality, other difficulties may be encountered. For example, data requirements may become excessive.

Data are needed in constructing a realistic model, in testing its validity, and in using it to control operations. The right data have to be brought to the point of use at the right time. If data requirements are too complex, a model that might in other respects be sound will prove impractical.

Finally, the concern must be prepared to deal with the situations where the limits of operation of the controlled system are exceeded. Hence forecasting may still be appropriate with respect to the problems not solved by operations research, or by scientific management in general, and particularly with respect to problems arising from changes in the broader environment outside the firm's control.

Forecasting may thus properly be regarded as a branch of research or analysis dealing with external influences of importance to the firm, whereas various kinds of scientific management research deal with matters that may be handled effectively by the firm's own policies or operating procedures. Where the two overlap, it will probably be found that differences in the particular circumstances encountered are sufficiently great that either can work well on occasion but neither can work well on all occasions. When the kinds of action called for by the two approaches would be opposed or inconsistent, specific consideration by top management of the best course of action would probably be called for, taking account of all the relevant factors entering into both kinds of analysis.

Forecasting and operations research, like budgeting, are aids to management rather than alternatives to it. They are activities that have to be fitted into the pattern of operations as a whole if they are to make any useful contribution to results. As a rule, the personnel in other parts of the organization will not be able to master the techniques of forecasting or analysis, but their cooperation is necessary if the fruits of those techniques are to be realized. Since the personal element is bound to be important in the situation in which the results of research are to be utilized, the research analyst should avoid all pretenses about the methods he uses. He should be the first to point out that there is no magic in the solutions proposed. It should be made clear that getting results in this field is a matter of plugging away at a job, as it is in any other phase of company activity.

PROGRAM PLANNING

In many large corporations, top management has come to recognize that keeping abreast of economic development is a time-consuming job, one that cannot readily be handled along with myriad other duties. A solution of the problem is frequently sought by appointing a staff economist to keep informed, define potential areas of stress, report from time to time on problems of importance, and hold himself in readiness at all times to answer any questions that may arise. Sometimes he is also expected to prepare periodic forecasts of the general economy.

Even apart from this last item, this is an assignment whose difficulty is frequently not appreciated. For what is wanted is not economic information in general but such information sorted, rearranged, and oriented so that its implications for the company's own position are clear. Moreover, the presentation must be adapted to the importance of the question at hand; small points must be covered briefly as well as understandably and accurately. Before one can even begin to meet these specific needs, he must acquire a sound working knowledge of current industry developments and must even be able to anticipate problems before they become acute, in order to gain time for preparation and revision of applicable data. Without close, day-to-day contact with top executives on a basis of mutual confidence, these prerequisites of timeliness and orientation may not exist, and the possibility of functioning in this way may therefore also be lacking.

Where good working relations are established, there tend to be rather wide limits to the range of activities assigned to the economic research staff. It is often found that a good research man is good for other tasks also. Many assignments not strictly in his province may then be thrust upon him. Great restraint in the expansion of his activities is usually desirable, since extraneous assignments may pose a dilemma, unless they are part of a definite change in position. The analytical functions have to be kept up, but perhaps they cannot be kept up adequately, so that mistakes begin to creep in and working relations are disrupted. Here, as in other operations, responsibility has to be fixed and resources either kept undiluted or expanded with increases in the work load.

The functions most commonly assigned to the central research staff are those in the general area covered by the term "program planning." This activity is a systematic, continuing appraisal of opportunities and operating needs. It involves a broad view of the company's position in the industry and the industry's position in the economy. It involves bringing together and developing the importance of information from various sources, external and internal, covering such topics as potential economic changes of significance for the company's operations; shifts in the character of company or industry markets; the development of new products in the company's own laboratories or the appearance of new competition from such developments elsewhere; and the advantages of new equipment or the possible loss of position to be incurred in the event such equipment is installed by competitors. The information used often has to be of an engineering or other noneconomic character, but it must be translated and interpreted so that its economic significance can be understood as the basis for decisions.

Altogether, program planning is a process of systematic study of developments, which are often just distantly related to company operations and perhaps not pressing for an immediate decision, but which are of potentially great importance over the longer term. The program planner in effect becomes the understudy for top management in acquiring an education, and he must condense its conclusions for use by the executive who "is so busy he hasn't time to think."

The forecasting appropriate to carrying out these functions is primarily of a general economic character and refers to the intermediate or long term rather than to current operating periods. Such functions as budgeting and scheduling are performed within the framework of policies and rules that program planning is intended to formulate. The longer, detached analysis that results in decisions as to product lines, construction or acquisition of new facilities, new areas of operation, and other broad policies must usually be given, and cannot be changed, in the scheduling period. Line management should, of course, participate in the making of such decisions. But the forecasts or analyses that provide the basis for them often lie outside the province of the line organization and may appropriately be set up in a separate department.

Whether or not the central research staff actually has responsibility for making forecasts, there is usually something to be gained by having this group review all forecasts made elsewhere. The research staff is oriented toward a body of information and a type of causal relationship that are not matters of concern to the line departments. Its efforts are usually directed toward bringing out the broader lines of reasoning or implicit assumptions embodied in the forecasts of the more specialized departmental analysts. Merely making these explicit may reveal inadequacies, and if a synthesis in terms of special and general economic considerations is possible, the work of the central research staff as well as that of the line departments may be improved.

A technique for reviewing the forecasts of operating divisions is described by Ashley Wright, of Standard Oil of New Jersey.[5] The central staff there makes a series of statistical projections for each product or area and sets up a band covering the range of two standard errors above and below the projections. If the forecast of any operating division falls within this band, it is accepted. If not, it is questioned, and the operating division is forced to justify its estimates. Occasionally this results in acceptance of an extreme forecast. More often, the forecast is modified toward the range that can be justified by the statistical projection. It

[5] C. Ashley Wright, *Improving the Accuracy of Economic Forecasts,* August, 1953. (Mimeographed.)

should be kept in mind that demand for the output of this industry is relatively stable, so that such projections offer a fairly high degree of reliability. The same method would not necessarily operate as well in other industries and might be particularly wanting in the highly variable durable-goods industries. Nevertheless, it shows how different approaches can validly supplement each other.

Similar values may often be realized by calling in experts from the outside as consultants on problems of this kind. The outside expert represents a new source of ideas, again with a different focus and orientation. He is usually capable of exercising a greater degree of independence with respect to the thinking of top management than are the lower echelons of company executives. He may do a given job more economically than would be possible if a full-time staff would otherwise have to be employed. For these and a variety of other reasons, many concerns prefer not to make internal forecasts of the general economy but to rely on outside consultants or research services for ideas in this field. With respect to the internal forecasts of a more specific character, the consultant can play the same role of reviewer, critic, and conciliator as a central research staff to whom these functions might be assigned.

ORGANIZING FORECASTING ACTIVITIES

Forecasting activities other than that of a general economic character may appropriately be assigned to the points of use. Sales forecasting is most commonly placed in the sales department, often under the director of market research. Sometimes it is placed in the finance department for better integration with budgeting, and occasionally even in the production department, as part of the scheduling process. Hardly ever is the forecasting of raw-materials markets placed anywhere but in the purchasing department, the exceptions again usually being attempts to integrate it with budgeting operations. The finance department almost invariably does some forecasting, because of the need for anticipating cash flows that might unduly affect the liquid position of the company if provision is not made in advance for handling them.

Attempts to centralize all forecasting in a separate department usually do not meet with complete success. Even where a good central staff is organized, as by promotion from within, the various departments continue to do the forecasting they consider necessary, merely describing it as something else for budgetary purposes. Or, worse still, they may refuse all cooperation, focusing responsibility on the central staff, and wait for the mistakes that will inevitably be made. The harm that may accrue from such developments is inestimable.

The allocation of responsibility for any kind of forecasting depends in part upon the availability of personnel with the qualifications and temperament suitable to this activity. It is futile to expect satisfactory forecasts from certain kinds of personnel who may nevertheless be excellent in the performance of the line duties for which they were employed.

Where only one economic-research staff is available, it is rarely desirable to assign both forecasting and public relations work to it. Necessary deviations of company policy or of its public statements from those appropriate in the light of accurate forecasts should not be permitted to influence the forecasts themselves. The attitudes of the good public relations man and the good forecaster are so divergent that they ordinarily can be mixed only to the detriment of both. The research staff may appropriately be asked for material to be included in speeches or in other public relations output; but if the latter is its primary function, not much in the way of realistic analysis or forecasts should be expected from it.

Only as forecasters and analysts are able to present the results of their work in such a way as to make it understandable to those with the power of decision can they expect to function effectively. This requirement is not unique to the economic analyst, of course; it is a basic condition affecting technicians, engineers, and specialists in general. Some things must perhaps be taken on faith by executives without specialized training, but at least the basic logic of the processes involved should be presented clearly, and to the extent that those processes give only partial indications or probabilities rather than assured results, proposals for their application should be tempered with judgment. In other words, the best results will usually be obtained when the analyst himself is capable of assuming the attitude of the executive, who of necessity considers proposals in the broad perspective of company activities as a whole.

Forecasters sometimes find it hard to endure the sad experience of having their best forecasts disregarded—with all the dire consequences they were able to foretell. There are occasions, however, when management may be unable to avoid such consequences even though it accepts the forecast. It may have to go along with a movement in order to protect its future standing in the business. As a rule, neither customers nor suppliers will be tolerant of efforts that restrain the fulfillment of their own programs. To avoid antagonizing them, actions contrary to the best policy may have to be taken. Even when it is perfectly aware of the danger of overstocking, a concern may have to build up work in process to the point where such danger becomes acute in order to meet the demands of customers, and it may have to overorder materials to be assured of adequate supplies. Such action is a management prerogative and cannot be effectively opposed by the forecaster.

Partly as a means of promoting good personal relations and preventing misunderstanding, many large corporations have arranged for interchange of personnel or training programs to acquaint younger executives with the methods and purposes of work in other divisions, both line and staff. Research men may be given temporary assignments in line divisions or even permanently transferred to line managerial positions when they have displayed ability to handle such work. Conversely, short courses in research or forecasting may be set up for line executives, and they too may be assigned temporarily or permanently to the research staff.

As another approach, task forces from various areas may be assigned to work closely together on problems of joint interest. Thus, economists and engineers may work with production men on problems relating to the introduction of new equipment, with the engineers primarily interested in the question of what is the best kind of equipment and the economists primarily interested in the questions of how many units are needed and when they should be installed. The process of working together may produce momentary disagreements, but the processes of discussion and weighing differences of opinion in the interest of a common goal makes for effective cooperation in the longer run.

If there is any acceptable generalization at all on the organization of forecasting activities, it is perhaps that they should be set up in such a way as to promote teamwork at top management levels. Each part of the organization must know what the others are planning to do in order to achieve coordination of efforts, and each must be willing to sacrifice its own special interests at times to the greater good of the organization as a whole. Discussion of divergent views and agreement on a line of action that appears best in the light of the various possibilities may well be more important than anything to be gained from forecasts as such.

FORECASTS SHOULD DEAL WITH SPECIFIC PROBLEMS

Three kinds of forecasting problems are typically encountered by business concerns. The first kind is encountered in connection with such activities as budgeting, production scheduling, and the handling of sales campaigns. It is usually of a very short term character, say, one-quarter of a year ahead. Because of its close tie to current operations, such forecasting lies primarily in the province of line management. The second kind is encountered as a result of general economic changes or limited changes in program, such as new-model introductions or rearrangement of work in existing facilities, for which special provision must be made. Such changes require forecasts running to a year or more ahead and are the special province of the financial and economic research staffs. The third kind involves basic decisions concerning the sphere of operations of the business as a whole, such as those relating to product lines and investment in new facilities. Such decisions are the province of top management. The forecasting involved is essentially long range in character and should embody the results of research and planning work throughout the organization.

This classification is not intended to be either complete or wholly accurate. There are numerous exceptions and special situations that cannot be briefly covered. The firm whose products require an exceptionally long production period may feel that the description does not fit its problems at all. The firm trading in sensitive farm commodities, whose purchases and sales have very short term aspects as well as some that run through an entire crop year or longer, may feel for entirely different reasons that the separation is artificial. Nevertheless, there are many firms for which these are typical problems, and the classification may serve to bring out some important distinctions as to the techniques appropriate in each case.

The term *sales forecasting* is loosely used to apply to work on all three of these types of problems. This term is not entirely inappropriate because future markets are an element invariably considered, regardless of the range or purpose of the forecast. Perhaps, however, this term might best be confined to the first type alone, the short-term operating forecasts, in order to avoid any implications that the same procedures are applicable to all three types of problems. Reports from the sales force, for example, have only very short term validity at best, and it is futile to think of applying them to the longer-term needs. If this suggestion were followed, other appropriate terms could be used to designate attempts to solve the other kinds of problems. For convenience in the following discussion, the second type, ranging a year or so into the future, will be referred to as *program forecasting*, and the third type will be designated *facilities forecasting*.

The most common source of fallacy in discussions which treat all these problems as if they were alike arises from the fact that unsupported judgment methods seemingly apply in all cases. The judgment technique most widely used is commonly referred to as the "panel-of-executive-opinion" method. The key executives of the concern—who are assumed to be best informed about developments in the industry, in its markets, and in other matters relevant to the prospects for future business—are brought together to consider all aspects of the situation and combine their individual judgments by reconciling diverse, and possibly conflicting, influences and points of view.

The advantages usually cited for this approach are of a twofold character: first, it is supposed to bring to bear on the problem the best available, up-to-the-minute appraisals of what is currently happening as well as the widest range of information about special factors which may be significant in the anticipated situation; second, it is supposed to result in a balanced point of view, by tempering the enthusiasm of some with the misgivings of others. Whether it actually produces these advantages is doubtful. In an actual situation, the views of each executive are affected to a large degree by questions of personal relations, by what he wants for his own department, and by what he thinks the others ought to be doing in theirs. The result of such discussions is ordinarily compromise rather than integration. Nevertheless, a good many firms have come to the conclusion that there is no satisfactory alternative and have gone back to this method after trying other approaches.

Reliance on this method partly derives from confusing forecasting and program setting. This confusion is expressed in what is thought to be a third advantage, namely, the fixing of responsibility on all who have participated in making the forecast. In most concerns that are not dictatorially operated, the committee approach is used in setting programs, and participation may provide an additional incentive to make things come out as desired. However, any executive, whether or not he participates, should feel responsible for helping to achieve the established goals. Even more important, it should be recognized that the primary purpose is not forecasting at all. The group may wish to use forecasts from various sources as one type of information bearing on their problem. But it should aim at modifying the results forecast rather than at incorporating them in the operating schedules.

Where forecasts are actually intended as the end product of committee action, perhaps being recorded and subsequently checked as such, all sorts of difficulties are encountered. Other interests invariably affect the discussion, sometimes in obscure ways. Members of the group necessarily vary greatly in training and background, in time spent in preparation, and in ability to present a point of view forcefully. None of these need be highly correlated with forecasting ability, and any consensus arrived at will be biased accordingly. But if extraneous matters may bias the forecast, the latter may also bias operations. Many participants come out of such meetings in a spirit of either "I'll show them!" or "This is it! I'm glad I don't have to go through that again for another three months!" The effects in either case are anything but harmless. All this is best avoided. Management should stick to the job of running the business and not open up another avenue of possible friction and additional personal pressure on key executives.

SALES FORECASTING

In sales forecasting, as in commodity and industry forecasting, one of the first things to be determined is the relation of the company's sales to business in general. This has to be accomplished by systematic investigation of past experience and basic factors, as in other fields of forecasting. However, for reasons to be discussed shortly, this phase is usually of a lower order of importance for very short term forecasts or projections. Reports from analysts actually engaged in forecasting for business concerns indicate that general business developments are considered important about half the time, but this probably overstates the case, since they were reporting on all their forecasts, long and short alike, and not just on those extending over scheduling periods. Nevertheless, underlying relationships should not be overlooked, even though primary reliance is placed on other methods.

For best results, both the timing and the range of forecasts should be explicitly considered. These should, of course, be adapted to the need and therefore made a function of the firm's operating schedules; forecasting periods should not be made to conform slavishly to calendar quarters or years. In fact, scheduling periods should themselves be adjusted in the light of any "natural" periodicity in the firm's operations. Seasonal factors may be of primary importance in this respect. Other important factors may be found in such conditions as procurement-contract periods for necessary raw materials or recruitment and training time for new workers. Since there is no reason why a firm should not break the year into fiscal periods to suit its own convenience for these purposes, the research that defines the forecasting method to be used may also contribute in other ways to the improvement of planning and control procedures.

Projecting Continuity and Irregularity. Perhaps the most important point to keep in mind in forecasting over very short periods is that results will be determined under conditions of temporary variation or deviation from established patterns. Both relationships and timing must bow before the changes temporarily imposed by irregularities beyond any possibility of control.

The sources of variation that may have no effect beyond a very brief interval are indeed numerous. Seasonal factors indicate "normal" movements only in the sense of a statistical average from which wide deviations may occur. Customers sometimes move simultaneously to place or to cancel orders; bulges of air-conditioner sales in extremely hot weather afford an illustration. Sales efforts may also vary sharply, and it is much easier by these means to shift the timing of orders than the ultimate total realized. If customers are piling up excess inventories, the movement is much more likely to continue for 3 months than for a whole year. Market shares may also gyrate wildly for a time; in the 1954 setback, Chrysler's share of the passenger-car market was cut in half in less than a year. All such possibilities make for a situation in which the considerations of the moment tend to gain precedence over the basic, and perhaps ultimately the more reliable, determinants of position.

In these circumstances, the main reliance is ordinarily on continuity, tempered by knowledge of special developments, many of which are of no lasting significance. The usual procedure is to project what is currently going on some distance into the future. Any method for doing this may be used, but for the analyst with judgment the simple extension of current movements from the last point of record is as good a procedure as any. As a rule, the next quarter year is still very much a part of the "specious present" in which the forecaster is doing his work.

Experience and understanding are, of course, essential. The mere character of the product—for example, whether it is durable rather than non-durable—may make an important difference in the kind of projection used. An accurate appraisal of the over-all situation is also helpful. But even when applied with the best of judgment, the techniques of projection are likely to be inadequate by themselves. Inside information of a relevant character has to be used to make modifications and adjustments, and in some periods, these will be the essence of defining the short-term movement. The switching of a single large account from another supplier may be decisive. Sales contests, new advertising campaigns, or other special stimuli should be taken into account. The progress of labor negotiations indicating the probable termination of a strike may be the key to near-term developments. The more completely and accurately such bits and pieces of special information can be utilized, the greater will be the possibility of anticipating the temporary jogs and jiggles that cannot properly be considered part of the statistically definable movement at all.

Since so much depends upon mere deviations and irregularities, it is important to distinguish between temporary and permanent shifts. The increase in sales resulting from a contest has different implications from the switch of a large account from a competitive source of supply, though possibly the latter may be tied up with the former. A gain of the former kind may produce only a momentary bulge in ordering, and an early reversal should then be looked for. In contrast, a gain of the latter kind may require a permanent adjustment of program.

Projecting the future course of an exceptional movement depends largely on being able to define its character in causal terms. Knowing the factors responsible for what has occurred may make it possible to say definitely that the move will continue or that it will soon reverse. If a certain kind of movement recurs from time to time, it may be possible to apply a pattern in making the projection. This is the usual procedure for seasonal movements, but other movements longer or shorter than a year can sometimes be defined in the same way, as, for example, when they are associated with a typical adjustment undertaken by customers from time to time. An attempt to reproduce past movements accurately by means of interpolation over periods defined by specific criteria may be helpful in developing such patterns.

Continuity of change may be utilized statistically as well as by direct projection or extrapolation. The means of approaching the problem in this way are provided by the techniques of serial correlation. Each period's sales may tend to be correlated with those of the preceding period. Or the change from one period to the next may be correlated with the preceding change. After such a correlation is established, it may be utilized by setting up a "naïve model" and simply computing the next observation as soon as the last needed as an independent variable is available.

As a rule, the results obtained by this method can be improved by the application of judgment and special information; therefore it is recommended not as the sole basis for a forecast but rather as a supplement to other methods. Several studies of actual forecasts have shown that greater accuracy could have been obtained by this method than by the methods actually used.[6] Chart 16–1 provides a comparison of the results obtained from a naïve model with the forecasts worked out by a company that makes detailed quarterly forecasts by geographical area and takes pride in the results it has obtained.[7] It is clear from this chart that the company's forecasters were not doing much better, on the average, than the results produced by a simple mechanical formula. The latter, incidentally, had the advantage of avoiding the problem of seasonal adjustment, since it utilized year-to-year percentage changes, merely carrying the last observed percentage into the next quarter.

In cases where the serial correlation is high enough, this procedure may eliminate the necessity for working out forecasts by other methods. Sometimes this approach gives good results at all but certain critical points, such as cyclical turns. A perfectly regular 40-month cycle of the type constructed by Newbury[8] would be accurately forecast by a naïve model in all but 1 month out of 20. Some forecasters therefore advocate use of some relatively simple method of projection to be used in routine circumstances, supplemented by special efforts to detect the approach of turning points. One approach to the latter problem is based upon the use of statistical indicators.[9] Another is simply to apply judgment in the

[6] See R. Ferber, *The Railroad Shippers Forecasts,* University of Illinois, Bureau of Economic and Business Research, Urbana, Ill., 1953.

[7] See C. M. Crawford, *Sales Forecasting: Methods of Selected Firms,* University of Illinois, Bureau of Economic and Business Research, Urbana, Ill., February, 1955.

[8] See Chap. 3, p. 63.

[9] See Chap. 4, pp. 118–125.

problem of timing, so that, after a movement has run for a while, the forecaster begins to look for a reversal.[10]

Although these simple techniques may work well at times, particularly for experienced forecasters who have developed a "feel" for the significance of various developments, they are at best an inadequate substitute for the search for causes that define the course being pursued into the period ahead.

Chart 16–1. Contrast between Company Forecast and Naïve Model on Sales of Product A, by Quarters, 1949–1952

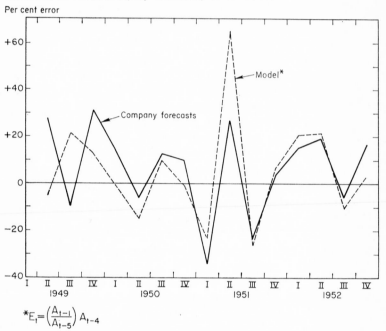

$$*E_t = \left(\frac{A_{t-1}}{A_{t-5}}\right) A_{t-4}$$

SOURCE: C. M. Crawford, Sales Forecasting: Methods of Selected Firms, University of Illinois, Bureau of Economic and Business Research, Urbana, Ill.; February, 1955, Bulletin 78, p. 44.

Using Outside Information. Ordinarily this kind of short-term forecasting is carried out in terms of the sales data themselves, with "sales" being variously defined as orders, billings, shipments, or receipts. Sometimes output is the strategic variable to forecast, and the exact objective or focus of the forecast may accordingly be shifted from time to time, as appears to be appropriate.

In any case, the differences between such measures as orders and out-

[10] See Wilson Wright, "Turning Points in Sales and Profits," *Forecasting for Profit,* John Wiley & Sons, Inc., New York, 1947, pp. 127–136.

put have to be taken into account in effecting coordination of operations. What will happen to inventories is almost always a matter of direct concern. In some lines of business, shifts in unfilled orders may also play an important role in reconciling the various items that enter into detailed operating budgets. When the changes in these balancing items are large, they may become the decisive elements in the picture, and forecasts of at least some of the other items will be dependent upon the adjustments undertaken to bring inventories or unfilled orders under control.

Finding an explanation in the latter terms may require reference to other data than those available in the firm's own records. Thus an advance in sales accompanied by a rise in distributors' inventories is different from an advance accompanied by a fall in such inventories. Similarly, a shift that affects the whole industry or the whole economy is likely to have a different impact from one affecting the company's business alone. A broader appraisal of the situation may therefore be useful. If the firm is not moving in line with the rest of the industry, every effort should be made to discover the factors underlying its exceptional performance, because only knowing what accounts for such a movement can provide a basis for making forecasts accurate or for taking effective management action.

The difficulty usually encountered in utilizing knowledge of distributors' stocks or competitors' sales is lack of up-to-date information. Even where statistics of the kind desired are compiled and published, they may be available only after too long a lapse of time. The operations of one of the foremost market-research organizations is based largely on an attempt to remedy this deficiency. It employs a field force to make prompt monthly checks of a sample of retail outlets in the drug and grocery fields and to determine sales and inventories of its client's products and also of competitive brands.[11] Other surveys of flows and stocks have also proved successful, usually where conditions for satisfactory sampling exist or other characteristics of the business make it possible for a limited number of reports to give satisfactory indications for other reasons.

Some companies or industries, through their trade associations, compile their own estimates of distributive stocks. The individual company is usually at a disadvantage in compiling data. It may have to rely on estimates by its sales force, which are seldom accurate, because salesmen are not statisticians and do not exercise proper care in compiling data; or it may have to accept reports from a group of wholesalers or re-

[11] A. C. Nielsen, "Evolution of Factual Techniques in Market Research," in *Market Research and Business Management,* Marketing Award Papers, 1951, Illinois Marketing Symposium, University of Illinois, Bureau of Economic and Business Research, Urbana, Ill., 1952.

tailers, and these reports may be subject to biases of various kinds. If comparatively accurate reports of sales at any succeeding stage are available, inventory changes in intermediate positions may be inferred by taking the difference between the sales estimates and the shipments. However, when the inventory change is computed as a residual, it may be subject to large errors as a result of minor errors in the sales estimates.

In the auto industry, where finished stocks are typically held by dealers or are in process of shipment to dealers, the various companies regularly compile data on retail sales and dealers' stocks at 10-day intervals. As soon as the reports from the individual companies are available, the Automobile Manufacturers' Association combines them into over-all totals for the industry and makes the results available to the companies. Even with the relatively elaborate reporting mechanism thus available, the data reveal a certain amount of inconsistency in that changes in stocks do not coincide with the difference between sales and shipments, and in particular periods the discrepancy may be substantial. On the whole, however, these data are very useful in forecasting any of the interrelated components.

Useful information from the outside need not be confined to distributive operations, of course. It may go beyond distributors to the final consumers or back in the flow of parts and materials to the "earliest" activities associated with the firm's products. Any item of information that gives valuable clues may justify the expense of compiling it, and surveys are therefore commonly employed by market-research analysts to obtain desired information. However, with certain exceptions, like those described in the preceding paragraphs, surveys are not well suited to recurring, short-term use. More commonly, they are designed to obtain information desired for programing activities, such as introducing a new model, changing packages or labels, and deciding other questions that do not recur from one scheduling interval to the next.

Forecasts by the Sales Force.[12] Another way to utilize information from the field of operations in forecasting sales is to draw upon the knowledge and judgment of the sales force. The most widely used procedure is to obtain forecasts of sales from each salesman in standard form and to compile these, with some adjustment, into a combined forecast for the firm as a whole. The result is commonly referred to as the "sales-force composite."

The individual salesman participating in this procedure might be regarded as a kind of survey interviewer. He is constantly in the field and makes regular contacts with the firm's customers. Once he has estab-

[12] For a more extended discussion of sales-force methods, see G. Clark Thompson, *Forecasting Sales*, National Industrial Conference Board, Studies in Business Policy, no. 25, New York, 1947.

lished satisfactory working relationships with buyers, he is bound to learn something about what their firms are doing and planning. Perhaps all he needs is a little training in systematic observation and reporting. Some firms make rather extensive efforts in this direction. Other firms, who are more skeptical of the approach, feel it is a waste of selling effort to convert the sales force into part-time interviewers or reporters.

The salesman also has specialized knowledge of a more or less personal character. He often knows where he can get additional orders if he has to. He may have a kitty of potential orders saved up, to be drawn upon only when some special incentive is offered or some emergency has to be met. Or he may know how to borrow from the future under such conditions. He is able in various ways to step up his selling effort for limited periods. Certain orders that he had considered hardly worth writing up take on real value during a contest. In other periods, the process works in reverse. Opportunities are exhausted. Quotas cannot be met by anything he can do. Resistance to pressure from above may even result in reduced effort for a while. The personal element in the situation may, therefore, invest his judgment with some value. For the same reason, however, his own biases are likely to creep into any forecasts he submits.

The basis for accepting this kind of judgment evidently lies in the intimate knowledge of the sales force about the activities of customers and salesmen and the relations between them. It may immediately be noted that this kind of knowledge produces advantages of a very short term character only. Its merit lies in providing a way to take account of the current adjustments being made by customers or by the salesmen themselves. Since their current operating adjustments are seldom effective for more than a brief interval—depending, of course, on the nature of the business—any longer extension of the forecast reduces the whole procedure to an unsupported-judgment technique. As such, its validity is open to question. The idea that the salesman's judgments about the future are better than those of any other group has never been validated. Most observers, in fact, lean toward the contrary opinion, which holds that the salesman's expectations are more unstable than business itself, swinging widely from extreme optimism to extreme pessimism.

Few firms that use this procedure accept the judgments of the individual salesmen as they are first reported. Usually they are adjusted in the district office, then adjusted again in the central sales office, and perhaps further modified in the light of information from other departments.

A variant of the method is known as the "sales-manager composite." In this case, the forecasts originate not with the individual salesmen but with the sales managers, who supervise groups of salesmen in each of the districts or areas established by the organization of the sales force. This method has the advantage of being much less expensive, since the number of participants is greatly reduced. In addition, the maturity and experience of the managers is presumed to introduce certain advantages, among them better perspective on current developments, greater stability of judgment, and less violent emotional response to market changes. On the other hand, something of the specialized, local, and personal knowledge of the individual salesmen may be lost, and sales managers, like the salesmen themselves, are selected for qualities almost entirely unrelated to forecasting ability.

One attraction of these sales-force procedures for many companies lies not in their ability to produce good forecasts but in their value as aids to sales administration. They provide an opportunity for regular discussion of current developments and exchange of ideas between central administration and the sales force. If over-all forecasts are worked out centrally, they must in any case be broken down by products, districts, and individual salesmen, and such breakdowns are automatically provided by this method. Moreover, if the sales force cannot live up to the forecasts, they cannot blame central administration for unrealistic quotas. It is then thought to be easier to "straighten them out." Pep talks and other pressure can be applied vigorously in good conscience.

Even as aids to sales administration, the value of these "forecasts" may be questioned. Attempts to shift responsibility are more likely to be destructive of morale than the reverse. Nothing is gained by impressing the salesman with the fact that he is a poor forecaster as well as a poor salesman. However, let that question be answered by each company as it may, it is clearly no more than confusion to think of any procedure worked out primarily for administrative purposes as a real forecasting effort.

Particularly destructive of any forecasting value are arrangements that tie salesmen's compensation to the "forecasts." The sales force quickly develops a cynical attitude toward the whole process and attempts to use it to its own advantage. Sales managers in particular develop an acute sense of what is politic under the circumstances. With objectivity lacking, the entire approach is rendered futile. The whole upward and downward flow of specious "forecasts" is best avoided under these circumstances.

Correlation Techniques. To be useful in sales forecasting, information does not have to be directly tied to the firm's own operations. Relevant information includes everything that is capable of providing valid indications of prospective changes. Whenever a correlation with a suitable statistical series can be set up, it is likely to be useful if that series leads the company's sales or is itself capable of being forecast. The possibility of using published statistical series in this way should not be overlooked.

An example of the correlation approach is given in Charts 16–2 and 16–3.[13] In this case, the lead of contract awards over construction activity is used to derive sales of plumbing equipment 4 months later. The seasonal variation in both series is well defined, as Chart 16–2 indicates. There is, however, a great deal of irregularity in the monthly data, so that the correlation is better if set up in terms of smoothed data, as shown in Chart 16–3. Then the ratio of sales to contracts may be applied

Chart 16–2. Seasonal Variations in Residential Contracts Awarded and ARCO Plumbing Sales

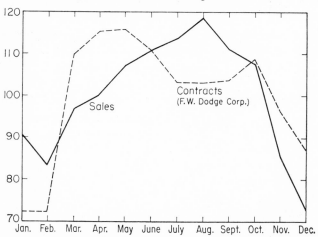

SOURCE: Reproduced from G. Clark Thompson, Forecasting Sales, National Industrial Conference Board, Studies in Business Policy, no. 25, New York, 1947, p. 19. Original data from American Radiator and Standard Sanitary Corporation and F. W. Dodge Corporation.

to obtain an estimate of sales for a year that includes 4 future months. Subtracting the actual sales for the last 8 months results in an estimate of sales for the 4 months ahead. Some practical difficulties are experienced in the actual use of this method, but the idea behind it is unquestionably sound.

The opportunities for use of correlations in short-term forecasting of this type are very restricted. The statistics used as independent variables become available only after a lag. Sometimes they can be projected more dependably than the sales data themselves, but the lack of dependability in the relationship tends to offset this advantage. Whether such relationships exist and whether the necessary data can be obtained to

[13] *Ibid.*, p. 19.

use them on a useful working schedule are questions to be answered in each specific case. Considerable ingenuity must be exercised in discovering and testing relationships and in establishing the data-transmission system needed to make them operative.

Forecasts may also be used to check each other. Systematic recording and checking of forecasts worked out by different methods is the basic procedure for determining the validity of any of them. If this procedure does not prove that one method is always better than the others, it may —perhaps better still—reveal the circumstances in which each gives its best performance.

Checking the sales forecasts against longer-range program forecasts is also useful. The current developments that reveal the accuracy of the

Chart 16–3. ARCO Plumbing Sales and Residential Contracts Awarded†
Index Numbers: 12-months moving averages

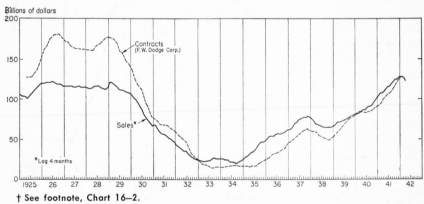

† See footnote, Chart 16–2.

short forecast are also the initial testing ground for the longer forecast. If there are inconsistencies between the forecasts, or between forecasts and current developments, attention is called to the need for research that will put both forecasts on the right track. In this way, the longer-term program forecast can lend stability to the series of short-term sales forecasts of which it is ultimately composed, and the latter can call early attention to the need for program revision.

PROGRAM FORECASTS

Program forecasts are usually desired in making decisions about activities that will have to be sustained for a year or more after the decision is made. The necessity for such decisions arises from time to time in all phases of company activity. Among them may be mentioned basic decisions on product lines, including model changes; sales and advertising campaigns requiring sustained effort for satisfactory results; procurement programs where materials are short or capacity for parts production is limited; and provision for peak financing needs, including both working capital and expansion of fixed assets.

There are bound to be mistakes in the programs adopted, of course, and these will vary in costliness. Usually adjustments can be made after the difficulty has made itself felt. In some cases, however, failure to prepare in advance may make it extremely difficult to carry out an assignment at all, and then a real emergency may be encountered.

The fact that such problems arise in all phases of activity does not mean that all departments have to engage in the over-all analysis needed for general forecasting. The specific information about the current situation available to each department is of much less value after the first few months ahead and may be worthless in delineating what the situation will be a year later. Hence this function is usually assigned to a single staff group, whose results may be modified by top-management discussion and adjusted in various respects to meet the needs of the various departments.

Where there is no central economics staff, the finance department is commonly assigned this function. That department has responsibility for providing adequate finances to carry out the programs decided upon, and the only way it can meet this responsibility is by anticipating the situations that will develop.

Another reason the finance department may be given an important role in this activity arises from the fact that it usually becomes custodian of the program forecasts, for purposes of budgeting and cost control, and subsequently prepares analyses of the financial results achieved. In large corporations, over-all program plans typically assign responsibility for results to divisions, or "profit centers," which may at times be run like separate independent businesses, often buying from each other and requiring competitive prices on the items purchased.

When results are subsequently reviewed, it is ordinarily evident that they were influenced by circumstances beyond control. To evaluate performance with respect to controllable factors, it is necessary to adjust for uncontrolled variation. For this purpose, some form of "break-even" analysis is usually adopted, ranging from relatively simple "standard-volume" adjustments to relatively complex "flexible" budgets.[14] The essence of such analysis is a determination of the relationship of costs and profits to sales volume or to some other measure of output. This makes possible a determination of what costs and profits would have been if

[14] For a more detailed discussion, see Joel Dean, *Managerial Economics,* Prentice-Hall, Inc., Englewood Cliffs, N.J., 1951.

output goals had been realized or, alternatively, a determination of what costs and profits should have been at the volume realized, and this provides a standard by which actual results may be judged.

Once the relationships necessary to break-even analysis are available, they may readily be put to forecasting use. The effects on profits of anticipated changes in volume, prices, and various elements of cost may readily be segregated from those of other factors and their special significance thus analyzed as a basis for program changes or other policy decisions. It should be recognized, however, that this kind of analysis does not automatically produce forecasts. The forecasting results obtained from it are dependent not only upon the various subsidiary forecasts entering into the computation but also upon unforeseen variation in the "other things assumed to remain equal."

Financial executives often find break-even analysis of approved programs useful in carrying out their own responsibilities. It may be used, for example, as the basis for cash forecasts, though departures from the strict application of this approach are commonly desirable. Cash inflows and outflows vary greatly in timing as well as in amplitude. As a result, funds may be extremely tight in one period and accumulate to an unreasonable surplus in another. If seasonal levels differ widely, provision has to be made at one period of the year for the requirements of another. Crises may arise over somewhat longer periods, as, for example, when a sudden downturn in demand makes it necessary to carry large inventories over a period in which other commitments undertaken in an earlier period are also at a peak level.

If such developments are not anticipated, financing has to be attempted in an atmosphere of emergency, and the financial position may look so shaky that loans are refused. When the need is anticipated, on the other hand, lines of bank credit may be prearranged and drawn upon without question over the period specified. Even then difficulties may be encountered. Bank loans are ordinarily regarded as short-term credit of a kind that will be self-liquidating. They may not prove to be so, however, and if a period of tight money develops, outstanding loans may be called or refused renewal at a time when company needs are acute, requiring additions to available funds rather than any curtailment. Such developments are a frequent cause of failure for small businesses. It is so important to avoid them that forecasting the cash position may be considered a requirement for sound financial management.

Ideally, the cash forecast should be based upon a complete forecast of all receipts and all outlays, including those resulting from capital and financial transactions. This would involve a forecast of the economy as a whole, of money-market developments, and of specific sectors relating to the company's business.

In practice, a much less exacting procedure is usually followed. Attention is concentrated on a limited number of major items. Outlays that are subject to management decision can be anticipated with reasonable accuracy. Some, like payrolls, are of a recurring character, and may be regarded as primarily determined by budgeting or scheduling procedures. Others, like payments on construction contracts, are known in advance. In contrast, receipts are likely to be much less subject to control. They are not entirely beyond control, because sales may be pushed at sacrifice prices; but such expedients may be costly, not only during the immediate emergency but also afterward, because of their reactions on the market.

Considerations of this kind often lead the financial executive to a cautious appraisal of prospective receipts, to ensure protection against the maximum discrepancy that might develop. This tends to place a check on the enthusiasm of sales or producing departments and helps to explain why financial policy is regarded in some concerns as an additional obstacle that has to be overcome in getting things done.

Under these circumstances, the "easy way" of making cash forecasts may be a source of friction, useful as those forecasts may be in themselves. This is particularly true if management attitudes in general are competitive rather than cooperative, so that other executives try to "show the forecaster up." In contrast, where all seek to make the best adjustments to the emerging situation, regardless of how well it conforms to the forecast, the longer look into the future may be of real value, not only in facilitating program decisions, but in helping to interpret interim developments and thus in making a contribution to program revisions.

In other words, forecasting as a continuous process, in which long- and short-term forecasts constantly interact, should help to eliminate conflicts between basic objectives of carrying programs through to completion and of maintaining flexibility of operations. There is a tendency for management to assume that the existing conditions will continue, so that decisions once made can be permitted to stand indefinitely. On the other hand, when the actual facts belatedly reveal incorrect expectations, there is a tendency to shift all the way to the other extreme for a while. This makes for instability and recurring crises. Sound forecasting should run counter to both tendencies. It should temper undue optimism or pessimism in the first instance; and it should also be kept flexible by conscious comparison of actual conditions with those forecast, so that deviations are detected early and made the basis of revisions if it appears that the emerging situation is inconsistent with the program adopted.

The kind of comprehensive forecasting that attempts to define prospective operating results as a whole is more nearly akin to the commodity and industry forecasting described in Chapter 15 than to sales forecasting more narrowly defined. The starting point is analysis of the factors affecting the company's business, with a view to determining those which are primarily dependent upon changes in other parts of the economy and those which must be treated as autonomous or independent variables. Included in the latter group are some factors subject to the company's own control.

The most important element added to the forecasting problem at the level of the individual firm is its relations with competitors. These are important even to the firm that is the sole producer of a product, to the extent that there are other products which serve the same kind of needs and therefore represent substitutes for it. The actions taken by competitors may modify the effects of both general economic relations and autonomous factors. Aggressive competition may make it impossible for the individual firm to gain anything from a rise in over-all income and the threat of competitors' retaliation may seriously restrict the firm's own freedom of action. This means that the definition of both kinds of factors must be made specific to the firm's own situation. In other words, the industry analysis must be carried one step further, to a definition of the firm's position in the industry.

The usual procedure, therefore, is as follows: Determine whether, or to what extent, autonomous analysis is applicable. If autonomous methods of projection are utilized, it is nevertheless essential to give due attention to the competitive situation in the industry or in closely related lines. If relationships are decisive in the forecast, on the other hand, it is generally best to proceed from the general to the specific, that is, first to work out or otherwise obtain an acceptable forecast for economic activity in general, then to translate it into an industry forecast, and finally to determine the individual concern's prospects in relation to the industry as a whole or in relation to key firms in the industry. An intermediate step may involve working out a geographic forecast if the company's area of operation is regional or local.

In making the appraisal of relative position in the industry, the most common approach is in terms of "market shares." This is simply an application of the ratio or percentage-distribution method at the level of the individual firm. Here again it may be more important to know the reasons for shifts in market shares than to record the mere fact that they have occurred.

One difficulty in obtaining realistic forecasts by this method is that executives tend to be unwilling, except in extraordinary circumstances, to concede the possibility of any reduction in the firm's market share until after the fact. They "know" they are "doing just as good a job as the other fellows."

For other reasons, also, the percentage method may be faulty in deciding whether a given share of the market is appropriate under particular circumstances. If products or markets are differentiated, there is no reason for shares to remain constant over the business cycle. In a period of rising income, the firm whose output is in the middle price and quality bracket may experience only a slight increase in share despite a good sales effort, and the low price and quality firm may suffer a reduction through no fault of its own, whereas the luxury-line firm that benefits from the shifting of consumers to higher brackets may congratulate itself on a sales effort that is not really good at all. The existence of such conditions may require a definition of market shares by correlation techniques rather than by a straight computation of percentages.

Correlation techniques may also be used to proceed directly from an over-all forecast, or from some broad aggregate derived as a major component of the over-all forecast, to a forecast for the individual firm. The greater time span covered by a program forecast than by a shorter-term sales forecast makes for greater validity in the results obtained by this method. Certain elements of variation are eliminated or moderated over a period of a full year. If a good relationship can be established, the surges and reactions that run their course in several weeks or months may not disturb the picture a year hence, and the relationship may be useful in identifying them as temporary in character. For various reasons, therefore, direct correlation techniques may be useful in preparing forecasts, even though the final appraisal of results will have to be carried out in terms of market shares or other criteria of competitive success.

Some of the other concepts appropriate to over-all forecasting are also applicable in forecasting for the individual concern. Adjustments for special factors affecting the industry may be important, even though they have no over-all significance. Inventory movements or changes in inventory policy on the part of the industry or its customers may make for a special course of development. The principles of inventory cycles may be applied to such movements, making due allowance in timing for the durability of products in use and for the conditions of production and distribution. If market shares are calculated from output data, every effort should be made to take into account the effects of inventory changes. Other factors specifically related to the exceptional circumstances of the industry may be equally deserving of attention.

In applying knowledge of special factors, it should be recognized that they are not necessarily decisive either for near-term forecasts or for operating decisions. For example, when inventories are high, they may tend to move to a more extreme position for a while rather than to make an early reversal. Moreover, even though surpluses exist all along the line, customers' orders have to be filled. The manufacturer who perceives the difficulty can warn his distributors and competitors; he can limit his commitments and take other steps to protect himself; but he may not be able entirely to avoid participating in the boom and bust.

The techniques of engineering and market research may also be applied in working out program forecasts. Frequently data are not available, or other circumstances prevent the use of procedures that would otherwise be preferred. New-product introductions typically pose such problems. In these circumstances, engineering or market information may be the primary sources on which a decision must rest. Again, however, qualifications of the same kind hold good.

Appraisals by engineers and designers ordinarily provide the basic approach to evaluating the comparative merits of a new product. Their efforts are also basic to achieving operating efficiency, and where new facilities are being put into operation, the only way of estimating prospective costs of production is through the engineering approach. Data from this source may therefore be of substantial help both in estimating market demand and in working out such supplementary elements of a complete program forecast as the cost functions used in break-even analysis.

Surveys and other market analyses also offer assistance in circumstances where experience is inadequate to provide knowledge of customer preferences or of other aspects of market acceptance. The significance of the direct approach—through statements obtained from customers of buying intentions or plans—dwindles as the period covered by the forecast is extended. Market surveys seeking to appraise market potentials a year or more ahead tend, therefore, toward the indirect approach—through the disclosure of customers' preferences, attitudes, or states of mind, which may bear upon prospective purchases of company or similar products. Surveys can also be useful in clarifying such aspects of the situation as the market position of company products relative to those of competitors and the over-all degree of market saturation as a factor affecting sales potentials. All such surveys are subject to error, of course, and the errors cannot be controlled simply by increasing the size of samples, since response errors are often far more important than sampling errors.

Engineering and market research findings may supplement and check each other, as well as supplement other methods of forecasting. Conflict in findings may serve as a moderating influence. If a product of high utility as measured by engineering standards will not be widely accepted by consumers for other reasons, enthusiasm should be restrained accordingly. If a product lacks the qualities that would give it continuing utility, any market success it achieves may be temporary. On the other hand, there may be no need to accept the initial findings of engineering research or market surveys as final. Deficiencies in design can be corrected. Consumer tastes may change, and they are, in fact, bound to change under the impact of experience and of new developments. The history of inventions shows that what was at first ignored or ridiculed may in time come to dominate.

The policy decisions required in such situations are difficult ones. Unreasonable cost increases should not be incurred in fighting adverse markets, and sales should not be lost through lack of adequate effort. Lack of a really sound basis for a forecast stresses the need for caution. An expedient commonly adopted under these conditions is experimentation in a local market area before any decision is made upon the program for the national market as a whole.

FACILITIES PLANNING

In deciding to build new facilities, a substantial degree of uncertainty is inescapable. The facilities will not be available for some time, and they will have to be used over a much longer period of time. Forecasting for this purpose cannot be realistic because it involves projecting many variables into a period too distant to afford any possibility of accuracy, and as a rule definite predictions are not attempted. True, long-term projections are made, but these usually abstract from so many factors that may change the situation in important respects that they represent hypothetical or assumed models rather than categorical forecasts.

The degree of confidence that should be placed in long-term projections is difficult to determine. The degree of confidence that is actually placed in them tends to vary inversely with their short-term validity. It rises to a peak just before the breakaway from the upward "trends" of the boom and falls to a low just before recovery from the trough of the depression gets under way. Acceptance of long-term forecasts is thus biased by what is currently taking place.

It is also biased by the spirit of rivalry that keeps most concerns moving in unison with their competitors. Each feels that it cannot afford to sit still while the others are moving ahead. Each projects its need for capacity into the future because it feels that, unless it is prepared to handle its share of whatever business there may be, competitors will move in and take over the market, and then it will never experience the increase in demand which would justify its own expansion. To put this another way, most concerns would rather run the risk of incurring excessive fixed charges for a while than of failing to pick up their share of new customers in future periods of peak load.

Under these circumstances, the "forecasts" are as likely to be cooked up in justification of what is decided on other grounds as they are to be the result of genuine efforts to predict the future. In facilities planning, as in other phases of business operation, forecasting may on occasion play an important role, and at other times its role may be negligible.

As a process of solving business problems, facilities planning may be regarded as consisting of three interrelated activities—establishing long-term objectives or goals, designing projects suitable to meeting those goals, and selecting, by some suitable system of priorities, the projects actually to be carried out in the immediate future.

Forecasting is usually thought of in connection with the first of these activities but is not essential to it. Objectives may be set on any basis from pure daydreaming to the most hardheaded appraisal of existing needs. If they are unrealistic, the possibility of approaching them is as a rule correspondingly remote. If they are realistic, the means of achieving them tend to emerge step by step with the developments that reveal their validity.

The distinction between the long and the short view is of critical importance. A concern may serve a small customer in an out-of-the-way place at a loss, hoping that he will grow large enough to make business with him profitable in the future. An airline may decide to operate an unprofitable route in order to realize the future profit which the route will produce after a period of further development of the communities served. If the financial resources of the firm are limited, the timing of the shift from red ink to black in situations of this kind may be the most important question to consider.

Costly errors are sometimes made in attempting to reach unattainable goals, but it is hardly ever apparent that they were unattainable at the time of decision. At the opposite extreme are the outstanding successes in which vigorous action coincides with an exceptional opportunity to make a dream come true. Most success stories lie between these extremes. Establishing realistic goals is usually accomplished in one or the other of two prosaic ways—making them extensions of past experience or keeping them in line with some measure of growth upon which success at least partly depends.

Converting goals into actualities requires the drafting of plans for specific projects. The projects must be practical if the goals are to be realized. In this context a wide range of problems is encountered. There are problems of general economic conditions and of special circumstances affecting the market for particular products. There are problems of alternative opportunities, new products, new markets, and possible improvements in the old to balance against the challenge of the new. There are problems of technology, of new processes and their comparative costs. There are problems of location, with various sites differing in kind and in degree of advantages offered. There are problems of competitive response, of possible strategy or tactics by competitors that might vitiate advantages gained. Some aspects of these problems can be partially resolved on a *status quo* basis. Others are dependent upon changes or actions whose nature cannot be foreseen.

In the third area of decision—the approval of capital expenditures for the period just ahead—there are also long-term questions to be answered. One common means of establishing priorities between projects is the "pay-back period." The difficulty with this measure lies in its emphasis on short-term considerations. A striking example of the fallacy involved is provided by the experience of a large meat-packing concern that expected the return of its capital within 2 years from a new plant built at the end of World War II. Before the plant was completed, however, product prices had fallen, and by the end of the 2-year pay-back period the plant had failed to return any profit at all. Ultimate success is determined not by the initial operating experience, of course, but by the return realized from the facilities over their whole useful life. The degree of success to be achieved may remain unpredictable even after several years of experience have been gained.

If all the specific forecasting problems involved in facilities planning were taken seriously, the task of the forecaster would indeed be insuperable. There is nothing to be said against considering all the various facets of the problem in as explicit a manner as possible. On the contrary, the best results will probably be obtained if research is moving well ahead of action. Time is needed to investigate the various alternatives and to explore the ramifications of each in terms of factors and conditions whose effects are not readily apparent. The necessary time will not be available if projects are drawn up hurriedly and rushed through to meet an urgent need that had not been anticipated. But when all is done that can be done, it has to be admitted that the answers arrived at are provisional in various respects. Potential margins of error are large, and results are bound to be disappointing at least part of the time. Unless these facts are accepted, disillusion may tend to destroy the basis for rational action in the future.

The uncertainty arising out of limitations on the accuracy of forecasting over long periods provides a partial explanation of what is reported by those who have participated in or had opportunity to observe actual investment decisions: That such decisions are more commonly based on judgment, intuition, or emotional states of mind than on detailed analysis of the problem. The insistence of an enthusiastic key executive is often the most important factor in a favorable decision.

The one essential requirement for expansion is that the future volume of business obtained will require rates of operation above the level of existing capacity. Most concerns go beyond this minimum. They want to be reasonably sure that the market as a whole will be large enough relative to the capacity they and their competitors are building to prevent the development of "excessive" competition. This means that total capacity should be held to the point where it will be in full use during periods of peak load, perhaps at moderate overtime rates of operation; and it should not be so substantially idled in periods of low demand as to induce price cutting, which, though perhaps merely aimed at keeping volume above the break-even point, has the effect of raising the break-even point for everybody. This caution may be set aside under certain conditions—as when various firms believe their chances of obtaining larger market shares are good or feel that the mechanisms of price administration can be relied upon to prevent undue price reductions.

Not all facilities decisions are concerned with expansion, of course. Some aim primarily at improving products or increasing efficiency, though some expansion is often obtained as a by-product when improvements are undertaken. Even though expansion is not the direct objective, however, many of the same considerations relating to the state of future markets, the distribution of market shares, and the potential reactions on price policy are still applicable. Competitors are usually free to undertake the same improvements. The one best assurance of a satisfactory return on any investment is a volume of business close to the output potential of the facilities created. Hence the one key item to be projected is the future volume of demand.

The basic technique for projecting market demand over long periods is the construction of trends fitted to past experience. The trends may be fitted directly to the data it is desired to forecast or to related data which may then be translated into the desired series. Even when past experience is lacking, trend techniques may be applicable. Thus an approach to the problem of market potential through the study of needs and of the ability of the product to satisfy those needs still requires, in effect, projecting trends of the needs themselves and of potential progress in displacing alternative means of satisfying those needs.

Since trends are so important to any long-term projection, it is essential to construct them properly and to make every effort to interpret them adequately in the light of all available information. Their validity ordinarily rests upon known causes which have displayed persistent effectiveness over a long period of time. It is important to consider whether those causes will continue to be effective or whether they will be modified by such factors as approaching market saturation or the development of competing products.

Considering separately the behavior of subsidiary product lines relative to each other may be helpful in this connection. If the firm has limited its output to one line, some indication of market shifts may be obtained by studying the reports of other firms specialized in various ways.

The value of this analysis is likely to be limited, however, by the large number of variables involved and the lack of any marked pattern persisting over long periods.

Perhaps the most common source of error in making trend projections consists in basing them on too short a record of experience. The progress of most economic variables during a postwar boom reflects strong cyclical components as well as underlying trend components. Hence lines measuring the progress of such variables through the decade following the end of World War II are not trends at all in the proper meaning of the term.

The error that results from projecting any phase of a cycle over long periods should be apparent, but it is frequently overlooked. In 1955, it was common to project the "postwar trends" in this way. These "trends" were sometimes supported by discussions of how business was planning its investment in facilities on a stable basis, with the result that the business cycle no longer had to be feared. This ignored the cyclical effects of the cumulative growth in capacity, which renders futile any hope that business could keep investment at peak rates indefinitely; for business to maintain peak investment after demand had ceased to expand would be suicidal. The "postwar trends" were also supported by the statement that rates of expansion were in line with those achieved in similar past periods of prosperity—apparently without any perception of the self-contradictory nature of this argument. The concept of a trend is one that abstracts from cyclical and other short-term influences, and the only way to make it valid is to fit to a period long enough to minimize the effects of such influences.

Another common error is one of interpretation. A trend projected a decade or two ahead may show a substantial increase from current levels. It is then sometimes assumed that this trend offers some assurance of continuing good business in the intervening years. It is startling to find this elementary error being made by people who ought to be better informed. Even the best of trends may be modified substantially by other influences over short periods, and the trend itself tells practically nothing about the probable short-term movements of cyclical or erratic variables.

Some assistance in avoiding both these errors is provided by the "highs-and-lows method" of trend fitting, which has frequently been used by stock-market analysts. One line is fitted to the high points of the past, that is, to data for prosperity periods alone; another is fitted to the lows experienced in depressed periods. If an intermediate line is desired, it can be established between these limits and with a slope appropriate to the use to be made of it. Whether or not this is done, any rise to or above the upper line represents a warning that the recent pace of development has been too fast, and any decline to the lower line is interpreted as bringing about a situation with less unfavorable implications than that preceding the decline. The causes or factors responsible for those movements should, of course, be considered.

In the case of producers of durable goods or capital equipment, the target-stock method is the only sound approach to long-term projection of market demand. The total number of units required at the target date is the key item to be forecast, since the demand for the services of equipment will be met by the cumulative production less retirements. When this approach is used, two components have to be separately analyzed: the growth component and the replacement component. Again, the estimates of these components will be averages for the period as a whole, so that their significance with respect to short-term movements in the intervening years may be negligible.

Correlation techniques are also frequently relied upon for long-term projections. This does not avoid the trend problem, because the result of the correlation depends upon the value assigned to the independent variable at the target date, and this value is itself usually the result of a trend projection. There may be some advantage in having the trend projection worked out by someone else who is regarded as an authority in the field of the independent variable, but the basic uncertainty remains, since even the most expert analysts are unable to guarantee accuracy in projections over long periods.

The variable most commonly used as the basis for a correlation is population. Its appeal as an independent variable derives from its continuing increase generation after generation. However, the contribution of population to many economic variables is a function not of its absolute magnitude but of its rate of change. Within the last generation, this rate of change has shown such substantial variation as to make the record of population forecasts a sorry one indeed. Moreover, there is every reason to expect such variation in the future, possibly with its violence increasing in future swings of the business cycle. The minimum precaution to be taken by the forecaster using this approach is to analyze carefully the relation of population changes to the variable he is projecting.

Other independent variables commonly used are the labor force, productivity, gross national product, and disposable personal income. All of these are, in different degrees, cyclical as well as trend variables, and they usually have to be projected on the basis of assumptions that exclude the cyclical elements of variation. Thought must therefore be given to how much could be gained by proceeding indirectly from a cyclical variable, modified by assumptions, through a correlation subject to additional errors of estimate. For the forecaster dealing with a product whose demand is suited to direct trend projection, these alternatives are dubious indeed.

Procedures have to be adapted in each case to the special circumstances of the problem. Since none is clearly superior to all others, the forecaster need not feel tied to any single approach. Whether he relies entirely upon his own efforts or calls upon outside experts for assistance, the validity of the result is likely to rest upon the soundness of the analysis underlying it. Exploring different approaches tends to broaden the analytical horizon and to minimize the possibility that relevant forces may be overlooked. The multiple approach is not a sure one just because the results obtained by various methods seem to confirm each other. The future is bound to produce surprises. But the only means available for minimizing the risks of moving ahead into the unknown is to develop as fully as possible the implications of what is known.

CHAPTER 17

Forecasting for the Investor

Investors and speculators have long made the stock market a focal point for economic forecasting. Perhaps more time and effort have been spent in attempts at forecasting stock prices than in all other kinds of economic forecasting combined.

Underlying these attempts, of course, are hopes of easy wealth. The market makes spectacular swings. Even when it has ended a long period no higher than it began, the total up-and-down movements within the period have usually been large enough to suggest the possibility of tremendous gains. It has always seemed evident that anyone who could find a way of forecasting its movements would hold the key to getting rich quick.

Most of those who chased this rainbow mirage in search of riches have suffered disappointment. This is almost inevitable by the nature of the situation. Each outstanding success is earned at the expense of many small failures. But the successes do not gain everything the failures lose. Operating and trading costs on each side have to be deducted before net profits are computed. There have been relatively brief intervals—at the heights of great booms—when almost everybody in the market is temporarily ahead of the game. Lasting successes are comparatively few.

Success in forecasting the market has also usually been short-lived. Promising procedures have been worked out—often belatedly, on the basis of past experience during periods in which they would have given good results. Most failed dismally when put to actual use, and on occasion they served merely to encourage unwise commitments.

Actual market action is made up of a multitude of diverse elements and theories. One kind may rule for a while, to the advantage of one forecasting system. Then another may take over, and what was previously an advantage may become a disadvantage in the new circumstances.

The tendency of the market to lead business through cyclical swings was observed almost as soon as the cycle itself was recognized. The financial panics that took place in the early stages of downturns were immediately evident in the market, and the break in the market was often held to be responsible for the entire recession. Out of this pattern of advance action evolved the theory of the stock market as a barometer of business.[1] This theory attempted to rationalize market action as the product of a kind of "composite mind" which had available all the inside information available to business. The market was sensitive to and could anticipate future changes in business and give them immediate effect in current prices.

Acceptance of the market as a leading, or even a causal, factor in the economy tended to divert attention away from business analysis as a means of forecasting the market. Beginning with the collapse of 1929, however, and especially after the Securities and Exchange Act became effective in 1934, the market has been wrong about as often as right, and thinking has turned more definitely toward the tie between business conditions and stock prices. It is clear that the market cannot remain high without the support of good business. The long depression and the sharp setback of 1938 emphasized its sensitivity to business declines. Today it is common to think of a general business forecast as a prerequisite to a stock-market forecast or to any other money-market forecast.

Even the strongest advocates of this position recognize, however, that it falls short of a full explanation. Anyone who observes stock-market extremes like those of 1929 and 1932 is forced to concede that the market at times gives effect to a wholly unreasonable interpretation of business prospects. The sharp break in the summer of 1946, at the beginning of a great postwar boom, illustrates a different kind of divergence. Even minor movements may, in the day or week they last, carry prices to an extreme not justified by the news that touched them off. Such mistaken moves cannot persist, however. Sooner or later there is sure to be a rebound, and it is the probability of the latter that provides an opportunity for the wise investor or speculator, though he is still faced with the problems of timing and selection.

The depression also helped subdue some of the wilder popular notions about the role of investment in personal finance. It taught that investment for gain or income—in real estate or industrial bonds as well as in stocks—might prove to be an unthinking disposition of funds. The money destined for payment of the mortgage was no longer there after the collapse in values. It was profitless to seek consolation in the thought that no one could have foreseen how drastic the deflation would be. The

[1] William Peter Hamilton, *Stock Market Barometer*, Harper & Brothers, New York, 1922.

public came to look askance on assuming the risks of investment, especially in stocks.

This attitude carried over into the period following World War II. Individuals stayed away from the market, leaving it to the professionals and the financial institutions. Savings were channeled into the market through the institutions, and by the end of the first postwar decade it was demonstrated that a market dominated by institutional and professional investors could, despite continued restriction of margin trading by the Federal Reserve Board, carry to excesses similar to those of the late 1920s.

Turning the job over to professional investment managers apparently has offered no sure solution—even granting their superior ability to forecast business and their better-informed procedures for selecting particular instruments and outlets for investment funds. When the nation is in the throes of rosy dreams about "prosperity unlimited," perhaps no group whose primary goal is to maximize gains can be expected to act with the restraint essential to sound investment. Excesses can be prevented only if operations are constantly guided by objectives that are not themselves inflated by the enthusiasm of the moment.

TAILORED INVESTMENT PROGRAMS

Definition of objectives, however well it may be practiced, or disregarded in practice, has become an almost universal precept of printed statements intended to advise or instruct the individual investor. This precept is based on the recognition that investments are not all equally good ways of putting funds ·to work. Most investments are suitable for accomplishing some things and not for others. Unless they are suited to doing what the investor wants done, they may not serve his needs at all. "Setting the program," therefore, is commonly regarded as the first step in sound investment procedure, taking logical precedence over appraising business prospects and dealing with specific problems of selecting instruments and timing their purchase.

Institutions as well as individuals need explicit programs to ensure the best results. As a rule, institutional programs are determined by the character of the organization. Some of the large financial institutions operate several departments, each of which has its own program, and there are circumstances in which one department may be doing almost the reverse of another. For example, a banking department may be selling government securities in order to obtain funds to accommodate borrowers at the same time a trust department of the bank is buying governments. Or the trust funds under the supervision of a trust company may be so divergent in character that similar securities are being eliminated from one fund and accumulated in another. These are matters that have to be determined by the organization in the light of its own circumstances.

Even in substantial financial concerns, however, there may be little in the way of a clearly thought-out program. In some institutions what passes for a program is a set of rather inflexible rules handed down through the decades; these may even be referred to with pride as "our conservative policies." At the other extreme are investment trusts whose primary aim is to "do better than the other fellow" in building asset values. In some cases, this is supplemented by the thought that policy will be reversed quickly if conditions change. On this basis, policy not only is speculative but also becomes a variant of the "bigger boob" theory, which stipulates that risky investments may be purchased because a bigger boob will be found on whom they can be unloaded at a profit. It is not intended here to review or analyze the programing problems of institutional investors. The point simply is that they, too, have such problems. Beyond this comment the discussion will be confined to the problems of the individual.

An individual's investment program is in effect his own personal answer to the question: "Why invest?" It should be based on a review of his position, to define what he hopes to accomplish by investing and to ensure that his investments are suitable to the objective. Specific investments differ so widely in income, in potential gain, and in safety of principal that their selection must be a function of the individual's personal situation if they are to meet his needs.

Another way of looking at the program is to view it as a matter of setting up priorities for the use of limited resources. Everyone has plans for improved living or for future activities and projects he wishes to carry out. He must decide whether these have a prior claim on his capital and therefore preclude at least some kinds of investments.

Some of these special needs may be considered briefly. The first is insurance. An income earner must buy insurance to protect his family's position against the possibility of his premature death. Most workers simply have no way of accumulating within a reasonable time an estate sufficient to make insurance protection unnecessary. The cheapest way to obtain pure protection, with no investment element, is to buy term insurance. The funds available to many workers are no more than sufficient to buy adequate protection in this form, and for them there is no investment problem. Others with a somewhat larger margin of income over current expenses may save and invest by buying insurance with an investment element included in the policy. The rate of interest on these savings is comparatively low, but many who buy this kind of insurance might find it difficult to save in any other way.

A second typical need is for cash reserves. The usual explanation offered for this item is that it will be on hand for meeting emergencies, but it really goes far beyond emergency needs. Many unexpected demands for cash arise from time to time, representing opportunities or desirable activities that are not in any sense emergencies. A liquid position confers the ability to do what the individual wants to do at the time he wants to do it and without explaining to a lender why he wants to do it. For most families, the advantages of being in such a position are worth paying for, and the costs are not high unless the mirage of forgone gains is given undue consideration.

Since government savings bonds are redeemable at fixed values on demand (after the initial waiting period), buying bonds on the payroll-deduction plan provides a means of accumulating a reserve through small installments for families who find it easier to save this way. The return over a period of time is by no means insignificant, so that these bonds combine the features of a reserve and an investment; but putting reserves in this form may tend to inhibit their use.

A third need assigned high priority by many families is provision for the children's education. This is a reasonably fixed need that can be anticipated well in advance. A similar need, even more distant in timing, is provision for retirement.

Needs of this kind must be provided for by systematic saving over a period of years. Once reasonable cash reserves are established, the same degree of liquidity is no longer required with respect to additional savings. Risks, especially of a short-term character, may then be assumed somewhat more freely in the interest of obtaining higher returns. In other words, the individual who is able to save beyond the minimum requirements of protection and reserves of necessity becomes an investor. It is then only a question of how he can best put his savings to work for the goals he has in mind.

Sometimes current need dictates the kind of investment to be undertaken. This is the situation of many families who bought houses because there was no other way to obtain satisfactory living quarters. Borrowed funds are the basis for the immediate investment, and the savings of a long period of years go into paying off the mortgage. Monthly payments in this form strain the budgets of many families, making other forms of saving impossible. Since the way the family lives tends to be so dependent on this expenditure, it is usually considered fully justified.

Any accumulation of cash over the amounts currently allocated to special needs becomes a potential investment fund. If future needs, like children's education or retirement, are fixed and can be met with savings supplemented by a sure but limited rate of interest, the individual might decide that the risk of declining stock values is best avoided. It is a generally sound proposition that, if funds are going to be needed at a particular time, they should not be put into stocks because no specific value can be depended on at that time. There are, however, two qualifications to this conclusion. First, there can be no assurance in this uncertain world that future financial needs will remain fixed. Second, the risks involved in systematically investing limited amounts in stocks year after year are much more limited than those incurred in putting a fixed total of capital in stocks at a given moment in time.

One may discount inflation prospects and write off the first of these qualifications. But the second is important and should be understood as a basis for planning an investment program. It is commonly referred to as "dollar averaging." When a fixed amount is put into stocks year after year, it purchases more shares when prices are low than when they are high, and average costs are weighted downward by the larger number of shares purchased at the lower prices. Thus $1,000 will buy 10 shares at $100 and in another year 20 shares at $50, making a total cost of $2,000, or an average of $67 for each of 30 shares; if the price settles at 75, midway between 100 and 50, a profit of over 10 percent will be earned on each share. This is in addition to any dividends paid while the stock is held. Over a period of years, therefore, this kind of saving and investment is likely to produce a good return, unless the investor is unfortunate in selecting stocks that tend steadily downward.

Presumably the time will come when any savings program has reached its maturity and the savings are withdrawn to be used for the purposes intended. At retirement age, the flow of savings ceases. What is there can be used but cannot be increased. The problem then is to get a satisfactory means of living from the accumulated capital. The total may be large enough to produce a satisfactory income without drawing upon the principal. Or it may be necessary to draw on capital as well as income. If the individual is healthy, a good medical risk for his age, an annuity may provide the right answer. In other cases, an annuity may be a poor investment, and there may be no other good alternative.

This position of an individual or family with a fixed capital fund, needing all the income the capital can produce or somewhat more, is a second typical investment situation. The investment program required is quite different from that of the steady saver. High yields are a primary objective, and stability of dividend payments is also an important consideration, but some risks of declining market values have to be assumed.

A recent development is designed to combine both of these situations into a single program. It is called the "variable annuity." The best known of the variable annuities is that established by the Teachers Insurance and Annuity Association, which operates a mutual-investment fund known as CREF (College Retirement Equities Fund). The individual joining this plan early in life makes a fixed schedule of payments into the fund. These payments are invested wholly or in part in equities, that is, common stocks. The accumulated value grows through the years, and upon retirement the individual receives an annuity based on the total available. That total includes not only the amounts paid in but also the dividends received and the gains from dollar averaging or from long-term growth in stock values. In a period of inflation, stock prices would tend to rise, enlarging the annuity to offset at least partially the increased income needs produced by rising living costs.

A secondary advantage of contractual arrangements of this kind is that they may reduce the likelihood that an individual will be enticed away from a sound program by hopes for speculative gains. Sometimes a person who has been following a sound saving and investment program for years decides to get into stocks and may convert the bulk of his assets for the shift. If he does this at the depression lows, it might be a very wise move. Most people, however, are more likely to be attracted toward such a move near the peak of the boom, when optimism is running high. Even if it is successful at first, it may wind up in disaster at some later point by creating a psychological bias toward speculation. It is usually as important to adhere to a sound investment program as it is to establish it in the first place.

A third investment situation is represented by the well-to-do individual who has a surplus above all his needs and wants to do the best he can with the funds on hand. His program is usually quite different from the others discussed above by reason of tax considerations. Additional income will put him in a higher tax bracket. Therefore, he seeks tax-exempt bonds and capital gains without large dividends. He is willing to hold stocks that pay little or no dividends if they promise to increase in value over the longer term. But he is also in a position to hold cash over extended periods of declining security values. For him, forecasting the swings of the market assumes greater importance than for the small investor, but he is likely to have a better sense of values and be more cautious than the small speculator. The latter usually has no program beyond the hope for a quick return on a gambler's chance.

MAKING INVESTMENT PROGRAMS EFFECTIVE

Assuming that the investor's program leaves him with funds to invest, there are two ways he may seek to obtain gains or to prevent losses. Either he can time his purchases so that price movements will be in his favor or he can select investments that will produce a return even though business and market conditions take an unfavorable turn. Both of these alternatives involve some forecasting: the first rests heavily upon forecasts; the second may disregard forecasts only by sacrificing the possibility of gain and assuming the risks of a decline in the value of money. The following discussion will be confined to securities, but the same principles apply to other kinds of earning assets.

The possibility of gain or loss is largely tied up with the fluctuations of stock prices. Fluctuations of bond prices are not insignificant, but if the investor is willing to hold the bonds to maturity, he can disregard interim price changes—provided, that is, that the quality of the bonds remains good throughout.

One of the first questions to be decided, therefore, is whether stocks should be purchased at all. This question tends to be confused with various ideas that are essentially extraneous to the issue. Some make it a moral issue; to them, buying stocks is speculation, or gambling, and gambling is wrong. Others with very limited experience, perhaps gained from some special incident, may generalize that experience into a fixed rule which has no genuine applicability to other situations.

Perhaps it is unnecessary to state that all such extraneous notions should be put aside. The only way to get sound results is to look at the question as a purely technical problem of determining the best investment values. From this point of view, stocks may be as good, better, or worse than bonds, depending on the situation. Gains or losses cannot be foretold with accuracy. Current yields are currently known but may not be maintained. With hindsight, after an extended period, the over-all results, including both yields and gains or losses, may be computed as annual rates of return for comparative purposes. Review of several decades of experience indicates that the best results—barring the possibility of fantastically good judgment in calling the turns—would have been obtained by policies that called for shifting from time to time between stocks and bonds.

The investor—who seeks security by confining his purchases to "real" investment values—does not necessarily sacrifice all possibility of gains. Two things in the early postwar period gave him definite incentive to seek higher returns—the low rates of interest on high-grade bonds and the inflation of prices with consequent depreciation of the value of the dollar. Nevertheless, he moves cautiously, his primary interest being yields, and ordinarily he makes no attempt to call the turning point.

The speculator, on the other hand, attempts to obtain the maximum return possible in a limited time. He takes risks but tries to avoid unnecessary or extreme risks. He usually takes a definite position and holds it until the time comes for a reversal, and then the reversal is complete. He may attempt to call the turns but soon learns he cannot do this consistently; hence his primary protection is to reverse himself promptly when the market is going against him. His attitude is perhaps best expressed in the old speculative maxims: "Buy low and sell high!" and

"Limit your losses, but let your profits run!"[2] Since his primary interest is gain, he tends to regard yields as incidental, but at times they may bulk large in his actual results.

Although these summary paragraphs seem to convey a sharp contrast, the differences between the investor and the speculator are not clear-cut. Both assume a certain amount of risk in order to obtain a return on capital. Both engage in a certain amount of forecasting. The whole concept of "real" or "intrinsic" investment value used by the investor must be forward-looking to be meaningful; past values have no significance other than the indication they may afford of future values. Some investors deny the possibility of making accurate forecasts but make them implicitly in such judgments as, "We have to take our chances on some stocks because of the long-term bias toward inflation." Perhaps the main difference is that the investor pursues a stable policy over a period of time whereas the speculator may go in for a quick killing on the basis of short-term turnover.

Certainly many speculators display what is one of the worst faults of their calling, namely, impatience. Anxiety undermines their judgment, so that they trade unwisely and too much, often on the spur of momentary decisions. It is hardly ever necessary to take action right now, today, as if the decision could not wait even a moment, and it is just about impossible to hit the precise highs or lows very often. But the signs that the market is approaching the highs or lows cumulate, and action confined to the general area of the turn, perhaps a little ahead of or beyond the point which hindsight shows to be the actual turn, will pay off handsomely. That is why a fairly stable policy is desirable. It is an advantage that most investors have over most speculators.

Almost all speculators have to take some losses in order to realize the greater gains obtained by "calling the market." The small investor incurs too many losses, partly because he excludes too many alternatives. Usually he asks, "What is the best buy now?" Then he takes a long position, even at the peak of the boom. Most speculators would be better off if they could find some way to consider the opposite possibility as well as the one they have decided upon. They should consider selling short as a routine procedure, even though no short sales are actually undertaken. This induces a balanced attitude of mind with respect to the possibilities of declines as well as advances.

It may be pointed out that circumstances are not balanced with respect to purchases and short sales. The latter are subject to several disadvantages. First, dividends are received by the buyer and have to be paid by the short seller; this double difference in yields imposes an im-

---

[2] For a discussion of rules to govern stock-market operations, see The Trader, *Commonsense Speculation,* published by *Barron's,* New York, 1938.

portant penalty. Second, the short seller is almost always in a loss position just after he trades; he has to sell on a "plus tick," and if the market rises to permit the sale, it usually rises at least a little further. Third, the risks of total loss are greater, because the short seller is, in effect, always on margin, no matter how much margin he actually puts up. Fourth, he incurs a tax disadvantage in that all gains are considered short term and therefore taxed as ordinary income. For all these reasons, short sales should be undertaken only when there is a high probability of price declines in a short period of time; many investors in the high-tax brackets refuse to consider short sales at all. But the attitude of thinking that prices are high enough to justify a short sale helps to put those prices in the proper perspective.

In attempting to forecast the stock market, the speculator should recognize that he is tackling one of the trickiest assignments in the entire realm of prediction. The market is sensitive and erratic. It gives effect to any real or suspected influence very quickly. It makes substantial moves on the sketchiest possible basis, and these moves tend to be inordinately large in relation to the influences they discount. From any given position, the market may move either up or down, and by any given date it cannot be depended upon to be either higher or lower. That is why anyone who is going to need his capital intact at a certain time for other purposes may be well advised to avoid stocks. Even though his forecast may be right from a longer-term point of view, it may be wrong for a period too long to tolerate.

It is not enough to be able to forecast business conditions with considerable accuracy. At times business developments dominate the market. At other times the market goes its own way. In 1946 business was running strong; there were tremendous backlogs of unfilled demand to keep it going; and price controls were about to be removed, eliminating a primary restraint on the advance in profits. But the market broke sharply and stayed low for almost 3 years. A partial explanation for this disparity lies in the fact that, although business conditions were favorable, sentiment about the future of business was unfavorable.

The interaction of business sentiment and the stock market is much more complete than the interaction of sentiment and actual business. But an explanation in these terms is not encouraging to the business forecaster who wants to play the market. Some analysts of the market go so far as to deny that business forecasting confers any advantage at all. An incident that occurred early in the spring of 1949 is illustrative. Stock prices had fallen to a point which not only raised earning and dividend yields to a record level but also in many cases put share prices below net-current-asset values. A market analyst who supported his pessimistic views with charts that "reveal all the secrets of market behavior" referred to such analysis of real values underlying corporate securities as "Pish-posh!" Here we have one of the most startling facts of financial history—the fact that the plant and equipment of the world's most productive economic machine were being given away free, in fact, with a bonus on current account—referred to as mere "pish-posh" because the aberrations of speculative psychology were held to be overwhelmingly important.

This is, of course, an extreme view and not one that can be supported in the broad perspective of market behavior. Nevertheless, it serves as a warning against too ready acceptance of any simple criterion for judging stock prices on the basis of current business reports.

FORMULA PLANS

Many attempts have been made to eliminate judgment from stock-market operations. Both investors and speculators have formulated rules of procedure to determine when they should enter or leave the market. These rules are most commonly stated in terms of the level of stock prices themselves, but other criteria are used to supplement the price data in some cases. The basic objective is to specify fixed points at which predetermined actions will be taken and thereby reduce the handling of investment funds to a routine. A set of rules of this kind is termed a "formula plan."

One of the most important advantages of this kind of procedure is its effect in removing discretion in situations where current developments may unduly influence judgment. Waves of optimism or pessimism are infectious, and few people are immune to the views and attitudes of their fellows. Another advantage is that it tends to reduce responsibility for management of the funds, by preagreement on specified actions. Whether in a broader sense judgment is actually eliminated, or responsibility avoided, may be a debatable point. While the immediate decisions are made mechanically, the question of the soundness of this approach at times when analysis and judgment dictate another course cannot be avoided.

The most common type of investment formula divides the funds between stocks and bonds. When stock prices are low, a larger proportion is put into stocks, and vice versa. Since stock prices are the volatile element, the formula usually sets its trading points in terms of a stock index. Thus, for example, suppose that a fair average for the Dow-Jones index over a long period of time is assumed to be 350, and at this level holdings are equally divided between stocks and bonds. Then, whenever the index moves up a certain distance, say 10 percent, stock holdings are reduced, say by 10 percent of the total fund. The first 10 percent increase in prices over 350 brings the proportion of stocks down to 40 percent, the second to 30 percent, and so on, until all stocks are sold off. When prices are falling, reverse shifts are made, possibly until the whole fund is in stocks. Variations on this basic pattern are almost infinite, introducing, for example, a trend factor to adjust the trading points. A growing literature is available to explain them.[3]

Some of these formula plans have produced excellent results for the investors who have used them. The way they make money is by obtaining the gains of advancing stock prices and avoiding the losses of falling stock prices. It works beautifully when stock prices are fluctuating around a fairly stable level, from which they move in either direction. This level does not have to be the mid-point of the formula's trading range, but the fluctuations must be large enough to carry prices over some of the trading points. Increases in the value of formula funds are sometimes substantial and might even exceed the gain on an outright investment in stocks over a long period in which the general trend was upward.

What these formulas miss are the profits from wide swings of the market, because stocks are held only through about half the formula's trading range, and the total range of the market is usually wider than the trading range of the formula. Proponents justify this limitation on the basis that playing the wide swings is "speculation" rather than investment—ignoring the fact that all these formulas are basically an effort to introduce an element of speculative gain into investment operations. They also justify it on the ground that any gains at the higher price levels will be lost on the next decline, assuming that eventually prices will drop back to the trading points. Aside from the fact that "eventually" may cover too much time for the ordinary investor, the profits forgone by being out of the market over a period of years may be substantial.

Proponents of formula operations also hold that, if everyone behaved in accordance with these plans, the stock market would be greatly stabilized—by concerted buying at the lower levels and concerted selling at the upper. But this appears to be a dubious contention. If basic economic conditions shifted in such a way as to justify a large rise in stock prices, concerted sales from the formula funds might keep prices from rising in line with their real value for a while, but their influence would eventually break down; when prices finally moved to eliminate the discrepancy, the total advance would not necessarily be any smaller.

Traders who feel that criteria of "real" investment values can be set up prefer to rely on their judgment of the circumstances to determine when shifts should be made. They may even feel at times that they can gain an advantage by taking over the stocks sold from formula portfolios. An investment-trust executive once stated: "We don't use a formula plan,

[3] See Lucille Tomlinson, *Practical Formulas for Successful Investing*, Wilfred Funk, Inc., New York, 1953.

but our operations are much the same as if we did. We need a lot of time to work out any substantial shift, and this alone makes it necessary to level the peaks and valleys a bit."

Speculators, too, may resort to formulas for speculation, especially if they are inclined toward "letting the market tell its own story." Perhaps the most widely known of such devices is the Dow theory, which becomes a formula when the secondary movements are defined arbitrarily so as to eliminate any question of whether or not a fluctuation is a secondary movement. It establishes the direction of the market, not at the first reversal of the primary trend but at the point where the extreme price of the first reversal is again exceeded in the new direction. A secondary movement may be defined as any fluctuation that exceeds a fixed percentage. Taking this percentage in a range that is small in comparison with the total range of prices in a major bull or bear market—say 3 to 7 percent—will at comparatively small sacrifice establish a position to be held throughout the major price swing, the bulk of which will then appear as gain. This formula produces good results when the market displays a high degree of continuity through long cyclical movements.

When such a formula is relied on, the type of market that produces losses is exactly the one that produces gains for the investment formula —sharp reversals around a fixed level. In the decade following the end of World War II, adherents of the Dow theory suffered substantial losses because the index gave a number of false signals. Those whose judgment enabled them to disregard the bear signals given by the theory in its simplest version made large profits as the market moved to new highs by the end of the decade. Nevertheless, the Dow theory approach, at least in its simpler forms, has steadily lost adherents to new methods of market analysis, which are discussed briefly later in this chapter.

An interesting aspect of this situation appears in the contrast between these two approaches to what is essentially the same problem. The former attempts to take advantage of fluctuations around a level, ignoring the possibility of large changes in level; the latter regards the limited fluctuations around a fixed level as inconsequential and aims at realizing on the wide changes in level. To some extent, the market must reflect this battle of the formulas. Advances are undoubtedly restrained as investment formulas call for shifting to bonds. This forces the speculators who have obtained a "buy" signal to work through the formula "sell" orders before prices can advance. These are, however, only two of the many influences that affect market action.

Investors and speculators who have met with success are not likely to be swayed from the course they have been pursuing. It may be doubted, however, that any relatively simple formula designed to eliminate judgment could hope to continue successful under all conditions. The level of prices must ultimately be determined by economic and political realities. Understanding the implications of changes in this real world, which is largely beyond the influence of the market, must represent a primary basis of success over the longer term. Formulas have to be revised from time to time in the light of such understanding.

SELECTING THE RIGHT STOCKS

Over-all forecasts and formulas are designed to tell *when* to buy; they tell little or nothing about *what* to buy. The investor tends to place great emphasis on the latter question; he can show that it would have been possible, with timely shifts in holdings, to remain in the market continuously over the years and realize tremendous capital appreciation. The speculator, on the other hand, may be overwhelmingly concerned with the former question; but he, too, must make his decisions specific, and the choice of a particular issue may have a decisive influence on the result.

The importance of divergent movements within the market is consistently pointed out by market observers. Individual issues and industry or other groups may show extreme differences in volatility and in direction of movement. Some issues show so little relation to the rest of the market, and even occasionally to other issues in the same industry, that the broader considerations governing market action seem hardly relevant to their behavior.

There may be real economic reasons for this divergent behavior, or it may be based on extraneous or irrational factors like struggles for management control or misinformation conveyed by tipsters and rumor mongers. One-day gains of 5 percent on the basis of unfounded expressions of optimism by one of a company's top executives are not uncommon. Sometimes such gains are based on matters almost wholly unrelated to profit prospects in the reasonably near future; an example is provided by the case of a coal company whose management merely mentioned the possibility that coal might someday be moved through pipelines with a saving of freight charges. The most extreme changes take place, of course, on days of panic. But the revelation of unsuspected weakness in a company's position may produce momentary panic in a single issue when the tone of the market as a whole is firm. The special circumstances of the individual issue or instrument cannot be ignored.

The basis for selection derives in large part from the buyer's program and from his view of future prospects. Responsibility to program objectives will probably rule out many possible investment outlets. The appraisal of general business prospects may also impose important restrictions. When prospects are unfavorable, "speculative" commitments may be avoided and funds may be shifted into bonds or into the stronger, more stable issues ordinarily called "defensive issues." The forecast also provides a basis of selection by indicating which industries will be particularly favored or hampered under the conditions forecast.

In the operation of a formula plan, it is often considered desirable policy to buy volatile stocks rather than conservative issues, because the plan itself is assumed to give adequate protection against price declines. Thus, established programs and policies go far toward determining selection; but any set of general principles can tell only part of the story.

Investment analysts commonly set up a set of supplementary rules to guide the investor. Most of these are helpful if properly applied. All of them, however, are subject to important qualifications.

One of the rules most frequently mentioned in the literature of the subject is, "Before you invest, investigate!" Hardly anyone would quarrel with the thought underlying this rule, that operations should be informed and not based on mere guesses or unjustified hopes of large gains. In practical application, however, it does not work out as well as the thought suggests, for effective investigation requires analytical resources which the average investor does not possess.

A cynical securities dealer remarked of this rule: "When clients come in with this attitude, we are glad to sell them something. Usually it's AT & T. But they never make much, and they hardly ever get what would really be the best thing for their situation."

The one place investigation is usually held to be unnecessary is investment in government bonds. It is presumed these bonds can always be paid off, because the government has power to issue money and could use this power for debt service if necessary. This view conveys a somewhat false implication, since, if the government had to create money for debt service, its bonds would probably be one of the worst forms of investment. The better view is that the financial community, including the Federal Reserve System, cannot afford to let government credit weaken, because to do so might lead to the inflation that would destroy values.

A second generally accepted rule is diversification: "Don't put too much in any one stock! Then if one stock should go sour, only a small proportion of the total can be lost." The theory behind this rule is that even the best analysis can establish only a probability of merit. Since probabilities cannot be depended upon in any one trial but will work out in a number of trials, operations should include a sufficient number of separate issues so that the off-chance of failure will not be overwhelming. For investors with large funds, another reason for diversifying is that holdings of any one issue should be kept to a level where a decision to switch will not unduly affect the market.

The trouble with diversification is that many investors tend to overdo it. They pick up dabs of this and that rather indiscriminately. Most investors justify this action as a way of protecting themselves against losses, but they ignore the possibility that they are using the principle of diversification to operate more or less in the dark. Diversification not only prevents losses but also works on the other side to prevent gains. The investor who really knows what he is doing does not have to diversify. He can confine his operations to the best opportunities under the circumstances. Most successful operators warn against spreading funds in small bits all over the list.

Another rule for "playing it safe" is to keep part of an investment fund in the form of cash or other liquid reserves. Maintaining liquidity day in and day out, however, is costly. Even the difference in return between long- and short-term governments is significant; for the long-term investor, it pays to be in short-term issues only for limited periods when interest rates seem likely to move up. For the speculator or formula-plan operator, there is no point in consistently maintaining substantial cash holdings; he may hold cash at times but should seek to be fully invested at other times.

Aside from rules of this kind, the usual effort of the careful investor is to search out securities that are undervalued. When the degree of undervaluation becomes sufficient to allow both for errors in the investor's judgment and for quirks in the market, these securities are good buys, because income over the longer term should be ample to justify the purchase even though the price fails to respond quickly or goes lower for a while.

The problem is to determine when a stock is "undervalued." This implies a comparison of market price with some concept of "real" value, and it is frequently difficult to ascertain what the "real," the "intrinsic," or the "underlying" value of any security may be. In actual practice, a change in market price may be the first notice to the investor that the real value of the stock has changed. On the other hand, a change in price may be of no significance whatever to the real value in this sense of the term; it may merely make the difference between real and market value more extreme. What this search for undervalued stocks reduces to, therefore, is a problem in research, and the findings must be good enough to give the investor confidence to maintain a position that may look rather shaky for some time after the decision is made.

Various procedures for security valuation have been worked out. These usually involve the analysis of economic data and corporate financial reports.[4] The simplest of such analytical procedures take account of the corporation's past record of sales, earnings, and dividends and of its current financial position. Some of the suggested procedures are quite detailed, going into many ramifications of a concern's position.

It is also frequently suggested that the analysis be specialized by industry. Certain kinds of industries—such as railroads, utilities, and financial institutions like banks and insurance companies—are so different that the procedures suitable for manufacturing corporations may not be considered appropriate for obtaining the desired results. Moreover, the markets for stocks in these industries are specialized and do not necessarily behave in the same way as the market for the industrials.

It should be recognized that this kind of analysis is essentially forecasting. Where it is merely a mechanical review of past data, it becomes a variant of the "dying horse" theory of investment. According to this theory, it is all right to back a dying horse if he has shown himself to be a great runner in earlier years. Past-performance records are indeed useful in horse racing and in investment, but only as indications of future performance and not as fixed standards of continuing worth.

Methods of forecasting the prospects for industries and individual firms have been discussed in earlier chapters. A point worthy of special emphasis here is that conclusions valid for an industry may not apply to the individual concern. Within a single industry some firms have good prospects and others do not. The differences here become a primary focus of attention.

Negative as well as positive aspects of a company's prospects should be considered. The most common cause of a stock's deterioration is a decline in corporate earnings. Anything that might affect earnings adversely is therefore a matter of concern. Financial weakness is a second adverse contingency. Alarm over potential declines in earnings may be tempered if the company has a strong financial position. If finances are so weak as to threaten insolvency, any potential loss in earnings would be a serious matter indeed, and the only sensible action in this case is to accept any losses already made effective in the market price and get out from under as quickly as possible. A third potential form of risk occurs when a particular issue temporarily gets out of line on the upside; the overvalued stock may be risky even though the corporation is perfectly sound. These and other negative factors must be combined with the positive to give a complete picture of a stock's investment value.

Among the positive criteria of merit commonly cited by stock-market analysts are the following:

1. Growth. The corporation with better than average prospects for

[4] For example, see Benjamin Graham and D. L. Dodd, *Security Analysis*, 3d ed., McGraw-Hill Book Company, Inc., New York, 1951.

growth is preferred. The "growth" company will produce the greatest gains over time, provide greater security by making the best recovery from periods of cyclical decline, and confer tax advantages by accumulating earnings so that they accrue as capital gains rather than dividend income.

Originally the growth concept was rather simple and straightforward. It referred to successful companies in industries whose development was just beginning, so that the autonomous factors making for expansion were decisive enough to create a probability of growth even in periods of cyclical decline. In the decade following World War II, however, the concept was almost continuously expanded. Some writers have included any or all of the following situations in this category:

a. Companies operating in growth areas, for example, in the Southwest or in Canada

b. Companies with an aggressive approach to research and product development

c. Companies whose activities relate to some growing portion of the economy, such as population, the number of school children, or the number of retired persons

d. The existence of backlogs of demand, measured in such terms as the average condition of dwelling units currently occupied

e. Undervalued stocks in stable companies strong enough to weather any probable depression

These items show progressively greater departures from the original concept. The last two are included primarily to show how a popular idea may be misapplied.

2. Stability of earnings and dividends. The mere record of consistent dividend payments over a long period of years—without regard to size or to their justification in some years—is frequently considered an indication of quality that puts a stock in the "prudent-man" category. A variety of background situations may be thought of as guarantees of stability:

a. Monopoly position. This advantage may be conferred by location, by franchise or license, by patents, or just by exceptional know-how.

b. Established position in a stratified market. The firm that can claim an important share in a continuing market in which entry is difficult and "repeat" business is important—for example, automobiles or cigarettes—can be considered to have an assured future.

c. Control of resources that enable production at lower than average cost.

3. Good management. Alertness and ability in management are intangibles that are hard to evaluate (it is generally more difficult than appraising the performance record of a forecaster). Judgment is of the

essence, and it may be suspected that the superficialities of financial importance and past success tend to bias the judgment of analysts who are most impressed with this aspect of corporate performance.

By far the most popular of these criteria is growth, and because of that popularity, growth stocks command considerable premiums on the market. In some cases, the extent of overvaluation is so great that a decade or two of growth may be required to get a return equivalent to that available on stocks not so well regarded. With the aid of hindsight, of course, it is possible to show that some growth companies have surpassed income companies within much shorter periods than a decade. Whether these performances could have been foretold is another question.

Even on the assumption that this basic criterion of an industry's future can be accurately predicted, the problem of selecting growth companies in any industry may still be difficult. In the mid-1920s, the automobile industry was a prominent growth industry. Within a decade, however, a large majority of the companies then operating in this industry had failed or been absorbed by others. Competition and the depression reduced the growth factor to naught.

More recently, industries like electronics and atomic energy have often been placed in the growth category. These are obviously important new fields, but it should be almost equally evident that not everybody operating in them will succeed. The industrial giants of the nation as well as the small, specialized concerns are aware of the opportunities in these fields, and their research facilities and financial strength give them a definite advantage. Just because some small company happens to have been started in one of these fields, there can be no guarantee that it is going to walk off with any prizes.

Whenever some principle like "growth" sets the fashion in the market, it is time to be cautious. The favorites of the day tend to be bid up almost out of reason. It is an old saying of the market that the leaders of a bull market become the leaders of the next bear market.

The trader who is not greatly taken in by the standard line of opinion being passed around the financial community can prosper by playing against the accepted gospel of the moment. He, too, must make a good analysis. He has to distinguish between the stocks that are low because they ought to be low and those that are low because of some temporary condition that will not persist. In so far as he can succeed in this, the stock that is temporarily underpriced will give him special gains or a large measure of protection against future market declines.

One further comment along this line: The characteristics of the market may be made a factor in selection. Fashions have a power and a life of their own. It does not pay to fight them when they are at peak strength. The shift may come quite gradually. At one point the market may favor the "blue chips" or other high-grade investment issues. Then it may begin to swing to the speculative side. The movement ordinarily will not be all the way over all at once. In the transition, the swing may be first to secondary or other intermediate grades and only at long last to the "cats and dogs." Playing against the fashion may best be done by stages.

WHO SHOULD DO THE INVESTING

Whether the investor places primary emphasis upon forecasting or upon selection, he is faced with analytical problems of no mean scope. Their solution requires time as well as intelligence. Anyone who studies the problem seriously may be able to handle it satisfactorily. But this is time-consuming work, and most investors, who are busy with other things, do not have the time to devote to it.

The individual investor who chooses to do the job himself should recognize that he is pitting his efforts against tough competition. Tremendous energy is always being spent on problems of investing or speculating. The really large investors, the institutions, have professional staffs with no other responsibility than getting the right answers.

Furthermore, there are differences in personal temperament that make it inappropriate for some persons to do their own investing. Some lack confidence and the power of decision. Some lack stability or perspective. Some find that responsibility and uncertainty create too much tension. Some are upset by losses, even minor losses. What any of these persons can accomplish may be so limited that they would be well advised to turn the job over to someone else.

To get competent advice and portfolio supervision usually costs something. An investment counselor charges fees on a specified scale for his services; the fees vary considerably, depending in part on the character of the services required. An investment trust usually charges a fixed markup over net asset value when shares are purchased—usually about $7\frac{1}{2}$ percent of the offering price. There are some mutual funds that do not impose this surcharge, but they do not have salesmen, and the investor may never hear of them.

There is a temptation to rely on free advice. Well-meaning friends who have had at least some success are usually more than free with suggestions. Even if they are wholly competent advisers, one difficulty frequently arises. The advice may be good only for the moment it is given. But it tends to be taken seriously with little regard to the time element and keeps working too long. When the situation changes, advice should change with it, but casual advice is not continuous, and there may be no communication of the shift.

Many published services are available at relatively small cost. These are highly variable in what they try to do and in how well they do it. Printed reports must, of course, be utilized as sources of information. Where specific recommendations are made, they may or may not be worth acting on. The kind of reports giving recommendations are sometimes of least value from the standpoint of information and analysis; they may give only the results of somebody's thinking. Review of several of these services does not suggest a high degree of reliability. Some of the most expensive are the worst. Advice in printed form is likely to be received too late to get maximum benefit from it. It is only by accident adapted to the program of the individual.

The investment counselor is presumably the answer to the latter problem. He can tailor his advice to the personal needs of the client. His relations to his clients vary considerably. He may assume the entire responsibility for one and merely inform him after the fact of actions taken. He may merely offer suggestions to another, and although these are usually taken, they may on occasion be rejected. The field includes everything from reliable, competent firms to the modern-day version of the old bucket shop. Out-and-out confidence men sometimes gain funds by presenting themselves in this guise; the legitimate firms do not take the money but merely take the limited powers of attorney needed to direct its disposition. If speculatively inclined, the investor who is willing to take big risks in the interest of big gains and does not wish to devote his own attention to the details, may find an imaginative counselor the best solution to his problem.

The other main resort of the investor who wishes to obtain professional supervision of his funds is the mutual investment trust. The popularity of this outlet is attested by the fast growth of these funds in the postwar years. When the investor buys shares in one of these companies, his funds are pooled with all the other funds placed with the company. He obtains the diversification provided by the entire shareholdings of the company and participates in gains and earnings share and share alike with all the others who have invested in it. The "open-end" companies are prepared to sell additional shares at any time, and these are usually redeemable at net asset value on demand; but the relatively high surcharge on purchases makes in-and-out transactions uneconomic.

One of the attractions of the mutual investment trusts is their great variety. There are over 200 of these companies currently in operation. The investor can in effect determine his program and then turn over the problems of forecasting and selection to a fund of the specified character for detailed supervision. He can buy into a common-stock fund, into a conservative bond and preferred-stock fund, or into a "balanced" fund that includes both bonds and stocks and shifts the proportions of each held. He can buy for growth or for stability. He can buy shares in a specific industry—such as chemical shares, oil shares, electronics, or atomic-energy shares. Some companies offer a variety of subsidiary funds and permit shifting from one to another at much lower cost than the charge for original entry.

If the investor wants high volatility, he may buy "closed-end" shares which are "leveraged." These are issued and sold on the open market like ordinary industrial shares. "Closed-end" means the company has a fixed capitalization, so that new shares are not constantly being sold or redeemed. These companies may operate with borrowed funds—bank loans or bonds—as well as with the receipts for sale of their own shares. Use of such funds gives the shares "leverage," so that gains or losses fluctuate more widely than they would if owned capital only were employed. In some cases warrants have been issued, and these fluctuate more widely still.

An evaluation of the performance record of these funds does not encourage the idea that they do wonders with the investor's money. Few have shown results as good over a period of time as a hypothetical straight investment in the Dow-Jones Industrial Average. On the other hand, most of them do fairly well, and it would be just about impossible for them to fail. If they do not represent an ideal solution of the investor's problem, they at least offer a reasonable solution, with relief from what might otherwise be a heavy burden.

FORECASTING THE STOCK MARKET

The most widely accepted approach to financial forecasting proceeds from two simple propositions—that stock prices vary directly with prospects for business and that bond prices vary inversely with the rate of interest. Almost invariably such propositions are coupled with statements indicating that certain intangibles have to be taken into account. These intangibles may be described as psychological or discretionary influences, such as "trends" in sentiment among traders or changes in policy on the part of the monetary authorities.

In the case of the stock market, the two sets of considerations are usually referred to as the "fundamentals" on the one hand and the "technical factors" on the other. The fundamentals include everything derived from statistical-economic analysis, with the main focus ordinarily on corporate earnings and dividends. The technical factors include everything relating to the autonomous behavior of the market itself; they include any number of items relating to traders' opinions about prices and to changes in the flow of funds into or out of the market. There is no need to confine a forecast to one or the other of these approaches. Even combining the two will probably leave something to be desired in the results.

The approach by way of the fundamentals is usually considered basic by those investing for the longer term. The deviations from "real" values established in these terms are regarded as temporary aberrations whose influence will be dissipated after a reasonable period of time. There is evidently little or no intention of gaining from the secondary movements when this approach is followed. Business changes are usually slower than market changes and cannot provide satisfactory indications of short-term fluctuations. Nor can the follower of this approach gain from the extremes reached at market peaks, when the market deviates widely from the norm set by earnings and dividends. Playing market patterns of these two types is more specifically the province of the speculators. In recent years, however, with conservative investors going more frequently into stocks, the technical analyst has increasingly been called upon to serve both groups.

A third branch of analysis frequently held to be important in forecasting stock prices is analysis of money and capital markets. Some writers hold interest-rate developments to be a primary influence on stock prices. It is difficult, however, to find verification for this thesis.

There are two commonly accepted ways to analyze the influence of interest-rate changes on stock prices. The first is to capitalize current and expected earnings or dividends by the rate of interest on high-grade bonds.[5] The idea has a great deal of logical plausibility. In addition, some stocks with relatively fixed dividends, such as utilities and preferred stocks, do appear to be influenced by changes in interest rates; these are referred to as "yield" stocks. With respect to most stocks, however, it is hard to demonstrate any dependable effect. The rate of interest changes slowly. The long-term trend has been downward, but stock prices did not move up 50 percent in relation to earnings and dividends over the period in which the rate was cut by one-third. The cyclical movements indicate that the conditions which make for high stock prices also make for tight money, so that the highs in interest rates have tended to coincide with the highs in stock prices rather than with the lows.

The second method of gauging the influence of interest rates is to compare yields. Usually this is done in terms of the differential between the current dividend yield on an index like the Dow-Jones Industrial Average and the yield on high-grade bonds. When this differential falls to a certain point, say below 1 percent, it is interpreted as a danger signal. There

[5] This approach is commonly used in securities analysis. See *ibid*. For a detailed exposition of the rationale of this approach, see John B. Williams, *Theory of Investment Value*, Harvard University Press, Cambridge, Mass., 1938.

is little doubt that it may, in boom periods, serve as an indication that stock prices are too high. Like other such indicators, it leaves the precise timing of the turn in considerable doubt. In the more usual situation, the size of the differential seems to be of little importance. Very large differentials in the late 1940s had very little effect in raising stock prices, and a very sharp lowering of the differential in 1954 and 1955 did not keep stock prices from continuing to rise.

A series of correlation studies attempting to relate stock prices and interest rates have been conducted, but all failed to produce significant results. Introduction of interest rates in varying ways and with varying treatment of time intervals gave no dependable indication of stock-price movements. The interest-rate variable typically improved the relationship in some years or periods and made it worse in others. Hence, except for the general comment that money- and capital-market developments may throw light on the character of business and speculative situations under certain conditions, the interest rate will not be considered further as a factor in forecasting the stock market. It is considered briefly in its own right in a later section.

Returning to the fundamentals, it seems clear that over the longer term the level of stock prices depends upon business prospects. The market conforms in a general way to the pattern of corporate earnings over the broad swings of the business cycle. Important departures occur on occasion, but these are always eliminated after a time, and in most cases the time interval through which they persist is relatively short. Corporate earnings may therefore be regarded as setting a norm around which prices fluctuate. It would seem, in other words, that the main thing the investor needs to know is what the general position of business is likely to be over an extended period of time, say something like a year at least; knowing this, he can ignore or take advantage of the minor ups and downs that are always taking place in the course of weeks or months within the year.

One of the most common methods of appraising the level of prices is in terms of price-earnings ratios. Some analysts have set up rules in these terms for judging when prices are too high or too low. However, the rates at which the market capitalizes earnings are very erratic. The ratio tends to move inversely with earnings; thus a stock earning $4 might sell at $50, with a ratio of 12.5, and fall to $25 when earnings were only $1, with a ratio of 25. But sometimes the actual movement is the opposite of what would be expected on this basis; the price movement at times greatly exceeds the earnings movement in percentage terms.

Timing introduces other elements of variation into price-earnings ratios. The fluctuations in market price within the course of a year are substantial. The high of an average like the Dow-Jones Industrials in a given year may exceed the low by 100 percent or more. Ratios to earnings computed on the basis of the reported aggregate for the year show corresponding variation. Moreover, in some years the highs were based on expectations of higher earnings than were actually realized; and in others the lows were based on expectations below the actual realization. With both numerator and denominator varying within the year, the ratio computed in terms of annual earnings and current prices provides only an uncertain index of whether prices are high or low. Despite the difficulty of establishing any valid criterion under these circumstances, it is commonly stated that a price-earnings ratio of 15 (or some similar figure) is a danger signal in booms and that a ratio only half as large represents a buying opportunity. This approach may be useful if applied with considerable judgment but is of little value in attempting to call the short-term swings.

Simple correlations of prices and earnings also have proved to be of limited value. The general cyclical correlation of the two series cannot readily be translated into high correlations of movements measured by changes in annual data or in those derived from smaller time intervals. The erratic movements of prices detract much from any such correlation, and there appears to be no way of breaking the time intervals to eliminate this effect. Adding other variables derived from corporate reports—such as dividends, book values, or measures of financial condition—tends to improve the correlation, but not much.

A good case can be made for substituting dividends for earnings or for including them with earnings as a basis for the correlation. Various studies of the movements of individual stocks show that the market places more emphasis on dividends than on earnings. A stock paying higher dividends usually sells above a similar stock with equal earnings but lower pay-out rate. The comparative market valuations of dividends and retained earnings vary considerably from industry to industry and even among stocks within industries, but on the average a definite premium is placed on dividends. Hence dividends may be given a greater weight than retained earnings, or dividends may be counted twice by averaging dividends and profits after taxes.

One reason most of the correlations of price changes do not give good results is that they fail to take account of the price position at the beginning of the period. If stocks were overvalued at the beginning of the year, they should be expected to make less than the average increase with a given change in earnings and dividends. If they were undervalued, a better than average performance should be expected.

The results of a correlation taking account of this factor are presented in Chart 17–1. The Standard & Poor's 480 Stock Index (1935–1939 = 100) was used in this computation; changes in the Dow-Jones Industrials are

Chart 17–1. Relation of Stock Prices to Corporate Earnings

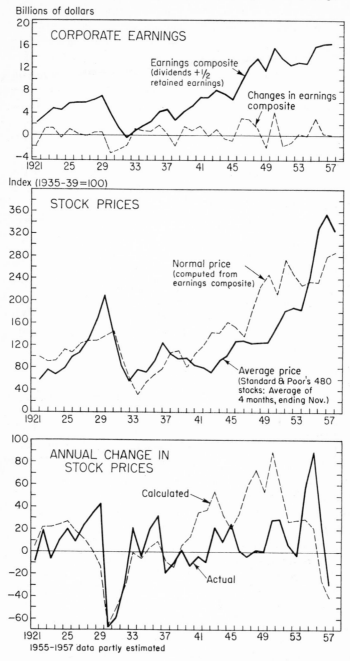

Billions of dollars

CORPORATE EARNINGS

Earnings composite
(dividends + ½
retained earnings)

Changes in earnings
composite

20
16
12
8
4
0
-4

1921   25   29   33   37   41   45   49   53   57

Index (1935-39=100)

STOCK PRICES

Normal price
(computed from
earnings composite)

Average price
(Standard & Poor's 480
stocks: Average of
4 months, ending Nov.)

360
320
280
240
200
160
120
80
40
0

1921   25   29   33   37   41   45   49   53   57

ANNUAL CHANGE IN
STOCK PRICES

Calculated

Actual

100
80
60
40
20
0
-20
-40
-60

1921   25   29   33   37   41   45   49   53   57

1955-1957 data partly estimated

633

very close to half again as large as the changes in this index. Earnings and dividends are Department of Commerce data for the economy as a whole; the composite is the average of dividends and of profits after tax, that is, dividends plus one-half of retained earnings.

It was found that prices in the fall of the year conform most nearly to the annual earnings. Average prices for the months August to November were therefore related to the annual-earnings composite in such a way as to bring out their implications for the change in prices to the same period of the following year. It was found on this basis that the "normal" price could be computed as 40 index points plus 15 times the earnings composite.

The actual and computed normal prices are compared in the middle section of Chart 17–1. It may be noted that in 1928 to 1929, 1933 to 1936, and 1954 to 1956 prices rose above the normal. Through the early 1920s actual prices remained well below normal. In the entire period from 1940 to 1952 prices were consistently below normal, with one exception: through the first half of 1946 they were moderately above normal.

The excess of actual price over normal in the fall of the preceding year and the change in the earnings composite were used as independent variables in estimating the change in stock prices. The earnings composite and the changes in that composite from the preceding year are shown in the upper part of the chart. Note that the upward trend in earnings is eliminated by taking the year-to-year changes; thus in a year like 1952 the change may be negative, although aggregate earnings remain high.

The change in stock prices is estimated as nine times the change in the earnings composite less six-tenths of the difference between actual and normal prices in the fall of the preceding year. The multiplier of nine is obviously a rounded figure; when one is dealing with a rather erratic series of this character, precision in estimating this parameter contributes little. Changes in earnings and dividends adjusted by this "normal" multiplier are carried fully into changes in stock prices. However, only a little more than half of any discrepancy between actual and "normal" price tends to be wiped out in the following year.

To use this relationship, it is necessary to forecast earnings and dividends. The basic approach to this problem was outlined in Chapter 13. The basic estimates given there were not, however, on the same basis as profits reported by business. They excluded price effects, both in neglecting to adjust the gross-national-product estimates to a current dollar base and in excluding inventory-revaluation profits from the computations. The forecasting of price changes was discussed in Chapter 14. The price changes forecast must be applied in order to recompute profits and to express the inventory series in current dollars. The difference between the inventory change in current dollars and the inventory change in constant dollars must then be added to the revised profit figure to obtain a profit estimate comparable to the corporate reports to which the stock market regularly devotes its attention. This is a rather complicated estimating procedure, but it appears to be the only way to a reasonably close approximation to corporate earnings in the desired terms. As another source of potential error, it emphasizes again the difficulty of forecasting the market.

This "year-ahead" profit analysis may be supplemented by short-term projections based on the quarterly data. The market reacts promptly to changes in reported earnings. To some extent, the reports are even anticipated in the price movements. Generally speaking, however, any method of anticipating what the earnings reports will show, even by as little as several weeks, confers a definite advantage on the trader who is able to make short-term projections of this kind.

One approach to this problem is illustrated in Chart 17–2, where actual quarterly profits are compared to estimates derived by means of a simple formula using data on sales and commodity prices. Quarterly changes in profits were correlated with changes in business sales, as reported by the Department of Commerce, and with changes in the BLS index of wholesale prices.[6] The estimated changes obtained from this relationship were chained to actual profits at two fixed starting points to obtain the profits estimates shown in the chart. During World War II, the estimated profits moved far out of line with the actual, and it was therefore necessary to make a new start, beginning from the second quarter of 1948. It should again be noted that the differences between actual and calculated values are large over relatively short intervals, so that careless use of such estimates could be very costly.

The approach has the advantage that it may often be applied to specific companies or industries where sales data are obtainable in advance. In many cases, monthly or weekly estimates of sales or production are available not only for such industries as steel, railroads, and department stores but also for particular companies within industries or for particular areas served by them. Since erratic elements are more likely to be important for a particular industry or company than for business as a whole, greater caution has to be used in interpreting the results.

The annual and quarterly estimates may to some extent be used to

[6] The estimating equation is

$$\Delta E = 0.37\Delta S + 0.55\Delta P$$

where ΔE = change in reported corporate profits before tax
ΔS = change in manufacturing and trade sales
ΔP = change in BLS index of wholesale prices

check each other. If the quarterly estimates showed an adverse movement to the longer-term forecast obtained by the method shown in Chart
17–1, less reliance might be placed upon them as a basis for trading.
Or in a general situation where prices showed a substantial degree of
overvaluation, indications of temporary further advances in profits for
a quarter or two might even be disregarded.

It may be noted from Chart 17–1 that in 1928 and 1929 prices remained
too high for more than 2 years. Moreover, they continued up when they

Chart 17–2. Short-term Projection of Quarterly Corporate Profits

Seasonally adjusted

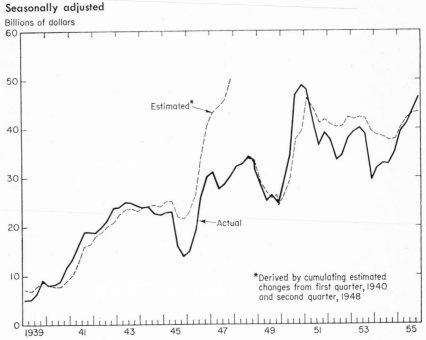

should have been going down. The speculative boom then going on in
the market contributed markedly to the character of the economic situation prevailing at that time and to the depression that followed. Not
until 1932 did prices get back to "normal." In the spring of 1932, they
fell well below normal in the period of most acute liquidation; after
a rebound from the lows, they approximated the normal in the latter
part of that year.

It may be seen from this relationship how prices deviate widely from
the norm set by earnings at the extremes of booms and depressions and
even to some extent in the intermediate swings of shorter duration. The
market affects sentiment more than it does business; when it moves up,
it tends to encourage optimism, leading to overvaluation. When it de-

clines, fears are aggravated, leading to undervaluation. Some short-term market moves disregard fundamental factors almost completely. In a study of the sharp break of September 3, 1946, the Securities and Exchange Commission found that the two primary reasons for sales by the public were the price weakness of the day and the Dow theory bear-market signal. A complete forecasting scheme would have to explain these self-induced movements as well as the changes explained by business conditions as such.

TECHNICAL ANALYSIS OF THE MARKET

Technical analysis of the market attempts to fill this gap. It usually proceeds on the theory that there are ways of objectively measuring the force of market behavior as a specific influence on prices. In following this approach, numerous indexes or other measures have been computed to interpret the character of the current market situation with a view to calling the turns. It would hardly be appropriate to embark on any detailed discussion of this material. All that is attempted, therefore, is a brief summary of some of the basic ideas underlying various kinds of technical analysis.

Much of this work had its beginnings in the Dow theory. According to this theory, whenever a movement of the market was halted, a "resistance point" was established. If the recovery from a secondary reversal subsequently carried through the prior upside resistance point, the bull market was confirmed (in the Dow theory, both the rail and the industrial indexes had to "break through" to confirm a trend). If the recovery failed to break through and the next decline broke the lower resistance point established on the first reaction, then the market had turned and a bear market was in progress.

A similar technique, designed for early detection of tops and bottoms in major price swings, made use of trend lines. During an upward movement, the bottoms of successive minor reactions formed a "trend" of the lows, along which a line was drawn; if any market reaction broke through this line, it was interpreted as a sign of weakness and the potential beginning of a reversal, even though the market continued at or above the last downside resistance point.

Moving averages have also been widely used in "trend analysis." The moving averages smooth out the irregularities; they are usually timed to cover intervals of past prices equivalent to periods from several weeks up to a year, thus comprising a group of moving averages centered on the last quotation, with the longest reflecting a half-year's lag. This longest moving average follows prices slowly; it may be taken as a lower extreme of the price movement on rising markets and as an upper extreme on declines. The shortest moving average turns first; when it breaks through the next longer average, it gives a signal of faltering progress. As the shorter moving averages break through the longer moving averages, they give successively stronger signals that the "major trend" has changed.

Patterns in the price formation have also been studied intensively to obtain indications of future changes. Sometimes the market remains for a period in a very narrow range, termed a "line." This represents, in effect, a type of situation where upper and lower resistance points are very close together. When the index breaks out of the range, the "direction" of the market is established, and the extent of the next move is supposed to bear a definite relationship to the duration of the "line."

The import of other patterns has also been explored. One of these is the "triangle," a formation in which successive secondary tops and bottoms are progressively closer together. Like the line, the triangle leaves the primary direction of the market undecided for a while, and both the timing of the breakaway and the extent of the succeeding movement are supposed to vary with the character of the movements making up the triangle.

Progress was made by considering the behavior of trading volume as well as the behavior of prices. When the market was in an indecisive state, as in a line or a triangle, if volume was strong on the advances and weak on the declines, the next move would be upward, and vice versa. The difference in volume was supposed to indicate on which side of the market the decisive influence of traders' opinions held sway. High volume on the advances represented "accumulation"; high volume on the declines, "liquidation."

Volume considerations were also applied to the problem of distinguishing major tops and bottoms. Volume of trading usually increased when prices advanced. It tended to rise to a peak of speculative excitement near the end of a bull market. But declining volume on successive advances gave a more dependable danger signal. Bull markets were held to end with a final rally on feeble volume, meaning simply that volume was reduced in comparison with the excited level of trading that had prevailed earlier, when the bull market was driving to a peak. At the depression lows, volume tended to dry up; a succession of dull, inactive days with sagging prices was held to mark the approach of a recovery movement.[7] Extremes of volume were in general credited with marking an unusual condition in the market; a sharp expansion of volume at the end of a secondary movement has commonly been referred to as a buying or selling "climax."

---

[7] For a more detailed discussion of the signs of major turning points, see L. H. Haney, *Business Forecasting*, Ginn & Company, Boston, 1931.

Another kind of analysis has been carried out in terms of the disparate behavior of different groups of stocks. Indexes of the blue chips are compared with indexes of speculative issues or with broad indexes of the total market. If the speculative issues forge ahead for a while and then weaken while the blue chips are still rising, a reversal is held to be near at hand.

Another danger signal to be noted at an approaching top may be obtained by counting the number of issues advancing and declining each day. If most stocks decline day after day while the price averages continue to rise, a dangerous market situation is developing.

Much of the present-day technical analysis. rests on these early foundations. New measures have been derived by students of market behavior, and new terms are used to describe them.[8] How much refinement adds to the older concepts and how far it goes toward eliminating the need for judgment is a question.

One of the most popular of the newer techniques is based on a study of volume of trading in individual issues. The price movement in each stock is presumed to indicate buying or selling initiative, and separate tabulations are made each day for the stocks that moved up and for those that moved down. The results appear as indexes of "buying power" and "selling pressure," which have given useful signals on various occasions.

A logical extension of this idea involves tabulating volume not merely for the individual issues but for the individual transactions in each issue. The author conducted a study of this type in which two samples of issues from the entire stock list were used to reduce the statistical burden of the project. The indexes obtained gave correct signals in some years—for example, at the 1949 low—and incorrect signals in others— for example, at the 1946 high. For the entire period studied, the results proved to be of such limited value that they were not considered worthy of publication.

Another approach to the problem of market analysis attempts to evaluate the behavior of various groups in the market. One of the earliest versions of this kind of analysis is based upon the odd-lot data. The essence of its underlying theory is that the odd-lot traders are always wrong. They sell in the early stages of a bull market and buy in the late stages, when most of the potential gains have already been realized. A bull market largely supported by odd-lot buyers is held to be near the breaking point. Conversely, such traders buy on the way down and only become discouraged enough to sell out when the market is approaching a bottom.

This type of analysis may be extended to take account of other market

[8] See N. Molodovsky, "New Tools for Stock Market Analysis," *Fortune*, April, 1949.

groups as well as the odd-lotters. In one study, a special survey was made of the transactions of financial institutions, such as investment trusts, pension funds, and life-insurance companies. The purchases and sales of the members of the exchanges were also analyzed, to appraise the operations of the group commonly referred to as "professionals."[9] This study threw considerable light on the character of the market in the early 1950s and helped provide the basis for forecasts of the strong advance from the 1953 lows. The data are not regularly available, but the potential importance of this approach is summed up in the statement of an investment trust executive: "Just tell me what the people with the money are doing and what they are planning to do, and you can keep all the rest of the thinking on the stock market." This statement obviously ignores the possibility that plans and policies may change without notice.

Occasionally outside data have been used to supplement market data as such in technical analysis. Sensitive commodity prices in particular have been used as barometers of an approaching turn. Prices of such commodities as steel scrap and copper tend to move up sharply near the end of the boom and then fall back just before the break. Recovery in sensitive prices is also held to be a necessary prelude to recovery from bear-market lows.

Most of the technical analysis of the market is presented in the form of charts. An endless flow of charts is published in financial periodicals or by special advisory services. There are trend and moving-average charts, ratio lines, point and figure charts, volume bars, vertical-line charts, and a number of other kinds of charts. Most of these charts, and the theories that have produced them, require a good deal of judgment in order to obtain a reasonable interpretation of market behavior from them. Most do not work consistently but are supposed to work often enough to create a distinct probability in their favor. Even when interpreted with judgment, they leave a great deal of uncertainty about the state of the market at important junctures.

FORECASTING OTHER FINANCIAL DEVELOPMENTS

Experts in the monetary field constantly point out that there is not just one money market but a series of markets, interrelated and yet highly stratified. Nevertheless, in discussions of financial developments, it is the common practice to talk of "tight" or "easy" money and of "the" interest rate. The actual forecasting methods used in most cases make a primary analysis in over-all terms and then proceed to develop the

[9] Irwin Friend, "New Influences in the Stock Market," *Fortune*, March, 1953.

implications of over-all tightening or easing on the various specific markets of interest.

The stratification of money markets has several aspects. One important distinction is between long- and short-term funds. Another is by type of borrower—whether Federal government, state and local governments, home builders, business (different kinds and for different purposes), or consumers. A third is by type of lender or investor—banks, consumer-credit agencies, savings-and-loan associations, insurance companies and pension funds, investment bankers, investment trusts, business investment of retained earnings outside the company, and disposition of accumulated savings by individual investors.

As a rule, the areas in which any borrower seeks funds and the areas in which any lender operates are subject to definite limits. The consumer, the individual home builder, and the small businessman almost of necessity deal with local banks, local loan associations, or the finance companies who handle the paper of local merchants. The large business concern has much wider banking connections and can tap the new-issue market. The local bank ordinarily does little direct lending outside its own area, the savings-and-loan association takes mortgages only on local buildings, and the credit union usually lends only to its own members. Insurance companies may acquire mortgages over a wide area and purchase a variety of bonds and stocks but avoid short-term loans. The investment bankers undertake to sell new issues of stocks and bonds on prearranged terms and may borrow to carry their "inventory," but they have little interest in most other lending operations.

This stratification affects the structure of interest rates to a considerable extent. Municipal and other tax-exempt bonds, for example, ordinarily dwell in a fenced-in pasture of their own and command a substantial differential in rates over taxable bonds. These bonds are preferred by investors in the higher tax brackets. At times, however, the pressure of projects breaks the fences, and the differential is lost. In boom times, the demand for funds is so great that the bonds issued cannot be sold to the group of investors primarily interested in them. Other kinds of investors then have to be brought into the market, and most other investors have far less interest in tax exemption. When it becomes necessary to sell the bonds to nonprofit or other institutions whose income is already tax-exempt, the differential may disappear completely. In fact, the going sometimes gets so tough that the investment bankers have to ration the new issues, and municipalities that insist on getting funds to push their projects quickly may have to pay a premium over taxable bonds. This makes for wider fluctuations of rates in this market than those that occur in the rates for other long-term funds.

In contrast, a special field in which rates have displayed unusual stability since the end of World War II is the financing of residential construction. The mortgages issued to finance the housing boom have in large part been guaranteed by the government and were subject to rates limited by law. For many years, the rates on these guaranteed-mortgage loans were well above the rate on government bonds, and there was little upward pressure on the mortgage market. Later, when rates tended to rise, buyer resistance curtailed the volume of building. The combination of circumstances, legal and economic, made the mortgage market in many respects more of a pegged market than any of the others.

The primary impact of business-cycle developments is in the short-term market and focuses most directly on the banks. Loans for carrying business inventories or for installment purchases draw heavily on bank credit, either directly or through other agencies, which in turn borrow from the banks. Business concerns may also finance some fixed-capital requirements by means of bank loans. When credit use appears to be excessive, restrictive monetary action is called for. The Federal Reserve then attempts to control the use of credit and operates to limit the available supply of bank funds. The combination of heavy demand and limited supply tends to drive up short-term rates. In a recession, the opposite kind of changes occurs. Demand for loans falls off, and the Federal Reserve contributes what it can to stabilizing the economy by making funds more readily available. Hence the short-term market is subject to extreme tightening or loosening over relatively short periods as business conditions change.

In the course of such movements, changes in pressure on long-term rates may be nowhere near as great. The funds flowing into the long-term market through insurance companies, pension funds, and other institutions may continue at a high level while bank funds are restricted. The long-term market also displays distinct resistance to changes in rates. Borrowers are reluctant to commit themselves to high interest payments over a long period of time, especially if they feel the high rates may be only temporary; they may therefore postpone entering the market when it is tight. Similarly, investors are reluctant to pay premiums for outstanding issues or to accept new issues at extremely low rates; they may prefer to hold cash for a while rather than to risk losses in market value when rates again move up.

For a variety of reasons, therefore, short-term rates may move while long-term rates remain comparatively stable. For most of the period since the depression of the 1930s, rates on short-term governments have remained consistently below long-term rates, reflecting in part the usefulness of these short-term securities as liquid reserves. The rate on long-term governments has represented a ceiling for short-term rates throughout this period. In the mid-1950s, the yield curve on government securities became very flat; that is, rates on short-term issues were about as high as on long-term issues. The longs then rose to over 3 percent. The main difference in the quarter century up to that point had appeared on the lower side. There had been a floor under long-term governments at about 2 percent and under high-grade corporates at about 2½ percent, but short-term governments at times approached zero.

The operations of banks and business concerns effect some transfers of funds between markets and to that extent restrict the movement of short-term rates in relation to long. The banks may sell off government securities in order to meet demands for short-term loans and keep their reserve positions adjusted. However, they prefer to let short-term governments run off before liquidating bond holdings; and to the extent that short-term holdings are adequate, as they were after World War II, this merely transfers funds from one short-term market to another. The banks have another alternative, which also tends to be rather limited. They may to some extent divert consumer savings out of long-term channels by raising rates of interest paid on savings deposits; the importance of this alternative derives partly from the fact that reserve requirements on time deposits are lower than on demand deposits.

Large corporations may shift funds between long and short markets by exercising their choice of methods of financing. They are in a position to shop around for favorable terms, and when costs of short-term borrowing rise, those needing funds may draw upon the long-term market.

At the same time, a rise in rates on short-term governments provides an added incentive for corporations to hold reserves in this form rather than as cash. They may minimize the need for loans by drawing down cash balances or reducing dividend payments. Reducing dividends in a period of high profits is frowned upon, but to some extent stock dividends may be substituted for cash. Finally, they have the option of adjusting operations, on both current and capital accounts, in such ways as to reduce total needs. In boom times, however, when expansion programs are at a peak and working capital demands are correspondingly inflated, these alternatives may serve to moderate pressure on the short-term market but not to dispel it.

Government-debt operations are another potential means of shifting funds between long and short markets. However, for several years after the Treasury–Federal Reserve "accord" of March, 1951, which eliminated the wartime policy of pegging the rates, market conditions did not favor any substantial lengthening of maturities. Several attempts to issue long-term bonds indicated that the market could be induced to take them only at too rapid an advance in rates. In these prosperity years, the competition for long-term funds was consistently strong, from state and local governments as well as from consumers and business concerns; and for a variety of reasons, such as the higher return on government guaranteed mortgages, investors preferred the alternative outlets for their funds to increased holdings of long-term governments.

Through the prosperity years of the early 1950s, therefore, pressure on the short-term rate built up but did not carry it distinctly above the long-term rate, as in 1929. In this situation, the government securities market was supported to some extent by shifting from stocks. Stock prices rose to levels where yields were low, and bond yields rose to a comparatively high level. With a large volume of low-coupon government bonds outstanding, not only was the actual yield available comparable to that on high-grade stocks but a substantial portion of it—perhaps the major portion if considered from a short-term point of view—could potentially be realized as capital gain rather than interest income. There were, in short, steadying as well as disturbing influences. These crosscurrents in the market made prediction difficult but maintained an effective ceiling even under the tight-money conditions of the mid-1950s.

In forecasting interest rates, attention tends to center on the area in which changes occur—the short-term rates which are the primary object of attention of the monetary authorities seeking to control the use of credit. The actions of the monetary authorities are not all-decisive, but certainly they cannot be ignored. The most widely accepted approach to forecasting interest-rate changes, therefore, is to try to determine what the "market" would do if left to itself and then supplement this statistical-economic analysis with "guesses" as to what official action will be.[10] In this approach, a general business forecast is needed both for the market analysis and as a basis for judging the official actions to be taken.

Most forecasters utilize some form of flow-of-funds analysis as the basis for their forecasts. Current savings and investment by various major groups constitute an important part of this analysis, but the data on income and product account have to be expanded to take account of financial transactions and of funds other than those realized as current income. These financial sources of funds, largely involving the creation and liquidation of debt, tend to be the central objective of this kind of analysis.

The consumer account, for example, must be broadened to take

---

[10] For an excellent short discussion of the problem, see Roland Robinson, "Forecasting Interest Rates," *Journal of Business*, University of Chicago, Chicago, January, 1954. This article discusses theoretical aspects and points out some inadequacies in interest-rate theory.

account of changes in consumer debt and of the accumulation or liquidation of liquid assets by consumers if it is to be meaningful in terms of impact on the money markets. Thus a reversal of consumer policy as to durable goods purchased on credit has a double impact: it reduces the demand for credit and increases the flow of savings. Two long-term trends—toward larger purchases of durables and a larger proportion of saving in contractual form—suggest that the consumer sector will have a constantly increasing impact on the money market.

The corporate account is the most difficult to analyze. It is usually undertaken in terms of the data on sources and uses of corporate funds. These data for the year 1954 are shown in Table 17–1. Each item in

Table 17–1. Sources and Uses of Corporate Funds, 1954
In billions of dollars

Uses, total	$21.2
Plant and equipment outlays	22.4
Inventories (change in book value)	−2.8
Change in customer net receivables	1.9
Cash and United States government securities	−1.0
Other assets	0.6
Sources, total	$20.8
Internal, total	$19.3
Retained profits and depletion allowances	6.2
Depreciation and amortization allowances	13.1
External, total	$ 1.4
Change in Federal income tax liability	−4.1
Other liabilities	0.3
Change in bank loans and mortgage loans	−0.9
Net new issues	6.1
Discrepancy (uses less sources)	0.4

SOURCE: *Economic Report of the President to Congress*, January, 1956, p. 227.

this table has to be projected in order to estimate the effects of business operations on money and capital markets in general and on the specific markets to which the various items relate. The most highly variable items in the corporate picture are inventories and profits. Any change in inventory valuation is matched by a corresponding change in profits, but an increase in inventory volume may result from a reduction in sales and, with profits also down, may produce a sharp loss in cash and a correspondingly heavy demand for loans.

The analysis of the government accounts proceeds along the lines indicated in Chapter 6. In the present context, attention focuses on the cash budget rather than on the administrative budget. In addition, con-

Table 17–2. Summary of Flow-of-funds Accounts for 1954

S = sources of funds, U = uses of funds

Annual flows, in billions of dollars

Sectors / Transactions	Consumer S	Consumer U	Corporate S	Corporate U	Non-corporate S	Non-corporate U	Farm S	Farm U	Federal S	Federal U	State and local S	State and local U	Banking S	Banking U	Insurance S	Insurance U	Other S	Other U	Rest of the world S	Rest of the world U	Total S	Total U
NONFINANCIAL																						
A Payroll	193.7			116.3		29.8		2.6		18.1		14.8		2.1				2.8			193.7	193.7
B Receipts from and payments on investment	64.9	17.2	9.6	21.8	17.8	40.9	1.1	15.1	1.1	5.7	0.8	1.1	6.4	2.3	4.2	0.3	1.9	1.7	0.4	2.2	108.2	108.2
C Insurance and grants	27.0	24.2	1.4	12.8	1.1	3.1	0.5	0.5	1.1	16.3	13.2	13.0	*	1.0	30.5	18.1	5.9	1.4	2.3	0.3	90.4	90.4
D Taxes and tax refunds	2.9	38.4	0.4	36.2		7.1		1.6	61.7	3.3	22.8	22.8		1.0	*	0.3		*			87.9	88.0
E Capital acquisitions	24.5	66.3	0.2	20.9	1.8	5.4	0.4	4.5	*	3.5	0.1	9.0	0.2	0.2			2.6	2.6				
F Net change in inventories				−3.0		−0.5		0.3		*												
G New fixed capital		40.2		23.7		5.9		4.2		3.4		8.4			*						805.7	798.9
H Other capital acquisitions	24.5	26.0	0.2	0.2	1.8		0.4		0.7	*	0.1	0.7			*	0.2						
I Purchases and sales of other goods and services	155.5		521.1	330.3	193.5	128.5	30.2	9.7	6.1	32.4	6.0	6.5	0.8	0.8	0.6	3.9	5.2	3.7	15.2	3.7		
J Total	313.0	304.1	532.8	538.4	214.2	214.5	32.2	33.3	77.3	79.7	42.9	44.5	7.3	6.8	35.3	26.3	13.0	14.1	18.0	17.7	1,285.9	1,279.3
FINANCIAL																						
K Currency and deposits		6.5		0.7		0.7		−0.3		0.4		0.8	9.7			*	0.2	0.7	0.2	0.7	9.7	10.1
L Federal obligations		−1.8		−1.7		−0.1			2.2			1.7		3.9		−0.5		0.5		0.5	2.2	2.4
M Mortgages	8.5	0.6	1.6	1.6	1.8	1.1	0.8	1.6		−0.1				3.7		2.7		4.4			12.5	12.5
N Corporate securities and state and local obligations				0.1							4.4	0.4				0.1						
O (obligations)	2.7	2.5	5.7	0.1	0.4	0.1			0.2	−0.3			0.2	2.1	0.4	8.4	0.5	−0.9	0.3	0.1	11.1	12.7
Other	.2	2.2	−2.2	−0.3	−0.4	−0.3		−0.3		−0.1			0.2	1.3	0.4	0.2	5.8	−0.6	1.0	0.5	8.2	9.0
P Total	10.6	13.6	5.1	1.3	2.2	1.6	2.9	1.6	2.4	2.9	4.4	4.2	10.2	11.0	0.4	10.7	6.3	10.7	1.5	1.8	43.8	46.8
Q Grand total	324.0	324.0	537.8	537.8	216.4	216.4	33.0	33.0	79.7	79.7	47.3	47.3	17.5	17.5	35.6	35.6	19.3	19.3	19.5	19.5	1,330.2	1,330.2
Memoranda:																						
R GNP identifiable in J		220.2		24.1		6.4		6.2		49.0		26.9						11.7		−0.3	11.3	345.8
S Bank credit in P	3.0		−1.1	−1.1	2.1		0.5		3.9		2.0		*	1.5		.1		.2	0.8		11.3	11.2

* Less than $50 million.

SOURCE: *Federal Reserve Bulletin*, October, 1955, p. 1122.

sideration must be given to refunding operations. The impact of heavy refunding may be decisive when the market is closely balanced. It may determine the precise moment at which changes occur. An underlying tendency toward tightness may, for example, become effective all at once, and there may even be a subsequent movement away from the extreme engendered on such an occasion.

The basis for analysis of refunding operations lies in regularly published tabulations of maturities on the Federal debt. The action to be taken on any issue is usually announced in advance. The forecaster versed in this field can frequently anticipate announcements concerning issues called in advance of maturity by analyzing the possible occasions on which it would be advantageous for the Treasury to move, given the rate on the outstanding issue, the current state of the market, and the general economic policies of the government.

Data summarizing the transactions of all sectors of the economy are brought together in a single flow-of-funds tabulation by the Federal Reserve Board.[11] These data, for the year 1954, are shown in Table 17–2. As the column heads indicate, separate accounts are provided for each of 10 economic sectors. In each case financial and nonfinancial transactions are separately reported. At the bottom a summary memorandum shows how much of the total of nonfinancial uses of funds is identifiable as gross national product and how much of the financial total is bank credit. In each case the gross transactions were about four times these important subsidiary items in 1954.

The data are useful in the form shown in this table in presenting the picture as a whole and in forcing a reconciliation of estimates for the various sectors. Analysis must actually proceed, however, sector by sector, in terms of projections of the various kinds of activity that constitute the operations of each. The objective of the analysis is to determine what the aggregate needs for funds will be and how much flexibility there will be in the system for meeting those needs.

THE ROLE OF MONETARY POLICY

One of the most important aspects of flexibility in the system lies in the potential for expansion of bank credit. Any excess of financial resources in the other sectors tends to be reflected in the availability of bank reserves through increases in deposits or reductions in bank loans. When the reserves available to the banks are ample, the potential

[11] See "A Flow of Funds System of National Accounts," *Federal Reserve Bulletin,* October, 1955. These data are not entirely comparable with those in Table 17–1. Background research is reported in Morris A. Copeland, *A Study of Moneyflows in the United States,* National Bureau of Economic Research, New York, 1952.

expansion of loans is correspondingly large, and any tendencies toward tightness in the money markets will be moderated.

The ability of the banks to expand credit may be limited, however, by the action of the Federal Reserve System, which is usually referred to more briefly as "The Fed." The Fed may limit the reserves available to the banks through its own operations, as by selling government securities in the open market, or by using its power to establish the level of reserve requirements. Usually the former approach, control of its own credit, would be the first kind of action undertaken, with the latter, which may change the banks' position drastically and quickly, being reserved for use in extraordinary situations.

It is customary to talk of the Fed as an independent agency and its policies as independent of those established by other government agencies. This is misleading, however, as no one agency could hope to take action contrary to national policy for more than a limited period. If it attempted to do this, it would soon lose any independence it might otherwise exercise. There is always support for the "independence" of the Fed in Congress, and it is frequently urged to take drastic action in bold speeches, but the actual votes taken in Congress do not encourage the idea that this is a realistic view.

In periods of emergency, national policy is clear-cut and there is hardly anything for the Fed to do but fall in line. War is, of course, a special case. Cold war or other aspects of international politics may be considered similar in character, but as a rule the resources involved are comparatively limited and therefore impose little restraint on monetary policy. If sizable Federal deficits were involved, the pressure on the Fed to create monetary conditions that facilitated financing of the established government programs would be severe.

The most important kind of domestic emergency arises from depressed activity and unemployment. Even a minor recession has become a matter of grave concern in recent years, and both major political parties view the matter in the same light. The government has accepted the responsibility, through the Employment Act of 1946 and in other ways, for preventing depressions. In this case, the Fed's own objective of stabilizing the economy is in accord with general government policy, so that both work in the same direction. Moreover, the Fed's policy is reinforced by tendencies elsewhere in the government to avoid direct counter-cyclical action, on the grounds that primary reliance should be placed on monetary and fiscal measures. Action to ease monetary conditions on a decline therefore tends to be pushed to extremes. Unfortunately, such action is relatively ineffective in bringing a downward movement to a halt.

These two situations may be taken as illustrating the dilemma of

Federal Reserve policy. On the one hand, its actions tend to be ineffective: they may create the possibility of recovery but not the actuality. On the other hand, action might be effective, but its application tends to come up against obstacles it cannot overcome, for such obstacles are encountered in any prosperity situation that involves a Federal deficit. What tends to save the day is that the requirements of government finance generally move inversely with business, owing to the high degree of variability in tax receipts, so that high business prosperity does present opportunities for restrictive action.

The specifics of government finance—provision of needed funds, interest-rate policy, debt management, and related matters—are ordinarily referred to as "the Treasury."

The objectives of the Treasury at times diverge from those of the Fed, most commonly when the Fed is applying restrictive measures and interest rates are moving up. The Treasury is interested in financing government operations at lowest cost and even more in making sure that adequate funds will be available when needed. The conflict between the Treasury and the Fed was a topic of wide interest in the period leading up to the "accord" of March, 1951.

Tight-money conditions create no great problem for the Treasury when prosperity conditions bring high revenues and a government surplus. Tight money does create a problem if the government is running a deficit. Under such conditions, all claimants for new money suffer a disadvantage. This is reflected in higher rates charged on new issues than on outstanding issues of similar quality. In addition, Federal-government securities tend to lose the advantage they ordinarily command by being "risk-free." This is not because they have become riskier but because nobody wants to put funds into them. Consumers, business, and other users of funds have other uses, on balance, for all their resources. Banks, insurance companies, and other institutional providers of funds prefer to channel them to the type of customers it is their primary duty to serve. Difficulties of goverment finance then pose problems for the Fed as well as for the Treasury. It is difficult to predict what the outcome of the conflict of objectives will be under such conditions.

The conflicts between the Treasury and the Fed need not be narrowly conceived. The Fed is the focal point of pressures from the financial community. It represents a wide variety of interests whose views are by no means unimportant. The persistent bias of those interests is toward preventing inflation and maintaining the "soundness of the dollar"; and although fears of inflation may be exaggerated, it behooves the government to handle its finances in such a way as to keep potential forces of inflation under control. The Treasury agrees with this, of course; its problems would become overwhelming with any loss of confidence in the government's credit. But the Treasury also represents the wider range of pressures that have made the government programs what they are at any given moment. Certain things have been demanded and approved, and until Congress is ready to act again, those things must be taken as the basis for fiscal operations. It is not farfetched to say that the interests of the whole economy bear upon the conflict.

If any definite tendency in government programs can be detected, it is the tendency toward recurring government deficits. The bias of government policy is toward high expenditures. It pursues objectives of preventing unemployment and of protecting producers' incomes, either directly through various kinds of subsidies or indirectly through maintaining markets for their products. These increases in expenditures tend to be restrained but not prevented by pressures for tax reduction. The latter are most effective in periods when the government budget is running a surplus. They prevent surpluses from becoming large enough to effect any substantial reduction of debt, so that the upward course of the latter is in effect set by the prevailing winds.

It is this tendency toward the accumulation of government deficits that gives rise to fears of inflation. The view underlying these fears is accurate, however, only to the extent that price levels will tend to be maintained at a higher level than would otherwise be the case. For government programs cannot be wholly effective in overcoming the forces of deflation and cannot even guarantee the maintenance of full employment year in and year out. There will always be cyclical fluctuations, bringing recurring waves of unemployment to be remedied by new deficits; but the latter will be discontinuous and primarily palliative in effect, so that no basis for continuing upward pressure on prices is likely to derive from them. Only if our tremendous capacity and productivity should somehow be rendered ineffective would there be a basis for all-out, continuing inflation. This might happen as a result of war, but hardly as a result of action to lift the economy out of depression.

The logical outcome of the policies envisaged is not inflation but a state of uneasy balance between inflationary and deflationary pressures. It will likely be characterized by partial employment—both in the sense that some unemployment will persist and in the sense that many will be less than satisfactorily employed. The producers who are able to retain employment in favorably situated industries will be able to command a good return, with more or less continuous advances in money incomes. The others, representing the greater number in unrestricted competition, will remain unemployed or enter less favorably situated industries or occupations where returns tend to be marginal. Even in the favored industries, price increases would be moderated by the tendency to take part of potential incomes in real rather than money terms. Many in these industries would feel that there was some advantage in passing on savings realized from increasing efficiency and avoiding extreme price disparities with other commodities. The end result would be the same, with the advantages of position appearing in higher real incomes. Divergent price trends might well be experienced, rather than any distinct, continuing price advance in over-all terms.

From this brief, imaginative look at future conditions in an economy in which the government struggles to keep unemployment at a minimum, it would appear that the occasions on which the Fed could put its really effective powers to use would be rather limited. It would have substantial discretion primarily in those intervals of prosperity in which the government budget was brought into balance by rapidly advancing tax receipts. More commonly, it would be charged, in accordance with the primary function of the Federal Reserve System, with creating the funds needed to assist recovery or to maintain an uneasy state of semiprosperity in which elements of inflation and deflation were continuously present.

The popular conception of the monetary function in periods of high prosperity is that it should increase the money supply sufficiently over a period of time to permit the normal growth of the economy without the disturbing effects of rising prices. Even in periods of prosperity, therefore, rather strong opposition to tight money would be encountered unless prices were rising rapidly enough to stimulate fears of inflation. A case for restriction might be made in terms of the speed of an upsurge in activity, but even this would find limited acceptance if it followed a period of deflation.

Looking at the problem in these broad terms provides the only approach to a solution. Although the role of the Fed appears in broad perspective to be a limited one, the degree of variability in its discretion may still occasionally be of urgent importance to the investor. Judging the manner in which that discretion will be exercised requires the broadest kind of appraisal of economic and political developments. The problem gives full play to the intelligence of the investor, since hardly any well-defined set of rules could be expected to hold good in all circumstances.

Interpolation Formulas for the Adjustment
of Index Numbers

There are many occasions in the construction or utilization of index numbers when adjustment of a monthly index based on a sample to more complete periodic surveys of the same field is desirable. It is also desirable on most occasions of this kind to preserve the characteristic pattern of the monthly index, though correction to the level of the more reliable data is the primary concern. The problem thus consists in holding to a minimum the necessary disturbances in the month-to-month pattern while the broad shifting of level is accomplished.

One situation of this kind arises when the only dependable data available are annual data and there is need for a monthly series representing the changes in the annual data. Where this is the problem, a smooth monthly interpolation with the required annual averages may represent an adequate solution in some instances. Ordinarily, however, a better solution can be obtained through the use of related data that are available monthly but not suitable for direct use in themselves. Such data can provide a more satisfactory monthly index after adjustment than the smooth type of interpolation.

A similar problem is encountered when periodic surveys, such as the censuses of manufactures, show somewhat different results from an index that is generally satisfactory over short periods. This may particularly be true in the case of indexes of the link type, where the links relating any month to the previous month are the percentage changes in a varying, though fairly adequate, sample of identical firms. In this case, adjustment of the monthly index by means of an appropriate interpolation formula is necessary to prevent bias and to bring the index averages in the census years to the level of the census data.

The method of adjustment described below applies to any problem of this type, but the discussion will be confined mainly to the particular situations described in the paragraph above. To put the problem in its simplest terms, the index and the census averages should be set equal in the first census year, and subsequent census averages should be expressed as percentages of the corresponding index averages. Chart A–1 presents a series of four hypothetical census averages expressed in this form; these averages are represented by the horizontal bars

Chart A–1. Assumed Census Averages as Percentages of Corresponding Index Averages and Three Interpolations for Adjusting the Index to the Census Level

Per cent of unadjusted index

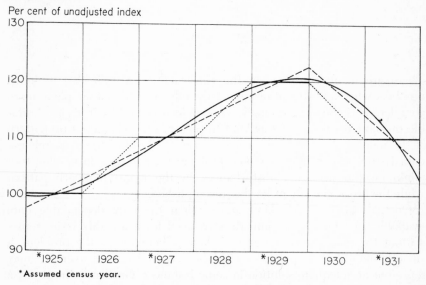

*Assumed census year.

in the odd-numbered years. The unadjusted index would be represented on this chart by a horizontal line at the 100 level. What is desired is a monthly interpolation series that will have the same averages as the census relatives in each of the census years.

Before discussion of such interpolations, attention may be called to the fact that the differences between the two sets of data, which may be looked upon as errors in the index, are expressed in relative rather than in absolute terms. Arithmetic corrections applied in absolute amounts by addition or subtraction may be satisfactory in a limited number of cases. But whenever (1) there is a marked trend in the index, (2) there is a marked seasonal pattern, or (3) there are wide fluctuations of a random character, this method produces wide variations in the percentage corrections applied to different months of the year, and such variations are quite illogical in order and in magnitude. Most of the series to which adjustments must be applied are strongly affected by trend and seasonal factors at least, and the use of arithmetic adjustments can therefore have little general validity.

Under the conditions outlined, the simplest interpolation that would equalize the averages would consist of the census averages themselves, joined by a series of straight lines connecting the end point of one with the beginning of the next, as indicated by the dotted lines in Chart A–1. This produces a series of steplike adjustments and has the effect of confining corrections to the intercensus years. While at first glance this may appear to be a good expedient, because our knowledge of those years is in any event the most limited, it is essentially an evasion of the problem. Its main disadvantage lies in the distortion of the pattern in intercensus years relative to that in census years.

Another straight-line method utilizes a series of lines drawn from the mid-points of the census averages and extended to the ends of the census years; where such an adjustment has previously been made, the next adjustment line begins from the last point previously corrected. This interpolation is represented by the dashed line in Chart A–1. It gives fairly satisfactory results when successive adjustments are similar in direction and magnitude, but results are far less satisfactory when successive adjustments are made in opposite directions. Under the latter circumstances, the corrections tend to deviate furthest from the average at the ends of the census years. This tendency is shown in the chart at the end of 1929, where fairly large and arbitrary modifications of the month-to-month changes occur. Moreover, the index level remains somewhat too high until after the next census adjustment is made.

From a causal point of view, either of these corrections is based upon arbitrary assumptions. Implicit in any interpolation is some assumption concerning the causes operating to produce the observed discrepancies. The first method assumes that such causes operate only in noncensus years. The second is based upon the assumption that the causes producing the observed discrepancy continue in operation at a constant rate to the end of a census year, when a new set of causes suddenly become effective and continues in operation at a constant rate until the end of the next census year. Such assumptions are not justified by our knowledge of actual economic forces. Changes in those forces are likely to be gradual or, if they occur as the result of sudden disturbances, to become effective at some unpredictable date. Since the possibility of taking account of the latter alternative is in most cases ruled out by lack of specific knowledge, the best procedure would seem to be one based upon the former. Hence a smooth interpolation, which would consistently represent a gradual shifting of the forces producing the observed discrepancies, might be expected to produce somewhat better results.

The curved line in Chart A–1 represents such an interpolation. It is fitted in such a way that its average value in each of the census years is equal to the corresponding census average. This curve gives a fairly satisfactory interpolation for the period covered, except in the last 2 years and particularly the last year. In this final year, the correction changes so rapidly from the beginning to the end that a serious distortion of trend is probable, with the final index considerably too low at the end of the period. The extreme degree of correction at this point follows from the use of a curve of high enough degree to provide the flexibility requisite to obtaining the many changes in level.

With somewhat different data, the curved interpolation would have given similarly unsatisfactory results in the opening year of the period and perhaps in one or more of the intercensus years. It is not at all difficult to set up examples where extreme, and wholly unreasonable, adjustments would be obtained in the intermediate years. Some control on the flexibility of the curve is clearly desirable.

The problem in the initial year becomes acute only when the adjusted index is to be spliced to previous data. Errors in the final year, on the other hand, are particularly important, for the index must be used without adjustment from the end of the period until the data from the next census become available. Such errors will be carried at least 2 years and may seriously distort the facts if comparisons of recent levels and those of previous years are made. The second straight-line interpolation also may be subject to serious criticism on this account, as already indicated. Hence some control on this tendency to overcarry at the end points is essential, and subsequent discussion will contain some implicit suggestions for obtaining such control when this type of interpolation is to be used.

It is not of primary interest at the moment to improve this curve, since the method has another limitation that restricts its usefulness. This further limitation is the practical necessity for conserving effort. Each problem and each set of adjustments require that a special curve be fitted. Hence in dealing with current problems, where new data are constantly being added to a series, this method would make necessary at the observation of each new discrepancy the computation of an entirely new, complex interpolation covering the entire period studied. Where new data are to be added and new adjustments are to be made, therefore, it is better to utilize a method which handles each successive adjustment as a single unit, without seriously affecting previous adjustments. The following discussion will present a method of the unit-adjustment type that retains the advantages of the smooth curve.

When each adjustment is to be made as a separate unit, only the data covering 2 successive census years and the intervening year need be considered. For convenience the problem will be formulated as above, except that differences from unity will be used instead of the actual relatives, so that a single formula may be applied to both positive and negative adjustments. The monthly corrections will then be represented by the terms of an interpolation from zero in the first census year to a factor K in the last of the 3 years considered. Assuming that the exact incidence of the discrepancy is indeterminate and that the corrections should begin not earlier than the first month of the 3-year period and cease not later than the last, it becomes necessary to consider the conditions to be placed upon the form of the interpolation. These conditions must determine the specific corrections, given the average correction to be made in the last year, and the logical validity of the whole process is therefore dependent upon the validity of the conditions specified. In the present instance, four such conditions are made the basis of the adjustment.

The first two conditions are identical in nature and arise from the fact that the index average must conform to the census average in the 2 census years. Thus any correction affecting the deviation of individual months from the adjusted average in one part of these years must be compensated by an offsetting correction in another part of the same year. In the first year the average correction must therefore be equal to zero; in the last year the average correction must be equal to K. There are various methods of fitting an adjustment formula to these conditions, but the simplest is by use of the integral calculus; in this process a curve is fitted so that the area under the curve is equal to the amount of the correction required. The definite integral of this curve over the first year should be set equal to zero, and over the last year equal to K.

The third condition arises from the necessity of splicing the adjusted series to the data for previous years. In order to avoid a break in the series at the beginning of the period, any adjustment at that point must be very small. Hence this condition merely specifies that the correction will be zero at the beginning of the first year and assures the continuity of the series with the items not subject to the current adjustment.

To meet these three conditions, a curve of greater than first degree is required. The course of such a curve, if not further controlled, would be particularly subject to error at the end of the period, as already indicated. It would be logically correct only in case the causes producing the observed discrepancy continued in operation with increasing effectiveness at the end of the period. Now, without further information, the assumption that such a situation exists is hardly justified. It might be assumed with equal validity that the observed tendency has ceased to be effective or even that a reverse tendency has set in by the time the end of the period is reached. The first of these alternative hypotheses is in fact the simplest of the various possibilities suggested; moreover, it ties in with the most reasonable assumption on which to carry the index forward from that point, namely, that the links obtained from the relative positions of the identical firms give the best indication of the subsequent course of change in the industry as a whole. The fourth condition, therefore, assumes that the tendency toward deviation has just ceased as the end of the period is reached—that, in other words, the curve levels off to become horizontal at the end of the period.

To give the conditions themselves precise mathematical formulation, let K_m—the correction factor for the month m—be expressed as a function of time:

$$K_m = f(t)$$

Take the beginning of the first year as the time origin and the unit as 1 year. The conditions may then be stated as follows:

(1) $$\int_0^1 f(t)dt = 0$$

(2) $$\int_2^3 f(t)dt = K$$

(3) $$f(0) = 0$$

(4) $$\frac{df(3)}{dt} = 0$$

The simplest curve type answering to these conditions is the cubic:

$$f(t) = a + bt + ct^2 + dt^3$$

If a function of this type is fitted according to the above specifications, the four basic equations reduce to

(1) $\qquad a + \tfrac{1}{2}b + \tfrac{1}{3}c + \tfrac{1}{4}d = 0$
(2) $\qquad a + \tfrac{5}{2}b + \tfrac{19}{3}c + \tfrac{65}{4}d = K$
(3) $\qquad a = 0$
(4) $\qquad b + 6c + 27d = 0$

and by simultaneous solution of these equations

$$a = 0$$
$$b = -0.34351K$$
$$c = +0.60687K$$
$$d = -0.12214K$$

so that

$$K_m = f(t) = K(-0.34351t + 0.60687t^2 - 0.12214t^3)$$

The required correction factors are obtained from this formula by substituting the observed K and computing the definite integrals over periods corresponding to the various months. In order to simplify the com-

putations, it is possible to divide through by K and tabulate the values
of the resulting function for the 36 values corresponding to the 36
months of the period. Then, to obtain the corrections applicable in any
particular case, it is necessaary only to multiply these tabled values by
the observed K. The values of the function K_m/K have been computed
in this way and may be obtained from the accompanying table.

The adjustment factors obtained by this method are presented graphically in Chart A–2 as three series of dots corresponding to three hypothetical adjustments. It is interesting to note the net effect of the combined adjustments in the census years, where there is an overlapping of

Chart A–2. The Multipliers Used to Adjust the Monthly Values of an Index
on Three Successive Occasions, Assuming That the Correction Is 10 Percent
in Each Case

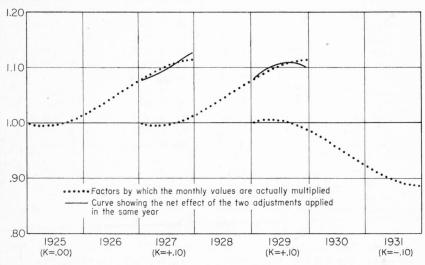

two successive adjustments. The curves in this chart represent the original correction factors multiplied by the corresponding correction factors
of the succeeding adjustment. There is clearly an averaging process
which makes the adjustments over long periods substantially linear
when successive adjustments are similar in direction and extent and
smoothly curved at the turning points when successive adjustments are
opposite in direction. In other words, the assumption upon which the
fourth condition is founded is relaxed, and the total correction at the
end of the period is automatically modified by the subsequent adjustment, in conformity with what subsequent events have revealed about
the nature of the situation that probably existed at that time.

Adjustment by this method will not bring the index average to the exact level of the census average in all cases, because variations of the index within the year represent differences in the weighting of the monthly adjustment factors. If there is a distinct upward or downward movement of the index, whether from seasonal or from longer-term types of fluctuations, a slight error will appear in the result. This error amounts to approximately 0.04 percent when the adjustment is 10 percent, and the difference between the first and last quarter is 10 percent of the

Table A–1.   Table of K_m/K*

Month	First year		Second year		Third year	
	m	K_m/K	m	K_m/K	m	K_m/K
January	1	−0.0129	13	0.1628	25	0.7888
February	2	−0.0334	14	0.2078	26	0.8383
March	3	−0.0460	15	0.2556	27	0.8855
April	4	−0.0513	16	0.3057	28	0.9298
May	5	−0.0496	17	0.3576	29	0.9710
June	6	−0.0415	18	0.4109	30	1.0083
July	7	−0.0272	19	0.4653	31	1.0417
August	8	−0.0072	20	0.5202	32	1.0706
September	9	0.0180	21	0.5753	33	1.0945
October	10	0.0480	22	0.6301	34	1.1131
November	11	0.0824	23	0.6843	35	1.1259
December	12	0.1208	24	0.7373	36	1.1325
Average		0.000		0.4427		1.0000

* K_m is the correction factor applied to the month m.
The factors here tabulated are proportional to the definite integrals of the function

$$f(t) = K_m/K = -0.34351t + 0.60687t^2 - 0.12214t^3$$

over intervals corresponding to the successive months. These intervals are the first thirty-six twelfths of t: first year, January, 0 to $\frac{1}{12}$; February, $\frac{1}{12}$ to $\frac{2}{12}$; etc.

larger, making a combined variation of 20 percent. It increases in proportion to increases in the variation of either of these factors. Thus, in problems stating the index values to one decimal place, an error of 0.1 percent may appear in the adjusted average whenever the combined variation is in the range of 20 to 40 percent. If it is desired to avoid this error where such variation is observed, K must be increased by 0.1 when the index moves downward within the year and decreased by 0.1 when the index moves upward.

The complete procedure in making the proposed adjustment may be summarized as follows:

1. Express the average of the index, in a census year where adjust-

ment is to be made, as a relative to (R_i) of the average in the preceding census year. Compute a similar relative for the census data (R_c).

2. Compute K from these relatives by the formula

$$K = \frac{R_c}{R_i} - 1$$

3. Multiply K by the values in the table of K_m/K.

4. Add 1 to each K_m thus obtained and use the resulting series as multipliers to adjust the monthly values of the index.

Note that it is not at any time necessary to transform the monthly values of the index to any base other than that customarily used for the published series. The simplicity of this process is quite evident, and the actual adjustment of the indexes could safely be turned over to a clerical force if desired. In cases where annual bench-mark data are available, the same procedure could be used with minor modifications.

The Nature of Inventory Cycles

The wavelike movements commonly termed "business cycles" are here viewed as the resultant of cyclical variations in various important segments of the economy. The forces inducing this form of variation are basically the same in all segments. They represent changes in the rates at which inventories are accumulated or liquidated, leading at the peak of the cycle to surpluses and at the low to deficiencies. The term "inventories" is broadly used to include not only business inventories in the usual sense but also stocks of durable goods, equipment, and structures held for use by consumers or business concerns.

The pattern of the cycle results from the interactions of imbalances on two different levels. On the one level there are imbalances of position: inventories may be either excessive or deficient relative to consumption. On the other level there are imbalances of flow: inventories may be either accumulated or liquidated at too fast a rate. (The latter kind of imbalance may be described alternatively as one in which the rate of production either exceeds or falls short of the rate of consumption by too great a margin.) As one kind of imbalance is corrected, it brings on the other. The processes of adjustment not only take time but involve interrelationships that make the creation of some imbalance of the other type unavoidable. The system as a whole must therefore keep changing to correct the kind of imbalance that prevails at the moment.

Once either kind of imbalance occurs for any reason, a whole cycle tends to follow—barring changes in other factors that would interfere with the usual cyclical movement. As an illustration of what happens in such a cycle, Chart B–1 depicts a situation arising out of an unexpected rise in consumption occurring at point A. This not only places

Chart B–1. Interrelated Phases of the Inventory Cycle

Billions of dollars

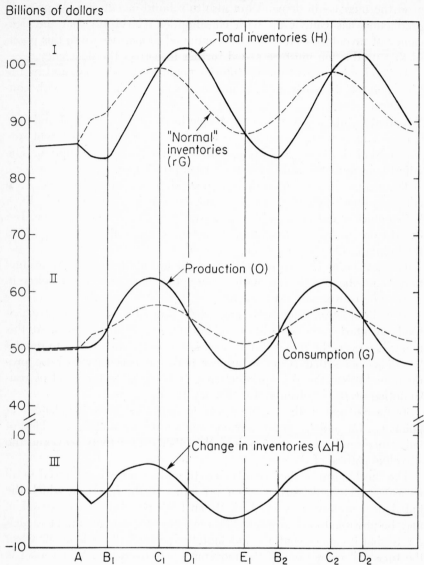

consumption above production (as shown on level II, the middle segment of the chart); it also produces some inventory liquidation (level
III) and a corresponding decline in total inventories (level I). The consumption line is reproduced on level I at a multiple of its actual value to
represent a norm for total inventories. Judged by this norm, inventories
have become deficient.

Business responds by raising production sharply; it seeks not only to meet the increase in demand but also to rebuild inventories. At point B, production has caught up with consumption (level II), but the deficiency of inventories (level I) has continued to increase up to this point, so that production must be raised further to correct the deficiency.

As production moves up, inventories begin to rise sharply; and by the time point C is reached, total inventories are again in line with consumption.

At that point, however, the imbalance in the flows (levels II and III) is near a maximum. Action has to be taken in an effort to prevent surpluses from developing. Nothing can be done about consumption. The adjustment must be made by cutting back production.

This action does not immediately succeed in its purpose, however. The cut in production reduces employment, income, and consumption. Even if inventories remained stable, they would be somewhat excessive. But the rise in stocks continues until production is cut all the way back to the falling level of consumption.

Then, at point D, a substantial excess of inventories exists. So production cannot be kept in line with consumption but must be cut below it, depressing consumption still further.

After liquidation progresses for a while, a point E is reached at which total inventories are brought down into line with consumption. At this point, however, the rate of liquidation is excessive. Attempting to restrict the deficiencies that begin to appear makes it necessary to raise production; but by the time production gets back up to the level of consumption at B_2, a substantial deficiency has developed.

From that point the whole cycle is repeated, with imbalances at points C_2, D_2, and E_2 succeeding one another. Correcting the one kind of imbalance tends always to produce the other, and activity moves in the wavelike pattern of the cycle.

The mechanism of the cycle is easy to understand when viewed in all its aspects. Difficulty arises whenever either of the levels on which the imbalances appear is overlooked. When level III alone is considered, it may be possible to say at times that a movement is progressing at so high a rate that it cannot continue indefinitely, but this tells little about when the turn will come or why the movement will overcarry. When level II alone is considered, it may again be said at times that production will have to be brought into line with consumption, but not that it will have to swing out of line again on the other side. Adding level I to the picture shows not only why the flows cannot remain in adjustment at the point where production comes back into line with consumption but why the excess or deficiency of inventories is greatest at almost that precise moment. But if level I is viewed by itself, there is no clear indication why the reversals occur when inventories reach the point of balance or why aggregate inventories lag at the turns.

There is a tendency on the part of economic analysts to disparage the business cycle by referring to it as a series of "herdlike" movements. In contrast, the cycle is here viewed as the resultant of the behavior of intelligent men doing the best they can under the circumstances. The pattern of motivations is as follows: on the upswing, to work off backlogs of demand; at the peak, to prevent the development of surpluses; on the downswing, to work off surpluses; and at the low, to bring output back into line with current demand after the surpluses have been liquidated.

The cycle in any particular type of product tends to be specific. Its timing and its magnitude depend upon the speed with which adjustments can be made. Their character depends upon the nature of the product and of the industry producing it.

The mechanisms of interaction in the economy transmit cycles from one industry or product to another. Any specific cycle that is important enough tends to swing the whole economy and thus to induce cycles in other products. Frequently these cycles conflict, and to some extent their movements cancel each other out. This kind of situation is commonly referred to as a "rolling readjustment"; it is illustrated by the mild recession of 1949, when the decline in business inventories freed supplies of steel and other resources needed to expand auto production and home building. The really big swings occur when many industries are moving together. At the beginning of a postwar cycle, both kinds of imbalance are working together; production is low and large backlogs of unsatisfied demand exist. The response is vigorous, affecting all parts of the economy.

How cycles of this kind affect capital goods, housing, and consumer durable goods has been brought out in the various chapters concerning these subjects. In all these cases, the condition for growth in the available stock of structures and equipment is production at a higher rate than consumption. It may or may not be possible to distinguish the part of new production which adds to stocks from the part which merely replaces what is retired or destroyed. But the logic of the saturation point in all these cases is clear. Once everybody who has the means to command a certain kind of services has been supplied with the item that provides those services, expansion in the stock in use must come to a halt. Halting it means not just the end of an upswing, but an actual reversal. Then stocks in use are likely to be too high, and in the process of liquidating them new production is correspondingly depressed.

The same principles also apply to military procurement programs or other programs that involve a target goal for durable stocks. The experience of World War II and the postwar decade including the Korean War gave ample evidence of this in the form of problems involving field equipment in the hands of the forces, stockpile requirements for critical materials, and large presses or other special machines for future armaments production. Once stocks are built to the required level, production has to be cut back to prevent accumulation of unneeded supplies. The government's failure to take such action in 1944 and early 1945 contributed to the instability and inflationary pressure of 1946. Taking it in 1953 was largely responsible for the letdown of 1954.

Some further light may be thrown on the relationships involved in inventory cycles by consideration of some simple equations. In simplest form, it may be assumed that inventory holdings at the end of the period are a linear function of the flow of goods into consumption during the period:

(1) $$H = a + bG$$

If this equation is expressed in terms of differences, by subtracting the similar equation for the previous period, the result indicates that the change in inventories is directly related to the change in the flow:

$$\Delta H = b\Delta G$$

This equation is a simple expression of the accelerator principle. It states that the rate of investment in inventories is a function of the change in the demand for goods. Various empirical tests of this relationship have indicated that it provides only an inadequate explanation.

The alternative that conforms to the type of cycles described above is derived from equation (1) by starting with the beginning-of-year inventories and the change in inventories on the left side:

$$H_{-1} + \Delta H = a + bG$$

where subscript $-1 =$ preceding period.

By simple algebra, the statistical form of the relationship then becomes

(2) $$\Delta H = a + bG - cH_{-1}$$

This may be described as the two-variable form of the relationship. It is the form in which most of the relationships are presented in earlier chapters.

If the flow of goods is treated in the same way as inventories, however, another variant is obtained:

(3)　　　　　　　$$\Delta H = a + b(G_{-1} + \Delta G) - cH_{-1}$$
or　　　　　　　$$\Delta H = a + b\Delta G + dG_{-1} - cH_{-1}$$

This may be described as the three-variable form of the relationship. Under certain conditions the parameters b and d prove to be approximately equal. Under other conditions they are not. The latter condition appears to hold, in general, if there is still another independent variable to be taken into account, as, for example, in the case of the automobile relationship (see Chart 11–1).

With some rearrangement, equation (3) becomes

$$\Delta H = a + b\Delta G - c(H_{-1} - rG_{-1})$$

where $r = d/c$

which may be regarded as the "normal" ratio of inventories to consumption or sales.

This equation states that the change in inventories is a function of the change in consumption and of the excess or deficiency of inventories at the beginning of the period. The first of the independent variables would appear to be a partial confirmation of the acceleration principle. It is modified by the second: If the excess or deficiency of stocks is large, the change in inventories may move in opposition to the change in comsumption.

Even this statement has to be qualified to the extent that the several terms are not independent. Reasons for thinking they are not may readily be found. For instance, sharp increase in consumption not only creates an incentive for higher inventories, but draws on inventories and tends to restrict holdings despite the incentive to enlarge them. Moreover, changes in the flow of goods tend to bear a definite relationship to the excess or deficiency of inventories over the cycle, with the latter lagged by roughly a quarter-cycle, as shown by Chart B–1. Hence, it is hardly valid to assume that the accelerator works in any simple manner.

This equation is the same as equation (3) if r is constant. However, r may vary, and does vary in some of the relationships investigated. This condition holds, for example, in the case of business inventories as such. (See Chart 7–6.) Assuming that r is a linear function of time, the equation may be written in four-variable form:

(4) $$\Delta H = a + b\Delta G + eG_{-1} + fG_{-1}T_{-1} - cH_{-1}$$

Statistical testing of these relationships with deflated data on business inventories and flow of goods, as described in Chapter 7, produced the following results:

(2) $\Delta H = 7.506 + 0.163G - 0.539H_{-1}$ $\qquad(R^2 = .574)$
(3) $\Delta H = 3.745 + 0.279\Delta G + 0.085G_{-1} - 0.284H_{-1}$ $\qquad.(R^2 = .635)$
(4) $\Delta H = -1.693 + 0.219\Delta G + 0.217G_{-1} - 0.0066T_{-1}H_{-1} - 0.348H_{-1}$
$\qquad\qquad(R^2 = .737)$

However, if inventories are adjusted to eliminate the disparity with the flow of goods, as shown in Chart 7–6, or if consumption is adjusted to

Chart B–2. Relationship of Change in Inventories to Change in Flow of Goods and Excess or Deficiency of Stocks

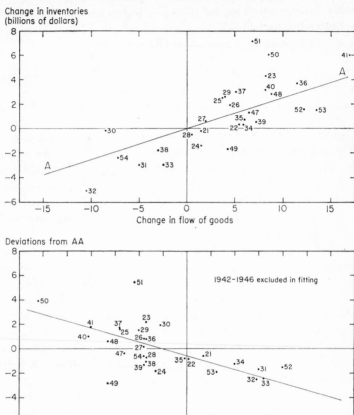

an equivalent trend with inventories, the following results are obtained:

$$(2') \qquad \Delta H = -0.598 + 0.251G - 0.562H'_{-1} \qquad (R^2 = .721)$$
$$= -0.598 + 251\Delta G - 0.562(H'_{-1} - 0.446G_{-1})$$

where H'_{-1} = adjusted inventories. The character of this relationship is depicted on Chart B–2.

$$(3') \qquad \overset{.}{H} = 0.395 + 0.292\Delta G - 0.459(H_{-1} - 0.424G'_{-1}) \quad (R^2 = .713)$$

where G'_{-1} = adjusted consumption

These equations may be used, together with an equation expressing the propensity to consume, to establish an "idealized" model of "the" inventory cycle. A solution carried out in terms of annual data provided a cycle of about 2 years' duration, violent in its initial swings but greatly damped in subsequent reactions. This model appeared unrealistic and uninformative in various respects, however, and the same promised to be true of any model expressed in terms of annual data.

To obtain a model in quarterly terms, it is necessary to make certain assumptions about appropriate lags and the precise treatment of the variables involved. The cycle presented in Chart B–1 may serve as an illustration. It was derived from the following equations:

$$\Delta G = 0.22\Delta O + 0.22\Delta O_{-1}$$
$$\Delta H = 0.27\Delta G_{-1} - 0.50(H_{-2} - 1.72G_{-2})$$
$$O = G + \Delta H$$
$$= G_{-1} + 0.63\Delta G_{-1} - 0.28\Delta H_{-2} - 0.64(H_{-2} - 1.72G_{-2})$$

The first equation, representing the propensity to consume, is based on the considerations detailed in Chapter 13. The multiplier is the 1.80 used in the third approximation shown in Table 13–4. The 44 percent of the change in output going into consumption was divided between the current and the preceding quarters. If a model showing growth as well as cyclical fluctuations were desired, a constant could be added to this equation. This would be entirely consistent with the findings of Chapters 12 and 13. For present purposes, however, it seems desirable to avoid complicating the cyclical model by introducing a trend.[1]

The second equation, representing the change in inventories, is derived from equations $(2')$ and $(3')$ by averaging, dropping the small negative constant, and rounding to indicate an attempt to eliminate just half of any excess or deficiency of total stocks in the following quarter. This attempt cannot be successful, of course, in phases of the cycle where lags and other influences dominate the outcome. It is assumed that the latest data available at the time production schedules for the current quarter are being set are the previous quarter's sales and the inventories on hand at the beginning of that quarter. The coefficient of quarterly sales in the last term of the equation was multiplied by 4 to express the sales criterion as an annual rate comparable to total inventory holdings.

The third equation represents a solution based on the first two. The result shown above was further modified to use year-to-year comparisons for sales and inventories. In actual practice, business firms commonly use this comparison in judging results. Using the change from the same

---

[1] If fixed capital instead of inventories were under consideration, it would be less easy to eliminate trend components, for reasons indicated in Chapters 9 and 10. Readers interested in "growth" models will no doubt wish to explore various alternatives. For a stimulating and suggestive discussion of the implications of growth, see Evsey Domar, *Essays in the Theory of Economic Growth*, Oxford University Press, New York, 1957.

quarter a year ago in effect adds 4 quarterly changes together, and the coefficients of these terms were accordingly divided by 4. The result, upon which Chart B–1 is actually based, is as follows:

$$O = G_{-1} + 0.16(G_{-1} - G_{-5}) - 0.07(H_{-2} - H_{-6}) - 0.64(H_{-2} - 1.72G_{-2})$$

It may be noted at this point that the relationships obtained in this manner, although derived empirically by the procedures described, are similar in many ways to those developed by Lloyd Metzler[2] and may be regarded as providing at least partial confirmation of his conclusions.

The illustrative cycle shown in Chart B–1 is essentially stable or invariant. It is not held to be a representation of what actually happens in the real world. It is obviously based on some very rough assumptions. The precise assumptions adopted are important, because relatively small variations may swing the model all the way from an explosive to a damped type. If it is assumed, for example, that output rather than consumption provides the criterion for size of inventory holdings, on the basis that business cannot tell whether orders are for consumption or inventory, the illustrative cycle would become highly explosive. On the other hand, if it is assumed that business does not attempt to eliminate so much as half of the existing surplus or deficiency of inventories within one quarter, the cycle would be damped; the damping would progress with the lowering of the percentage which was assumed to represent the desired correction.

Experimentation with various assumptions and alternative models suggests that the economy in fact operates near the margin of instability. It would be appropriate in forecasting, therefore, to expect violent movements at times and restricted movements at other times, depending upon other aspects of the situation.

Study of the actual data presented in Chart 7–7 suggests that movements tend to start with explosive force but shortly become self-limiting. A sharp, 1-year movement to accumulate or liquidate inventories tends to come to a rather abrupt halt and to be followed by a compensating liquidation or accumulation, but there is nothing to suggest a progression toward more explosive swings. None of the models developed could be considered an even fairly realistic representation of the actual data through both short swings and major movements like those of the Great Depression. The irregularities introduced in the actual data by disturbances, including changes in speculative psychology, or by other factors rule out any definitive representation of actual experience by smooth models of this kind.

[2] "Nature and Stability of Inventory Cycles," *Review of Economic Statistics*, August, 1941.

Factors Affecting
Residential Construction

A study of housing demand was conducted to test the hypothesis that the construction cycle is a form of inventory cycle governed by the relationship of the supply of housing units available to the aggregate demand for houses under the existing demographic and economic conditions. To test the hypothesis fully, in view of the length of the housing cycle, annual data covering these subjects would be needed over a long period of time. Unfortunately, such data are not available, but research indicated that partial data could be approximated back to 1920, or roughly to the beginning of the major cycle which followed World War I.[1]

The total supply of housing units available was estimated by use of the data on new construction reported by the Department of Labor. These data represent only one kind of change in one segment of the total. They cover only additions of permanent, nonfarm dwelling units. They leave out of account farm units constructed and marginal types of nonfarm units obtained by conversion or other expedients. They also ignore demolitions and other deductions from the housing stock.[2]

Some of the omissions are not so serious as might first appear. The downtrend in farm population has limited new farm-building, and neither replacement of existing units nor renovation of old farmhouses affects

[1] The study was completed before the results of the 1950 Census of Housing were available. The relationships developed in this study were not adjusted to the census results but were subsequently carried forward and revised on the basis of additional data for the early 1950s.

[2] For a reconciliation of the housing count of 1950 with the data on new residential construction, see H. E. Riley, *Change in Nonfarm Housing Inventory, 1940–50,* U.S. Bureau of Labor Statistics, Construction Division, February, 1952.

the total supply available. The omission of temporary, conversion, and other marginal living quarters no doubt involves a larger number of units. However, such units are largely brought into being by two kinds of special conditions: the first involves emergency or other temporary needs that will not affect the longer-run picture; the second involves special additions to the number of quasi families or primary individuals in separate households, in which case the changes in occupied units are matched by special additions to the number of family units. Since neither of these would have important effects on the kind of basic relationship used in analyzing the cycle, the housing measure computed from the basic construction data may be considered a reasonable approximation of the total supply for this purpose.

Furthermore, basic living standards may be expected to exert themselves over a period of time, so that any marginal units temporarily occupied fall into disuse and are no longer regarded as part of the normal housing supply. This implies a volume of building, on the average, as high as if those units did not exist in the first place.

Demolitions, accidental destruction, and other losses appear to present a more serious problem, since these deductions affect standard housing units as well as those that are marginal. Unfortunately, data on this point are not available. Examination of the problem suggested that demolitions and other losses tend to be high when there is a surplus of dwelling units, so that many are disused and provide no economic return as living quarters. They also tend to be high when construction is high, so that sites are required for other use. On this basis, estimates of losses were worked out by means of a formula using these factors as independent variables (see note c to Table C–1). Much more needs to be known before it could be said that this formula provides good estimates. However, two things can be said in justification for its use: It serves to bring the trends in houses available and in married couples into alignment, and it gives results generally consistent with the scattered information available. It explains why demolitions tend to remain comparatively stable for a period of years, as a rising surplus offsets falling construction or vice versa. The negative figures obtained for the war years are obviously unrealistic as a measure of losses as such; but since that was a period in which housing units were created in large numbers by splitting up or converting existing structures, it is not inappropriate to make additions to the housing supply in the war years larger than those provided by new construction alone.

The estimated number of nonfarm dwelling units available at the beginning of each year appears in the fourth column of Table C–1. These estimates were obtained by chaining year-to-year changes in available units both ways from the total for April, 1940, as enumerated in the Census of Housing. Each year's change was taken as the number of new

Table C–1.   Nonfarm Dwelling Units and Unemployment

In thousands

Year	Houses available, April[a]	Housing starts[b]	Estimated losses[c]	Houses available, January[d]	Unemployment[e]	Estimated housing starts[f]
1920	21,049	247	−19	20,989	1,700	812
1921	21,314	449	− 5	21,248	5,000	753
1922	21,768	716	30	21,654	3,200	746
1923	22,454	871	59	22,282	1,400	847
1924	23,266	893	77	23,063	2,400	867
1925	24,083	937	102	23,879	1,800	819
1926	24,918	849	112	24,709	900	814
1927	25,655	810	126	25,471	1,900	761
1928	26,346	753	135	26,175	2,100	691
1929	26,964	509	113	26,810	1,550	661
1930	27,360	330	86	27,261	4,340	582
1931	27,603	254	72	27,542	8,020	396
1932	27,785	134	51	27,739	12,060	177
1933	27,868	93	38	27,847	12,830	45
1934	27,923	126	28	27,909	11,340	102
1935	28,020	221	25	27,996	10,610	233
1936	28,216	319	27	28,167	9,030	357
1937	28,507	336	21	28,434	7,700	482
1938	28,822	406	22	28,743	10,390	491
1939	29,206	515	38	29,110	9,480	463
1940	29,683	603	49	29,564	8,120	554
1941	30,237	706	59	30,098	5,560	715
1942	30,884	356	−15	30,722	2,660	919
1943	31,255	191	−70	31,162	1,070	1,112
1944	31,516	142	−97	31,451	670	1,210
1945	31,755	209	−98	31,695	1,050	1,242
1946	32,062	670	−32	31,985	2,270	1,245
1947	32,764	849	−20	32,588	2,142	1,334
1948	33,633	932	− 3	33,416	2,064	1,386
1949	34,568	1,025	30	34,334	3,395	1,352
1950	35,563	1,396	139	35,314	3,142	1,280
1951	36,820	1,091	122	36,506	1,879	1,271
1952	37,789	1,127	163	37,547	1,673	1,248
1953	38,753	1,104	197	38,512	1,524	1,196
1954	39,660	1,220	263	39,433	3,230	1,092
1955	40,617	1,329	337	40,378	2,654	1,007

[a] Estimated by chaining housing starts less losses to nonfarm houses available in April, 1940, as reported in the Census of Housing.

[b] U.S. Bureau of Labor Statistics.

[c] Estimated from formula

$$D = -0.001 + 0.002(H - M) + 0.006S$$

where D = proportion of houses lost through demolition and other causes

$H - M$ = number of houses available less number of married couples in April, millions

S = housing starts, millions

[d] Houses available as of April interpolated to January.

[e] *Potential Economic Growth of the United States during the Next Decade*, materials prepared for the Joint Committee on the Economic Report, 83d Cong., 2d Sess., 1954, p. 33.

[f] Calculated from equation described on p. 680.

permanent nonfarm dwelling units started in the calendar year less estimated losses. This assumes that the units started in each calendar year
were available by the following April. The April-to-April series was then
converted to a January basis by straight-line interpolation.

The number of families was taken as the basic criterion of requirements for housing units, but demand was assumed to be restricted by
lack of means for making family needs effective. Data on annual changes
in the number of families of various types are available only since the
Census Bureau began its annual surveys following World War II. For
earlier years no satisfactory method of estimating numbers of most kinds
of families could be found. The study was therefore focused on married
couples instead of on families as such. Year-to-year changes in the number of married couples were estimated from marriages, divorces, married
immigrants, and deaths of married persons.

Use of the number of married couples as an index of families omits
consideration of other family groups—related persons other than married
couples living together and unrelated individuals who set up in living
quarters apart from their relatives. Various factors, both demographic
and economic, affect the number of such quasi families forming separate
households, just as they do the number of married couples living
"doubled-up" in joint quarters with others.

There are several reasons why the use of married couples to represent
the total demand for housing may be justified in this context. First,
most families are of this basic type. Second, the relationship of other
"family" types to married couples is controlled over long periods by social norms, so that deviations tend to be eliminated. In the 1930s, when
marriage rates were low, the number of other kinds of households showed
a relative increase, but in the immediate postwar years the proportion of
such households dropped to the 1930 level. Finally, the measure of
houses used includes only the standard units, and a basic measure of
families is therefore apropriate in the comparison. Deviations, such as
those occurring during the war, appear simultaneously in both families
and dwelling units, so that the relationship is not greatly affected; in
other words, omission of families of various special types tends to be
accompanied by a corresponding omission of dwelling units.[3]

One exceptional form of household formation not subject to ultimate
limitation by social norms is evident in the striking increase in the num-

---

[3] The extraordinary increase in households reported in the census of 1950 involved
both dwelling units and families or individuals occupying those units. Any adjustment based on the census would therefore affect both of these variables, with the
effect of spreading the scatters without necessarily changing the relationship (see
Chart C–2 below). Where the effects of any kind of omission are closely correlated
with those of other variables explicitly measured, the relationship remains useful
even though it is subject to additional qualification.

ber of elderly persons living on pensions.[4] These would only in part be offset by corresponding changes in the housing supply: some widows living on pensions may obtain separate living quarters by splitting the homestead, retaining part for their own use and renting the other part; others prefer neither to move nor to convert a house that is overly large for their own needs. What effect this may ultimately have on the demand for dwelling units is difficult to estimate.

The crosscurrents of the World War II years and the first postwar decade may require serious modification of the specific relationship obtained, but not necessarily of its basic form. Erratic movements have been experienced but apparently do not involve any continuing bias; the pattern of deviations, allowing for disturbances, may be interpreted as analogous to that of the 1920s. Future experience may require that the entire study be recast, but in the meantime the relationship between these estimates of dwelling units and married couples may be assumed to provide a generally sound indication of the forces affecting new construction.

The computation of the estimates of numbers of married couples is shown in Table C–2. The data do not represent married couples living together as such but rather the averages of the number of married men and married women reported in each year. Marriage and divorce data are those of the National Office of Vital Statistics.[5] Data on married immigrants and emigrants for the period 1930 to 1950 were prepared by the Department of Justice, Immigration and Naturalization Service, Research Education, and Information Division. For other years, data were obtained from annual reports of the Commissioner of Immigration. These data were converted from a fiscal-year to a calendar-year basis by means of interpolation formulas.

The number of married deaths for each year was computed by applying an estimated death rate to the average number of married persons. To facilitate the computations, the death rate was based on married couples rather than on total married men and women. The average number for each year was taken as the number at the beginning of the year less the number of divorces plus one-half the marriages and one-half the net immigration for the year. After deduction of the estimated deaths, the remainder of marriages and net immigration were added to arrive at the estimate of the number of married couples at the beginning of the next year.

[4] *Projections of the Number of Households and Families, 1955 and 1960*, U.S. Bureau of the Census, ser. P-20, no. 42.

[5] See *Summary of Marriage and Divorce Statistics: United States, 1950*, vol. 37, no. 3, p. 57, Federal Security Agency, Public Health Service, National Office of Vital Statistics, Oct. 29, 1952. See also subsequent releases.

Table C–2. Married Couples

In thousands

Year	Mar- riages*	Di- vorces*	Married immi- grant couples†	Married emi- grant couples†	Married deaths‡ Rate	Married deaths‡ Num- ber	Married couples, January§ Prelimi- nary	Married couples, January§ Ad- justed	Married couples, January§ Ad- justed to census
1920	1,274	170	115	98	0.02376	524	21,588	0	21,588
1921	1,164	160	93	78	0.02179	493	22,184	− 26	22,158
1922	1,134	149	63	42	0.02300	532	22,710	− 51	22,659
1923	1,230	165	119	22	0.02377	563	23,184	− 79	23,105
1924	1,185	171	89	27	0.02284	554	23,783	−106	23,677
1925	1,188	175	47	27	0.02316	573	24,306	−133	24,173
1926	1,203	185	54	22	0.02409	607	24,766	−160	24,606
1927	1,201	196	54	22	0.02271	582	25,209	−187	25,022
1928	1,182	200	47	21	0.02420	631	25,664	−214	25,450
1929	1,233	206	42	15	0.02399	635	26,041	−240	25,801
1930	1,127	196	30	14	0.02277	611	26,460	−267	26,193
1931	1,061	188	11	21	0.02228	604	26,796	−296	26,500
1932	982	164	6	26	0.02223	609	27,054	−326	26,728
1933	1,098	165	6	14	0.02181	602	27,243	−355	26,888
1934	1,302	204	8	10	0.02217	621	27,566	−384	27,182
1935	1,327	218	8	10	0.02190	624	28,040	−414	27,626
1936	1,369	236	9	8	0.02302	667	28,523	−443	28,080
1937	1,451	249	13	6	0.02224	655	28,991	−472	28,519
1938	1,331	244	18	7	0.02094	628	29,554	−501	29,043
1939	1,404	251	20	6	0.02092	637	30,014	−531	29,483
1940	1,596	264	17	5	0.02089	649	30,543	−560	29,983
1941	1,696	293	10	3	0.02014	640	31,237	−544	30,693
1942	1,772	321	6	1	0.01965	640	32,007	−528	31,479
1943	1,577	359	6	1	0.02038	678	32,823	−512	32,311
1944	1,452	400	8	1	0.01946	656	33,368	−496	32,872
1945	1,613	485	24	3	0.01907	650	33,771	−480	33,291
1946	2,291	610	38	6	0.01836	639	34,269	−464	33,805
1947	1,992	483	39	6	0.01864	669	35,342	−448	34,894
1948	1,811	408	45	6	0.01829	672	36,215	−432	35,783
1949	1,580	397	54	5	0.01789	669	36,975	−416	36 559
1950	1,667	385	55	6	0.01770	666	37,537	−400	37,137
1951	1,595	381	56	5	0.01773	678	37,793	.....	37,793
1952	1,539	392	50	4	0.01750	678	38,380	.....	38,380
1953	1,546	390	70	7	0.01776	698	38,895	.....	38,895
1954	1,476	376	112	19	0.01765	701	39,416	.....	39,416
1955	.....	...	...	..	....	...	39,908	.....	39,908

* *Summary of Marriage and Divorce Statistics: United States, 1950*, vol. 37, no. 3, p. 57, Federal Security Agency, Public Health Service, National Office of Vital Statistics, Oct. 29, 1952. Also subsequent reports.

† *Annual Reports of Commissioner General of Immigration, 1919–1954*, U.S. Department of Justice, Immigration and Naturalization Service (reported fiscal-year married female and male immigrants and emigrants were averaged and interpolated to calendar-year basis).

‡ Rates estimated from data on death rates in various age groups, adjusted to actual married deaths in 1940 and 1949 (see p. 677).

§ Preliminary estimate computed from data in columns 1 to 4 and column 6 chained to January, 1920. Adjustments represent an interpolation to bring data for subsequent census years into correspondence with actual census reports (see pp. 677–678).

Annual death rates for married persons were derived from death rates by age groups as reported by F. G. Dickinson and E. L. Welker in *Mortality Trends in the United States, 1900–1949.*[6] Since married deaths are generally lower than those of other persons in the same age group, the married death rates had to be represented by the mortality experience of lower-age groups in the population as a whole. This required assigning a set of weights to the over-all death rates in each age group, so that the weighted average would correspond to the married death rate. The desired weights were computed initially on the basis of percents of married deaths in each age group in 1940, as reported by the Office of Vital Statistics. These initial weights were then adjusted so as to equalize in both 1940 and 1949 the weighted average death rate by age group without regard to marital status and the reported actual death rate for married couples alone. The following weights were obtained in this way:

Age group	Percent of married deaths	Weight assigned to over-all death rate
25–34	6.5	16.3
35–44	11.0	20.0
45–54	18.5	23.5
55–64	24.0	23.0
65–74	24.5	12.0
75–84	15.0	5.0
85 and over	0.5	0.2

The reported death rates of earlier years for the whole population in each age group were combined by means of these weights to obtain a continuous series of estimated death rates for married persons. The results—shown in Chart C–1—agree closely with actual married deaths reported by the Office of Vital Statistics for the years 1936 to 1940 and 1949 to 1951, these being the only years for which such data were available.

Preliminary estimates of the number of married couples were obtained by chaining together the changes shown in the first six columns of Table C–2 from number of married couples reported by the Census Bureau for January, 1920. These preliminary estimates were obviously subject to various kinds of error, since the procedures used in computing them involved a number of expedients that could not be considered highly accurate. As a final step, therefore, the entire series was adjusted to the Census Bureau bench marks for 1930, 1940, and 1950. The adjustments were based on an interpolation of differences between preliminary esti-

[6] Bulletin 92, American Medical Association, Chicago, 1952, p. 10.

mates and actual data reported for each of the census years, after shifting the census figures in each case by a similar interpolation to represent January rather than the month in which the census was actually taken. The adjustments necessary were small, since the 1950 total arrived at by the preliminary computation was only 400,000, or 1 percent, higher than the actual 1950 census figure adjusted to January.

To supplement the basic series on housing needs provided by the number of married couples, unemployment data were used as a measure of income and other economic effects. The Census Bureau survey of the

Chart C-1. Married Death Rate

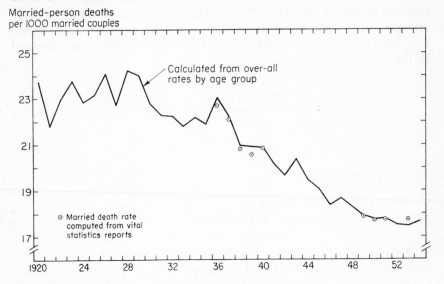

Married-person deaths
per 1000 married couples

labor force provides unemployment data back to 1939; comparable estimates for previous years were prepared by the Bureau of Labor Statistics for years 1929 to 1938 and by Stanley Lebergott for the 1920s.[7]

Problems of the time phasing of the variables were resolved largely on a pragmatic basis but in accordance with the lag relationships inherent in inventory cycles. The number of married couples at the beginning of the year—or the change during the preceding year—provided the primary determinant of housing starts during the year. The number of dwelling units at a somewhat earlier date was found to provide the comparable variable, as in other flow-stock relationships of this character; the mid-point of the preceding year appeared to allow an acceptable

[7] See *Potential Economic Growth of the United States during the Next Decade,* materials prepared for the Joint Committee on the Economic Report, 83d Cong., 2d Sess., 1954, p. 33.

lag. Any precise determination of the lag is difficult in dealing with stable variables of this kind. Unemployment in either the current or the preceding year appeared to affect housing starts adversely, and the average number unemployed in these years was therefore adopted as the ap-

Chart C–2. Relationship of Housing Starts to Married Couples, Unemployment, and Houses Available

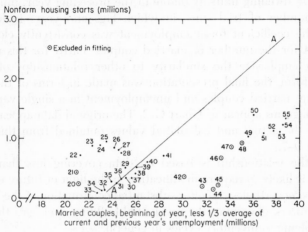

Nonfarm housing starts (millions)

Married couples, beginning of year, less 1/3 average of current and previous year's unemployment (millions)

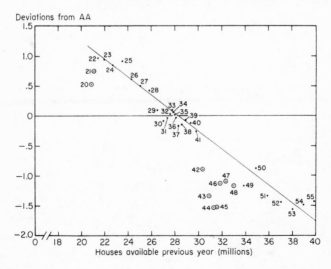

Deviations from AA

Houses available previous year (millions)

propriate variable. This might also be regarded as the measure of unemployment that coincided in timing with the number of married couples at the beginning of the year.

The relationship obtained from the correlation of these data for the years 1922 to 1941 and 1949 to 1955 is

$$Y = 302 + 172(X_1 - \tfrac{1}{3}X_2) - 150X_3 \qquad (R^2 = .905)$$

where Y = new-housing starts, thousands

X_1 = married couples at the beginning of the year, millions

X_2 = workers unemployed, average in the current and preceding year, millions

X_3 = dwelling units available in the preceding year, millions

In a number of trial runs, in which lags and years included were varied, the coefficient for unemployment was consistently close to one-third that for the number of married couples. Partly for this reason and partly to emphasize the similarity to other relationships of the two-variable form, the final presentation was made in terms of the equation combining married couples and unemployment in a single variable. The scatter diagrams appear as Chart C–2. The original data appear on Chart 9–6, and the actual and calculated values obtained from this equation on Chart 9–7.

Since the relationship is based on data covering less than two full cycles, it is likely to require modification in the light of future experience. It appears, nevertheless, to offer substantial confirmation of the hypothesis that the forces governing the residential-building cycle are the same as those applying to inventory cycles in general.

Investment in Plant

and Equipment

This appendix presents a summary of a study testing the hypothesis that industrial capital-goods investment is determined by the volume of industrial output demanded in relation to the industrial capacity available for producing that output. According to this hypothesis, the higher the current level of production relative to existing capacity, the higher will be new investment expenditures, and the lower the level of production relative to capacity, the less will be new investment.[1]

Data to represent the three variables called for by the hypothesis were derived for the period 1919 to 1954. The dependent variable is new industrial investment in millions of 1947 dollars. The independent variables are production, represented by a weighted average of quarterly averages of the Federal Reserve Board index of industrial production, and an index of capacity constructed for comparability with the production index.

The data for industrial capital expenditures are the Department of Commerce–Securities and Exchange Commission plant and equipment series[2] carried back to 1919 with estimates of the Federal Reserve Board.[3] The Commerce Department–SEC series is available from 1945 with a

[1] D. C. Streever, Jr., "A Study of the Relationship between New Investment Expenditures and the Utilization of Productive Capacity by the Manufacturing and Mining Industries, 1919–53," unpublished master's thesis, University of Illinois, Urbana, Ill., 1954. Some of the data have been revised, price indexes on a 1947 base have been substituted for earlier data on a 1939 base, and the final relationships have been recalculated for presentation here.

[2] *Business Statistics, 1955 Biennial Edition*, supplement to *Survey of Current Business*, U.S. Department of Commerce, p. 5.

[3] *Federal Reserve Bulletin*, September, 1939, pp. 731–736; *ibid.*, February, 1940, p. 116; *ibid.*, February, 1941, p. 103; *ibid.*, September, 1946, p. 967.

comparable estimate for 1939, and the Federal Reserve Board series is available for the period 1919 to 1945. The differences in the 1939 estimates are practically negligible, but the Commerce Department–SEC estimate is $600 million higher than the Federal Reserve estimate in 1945. The latter was adjusted to the former over the period 1942 to 1945 by means of an interpolation formula that progressively increased successive years to equalize the 1945 figures. This retains the original levels and year-to-year movements of both series, except for the war years, which are so disturbed that they do not contribute to statistical testing of the hypothesis.

The Federal Reserve data were published in separate plant and equipment classifications, whereas the Commerce Department–SEC series gives total expenditures only. The latter were divided into subtotals on the basis of the ratios of plant and equipment to total outlays as computed from the 1947 *Census of Manufactures* and the subsequent *Annual Survey of Manufactures* publications. The estimates of plant and of equipment were then deflated separately by the Boeckh construction-costs index of commercial and factory buildings[4] and by the Department of Commerce implicit price index of producers' equipment for 1929 to 1954.[5] The weighted index of prices of producers' durable goods of the National Bureau of Economic Research[6] was chained to the latter index in 1929 for earlier years.

The first independent variable, production, is a composite of quarterly averages of the Federal Reserve Board seasonally adjusted index of industrial production. The composite is designed to account for the fact that changes in investment outlays lag behind changes in production both on advances and declines: when output is rising, it takes time before decisions based on the current rate of output can pass through design and construction stages into operating facilities, and when output is declining, before work in progress can be completed.

The weights used in the composite were derived on the assumption that investment decisions made in a given quarter will result in actual expenditures spread out over the following year. A number of other assumptions were tested, using periods other than a year and different weights for quarters within the year. The one which yielded the best results was that 20 percent of the planned investment would be put in

[4] *Construction and Building Materials: Statistical Supplement*, U.S. Department of Commerce, May, 1954, p. 32; and *Business Statistics, 1955 Biennial Edition*, U.S. Department of Commerce, p. 39.

[5] *National Income, 1954 Edition*, supplement to *Survey of Current Business*, U.S. Department of Commerce, pp. 216–217, and *Survey of Current Business*, July, 1955, pp. 22–23.

[6] Solomon Fabricant, *Capital Consumption and Adjustment*, National Bureau of Economic Research, Inc., New York, 1938, pp. 178–179.

place in the quarter the investment decision is made, 40 percent in the next quarter, 30 percent in the next, and 10 percent in the last quarter. Under this assumption, the investment in any quarter is dependent on decisions made partly in that quarter and partly in each of the 3 preceding quarters. For a given year, the volume of investment reflects investment decisions made in the last 3 quarters of the previous year and each of the 4 quarters of the current year. Table D–1 shows the

Table D–1.   Output Levels Related to Current Investment

| Investment decision made | Investment outlay occurs | | | | | | | Total, current year |
| | Previous year | | | Current year | | | | |
	Q_2	Q_3	Q_4	Q_1	Q_2	Q_3	Q_4	
Previous year:								
Q_2	20	40	30	10	...	...	...	10
Q_3	...	20	40	30	10	...	...	40
Q_4	...	...	20	40	30	10	...	80
Current year:								
Q_1	...	...	...	20	40	30	10	100
Q_2	...	...	...	...	20	40	30	90
Q_3	...	...	...	...	...	20	40	60
Q_4	...	...	...	...	...	...	20	20
Total				100	100	100	100	400

derivation of the weights applicable to relevant quarterly production estimates in computation of the annual composite.

The second independent variable, capacity, is an index comparable with the FRB production index, changes in which were estimated from deflated net-investment expenditures. Net expenditures were computed by deducting industrial depreciation charges from gross expenditures, both in 1947 dollars. The depreciation data for industrial firms were estimates by the Department of Commerce for 1934 to 1954[7] with estimates by Fabricant[8] chained in 1934 for earlier years. These data are based on corporate income tax reports and were adjusted for unincorporated businesses by the compilers.

These estimates of capital-consumption allowances are based on original cost. Depreciation charges therefore had to be adjusted for price changes by an especially constructed deflator, which takes account of the estimated normal life of the capital goods being depreciated. Current depreciation charges represent write-offs on past investments made over a long series of years at prices prevailing, by and large, in the years

[7] National Income Division.

[8] *Op. cit.*, pp. 32–33.

the original investments were made. Deflation of these charges requires an index which weights the price in the year of acquisition by the portion of the investment made in that year that still exists in the sense of contributing to the current depreciation charges.

Fabricant's distribution of the life of plant and equipment[9] by age group was modified into 5-year classes and used to allocate past expenditures to current periods of depreciation (see Table D–2). Because of

Table D–2. Age Distribution of Plant and Equipment

Life in years	Percent of total expenditures
46–50	2
41–45	4
36–40	8
31–35	8
26–30	7
21–25	7
16–20	15
11–15	20
6–10	16
0– 5	13
Total	100

the 50-year life of some capital facilities, it was necessary to estimate plant and equipment expenditures and prices back into the 1860s. Capital-goods expenditures back to 1868 were estimated by projecting capital outlays back from the 1919-to-1955 period in accordance with the trend indicated by Kuznets' decade averages of capital formation.[10] To obtain prices corresponding to these outlays, Warren and Pearson's wholesale price indexes of building materials and metals and metal products[11] were combined with weights of 1 and 3 respectively and chained to the index implicit in the separate deflation of plant and equipment expenditures for the 1919-to-1954 period to get a continuous price index back to 1868, the earliest year indicated by the life of plant and equipment to enter into the 1913-to-1917 depreciation base. Both expenditures and deflators were compiled by 5-year intervals. Rough price and expenditures data for this early period proved to be adequate, since they receive only minor weight in the depreciation deflator for the 1917-to-1954 period.

The portion of each 5-year period's expenditures falling into respective age classes was computed and then distributed over future periods by straight-line amortization of the estimated original cost. This procedure

[9] *Ibid.,* p. 181.
[10] *Historical Statistics of the United States, 1789–1945,* U.S. Bureau of the Census, p. 15.
[11] *Ibid.,* p. 231.

yields subtotals of current depreciation by the period depreciated facilities were purchased. The subtotals constitute the weights given to year-
of-acquisition prices in computing the depreciation deflator for current
periods. Though total depreciation computed from the estimated age
distribution of facilities, estimated historical expenditures and prices,
and straight-line depreciation gave depreciation figures in excess of adjusted charges reported for tax purposes, the movement of the computed
and actual series from period to period was basically the same, and the
weights arrived at are believed to be of approximately the correct relative orders of magnitude.

Table D–3 shows a portion of the complete table used in computing
the depreciation weights. The deflator was computed at 5-year intervals
beginning with 1915, and annual values were subsequently obtained by
interpolation. All the values for depreciation and expenditures are shown
in the table for the 1948-to-1952 estimate, and the data from earlier
years necessary for computing the 1953-to-1957 and subsequent periods
are included. The columns in this table show the allocation of each
period's investment to the future periods in which the expenditures are
written off. The rows show the distribution of total depreciation for each
period by the period in which facilities being written off were purchased.
Also shown are the percentages of total depreciation which are applied
as weights to the price averages of the respective past periods in arriving at the deflator for total current depreciation.

The computed deflator thus represents a long-term moving average of
plant and equipment prices using shifting weights. It is a smooth series
with changes in the most recent period being predominantly a function
of the level of recent depreciable investment. In most periods, 50 to 75
percent of the weight derives from expenditures made in the most recent 10 years. Because of these factors, accurate interpolations between
the 5-year indexes are possible. The interpolations were made on the
basis of the following formula:

$$p_i = p_{i-1} + \frac{P_i - p_{i-5}}{10}$$

where p_i = current depreciation deflator
$\quad p_{i-1}$ = previous year's deflator
$\quad P_i$ = current implicit plant and equipment price index
$\quad p_{i-5}$ = depreciation deflator 5 years earlier

This assumes that the current plant and equipment price index pulls the
depreciation price index along by one-tenth of the change from the level
prevailing 5 years earlier. On the whole, the result given by the interpolation formula at the fifth year was very close to that computed by the
more detailed procedure described above, yielding an average error of
less than 2 percent. The error evident at the fifth year was removed by

Table D–3. Derivation of Weights Applied to Plant and Equipment Prices in Computation of Depreciation Deflator

Year depreciation is charged		Years expenditures are made										Estimated total depreciation
		1903–1907	1908–1912	1913–1917	1918–1922	1923–1927	1928–1932	1933–1937	1938–1942	1943–1947	1948–1952	
1933– 1937	$	109	205	411	1,184	2,173	2,748	3,686				10,586
	%	1.0	1.9	3.9	11.2	20.5	26.0	34.8				100.0
1938– 1942	$	64	149	304	697	1,254	1,823	2,382	5,399			12,093
	%	0.5	1.2	2.5	5.8	10.4	15.1	19.7	44.6			100.0
1943– 1947	$	25	85	214	514	738	1,052	1,580	3,489	10,010		17,713
	%	0.1	0.5	1.2	2.9	4.2	5.9	8.9	19.7	56.6		100.0
1948– 1952	$	8	34	126	363	545	619	912	2,315	6,471	18,586	29,979
	%		0.1	0.4	1.2	1.8	2.1	3.0	7.7	21.6	62.1	100.0
1953– 1957	$		10	50	214	384	457	537	1,336	4,293	12,015	18,586
	%											62.1
1958– 1962	$			15	84	227	322	396	786	2,478	7,972	12,015
1963– 1967	$				26	89	190	279	580	1,457	4,602	7,972
1968– 1972	$					28	75	165	409	1,076	2,706	4,602
1973– 1977	$						23	65	241	759	1,998	2,706
1978– 1982	$							20	95	448	1,409	1,998
1983– 1987	$								29	176	831	1,409
1988– 1992	$									54	326	831
1993– 2007	$										101	326
Total expenditures		$3,920	$5,190	$7,685	$13,012	$13,781	$11,559	$10,022	$14,679	$27,222	$50,546	

making interpolations to raise or lower the annual changes in the preliminary interpolations by the ratio of the 5-year change in the interpolated value to the 5-year change in the computed value. Finally, a 2-year moving average of the index was computed to convert the year-end figures to mid-year. The interpolation formula is also used to extrapolate the depreciation deflator currently until the next 5-year figure can be computed, whereupon the extrapolations are corrected as described.

A separate deflator was constructed, following the same principal as above, for adjusting emergency amortization allowed during World War II. These deflated deductions were added to "normal" depreciation. It may be noted that these 60-month write-offs, by making larger than "normal" deductions from gross expenditures over a short period, may cause some understatement of capacity changes. However, it is probably true that some of the investment made under the World War II fast-write-off plan was not fully suited to peacetime production and also that some of it had deteriorated at a faster than "normal" rate by intensive wartime use, thus making the apparent bias less significant. No bias appears in the final correlations that can be attributed to this item or to the fact that no special treatment was given rapid amortization allowed in connection with the Korean War.

Net expenditures in constant dollars represent the base from which capacity changes were computed. According to the Brookings Institution's study *America's Capacity to Produce,* industrial firms operated productive facilities at 83 percent of capacity in 1929.[12] FRB production in that year was 59 (1947 to 1949 = 100). Application of the 83 percent to this production figure leads to a bench mark for capacity in 1929 of 71.1 relative to the production base.

Changes in the capacity index were estimated as $\frac{1}{455}$ of annual net expenditures. The constant divisor, 455, controls the slope of the capacity index. Since no data comparable with the Brookings figure are available for the percent of industrial capacity operated, the constant had to be determined by approximation methods. A major consideration in this respect was that no long-run trend should appear in the percentages of capacity-operated series. Using 455 makes the ratios in years of peak-level activity, such as 1923 and 1948, about equal. It also yields reasonable utilization figures over the entire period of observation, as judged by general economic knowledge about the period. It actually makes little difference in the final correlations if any constant in the range of 400 to 500 is used, but at the outer margins of this range, utilization estimates become unreasonable. For a comparison of the capacity and production series, see Chart 10-1.

[12] E. G. Nourse et al., *America's Capacity to Produce,* Brookings Institution, Washington, 1934, p. 307.

Table D–4. Variables Used in Computation of Industrial Capacity and of Calculated Investment Expenditures

Year	Gross industrial-investment expenditures	Industrial depreciation	Net Expenditures	Industrial capacity, beginning of year	Production composite	Implicit plant and equipment prices,	Depreciation
	In millions of 1947 dollars			FRB production, 1947–1949 = 100		1947 = 100*	deflator
1920	$4,630	$2,798	$1,832	43.4	41.3	76.4	44.1
1921	3,321	2,819	502	47.5	33.0	61.2	48.0
1922	3,813	3,057	756	48.6	35.9	56.9	50.7
1923	4,171	3,135	1,036	50.2	45.9	64.3	52.7
1924	3,726	2,998	728	52.5	45.0	63.1	54.2
1925	4,367	2,989	1,378	54.1	46.9	62.4	55.3
1926	5,100	3,100	2,000	57.1	50.5	62.1	56.2
1927	4,608	3,179	1,429	61.5	51.8	61.9	57.0
1928	4,959	3,216	1,743	64.7	51.8	61.5	57.8
1929	5,679	3,328	2,351	68.5	58.0	63.3	58.8
1930	4,134	3,343	791	73.7	53.0	61.5	59.4
1931	2,469	3,188	− 719	75.4	42.7	58.1	59.5
1932	1,789	2,918	−1,121	73.8	33.5	52.0	58.9
1933	1,925	2,849	− 924	71.4	34.3	51.5	58.1
1934	2,628	2,723	− 95	69.4	40.2	55.6	57.8
1935	3,215	2,661	554	69.1	43.6	55.7	57.6
1936	4,359	2,700	1,659	70.4	52.2	56.2	57.4
1937	5,470	2,828	2,642	74.0	61.7	60.9	57.4
1938	2,919	2,863	56	79.8	49.4	62.7	57.7
1939	3,713	2,914	799	79.9	54.4	62.2	58.1
1940	4,921	3,054	1,867	81.7	64.3	63.8	58.6
1941	6,021	3,330	2,691	85.8	79.8	67.8	59.4
1942	4,576	3,888	688	91.7	99.2	72.5	60.4
1943	3,924	4,045	− 121	93.2	122.0	74.1	61.9
1944	4,354	4,193	161	93.0	127.4	76.6	63.8
1945	5,534	4,448	1,086	93.3	117.4	78.9	65.8
1946	8,328	4,438	3,389	95.7	91.5	86.7	68.2
1947	9,394	4,735	4,659	104.1	97.9	100.0	71.6
1948	9,135	4,855	4,280	114.4	102.8	109.6	76.3
1949	6,990	4,822	2,168	123.8	99.1	113.6	81.6
1950	7,025	4,841	2,184	125.5	105.0	116.7	87.0
1951	9,306	5,231	4,075	133.3	120.3	126.6	92.9
1952	9,823	5,539	4,284	142.3	121.6	128.4	99.0
1953	9,862	5,935	3,927	151.7	132.9	130.7	104.6
1954	9,145	6,186	2,959	160.4	126.6	131.4	109.5

* Average prices for the 5-year periods 1908 to 1912 and 1913 to 1917 which receive some weight in the 1953-to-1957 depreciation deflator are 33.4 and 38.3 respectively.

Capacity was placed on a beginning-of-year basis by deducting half of the 1929 change from 71.1, the mid-year bench mark. The year-to-year changes were then cumulated on to this figure. Beginning-of-year capacity is appropriate for comparison with the production composite. Since capacity changes occur smoothly, the ratio of the production composite to beginning-of-year capacity is essentially a weighted average of 7 quarterly ratios centered on the first quarter of the year.

Chart D–1. Relationship of Manufacturing and Mining Investment Expenditures to Percentage of Capacity Operated

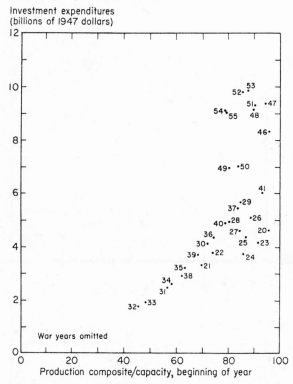

The data described above appear in Table D–4. The hypothesis that investment is dependent on production in relation to capacity may be formulated in several ways. The simplest formulation is the following:

$$I = a + b(P/C)$$

where investment is expressed as a linear function of the percent of capacity operated. The scatter diagram is shown as Chart D–1. Clearly a straight line is inadequate as an explanation of the relationship. As production moves from low to higher levels of capacity utilization, expenditures increase by more than a constant absolute amount. Closer inspection of the chart shows also an upward bias over time. Thus in the

Chart D–2. Relationship of Manufacturing and Mining Investment per Unit of Capacity to Percentage of Capacity Operated

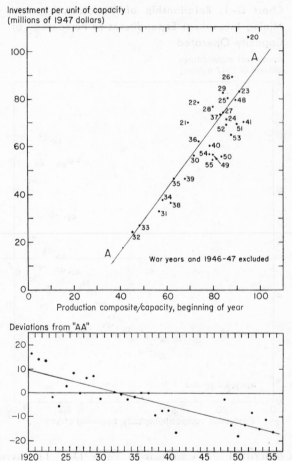

period 1924 to 1927, when percent operated ranged between 85 and 90 percent of capacity, investment averaged about $4.5 billion annually. However, in the years 1951 to 1953, when capacity utilization was again in this range, investment averaged close to $10 billion annually.

The explanation of the upward shift seems to lie in the tremendous increase in the size of the economy between the two periods—capacity tripled between 1922 and 1953. The same utilization rate when the existing capacity base is large will require more new investment to achieve the needed addition to capacity than when the base is small. New investment of $4 billion in 1925 (at 1947 prices) produced a 5 percent increase in capacity. The same amount of new investment in 1952, when utilization was approximately the same, would not have been large enough to offset estimated capital consumption in that year.

The defect in Chart D–1 may be corrected by adjusting new investment by the amount of capacity in existence each year. This leads to the following formula:

$$\frac{I}{C} = a + b\frac{P}{C}$$

where investment per unit of capacity is a straight-line function of percent operated. The relationship is shown in the upper panel of Chart D–2. In this case the regression is linear, but correlation of the deviations with time is evident, as shown by the lower panel. Since time per se is not a functional variable but is only representative of some consistent factor or bias which is present but has not been accounted for directly, it appeared desirable to use a third formulation which retains the good features of this correlation but dispenses with the need for a time variable. This was done by expressing production and capacity as separate independent variables in an equation of the following form:

$$I = a + bP - dC$$

The results of this correlation are shown in Chart D–3. They are better than, though not greatly different from, those obtained from the previous formulation. The similarity of the two approaches may be brought out by simple algebra. If the equation $I = a + bP - dC$ is divided through by capacity, the following results:

$$\frac{I}{C} = a\frac{1}{C} + b\frac{P}{C} - d$$

Comparison of this formula with that using time

$$\frac{I}{C} = a' + b'\left(\frac{P}{C}\right) - d'T$$

indicates that a positive decreasing variable, the reciprocal of capacity, is substituted for a negative increasing variable, time. But the correlation is improved, both logically and empirically, by using the more flexible trend variable, capacity.

Chart D–3. Relationship of Manufacturing and Mining Investment to Production and Capacity

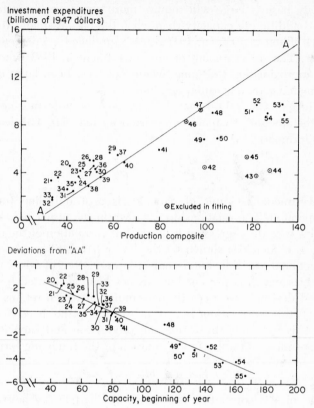

Investment expenditures
(billions of 1947 dollars)

Production composite

Deviations from "AA"

Capacity, beginning of year

The estimating equation calculated from Chart D–3 is

$$I = 1,496 + 130.4P - 57.8C$$

where I = new investment, millions of 1947 dollars
P = production composite
C = index of capacity in existence at beginning of year

This equation simply states that high production stimulates new investment and high capacity restrains new investment. The correlation is highly significant ($R^2 = .97$). That it gives good estimates for most peacetime years is shown by Chart 10–1.

Index